VICTORIA FORNER

PROSCRIBED HISTORY
The Role of Jewish Agents in Contemporary History

I

BANKERS AND REVOLUTIONS

ⒺMNIA VERITAS.

VICTORIA FORNER

PROSCRIBED HISTORY
The Role of Jewish Agents
in Contemporary History
I
BANKERS AND REVOLUTIONS

Cover illustration:
"The Rothschild family praying".
Painted by Moritz Daniel Oppenheim (1800-1882).
London, Roy Miles Gallery

HISTORIA PROSCRITA I
La actuación de agentes judíos en la Hª Contemporánea
Los banqueros y las revoluciones
First published by Omnia Veritas in 2017

Translated from Spanish and published by
OMNIA VERITAS LTD
ΘMNIA VERITAS.
www.omnia-veritas.com

To Ernst Zündel, Robert Faurisson, Germar Rudolf, Fredrick Töben, Horst Mahler, Sylvia Stolz and all the revisionists harassed and imprisoned for exposing the falsification of historical reality. Among them in Spain is the bookseller and publisher Pedro Varela, a victim of hatred and violence by sectarian groups and of an ignominious judicial persecution that violates the Constitution and perverts Spanish democracy. In solidarity with him, we will donate the dividends we receive from this Spanish edition to Mr. Varela for two years in order to contribute to his defence.

INTRODUCTION

"That life was serious, one begins to understand it later...". In these verses the poet warned, and he was right. Certainly, many things in life are understood "later". I began to realise that I was serious about this work some time ago. Now, at the time of writing, I can't say whether nine or ten years have passed since I started it without knowing exactly how it would end. I realised that I was serious for two reasons: first, because as I progressed, the path I followed offered no shortcuts, but widened and lengthened, forcing an overwhelming journey, whose end on a distant horizon seemed almost unattainable; second, because of the risk involved in reaching the end. Knowing that the thoughts and reflections that drove me are forbidden, that they are thought crimes in many European countries, invited me not to go forward in order to avoid unnecessary contingencies. Yes, it was only later that I realised that I was serious, that I was not going to turn back and that I was determined to pursue the route of this *Proscribed History*.

The fact that those who dare to criticise Jews are relentlessly harassed with stale accusations of anti-Semitism suggests that our book will not be well received by those who feel untouchable and persecute freedom of speech and thought, for it reveals the role played by countless Jews in the service of an elite of Jewish bankers and other capitulators who have been shaping modern history. The subtitle, *The Covert Action of Jewish Agents in Contemporary History*, was a working hypothesis which, if well founded, was to become a thesis as the events narrated confirmed it in the more than 250 years of history contained in the work. The continuous presentation of the actions of Jewish agents over hundreds of pages would not have been possible if they had not taken place.

What these men and women were used for and what their missions were is explained in detail in the book. We already anticipate that the French and Bolshevik revolutions were carried out by means of these agents. In the former, Freemasonry was used, impregnated and managed by the Illuminati founded by Adam Weishaupt, an agent of the Rothschild dynasty. As for internationalist communism, it will be seen that it was from the beginning a fraud involving the exploitation and oppression of the working masses, a gigantic hoax devised for the purpose of perpetrating a robbery on a planetary scale, the greatest in history. In order to execute such an ambitious coup, in Russia and China the greatest massacres in living memory were committed. If communism had been imposed in Asia and Europe as intended, there would have been no need for neoliberal globalism, because the resources and wealth of the whole world would have ended up in the hands of those who had financed the revolutions for this purpose.

Since we are likely to be accused of anti-Semitism, racial hatred, denialism and the like, it goes without saying that of course we are not anti-Semitic, nor do we hate anyone, although we do question whether the Holocaust is a historical reality. Our work abounds with names of Jewish authors, it is full of them. With some we share nothing at all and have only turned to their books and articles to learn about their views or to gain information and learn from them. Instead, we fraternally embrace all those non-racist Jews who, far from seeing themselves as beings chosen by an exclusive god, wish to share their lives with the rest of humanity. We will use part of this introduction to mention those with whom we most identify and with whom we share ideas and attitudes. We owe them a debt of gratitude, for they have been indispensable sources from which we have drawn during the years of our work. We wish to pay tribute to them in admiration for their courage and honesty, for their contribution to historical truth and for their willingness to "contaminate" themselves with other human beings.

The Jewish billionaire Benjamin H. Freedman, an astonishing figure, is one such source who deserves a paragraph of his own. Having lived with the main perpetrators of the two world wars (he even collaborated with Bernard Mannes Baruch), Freedman converted to Christianity and devoted the rest of his life and part of his fortune to denouncing Talmudist Jews and Zionism. He warned the world about a hidden tyranny (*The Hidden Tyranny*) that has falsified history. He announced that it was the Zionists who brought America into World War I in order to obtain Palestine (Balfour Declaration). Freedman was one of the first to publicly reveal the Khazarian origin of Ashkenazi Jews (*Facts are facts*). In 1961 he gave a landmark speech at the Willard Hotel in Washington D.C., which has become known as "A Jewish Defector Warns America". In it he warned as an American patriot that the United States would be used as the enforcement arm of Zionism for future wars in the Middle East, which could trigger World War III.

Another Jew who blew the whistle on the world conspiracy before his death in 1955 was Henry H. Klein, who like Freedman converted to Christianity. He served as a lawyer in the Great Sedition Trial of 1944, a trial we have been tempted to write about in the chapter on World War II. It was a trial orchestrated by the American Jewish Committee and the Jewish lodge B'nai B'rith for the purpose of imprisoning some hundred anti-communist American patriots who opposed Roosevelt's policies. Klein was sentenced by the judge to ninety days in jail for disrespecting the court and had to leave the trial after receiving several death threats. In 1946 he denounced in a 24-page opuscule the plan for world domination outlined in the *Protocols of the Elders of Zion*, the authenticity of which he considered indisputable. Klein referred to the existence of an international political and financial Sanhedrin controlled by the money masters, headed by the Rothschilds.

Our Jewish sources are scattered throughout the thirteen chapters; but in this paragraph we want to group together in a few lines the names of those most dear to us, which are not few. Here are some of them: Israel Shamir, a convert to Christianity, author of *The Masters of Discourse*, a trilogy translated into Spanish in which he unmasks Zionism and the international Jewish lobby. Israel Shahak, who denounced Talmudism, Zionist messianism and Israel's imperialist policy from Jerusalem. Gilad Atzmon, former soldier, philosopher, jazzman, pro-Palestinian activist, author of several works. Joseph Ginsburg, revisionist known as Joseph Burg, who was denied the right to be buried in a Jewish cemetery. Haviv Schieber, revisionist, former mayor of Beersheba, persecuted by the Zionist state, activist and tireless fighter for equal rights and peaceful coexistence of Muslims, Jews and Christians in Palestine. David Cole, a young revisionist forced to recant in the face of intimidation against his family. Ilan Pappé, historian exiled to England after being threatened with death in Israel for exposing ethnic cleansing in Palestine in a now classic book. Alfred Lilienthal, author of major works on Israel and the Middle East, friend of the Palestinian people and extreme critic of Zionism. Paul Eisen, revisionist who denounces the secular religion of the Holocaust, founder of an association to remember the massacre of Palestinians in Deir Yassin. Jeffrey Blankfort, journalist and pro-Palestinian activist, highly critical of Noam Chomsky, whom he considers a crypto-Zionist, has identified the state of Israel as the greatest threat to the planet. Jonathan Cook, an award-winning journalist who writes from Nazareth for several Western media outlets, whose articles in *The Electronic Intifada* show his unequivocal commitment to the Palestinian people. Roger Guy Dommergue Polacco de Menasce, who collaborated with Ernst Zündel and spoke publicly in defence of Robert Faurisson.

We could write another long paragraph with names of Jews who despise Zionist and Talmudist supremacism, whose texts have contributed ideas to our work: Brother Nathanael Kapner, a convert to Christianity, whose *Real Jew News* website is a veritable treasure trove of information; Henry Makow, Jonathan Offir, Miko Peled, son of General Matti Peled. And there are more. Revisionists such as Ditlieb Felderer or David Irving usually pass for gentile authors; however, their mothers were Jewish and, consequently, so are they. We feel indebted to all of them. They cannot be called anti-Semitic, but Zionists often accuse them of being Jews who hate themselves because they are Jews.

Before going on to other things, it is also pertinent to note that the plans for world domination have not only been revealed by critical Jews. They have also been recognised from militant positions. In 1924, for example, the Zionist intellectual Maurice Samuels published the famous book *You Gentiles,* in which he proclaims the absolute superiority of his race over others and the impossibility of reconciliation between Jews and gentiles, since assimilation would be seen as a humiliation. Another famous case is that of Harold W. Rosenthal, whose statements are contained in an interview that has gone down in history as the "Rosenthal Document". On 12 August 1976, thirty days after having spoken out of turn, naively and for money, this loud-mouthed young man was killed in Istanbul during an alleged attempt to hijack an El-Al plane. Rosenthal, 29, was travelling in the entourage of Zionist Senator Jacob Javits, to whom he was a personal assistant in New York. The interview, conducted by Walter White, editor of the monthly magazine *Western Front,* is not to be missed. It was published after the assassination and edited into a seventeen-page booklet. White and other observers interpreted the assassination as a false flag operation. The Jewish lobbies were, as always, quick to disqualify White and proclaim him an impostor. Rosenthal admitted in the interview that the Federal Reserve was in their hands, that the media was in their hands, that President Franklin D. Roosevelt was one of theirs, that they were the super-government of the world..., and other more serious things that we prefer to keep quiet now.

Regarding the content and structure of our work, we have said that it covers some 250 years of history, but in reality the period studied is longer, since the first chapter, which serves as a permanent backdrop throughout the entire historical journey, presents fundamental facts regarding the origin of the Jews, essential for an in-depth understanding of the facts and the magnitude of the historical lie that has been imposed. Thus, of the thirteen chapters, the first is devoted to presenting the genesis of an imposture. It will show that Semitic Jews today represent a minority, since more than eighty percent of present-day Jewry is of Ashkenazi origin. This percentage is higher in Israel, where about ninety percent of the Jewish population is believed to be of Ashkenazi origin. This means that the ancestors of the Zionists were never in Palestine, for Ashkenazi Jews are not Semites, not descended from the ancient Hebrews, but from a people of Turkic-Mongol origin, the Khazars, who entered Europe from Asia some centuries after Christ. The main source of this first chapter is once again a Jewish author, Arthur Koestler, whose book *The Thirteenth Tribe* is a classic.

This first chapter is followed by a further twelve chapters, in which events from the founding of the Bavarian Order of Illuminati in 1776 to the attacks of 11 September 2001 and their aftermath are examined. The first part of the chapter, entitled "Cromwell, Agent of the Jewish Bankers of Amsterdam", is devoted as briefly as possible to the fifty years from Oliver Cromwell's seizure of power to the founding of the Bank of England. We are aware that in the four pages which make up this part we offer only a brief outline of what happened; but we could not cover more if we wished to avoid an inordinate length of this *proscribed History.* In any case, we felt that they could serve as a preliminary part of the chapter, and so there they are.

The chapters consist of several parts where necessary, and these are divided into sections which break up the text according to the subject matter or other aspects. In order to save pages in an already excessively long work, we have chosen to dispense with abbreviations such as "ib/ibid.", "op.cit.", "cf/cfr.", typical of scientific work, which repeatedly refer to cumbersome comparisons or comparisons, quotations or other notes, thus unnecessarily increasing the number of pages. The titles of reference books appear in italics inside the text, and if the use of a work is recurrent, we refer to it so that we cannot be attributed credit or demerit for things that have been written by others. Textual quotations, if they are long or lengthy, are inserted in a separate paragraph, in quotation marks, and are somewhat reduced in length. Only in Chapter II have we kept the quotations from John Robison's work within the text, despite its length, because the "Robison" section required it.

As for the notes, the purpose of which is to expand or complement the text, we refer to them with a number and we have chosen to place them at the foot of the page on which they appear. We invite the reader not to dispense with them, as in general, but not always, their content is necessary and useful for a better understanding of what is being narrated. We are aware that some of them have slipped through our fingers and are exaggeratedly long. We apologise for this, but we have found them to be of interest and have decided to keep them.

In relation to other formal aspects of the text, it should be noted that the onomastic index does not include the names of places, institutions or organisations. Only the surnames of the characters appear in it. For this reason, sometimes a surname includes different people. We would have liked to specify the proper names, but this was not possible in this edition. The reader will therefore have to take a little time in his or her research. We had doubts about the accentuation of the names, as we considered the convenience of keeping them without accent marks when they are homographs with the Spanish ones and do not have them in their original language. In the end, perhaps erroneously, we opted to accentuate them according to our orthographic rules. In any case, there will be cases in which we did not know how to maintain the criterion. We have also decided to mark the stressed syllable in many of the Russian names and surnames in order to indicate their correct pronunciation. Thus, for example, in the surnames "Kamenev" or "Zinoviev" the stressed syllables are the first and second syllables respectively. In order to point this out, "Kamenev" and "Zinoviev" have been written as "Kamenev" and "Zinoviev". The fact that names and surnames are written differently in the different languages we have read has meant that some of them may appear in the text with some formal variations, for which we apologise. Let us consider a sample name. Nikita Khrushchev, for example, in the English transcription also appears as "Khrushchev"; in English it appears as "Khrushchev"; in French, Khrouchtchev"; in German,

"Chruschtschow". We think that in this case we have been able to keep the spelling the same, but we fear that this was not always the case.

Since we have read works and used sources written in English, French and German, the titles of the books in the original language in which they were consulted are given in the text and in the bibliography at the end of the work. In the case of David L. Hoggan's *Der erzwungene Krieg, a fundamental work for understanding the war*. Hoggan's Der erzwungene Krieg, a fundamental work for understanding the beginning of the Second World War, we have used the German edition, but since our command of the German language did not allow us to read this work of over 800 pages fluently and in its entirety, we have also used the English edition, *The Forced War: When Peaceful Revision Failed*, published by the Institute for Historical Review (IHR). Only when the titles of the works cited within the text are not easily understood by readers with a basic level of language proficiency have we chosen to offer a translation of them in brackets.

Finally, we would like to anticipate with a few words what may happen in the future as a consequence of having freely exposed the result of so many years of intellectual work. It is certain that Jewish and/or Zionist organisations will resort to the usual stereotypes in order to disqualify the work: justification of genocide, anti-Semitism, racial hatred, neo-Nazism, etc. Of course, we could not accept any of these imputations because they are false. Our Christianity is a vaccine against hatred and the justification of any crime, however small. On the other hand, the Constitutional Court (STC 235/2007) ruled on 7 November 2007 that questioning the Holocaust is not a crime in Spain, although justifying genocide would be. Years later, on 12 April 2011, the Supreme Court issued Ruling 259/2011, according to which the publication of works such as ours does not imply the justification of genocide or incitement to hatred. In any case, in the part of Chapter XII dealing with the persecution of revisionists in Europe for thought crimes, we have made it crystal clear what the sad reality is in many countries.

We are well aware of the power wielded by those who, with banal excuses, do not accept criticism, attack freedom of expression and ruthlessly persecute those who dare to expose objective historical facts, which are demonstrable if the existing evidence is accepted. We would therefore like to thank Omnia Veritas for the welcome they have given to our work and for their determination to publish it in its entirety, without any objection to its contents.

We recognise, on the other hand, that history is interpretable and that the authors' views on certain episodes vary. We therefore claim the right to express our interpretation. All historians, for example, agree that Hitler did not want to imprison the British at Dunkirk and allowed them to evacuate. This is an objective fact that no one denies. What is debatable or open to interpretation is why he did so. Let us consider a second case: Eisenhower's death camps are a historical reality, albeit a largely unknown one because they have been ignored or concealed by official historiography. It is an objective fact that the future president of the United States facilitated the death of nearly one million German prisoners in 1945. What admits of different opinions and can be debated is why the general allowed the death camps, but not their existence. The reader will know our views on these and many other events and will have the opportunity to judge their appropriateness.

The main purpose of presenting and denouncing the actions of Jewish agents in all the historical events recounted is to offer readers a revisionist version ignored by orthodox historians. This desire alone has spurred our will over the years to write this *Proscribed History*. Without needing to comment any further, we are left with the satisfaction of having worked honestly in the search for historical truth. As Rémy de Gourmont rightly warned, "Ce qu'il y a de terrible quand on cherche la vérité, c'est qu'on la trouve". ("What is terrible when one seeks the truth, is that one finds it").

CHAPTER I

ZIONISTS ARE NOT SEMITES

PART 1
ABOUT SEMITIC JEWS

Two main groups make up world Jewry: Sephardim or Sephardim (Sepharad means Spain in Hebrew) and Ashkenazi or Ashkenazi (Askenaz is the Hebrew word for Germany). The former are descended from the Jews expelled from Spain by the Catholic Monarchs; they are of Canaanite origin and therefore Semitic. The latter, however, are not ethnically Jewish, but come from an Asian tribe of Turko-Mongoloid origin, the Khazars, who converted to Judaism in the 8th century AD and are not Semites. This is one of the great mix-ups of history, no doubt astonishing to the reader who is hearing about it for the first time. The Zionists, the usurpers of Palestine, are mostly (ninety percent) of Ashkenazi origin and none of their ancestors, therefore, come from Canaan. We are thus faced with a fraud of historical significance, with a macabre imposture: those who accuse those who dare to criticise Zionism and the Jewish state of anti-Semitism are not Semites.

Before dealing with the history of the Ashkenazi Jews and therefore of the Khazars, it is useful to outline very succinctly, but with deep and meaningful strokes, the history of the real Jews, the Semites. And the first thing to say is that the Bible is not written by a series of chroniclers who recounted the events shortly after they occurred, but by a sect of priests of the tribe of Judah, the Levites, who, many centuries after the alleged events narrated, offered their version according to their own purposes and interests. In any case, no trace remains of the original texts, and the oldest extant copies are partial versions found in the Dead Sea Scrolls (200 B.C. to A.D. 100).

Archaeology is now providing evidence that is forcing biblical stories to be revised. Paradoxically, archaeological excavations in Palestine were started by militant Christians and Jews who wanted to prove the veracity of the biblical accounts, but the discoveries are serving the opposite purpose. Ze'ev Herzog, a leading Israeli archaeologist at Tel Aviv University, claims that the Israelites were never in Egypt, that they did not conquer the land in a military campaign and that the "united monarchy" (Israel and Judah) of David and Solomon was at best a small chiefdom with little territory and influence. The latter must be very hard for Israel's Zionists, whose flag symbolises their expansionist delusion: the Star of David encircled by two blue bars representing the Nile and Euphrates rivers alludes to the purported empire of the "united monarchy". Ultra-Orthodox Jews, supported by secular Zionists, claim that the land of Israel, from Egypt to Mesopotamia, was given to them by God (their Jehovah) and cannot be allowed to fall into other hands. "Every attempt to question the reliability of biblical descriptions," says Professor Herzog, "is perceived by the public conscience of Israel as an attempt to undermine our historical rights to the land.

But if the Hebrews did not come from Egypt, where did the idea of the Exodus come from and how did they appear in Palestine? Niels Peter Lemche, professor of Old Testament studies at the Department of Biblical Studies at the University of Copenhagen, answers the first part of the question: "the authors of the biblical narratives must have taken the story from the memories of some small group of people who were once in Egypt". Other authors propose that it could be more than one group that came to Canaan from Egypt, and suggest that Moses would be the leader of one of these groups; although he could also be the leader of a nomadic tribe, the 'Apiru, who had entered Canaan from Mesopotamia. This second hypothesis has a stronger historical basis.

John C. H. Laughlin clarifies who these 'apiru' or 'habiru' were in his work *Archaeology and the Bible*. He writes that the political situation in the Near East during the period 1400-1200 BC (Late Bronze Age II) has been illuminated by a group of clay tablets written in Akkadian, discovered in 1887 at Tell el-Amarna, a site on the eastern bank of the Nile, some 305 km from Cairo. The significance of the find led to the period being known as the 'Amarna Epoch'. Of these tablets, 350 are letters between various kings and vassals and the Pharaoh. About 150 of them come from Palestine itself. The letters from Palestinian vassals describe "a picture of constant rivalries, shifting coalitions, and attacks and counter-attacks between the small city-states". In a letter from Abdu-Heba of Jerusalem, Lab'ayu is accused of giving the land of Shechem to the Apiru, who in turn are accused of plundering "all the king's lands". The letters thus paint a picture of political deterioration with local leaders fighting among themselves, sometimes incited by a group identified as 'apiru'. These references to the Apiru (originally Hab/piru), C. H. Laughlin continues, immediately attracted the attention of scholars, many of whom thought that the Apiru were related to the Hebrews (F. Bruce, 1967; N. P. Lemche, 1992). Some (E. F. Campbell, 1960) equated the Apiru attacks with the biblical account of Joshua and the invasion of Canaan. The phonetic relationship hapiru>habiru>Hebrew or Hebrew seems obvious. M. L. Chaney (1983) concluded that "the best paradigm with which to describe the Apiru in the Amarna letters, and in other texts, is social banditry". Chaney argued that there was a socio-political continuity between the Amarna-era Apiru and the pre-monarchic 'Israelites' of the Iron Age I (1200 to 1000 BC), who occupied the same territory in

Palestine that had previously been inhabited by the Apiru. Chaney asks: "Can there be no continuity, therefore, between the social dynamics of Amarna-era Palestine and those of the formation of Israel, when the areas of strength of pre-monarchic Israel, its enemies and its forms of social organisation were all coincident with those of the Amarna Apiru and their allies?" John C. H. Laughlin concludes that the political and military disorder associated with the Apiru in the Amarna letters certainly helps to generate the social and political upheaval that made possible the emergence of Israel 200 or so years later.

The picture is thus as follows: Amorites and Canaanites, from whom the Palestinians are originally descended, constituted the indigenous population of the country, which was then joined by successive waves of neighbouring peoples or nomadic groups such as the Apiru. The Philistines, a people of the sea who controlled the coastal region of Palestine during the 12th century BC, must also be included. *Judges* says: "And the Israelites dwelt among the Canaanites, Hittites, Amorites, Perizzites, Perizzites, Hivites, and Jebusites; they married their daughters, gave their daughters to their sons, and worshipped their gods. Here the Bible agrees with the scholars we have been quoting, i.e. the Hebrews neither escaped from Egypt nor entered the area with a religion received during their wandering in the desert. Nor did they conquer Canaan, or even attempt to. For whatever reasons, they settled in the central highlands of Palestine. Israel Finkelstein, a prominent figure in current archaeological research in the Middle East and head of the Department of Archaeology at Tel Aviv University, in *From Nomadism to Monarchy. Archeological and Historical Aspects* (1994) says: "Israel did not exist until the 11th century BC, when new monarchies (Moab, Ammon, Philistia) were also founded on both sides of the Jordan". However, in *The Archaeology of the Israelite Settlement* (1996) he speaks of proto-Israelites, pushes back the dates and rectifies by saying that the "true Israel" did not come into existence before the 9th-8th centuries BC.

With these principles established, the question of the united monarchy of David and Solomon remains to be clarified. Biblical storytellers claim that the northern kingdom of Israel, with its capital at Samaria, and the southern kingdom of Judah, with its capital at Jerusalem, united to create the great empire between the Nile and the Euphrates. But Thomas L. Thompson, professor of biblical studies at the University of Copenhagen, in his work *The Mythic Past. Biblical Archaeology and the Myth of Israel* states that "there is no evidence whatsoever of a United Monarchy, nor of a capital at Jerusalem, nor of any coherent unified political force that dominated western Palestine". Thompson is surprised that there was an empire surrounded by neighbours and vassals and that there is not a single document to report it. There is no space or context," he adds, "artifact or archive that points to the stories described in the Bible about tenth-century Palestine.

In any case, there is no choice but to try to interpret what the Bible says in order to follow the historical trajectory of the Canaanite Jews, which is the purpose of this first part. We shall start, then, from the union between the kingdoms of Israel and Judah, which certainly had a short-lived existence, since at the death of Solomon there was a schism and in 937 B.C. the ten tribes of Israel broke away from those of Judah and Benjamin, which formed a separate kingdom in southern Israel that lasted until 587-86 B.C., when they were deported to Babylon. It should be remembered that Judah, after whom the tribe is named, was the fourth son of Jacob, who sold his brother Joseph to the Ishmaelites for twenty pieces of silver (much later Judas, the only apostle of the tribe of Judah, betrayed Jesus for thirty pieces of silver). The small tribe of Judah was identified as the Levites, the priestly sect who claimed to have received their power directly from Jehovah at Sinai.

The source of the problem

In his *History and destiny of the Jews*, Dr. Josef Kastein writes: "The two states had nothing more in common, for better or worse, than two countries with a border separating them. From time to time they were at war with each other or signed treaties, but they were completely separate. The Israelites had ceased to think of themselves as having a different destiny from other neighbouring peoples, and King Jeroboam separated himself from Judah completely, both politically and religiously". Then Dr. Kastein says the following about the Judahites: "They decided that they were destined to develop a separate race... they demanded a different way of life from the neighbouring peoples around them. These were differences which forbade them any process of assimilation with others. They claimed for themselves absolute differentiation and separation".

Here in a nutshell is the origin of a problem that has lasted for three thousand years. The priestly sect of the Levites imposed a creed of racial discrimination and segregation unknown to the other tribes during the days of the association between Israel and Judah. Recall that the Bible gives us multiple examples of racial fraternisation. Indeed, the most prominent Israelites set an example time and again: Abraham cohabited with Hagar, an Egyptian. Joseph married Ashtoreth, who was not only an Egyptian but also the daughter of a priest. Moses married a Midianite, Zipporah, one of the seven daughters of Jethro, who was also a priest and initiator of Moses. King David's mother was a Moabite and he himself married a princess of Geshur. Solomon, whose mother was a Hittite, loved many foreign women, including the daughter of Pharaoh, whom he married, married Moabite, Edomite, Hittite, Ammonite women and had hundreds of wives. And so the "scandalous chronicle" would go on.

In 722 BC the northern kingdom, Israel, was attacked and conquered by Assyria and the Israelites were taken into captivity. Finkelstein says that the northern kingdom was a wealthy state, unlike Judah, which was so poor and isolated that it had not even developed administrative organisation. According to Finkelstein Judah suddenly received large numbers of refugees to such an extent that in fifteen years it grew demographically about fifteenfold. Judah was thus spared at that time and for more than a century was a vassal first of Assyria and then of Egypt. The Levite sect continued to have Judah as its stronghold. Dr. Kastein interprets that Israel was "totally, deservedly lost because it rejected the creed of the Levites and chose rapprochement with neighbouring peoples", words that reveal his Zionist ideology.

During the years following the Assyrian conquest of Israel, the Levites in Judah began to compile the written Law. By 621 BC they had written *Deuteronomy* and read it to the people in the temple in Jerusalem. Thus was born the Mosaic Law, which Moses never knew. It is so called because it is attributed to Moses, but the authorities agree that it is a product of the Levites, who from then on repeatedly made Moses (and through him Jehovah) say what suited them. In reality, then, we should speak of the Levitical Law or the Judaic Law. Before the compilation of *Deuteronomy*, there was only the oral tradition of what God had said to Moses. The Levites claimed to be consecrated as the repositories and guardians of this tradition. From that time on *Deuteronomy* became the basis of the Torah, the Law, contained in the Pentateuch, which is also the unrefined material of the *Talmud*. The new orthodoxy fiercely fought the competing cults of Jehovah and exterminated their priests. Around 587 B.C., some thirty years after the reading of the Law in Jerusalem, Judah was conquered by the king of Babylon, and there was every indication that the matter would be settled.

However, the Babylonian episode had decisive consequences not only for the tribe of Judah at that time, but for the Western world today. During the Babylonian period the Levites added to *Deuteronomy* the four books that were to make up the Pentateuch and thus composed a Law of racial and religious intolerance which, suitably reinforced, was to separate the Judahites from the rest of humanity. There the chains that were to bind the Jewish people forever were forged. In Babylon the Levites found through experimentation mechanisms to strengthen the Law and succeeded in keeping their followers segregated, separated from those among whom they lived. There is a tendency to think that the Babylonian captivity was a black period, with no possibility of freedom. Nothing could be further from the truth. The benevolent behaviour of the Babylonian conquerors towards the Judaean prisoners allowed them, in the words of Dr. Kastein, "complete freedom of residence, worship, work and their own administration".

Douglas Reed, a master journalist and revisionist historian accused of anti-Semitism, as are all those who, while being friends of the Jews, dare to denounce the crimes of Zionism and Israel's exclusionary racism, writes in his work *The Controversy of Zion* that "the freedom granted to them allowed the Levites to constrain their own people into closed communities and to experience self-segregation. Thus the ghetto and the power of the priestly sect were born".

Although *Genesis* and *Exodus* were composed after *Deuteronomy*, the theme of tribal fanaticism is weaker in them. The crescendo occurs in *Deuteronomy*, *Leviticus* and *Numbers*. In *Exodus*, however, something of great importance appears: Jehovah's promise to "his people" is sealed with blood. From this point on, blood flows in torrents throughout the books of the Law. A good example is when the Levites write how they were chosen by Moses after the worship of the golden calf. Here is the passage from *Exodus*:

> "All the sons of Levi gathered around him. Thus says the LORD, the God of Israel," he said to them, "Gird each of you his sword on his thigh. Go through the camp from one end to the other, and slay every man his brother, his friend, and his kinsman. The Levites carried out Moses' command and that day about three thousand men fell. Moses said, 'Today you have consecrated yourselves as priests of the LORD, because each of you has attacked his son, his brother; therefore he gives you a blessing today."

Douglas Reed reflects on the image of the blood-spattered priests and from a distance wonders why the books of the Law insist again and again on blood sacrifices. "The answer seems to lie," he writes, "in the mysterious genius of the sect to install fear through terror.

It is in the last book, *Numbers*, that Jehovah fixes all the functions of the Levites and puts the finishing touches to the Law. Then it is recalled that Moses himself has become a transgressor, for in *Exodus* it is related that he has sought refuge among the Midianites, married the daughter of the high priest and received instructions from the high priest as to his priestly rites. Since the whole structure of the Law resides in Moses, in whose name the injunctions against such actions have been laid down, something must be done with him before the Books are completed. In these last chapters Moses, after showing his conformity to all the statutes and commandments of the Law, in order to redeem his iniquities and transgressions must slaughter the entire tribe of the Midianites, except for the virgins. In this way he dishonours his saviours, his wife, his two sons and his father-in-law, but he is redeemed from his sin and can validate the racial and religious dogma that the Levites have invented. In this way the benevolent patriarch of the primitive oral legends prior to the written Law, the one who receives the ten commandments that are taken up by all mankind, the one who is recognised by Islam and Christianity, the one of the Thou shalt not kill whom Jesus recalls again and again throughout his life, is transformed into the founding father of the Law of racial hatred and exclusion, since those who do not belong to the tribe cease to be his neighbour, as the *Talmud* will scandalously ratify hundreds of years later.

Ethnic cleansing

After the fall of Babylon, the Judahites returned to Jerusalem around 538 and the impact of the Law on other peoples began. This was possible because Cyrus, king of the Persians and founder of an empire that spread throughout western Asia, gave the nations he subjugated freedom to practise their religion and maintain their institutions. The historical book that records the fall of Babylon, also composed several centuries after the fact, is the one attributed to Daniel. He is said to have been a captive who rose to the highest place in Nebuchadnezzar's court through his ability to interpret dreams.

When King Cyrus conquered Babylon and allowed the Jews to return to Judea, the five books of the Law had not been completed and the Levite sect was still working on them. This is why a select group did not return and remained in Babylon finishing the writing. The mass of the Judahites knew nothing yet of the law of racial intolerance that had been prepared for them, though religious intolerance was familiar to them. The first to experience the impact of the Mosaic Law were the Samaritans, who warmly welcomed the returnees and in token of friendship offered them help in rebuilding the temple destroyed by the Babylonians; but they were rejected by order of the Levites and the restoration was thus delayed until 520 B.C. The Samaritans were Israelites who had probably mixed their blood with others. They worshipped Jehovah, but did not recognise the supremacy of Jerusalem, and perhaps this was the reason for the distrust of the Levites, who feared being absorbed again. The Samaritans were thus outlawed to the extent that just by taking a piece of bread from the hand of a Samaritan, a Jew broke the Law and defiled himself in an abominable way. Racial hatred against them continued down the centuries to the present day.

It is estimated that there were about forty thousand who returned from Babylon to Judea, which was not much, perhaps ten or twenty percent of the total number of people who had voluntarily dispersed to other lands. Reed comments that the Levites had the same difficulty as the Zionists in the 20th century in convincing their co-religionists to go to the Promised Land. Moreover, the leaders themselves did not spearhead the return, but wanted to remain in Babylon, just as today's Zionist leaders want to remain in New York. The solution was similar to that found in 1946: the zealots were willing to go and a few unfortunates who were too poor to be able to choose were recruited to accompany the masses. Those who asked for the privilege of remaining in Babylon with their prince, the Exilarch, were required to contribute money, exactly as American Jewish millionaires are required to contribute funds to the Zionist cause.

One of Douglas Reed's sources is Professor J. Welhausen, who in his *History of the Israelites and the Judahites,* published in German in 1897, points out that the Jewish nation was hopelessly dispersed and obviously could not be regrouped in Canaan. Welhausen insists that "from exile did not return the nation, but only a religious sect"; but this symbolic "return" was of the utmost importance for the priests who were able to establish their power over the frightened masses. Thus the sect that "returned" to Jerusalem was also the heart of the nation within nations, the state within states. The priestly sect had proved itself capable of maintaining its theocracy without a territory of its own and under a foreign king. It had ruled its own with its own Law. Dr Kastein says: "In place of the power of the State, another, more secure and more lasting power was eventually established: the stern and inexorable regime reinforced by the obligation of unquestioning obedience to the rules of ritual.

Among the most important priests was Ezekiel, who lived through the fall of Judah and the move to Babylon. He was undoubtedly one of the architects of the Law, for his book is one of the most significant in the Old Testament. It contains the fiercest penalties for those who do not keep the Law. Page after page of Jehovah's curses and promises to use the Gentiles as an instrument of punishment. Worshipping other gods brings unrelenting reprisals. This passage is a case in point:

> "The God of Israel called the man clothed in linen who had the scribe's purse around his waist and said to him, 'Go through the city, go through Jerusalem, and put a mark on the foreheads of the men who groan and weep because of the abominations that are done within it.' And I could hear what he said to them: 'Go through the city after him and strike. Do not pity your eyes and have no pity. Kill old men, young men, maidens, children and women, to the point of extermination. But do not touch those who have the sign on their foreheads'".

While the scribal school founded by Ezekiel continued for eighty years in Babylon to finish the compilation of the Law, the repatriated Judahites, who had never before known the regime of bigotry and exclusion that had been prepared for them, gradually developed normal relations with their neighbours. Then came an event of momentous importance: the priestly sect in Babylon was to get a foreign ruler, the Persian king who was their overlord, to put soldiers and money at their disposal so that they could enforce their Law. It was the first time they had done so. Subsequently they have repeated the same stratagem: during the twentieth century they have succeeded several times, as we shall see in other chapters, and in the twenty-first century the Iraq war is the latest example of the use of foreign soldiers and money.

In 458 B.C., the Levites set out to enforce their Law, which had already been completed. From this date the Judahites in Jerusalem were finally segregated, excluded from the rest of humanity. This was the real beginning of an affair that continues to this day. The story is told in the books of Ezra and Nehemiah, the Levite emissaries from Babylon who were sent to Jerusalem to enforce the Law. Ezra, a high priest, arrived with about fifteen hundred followers and did so in the name of the Persian king Artaxerxes I, nicknamed the Longimanus in Latin sources, with Persian soldiers and Persian gold. By what means the sect managed to bend Artaxerxes to their will no one can now discover. Ezra brought with him the new racial Law, which came into force among his fellow-travellers who, only after they had been able to prove that they were descendants of Judah or Levites, had been allowed to go with him. To anyone who does not keep the law of your God and the law of the king," the text of Artaxerxes read, "let rigorous justice be meted out: death, banishment, a monetary fine or imprisonment". Dr. Kastein writes that when Ezra arrived in Jerusalem "he found to his dismay and horror that intermarriage predominated.... By tolerating racial intermarriage with neighbouring tribes, they had established peaceful relations based on family ties". The biblical text tells it like this:

> "... 'They and their sons have married the wives of these people, and the counsellors have been the first to transgress'. When I heard this, I tore my garments and my cloak, and I brushed my hair and my beard, and I was overwhelmed. At this prevarication of the returnees, all those who feared the words of the God of Israel came to me, and I was overwhelmed until the evening sacrifice."

Dr. Kastein admits that the Judahites in intermarrying "observed their tradition as they understood it at the time". As emissary of the Persian king, Ezra assembled the Jerusalemites and announced that all mixed marriages were to be dissolved; henceforth "strangers" and foreigners were to be strictly excluded. A commission of elders was set up to break up the marriages and put an end to "peaceful relations based on family ties". Kastein acknowledges that "Ezra's measure was undoubtedly reactionary and was not then included in the Torah".

Thirteen years later, in 445 BC, the elders in Babylon sent Nehemiah, Artaxerxes' cupbearer, who was appointed Persian governor of Judea, with even more powers to finish the reforms begun by Ezra. He arrived in Jerusalem with dictatorial power and enough money to rebuild the city walls. When they were finished, Nehemiah ordered that every tenth Judahite be chosen by lot to reside within them. Then, in 444 BC, Nehemiah and Ezra introduced the prohibition of intermarriage into the Torah. The heads of the clans and families were assembled and required to sign a pledge that they would keep the statutes and commandments of the Torah, especially the latter prohibition.

In *Leviticus* came this necessary insertion: "I have separated you from other peoples that you may be mine". Henceforth no Jew could marry foreigners on pain of death. In Nehemiah it is said that any man who marries a foreign woman commits a sin against God (so the law remains today in the Zionist state). Strangers were forbidden to enter the city so that the Judahites would be purified of anything foreign. Thus the first ghetto was born. Nehemiah stayed twelve years in Jerusalem and then returned to the Babylonian court.

The artificial structure he had set up began to disintegrate at once and so, years later, he had to go down to the city again, where mixed marriages had once more been contracted. He forcibly dissolved them and ordered severe punishments against future transgressions. Next, in order to rigorously apply the selective principle, he again studied the birth register and expelled all those in whose descendants the slightest imperfection or defect could be detected. Finally, he ruthlessly purged the community of those who had transgressed the law on intermarriage and compelled all to renew the pledge. When he considered his work finished, he returned to his home in Babylon. These events constitute "the New Covenant". Thus the insignificant tribe of Judah, formerly disowned by the Israelites, produced a racial creed more devastating in its effects than any epidemic; thus the chosen race theory became "the Law".

Douglas Reed lucidly denounces the fact that it is often claimed that Christians, Muslims or other religious people must respect Judaism because of the supposedly incontrovertible fact that it was the first universal religion, in the sense that all universal religions are descended from it. In reality," Reed writes, "the idea of one God for all men was known long before the tribe of Judah was formed and Judaism became above all else the denial of this idea. *The Book of the Dead* (manuscripts of which were found in tombs of Egyptian pharaohs who lived 2600 years BC) contains the following passage: "You are the one, the God of the beginning of time, the heir of immortality, originated and born by yourself, you created the Earth and made man". Precisely," Reed continues, "the sect that forged the chains of the tribe of Judah took this concept of one God for all peoples and destroyed it to forge a creed based on its denial. The universal God is subtly but contemptuously denied, and as their creed is based on the chosen race theory, its denial is necessary and inevitable. A chosen race, if there were one, should itself be God".

The oral tradition of the Israelites contained the idea of one God for all humanity, the one whose voice was heard briefly in the burning bush; but throughout the five books of the Law it is transformed into another racial God, Jehovah, who promises them territory, treasure, blood and power over others in exchange for a ritual sacrifice to be performed at a specific place and in a specific land. Thus they found the permanent counter-movement to all universal religions and identified Judah with the doctrine of humanity's self-exclusion and racial hatred.

Apparition of Jesus

The most important event in the three hundred years that followed was the translation of the Jewish scriptures (the Old Testament) into a foreign language, Greek, which made it possible for the Gentiles to become partially acquainted with the Law that ordained their slavery and the supremacy of Judah. It is therefore somewhat surprising that the translation was made, tradition says, by seventy-two Jewish scholars in Alexandria between 275 and 150 BC. The Jewish Encyclopaedia notes that the *Talmud* even forbade the teaching of the Torah to gentiles. Anyone who taught it would therefore be "deserving of death". Certainly, the *Talmud* saw the danger of Gentiles acquiring knowledge of the Law.

The Greek translation was almost certainly because the Jews themselves needed it. The Judahites had lost their Hebrew language in Babylon and spoke Chaldee. However, the largest concentration of Jews was in Alexandria, where they adopted Greek as their daily language. Most could no longer understand Hebrew, so a Greek version of the Law became necessary as a basis for rabbinic interpretations of it. The old rabbis could not have foreseen that a few centuries later a new religion would be born that would take their scriptures as part of its own Bible. Perhaps if they had known this, the Greek translation would never have been made.

As we approach the appearance of Jesus in Palestine, it is necessary to pay attention to another particularly significant event: the rise of the Pharisees, who were to form the main political party in the small Roman province of Judea,. The word Pharisee means "one who separates himself" or keeps himself from impure persons or things. They were the dominant sect and claimed to carry the ideology of the Levites in its most fanatical form. "They had sworn - says the Jewish Encyclopaedia - to the strict observance of Levitical purity". However, the instinctive impulse to free themselves from this bondage has always had its reflection in a moderate party, which at that time was that of the Sadducees, the declared enemies of the Pharisees, although the Essenes also opposed them. Today the rabbis of Neturei Karta are declared enemies of the Zionist state, which they accuse of oppressing the Jews. Neturei Karta denounces Israel's crimes and demands its demise. During the first half of the 20th century, Jewish communities in Britain, Germany and the United States were hostile to the Zionists in Russia, but Zionism succeeded in silencing any opposition. In other words, despite the existence of moderate tendencies, the advocates of segregation and destruction have always prevailed, as we shall see.

It is in this context that Jesus of Galilee, the Nazarene, appears. The Zionists claim for political reasons that Jesus was a Jew: "Jesus was a jew". Incomprehensibly, Christian priests and theologians also subscribe to this assertion. Jewish scholars, however, reject the idea. Before we continue our historical tour, a clarifying aside on this subject is in order. The English abbreviation "jew" is recent and does not correspond to what the Greeks and Romans understood by "Judaite" or "Judean", a term derived from Judea. In fact, some dictionaries offer absurd definitions of the word "jew", such as: "A person of Hebrew race". The assertion "Jesus was a Jew" could mean three things at the time: that Jesus was of the tribe of Judah (hence a Judahite), that he was domiciled in Judea (hence an inhabitant of Judea) or that he practised the Jewish religion (like the Khazars, who were not Hebrews, nor are their Zionist descendants). The Jewish Encyclopaedia insists that Jesus was a native of the city of Nazareth and it is accepted without discrepancy that he was a Galilean, even though he was born in Bethlehem of Judea. Galilee, where he spent most of his life, was politically separate from Judea, had its own Roman tetrarch, and its relationship to Judea was equivalent to that of "a foreign country" (Heinrich Graetz). Marriage between a Judean (supposedly the virgin Mary) and a Galilean (Joseph) was forbidden. Moreover, before the birth of Jesus the members of the tribe of Judah living in Galilee had been forced by Shimon Tharsi, one of the Maccabean princes, to emigrate to Judea. Thus the Galileans were racially and politically distinct from the Jews of Judea.

The son of a carpenter from Galilee was evidently uneducated and it was not understood how Jesus could know without having studied. His enemies, the Pharisees, asked, "Where does the wisdom of this man come from?" Douglas Reed believes that what gives Jesus' teachings an unprecedented light, for the first time revealed, is the black background of Levitical law and Pharisaic tradition, against which he took a stand when he went to Judea, and adds, "Even today the sudden fullness of light in the Sermon on the Mount astonishes the student who emerges from the critical reading of the Old Testament; it is as if midnight becomes noon." Jesus reduces the whole Law to two commandments: "Love God with all your heart and your neighbour as yourself". This amounted to the unmasking and condemnation of the basic heresy that the Levites and Pharisees had, over the centuries, woven into the Law. In *Leviticus* there is the command: "Love your neighbour as yourself"; but the neighbour, in classical and modern orthodox Judaism, is restricted to those of your own race. Jesus went even further: "You have heard that it was said, 'Hate your enemy. But I say to you, love your enemies". It was certainly a total challenge to the Law that the Pharisees represented. The end is known.

After the death of Jesus the Pharisees, according to the Jewish Encyclopaedia, found in Agrippa I, the last king of Judea, the support they needed to get rid of the Sadducees, who disappeared from the scene. Thus all power fell to them in the same way as it had fallen to the Levites when Judah separated from Israel. Before the destruction of the second temple in Jerusalem in A.D. 70, foreseeing what was to happen, the Pharisees moved to the new headquarters at Jamnia (still in Palestine), from which the ruling sect would exercise its power. From the beginning they understood that the new religion would have to be destroyed if their Law was to prevail, and they were not deterred by voices from within their own ranks. Gamaliel, for example, when the priests and council considered whether to flog Peter and John for preaching in the temple said to them, "Consider well what you are about to do. If this is the work of men, it will soon come to nothing; but if it is the work of God, you will not be able to destroy it". The majority of the Pharisees, in keeping their Law, felt that they had the strength to destroy it, even if they had to work for centuries to do so.

The Talmud

The Law needed to be constantly reinterpreted so that it could be applied as events required. The Pharisees at Jamnia once again invoked their claim to possess God's oral secrets and began to reinterpret the statutes and commandments. Thus was to emerge *the Talmud*, the anti-Christian extension of the Torah, which over the centuries was to become "the fence around the Law". Dr. Kastein explains the importance of Jamnia:

> "A group of teachers, scholars and educators set out for Jamnia carrying the destiny of their people on their shoulders to be responsible for it through the centuries.... In Jamnia the central body for the administration of the Jews was established..... As a rule, when a nation has been completely defeated as the Jews were on this occasion, they all perish. But the Jewish people did not perish..... They had learned how to change their attitude during the Babylonian captivity.... And they followed a similar path now".

The old Sanhedrin, the source of all legislative, administrative and judicial authority, was established at Jamnia. An academy was also established for the further development of the Law. Here the scribes continued the revelation of Jehovah's thought and the interpretation of the Law, which was administered from there and erected as an impenetrable barrier against the outside world. Discipline was reinforced with the aim of making the life of the Jews completely different from that of the Gentiles. Any law that was passed with a majority vote of the Sanhedrin became a binding imposition on all the scattered communities. Opponents were threatened with an edict that meant exclusion from the community. The period of rule from Jamnia lasted about a century and was then transferred to Usha in Galilee, where the Sanhedrin was installed. From there, laws continued to emanate which, according to Dr. Kastein, "set further limitations on Judaism that made it even more exclusive".

In 320 AD, Emperor Constantine converted to Christianity and enacted laws prohibiting Jews from owning Christian slaves. Constantine also forbade marriage between Jews and Christians. This was in response to the Exclusion Law administered by the Usha government. Then, claiming it was persecution, they moved the centre back to Babylon, where the colony that eight centuries earlier had preferred to remain rather than return to Jerusalem was still intact. Eventually the Talmudic government settled in Sura. Academies were established there and in Pumbedita.

The *Talmud* took the place of the Torah, just as the Torah had previously supplanted the oral traditions. The spiritual leaders or heads of the academies of Sura and Pumbedita were called gaonim (gaon meaning eminence or excellence) and began to exercise autocratic authority. In fact the Talmudic schools of Sura and Pumbedita, along the Euphrates River, have been called the Oxford and Cambridge Universities of Mesopotamian Judaism. The Shadow Exilarchs (later Nasim or Prince) depended on the approval of the gaonim and even the Sanhedrin relinquished or perhaps was deprived of its functions. This period is known as the Gaonite period.

At this point it is essential to explain as concisely as possible what the *Talmud* is, since experience shows that few people are aware of its content and its importance for Judaism. In *Jewish History, Jewish Religion*, Israel Shahak warns us that "the first thing to be clear about is that the source of authority for all the practices of classical Judaism and orthodox Judaism today, the determining basis of its legal structure, is the *Talmud*". Specifically, he is referring to the Babylonian *Talmud*, as there is also a Palestinian Talmud. The legal interpretation of the sacred texts is rigidly fixed by the *Talmud* rather than by the Bible.

There are two parts to *the Talmud*. The first, the *Mishnah*, written in Hebrew and Aramaic when Pharisaism had already become Talmudism, was written in Palestine around 200 AD from much more extensive oral material accumulated during the first two centuries of our era. It consists of six volumes, each of which is subdivided into several treatises. The second and predominant part, the *Gemarah*, is a voluminous collection of discussions of and about the Mishnah. There are two collections of *Gemarah*: one composed in Babylonia between AD 200 and 500 and another composed in Palestine between AD 200 and an unknown date well before AD 500. The Babylonian *Talmud*, i.e. the Mesopotamian *Mishnah* plus the Mesopotamian *Gemarah*, is much more extensive and better organised than the Palestinian Talmud. It is considered definitive and its authority is undisputed. The predominant language of the Babylonian *Talmud* is Aramaic. Having said that, the next thing to say is that in the *Talmud* the racism is repugnant beyond belief and the hatred of Christianity is visceral. We cannot now exemplify at length, since our aim is to demonstrate the racial imposture of the Zionists. However, some samples of the above statement follow.

The insidious sexual allegations against Jesus are numerous. The *Talmud* states that his punishment in hell is to be immersed in burning excrement. There is a precept that Jews are commanded to burn, in public if possible, any copy of the New Testament that falls into their hands. Those who think that there is a long way to go are mistaken: on 23 March 1980 hundreds of copies of the New Testament were publicly and ceremonially burned in Jerusalem under the auspices of Yad Le'akhin, a Jewish religious organisation subsidised by Israel's Ministry for Religions. More recently, on 22 May 2008, the Reverend Ted Pike publicly denounced in the United States that on 20 May 2008, in compliance with the obligation imposed in the *Talmud* (Shabbethai 116), copies of the New Testament were burned in the Israeli town of Or Yehuda. The event took place in response to an order from the mayor, Uzi Aharon, who drove around the town in a car with a loudspeaker, ordering young people to collect all the books they could find and summoning them to burn them in public. It is easy to imagine the uproar that the submissive press (almost all of it) would have raised if any state (anti-Semitic of course) had publicly burned the *Talmud*. In the Zionist state, children today learn the Talmudic precept that when they pass a Jewish cemetery they must say a blessing, but if the cemetery is non-Jewish they must curse the mothers of the dead. It should not be forgotten that Jewish children in Israel learn the *Talmud* in schools. Professor Daniel Bar-Tal of Tel Aviv University recently conducted a study of one hundred and twenty-four primary, secondary and higher education textbooks and concluded that racial hatred is at the root of the education.

The examples of racism in the *Talmud* are endless. We gentiles are also called goyim. The word apparently comes from the onomatopoeia goy, which is intended to reproduce the grunting of pigs. Let us look at a few examples: "a Jewish woman defiles herself if she associates with Christians" (Iore Dea 198,48). "Christians and animals are comparable" (Orach Chaiim 225,10) "The seed of Christians is worth the same as that of animals" (Kethuboth, 3b). "Jews possess a dignity that even angels cannot share" (Chullin, 91b). "A Jew is considered good despite the sins he may commit" (Chagigah, 15b). "The property of a Christian belongs to the first one who claims it" (Babha Bathra, 54b). "It is permitted to cheat Christians" (Babha Kama, 113b). "A Jew may lie and perjure himself to condemn a Christian" (Babha Kama, 113a). "Do not save Christians in danger of death" (Hilkkoth Akun, X,1). "Christians must be destroyed by idolaters" (Zohar I, 25a). "Even the best of the goyim should be killed" (Abhodah Zarah (26b)T.). "If a Jew kills a Christian, he does not sin" (Sepher Or Israel, 177b.). "The extermination of Christians is a necessary sacrifice" (Zohar II,43a). These dechados translated from English are from the Soncino edition (London 1935).

A movement such as Hasidism, clearly Talmudist in inspiration, has hundreds of thousands of adherents around the world who fanatically follow their holy rabbis, some of whom - Israel Shahak comments in his *Jewish History, Jewish Religion* - have acquired considerable political influence in Israel among the leaders of all parties, and even more so among the top brass of the army (Tsahal). Their seminal book, the famous *Hatanya*, teaches that "all non-Jews are totally satanic creatures in whom there is absolutely nothing good". Even a non-Jewish embryo is qualitatively different from a Jewish one. The very existence of a non-Jew is "inessential", whereas all creation took place exclusively for the sake of the Jews. In Israel," insists Israel Shahak, "these ideas are widespread among the general public, in schools and in the army".

The intellectual honesty and moral rigour of Israel Shahak, one of the many anti-Zionist Jews worthy of admiration who appear in this work which aims to unveil the great impostures of history, lead him to denounce in his observations on Hasidism the philosopher Martin Buber (Goethe Prize of the University of Hamburg 1951. Peace Prize of the German Chamber of Books 1953. Erasmus Prize 1963). Shahak writes these words about Buber:

"A prime impostor in this case, and a good example of the power of deception, was Martin Buber. The numerous works in which he praises the entire Hasidic movement do not even hint at the true doctrines of Hasidism in relation to non-Jews. The crime of fraud is all the greater when one takes into account the fact that Buber's praise of Hasidism was first published in Germany during the period of the rise of National Socialism.... But while ostensibly confronting Nazism, Buber glorified a movement that held and, in fact, taught doctrines concerning non-Jews that were no different from Nazi doctrines concerning Jews".

Spain, centre of Talmudic Judaism

Having made this necessary digression on the *Talmud*, we can pick up the thread of the narrative where we left off. For hundreds of years the Talmudic government, in Jamnia, in Usha, in Sura, remained close to its native eastern clime, but with the coming of Islam it was to be transferred to Europe, specifically to Spain. The Caliph's instructions to the Arab conquerors in 637 were as follows: "You shall not act treacherously, dishonestly, you shall not commit any excess or mutilation, you shall not kill either children or old people, you shall not cut down or burn palm or fruit trees, you shall not kill any sheep, cow or camel and you shall leave alone those whom you find engaged in prayer in their cells". Compare this command with Jehovah's command in *Deuteronomy*: "Of the cities of these nations which the Lord your God is giving you as an inheritance, you shall not leave alive anything that breathes". Thus, thanks to the humanity of the Arabs, the native inhabitants of Palestine, the Palestinians, who had lived there for two thousand years before the entry of the Hebrews, either converted to Islam freely or continued to be Christians without hindrance.

The Spanish Jews, the Sephardim who lived in Spain at the beginning of the 8th century, played a decisive role in the Arab conquest of the

Peninsula. In *Orígenes de la Nación Española. The Kingdom of Asturias*, Claudio Sánchez Albornoz writes:

"Without the collaboration of the Jews and the Vitians..., even after the defeat of Guadalete, the Muslim conquest would have been much more difficult and much slower and perhaps would not have been completed. If Tariq had not been able to leave Toledo garrisoned by the Jews and a handful of his men, would he have been able to pursue the patricians who took refuge in Amaya and then cross the Gothic Fields? It is doubtful that Abd al-Aziz, son of Muza, would have succeeded in conquering the southeast without the help of the Jews of Granada and the other cities in the area? It would not have been possible for Muza to advance on Merida, the capital of Lusitania, if he had not secured the citadel of Seville with a Hebrew garrison".

The Jews supported the conquest of Spain not only with men, but also with money, and were therefore treated in a very special way by the Arabs, who brought city after city under their control. Due to the very propitious circumstances following the invasion, the Talmudic government was eventually transferred from Babylon to Spain. Dr. Kastein explains that Judaism, dispersed as it was on the face of the earth, was always keen to establish itself in a fictitious state to replace the one it had lost, and therefore aspired to a centre from which it could guide the Jews. This centre was then located in Spain," says Dr. Kastein, "to which national hegemony was transferred from the East. Just as Babylon had taken the place of Palestine, so now Spain was opportunely replacing Babylon, which, as the centre of Judaism, was no longer able to function".

Thus, the government of the nation within nations continued in Cordoba, where the gaonate moved and established the Talmudic academy. It is likely that at some point a shadow exilarch reigned over Jewry. All this may have been done under the protection of Islam. The Arabs and Moors, as had happened earlier in Babylonia and Persia, were extremely benevolent towards a force embedded among them, which progressively took over more and more power. During the caliphate of Abd-al-Rahman III, the highest power in Spain was held by a Jew, Hasdai Ibn Shaprut. He was the creator of the school of Talmudic studies in Cordoba, which would eventually break the hegemony of the Babylonian schools of Sura and Pumbedita. The school later moved to Lucena and finally to Toledo. This character is a key figure in the second part of this narration, in which we will finish commenting on the fate of the Sephardic Jews after the expulsion decreed by the Catholic Monarchs.

A document indicative of the hatred that the expulsion was to generate is found in the *Silva curiosa*, by Julián de Medrano, published in Paris in 1583 by Nicolas Chesneau. From it, with updated spelling, comes this correspondence:

"The following letter was found by the Hermit of Salamanca in the archives of Toledo, looking for the antiquities of the Kingdoms of Spain; and since it is heartfelt and remarkable, I want to write it to you here
Letter from the Jews of Spain to the Jews of Constantinople.

Honourable Jews, health and grace. You know that the King of Spain by public proclamation makes us become Christians, and they take away our property and our lives, and destroy our synagogues, and do us other humiliations, which make us confused and uncertain as to what we are to do. By the Law of Moysen we beseech you, and entreat you to be good enough to hold a town hall, and to send us with all speed the deliberation that you have made thereon.
CHAMORRA, Prince of the Jews of Spain'.

Reply of the Jews of Constantinople, to the Jews of Spain.

Beloved brethren in Moysen we have received your letter, in which you tell us of the troubles and misfortunes you are suffering, of which we are as much a part as you are. The opinion of the great Satraps and Rabbi is as follows.
To what you say that the King of Spain makes you become Christians, do it, for you can do no other. To what you say that they order you to take away your property, make your sons merchants, so that little by little they may take away theirs. To what you say they take away your lives, make your sons doctors and apothecaries, that they may take away theirs. To what you say they destroy your synagogues, make your sons clergymen and theologians, that they may destroy their temples. And to what you say that they do you vexations, see to it that your sons are lawyers, solicitors, notaries, counsellors who understand the business of the Republics, so that by subjecting them you may gain land, and be able to take revenge on them, and do not leave this order that we give you, because by experience you will see that from being depressed, you will come to be held in something.
USSUS FF., Prince of the Jews of Constantinople'".

The expulsion of the Jews from Spain is the beginning of the mystery for many historians, since the Talmudic government was transferred to Poland. But why was it transferred to Poland? There is not a single document that refers to a large migration of Jews from Western Europe to Poland. After leaving Sepharad the Sephardim spread mainly to North Africa, Italy, Greece and Turkey. Colonies were also formed in France, England, Holland and Germany. However, by the time the centre of government settled in Poland in the 16th century, more than half a million Jews were already in the area. Populations of this magnitude do not appear by magic. Where did they come from?

Dr. Kastein understands that something is wrong and that an explanation is needed; but he is reluctant to look for one, ruling out any cause for this "mysterious" fact other than immigration from France, Germany and Bohemia. When a Zionist historian passes over such an important fact with haphazard conjecture, one would think that something is being concealed. And what is being concealed is that the Talmudic government, after having made the racial creed the basis of its doctrine, incredibly, passed into the hands of a large community of "Jews" who had no Semitic blood at all: the Khazars of Turko-Mongoloid origin, a people whose ancestors had never known Judea, but who had converted to Judaism in the eighth century. This autonomous Talmudic government was called the Kahal. In its own territory the Kahal was a government empowered to exercise its power under Polish sovereignty: it had the independent capacity to levy its own taxes in its ghettos and communities, of which it had to hand over a part to the Polish government. But all of this will be covered in the second part, which tells the story of the Khazars.

PART 2
THE NON-SEMITIC JEWS: THE KHAZARS

For centuries everything, or almost everything, about the Khazars was concealed. Douglas Reed recounts in *The Controversy of Zion* that in 1951 a New York publisher was pressured by the Jewish head of a political office not to publish one of his books on the grounds that Reed had invented the Khazars. It had to be a Jewish defector, the multimillionaire Benjamin Freedman, who, after converting to Catholicism in 1945, publicly revealed one of history's best-kept secrets. In his famous and significant letter to Dr. David Goldstein, dated 10 October 1954 and later published in English as *Facts are facts*, Freedman explains that in 1948, at the Pentagon in Washington, addressed a large gathering of high-ranking US Army officers, many of whom belonged to a branch of Military Intelligence, to discuss the explosive situation in Europe and the Middle East. There he spoke to the military attendees about the kingdom of Kazaria and the Khazars. At the end of his speech, he was approached by a colonel who told him that he was head of the history department of one of the largest institutions of higher education in North America, that he had taught history for sixteen years and that he had never heard the word Khazars during his teaching career. This anecdote gives us, Freedman writes in his letter, "an idea of the success achieved by this mysterious secret power in its conspiracy to cover up the origin and history of the Khazars in order to conceal from the world the true origin of the Jews of Eastern Europe".

The information that Benjamin Freedman offers on the Khazars in *Facts are facts,* taken mainly from the *Jewish Encyclopaedia*, has already been largely superseded; but even so, as we shall see, his assessments are still of interest. In any case, the fundamental work for a detailed knowledge of the history of these Khazars or Khazars is Arthur Koestler's *The Thirteenth Tribe*, published in 1976. From it we will summarise the information relevant to the thesis. It should be said first of all that Koestler was himself a Zionist in his youth. Born into a Jewish family in Budapest in 1905, his first idol was Wladimir Jabotinsky (the founder of the Jewish Legion and the terrorist groups Irgun Zvai Leumi and Stern). On 14 May 1948, he even attended the proclamation of the State of Israel in Tel Aviv. Fortunately, he eventually distanced himself from the madness of Zionism, and in his work *The Shadow of the Dinosaur* he wrote: 'I consider myself a member of the European community, a naturalised British citizen, of uncertain and mixed racial origin. I accept the ethical values, but I renounce the dogmas of our Greco-Latin-Judeo-Christian tradition. I do not consider myself a racial Hebrew and I do not believe in the Jewish religion". Since then he never returned to Israel, although he continued to defend the Jewish state's right to exist, implying that he never ceased to be a Zionist at heart.

Sick with leukaemia and Parkinson's disease and having advocated euthanasia, he committed suicide with his wife in 1983.

So who were these Khazars, of Turkic descent, and where did they build their empire is the first thing to know in order to examine their history. Three magnificent natural borders delimited the territory of Kazaria: to the south, the great mountain barrier of the Caucasus; to the west, the Black Sea and the Sea of Azov; to the east, the Caspian or Sea of the Khazars. The steppes and the Volga, Don and Dnieper rivers opened up to the north, into which they expanded their domain. At the height of their power they controlled or exacted tribute from more than thirty different nations and tribes inhabiting the vast territories between the Caucasus, the Aral Sea, the Urals, the city of Kiev and the Ukrainian steppes. From the north, the main cities of the empire were reached via the narrow passage between the Don and the Volga, known as the Khazars' route. From this strategic position they served as a buffer to Byzantium, as they stood in the way of the barbarian tribes of the steppes: Bulgars, Pechenegs, Magyars, and later the Russians and Vikings, who came down the rivers from the north. In addition, they also safeguarded the Byzantines from the Arabs.

Among the authors Koestler cites in his select bibliography is the renowned orientalist Douglas Morton Dunlop. From his *The History of the Jewish Khazars*, (Princeton, 1954) he reproduces the following:

> "The country of the Khazars stretched along the natural line of advance of the Arabs. Within a few years of the death of Mohammed, the armies of the Caliphate swept northward between the ruins of two empires... and reached the great mountain barrier of the Caucasus. Once through this barrier, the way was open to the lands of eastern Europe. Thus it was that on the borders of the Caucasus the Arabs encountered the well-organised forces of a military power which effectively prevented them from extending their conquests in this direction. The wars between Arabs and Khazars, which lasted over a hundred years, although little known, are of considerable historical importance.... The victorious Muslims were stopped by the forces of the kingdom of Khazaria... Without the existence of the Khazars in the North Caucasus region, Byzantium, the bulwark of European civilisation in the east, would have found itself flanked by the Arabs and the history of Christianity and Islam might have been very different."

It is not surprising in these circumstances that in 732 - after a resounding victory of the Khazars over the Arabs - the future Emperor Constantine V married a Khazar princess. Eventually the son born of this marriage became Emperor Leo IV, known as Leo the Khazara. Ironically the last battle of the war, in 737, ended in defeat for the Khazars; but by this time the momentum of the holy war had passed and the Caliphate was already shaken by internal dissension.

A few years later, probably in 740, Koestler reports, the king, his court and the ruling military class embraced the Jewish creed and Judaism became the religion of the Khazars. No doubt his contemporaries were as perplexed by the decision," Koestler writes, "as modern scholars are when they check the evidence through Arabic, Byzantine, Russian and Hebrew sources. All these sources differ only in minor details and most of the facts are undisputed.

What is disputed is the fate of the Jewish Khazars after the destruction of their empire in the 12th-13th centuries, as sources on this issue are scarce. There are known Khazar colonies in the Crimea, Ukraine, Hungary, Poland and Lithuania. I reproduce here Koestler's text: "The general picture that emerges from the fragmentary pieces of information is that of a migration of Khazar tribes and communities to these regions of Eastern Europe - mainly Russia and Poland - where in early modern history the largest concentrations of Jews were to be found. This has led several historians to conjecture that a substantial part, and perhaps the majority, of the Jews of Eastern Europe - and thus of world Jewry - would be of Khazar rather than Semitic origin.

The extent of the implications of this hypothesis for believers in the dogma of the chosen race would explain the great caution of historians in their approach to this issue, when they do not seek to avoid it. Among the most vehement proponents of this idea of the Khazar origins of the Jews is the Professor of Medieval Jewish History A. N. Poliak , a professor of medieval Jewish history. N. Poliak[1], of Tel Aviv University. From his book *Kazaria* (Hebrew), published in Tel Aviv in 1944 and reprinted in 1951. Koestler quotes this excerpt from the introduction:

> "The facts demand a new approach, both to the problem of relations between the Khazarian Jews and other Jewish communities, and to the question of how far we can regard the Khazarian Jews as the nucleus of the vast Jewish colony of Eastern Europe.... The descendants of this colony - those who remained where they were, those who emigrated to the United States or other countries, and those who went to Israel - now constitute the vast majority of world Jewry."

If this is so, it would mean that the ancestors of the Zionists come not from the Jordan but from the Volga; not from Canaan but from the Caucasus. Genetically they are closer to the Huns and the Magyar tribes than to the seed

---

[1] Abraham N. Poliak was born in 1910 in Kiev. He arrived with his family in Palestine in 1923. Held the chair of Medieval Jewish History at Tel Aviv University. Author of numerous books. His essay *The Khazar Conversion to Judaism,* which appeared in the Hebrew newspaper *Zion* in 1941, sparked lively controversy. So did his book *Kazaria,* which was met with hostility and was seen as an attempt to undermine the sacred tradition linking the descent of world Jewry to the biblical tribe. His theory is not mentioned in the 1971-72 edition of the *Encyclopaedia Judaica.*

of Abraham, Isaac and Jacob, in which case, Koestler argues, the term anti-Semitism would be devoid of meaning. According to him, as it emerges from the past, the history of the Khazar Empire would be the origin of the cruelest farce ever perpetrated by history.

The chronicles

The earliest records come from Georgian or Armenian scribes, whose countries, of older cultures, had been repeatedly devastated by Khazar horsemen. One Georgian chronicler refers to them as "savages with frightful faces and the manners of untamed beasts, drinkers of blood". An Armenian scribe speaks of "horrible multitudes of Khazars with insolent and imperturbable expressions and with long hair like women". Later, the Arab geographer Istakhri, one of the main Arab sources, writes: "The Khazars do not resemble the Turks. They have black hair and are of two kinds: the so-called Kara-Kazars (black Khazars), who are as dark brown as the Hindus; and the Ak-Kazars (white Khazars), who are strikingly handsome".

Anthropology and linguistics appear to be essential sciences for clarifying the many questions about the origins of dozens of tribes such as the Huns, Alans, Avars, Bulgars, Magyars, Uighurs, Kyrgyz, Pechenegs, etc., who came to be related at one time or another to the Khazar Empire in their migrations. In *The Thirteenth Tribe*, Koestler notes that even the Huns, whom we know best, are of uncertain origin. Apparently their name would derive from the Chinese Hiung-un, which would designate nomadic warriors in general. From the 5th century onwards many of these westward-moving tribes were generically called "Turks". The term is also supposedly of Chinese origin and was used to refer to all tribes speaking languages with characteristics common to this linguistic group. Thus the term Turk, in the sense in which it was used by medieval writers, would essentially refer to language and not race. In this sense the Huns and the Khazars were Turkic peoples, but not the Magyars, whose language belongs to the Finno-Ugric (not Indo-European) group. The language of the Khazars was therefore probably a dialect of Turkic. The name Khazars is probably derived from the Turkic root gaz, meaning nomad.

One of the earliest references to the Khazars is found in a mid-6th century Syriac chronicle by Zacharia Rhetor, which mentions them as inhabitants of the Caucasus region. Other sources indicate, however, that they had already arrived in the area a century earlier and were closely related to the Huns. In 448 the Byzantine Emperor Theodosius II sent an embassy to Attila with a famous rhetorician named Priscus. Thanks to him we have information about the habits and customs of the Huns. But Koestler quotes him because Priscus also has something to tell about a people subject to the Huns whom he calls Akatzirs, who are very similar to Ak-Kazars (White Khazars). According to Priscus the emperor of Byzantium tried to win over this race of warriors, but a greedy Khazar chieftain named Karidach considered the bribe offered to him inadequate and chose to remain with the Huns. Attila defeated Karidach's rival chieftain and made him sole ruler of the Akatzirs. In short, Koestler concludes in his work, Priscus' chronicle confirms that the Khazars appear on the European scene in the mid-5th century as a tribe subordinate to the sovereignty of the Huns and must be seen alongside the Magyars and other tribes as late descendants of Attila's horde.

After the death of Attila, the collapse of the Hun empire left a power vacuum in eastern Europe. The Khazars during this time raided and plundered the rich trans-Caucasian regions of Georgia and Armenia, where they reaped huge spoils. It was during the second half of the 6th century that they became the dominant force among the tribes of the North Caucasus. It was perhaps the mighty Bulgars who offered the stiffest resistance; but they too were eventually crushingly defeated (around 641). As a result of the debacle, the Bulgar nation split in two: some of them migrated westwards to the Danube and settled in the region where modern Bulgaria is today. Others moved north-east to the middle reaches of the Volga and became subject to the Khazars.

But before gaining full sovereignty, the Khazars had apprenticed under another short-lived power of which they were the main shock force, the so-called Western Turkic Empire, which was a confederation of tribes ruled by a Kagan or Khagan, a title that future Khazar monarchs were to adopt in the future. This early Turkic state, which predated the Seljuk and Ottoman Turkic dynasties that dominated Asia Minor and the Middle East from the 11th century onwards, lasted about a century (ca. 550-650). The Khazars had thus been under the tutelage of the Huns and the said Turks. After the eclipse of the latter in the mid-7th century, it was their turn to become the Northern Kingdom, as the Persians and Byzantines called it.

Arthur Koestler sees this as the beginning of the rise to power of the Khazars, which for him began in 627. In this year the Roman Emperor of Byzantium, Heraclius, entered into a military alliance with them - the first of a series to follow - in order to prepare for his decisive campaign against the Persia of Cosroes, allied with the Avars. The Khazars provided Heraclius with a force of 40,000 mounted men commanded by a chief named Ziebel. Koestler reproduces a passage from Volume V of E. Gibbon's *The History of the Decline and Fall of the Roman Empire*, which, based on Theophanes, describes the first encounter between the Byzantine emperor and this Ziebel. The forty thousand warriors were apparently obtained after Heraclius had promised to offer his only daughter, Eudocia, in marriage to the barbarian chief, which would indicate the high value that the Byzantine court placed on the alliance with the Khazars. However, the wedding came to nothing because Ziebel died while Eudocia and her retinue were on their way to meet him.

Koestler also reports a mobilisation order for a second campaign against the Persians issued by the ruler of the Khazars and reproduces an excerpt from an Armenian chronicler, Moses of Kalankatuk, quoted by D. M. Dunlop in the above-mentioned work. The order is addressed "to all tribes and peoples (it is understood that they are subject to the authority of the Khazars) who dwell in the mountains or in the great plains, who live under roof or under the open sky, who have shaved heads or wear their hair long". This text gives an idea of the heterogeneous ethnic mosaic that made up the Khazar Empire. The true Khazars, the ruling class, Koestler believes, were probably a minority, as was the case with the Austrians in the Austro-Hungarian monarchy.

The Persian state never recovered from its defeats against Emperor Heraclius. There was a revolution and the king was assassinated by his own son, who in turn died months later. A child was raised to the throne and after ten years of chaos the first Arab armies burst onto the scene and dealt the Sassanid Empire the coup de grace. Twenty years after the Hegira the Muslims had conquered Persia, Syria, Mesopotamia, Egypt and had encircled Byzantium in a semicircle stretching from the Mediterranean to the Caucasus and the southern shores of the Caspian. A triangle of three powers was thus formed: the Islamic Caliphate, Christian Byzantium and the pagan kingdom of Kazaria in the north.

The Arabs did not stop at the formidable natural obstacle of the Caucasus, any more than they did at the Pyrenees. There were two traditional gateways through the formidable mountain range: the Dariel Pass in the centre, and the Darband Gorge in the east. The Darband Gate, near the shore of the Caspian Sea, called by the Arabs Bab al-Abwab, the Gate of Gates, was the passage through which the Muslims broke through time and again between 642 and 652 into the interior of Kazaria with the intention of taking the city of Balanjar. Their intention was to settle in the European part of the Caucasus. They did not succeed. There are records of a major battle in 652 in which both sides used artillery (catapults). Four thousand Arabs were killed, including their commander, Abd-al-Rahman ibn-Rabiah; the rest fled in disorder across the mountains. After this defeat they did not attempt any further raids for thirty or forty years. Their main attacks were then directed against Byzantium and on several occasions they laid siege to Constantinople by sea and land.

Meanwhile the Khazars, having subdued the Bulgars and Magyars, completed their westward expansion into the Crimea and Ukraine. These were no longer random raids to amass booty and capture prisoners, but wars of conquest that incorporated the defeated peoples into the Empire, which had established a stable administration and was led by an all-powerful Kagan. By the beginning of the 8th century his state was sufficiently consolidated to launch an offensive against the Arabs.

The second period of warfare (between 722-37) repeated the same script over and over again: Khazara cavalry, through the Darband Gate or through the Dariel Pass, broke into the Caliphate's domain to the south and the Arabs responded with counter-attacks through the same passes towards the Volga. And it was back to square one. In one of the most important raids, the Khazars invaded Georgia and Armenia, inflicted a resounding defeat on the Arab armies at the Battle of Ardabil (730) and reached Mosul in the direction of Damascus, the capital of the Caliphate. The mobilisation of a fresh Muslim army turned the tide of events and the Khazars were forced to retreat through the mountains. The following year Maslamah ibn-Abd-al-Malik, the most prestigious Arab general of his time, who years earlier had led the siege of Constantinople, crossed the Caucasus, finally took the city of Balanjar and even reached Samandar, another important city further north; but he failed to establish permanent garrisons and had to retreat. It is possible that the stronghold of Balanjar, in the foothills of the northern Caucasus, was the first capital of the Khazars and that as a result of these raids it was moved to Samandar on the western banks of the Caspian. Later the capital would be Itil on the Volga estuary, a city built on both sides of the river and described in detail by the chroniclers.

The last Arab campaign was led by the future Caliph Marwan II and ended in a Pyrrhic victory. Marwan made an offer of alliance to the Khazar Kagan and then made a surprise attack through the two passes. The Khazar army, unable to recover from the initial surprise, had to retreat to the Volga and the Kagan was forced to ask for peace terms. Marwan, following the routine pattern of previous conquests, demanded the Kagan's conversion to Islam. The Kagan complied, but his conversion must have been lip service, since nothing more is said of this episode in Arab or Byzantine sources, in contrast to the lasting effects of the adoption of Judaism as the state religion, which occurred a few years later (around 740), as we shall see.

In any case, what happened can be summarised as follows: Marwan, pleased with the results achieved took leave of Kazaria and returned with his army to Transcaucasia without leaving behind garrisons, governor or an administrative apparatus. The reasons for his magnanimity are a matter of conjecture. Perhaps the Arabs realised that, unlike the civilised Persians, Armenians or Georgians, these fierce northern barbarians could not be ruled by a Muslim puppet prince and a small garrison. Consider also that Marwan needed every man in his army to deal with the rebellions that were underway in Syria and other parts of the Umayyad Caliphate. Marwan himself led the ensuing civil war and became the last Umayyad Caliph in 744. Six years later he was assassinated and the Caliphate passed into the hands of the Abbasid dynasty.

With this brief introduction, we can now understand who the Khazars were and in what historical context their conversion to Judaism took place. However, before addressing the main question, it is worth considering a few final points that may help to understand better. Koestler states without a doubt that the Kagan was eventually given or attributed a divine role that led to a kind of veneration of his person. Thus, the Kagan would live in jealous seclusion and his contact with the people would be extremely limited until the moment of his burial, which was clothed in extraordinary ceremonial. The affairs of state, including the leadership of the army, were in the hands of a Bek (a kind of prime minister), sometimes called Kagan Bek, who held de facto effective power. Modern historians agree with the Arabic sources. They describe the system of government as a "double kingship", i.e. a double dignity or dual kingship or monarchy in which the Kagan would represent divine power and the Bek, secular or lay power. This system, Koestler believes, could be compared to the Japanese system from the Middle Ages until 1867, when secular power was concentrated in the hands of the Shogun, while the Mikado was revered from a distance as a divine figure.

Paulus Cassel, a Protestant theologian of Jewish origin, suggests an analogy between this system of government and the game of chess. The double dignity is represented by the king (the Kagan) and the queen (the Bek). For the duration of the game, the king is kept out of the way and protected as much as possible. He has little power and can only move to a very limited extent. The queen, on the other hand, is the most powerful piece on the board and dominates. The queen can be lost and the game continues; but if the king falls, it is the ultimate disaster and all is over. This system of dual dignity thus indicates a categorical distinction between the sacred and the profane in the mentality of the Khazars. The divine attributes of the Kagan are highlighted in the following text by Ibn Hawkal, a 10th century Arab historian and geographer:

> "The Kagan must always be of the imperial race (family of notables). No one may approach him except on a matter of great importance: if need be, they will prostrate themselves before him and rub their faces on the ground until he gives permission for them to approach him. When a Kagan... dies, whoever passes near his grave must do so on foot and pay his respects; and when he departs he must not ride on horseback until he is at a distance from which the grave is out of sight. So absolute is the authority of this sovereign, and to such an extent are his commands obeyed, that if it seems to him expedient that one of his nobles should die, with saying to him, 'Go and take your life,' the man will immediately go home and kill himself without hesitation."

Thus, the Kagan had to be chosen from among the members of the "imperial race" or the "family of notables". This is also the view of M. I. Artamanov, an archaeologist who excavated the Khazar fortress of Sarkel in Russia in the 1930s. Artamanov argues that the Khazars and other Turkic peoples were ruled by descendants of the Turkut dynasty, a dynasty of the defunct Western Turkic Empire (550-650), mentioned above. Other scholars suggest that the 'imperial race' or 'family of notables', to which the Kagan must belong, refers to the ancient Asena dynasty mentioned in Chinese sources, a kind of merit-based aristocracy from which Turkic and Mongol rulers claimed to be descended. However, in Koestler's view, all this would not satisfactorily explain the division of powers (divine and secular) unique to the region at the time.

Artamanov himself proposes a speculative response to this allegation. He suggests that the acceptance of Judaism as a state religion was the result of a coup d'etat, which at the same time reduced the Kagan, the descendant of a pagan dynasty whose allegiance to the law of Moses was uncertain, to a token role. For Koestler this is as good a hypothesis as any, but with little evidence to support it. However, he admits that it seems likely that the two events - the adoption of Judaism and the dual dignity - may be connected in some way. In any case, prior to the conversion there is information about the active role played by the Kagan, such as his relations with Justinian.

Conversion to Judaism

The conversion of the Khazars to Judaism is a unique event in history. How it came about and why is the subject of this section. We will see that the reasons for this momentous decision are plausibly explained in terms of political power. At the beginning of the 8th century the world was polarised between two great superpowers representing Christianity and Islam. These two religions were ideologically linked to political powers that proceeded according to the classical methods of propaganda, subversion and military conquest. The Khazar Empire represented the third force; but it could only remain independent, Koestler argues, if it rejected both Christianity and Islam, since acceptance of one of the two faiths automatically implied subordination to the authority of the Caliph of Baghdad or the Roman Emperor. There had been various attempts by both courts to convert the Khazars: military alliances, marriages and even, as we have seen, impositions. Relying on its military strength and the vassalage of the steppe tribes (its "hinterland"), lacking religious commitment, the kingdom of Kazaria was determined to maintain its position as a third force.

At the same time, however, their close contacts with Byzantium and the Caliphate had taught the Khazars that their primitive shamanism was not only barbaric and outdated in comparison with the great monotheistic faiths, but also incapable of conferring on their leaders the spiritual and legal authority held by the rulers of the two theocratic powers. Since conversion to either religion entailed submission and loss of independence, embracing a third creed uncompromised by either of the other two must surely have seemed the most logical solution.

Although the conversion was politically motivated, it would be absurd to imagine that the Khazars blindly, overnight, embraced a religion whose dogmas were unknown to them. In fact, Koestler asserts, they had had relations with Jews and had known about their religious precepts for at least a century before the conversion, thanks to the continuous flow of refugees fleeing religious persecution from Byzantium. The persecutions, which had begun under Justinian (527-565) and had hardened under Heraclius in the 7th century, continued under Leo III in the 8th century and Leo IV in the 9th century. In fact Leo III, who ruled during the two decades preceding the conversion to Judaism, in an attempt to end at a stroke the anomaly of the tolerated status of the Jews, ordered that all his Jewish subjects be baptised. This order undoubtedly contributed to the increase in emigration to Kazaria. These exiles possessed a superior culture and were an important factor in creating an atmosphere of tolerance and cosmopolitanism. Their influence and proselytising zeal would have been felt mainly at court and among the ruling nobility. In their missionary efforts, the refugees would have combined theological arguments and messianic prophecies with astute assessments of the political advantages of adopting a "neutral" religion.

These Jews would have brought with them craftsmanship, Byzantine art, superior methods of trade and agriculture, and, in addition, the Hebrew alphabet. What kind of script the Khazars used earlier is unknown at, but both Dunlop and Poliak, to whom Koestler frequently refers, cite Ibn Nadim's *Kitab al Fihrist*, a kind of bibliographical encyclopaedia written around 987, to confirm that by the end of the 10th century the Khazars were using the Hebrew alphabet. It served a dual function: scholarly discourse (analogous to the use of Latin in Western Europe) and as a written alphabet for the various languages spoken in Kazaria (just as the Latin alphabet was used by the vernacular languages of Western Europe). From Kazaria the Hebrew script seems to have spread to neighbouring countries. Epitaphs have been found in Crimea in two graves written in Hebrew scripts, but with contents corresponding to non-Semitic languages that could not be deciphered. We hispanists understand these linguistic issues well, since in Spain there is a literature called aljamiada (aljamía, from the Arabic ayamiya: foreign language) which refers to writings in Castilian or Mozarabic with Arabic characters. Our Mozarabic jarchas are the best example of what we have been talking about, as they are considered the first lyrical manifestations in the Romance language. Written in Mozarabic, they are transcribed in Arabic or Hebrew characters and were found in Hebrew moaxajas (Stern 1948) and in Arabic moaxajas (E. García Gómez 1951).

The conversion was thus inspired by expediency and conceived as a shrewd political manoeuvre; but at the same time it brought about developments that could hardly have been foreseen by those who initiated it. The Hebrew alphabet was the beginning; but three centuries later, Koestler reports, the decline of the Khazarian state was marked by outbursts of messianic Zionism, as in the case of David El-Roi, hero of Benjamin's novel Disraeli, who led crusades of fanatical Jews to reconquer Jerusalem.[2]

The circumstances of the conversion are obscured by legend, but the main Arabic and Hebrew accounts of the event share the basic features. One of the Arabic sources cited by Koestler is al-Masudi, which confirms that during the Caliphate of Harum al-Rashid (786-809) the king of the Khazars had already converted to Judaism and that Jews from all the lands of Islam and from the land of the Greeks (Byzantium) had converged on him. It seems that an earlier book by al-Masudi describing exactly what had happened was lost; however, there are narratives based on it. Koestler reproduces that of al-Bakri, contained in an 11th-century book entitled *Book of Kingdoms and Roads*.

The reason for the conversion to Judaism of the king of the Khazars, who had previously been a pagan, is as follows. He had adopted Christianity (here Koestler points out that he knows of no other source mentioning this fact and considers this to be a version more acceptable to Muslim readers which would replace the short period of adoption of Islam imposed by

---

[2] Benjamin Disraeli (1804-1881), born into a Sephardic family, was Prime Minister of Great Britain twice for the Tory party (1867-68 and 1874-80). His terms of office were characterised by aggressiveness in foreign policy: control of the Suez Canal, colonial wars in Afghanistan and South Africa, curbing Russian expansionism by supporting the Ottoman Empire, which compensated with the surrender of Cyprus in 1878, etc... It could be said that Disraeli, like the hero of his novel, was a Zionist "avant la lettre". Regarded as the most powerful and influential Jewish leader ever to steer the destinies of a nation of gentiles, it is said that on one occasion the Queen asked him, "Are you a Jew or a Christian?" and his reply was, "Madam, I am the missing page between the Old and New Testaments". In Zionist circles, it is unambiguously asserted that he aspired to the restoration of the Jews to the Promised Land. Benjamin Disraeli wrote *The Wondrous Tale of Alroy* (1833) and *Coningsby* (1844). Alroy (El-Roi), a wonderful character for Disraeli, was in fact the leader of a messianic movement born in Kazaria in the 12th century that led a Jewish crusade to reconquer Palestine by force of arms. This Khazarian Jew, Solomon ben Duji (or Ruhi or Roy), wrote letters to Jews in nearby lands telling them that the time had come when God would bring them to Israel. In Kurdistan he assembled an army of local Jews, probably reinforced with Khazars, and managed to take the fortress of Amadie near Mosul. From there through Syria he intended to enter the Promised Land. It seems that one of his messengers travelled to Baghdad, where the rabbinical hierarchy, fearing reprisals from the authorities, adopted a hostile attitude towards the false Messiah and threatened him with an edict of expulsion. Not surprisingly, David El-Roi was eventually assassinated. In *Coningsby* Disraeli presents a picture in which the Jews rule the world behind the thrones. In a significant passage Sidonia, who represents Lionel Rothschild, tells Coningsby about a journey through several European countries in which she meets Jews who hold power in all of them. When he arrives in Spain from Russia, the person with whom he has to negotiate a loan is Mendizábal (President of the Government between 1835-36 and Minister of Finance on two occasions, linked to Freemasonry, he was the author of the law of disentailment of ecclesiastical property, which stripped the Church of its property). "A new Christian - says Sidonia - the son of a Jew from Aragon".

Marwan II discussed above). He then recognised its falsity and discussed this matter of great concern to him with a high official, who said to him: "O king, those who possess the holy scriptures form three groups. Gather them together and ask them to inform you each of their creed. Then follow the one who is in possession of the truth". Then he sent for a bishop among the Christians. There was with the king a Jew skilled in argumentation who entered into a dispute with him. He asked the bishop, "What do you say about Moses, the son of Amran, and the Torah, which was revealed to him?" The bishop replied, "Moses is a prophet and the Torah speaks the truth." Then the Jew said to the king, "He has just admitted the truth of my creed: ask him now what he believes." So the king asked him and he answered: "I say that Jesus, the Messiah, is the son of Mary, he is the Word and he has revealed the mysteries on behalf of God". Then the Jew said to the king of the Khazars: "He preaches a doctrine that I do not know, while he accepts my propositions". The bishop was then unable to prove what he preached. So the king ordered a Muslim to be brought to him. They sent him a scholar, an intelligent man, skilled in argumentation. But the Jew hired someone who poisoned him on the journey and he died. In this way the Jew succeeded in winning the king to his faith and embraced Judaism.

Certainly the Arab historians, Koestler warns, had a gift for sugaring the pill. Had the Muslim scholar been able to participate in the debate, he would have fallen into the same trap as the bishop, since both would have accepted the Old Testament, while they would have been pitted against each other, one defending the Qur'an and the other the New Testament. According to him, the king's acceptance of this reasoning is symbolic: he is only willing to accept doctrines that are shared by all three - their common denominator - and refuses to engage with any of the rivals' claims that go beyond that. This is once again the principle of the uncompromising world, applied to theology. Koestler relies on John Barnell Bury, who, in his *A History of the Roman Eastern Empire*, points out that this whole conversion story implies that Jewish influence at the court of Kazaria must have been very strong even before the formal conversion, since the bishop and the Muslim scholar had to be sought out, while the Jew was already with the king.

Another modern version of the details of the conversion is given by Alfred Lilienthal, a historian and journalist of Jewish origin, a prominent anti-Zionist and friend of the Palestinian people, who was a consultant to the US delegation to the founding meeting of the UN in San Francisco. Lilienthal, in his *What Price Israel?* confirms that the name of the Kagan who converted to Judaism was Bulan, and that he was followed first by his nobles and then by his people. The correspondence between Joseph of Kazaria and the Cordovan Jew Hasdai Ibn Shaprut, prime minister of the Caliph of Spain Abd-al-Rahman III, which we shall see at length below, serves as his source for a slight variant of how the debate went. Lilienthal explains that Bulan gathered representatives of the three monotheistic faiths and had them discuss in his presence; but none of them could convince the others or the sovereign himself that their religion was the best. Bulan then decided to speak to each of them separately. To the Christian bishop he asked: "If you were not a Christian or had to stop being a Christian, which would you choose, Islam or Judaism? The bishop replied: "If I had to leave Christianity then I would choose Judaism". He then asked the Muslim the same question and he too chose Judaism. So Bulan decided to convert to the religion of the Jews.

Bulan's successor already adopted a Hebrew name and was called Obadiah. Under his reign, Judaism became very strong in Kazaria. Synagogues and schools were built to teach the Bible and the *Talmud*. Lilienthal adds that Professor H. Graez in his *History of the Jews* confirms that Obadiah made serious efforts to promote the new religion by inviting Jewish scholars to settle in his domain and rewarding them generously. He also established a fundamental law according to which it was an indispensable condition for accession to the throne to be a Jew.

The Khazara Correspondence: Hasdai Ibn Shaprut

The main Jewish source is thus the so-called Khazara Correspondence, an exchange of letters in Hebrew between Hasdai Ibn Shaprut, prime minister of the Caliph of Córdoba, and Joseph, the King of Kazaria. This epistolary exchange took place between 954-61, according to Koestler, who describes Hasdai Ibn Shaprut as perhaps the most brilliant figure of the "Golden Age" (900-1200) of the Jews in Spain.

In 929, Abd-al-Rahman III of the Umayyad dynasty founded the western Caliphate, whose capital, Córdoba, with a library of 400,000 catalogued volumes, became the glory of Spain and a centre of European culture. Hasdai, born in 910 in Córdoba into a distinguished Jewish family, first attracted the attention of Abd-al-Rahman for his practical knowledge of medicine and appointed him as his court physician. So much did he trust his judgements and opinions that Hasdai was called upon to put the state's finances in order and later to act as the Caliphate's foreign minister. Koestler considers Ibn Shaprut a true "uomo universale" centuries before the Renaissance, for among the complicated affairs of state he still found time to translate medical books into Arabic, correspond with Baghdad's most learned rabbis and act as patron to Hebrew poets and grammarians.

This enlightened and devout Jew (it has already been mentioned in the first part that he had founded the Talmudic academy in Cordoba) used his diplomatic contacts to obtain information about the Jewish communities scattered around the world and to intervene on their behalf when possible. The persecutions in the Byzantine Empire under Romanus concerned him. Ibn Shaprut used his influence to intercede on behalf of his co-religionists and apparently succeeded because the Byzantine court was interested in

Cordoba's benevolent neutrality during Byzantium's campaigns against the Muslims in the east. According to his own account, Hasdai Ibn Shaprut first heard of an independent Jewish kingdom from Persian merchants; but he doubted the veracity of the story. He subsequently asked members of a Byzantine diplomatic mission in Cordoba and they not only confirmed it, but provided him with multiple details, including the name of Joseph, then the King. He therefore decided to send couriers with a letter.

The letter contains a series of questions about the Khazar state, its people, its method of government, armed forces etc. It also includes a question about which of the twelve tribes they belonged to. This question indicates that Ibn Shaprut thought that the Khazar Jews came from Palestine, as was the case with the Spanish Jews, and that perhaps they could be one of the lost tribes. Logically, not being of Jewish descent, they did not belong to any of the tribes. In his reply to Hasdai, Joseph provides him with genealogical information, but the main issue is that of the conversion, which had occurred two hundred years earlier, and the circumstances in which it took place.

Joseph's text begins by praising his ancestor, King Bulan, a great conqueror and an intelligent man who drove out the sorcerers and idolaters from his land (Benjamin Freedman specifies that they worshipped the phallus among other forms of worship practised in Asia by pagan peoples). Subsequently, the story asserts, an angel appeared to him in a dream and exhorted him to worship the one true God, promising him in return that he would multiply his offspring, put his enemies in his hands and make his kingdom last until the end of time. All this is, of course, inspired by the story of the Covenant in Genesis and implies that the Khazars too, though not Abraham's descendants, also claimed the status of a chosen race who made their own Covenant with the God. At this point, Koestler warns with subtle insight, the story takes an unexpected turn. Bulan shows himself willing to serve the Almighty, but he glimpses a difficulty. Koestler reproduces this excerpt from the letter: "My lord knows the secret thoughts of my heart and the depth of my trust, but the people over whom I rule have a heathen mind and I do not know whether they will believe me. If I am worthy in your eyes of favour and mercy, then I beseech you to appear also to his Great Prince to persuade him to support me. The Eternal One granted Bulan's request, appeared to this Prince in a dream, and when he arose in the morning he went to the King and let him know....

Koestler comments that there is nothing in either Genesis or the Arabic conversion narratives about a great prince whose consent has to be obtained. According to him this is an unmistakable reference to the Khazarian system of dual dignity or dual kingship. The Great Prince is apparently the Bek; but it is also possible that the King was the Bek and the Prince the Kagan. On the other hand, Koestler recalls, according to Arab and

Armenian sources the leader of the Arab army that invaded Transcaucasia in 731 (a few years before the conversion) was called Bulkan.

In our humble opinion, if the thesis that the conversion was politically motivated and that it was basically a cunning manoeuvre in the face of pressure from the other two powers (Byzantium and the Caliphate) has been maintained up to this point, it is most logical to think that the decision was taken in the political sphere, therefore in the sphere of decisions of the Bek, who was in charge of the army and the management of the affairs of state. Bulan would therefore be the Kagan Bek, and the Grand Prince who had to be convinced of the appropriateness of the measure would be the Kagan, the undisputed symbol in the eyes of the people, indispensable to the Bek for the credibility and acceptance of the decision to be taken.

Ibn Shaprut's letter, extensively discussed by Koestler, begins with a Hebrew poem (piyut) containing hidden allusions or riddles. The poem extols the military victories of King Joseph and at the same time the initial letters of the verses form an acrostic in which one reads the full name of Hasdai bar Isaac bar Ezra bar Shaprut, followed by the name of Menahen ben-Sharuk. The latter was a famous poet, lexicographer and grammarian, secretary and protégé of Ibn Shaprut, who would have been entrusted with the job of drafting the epistle to the Khazar king and embellishing it with the best calligraphic ornamentation. Ben Sharuk did not miss the opportunity to immortalise himself by inserting his own name in the acrostic after that of his patron.

After the poem, compliments and other diplomatic flourishes, the letter gives a glowing account of the prosperity of Arab Spain and the excellent living conditions of the Jews under the caliph Abd-al-Rahman. The country in which they live is said to be called Sepharad in Hebrew, but the Ismailis who live there call it al-Andalus.

Hasdai Ibn Shaprut then tells King Joseph of his first efforts to contact him. He had first sent a messenger, one Isaac bar Nathan, with instructions to present himself to the Khazara court; but Isaac got only as far as Constantinople, where, although courteously treated, he was prevented from continuing his journey (here Koestler comments that this is understandable given the ambivalent attitude of the Byzantine empire towards the Jewish kingdom. No doubt Emperor Constantine was not at all interested in facilitating an alliance between Kazaria and the Caliphate of Cordoba with its Jewish prime minister). Thus, Ibn Shaprut's messenger had to return to Spain without having fulfilled his mission. However, a new opportunity soon presented itself with the arrival in Cordoba of an Eastern European embassy whose members included two Jews, Mar Saul and Maar Joseph, who offered to deliver the missive to the Khazar king. It was, however, a third person, Isaac ben Eliecer, who eventually presented the letter, according to King Joseph's reply.

The content of the epistle is extremely interesting. Hasdai asks a series of questions that demonstrate an eagerness for information on many subjects, including the rites of Sabbath observance. Here is one of the paragraphs that Koestler reproduces in his work:

"I feel an urgent need to know the truth as to whether there really exists in this world a place where harassed Israel can rule itself, where it is not subjugated by anyone. If I were to learn that this is indeed the case, I would not hesitate to abandon all honours, to resign my high office, to leave my family and travel over mountains and plains, over sea and land, until I reached the place where my lord the King rules.... And I have yet one more question, concerning whether there is any information about (a possible date) for the Final Miracle (the coming of the Messiah), which, wandering from country to country, we are all waiting for. Dishonoured and humiliated in our dispersion, we have to listen in silence to those who say: every nation has its own land, only you do not possess even a semblance of a country on this earth".

Koestler comments after the quotation: 'The beginning of the letter praises the welfare of the Jews in Spain; the end breathes the bitterness of exile, Zionist fervour, and messianic hope. But these opposing attitudes have always coexisted in the divided hearts of Jews throughout their history. The contradiction in Hasdai's letter gives it an added touch of authenticity. How far the implicit offer to enter the service of the king of Kazaria is to be taken seriously is another question which we cannot answer. Perhaps he himself could not do so.

The one who did respond with pride was King Joseph, who assured Ibn Shaprut that the kingdom of Khazaria disproved all those who said that the sceptre of Judah had fallen forever from the hands of the Jews and that there was no place on earth for their own kingdom. However, in tracing the genealogy of the Khazars, he cannot and does not claim Semitic descent for his people. He alludes to their ancestry not from Shem, but from Noah's third son Japheth, or more specifically from a grandson of Japheth, Togarma, the ancestor of all the Turkic tribes. "We have found in the family records of our fathers," Joseph boldly declares, "that Togarma had ten sons whose names are: Uigur, Dursu, Avars, Huns, Huns, Basili, Tarniakh, Kazars, Zagora, Bulgars, Sabir. We are the sons of Kazar, the seventh".

The reign of Obadiah, of which, as we have already noted, details are given in King Joseph's letter, seems to mark a turning point in the process of Judaisation of the Khazars, which occurred in several stages. The conversion of King Bulan and his followers would have been an intermediate step, a stage during which a primitive or rudimentary form of Judaism based exclusively on the Bible was embraced. The *Talmud* and all rabbinic literature and the teachings derived from it were thus dispensed with. In this respect the early Jewish Khazars would resemble the Karaites, a fundamentalist sect that arose in Persia in the 8th century, accepting no doctrine other than the Bible and ignoring the *Talmud* and rabbinic literature. These Karaites spread among Jews all over the world and abounded in the Crimea. Dunlop and other authorities assume that between the reigns of Bulan and Obadiah (ca. 740-800) some form of Karaism prevailed in the country, so that orthodox, Talmudic, rabbinic Judaism was introduced only after Obadiah's religious reforms.

Thus, the Judaisation of the Khazars was a gradual process, triggered by political expediency, which then slowly penetrated the minds of the Khazars and eventually produced messianic phenomena in the period of decline. Religious commitment survived the collapse of the Khazar state and persisted, as we shall see, in the settlements of Jewish Khazars in Russia and Poland.

Regarding Ibn Shaprut's question about news of the possible coming of the Messiah, King Joseph's letter states: "We have our eyes on the wise men of Jerusalem and Babylon, and although we live far away from Zion, we have nevertheless heard that the calculations are wrong because of the great profusion of sins, and we know nothing (of the coming of the Messiah). Only the Eternal One knows how to calculate the time that remains".

The exchange of letters between the Spanish statesman and the king of Kazaria, the so-called Khazara Correspondence, has long fascinated historians and its authenticity is today undisputed. The first mentions of the Correspondence are in the 11th and 12th centuries by Rabbi Jehuda ben Barzillai of Barcelona, who around 1100 wrote in Hebrew his *Book of Festivals*, in which there is a long reference. The first printing is found in a Hebrew pamphlet, *Kol Mebaser*, published in Constatinopla around 1577 by Isaac Abraham Akrish. Two copies belonging to two different editions are kept in the Bodleian Library. The only manuscript version containing both letters, Ibn Shaprut's and King Joseph's replica, is in the library of Christ Church in Oxford.

More Hebrew and Christian sources

Let us look at other Hebrew sources cited by Koestler that allude to the Jewish Khazars. A century after the Khazara Correspondence, another Spanish Jew, Jehuda Halevi (1085-1141), considered the greatest Hebrew poet in Spain, wrote in Arabic the book entitled *Kuzari*, (the Khazars), later translated into Hebrew. Halevi was also a Zionist avant la lettre who died on a pilgrimage to Jerusalem. *Kuzari*, written a year before his death, is a philosophical treatise which asserts that the Jewish nation is the sole mediator between God and the rest of humanity. In the end all nations will eventually convert to Judaism. The conversion of the Khazars is for Halevi a symbol, a premonition. Despite the title, rather little is said about the Khazars, but it serves as a backdrop for yet another version of the legendary conversion story: the angel, the king, the Jewish scholar and the philosophical and religious dialogues between the monarch and the representatives of the three religions.

There are, however, references indicating that Halevi had read the correspondence between Ibn Shaprut and Joseph or, if not, that he had other sources of information about the Khazars. Halevi relates that after the angel's appearance, the King revealed the secret of his dream to the first general of his army, and the latter played a decisive or major role thereafter. Here Koestler is of the opinion that this is again an obvious reference to the dual dignity between the Kagan and the Bek. Halevi also mentions stories and books of the Khazars, which recalls Joseph's allusions to "our archives" where state documents are kept. Finally, twice, in different parts of the book, Jehuda Halevi gives the date of the conversion, which would have occurred "400 years earlier", in the year 4500 according to the Jewish calendar, which brings us back to the already given date of 740.

On the idea outlined above that a Karaite sect of Jewish Khazars would have settled in the Crimea, there is the testimony of a famous German Jewish traveller, Rabbi Petachia of Regensburg, who visited eastern Europe and western Asia between 1170 and 1185. In his work *Sibub Ha'olam* (*Journey around the World*), he recounts his amazement at the primitive observances of the Jewish Khazars of northern Crimea, which he attributes to their adherence to the Karaite heresy. Another 11th century Jewish author, Japheth ibn-Ali, who also participated in the beliefs of the Karaite sect, explains that the Jewish Khazars were called mamzer (bastards), since they had become Jews without belonging to the chosen race.

Christian sources also report that the Khazars were Jews. One of them is even older than those just cited. Sometime before 864, the Westphalian monk Christian Druthmar of Aquitaine wrote *Expositio in Evangelium Mattei,* a treatise in Latin in which he reports that "there are people under heaven in regions where Christians are not found, whose name is Gog and Magog, and who are Huns; among them are some, called Gazari, who are circumcised and practise Judaism in its entirety".

Around the same time as the Westphalian monk wrote the above, a renowned Christian missionary sent by the emperor of Byzantium attempted to convert the Jewish Khazars to Christianity. This was Saint Cyril, apostle of the Slavs, who is credited with the creation of the Cyrillic alphabet. He and his elder brother, St Metodius, were entrusted with proselytising missions by Emperor Michael III. As is well known, Cyril's proselytising efforts were successful among the Slavic peoples of Eastern Europe, but not among the Khazars, to whose country he travelled via Cherson in the Crimea, where he stopped for six months to prepare his mission and learn Hebrew. He then set out on the Khazarian road (the passage between the Don and the Volga) to the capital Itil. It is known that he met with the Kagan and that the well-known theological discussions took place, which had little impact on the Jewish Khazars. Cyril, however, made a good impression on the Khagan: a few people were baptised and about 200 Christian prisoners were released as a gesture of goodwill.

The Vikings appear

Historians agree that in the second half of the 8th century, between the conversion of Bulan and the religious reforms of Obadiah, the Khazar empire reached the height of its glory. However, according to Arab sources, incidents with the Arabs recurred at the end of this century. The most serious of these occurred around 798. The Caliph ordered the governor of Armenia, a member of the powerful Barmecide family, to marry the daughter of the Kagan in order to make the northern borders more secure. The Kazarian princess was sent to him with her retinue and dowry in a luxurious cavalcade; but she and the child she had borne died in childbirth. Her couriers on her return to Kazaria hinted that she had been poisoned. The Kagan lacked time to invade Armenia and, according to Arab sources, captured about 50,000 prisoners. The incursion forced the Caliph to release thousands of criminals from prisons and give them weapons to contain the Khazars' advance.

Thus, with no further news of fighting between Arabs and Khazars, the century came to an end. Friendly relations with Byzantium and a tacit non-aggression pact with the Arabs led to decades of peace in the first half of the 9th century. During this idyllic period one event deserves mention. In 833 the Khazars sent an embassy to the Byzantine emperor, Theophilus, and asked him for good architects and workmen to build them a fortress on the banks of the Don. The emperor was very willing and sent a fleet across the Black Sea and the Sea of Azov to the mouth of the Don to sail up the river to the strategic place where the fortification was to be built. Thus was born Sarkel, the famous fortress that would eventually become a site of priceless archaeological value, providing clues and clues to the history of the Khazars. Constantine Porphyrogenitus relates the episode in some detail and from him we know that, since there were no stones available in the region, Sarkel was built with bricks hardened in specially made kilns. He does not mention, however, the fact (discovered by Soviet archaeologists) that the builders also used 6th-century marble columns recovered from some Byzantine ruin.

The potential enemies against whom, with the combined efforts of Byzantines and Khazars, this impressive fortification was built were newcomers on the international scene: the Vikings to Westerners, the Varangians to Arab chroniclers, or the Rus to Eastern European historians. While Sarkel was being erected on the banks of the Don to prevent Viking attacks from the east, the Viking branch from the west had broken into the sea lanes of Europe and conquered half of Ireland. In the following decades they colonised Iceland, conquered Normandy, repeatedly sacked Paris, raided Germany, the Rhine delta, the Gulf of Genoa, circumnavigated the

Iberian peninsula and attacked Constantinople via the Mediterranean and the Dardanelles. No wonder, then, that a special prayer was inserted into the litanies of Western Europe: "A furore Normannorum, libera nos Domine". Nor is it strange, then, that Constantinople needed its Khazar allies as a protective shield against the dragons carved on the bows of Viking ships, as it had needed them centuries before against the green banners of the Prophet. The Khazars would therefore have to withstand the onslaught of the attack and eventually, as we shall see, would see their capital in ruins.

The branch of the Vikings whom the Byzantines called Rus and the Arabs called Varangians came from eastern Sweden, while those who came to Spain and wreaked havoc in Asturias, Galicia, Lisbon, Algeciras, Murcia and ravaged the Balearic Islands came from Norway and Denmark, according to C. Sánchez Albornoz in the work cited in the first part. The word rus reports A. J. Toynbee, whose work *Constantine Porphyrogenitus and His World* is one of Koestler's sources for narrating this historical period, would come from the Swedish word "rhoder" (oarsman). The Finnish word "Ruotsi", which means Sweden in Finnish, could perhaps come from the lexeme rus. Finally, it was these Vikings, who had initially settled near Lake Ladoga, who in the 9th century subdued the Slavs of the city of Novgorod (852) and then those of Kiev (858). From Kiev in 860 they launched their first attack on Constantinople after entering the Black Sea via the Dnieper River. The earliest Russian chronicle, the *Chronicle of Nestor*, reports that the Varangians demanded tribute payments from the Slavic and Finno-Ugric tribes of central and northern present-day Russia.

With the arrival of good weather and the thaw, the Rus' convoys sailed the rivers southwards and were both trading fleets and military armies. It was impossible to know at what point the merchants became warriors. The size of these fleets was formidable. Masudi, the Arab chronicler, writes of an armada of about five hundred ships, each with a hundred men on board, which in 912-13 entered the Caspian via the Volga, on whose estuary stood Itil, the capital of Kazaria, but let us not anticipate events.

Given the formidable threat of the new invaders, Byzantines and Khazars had to tread very carefully. For a century and a half after the construction of the Sarkel fortress, trade agreements and the exchange of embassies alternated with savage wars. Gradually the Russians built permanent settlements and gradually became more and more slavic as they intermingled with their subjugated vassals. Eventually, through the efforts of St Cyril, they would adopt the faith of the Byzantine church. By the end of the 10th century, the Russians had become Russians. The first Russian princesses and nobles, Koestler notes to reinforce this thesis, the subject of several discussions among historians, bore Scandinavian names that had been Slavicised: from Hrörekr, Rurik; from Helgi, Oleg; from Ingvar-Igor; from Helga, Olga, and so on. Toynbee, in the above-mentioned work, refers to a trade treaty in 945 between the Byzantines and Prince Ingvar-Igor, which contains a list of names of the prince's companions: only three are of Slavic origin as opposed to fifty of Scandinavian origin. According to Koestler, who follows Toynbee, the Varangians gradually lost their identity as a people and their Nordic tradition faded into Russian history.

Sarkel was built just in time. It enabled the Khazars to guard the Russian flotillas on the lower reaches of the Don and also to control the passage between the Don and the Volga (the Khazar route). During the first century of their appearance on the scene, the plundering raids of the fierce Russians were mainly aimed at Byzantium, where obviously richer booty could be obtained. Meanwhile their relations with the Khazars were based on trade. Despite this, there were frictions and some clashes. However, Koestler points out that at first the Khazars were able to control the Rus trade routes to the extent that they demanded a passage tax of ten percent on goods going through their country to Byzantium or to the Arab lands.

The Khazars also exerted a certain cultural influence on these northerners, who, despite their violent and coarse manners, showed a willingness to learn from the peoples with whom they came into contact. The fact that the early rulers of Novgorod adopted the title of Kagan is indicative of the extent of this influence. Arabic and Byzantine sources confirm this. For example, Ibn Rusta reports that they had a king who was called Kagan Rus. Furthermore, Ibn Fadlan states that Kagan Rus had a general who commanded the army and represented him. This delegation of army command was unknown among the northern Germanic peoples, among whom the king had to be the first warrior. Some historians believe that the Rus imitated the Khazar system of dual dignity. This is not unlikely, considering that the Khazars were the most prosperous and culturally advanced people with whom the Russians came into contact in the early years of their conquests. This contact must have been quite intense, since there was a colony of Varangian merchants in Itil, and a community of Jewish Khazars also settled in Kiev.

Intense trade and cultural exchanges did not prevent the Russians from progressively eroding the territory of the Khazars while taking over their Slavic vassals. According to the *Chronicle of Nestor,* by 859, some 25 years after the construction of Sarkel, the tribute of the Slavic peoples was divided between the Khazars and the Varangians. The latter collected tribute from the North Slav tribes: Krivichi, Chuds, etc., while the Khazars exacted it from the Vyatichi, Severyane and especially from the Polyane of the central Kievan region, though not for long. Three years later, if one accepts the dates of the first Russian chronicle, Kiev, the key city on the Dnieper River under Khazara sovereignty, passed into Russian hands.

According to the *Chronicle of Nestor,* at this time Novgorod was ruled by the semi-legendary Prince Rurik (Hrörekr), who had under his rule the Northern Slavs, several ethnic Finnish tribes and all the Viking settlements. Two men from Rurik, Oskold and Dir, sailing on the Dnieper, saw a fortified place on a mountain that they liked. They found out that it was Kiev, a tributary of the Khazars. They settled in the city with their families and gathered many men from the north around them. They soon succeeded in ruling over their Slav neighbours, although Rurik still ruled Novgorod. Some twenty years later Rurik's son Oleg (Helgi) came down to the city, killed Oskold and Dir and annexed Kiev to his domain. Soon Kiev eclipsed Novgorod, surpassed it in importance and became the capital of the Varangians and the mother of Russian cities. The principality of Kiev became the cradle of the first Russian state.

The letter of King Joseph discussed above, written almost a century after the Rus occupation of Kiev without a fight, does not mention the city in the list of possessions. However, the influence of the Jewish Khazar communities survived both in the city and in the province of Kiev. After the final destruction of the kingdom of Kazaria, these communities were reinforced by numerous emigrants who moved westwards.

The Magyars and the Khazars

Arthur Koestler's *The Tthirteenth Tribe,* the work we have been following, not only illuminates the obscure origins of the Ashkenazi Jews, but also sheds light on the vicissitudes of another European people: the Magyars, who make up present-day Hungary. What happened to them occurs parallel to the rise to power of the Rus and affects the history of the Khazars. Before explaining the fall of the Kazaria empire, it is therefore necessary to look briefly at what Koestler, himself born into a Jewish family in Budapest in 1905, has to say about them.

The Magyars had been allies and vassals of the Khazars from the beginning. Their origin is a historical enigma that has always troubled researchers. What is known for certain is that they were related to the Finns and that their language belongs to the Finno-Ugric group. Originally, therefore, they were related neither to the Slavic peoples of the steppes nor to those of Turkic origin. They and the Finns, their distant cousins in time and space, are an ethnic curiosity that remains to this day. At an unknown date, perhaps near the beginning of the Christian era, this nomadic tribe migrated from the Urals south across the steppes and settled in the region between the Don and Kuban rivers, in the vicinity of the Sea of Azov. They were thus neighbours of the Khazars even before the Khazars came to prominence. From the mid-7th to the end of the 9th century, they were part of the Khazar empire. Koestler stresses the fact that during this period there was not a single conflict between the Magyars and the Khazars and again quotes Toynbee to clarify that the Magyars dominated the neighbouring Slavic tribes and the Khazars used them as agents to collect tribute, from which they undoubtedly profited.

The arrival of the Russians radically changed things. Around the time the Sarkel fortress was built, there was a major movement of Magyars across the Don to the west. From 830 onwards the bulk of the Magyar nation resettled in a region between the Don and the Dnieper later known as Lebedia. Toynbee argues that the decision was made in agreement with the Khazars for tactical and defensive reasons related to the construction of Sarkel.

For half a century this realignment worked quite well: it improved relations between the two peoples and culminated in two events that were to leave a lasting impression on the Hungarian nation. The first was that the Khazars gave them a king who founded the first Magyar dynasty. The second was that several Khazar tribes joined the Magyars and profoundly transformed their ethnic character. The first event is described by Constantine Porphyrogenitus in *De Administrando Imperio* (about 950) and is confirmed by the fact that the names he mentions appear independently in the first Hungarian Chronicle (11th century). Constantine tells us that before the Khazars intervened in their internal affairs, the Magyar tribes had not had a supreme king, but only tribal chiefs, of whom the most prominent was called Lebedia (hence the name of the region where they settled). On the second event, Constantine reports that there was a rebellion (apostasy) against the rulers. The insurgents were three tribes, called Kavars or Kabars, of the Khazars' own race. Some of these rebels were killed and others fled the country and settled with the Magyars.

The influence these Kabars exerted on the Magyars was considerable: not only did they teach them the Kazar language, which they shared with their own, but the Magyars also adopted, like the Rus, a modified form of the dual dignity or dual monarchy system, indicating that the Kabars exercised some de facto leadership over the Magyar tribes. There is evidence that among the dissident Kabar tribes there were Jews or adherents of Judaism. Artamanov, the Russian historian and archaeologist already cited, has suggested that the Kabar apostasy was in some way connected with, or was a reaction against, the religious reforms initiated by King Obadiah. Rabbinic law, the strict daily rules, the *Talmud* would have been too much for these warriors of the steppes. Koestler speculates by suggesting that if they professed the Jewish religion, it must have been a Judaism close to the faith of the ancient Hebrews and far removed from the rabbinic orthodoxy. He concludes that they may have been Karaites and thus considered heretics.

Cooperation between the Khazars and Magyars ended when the latter left the Eurasian steppes for good at the end of the 9th century, crossed the Carpathian Mountains and conquered the territory they occupy today. The circumstances of this migration have been the subject of controversy. According to Koestler, another actor burst onto the scene in the last decades of the 9th century, the Pechenegs. What is known of this tribe of Turkic origin, one more, is summarised by Constantine, who describes them as a barbarian tribe of insatiable greed, who for money could fight the Rus or other barbarians. They lived between the Volga and the Urals under the sovereignty of the Khazars, who often raided them to force them to pay tribute.

Towards the end of the 9th century a catastrophe befell the Pechenegs: they were driven from their territory by their eastern neighbours, the Ghuzz, another of the endless tribes of Turkic origin that from time to time moved westwards from Central Asia. The displaced Pechenegs tried to settle among the Khazars, who rejected them and forced them to continue their migration. They finally crossed the Don and invaded the territory of the Magyars, who as a result of the clash were pushed westwards into the region between the Dnieper and Sereth rivers. The Pechenegs, however, now allied with the Danube Bulgars, continued to press them, and the Magyars eventually retreated across the Carpathians to the territories that make up present-day Hungary.

In spite of everything, i.e. the integration of the Kabars and nearly sixty years of onslaught and migration, the Hungarians were able to maintain their identity and after a period of bilingualism also managed to preserve their original Finno-Ugric language despite being surrounded by Germanic and Slavic peoples. The Bulgarians, for example, who lost their original Turkish language and today speak a Slavic language, did not have the same success. Nevertheless, the influence of the Kabars continued and across the Carpathians the Khazar-Magyar connection was not entirely severed. In the 10th century the Hungarian duke Taksony invited an unspecified number of Khazars to settle in his domain. It is likely that among them there was a majority of Jewish Khazars.

From the Russians to the Russians

We can now return to the story of the Rus' rise to power where we left off: the bloodless annexation of Kiev around 862. Around the same time the Magyars were being pushed westwards by the Pechenegs and the Khazars were left without their protection on the western flank. Perhaps this explains why the Russians gained control of Kiev so easily. On the other hand, the weakening of the military power of the Khazars left the Byzantine exposed to attack by the Rus, whose ships, sailing down the Dnieper River from the newly annexed city, entered the Black Sea and attacked Constantinople. At this point in the historical events, Arthur Koestler reintroduces a commentary by Toynbee, who writes that in 860 the Russians (note that he no longer alludes to the Russians, but to the Russians), were on the verge of conquering Constantinople. Toynbee shares the thesis, along with other Russian historians, that "the attack of the Northmen's flotilla across the Black Sea was co-ordinated with a simultaneous attack by the

Viking armada from the West, which approached Constantinople via the Mediterranean and the Dardanelles".

The size of the new power that was emerging was noticed by Byzantine diplomacy. Constantinople, as the situation allowed, played a double game alternating between war, if nothing else, and appeasement in the hope that the Russians would eventually be converted to Christianity and incorporated into the fold of the Patriarch of the East. The Jewish Khazars were left in a delicate situation. For almost two hundred years relations between Byzantines and Russians thus alternated between friendly treaties and armed conflicts. After the siege of Constantinople they were at war in 907, 941, 944, 944, 969-71, clashes that ended in treaties of friendship.

For a hundred years there was no significant progress in the process of Christianisation of the Russians; but their visits to Constantinople and contacts with Byzantium would eventually bear fruit. In the early 10th century Scandinavian sailors were recruited to serve in the Byzantine fleets. The rulers of Kiev even supplied troops to the Byzantine emperor. Famous in its time was the "Varangian Guard", an elite corps of Rus and other Norse mercenaries. In the mid-10th century it was common to see the sails of the navies of the Principality of Kiev deployed on the Bosphorus. Trade was meticulously regulated, and treaties even regulated access to Constantinople for Russians through a specific gate, which no more than fifty people could pass through at any one time. To ensure that all transactions were clean and decent, black market deals were punishable by the amputation of a hand.

In 957 a significant event finally occurred: Princess Olga of Kiev, widow of Prince Igor, was baptised on the occasion of her state visit to Constantinople. There was a further setback when Olga's son Svyatoslav rejected his mother's insistent pleas and returned to paganism. Svyatoslav organised a battle-hardened fleet and launched several campaigns, including a decisive war against the Khazars and another against the Byzantines. It was not until 988, in the reign of his son Vladimir, as we shall see below, that the reigning dynasty of the Russians definitively adopted the faith of the Greek Orthodox Church. Around the same time Hungarians, Poles and Scandinavians converted to the Christianity of the Church of Rome.

The growing rapprochement between Kiev and Constantinople meant that the importance of Itil gradually declined, and the cross-cutting presence of the Khazars on the trade routes, demanding payment of ten percent on the ever-increasing flow of goods, eventually irritated both the Byzantine treasury and the Russian warrior-merchants. The policy of alliances with the Khazars was coming to an end. In 988 Vladimir occupied the Byzantine city of Cherson, the all-important port on the Crimean peninsula that had been disputed for centuries between the Khazars and the Byzantines.

The collapse of the Khazar Empire

Russian-Byzantine relations in the 9th and 10th centuries have two good sources in the *First* Russian *Chronicle* and *De Administrando Imperio*. But for the Russo-Kazar confrontation, which occurs during the same period, no such materials exist. The Itil archives, if there ever were any, do not exist, and only through Arabic sources are some episodes known. The period in question runs from 862, the date of the Russian occupation of Kiev, to 965, when Svyatoslav, Olga's son who rejected Christianity, destroyed Itil. After the loss of Kiev and the movement of the Magyars towards Hungary, the Khazars gradually lost control of the western territories and the prince of Kiev was able to address the Slavic tribes without hindrance, telling them not to pay any more money to the Khazars.

But access to the Caspian was controlled by the Khazars, since it inevitably passed through the Kazarian capital of Itil in the Volga delta. The Russians therefore had to ask permission for their flotillas to pass through and pay a ten percent customs duty. For a time there was a precarious modus vivendi. It was in 912-13 that an important incident took place, described in considerable detail by Masudi. As mentioned above, an armada of five hundred ships with one hundred people on board each, equivalent to fifty thousand men, approached Khazar territory. They sent a letter to the king of the Khazars asking for permission to sail down the Volga and enter the Sea of the Khazars (as they called the Caspian) on condition that they would hand over half of the booty they had taken at the expense of the coastal peoples. Having obtained permission, the Russians' ships spread out over the sea and attacked Khilan, Jurjan, Tabaristan, Azerbaijan.... The Russians," writes Masuki, "shed blood, killed women and children, took booty, and ravaged and burned in all directions. They even plundered the city of Ardabil, which was three days inland.

According to Masudi, when they wanted to deliver their promised share of the booty to the king of the Khazars and return north, things did not go according to plan: the arsiyah (Arab mercenaries in the Khazar army) and other Muslims living in Kazaria, after learning of the massacres and outrages committed against their brothers, asked the king to let them settle accounts with the Russians. The king could not refuse, but sent a message to the Norsemen informing them of the Muslims' determination to fight them. So the Muslims of Kazaria, joined by some Christians living in Itil, gathered an army of about 15,000 men at the Volga estuary and confronted the Russians. The fighting lasted three days. God helped the Muslims," says Masudi. The Russ were put to the sword. Some were killed and some drowned. Thirty thousand dead were counted on the banks of the river of the Khazars". Once again Koestler considers the information from the Arab source to be biased, although he admits that it gives a clear picture of the dilemma the Khazars were to face.

In 943 an even larger fleet repeated the raid, and on this occasion the Arab sources do not mention that the Khazars were to share the booty. By contrast, King Joseph's letter to Ibn Shaprut, written a few years later, states: "I guard the mouth of the river and do not allow the Rus, who come with their ships, to invade the lands of the Arabs.... I wage fierce wars with them". The campaign that marked the beginning of the collapse of Kazaria occurred in 965 and was led, as mentioned above, by Prince Svyatoslav, son of Igor and Olga. The Russian Chronicle reads as follows:

> "Svyatoslav went to the Volga, contacted the Vyatichians (a Slavic tribe inhabiting a region south of modern Moscow) and asked them to whom they paid tribute. They replied that they paid tribute for ploughing the land to the Khazars. When the Khazars heard of the approach, they went to meet their prince, the Kagan.... When the battle broke out, Svyatoslav defeated the Khazars and took their city of Biela Viezha".

Biela Viezha was the Slavic name for the famous fortress of Sarkel on the Don. The Chronicle reports that Svyatoslav also conquered Ossetians and Circassians while defeating the Bulgars on the Danube; but the Byzantines defeated him and on the way back to Kiev he was killed by a horde of Pechenegs, who: "cut off his head, made a cup of his skull, covered it with a layer of gold, and drank from it". The destruction of Sarkel in 965 marked the end of the Khazar empire, but not of the Khazar state. The control of the Slavic tribes ended, but the territorial heartland of Kazaria between the Caucasus, the Don and the Volga remained intact.

After Svyatoslav's death, civil war broke out between his sons, and the youngest, Vladimir, emerged the victor. He began as a pagan like his father, but eventually accepted baptism like his grandmother Olga. If the conversion of the Khazars to Judaism was momentous for the history of the world, so was Vladimir's baptism in 989, which was preceded by a series of diplomatic manoeuvres and theological discussions similar to those of the Khazars.

The Russian Chronicle relates that after a victory achieved against the Volga Bulgarians (remember that centuries earlier the Bulgarian nation had split in two) a treaty of friendship was signed in which the Bulgarians declared: "May peace prevail between us until the stones float and the straws sink". Vladimir then returned to Kiev and shortly afterwards the Bulgarians sent a Muslim religious mission with the intention of converting him to Islam. They described to him the delights of Paradise, where every man would enjoy seventy beautiful women, but when warned of abstinence from pork and wine, he said: "Drinking is the joy of Russians. We cannot exist without this pleasure. A Germanic delegation of practising Catholics of the Latin rite from Rome then turned up and had no better luck when they brought up the subject of fasting. Vladimir replied: "Get out of here; our fathers would not accept such a principle. The third mission was that of the

Jewish Khazars. Vladimir asked them why they no longer ruled in Jerusalem. They replied that God was angry with their ancestors and scattered them among the Gentiles because of their sins. The prince then asked them, "How can you pretend to teach others when you yourselves have been cast off and scattered by God? Do you intend for us to accept this fate as well?" At last came the fourth and last delegation sent by the Greeks from Byzantium, whose scholars accused the Muslims of eschatological filth, the Jews of having crucified Christ, and the Catholics of Rome of having modified the rites. Only after these preliminaries did they begin the exposition of their creed. In the end, however, Vladimir was unconvinced and expressed his willingness to procrastinate a little. He then sent a delegation of wise and virtuous men to various countries to observe their religious practices. In due course, this commission informed him that the Byzantine rite surpassed the ceremonies of other nations "and we did not know whether we were in heaven or on earth".

Vladimir sent messages to the emperors Basil and Constantine, who ruled jointly at the time, and asked them to give him his sister to marry her. The emperors replied: "If you are baptised, we will give her to you as a wife, you will inherit the kingdom of God and be our companion in the faith". So Vladimir accepted baptism and married the Byzantine princess Anna. A few years later the Christianity of the Greek Orthodox became not only the religion of the rulers, but also of the Russian people, and from 1037 onwards the Russian Church was ruled by the Patriarch of Constantinople. Undoubtedly, regardless of the naive accounts in the Russian Chronicle, Byzantium's assumption of the loss of the important port of Cherson was part of the price Byzantine diplomacy agreed to pay for the new alliance against the Khazars.

In discussing the importance of Svyatoslav's capture of Sarkel above, what happened to the capital of Kazaria, Itil, remains to be seen. There is some confusion about the destruction of Itil, as the sources do not agree on the explanation of the events. The Russian Chronicle mentions only the destruction of Sarkel, but not that of Itil. From various Arabic sources, however, it is known that the capital of the Khazars was sacked and devastated, although there are differences of opinion as to how and when this happened. Ibn Hawkal, the main source in Koestler's opinion, says that it was the Rus who ravaged Itil and Samandar in 965. However, another historian, J. Marquart, suggests that Itil was not ravaged by Svyatoslav, who would only have gone as far as Sarkel, but by another wave of Viking refreshment. To complicate matters further, other sources point to a tribe of Turkic origin, the Pechenegs, a horde of whom would have descended on the capital in that critical year for the Khazars.

Although the sources agree that Itil was razed to the ground in 965, it appears from later writings that the city was more or less rebuilt. But Kazaria's weakness was already evident and in 1016 the Khazars were again defeated in a joint Byzantine-Russian campaign. During the 11th century, despite the decline that was to lead to their ultimate collapse, the Khazars continued to appear on the scene in one form or another. The Russian Chronicle, for example, mentions in a terse entry that in 1079 they seized the Russian prince Oleg and took him to Constantinople. Koestler speculates on the intrigues latent in this action, but anecdotes and digressions are no longer of interest.

The sources that speak of the Khazars in the 12th century are increasingly scarce, indicating that they had less and less influence on international events. On the other hand, new actors continued to emerge. The Seljuks, a tribe of Turkic origin settled near the Aral Sea and who embraced Islam in the 10th century, were the main protagonists east and south of Kazaria. During the 11th century they had built up an empire with its capital in Tehran, occupied Jerusalem, pushed into Anatolia and even threatened Constantinople. They were to be the true founders of the Muslim Turkey that the Ottoman Turks were to consolidate centuries later. Their relationship with the Khazars had some interesting episodes, but they are not directly relevant to our history and we cannot dwell on them. During the 12th century, the Seljuk empire was dismembered and they would end up as vassals of the Mongols.

Of the Mongols, it should be briefly noted that the empire established by Genghis Kahn in 1206 eventually stretched from Hungary to China and was, at the time of its greatest expansion, one of the largest in human history. According to some sources it encompassed almost half of the world's population at the time,. In its unstoppable westward advance, all the territories of the kingdom of Kazaria came under its rule in the 1250s. It is therefore not surprising that the already scarce sources of information about the Khazars dried up almost completely in the 13th century.

The last known reference to them dates from 1245-47. At this date Pope Innocent IV sent a mission to Batu Khan, the grandson of Genghis Khan, who ruled the western part of the Mongol empire, in order to explore the possibilities of understanding with the new world power. The leader of this mission, Koestler reports, was a sixty-year-old Franciscan, John of Plano Carpini, a contemporary and disciple of St Francis of Assisi, an experienced traveller and seasoned diplomat who had held many positions in the ecclesiastical hierarchy. The mission started on Easter 1245 from Cologne and arrived a year later at the capital of Batu Khan's horde on the Volga estuary. The name of the city was Sarai Batu, i.e. ancient Itil. Thus the Mongols established the centre of their empire on Khazar territory. On his return to Europe, Carpini wrote the *Historia Mongolorum,* which contains a list of the peoples who inhabited the regions he visited. In it he mentions various peoples of the North Caucasus, and along with the Alans and Circassians he mentions the Khazars who professed the Jewish religion. This is the last time they are mentioned before the curtain comes down for good.

Migration and the ghetto mentality

Just as the Semitic Jews had already begun their diaspora before the destruction of Jerusalem, so too, before the Mongol cataclysm, the Jewish Khazars had begun to move to the lands of the unsubdued Slavic peoples of the West. There they established the great Jewish centres of Eastern Europe, which were to become the largest and most culturally dominant part of world Jewry in the future. Their religion, based as we have seen on exclusivism, fostered the tendency to stick together to establish their communities with their own places of prayer, their own schools, their own neighbourhoods; that is, the Jewish quarters or ghettos, which they themselves, of their own free will, imposed on themselves in the countries or cities where they settled. Both the Semitic Jews and the Jewish Khazars thus shared the ghetto mentality, which both groups reinforced with messianic hopes and the pride of considering themselves the chosen race, even though the latter did not come from Shem, as we have seen, but from Japheth. The meanings of some dictionaries that define the ghetto as a neighbourhood in which the Jews were forced to live are therefore mistaken.

Arthur Koestler follows in the footsteps of the first Jewish Khazars, his own ancestors, in his native Hungary. As he reports, the Kabars, the Kazar tribes who migrated with the Magyars, and who, it will be recalled, were invited by Duke Taksony to settle in his domain in the 10th century, played an important role in Hungary's earliest history. John Cinnamus, a Byzantine chronicler, two centuries later writes of troops observing Jewish Law fighting in 1154 against the Hungarian army in Dalmatia. Koestler asserts that there would be very few "real Jews" from Palestine living in Hungary, and he has no doubt that it was the Khazars-Kabars who were at the centre of the fighting. The fact that the Hungarian Magna Carta of 1222, promulgated by Endre II (Andrew), forbade Jews to act as minters of coin, tax collectors and controllers of the royal salt monopoly, indicates that before the edict Jewish Khazars held these and perhaps even more influential positions.

The Khazar origin of the Jewish population of Hungary during the Middle Ages is relatively well documented and it may seem that Hungary constitutes a special case in view of the Magyar-Kazar connection; however, this is not the case. In the 12th century there are already established settlements and colonies of Khazars in various parts of the Ukraine and in southern Russia. It has already been mentioned that a community of Jewish Khazars flourished in Kiev. There are many place names in Ukraine and Poland derived from "kazar" or "zhid" (Jewish): Zydovo, Kozarzewek, Kozara, Kozarzov, Zhydowska Vola, Zydaticze, etc. These places were probably, in Koestler's opinion, temporary villages or camps of communities of Jewish Khazars on their long journey to the west. Similar place names are also found in the Carpathian Mountains and in the eastern provinces of

Austria. While the main route of the Khazar exodus led west, some groups were left behind, especially in the Crimea and the Caucasus, where they formed Jewish enclaves that remain today. But the main migration flow of the Khazars settled in Poland and Lithuania, as noted in the first part of this chapter.

On this issue of the Khazar migration to Poland, Koestler provides important information that allows us to consolidate some earlier assessments and assertions made about Poland as the centre of Judaism after the expulsion of the Jews from Spain in 1492. In *The Thirteenth Tribe* he explains that around 962 several Slavic tribes formed an alliance led by the strongest, the Polans, which was to become the nucleus of the Polish state. The importance of the Polans thus began at the same time that the power of the Khazars declined with the destruction of Sarkel in 965. It is significant, Koestler remarks, that the Jews played an important role in one of the early legends that allude to the founding of the Polish kingdom. It seems that when the coalition tribes wanted to elect a king, they chose a Jew named Abraham Prokownik (Koestler's source is Professor A. N. Poliak), who must have been a wealthy Khazar merchant. Prokownik renounced the crown in favour of a native peasant named Piast, who thus became the founder of the historic Piast dynasty, which ruled Poland from 962 to about 1370.

Whether the legend is true or not, whether Prokownik existed or not, is relatively unimportant, for it is certain that the Jewish immigrants from Kazaria were well received for their contributions to the country's economy and government administration. Coins minted in the 12th and 13th centuries bore inscriptions in the Polish language written in Hebrew script. Under the Piast dynasty the Poles and their Baltic neighbours, the Lithuanians, who by a series of treaties became part of the Polish kingdom from 1386, rapidly expanded their territory and needed immigrants to colonise the territories and develop the towns. They first encouraged German farmers, burghers and craftsmen, and then emigrants from the Mongol-occupied territories, among whom the Khazars abounded (Poland and Hungary were only briefly invaded by the Mongols in 1241-42, but were not occupied).

From the beginning, Poland turned westward and adopted Catholicism, but this did not prevent the granting of all kinds of privileges to the Jewish Khazars. In the Charter promulgated by Boleslav the Pious in 1264 and confirmed by Casimir the Great in 1334, the Jews were allowed the right to maintain their own synagogues, schools and courts, their own estates, and to engage in whatever commercial activities they wished. Under the reign of Stephen Bathory (1575-86) they were granted their own parliament, which met twice a year and had the power to levy tribute on their own co-religionists. Undoubtedly, in Koestler's opinion, Kazar Jewry had entered a new chapter in its history.

That the Church of Rome was aware of the power of the Jews in Poland is shown by a papal document, a brief from the second half of the

13th century, probably by Pope Clement IV, addressed to an unnamed Polish prince. It states that the ecclesiastical authorities in Rome are aware of the existence of numerous synagogues in several Polish cities, namely no less than five in one city. The Pope deplores the fact that these synagogues are taller than the churches, more majestic and better decorated, with ceilings covered with painted plaques, which makes the adjacent Catholic churches look poor by comparison. The complaints contained in the papal brief are later endorsed by a decision of the papal legate, Cardinal Guido, dated 1267, stipulating that Jews should not be allowed more than one synagogue per town. From these documents contemporary to the Mongol conquest of Kazaria, it is certain that already in the 13th century, the presence of Khazar Jews was very numerous in Poland.

It is known that in the 17th century the number of Jews in the Polish-Lithuanian kingdom exceeded half a million. According to the article "Statistics" in the *Jewish Encyclopaedia,* in the 16th century the Jewish population worldwide amounted to one million people, which indicates, according to Koestler, who quotes Poliak and Kutschera[3], that during the Middle Ages most of the non-Sephardic Jews who professed Judaism were Khazars. A substantial part of this majority went to Poland, Lithuania, Hungary and the Balkans, where they founded the community of Eastern Jews that was to become the majority of world Jewry. There is every reason to attribute leadership to the Jewish community in Poland, which was of Khazar origin, and not to the immigrants who came from the West after the expulsion from Spain, as we shall see below.

The Sephardim in Western Europe

The transformation of the Khazar Jews into Polish Jews was not a brutal break with their past. It was a gradual process of change that allowed them to preserve ways of life that corroborate their origin; ways of life found nowhere else in the world Diaspora. We refer to the small Jewish towns: "ayarah" in Hebrew, "shtetl" in Yiddish, "miastecko" in Polish. All three names are diminutives; however, in some cases they were quite large towns.

---

[3] Hugo Baron de Kutschera (1847-1910) was one of the first to propose the theory of the Khazar origin of Eastern Jews. A career diplomat, he studied at the Oriental Academy in Vienna, where he became an expert linguist who became fluent in Turkish, Arabic, Persian and other Eastern languages. After serving as an attaché at the Austro-Hungarian embassy in Constantinople, he became director of the administration in Sarajevo. After retiring in 1909, he devoted his last days to what had been his lifelong preoccupation: the connection between European Jews and the Khazars. As a young man he had been impressed by the contrast between Sephardic Jews and Ashkenazi Jews in Turkey and the Balkans. His study of the ancient sources on the history of the Khazars led him to the conviction that they offered at least a partial answer to the problem. His Study of the History of the Khazars was published posthumously and is rarely mentioned by historians.

The shtetl is not to be confused with the ghetto, which, as mentioned above, was a neighbourhood within the city of the gentiles in which Jews were forced to live in order to avoid being contaminated by beliefs and ways of life they repudiated. The shtetl, which exists only in Poland-Lithuania and nowhere else in the world, was a village with an exclusively Jewish population. Its origins date back to the 13th century and it is certainly the connection between the Khazar market towns and the Jewish colonies in Poland. The economic and social functions of these semi-urban, semi-rural agglomerations were similar in Kazaria and in Poland, i.e. they constituted a network of commercial centres supplying the needs of the large towns and the countryside.

According to Poliak, these towns arose as a consequence of the general migration that resulted from the Mongol conquest, when the Slavic towns and the Khazar shtetl were wandering westward. The pioneers of these settlements were probably wealthy Khazar merchants who were constantly travelling to Hungary via the trade routes of Poland, which was thus becoming a transit territory between the two Jewish communities. Poliak argues that in this way the Khazar shtetl was transplanted and became the Polish shtetl, which gradually abandoned agriculture.

The disappearance of the Kazara nation from its historical habitat and the simultaneous appearance of large concentrations of Jews in adjacent regions of the northwest are two connected facts. Historians agree that immigration from Kazaria contributed to the increase in the number of Jews in Poland. The dispute is whether these Khazarian Jews actually constituted the bulk of the settlements. To answer this question, Koestler examines the possibilities and size of a possible migration of "real Jews" from Western Europe to Poland.

Towards the end of the first millennium, the Jewish communities of Western Europe resided in France and in the vicinity of the Rhine (the Jews of Spain should not be taken into account for this historical research, since they were living their "Golden Age" in Sepharad at that time and did not participate in any migratory movement until 1492). Some of these communities had probably been established in Roman times, since between the destruction of Jerusalem and the fall of Rome, Jews had settled in many of the great cities of the Empire. These communities were later reinforced by new immigrants from Italy and North Africa. Jewish communities are recorded from the 9th century onwards throughout France, from Normandy to Provence and the Mediterranean. One group even crossed the English Channel in the wake of the Norman invasion, invited by William the Conqueror, who needed their capital and initiative. Their history has been summarised by A. W. Baron:

> "They were subsequently converted into a class of royal usurers whose main function was to provide credit for political and economic

enterprises. After accumulating great wealth at high interest rates, these moneylenders were obliged to repay it in one way or another for the benefit of the royal treasury. The prolonged well-being of many Jewish families, the splendour of their residences and their influence in public affairs blinded even experienced observers, who failed to see the danger hidden in the growing resentment of debtors of all classes and in the exclusive reliance of the royal household on their protection.... Dissatisfaction grew and culminated in outbreaks of violence in 1189-90 that foreshadowed the final tragedy: the expulsion of 1290. The meteoric rise and even more rapid decline of English Jewry in the brief space of just over two centuries (1066-1290) highlighted the fundamental factors that shaped the destinies of western Jewry in the crucial first part of the second millennium".

The main lesson Koestler draws from the events in England is that the social and economic influence of the Jews was totally disproportionate to their small demographic weight. There were apparently no more than 2500 Jews in England at the time of their expulsion, and this tiny community in medieval England played a leading role in the country's economy. What happened encapsulated the events that were to come later when Jews in France and Germany faced the same situation. Cecil Roth writes that trade in western Europe was largely in the hands of Jews, including the slave trade, and in the Carolingian cartularies the terms Jew and merchant were interchangeable. The boom period in France ended in 1306 when Philip the Fair banished the Jews from his kingdom. Some returned, but there were further expulsions and by the end of the century the Jewish community in France was extinct. The modern Jewish community in France was founded by exiles from Spain fleeing the Inquisition in the 16th and 17th centuries.

There are incomplete references to the history of the Jews in Germany. The *Germanica judaica* is one of the works that provides historical references to certain communities in 1238. Thanks to it, we know the territorial distribution of these groups of German Jews during the period when the immigration of Khazar Jews to Poland was at its peak. It is known that in the 10th, 11th and 12th centuries there were Jews in Spira, Worms, Trèves, Metz, Strasbourg, Cologne, i.e. in a narrow strip in Alsace and along the Rhine. Benjamin of Tudela visited these cities in the 12th century and wrote that there were many educated and wealthy Israelites in them. Koestler wonders how many there were and ends up answering that there were actually very few.

Koestler claims that at the end of the 11th century the Jews of the communities in Germany, as a consequence of the First Crusade (1096), were persecuted and killed en masse by the mob, whose outbursts of hysteria were uncontrollable. He cites a Hebrew source he considers reliable, the chronicler Solomon Bar Simon, to highlight the case of the Jews of Mainz, who, faced with the alternative of baptism or death at the hands of the mobs, decided to commit collective suicide, setting an example to other groups. Hebrew sources give the figure of 800 dead between massacres and suicides in Worms and between 900 and 1200 in Mainz, although no doubt many preferred baptism. Again, it would be necessary to know how many there were, but the sources do not mention the number of survivors, although A. W. Baron estimates them to be in the hundreds. Nor can we be sure, Koestler admits, that the number of martyrs is not exaggerated.

In any case, it seems clear that before the First Crusade the number of Jews in the above-mentioned areas of Germany was small. There were no Jewish communities in central and northern Germany, nor would there be for a long time. Koestler completely rejects the traditional thesis of many Jewish historians that the Crusade of 1096 resulted in a mass migration of German Jews to Poland. He considers this to be simply a legend or a hypothesis invented ad hoc, since little or nothing was known about the history of the Khazars and there was no other possible way to explain the impressive concentration of Jews in Eastern Europe. Moreover, Koestler concludes, "there is no contemporary source of a migration, large or small, from the Rhine to eastern Germany, let alone to distant Poland".

In this regard, a group of Jewish geneticists recently came to the aid of traditional historians. Harry Oster of Yeshiva University published in 2012 the book *Legacy: A Genetic History of the Jewish People*, which maintains the thesis that Jews belong to a single ethnic group. These scientists, committed to the official historiography, insisted on maintaining the theory that the Jews of Eastern Europe came from the Rhine area. They received a strong response from a young Jewish researcher at Johns Hopkins University, Eran Elhaik, who specialises in molecular genetics, who called the assertions of Oster and company "nonsense". On 4 December 2012, Elhaik published *The Missing Link of Jewish European Ancestry: Contrasting The Rhineland and the Khazarian Hypotheses*, a research paper of some forty pages published in the online journal *Genome Biology and Evolution*, in which he provided compelling evidence for the Khazarian provenance of Ashkenazi Jews. Elhaik's article was commented on in December 2012 by Shlomo Sand, professor of history at Tel Aviv University. Author of the book *The Invention of the Jewish People*, Sand welcomed Elhaik's scientific contribution as confirming his thesis. "It is obvious to me," said Sand, "that some people, historians and even scientists, close their eyes to the truth. Sometimes saying the Jews were a race was anti-Semitic, now saying they are not a race is anti-Semitic. It is absurd how history plays with us". In his article, Elhaik argues that the conversion of the Khazars to Judaism in the eighth century must necessarily have been widespread, as the eight million Jews in Europe in the early twentieth century cannot be explained by the small populations of the Middle Ages.

Simon Dubnov, one of the historians of the old school, goes so far as to say that the first Crusade moved masses of Christians to East Asia and at the same time masses of Jews to Eastern Europe. However, he later admits that there is no information about this migration movement, which is so important for Jewish history, and it is clear that his assertions are mere speculation. In contrast, there is knowledge of what the harassed Jewish communities did during the successive crusades that followed the 1096 crusade. Those who managed to escape the angry mobs sought refuge during periods of emergency in the fortified castle of the bishop, who in theory was responsible for their protection. Once the crusading hordes had passed, the survivors invariably returned to their ransacked homes to start afresh. This pattern of behaviour is repeatedly documented in various chronicles: in Trèves, in Metz and in many other places. During the time of the Crusades it became almost routine. When the agitation for a new crusade began, many Jews from Mainz, Worms, Spira, Strasbourg, Würzburg and other cities escaped to neighbouring castles, leaving their possessions in the custody of gentiles considered to be friends. One of the main sources cited by Koestler is the *Book of Remembrance* of Ephraim Bar Jacob, who at the age of thirteen had been among the refugees from Cologne who took refuge in the protection of Wolkenburg Castle. Solomon Bar Simon reports that during the Second Crusade the survivors of Mainz found refuge in Spira and then returned to their city and built a new synagogue. This is what the chronicles repeat over and over again, and not a single word is found about groups migrating to eastern Germany, which remained without a Jewish population for several centuries.

The 13th century was a period of partial recovery, and Jews are first recorded in regions adjacent to the Rhine: the Palatinate (1225), Freiburg (1230), Ulm (1243), Heildelberg (1255), etc... But at the beginning of the 14th century things became more complicated in France, as mentioned above, with the expulsion decreed by Philip le Bel (Philip the Fair). Refugees migrated to other French regions such as Provence, Burgundy, Aquitaine, which were outside the King's domain; but there is no historical record to conclude that Germany saw an increase in the number of Jews with co-religionists from France. Of course no historian has ever suggested the possibility that French Jews emigrated to Poland via Germany on this or any other occasion.

The worst catastrophe of the 14th century was the Black Death, which between 1348 and 1350 killed a third of Europe's population and in some regions two-thirds. Jews, who had been accused of ritual sacrifices of Christian children, were blamed for poisoning wells to spread the Black Death. The rumour spread and the consequence was the burning of Jews across Europe. The decimated population of western Europe did not reach its pre-plague demographic level until the 16th century. As for the Jewish population, which had suffered the onslaught of rats and men, only a fraction survived. According to Kutschera, who cites contemporary historians, there were virtually no Jews left in Germany when the epidemic subsided. He notes that they never prospered there, where they were never able to establish significant communities, and wonders how in such circumstances one can sustain the thesis that they were able to establish densely populated colonies in Poland.

Koestler considers that after the Crusades and the Black Death, the number of Jews in Western Europe was negligible. Only in Spain and Portugal was there a large Jewish population. It was therefore the Sephardim who, after being expelled from the Peninsula, founded the modern communities in France, Holland and England in the 16th and 17th centuries. The traditional idea of an exodus to Poland via Germany is historically untenable.

Before proclaiming that one hundred percent of the Jews of the East are of Khazar origin, there remains one last group of Jews in Europe to be examined: those who in the late Middle Ages were located in Vienna, in Prague, in the Balkans, in the Carinthian Alps and in the mountains of Stiria. Koestler wonders where they came from. "Certainly not from the West" is his answer. Koestler admits that among the Jewish immigrants to Austria there was certainly a component of genuine Semitic Jews from Italy, a country which, like Kazaria, had received its share of Hebrew immigrants from Byzantium. However, there is no documentary evidence of such migration and it must therefore be assumed to have been insignificant. On the contrary, there is ample evidence and proof of a migration in the opposite direction, i.e. of Jews entering Italy at the end of the 15th century as a result of their expulsion from the Alpine provinces. The outlines of the migratory process are clearly discernible to Koestler, for whom the Alpine settlements were most probably offshoots of the general migration of the Khazars to Poland that spread over several centuries and followed different routes: through the Ukraine, the Slavic regions, northern Hungary and perhaps also the Balkans. The *Jewish Encyclopaedia* reports an invasion of Romania by armed Jews.

There is also a legend about the Jews of Austria, launched by Christian chroniclers during the Middle Ages, but repeated in all seriousness by other historians at the beginning of the 18th century. According to this legend, the Austrian provinces were ruled by a succession of Jewish princes. The *Austrian Chronicle*, compiled by a Viennese scribe in the reign of Albert III (1350-95), contains a list of no less than twenty names, some of which phonetically denote an Ural-Altaic origin, even mentioning the extent of the reign and the site of their burial. The legend is repeated with some variations by Henricus Gundelfingus in 1474 and by several others, the last of whom is Anselmus Schram in his *Flores Chronicorum Austriae* of 1702.

The origin of the legend is clear to Koestler, who recalls that for more than half a century, until 955, a part of Austria was under the rule of the Magyars, who had arrived in their new country in 896 in company of the tribes of Khazars-Kabars, who, as has been seen, had much influence on the

Magyar nation. The Hungarians at that time had not yet converted to Christianity, which happened a century later, and the only monotheistic religion they knew was Khazar Judaism. Let us recall that the Byzantine chronicler John Cinnamus mentions the clash of Jewish troops with the Hungarian army. It all seems to fit together.

Contribution of linguistics: Yiddish lexical items

Further evidence against the theory of the Western origin of Eastern European Jewry is provided by the structure of Yiddish, the popular language of millions of Jews still in use today among some traditionalist minorities in the United States and Russia. Yiddish is a curious amalgam of Hebrew, medieval German, Slavic and other characters, written in Hebrew scripts. Now on its way to extinction, it has been the subject of much study in the United States and Israel, but until the 20th century it was considered by Western linguists to be a bizarre jargon. Except for a few newspaper articles, it did not receive much attention until 1924, when M. Mieses published the first serious scientific study, *Die Jiddische Sprache*, a historical grammar.

At first sight, the predominance of German borrowings in Yiddish seems to contradict Koestler's thesis about the origin of Eastern European Jews. The first thing Koestler investigates is which of the German dialects entered the Yiddish lexicon, and for this he turns to the aforementioned M. Mieses, who was the first to pay attention to this question. On the basis of the study of vocabulary, phonetics and syntax in comparison with the main German dialects in the Middle Ages, Mieses concludes that there are no linguistic elements from the parts of Germany bordering France, nor are there any from the central regions of the Frankfurt area, and he therefore rules out any influence on Yiddish from the West German regions. He then writes: "Could it be that the generally accepted theory, according to which German Jews at some time in the past migrated across the Rhine to the east, is wrong? The history of the German Jews, of Ashkenazi Jewry, needs to be revised. Errors in history are often rectified by linguistic research. The conventional view of the migration of Ashkenazi Jews from France and Germany belongs to the category of historical errors that need to be revised".

This is precisely the mistake made by Joan Ferrer, professor at the University of Girona, who in a work entitled *History of the Yiddish language* tries to explain its origin on the basis of the traditional theory of the emigration of Jews from Western Europe, many of whom must have spoken Romance languages. It is likely that this professor does not even know about the Khazarian Jews, as he does not even mention them in his study,.

Mieses confirms that the German component in Yiddish comes from the East German regions adjacent to the East European Slavic belt, which is further evidence against the Western origin of Polish Jewry and East European Jewry in general. This does not, however, explain how an East

German dialect combined with Slavic elements and Hebrew became the language of the Khazarian Jewry.

The evolution of Yiddish was a long and complex process that presumably began before the 15th century. For a long time it remained an oral language, a kind of lingua franca, which only appeared in writing in the 19th century. There was thus no grammar and it was also left to individuals to introduce foreign words as they wished. There were no rules on pronunciation or spelling. The rules laid down by the *Jüdische Volks-Bibliothek* illustrate the spelling chaos: (1) Write the way you speak. (2) Write in a way that Polish and Lithuanian Jews can understand you. (3) Write words that sound the same and have different meanings differently.

In this way Yiddish developed through the centuries unhindered, eagerly absorbing words, idioms, syntagmatic or sentence constructions from the social environments that surrounded it. Socially and culturally, the dominant element around medieval Poland was the Germans. They alone among the immigrant populations were more influential than the Jews from an intellectual and economic point of view. Kutschera claims that no less than four million Germans moved to Poland and constituted an urban middle class such as the country had never had before. Not only the educated bourgeoisie, but also the clergy was predominantly German, which was a natural consequence of the adoption of Catholicism and Poland's westward tilt. The first Polish university was founded in 1364 in Kraków, then a predominantly German city (Koestler recalls that a century later Nicolaus Copernicus studied there, and Poles and Germans claim him as one of their own). Although the German settlers were initially regarded with suspicion, they soon gained a firm foothold and introduced the German education system to Poland. The Poles learned to appreciate the advantages of the superior culture introduced by these immigrants and imitated their ways. The aristocracy became fond of German customs and found everything that came from Germany beautiful and pleasant.

It is therefore understandable why the Khazarian immigrants who settled in the country had to learn German if they wanted to prosper. Those who had dealings with the local population certainly had to learn a little Polish, Ukrainian, Lithuanian or Slovenian. German, however, was of prime necessity for any contact in the cities. To all this must be added the synagogue and the study of the Torah in Hebrew. It is easy to visualise, writes Koestler, a craftsman in a Shtetl or a wood merchant trying to speak German with his customers, Polish with his neighbours and then at home mixing both languages with a little Hebrew. In this way an intimate language was formed. How this hodgepodge managed to become a standardised common code is a question for linguists.

Koestler recalls that the descendants of the twelve tribes are an example of linguistic adaptability. First they spoke Hebrew. In the Babylonian exile, Chaldean. At the time of Jesus, Aramaic. In Alexandria,

Greek. In Spain, Arabic; but later Ladino, which is a mixture of Spanish and Hebrew written with Hebrew spellings: for Sephardic Jews Ladino would be the equivalent of Yiddish. The Khazars were not descendants of the twelve tribes, but, as we have seen, they shared with their co-religionists the facility to change languages as they saw fit.

Today, the Santillana publishing house unwisely includes Yiddish among the Germanic languages in its high school textbooks. Paul Wexler of Tel Aviv University, who has published several studies (the most important in 1992 and 2002), which Arthur Koestler was not aware of, categorically denies that Yiddish is a dialect of German. This is neither the place nor the time to delve into linguistic issues; but let us look very briefly at some of his conclusions. According to Wexler, Yiddish can only come from the Turkic-Iranian-speaking Khazars, since the lexicon and grammar of Yiddish reveal connections with Turkic-Iranian languages that have not been assessed. This linguist claims that Yiddish began as a Slavic language with the unusual feature of having a predominantly German lexicon. Interestingly, the only major component of Yiddish that did not develop significant innovations in its formal or semantic features is the Slavic component, suggesting that Yiddish was a Slavic language that exploited only its two non-Slavic components: German and Hebrew (we have seen with Koestler how and why this was the case). Wexler argues that several studies of Yiddish morphosyntax and phonology have demonstrated the similarities between Yiddish and Slavic grammars and claims that the consideration of German as the original component of Yiddish and the Slavic component as non-original is erroneous.

Although he is not a linguist, Benjamin Freedman warns in *Facts are facts* that, for obvious reasons, many people are keen for Yiddish to be believed to be a German dialect and asks: "If Yiddish is a German dialect acquired from the Germans, then what language did the Khazars speak for almost a thousand years? The Khazars must have spoken some language when they penetrated Eastern Europe. What was this language? When did they reject it? How could the entire Khazar population suddenly discard one language and adopt another? The idea is too absurd for to discuss. Yiddish is the modern name for the ancient mother tongue of the Khazars with the addition of German, Slavic and Baltic languages".

Having outlined the contribution of linguistics to the subject, it only remains to comment in a few lines on the last phase of the migration of the Khazarian Jews, whose communities, whether in the ghettos or in the shtetls, had to face problems of overpopulation, as they had to absorb new immigrants fleeing from the Cossacks in the Ukrainian cities. Deteriorating living conditions led to a new wave of mass emigration to Hungary, Bohemia, Germany and Romania, where the Jews who had survived the Black Death were scattered in small groups. Thus the great westward journey that was to continue for another three centuries was resumed and became the main source for the remaining populations of Semitic Jews in Europe, America and Palestine.

The facts are clear, and modern Austrian, Israeli and Polish historians agree that most of world Jewry is not of Palestinian origin, but of Caucasian origin. The main stream of Jewish migration does not flow from the Mediterranean through France and Germany to the east of the continent and then back again. The stream moves without reversal in a westerly direction, from the Caucasus through the Ukraine to Poland and from there to Central Europe and America. The eastward journey (Palestine) of the Zionists in the 20th century is a subject that will be dealt with separately. These "Jews" of Turko-Mongolian origin have ended up completely imposing their theses on the Sephardim, who during the 19th century were mostly in favour of emancipation and progressive assimilation into the societies in which they resided.

CHAPTER II

BANKERS AND REVOLUTIONS (1)

PART 1
CROMWELL, AGENT OF THE
AMSTERDAM JEWISH BANKERS

Having explained the racial origins of the Zionists, we will now see how an elite of Sephardic and Ashkenazi Jews, united in their desire to subjugate and dominate the world, have formed a hidden power that has been decisive in all historical events. This power now acts in the open, as it considers its global hegemony irreversible.

The following pages will explore how this hidden force, of which nothing is said in the history books used in high schools and universities, has become an omnipotent power, an absolute tyranny, exercised through its economic power, the media and the manipulated teaching of all academic disciplines that create opinion, especially history, which has been completely misrepresented. As George Orwell wrote, "He who controls the past controls the future. He who controls the present controls the past". The historical review undertaken in this book actually begins with the Rothschilds' emergence on the stage of European politics and finance; however, to see how an elite of Talmudic Jews had long been conditioning and programming historical events according to their interests, we will see briefly how in the 17th century Cromwell seized power in England.

To most Europeans Cromwell is best known for beheading King Charles I and for repealing in 1655 the edict of expulsion of the Jews[4], which

---

[4] The Jews had come to England in 1066 and installed William I on the throne, who to reward their support allowed and protected the practice of usury, which had disastrous consequences for the people, since within two generations a quarter of English land was in the hands of Jewish usurers. King Offa, one of the seven kings of the Anglo-Saxon heptarchy, had banned usury in 787. The laws against usury had subsequently been entrenched by King Alfred the Great (865-99), who ordered the property of usurers to be confiscated. In 1050 Edward the Confessor decreed not only the seizure of property, but also that the usurer should be declared a bandit and banished for life. After the expulsion of the 16,000 Jews from England by Edward I in 1290, further measures were taken against usury: in 1364 Edward III granted the City of London an "Ordinatio contra Usurarios". A new law was passed in 1390.

had been promulgated by Edward I in 1290 (they had been expelled on paper, but had never actually left England and their 'readmission' required legal formalism). More enlightened students may also know that Cromwell ordered the massacre of 40,000 Irish Catholics; but let us see who was behind it.

Taking advantage of a conveniently prepared disagreement between the king and Parliament, the plan was hatched in Holland that was to put an end years later to the Stuart dynasty and the establishment of the Dutch Orange. Rabbi Manasseh Ben Israel, one of the money barons then based in Amsterdam, contacted Oliver Cromwell through his agents and offered him huge sums of money if he dared to lead a conspiracy to overthrow the king. As soon as Cromwell agreed to the plan, Manasseh Ben Israel and other Jewish moneylenders from Germany and France financed Cromwell. According to John Buchan, author of *Oliver Cromwell*, the Amsterdam Jews controlled the trade in Spain, Portugal and much of the Levant, as well as dominating the flow of gold bullion.

In his *Pawns in the Game*, William Guy Carr explains that the Portuguese Jew Antonio Fernández Carvajal, known as "The Great Jew", became Cromwell's military contractor. It was he who reorganised the parliamentarians opposed to the king (mostly Puritans and Presbyterians). Thanks to his money, he turned them into a modern army, with the best equipment and the best weapons. Once the conspiracy was set in motion, hundreds of trained revolutionaries went underground to England and camouflaged themselves in the Jewish underground, whose top leader was the Portuguese ambassador Francisco de Sousa Coutinho, who, after having been Portugal's representative in The Hague during the 1640s, had been sent to London thanks to the influence exerted by Fernández Carvajal. It was in his house that, protected by diplomatic immunity, the Jewish revolutionary leaders met to secretly weave the threads of the plot.

The absolute evidence that confirms beyond doubt that Cromwell was a pawn in the interests of the Jewish revolutionary plot is contained in a weekly publication edited by Lord Alfred Douglas, *Plain English*, a weekly published by the North British Publishing Co. In an article dated 3 September 1921, Lord Alfred Douglas explains how his friend L. D. Van Valckert of Amsterdam was in possession of a volume of archives of the Mulheim synagogue that had been lost. This volume, lost during the Napoleonic wars, contained documents, namely letters, addressed to and answered by the directors of the synagogue. William Guy Carr, in the aforementioned work, reproduces two of them verbatim. The first, dated 16 June 1647, is from O. C. (Oliver Cromwell) to Ebenezer Pratt. It reads:

"In return for financial aid, we will advocate the admission of Jews into England; however, this is impossible as long as Charles lives. Charles cannot be executed without trial, for which there are no grounds at present. I therefore advise that Charles be killed, but we shall have nothing to do with the preparations for finding an assassin, although we are willing to help him to escape."

In response to this dispatch, E. Pratt wrote a letter to Oliver Cromwell dated 12 July 1647:

"We guarantee financial aid as soon as Carlos is removed and the Jews are admitted. Murder, too dangerous. We should give Charles a chance to escape. His recapture would then make trial and execution possible. The aid will be generous, but it is useless to discuss terms until the trial begins."

On 12 November of the same year, 1647, Charles I was given the opportunity to escape. Naturally, he was immediately recaptured. After his re-arrest, events moved swiftly. Cromwell set about purging Parliament of members loyal to the king. Despite this drastic action, when the House of Commons met through the night on 5 December 1648, the majority of MPs felt that "the concessions offered by the king were satisfactory for a settlement."

Such an agreement would have disqualified Cromwell from receiving the blood money he had been promised by the international money barons through their agent Ebenezer Pratt, so Cromwell struck again. He ordered Colonel Pryde to carry out a new purge, "Pryde's Purge", of those members of the Commons who had voted in favour of the agreement. After the purge, only fifty MPs remained, "The Rump Parliament", which usurped absolute power. In January 1649 a "High Court of Justice" was proclaimed for the purpose of trying the King of England, two-thirds of whose members were drawn from Cromwell's army. The conspirators could find no English lawyer who could bring a criminal charge against the king. Fernandez Carvajal then instructed a foreign Jew, Isaac Dorislaus, agent of Manasseh Ben Israel in England, to draft an indictment by which Charles I could be tried. Predictably, Charles was found guilty of the charges brought against him by the international Jewish moneylenders, but not by the English people. On 30 January 1649, the King of England was publicly beheaded. Cromwell, like Judas, got his money and also received new funding to extend the war to Catholic Ireland.

From 7 to 18 December 1655, Cromwell organised a conference at Whitehall (London) in order to get the go-ahead for a large-scale immigration of Jews. Although the conference was packed with staunch Cromwell supporters, the delegates, who were mainly priests, lawyers and merchants, decided by overwhelming consensus that Jews should not be allowed to enter England. Despite strong protests from the sub-committee of the Council of State, which had declared that these Jews "would be a grave menace to the state and to the Christian religion", the first Jews were surreptitiously allowed to enter in October 1656. A. M. Hyamson in his *A History of the Jews in England* confirms that "the merchants without exception spoke out against the admission of the Jews. They declared that the proposed immigrants would be morally injurious to the state and that their admission would enrich foreigners at the expense of the English".

England and Holland were soon involved in a series of wars which ended with the proclamation of William of Orange as King of England. When Cromwell, who in 1653 had proclaimed himself Lord Protector of England, died in 1658, it was the turn of his son Richard, also called Protector; but in 1659, after nine months in office and disgusted with so much intrigue, he resigned. In 1660 General Monk occupied London and Charles II, son of the beheaded monarch, was proclaimed king. The Dutch Jews continued to provide temporary financial support, but soon bore the costs of William of Orange's expedition against Charles II's brother and successor, the Duke of York, who reigned as James II from 1685-88.

Very succinctly stated, things happened like this. When in 1674 England and Holland made peace, those behind the machinations that had brought about the English civil wars became matchmakers: they elevated William Stradholder to the rank of captain-general of the Dutch forces, and he became Prince of Orange. All had been arranged for him to meet Mary, the eldest daughter of the Duke of York, the King's brother, who was intended to succeed him on the throne. In 1677 Mary and William Stradholder, Prince of Orange, were married. To place the latter on the English throne it was necessary to get rid of both Charles II and the Duke of York. In 1683 the plot to assassinate them both at once, "The Rye House Plot", had already been hatched, but failed. In 1685 Charles II died and the Duke of York, who had converted to Catholicism, reigned as James II. A campaign of infamy began immediately, followed by insurrections and rebellions orchestrated by the "Secret Powers", who once again pulled the strings of the new conspiracy by their favourite means of yesterday and today: bribery and blackmail. The first to succumb was the Duke of Marlborough, John Churchill, Winston Churchill's ancestor, who was head of the army, making his support crucial. Eustace Mullins, in his *The Curse of Canaan,* claims that John Churchill was bribed with £350,000 by Medina and Machado, two Sephardic bankers from Amsterdam. The Duke of Marlborough's gall was such that on 10 November 1688 he signed a renewed oath of allegiance to the king and two weeks later, on the 24th of the same month, he joined the forces of William of Orange. The *Jewish Encyclopaedia* reports that "for his many services, the Duke of Marlborough received from the Dutch Jewish banker Solomon Medina no less than £6000 per annum." William of Orange landed in England in 1688 and in 1689 he and his wife Mary were proclaimed kings of England. James II did not want to give up the throne without a fight and had landed in Ireland on 15 February. Since the king was a Catholic, William of Orange was proclaimed champion of the

Protestant Calvinist faith. On 12 July of the same year came the famous Battle of the Boyne, which the Orangemen have celebrated annually ever since with provocative commemorative parades.

One of the purposes of importing Calvinism into England was to drive a wedge between church and state. Calvinism emphasised that usurious lending and the accumulation of wealth were new ways of serving the Lord. The big news for the moneylenders and the newly emerging merchant class was that God wanted us to get rich. "Get rich" was the battle cry proposed by the Calvinists. The prophet of the sect was a French crypto-Jew named Jean Cauin, who founded Calvinism in Geneva, where he was at first known as Cohen (pronounced Cauin). He then gave English form to his name and became John Calvin. Calvinism was based on the literal Jewish interpretation of the Commandments and the Old Testament. The early disciples were known as Christian Hebraists. Calvinism made work easier for Jewish moneylenders and facilitated their expansion into European trade. Hence the phrase: "Calvin blessed the Jews". From its inception Calvinism was brutally despotic and proved to be the most tyrannical and autocratic sect in Europe. In November 1541 Calvin published his Ecclesiastical Ordinances, a body of instructions imposing absolute discipline on citizens on pain of death. His main critic, Jacques Gruet, was beheaded for blasphemy. Michael Servetus, another of his opponents, was burned on a stake. As a rule, critics were tortured and beheaded.

All the wars and rebellions between 1640 and 1689 were fomented by the international Jewish moneylenders for the purpose of controlling British politics and the British economy. Their main objective was to obtain permission to found the Bank of England (1694), in order to secure the debts Britain owed to them for loans they had made to them to wage wars instigated by themselves. The history books attribute its foundation to William Patterson and Sir John Houblen; but in reality both acted as representatives of the government in negotiating with the lenders. As soon as the Dutch general sat on the throne of England, he persuaded the British Treasury to borrow £1,250,000 from the Jewish bankers who had put him there. The international lenders agreed to lodge this provision in the Treasury's coffers, but imposed their conditions. One condition was the granting of a charter to establish the Bank of England[5]. Another condition was the secrecy of the names of those who granted the loan. The identity of the people controlling the Bank of England remains secret. A committee, the Macmillan Committee, was set up in 1929 to try to shed some light on the matter, but it failed because of the continued evasiveness of its then head,

---

[5] In 1694 the House of Commons had 512 members: 243 Tories, 241 Whigs and 28 of unknown affiliation. Two-thirds were landowners and it is believed that 20% of MPs were illiterate. The bill was debated in July, when most MPs were in the fields harvesting crops. On 27 July, when the vote was taken to grant the bank's charter, only 42 members were present, all of them Whigs who voted in favour. The Tories opposed the bill.

Norman Montagu. In conclusion, it remains to add that the international lenders demanded that the directors of the Bank of England should have the right to adopt the gold standard and the special privilege of issuing banknotes. Also, in order to consolidate the nation's debt and to ensure the payment of the amounts and their interest, they succeeded in imposing direct taxes on the people. The present system, based on debt and taxes of all kinds on the people, was thus established. From then until today, those who control credit and speculate with money have progressively usurped the functions of sovereign states. Democracy is the name given to a system which, in reality, is nothing more than the corrupt regime that allows the lenders' and international speculators' paradise to be covered up. Between 1698 and 1815 the national debt of Great Britain was increased to 885,000,000. Pounds sterling.

In addition to the Bank of England, the first privately owned central bank in the modern world, two other joint-stock companies associated with state finance were created: in 1698, the new East India Company, which was to monopolise trade beyond the Cape of Good Hope, and in 1711, the Pacific Company, which was to have the privilege of trade in South American waters.

PART 2
ADAM WEISHAUPT, ROTHSCHILD AGENT

Freedom, democracy, independence are prestigious words to which no one would associate any negative connotations. The term revolution is another of those words whose connotations are positive and therefore it enjoys a generally accepted prestige. Who has not thought at some time that a revolution is needed to change everything? History teaches students that revolutions happen because the people, fed up with suffering and arbitrariness, rise up against a series of unacceptable events or things that provoke revolution. No matter how many crimes the revolutionaries had to commit to achieve their goals, the end will justify the means. History explains that revolutions lead to the establishment of a new order that puts an end to the previous injustice and constitutes an advance towards freedom, democracy or independence.

Isaac Disraeli, father of Benjamin Disraeli (Lord Beaconsfield), from whom we have already quoted some texts in the first chapter and to whom we shall return later, writes in detail about the English Revolution in his two-volume *The Life of Charles I*. The second volume begins with this cryptic sentence: "It was predestined that England would be the first of a series of revolutions, which has not yet ended". Since when he wrote these words the French Revolution had already taken place, it seems clear that he was alluding to a later one, which would become known as the Bolshevik Revolution. In this work Disraeli states that when the Calvinists took the country into their power "it seemed that religion consisted chiefly in the rigours of the Sabbath, and that the British Senate had been transformed into a company of Hebrew rabbis". Further on he states: "In 1650, after the execution of the king, a law was passed imposing penalties for Sabbath-breaking". Isaac Disraeli points out the great similarities in the patterns of activities which preceded the English and French revolutions, thus, in a sense, uncovering the preparations of the secret directors of the World Revolutionary Movement.

As we have seen in the case of the English revolution, things are sometimes not what they appear to be. Revolutionary processes need agents, organisation and, above all, financing, money. It will be seen in due course that the paradigmatic example is the Bolshevik Revolution, financed by Jewish Wall Street bankers. However, the international left is unable to glimpse the truth. Marx, Trotsky, Lenin remain for "progressives" all over the world untouchable saints, benefactors of humanity. Yet Trotsky (Bronstein) was an agent of the Zionist banker Jacob Schiff, who proudly declared in public that thanks to his financial help the revolution had succeeded. Max Warburg, another Zionist banker, on 21 September 1917 opened by cable from Hamburg an account at Nya Banken in Stockholm

(Rothschild's bank) in Trotsky's name. Olaf Aschberg, also a Jew and the top manager of the Nya Banken, was to found the Russian Commercial Bank in 1921 and thus become the head of Soviet finance. All this will be recounted in detail in the chapter on the revolution in Russia. Let us now go step by step and see how the revolution in France was prepared.

The Rothschilds, a family of Jewish Talmudists from Frankfurt, came on the scene in the last third of the 18th century. They quickly became the masters of international finance and politics in the course of the 19th century. Mayer Amschel Bauer (1744-1812), a man of extraordinary intelligence, founded the dynasty and adopted the name Rothschild. Before his death, he forced his five sons to inbreed among themselves and their descendants. All of this will be recounted in detail below. According to William Guy Carr (*Pawns in the Game*), in 1773 Mayer Amschel Rothschild was reportedly the organiser of a meeting in Frankfurt attended by twelve other very wealthy and influential people. Their purpose was to convince the families represented there that if they pooled their resources they could finance and direct the World Revolutionary Movement and use it as a manual for action to gain total control of wealth, natural resources and power throughout the world. The analysis of how the British revolution had been organised revealed the mistakes and errors that had been made: the revolutionary period had been too long and the elimination of the reactionaries had not been carried out quickly enough. According to Guy Carr, who does not cite his source, it was at this meeting that a plan of action was drawn up which was to be refined over the years. Many of the essential ideas of the project were to appear in the documents that years later were seized from the Bavarian Illuminati and have since reappeared in the manuals of various secret societies. Finally, expanded and with few modifications, the programme would be embodied in the *Protocols of the Learned Elders of Zion*, which consists of twenty-four sections and was published at the beginning of the twentieth century. It can therefore be deduced that in reality the famous *Protocols* are nothing more than a paraphrase of a conspiracy to control the world that had been latent since the end of the 18th century.

The proposed plan of action was based on the assumption that the end justifies the means. Consequently, honesty and morality were considered to be political vices, and violence and terror were used to achieve objectives and liberalism to obtain political power. The idea of Liberty was to be used to provoke class struggle. Another fundamental idea had to do with the need to keep power (theirs) hidden until the final triumph. According to Guy Carr, the meeting at Frankfurt would have considered for the first time the importance of understanding the psychology of the masses in order to modify their behaviour and control them despotically. Among the most relevant ideas pointed out by the thirteen families that have been standard practice since then, the following stand out: the right to seize property by any means; the financing of both sides in wars and the control of subsequent peace conferences; the use of the power of money to place subservient and obedient politicians in governments; the use of propaganda through control of the press and books; the use of Freemasonry to carry out subversion and to spread materialistic and atheistic ideology; revolution and the subsequent reign of terror as the most economical means of rapidly subduing the people; the control of nations and international affairs through secret agent diplomacy; the establishment of large monopolies and colossal reserves of wealth in order to establish World Government; the tailoring of national and international laws to the interests of the "Secret Power".

Three years after the Frankfurt meeting, on May 1, 1776, the Order of the Perfectibilists was born in Ingolstadt, better known as the Order of the Bavarian Illuminati, the Illuminati, the secret society which was to implement the revolutionary programme conceived in Frankfurt and which Rothschild had commissioned Adam Weishaupt (1748-1830), a crypto-Jew, son of Rabbi George Weishaupt, who died when he was only five years old, to found. In 1771 Adam had met a Danish Jewish Kabbalist, Kölmer, who had just arrived from Egypt and deeply impressed him with his occult knowledge and initiated him into the secrets of the magic of Osiris and the Kabbalah. Weishaupt would later choose the pyramid as the symbol of the Illuminati, whose emblem, now famous throughout the world, is "The All Seeing Eye". The founding ceremony took place in the Bavarian forests on the famous Walpurgis night (30 April - 1 May). This date was no coincidence, because among the Jewish Kabbalists May 1st symbolised the sacred number of Yahweh and had become a hidden holiday for them. According to Johann Wolfgang Goethe, the first of May, the day after Walpurgis Night, is when the dark mystical forces are celebrated. It is known that among the group of strangers who attended the event were several students, subjugated by the ideas of their teacher: Weishaupt, born in the same town, had become professor of canon and civil law at the University of Ingolstadt in 1772. In 1773, after the dissolution of the Society of Jesus by Pope Clement XIV, Weishaupt became dean of the Faculty of Law, which had been held by Jesuits for ninety years. The fact that Weishaupt had been educated by the Jesuits, which enabled him to penetrate their organisational system and to know the inner workings of the order in detail, was certainly a factor in entrusting him with the creation of the Order of the Illuminati of Bavaria. In fact, he adopted for the Illuminati the organisational chart of the Company, of which he became its worst enemy.

Frankists and Illuminati

That Adam Weishaupt was an agent of the Frankfurt bankers is a fact that is agreed upon by numerous authors to whom we will refer in the course of our discussion. However, there is one source that has been little cited and is of great interest because it is a very significant authority. This is Rabbi

Marvin S. Antelman, who from 1974 served as chief judge of the Supreme Rabbinic Court of America (SRCA). Antelman, in his work *To Eliminate the Opiate* (a two-volume work published twenty-eight years apart in 1974 and 2002), states that it was the founder of the Rothschild dynasty, Mayer Amschel, who convinced Adam Weishaupt to accept the doctrine of Jacob Frank (Frankists) and who later financed the Bavarian Illuminati. The Frankists, a pre-Illuminati sect to which Europe's most influential Jewish financiers and intellectuals belonged, were themselves followers of Shabbetay Zeví[6] and only intermarried. Jacob Frank (1726-1791), whose original name was Jacob Leibowicz, was born in Galicia, Poland, into a Shabbetaic family. At the age of 25 he proclaimed himself to be a reincarnation of Zeví.

Gershom Scholem in his work *Le messianisme juif* defines Frank as "the most appalling case in the history of Judaism". Frank's thought, Scholem explains, is situated in the Kabbalistic interpretation of Shabbetay Zeví: Cosmic redemption (ticún) is realised through sin (Erlösung durch Sünde): "it is by violating the Torah that it is fulfilled." His doctrine is

---

[6] The doctrines of Shabbetay Zeví (1626-1676) and Jacob Frank are considered by rabbis such as Marvin S. Antelman to be a satanic movement that turned Jewish teachings upside down. Shabbetay Zeví, of Sephardic origin, was born in Smyrna in 1626. He studied to become a rabbi, but soon became interested in Kabbalah. Yitshac Luria had announced in the 16th century that the Messiah would reign from 1648. On the same date, in the synagogue of his hometown, Shabbetay Zeví proclaimed that he was the awaited Messiah. Excommunicated, he went to Thessalonica, from where he was expelled. He went to Egypt and there contacted a Kabbalist group led by the Jew Raphael Joseph, who was the viceroy's treasurer and controlled the banking activities in Egypt, an Ottoman province. In 1662, with a lot of money, he arrived in Jerusalem where he stayed for two years. In 1664 he returned to Egypt and married a Jewish prostitute named Sarah, who seven years earlier had claimed in Amsterdam that God had commanded her to marry the new Messiah. This marriage was consummated to fulfil the legend that the Messiah would marry an impure woman. Shabbetay needed a prophet and this was Nathan of Gaza, who claimed to have visions in which God confirmed that Shabbetay Zeví was the Messiah. In 1665 the two got together and began to teach the Jerusalem rabbis and their followers that Shabbetay had divine permission to break the commandments of Moses and that incest and fornication were not a sin. He was expelled once again, but many Jews began to believe in him. He went on to Aleppo and from there returned to Smyrna, where there was a split between those who followed the rabbis and those who proclaimed him Messiah. On 30 December 1665 he embarked for Constantinople, for according to a prophecy the sultan would surrender and thus begin his reign. When he arrived on 8 February 1666, the sultan was waiting for him and imprisoned him. He then presented him with an ultimatum: either he converted to Islam or he would be executed. Shabbetay, in front of the sultan and his court, took off his hat, spat on him and renounced his Jewish faith. His wife and those with him in prison also converted. There was a worldwide commotion among those who had accepted him. It was Nathan of Gaza who explained that by committing apostasy Shabbetay saved all the Jews who believed he was the Messiah. Shabbetay died on the Day of Atonement in 1676 and his inner circle spread the word that he had risen on the third day.

summarised in his book *The Words of the Lord,* in which he asserts that the creator God was not the same as the one who had revealed himself to the Israelites. Frank believed that God was Satan and vowed not to tell the truth and to reject any moral law. He declared that the only way to a new society was through the destruction of the present civilisation. Murder, rape, incest and blood drinking were perfectly acceptable and necessary ritual actions.

Frank founded his own sect, evidently satanic, based on transgression and orgiastic debauchery. In 1752 he married a beautiful Jewish woman of Bulgarian origin named Hanna, whom he used, according to the custom of the sect's members, to captivate and entrap dozens of men who engaged in licentious activities with her. Hanna had two sons, Joseph and Jacob, and a daughter, Eva, who, according to the *Jewish Encyclopaedia,* following her mother's example, was to sleep years later with the most prominent men of the time, including the Emperor of Austria, Joseph II. In Turkey, in imitation of Shabbetay Zeví, Frank converted to Islam and became a "doenmé"[7]. He then organised an underground Shabbetaic network in Poland, which spread to Ukraine and Hungary. To protect himself from the orthodox rabbis, Jacob Frank even sought the protection of the Catholic Church. Frank claimed that in order to complete the messianic mission, one must act with double-speak: one acts as one believes, but does not say what one believes (Weishaupt would say exactly the same thing). This strategy of lying went so far that he was baptised in the Catholic rite. Thus, while in 1683 Shabbetaism penetrated Islam, the Frankists did the same with Catholicism in 1759. Frank was baptised in Warsaw Cathedral, and his godfather was none other than King Augustus III,. Jacob Frank even conceived a plan to penetrate the Orthodox Church and subvert the Russian imperial regime.

The Polish authorities soon discovered his double-dealing and imprisoned him in the Czenstockova citadel. Released in 1773 by the Russians on the eve of the first partition of Poland. Jakob Frank then took the name Dobrushka and settled in Brno. A consummate master of political subversion and propaganda manipulation, he organised a movement in Brno with paramilitary training camps where 600 of his supporters were trained as terrorists. It is safe to assume, then, that he had plenty of money, and everything suggests that it came from his friend Mayer Amschel Rothschild.

---

[7] In Spain, the name Marranos was given to Jewish converts, many of them infiltrators of the Church and the State, who continued to practise Judaism. In Turkey, following the famous conversion to Islam of Shabbetay Zeví, the name doenmé (apostate) was given to crypto-Jews who outwardly behaved as Muslims, but in reality remained faithful to the Jewish religion. Mustafa Kemal Atatürk and the Young Turks who established the secular state in Turkey in 1923 were Shabbetayans, Doenmés. For Shabbetay Zeví and Jakob Frank, apostasy and Marranism are necessary, with the obligation of secrecy about the true Jewish faith kept by the false convert. Frank explained to his disciples that "baptism would be the beginning of the end of the Church and of society, and they, the Frankists, had been chosen to bring about the destruction from within, like soldiers storming a city by passing through the sewers".

Gershom Scholem acknowledges that in 1786 Frank had set up an international subversion centre specialising in infiltration, terrorism and enrichment by blackmail in the vicinity of Frankfurt, in Offenbach Castle. In an article entitled "The Deutsch Devils" dated 31 December 2003, Barry Chamish[8], another Jewish and Zionist author, confirms this: "At that time Frankfurt was the headquarters of the Rothschild empire and of Adam Weishaupt, founder of the Illuminati. When Jacob Frank entered the city, the alliance between the two had already begun. Weishaupt provided the Jesuits' conspiratorial resources, while the Rothschilds provided the money. All that remained was the means to expand the Illuminati programme. Then the Frankists added their network of agents scattered in Christian and Islamic countries. Jacob Frank was suddenly rich because he received a nice gift from the Rothschilds. There is no other explanation.

Rabbi Antelman makes it clear: "It must be pointed out that when the Illuminati and the Frankists infiltrated the Freemasons, it did not mean that they harboured any particular feeling of love for Freemasonry. On the contrary, they hated it and only wished to use its cover as a means of spreading their revolutionary doctrine and providing a place where they could meet without arousing suspicion." It is worth bearing these words in mind, for it is explained below how the infiltration took place.

Years later, in 1818, Mary Shelley, wife of the poet Percy Bysshe Shelley, would also place Professor Victor Frankenstein, a novel character who was the creator of another uncontrolled monster, at the University of Ingolstadt. Let us see, although the quotation is somewhat lengthy, what Rabbi Antelman says about this in *To Eliminate the Opiate*:

"We can see from our study of the Frankists and their elite that they were real monsters. Indeed the concept was retained, and not by accident, in the novel *Frankenstein*. Mary Shelley and her husband, the famous poet Shelley, were members of the Illuminati. The symbolism inherent in the name Frankenstein is as follows: The name Frank comes from Jacob Frank, founder of the Frankists. The EN is an English abbreviation of the three-letter Hebrew word 'Ayin', which means eye. Stein in German means stone. In the symbol of the all-seeing eye cult and in the seal found on the US dollar, the eye is on the stones that form the base of the pyramid. Thus Frankenstein=Frank+eye+stone. But what is the symbolism of the Frankenstein monster? As we have pointed out, the Frankists were linked to mystical kabbalism and there is a kabbalistic tradition of monsters called Golems. The concept of the Golem is discussed in detail in Professor Scohlem's book *Kabbalah and its*

---

[8] Barry Chamish, who died on 23 August 2016, popularised Rabbi Antelman's revelations about Shabbetaic Jews and the Illuminati. In the book *Who Murdered Yitzhak Rabin?* Chamish revealed the involvement of the "Shin Bet" in the assassination of Yitzhak Rabin.

Symbolism. [...] In the classic construction of a Golem, the Kabbalists form a human figure out of earth or clay, write one of God's secret names on a scroll and place it in a cavity in the Golem's head. After writing the relevant code, the Golem comes to life. The cryptic symbolism of the Frankenstein monster is that wise mystics, purveyors of wisdom, using the great secrets of the universe, are to give new life to the dead and decrepit ideas of the old world".

The well-known Jewish author Bernard Lazare wrote in his work *L'Antisemitisme* (1894) that mostly Jewish cabalists surrounded Weishaupt. Confiscated documents show unequivocally that half of the Illuminati in important positions were Jews, a proportion that increases the higher the rank. As reported by the publication *La Vieille France* in its issue of 31 March 1921, there were four particularly important Jews in the leadership of the Bavarian Illuminati: Naphtali Herz, Moses Mendelssohn, Isaac Daniel von Itzig (banker) and his son-in-law David Friedländer. Both Itzig and Friedländer were prominent Frankists. It is of interest to note that the Itzigs supplied Prussia with silver for minting coinage. Rabbi Antelman traces the successive marriages of this family of enlightened-Frankists in the above-mentioned work to demonstrate the political intrigues of this elite, whose strategy of liaising with each other played a key role in their power grab.

Between 1773 and 1775 Weishaupt had travelled to France, where he befriended two Freemasons, Maximilien Robespierre, who in 1794 would end up on the guillotine after daring to denounce the conspiracy of the Illuminati, and the Marquis de Lafayette, who would later intervene in the American Revolution and play a prominent role during the first three years of the Revolution in France. Lafayette also publicly accused the sect, as will be seen below. In 1777, almost two years after founding the Bavarian Order of the Illuminati, Weishaupt became a Freemason and joined the Munich lodge Theodore of Good Counsel through his friendship with the Protestant Baron Adolph Franz Friedrich Ludwig von Knigge. No doubt all these experiences were used to imbue Freemasonry with the programme of the Bavarian Enlightenment, for as early as 1778 Weishaupt made known his plan to amalgamate the two societies.

Thirteen members composed the Supreme Council of the Order of the Illuminati, which constituted the executive body of the Council of Thirty-Three. The Supreme Council decided that the Ingolstadt lodge would be used to organise the campaign to penetrate continental Freemasonry through its agents or cells, who could even found new lodges for the purpose of proselytising and contacting wealthy or well-established non-Jews in the Church or State. Lodges founded in France had to be associated with the Grand Orient, which grouped together almost all the lodges in the country and had as its Grand Master the Duke of Orleans, cousin of King Louis XVI. The event that was to mark a turning point in achieving the aim of controlling Freemasonry was the Wilhelmsbad Congress.

Mirabeau

Among the noteworthy contacts established was Honoré-Gabriel Riquetti, Count de Mirabeau (1749-1791), who, on the death of his father in 1789, became the fourth Marquis de Mirabeau. A few brief biographical sketches will help us to understand his recruitment by Weishaupt's agents. Honoré-Gabriel's bad relationship with his father, the third Marquis, marked his life. When he joined the army in 1767, his father refused to buy him a commission and he began to accumulate debts. After an intrigue with his colonel's mistress, he was arrested and imprisoned. Nevertheless, in 1771 he was received at the court of Versailles, but after a serious quarrel with his father, he left it. In 1772 he married Emilie de Marignane, daughter of the Marquis de Marignane, without a dowry. Hoping to inherit on the death of Emilie's stepmother, he ran up scandalous debts, for which his father brought a prohibition suit against him and he ended up in prison again. When he regained his freedom, he fought a duel with a nobleman from Grasse and, again pursued by his father, ended up in the fort of Joux in semi-liberty. He was soon captivated by the charms of the Marquise Sophie de Monnier, a young woman married to a fifty-year-old man, whom he followed to Dijon when she left her husband. There he was arrested. His father asked for him to be interned in Lyon. After many vicissitudes, he embarked for Holland and was received by the members of the lodge "The Well Beloved" in Amsterdam, where he wrote a *Plan for the Reorganisation of Freemasonry*, in which he advised against the admission of people of no importance and without purchasing power. After a violent dispute with his father, Mirabeau was condemned to be beheaded by the justice of Pontarlier and to pay a fine of 40,000 livres for "abduction" to the Marquis de Monnier. Poor Sophie was sentenced to life imprisonment in a correctional institution and her marriage contract was annulled. Mirabeau narrowly escaped execution thanks to an extradition that led to a new imprisonment. Finally, in 1782, through "transactions" with Monnier, he obtained the annulment of Pontarlier's sentence. A year later, he sued his wife, who had finally inherited a large fortune, for desertion of the marital home. Unfortunately for him, the lawsuit was rejected.

It is understandable that people like Mirabeau were ideal prey for Weishaupt's agents. When Mirabeau was recruited by the Illuminati is not easy to say, for in the whirlwind of events outlined above there is no mention of his escapes and journeys abroad: Amsterdam, Geneva, Potsdam, Vienna and Berlin, where Minister Calonne had sent him on an official mission that caused a great deal of discussion. In any case, it is certain that Mirabeau belonged to the Order and knew the leader. John Robison, whose *Proofs of a Conspiracy Against All the Religions and Governments of Europe* will be discussed below, makes it clear that Weishaupt himself was watching him and that he finally decided to contact him through a lieutenant colonel named

Mauvillon, who was in the service of the Duke of Brunswick. Robison explains that Mirabeau brazenly published a pamphlet of ambiguous intentions, *Essai sur la secte des illuminés (Essay on the sect of the Illuminati),* in which he seems not to have realised what he had got himself into, for he recklessly refers to the Illuminati as absurd fanatics full of superstitions and even comments on some of the rituals and ceremonies of the Order. In the essay he even shows that he was aware of Weishaupt's intention to infiltrate the lodges and of his motives. In another controversial work that also made him enemies in Germany, *Secret History of the Berlin Court,* he refers to Weishaupt and the illuminati and says: "The lodge Theodore of Good Counsel in Munich, where there were a few men with heads and hearts, was tired of being at the mercy of the vain promises and quarrels of Freemasonry. The leaders decided to graft onto it another secret association to which they gave the name of the Order of the Illuminati. They used as their model the Society of Jesus, although their purposes were diametrically opposed." These words of Mirabeau invite one to think that he knew practically from the beginning what was being prepared, for he knew that the intention of the secret society was to gain control of Freemasonry and to use it to instigate and direct the revolution through it. Thanks to documents later seized by the Bavarian police, it became known that Mirabeau's secret name in the Order was first Arcesilas and later Leonidas. It is likely that Mirabeau, resentful of the social problems he had experienced and perhaps in a spirit of revenge, even took the oath of unlimited obedience on pain of death.

The Supreme Council of the Order must have considered that Mirabeau could be of great use to them in achieving their aims: he belonged to the nobility, knew court circles, was an extraordinary orator, and was intimate with Louis Philippe Joseph, one of the richest men in France, who had been Duke of Montpensier until the age of five and then Duke of Chartres until 1785, when his father died and he finally became Duke of Orléans. The Duke of Chartres had signed a document on 5 April 1772 in which he accepted the proclamation "for Grand Master of all the Scottish Councils, Chapters and Lodges of the great globe of France, offices which His Serene Highness has deigned to accept for the love of the royal art and in order to concentrate all Masonic operations under a single authority". Louis-Philippe d'Orléans (1747-1793) had been chosen as the ringleader to lead the revolution in France and Mirabeau was the ideal liaison. Surely, under the pretext of friendship and admiration, agents of the lending bankers who financed the Enlightenment offered Mirabeau help to get out of financial difficulties. When they had him in their possession, he was introduced to Moses Ben Mendel, who had Germanised his name and called himself Moses Mendelssohn (1729-1786), who became his mentor. So much so that shortly after his death in 1787, Mirabeau published a memoir on *Moses Mendelssohn and the political reform of the Jews.* Perhaps it was

Mendelssohn himself who introduced him to Henrietta de Lemos, wife of Dr. Herz, a Jewess of Sephardic origin famous for her beauty and personal charm. For a guy like Mirabeau, the fact that this attractive woman was married only made her more interesting and desirable. Madame Herz entertained her friends in open salons in Berlin, Paris and Vienna. Disciples of Moses Mendelssohn who were part of the conspiracy frequented them.

In *Under the Sign of the Scorpion*, Jüri Lina attributes great importance to Moses Mendelssohn within the Order *of* the Illuminati. According to him, Mendelssohn was "Weishaupt's invisible guide". In 1776 he had founded the Haskala movement (the importance of this movement will be discussed in more detail in another chapter), whose ostensible aim was to modernise Judaism so that people would accept Jews when they abandoned Talmudism and assimilated Western culture. The book Mirabeau wrote about his plan for political reform was at the same time intended to enshrine the figure of Mendelssohn, who, according to Lina and other authors, was the leader of the Illuminati in Berlin. While officially Mendelssohn preached assimilation, he secretly continued to encourage his co-religionists to faithfully maintain the Talmudic racial beliefs of their fathers.

Everything indicates that Mirabeau's essential job was to convince the Duke of Orleans, Grand Master of French Freemasonry, who would later be called Philippe Egalité (Philippe Equality), to put himself at the head of the Revolutionary Movement in France. It was understood that once the king had been forced to abdicate, he would become the democratic sovereign of the nation. It should be added here that in 1780 Louis-Philippe d'Orléans was also heavily in debt and that, despite his lack of scruples about the deals he was offered, his debts were growing all the time. Bankers and moneylenders had also offered him advice and financial help. Of course, to secure their loans, they had asked him for his property (estates, palaces, houses and the Palais Royal) as collateral. The Duke of Orleans even signed an agreement with his Jewish financiers whereby they were authorised to administer his properties or estates in order to secure him the sufficient funds he needed to meet his financial obligations and to live adequately at the same time. Eustace Mullins (*The Curse of Canaan)* and William Guy Carr (*Pawns in the game)* agree in reporting that Choderlos de Laclos, author of *Les Liaisons Dangereuses*, was appointed to administer and manage the Palais Royal and the estates of the Duke of Orleans. Laclos had a Jew from Palermo, the famous Cagliostro (Giuseppe Balsamo), who had had as his Kabbalist master a certain Altotas, who, according to some authors, was the same person who had initiated Weishaupt, i.e. Kölmer, travel to Paris to help him. Cagliostro was the Grand Master of the Rosicrucian Knights of Malta. According to Mullins and Guy, between them they turned the palace into "one of the finest brothels in the world" and used it as a headquarters for revolutionary propaganda. Thousands of inflammatory pamphlets were printed there and flooded Paris. When the revolution broke out, the palace became the centre of operations. Hippolyte Taine recounts in his *History of the French Revolution* that the agitators were in permanent session there: "The Palais Royal is an open-air club where day and night the agitators excite each other and provoke the crowd to outbursts of violence. In its enclosure, protected by the privileges of the House of Orleans, the police dare not enter. [...] The palace, a centre of prostitution, gambling, leisure and pamphleteering, attracts the whole uprooted population that moves about the big city without home or occupation".

In *Memoires pour servir à l'Histoire du Jacobinisme*, the Abbe Augustin Barruel also asserts that Mirabeau belonged to the Illuminati. Barruel maintains that in 1788 Mirabeau and Charles -Maurice de Talleyrand-Périgord, who were the directors of the "Amis Reunis" lodge, wrote to their brothers in Germany asking for assistance and instruction. The indefatigable Talleyrand, also known as "le diable boiteaux" (the lame devil), was to be Napoleon's discoverer and it was he who was to put him in touch with Mayer Amschel Rothschild. Two leading sectarians of the Order, Bode, known as Amelius, and Baron de Busche, alias Bayardo, travelled to France to help them introduce Illuminism into the lodges of their country. Barruel says that at the lodge of the "Amis Réunis", where members of all the Masonic lodges of France were gathered, Weishaupt's emissaries made known the mysteries of Illuminism. He thus confirms that, without the Masons in general knowing even the name of the sect, since only a small number had been initiated into the true secrets, by the beginning of 1789 the two hundred and sixty-six lodges under the control of the Grand Orient had been enlightened.

The Wilhelmsbad Congress

According to Nesta Webster, the importance of the Wilhelmsbad Congress for understanding the historical development has never been properly appreciated by historians. At the Wilhelmsbad Congress, held in a convent near Hanau in Hesse, the alliance between the Enlightenment and Freemasonry was definitively sealed. Jüri Lina states in *Under the Sign of the Scorpion* that the congress premises were actually in a castle owned by Mayer Amschel Rothschild. The congress, which opened on 16 July 1782 and ended in early September, was attended by representatives of secret societies from all over the world, grouped into three main tendencies: Martinists, Freemasons and Illuminati. A Portuguese Jew named Martinez Pasqualis is said to have founded the secret society of the Martinists in 1754, based on a system inspired by Judaising Christianity and Greco-Eastern philosophies. In Nesta Webster's opinion, the sect had split into two branches: the followers of Saint Martin, from which the name derives, and a more revolutionary one that had founded the Philalethes lodge in Paris. Saint

Martin in his book *Des erreurs et de la verité (On Errors and Truth)*, published in 1775, mentions the formula "liberty, equality, fraternity" and considers it as "the sacred triad". David Livingstone, in *Terrorism and the Illuminati*, reinforces this thesis, saying that Pasqualis was a Jewish mystic who was known to have organised a movement by the name of *Ordre des Chevaliers Maçons Elus-Coën de L'Univers (Order of the Chosen Masonic Knights Priests of the Universe)*. According to Livingstone, Pasqualis' work was continued by his disciple Louis-Claude de Saint Martin, who later founded the order of Martinists.

At Wilhelmsbad, ideas about the emancipation of the Jews soon surfaced. In August 1781, under the influence of Moses Mendelssohn, Christian Wilhelm von Dohm (1751-1820) had published *On the Improvement of the Civil Condition of the Jews*, a work of great influence on the revolutionary movement which, according to the Jewish historian Heinrich Graetz, "described the Christians as cruel barbarians and the Jews as illustrious martyrs". Dohm, a regular visitor to the salons of Henrietta de Lemos, where he befriended Mirabeau, demonstrated with this work the existence of a complete project in favour of Judaism. Also at 1781, the Prussian Baron Jean Baptiste Cloots (Anacarsis), an enlightened man of Jewish origin who had declared himself a "personal enemy of Christ" and whom Robespierre had ordered to be beheaded, had published a prosemitic pamphlet, *Letters about the Jews*. The first consequence of so much propaganda in favour of the Jews was their immediate admission to all the lodges.

The Bavarian Illuminati knew very well how to manoeuvre at the congress, since they were the only ones who had come to it with a preconceived plan to take control of Freemasonry. Cushman Cunningham, in *The Secret Empire*, considers that after 1782 European Freemasonry became dominated by the Illuminati. One notable recruit at Wilhelmsbad was Duke Ferdinand of Brunswick, Grand Master of German Freemasonry, called Isch Zadik (just man), although he later repented. Another personality who confirmed his membership of the Illuminati was Prince Karl of Hesse-Kassel, who together with Daniel Itzig, the Berlin Frankist banker, were the most prominent leaders of the Asiatic Brethren or Asiatic Order, whose full name was the Order of the Brethren of St. John Evangelist of Asia in Europe ("Die Brüder St. Johannes des Evangelisten aus Asien in Europa"), which was largely composed of Jews, Turks, Persians and Armenians. Four of the Illuminati lodges in Vienna belonged to the Asiatic Order, also known as the Order of Abraham. According to Rabbi Marvin S. Antelman, a key man for the connection between the Illuminati, the Jacobites and the Asiatic Order was the Frankist Moses Dobrushka (1753-1794), second cousin of Jacob Frank, alias Schönfeld, alias ben Joseph, alias Junius Frey, who in 1780-81 was one of the founders of the Asiatic Order in Vienna.

In the first volume of *To Eliminate the Opiate*, Rabbi Antelman, drawing on Stanley Loomis's *Paris in the Terror* and Jacob Katz's *Jews and Freemasons in Europe 1723-1939*, attributes the creation of the Asiatic Order to the Frankist Moses Dobrushka. Dobrushka, who was related to Jacob Frank, followed the example of the sect's leader and converted to Catholicism in 1775 so that he could prosper at the court of Joseph II of Austria, where he took the name Franz Thomas von Schönfeld. As a Freemason he called himself Isaac ben Joseph. He later joined the French Revolution under the name of Junius Frey and was a fervent Jacobin. Accused of espionage and of being in the service of the East India Company, he was finally guillotined with the Dantonists in 1794. An almost definitive book on Jacob Frank and his relative Moses Dobrushka is Arthur Mandel's *Le Messie Militant ou la Fuite du Ghetto* (*The Militant Messiah or the Flight from the Ghetto*). This seminal work explains in detail the vicissitudes of Dobrushka-Schönfeld-Frey, who was the son of a cousin of Jacob Frank's named Sheindel Hirschel. Jacob Frank came into contact with them when he moved to Brno, having initially stayed with his cousin, whom the ultra-orthodox rabbi Jacob Endem calls "this great whore from Brno" ("cette grosse putain de Brünn"). In this work it is fully confirmed that Dobrushka, under the name of Franz Thomas von Schönfeld, is listed as one of the founders of the Asiatic Order. His role was of the utmost importance, for it was he who translated the original texts written in Hebrew and Chaldee, from which the Eastern and Kabbalistic mysteries that so dazzled some of the nobles came. The leadership of the Order after the Congress of Wilhelmsbad was exercised by a Sanhedrin which included the banker Daniel Itzig and Charles of Hesse. Below this all-powerful Sanhedrin was the General Chapter. Charles of Hesse, designated in the Order as Ben Our Ben Mizram, was the brother of Wilhelm (1743-1821), who was Landgrave of Hesse-Kassel from 1785 under the name of Wilhelm IX and Prince Elector of Hesse-Kassel from 1803 to 1821 under the name of Wilhelm I. The Rothschilds owe their supremacy to the Rothschilds. The Rothschilds owe their absolute supremacy in the world of finance and banking to their relationship with Wilhelm IX. This will be explained in the next chapter.

Nesta Webster explains how the Enlightenment spread throughout Germany after the Wilhelmsbad Congress : "The Eichstadt lodge enlightened Bayreuth and other imperial cities. Berlin enlightened the provinces of Brandenburg and Pomerania. Frankfurt illuminated Hanover, etc. All these sections were directed by Weishaupt, who from the Munich lodge held all the strings of the conspiracy in his hands." Professors Cossandey and Renner, forced to give evidence because of the seizure by the Bavarian police of documents revealing the plot, testified in Munich in April 1785 that "all the Illuminati were Freemasons, but by no means all Freemasons were Illuminati." Professor Renner confessed in court that "the illuminati feared nothing so much as to be known by that name." This was because those who did not keep the secret were threatened with terrible punishments.

Among the important decisions taken at Wilhelmsbad was the decision to move the headquarters of Enlightened Freemasonry to Frankfurt, where the most prominent members of Jewish finance lived: Rothschild, Oppenheimer, Wertheimer, Speyer, Stern. Eustace Mullins mentions as members of the Frankfurt lodge in 1811 Sigismund Geisenheimer, administrative head of the house of Rothschild, the bankers Adler, Speyer, Hanauer, Goldschmidt and Zevi Hirsch Kalisher (1795-1874), one of the pioneers of Zionism who would later become Frankfurt's chief rabbi. Niall Ferguson, in his *The House of Rothschild*, adds that Salomon Rothschild himself, the second son of Mayer Amschel, attended the sessions. It may be surprising that Zevi Hirsch Kalisher in 1811, at the age of sixteen, was already attending lodge meetings, but it is credible. In any case, his *Drishal Zion (The Quest for Zion)*, along with Moses Hess's *Rome and Jerusalem*, are considered the two precursor books of Zionism, which will be discussed in chapter four of this work. In *The World Revolution*, Nesta Webster, who in turn cites A. Cowan's *The X-Rays in Freemasonry* and the *Israelite Archives*, states that it was in the main lodge in Frankfurt, the headquarters of the Rothschilds, that the gigantic plan of the world revolution was carried out, and that it was there, on the occasion of the Masonic congress held in 1786, that the death of Louis XVI and Gustav III was finally decreed, as well as the creation of the Republican National Guard for the protection of the new regime. Jüri Lina adds that the assassination of Emperor Leopold II of Austria, brother of Queen Marie Antoinette of France, who was poisoned on 1 March 1792 by the Jew Martinowitz, was also decided, according to the Estonian author.

Gustav III of Sweden, who was a Freemason, was indeed assassinated: he was shot dead by another Freemason, Jacob Johan Anckarström, on 16 March 1792 in the Royal Theatre in Stockholm. Verdi's opera, *Un ballo in maschera*, is based on this crime. Gustav III, an ally of the French royal family, was planning to fight the Jacobins by organising a coalition of the monarchies of Europe. King Louis XVI, as is well known, was guillotined on 21 January 1793.

The conspiracy uncovered

The first revelations about the existence of the Bavarian Order of Illuminati came in 1783. Johann Baptist Strobl, a Munich bookseller who had been rejected as a candidate, made the first complaint. Weishaupt accused him of being an uninformed slanderer; but in the same year, according to a Swedish publication (*Guidance for Freemasons*) published in Stockholm in 1906 and quoted in *Under the Sign of the Scorpion*, Professor

Westenrieder, Duchess Maria Anna and Professor Utzschneider, who had left the sect, also raised the alarm.

Also a personality within the Illuminati, Freiherr von Knigge, alias Philo, who had joined the organisation in 1780 and had become one of the key men in Weishaupt's attempts to infiltrate Freemasonry, clashed with the leader and temporarily left the organisation, but later rejoined it. Knigge had made a pact with Weishaupt that the Illuminati would receive the first three degrees of Freemasonry, but he could not get Weishaupt to reveal any of his secrets. On 20 January 1783 he wrote these words to Cato, lawyer Zwack's secret name: "The cause of our divisions is the Jesuitism of Weishaupt and the tyranny he exercises over men who perhaps are not as imaginative and cunning as he is. [...] I declare that nothing can make me deal with Spartacus (Weishaupt) in the same way as I did before". Later, perhaps as early as 1784, another letter from Philo to Cato confirmed that relations with Spartacus had worsened: "I abhor perfidy and wickedness, and therefore I abandon him and his order to the snare."

By 1784 the Order had more than three thousand members scattered throughout Europe and, predictably, some decided to turn back. Among these were Professors Grünberg, Renner, Cossandey and Utzchneider of the Marian Academy in Munich, whose statements left no doubt about the diabolical nature of Illuminism. The firm of the bookseller Strobl began to publish polemical articles directed at the Illuminati. Jüri Lina cites one of them as an example, entitled *Babo, Gemälde aus dem menschlichen Leben (Babo, impressions of human life)*. This coincided with the accession to power in Bavaria of Duke Charles Philipp Theodore, a more patriotic and conservative regent, who on 22 June 1784 banned all secret societies.

A book published in Moscow in 2000, *The Brothers of the Night*, written by Countess Sofia Toll, is the source Jüri Lina cites in her book for the information below. All sources allude to the lightning that struck the Illuminati mail-rider in Regensburg (Regensburg) in 1785, but none of them give details. Let us look at these novel details. On 11 February 1785, Weishaupt had been dismissed from office and forbidden to live in Ingolstadt. At the same time the university had been informed that he was to be arrested. On the 16th of the same month he went underground and was hidden by his enlightened brother Joseph Martin, who was a locksmith. A few days later he escaped from Ingolstadt to Nuremberg disguised as a craftsman. He remained there for a short time and then travelled to the free city of Regensburg, where he continued his work. In the course of the investigation, more and more evidence came to light against the Illuminati, who continued their activities despite the ban. On 2 March, therefore, a new decree was issued which made it possible to confiscate the property of the Illuminati Order. As fate would have it, on 20 July 1785, an event occurred that put the police on the trail for good. Jakob Lanz, a priest, a courier for the Order who intended to travel to Berlin and Silesia, was struck by lightning in Regensburg and died. Everything suggests that Weishaupt, who was living in hiding in the city, and Lanz had seen each other and Lanz had received instructions from his leader. Compromising papers and a list of names were found sewn into Lanz's clothes. The local police then searched the priest's house and discovered other important documents, including instructions concerning the revolution in France addressed to the Grand Master of the Grand Orient. Everything was handed over to the Bavarian authorities, who on 4 August 1785 enacted a new ban on secret societies. On the 31st of the same month they ordered Weishaupt's arrest and even put a price on his head in Bavaria. Weishaupt fled to Gotha where the enlightened Ernest, Grand Duke of Saxe-Gotha, granted him the title of Privy Councillor and was able to protect him in his sanctuary until his death on 18 November 1830. A bust of Weishaupt is on display in the Germanic Museum in Nuremberg.

Jüri Lina states in his book that in the summer of 1986 he worked in the Ingolstadt archives and was able to carefully study some of the documents related to the case. She found out that the search for other important members of the Order was proceeding slowly. The papers found in Lanz's house were compromising for Dr. Franz Xaver Zwack, Cato, whose house in Landshut, where the Illuminati kept important documents, was searched on 11 and 12 October 1786. In 1787 the castle of Baron Bassus, Hannibal, was also searched by the police. Further papers were confiscated there relating to the conspiracy of the Bavarian Illuminati, in which plans for a world revolution carried out by secret societies were set out. The private correspondence found in Landshut and in the castle of Baron Bassus was published and commented on a decade later by the Scottish professor John Robison. We will have the opportunity to examine it below

Among the texts and documents published in those years about the Illuminati, two books stand out in 1786: *Drei merkwürdige Aussagen (Three Curious Expositions)*, containing the statements made by Professors Grünberg, Cossandey and Rener, and *Grosse Absichten des Ordens der Illuminaten (Great Intentions of the Order of the Illuminati)*, with the testimony of Professor Joseph Utzschneider. The Elector of Bavaria, Karl Theodor, also ordered in 1787 the printing of two works containing the confiscated secret documents: *Einige Originalschrifften des Illuminaten-Ordens (Some Original Documents of the Order of the Illuminati)* and *Nachtrag von weitern Originalschrifften (Supplement of New Original Documents)*. Finally, the bookseller Johann Baptist Strobl also published a new collection of documents concerning the Illuminati in 1787. These books were sent by the Bavarian authorities to the governments in Paris, London, St. Petersburg and others, but only when it was too late were they taken seriously.

In Ingolstadt and Munich, therefore, the documents are available for anyone who wants to see them. There is no denying the existence of a powerful secret organisation which planned a world revolution which was to do away with all religions and all governments. Obviously, secret societies cannot be suppressed by decree. Therefore, after being discovered, the conspirators hid in their dens and apparently disappeared, although their plan survived, as we shall see as we proceed in our exposition. The basic aims of the Bavarian Illuminati were these: 1. Abolition of all established governments. 2. Abolition of private property. 3. 3. Abolition of inheritance. 4. Abolition of all religion. Abolition of patriotism. 6. 6. Abolition of the family. 7. Creation of a new World Order or World Government. One does not have to be very suspicious to notice that these points reappear in 1848 in the *Communist Manifesto*, written by the Jewish Karl Marx, a 31st degree Freemason, on behalf of the League of the Righteous ("Der Bund der Gerechten"), a secret society sponsored by the Illuminati from which the Communist Party originated. These same points were in 1917 the aspiration of the internationalists who implemented the programme in the USSR. Today the goal of the "New World Order" (Novus Ordo Seclorum) is the highest aspiration of the bankers who hold the real power in the world. Paul Warburg, the Zionist banker who designed the Federal Reserve project, put it in these words on 17 February 1950 in testimony before the US Senate: "We will have a world government whether you like it or not. The only question is whether that government will be achieved by conquest or consent" ("We will have a world government whether you like it or not. The only question is whether it will be established by concession or by compulsion".)

Can anyone believe that such a gigantic plan, the plan of the World Revolution, could be devised in the mind of a single man, who, moreover, has remained practically unknown? There is no doubt that Adam Weishaupt was a super-agent, as we have explained throughout these pages, who worked for powerful men, mainly Jewish bankers, to whom we shall henceforth refer assiduously, for they are behind all the decisive events of contemporary history.

Robison, Barruel and Scott

As it took shape, the World Revolutionary Movement left, as we have just seen, evidence of its existence, but few dared to denounce it and expose it publicly. Among the contemporaries who left to posterity works that reveal the true nature of the revolutionary events are three great intellectuals who had the courage to write down what they knew about the conspiracy. Today they are indispensable sources to which scholars should turn.

The first is John Robison (1739-1805), professor of Natural Philosophy at the University of Edinburgh and general secretary of the Royal Society of Edinburgh. Des Griffin in *Fourth Reich of the Rich* states that Adam Weishaupt himself, seeing in this professor the ideal person to expand Illuminism in Britain, invited Robison to join his organisation. In Griffin's words, "Weishaupt completely misunderstood Robison's character. Instead of discovering a vain man with an unquenchable thirst for power, he found a person of great integrity, deeply committed to the welfare of human beings and to that of his own nation in particular. Robison was a man who could not be bought." That is to say, John Robison, who was a high degree Freemason and had frequented on the Continent various lodges in Belgium, France, Germany and Russia, did not fall into the trap and did not believe that the aims of the Illuminati were clean and honourable. He kept his thoughts to himself, however, and met the conspirators. As a result of his experience, Robison wrote a surprising and unexpected book: *Proofs of a Conspiracy Against All the Religions and Governments of Europe Carried on in the Secret Meetings of Freemasons, Illuminati and Reading Societies.* The book was published in London in 1797 and in New York in 1798.

The second is Abbot Augustin Barruel (1741-1820), a Jesuit who also in 1797 published in French *Mémoires pour servir à l'Histoire du Jacobinisme (Memoirs to serve the History of Jacobinism)*, a work that was translated into English and published in London in 1798. Robison and Barruel, without knowing each other, offer a similar view of the organisation of the sect or Order of the Bavarian Illuminati. Barruel's book was translated into Spanish by a religious from Santoña, Simón Antonio de Rentería (1762-1825), who died in Santiago de Compostela as its archbishop. As far as we know, this translation cannot be found; however, Raymundo Strauch i Vidal, bishop of Vich, made a second translation into Spanish and Abbé Barruel's work was published in Vich in 1870 in two volumes.

The third man is Sir Walter Scott (1771-1832), the famous Scottish novelist, who, incidentally, was also a Freemason. Scott offers in *The Life of Napoleon Buonaparte* (1820) a preliminary study of the French Revolution, in which he reveals that the events that led to the revolution and ushered in the reign of terror were orchestrated by Frankfurt bankers, whose agents guided the masses. Walter Scott reveals that the Secret Power behind the conspiracy was of Jewish origin and points out that the leading figures in the revolution were foreigners. Scott notes that typically Jewish words were used, such as "directors" or "elders", and uses the terms "Sanhedrin" to refer to the Paris Deputation during the massacres of September 1792 and "synagogue" to refer to the Jacobin clubs, whose leaders were Danton, Marat and Robespierre. The *Israelite Archives* admits with calculated ambiguity or perhaps with disguised pride the Jewish hand behind the events and textually acknowledges: "The French Revolution has a very expressive Hebrew character". Curiously, this work by Walter Scott, whose fame as a novelist is universal, is virtually unknown.

Robison's and Barruel's books, by contrast, saw numerous editions and deserved the attention of their contemporaries, although they were soon attacked with disqualifications and insults intended to discredit them. Both writers were accused of being witch-hunters, alarmists, bigots who persecuted freedom of opinion or academic freedom. In those days newspapers were moving beyond their birth or early development stage and were beginning to be coveted by those who sought to create and control people's opinion. The concentrated attacks on these two authors for saying that the Bavarian Illuminati had triggered the revolution in France show that control of the press, which today is absolute, was beginning to be effective in America and England. If one now searches Wikipedia, for example, for information about Barruel, accusations of falsehood and anti-Semitism soon appear. Even today, researchers who attempt to revise history are immediately accused of being anti-Semitic, reactionary or neo-Nazi.

It is precisely in the chapter of John Robison's work where he explains all about the Reading Societies that the importance attached by the Illuminati to the control of the writing, publishing and sale of books becomes clear. These are the words of Adam Weishaupt: "With our writers we must take care that we puff them up and that the critics do not demean them; we must endeavour by all possible means to win over the critics and the journalists; and we must also endeavour to win over the booksellers, who in time will find that it is in their interest to take our side. [...] If any writer publishes something that attracts attention and what he says is good, but does not agree with our plans, we must endeavour to win him over or discredit him". Weishaupt's ideas were continued a century later in the *Protocols of the Elders of Zion*, the authenticity of which has been unsuccessfully challenged by Zionists throughout the 20th century. They state: "We will hold the reins of the press in our hands. We shall also endeavour to control all other publications. [...] From all parts of the world all the news is received by a few agencies in which it is concentrated. When we have acquired power, these agencies will be entirely ours and will publish only such news as we allow them to publish. [...] None of those who would try to attack us with their pen would find anyone to publish it for them. [...] If any people want to write against us, they will find no publisher."

Robison

The availability of a facsimile reprint of Robison's book in English allows us to translate some texts that will help us to understand the project that the Illuminati set in motion. So let us look at some essential ideas that show the true nature of the conspiracy and its deeper aims. In the introduction Robison warns that, despite being officially disbanded, the Order of the Illuminati was still active in 1797: "I have seen this Association systematically working with enthusiasm and becoming almost irresistible. And I have seen that the most active leaders of the French Revolution were members of this Association and led the first movements according to its principles, through its instructions and through assistance, previously requested and obtained. And finally I have seen that this Association still exists, it still works in secret...". The Scottish professor confirms that the illuminati ascended by taking advantage of the lodges and their protection; he denounces that they introduced into them innovations fraught with corruption and violence; he notes that uncertainty and darkness hang over the mysterious Association, which is different from Freemasonry.

As we have been pointing out, the members of the sect had secret names that concealed their real names. Also all the Bolshevik leaders in 1917 concealed their Jewish names and changed them to Russian ones. Robison gives the list of the main "aliases" adopted by the most conspicuous members of the sect and also explains the organisational diagram in the form of a pyramid structure, so often reproduced in numerous publications. The way it worked was as follows: at the top, the "general" of the Order had two trusted men, who in turn each had two others, each of whom in turn had two others under him, and so on. In the lower echelons, each individual knew only one person or mentor to whom he reported and from whom he received training and instructions. It could be known that there were superiors of different ranks, but they were usually never seen or known. The whole process of information and training was filtered as one moved up and down the pyramid structure. Logically, the members of the lower rungs of the pyramid knew nothing about the organisation they worked for and only became more trustworthy as they moved up the ladder by merit and after careful observation.

Among the ideas inculcated in the novices or minervals was that of universal happiness, to be achieved by the abolition of nations and the union of the human race and all the inhabitants of the earth in one great society. Concepts such as patriotism or loyalty were considered narrow-minded prejudices incompatible with universal benevolence. Suicide was justified: it had to be introduced into the minds of men that the act of depriving oneself of life provided a certain voluptuous pleasure (nowadays, social networks or clubs promoting suicide among young people proliferate on the internet). At a certain point, those who had been admitted to higher ranks could already be told that the Illuminati would rule the world.

In the correspondence between the leaders things were much clearer. In a letter of 6 February 1778 to Cato (Zwack), Spartacus (Weishaupt) writes: "Only those who are surely suitable will be chosen from among the lower classes to know the higher mysteries, which contain the principles and the means of attaining a happy life. In no case are religious principles to be accepted among these. [...] Each person is to become a spy on another and on all those around him. Nothing must escape our gaze. [...] No man is fit for our Order unless he is a Brutus or a Catiline" (i.e. capable of the worst crimes). In another letter of March 1778, Spartacus proposes to Cato a series of "inventions" typical of "benefactors of humanity", among which the following stand out: a box-bomb that would explode when forced, a drink to cause miscarriages, a liquid that would blind or kill when thrown in the face, recipes for a kind of "aqua toffana" with deadly effects, poisonous perfumes that would fill rooms with pestilent vapours, and a recipe "ad excitandum furorem uterinum".

In another text from Spartacus to Cato, the date of which is not specified, but which is already after the years of the prohibition of the Order, Weishaupt writes: "...By this plan we shall lead the whole of humanity. In this way and by the simplest means, we shall set everything in operation and on fire. The employments (offices) are to be assigned and conceived in such a way that we can, in secret, influence all political operations." The historical facts show that this objective has been absolutely fulfilled: the agents who surrounded Wilson and Roosevelt, as will be seen in due course, obeyed the orders of the Secret Power and brought about the entry of the United States into the two world wars. They were men placed in key positions, conceived and prepared for such purposes. In the same letter Spartacus says: "I have considered all things and prepared everything so that if the Order goes to ruin today, I shall restore it in a year and stronger and brighter than ever." Here Professor Robison interrupts the text and makes an aside to point out that it did indeed re-emerge as predicted in the time foretold under the name of "Deutsche Union" (German Union) and the form of "Reading Societies". It must therefore be understood that this new secret society was an extension of the Illuminati. The letter continues: "I am so sure of success, in spite of all obstacles, that it is indifferent to me whether it should cost me my life or my freedom. [...] But I possess the art of taking advantage even of misfortune; and when you think me sunk to the bottom, I will rise with new energy. Who would have thought that a professor from Ingolstadt would become the instructor of the professors of Göttingen and of the greatest men of Germany?"

In another text Spartacus, after recalling the need to impress upon those who claim moral pretexts that the end justifies the means, acknowledges the importance of Knigge (Philo) in infiltrating Freemasonry and gaining proselytes. Spartacus explains to Diomedes (the Marquis of Constance) that Philo is one of the most usable and practical men in the Order, and that it was mainly through his efforts among the Masons of the Protestant countries that the "Eclectic System" was introduced and they were brought to accept the leadership of the Illuminati, an achievement whose merit is entirely attributable to Philo's extensive connections in Freemasonry. Spartacus admits that Knigge, before his enlightenment, travelled as a philosopher from town to town, lodge to lodge, and even from house to house.

Weishaupt was building up the idea that the Reading Societies would be a basic structural element of the German Union. The following text, quoted by Robison without specifying date or addressee, is very significant: "The great strength of our Order lies in its concealment. It must never appear anywhere under its real name, but always hidden under another name and another task. [...] In this connection, the form of a learned or literary society is the one best suited to our purposes; and if Freemasonry had not existed, this cover would have been employed; but it must be much more than a screen, it can be a powerful machine in our hands. By establishing reading societies, and subscribing bookshops, and having them under our management, and supplying them with our works, we can mould the public thought as we will. It is in this way that we must try to influence military academies (this may have tremendous consequences), printing presses, bookshops, town halls, in short, wherever we can have an effect on the training or the management or even the direction of people's minds. Printing and engraving deserve our utmost concern. A Literary Society is the most suitable form for the introduction of our Order into a State where we have not yet been introduced (note this!)". Seeing how the culture industry and in particular the literary business and its market function today, it is evident that everything has been fulfilled: it is objectively proven that television channels, information agencies and publishing houses, which include newspapers, magazines and books, are mostly in the hands of Jewish capitalists and their friends. It is undeniable that we read what we read, i.e. what they want us to read.

In relation to how the Illuminati were taking over key positions in various institutions, Robison reproduces a handwritten letter from Cato (Zwack) addressed to an unknown addressee, who could well be Spartacus himself. It says that they have bought a house in Munich and that the garden is occupied by botanical species which give the house (a lodge) the appearance of a society of enthusiastic naturalists. In this house the Illuminati system has been established and the lodges of Poland have been taken in. The letter reads as follows: "Thanks to the activity of our brethren, the Jesuits have been relieved of all their offices in Ingolstadt and all the professors belong to the Order. Five of them are excellent and the students will be prepared by us. [...] We have been very successful against the Jesuits and things have come to the point that their revenues, such as the mission, the alms in gold, the exercises and the archives of the conversions are now under the control of our friends. All the German schools and the Benevolent Society are at last run by us. We have several stalwart members in the courts of justice and can afford to give them a salary and other good advantages. We have lately succeeded in placing a young clergyman in the Foundation of St. Bartholomew's and have thus secured his supporters. In this way we will be able to supply suitable priests for Bavaria. Thanks to a letter from Philo, we have learned that we have secured one of the highest offices in the Church for a fervent enlightened one, despite the opposition of the Bishop of Spire, who happens to be an intolerant and tyrannical priest."

Two publications of the period are cited by Professor Robison in relation to the German Union and the creation of the Reading Societies. The first, *More notes than text or the German Union of the XXII, a new secret society for the good of mankind,* was published by the bookseller Goschen in Leipzig in 1789, who says that the text came to him through an unknown hand and that he published it quickly considering the damage that this society, of which he had already heard certain reports, could produce in the world and in commerce if it were allowed to work in secret. Also in 1789 the second book was published, the German title of which was *Nähere Beleuchtung der Deutsche Union (More Information about the German Union).* The first publication contained plans and letters for trusted or secure members only, the printing of which had been authorised by the Twenty-two United Brethren. The first pages introduce the Twenty-two's Plan: "We work first of all to attract all good writers to our association. We imagine that this will be easy to achieve, for they can obtain obvious advantages. In addition we intend to win over the postmasters and clerks of the post offices so that they will facilitate our correspondence". Further on, the enormous benefits that humanity will achieve through the "altruistic" purposes of the Union are set forth: "Everyone will be able to note the progressive moral influence that the Union will acquire within the nation. Let us see what superstition will be lost and what learning will be gained when, 1. In every Reading Society the books are selected by our Brotherhood. 2. When we have trustworthy persons in every neighbourhood who are concerned to extend to every home the purposes of enlightenment to humanity. 3. When we have the voice of the public on our side, and when we are able to eliminate the fanatical writings which appear in the magazines which are usually read, or to warn the public against them; and, on the other hand, when we are able to publicise and recommend the works which enlighten the minds of men. 4. When we shall gradually have the whole book trade in our hands (for good writers will bring their works into the market through us), we shall make it so that writers who work in the cause of superstition and moderation will have neither publishers nor readers. 5. When our Brotherhood finally spreads, and all sensitive hearts and good people adhere to us, we will enable them to work quietly to influence administrators, stewards, secretaries, court officers, parish priests, public officials, private tutors....."

It is surprising to note that indeed great writers and talented artists were initially taken in by the Illuminati. The English poet Percy Bysshe Shelley and his wife, Mary Shelley, as we have seen above, were dazzled by the propaganda. Luckily a book by Barruel fell into Shelley's hands. On discovering the true nature of the conspiracy, he took care to warn his friends, among whom was the poet and essayist Leigh Hunt. The great Johann Wolfgang Göthe, alias Abaris, also fell into the trap, as a leading illuminist, Leopold Engel, revealed in 1906 in *Geschichte des Illuminaten Ordens (History of the Order of the Illuminati).* Fortunately, he too was suspicious of the true nature of the sect. In a letter of his to Bode, alias Amelius, he writes: "Believe me, our moral world is undermined by underground tunnels, cellars and sewers, as a large city usually is, without anyone suspecting its connections. It is understandable to me or to any other enlightened person that sometimes smoke seeps through the cracks or strange voices are heard..." Friedrich von Schiller, a poet and playwright who had also been bamboozled by the Order, was planning to write a play, *Demetrius*, which was intended to unveil some atrocities. Weishaupt learned of this from Heinrich Voss, a "hinting brother" (the "hinting brothers" were in a sense Weishaupt's secret police), and wanted to prevent it at all costs. Schiller died after a long illness on 9 May 1805. Hermann Ahlwardt in his book *Mehr Licht (More Light)* claims that Schiller was murdered by the Illuminati.

John Robison's work and the texts published in it would perhaps deserve more space, but we must move on. It is clear that wolves in sheep's clothing sought to supervise and control literary and intellectual creation. They planned to ostracise those who did not agree with their ideas, on the pretext that they produced writings pernicious to humanity, which they, enlightened philanthropists, intended to improve. Anyone can note, however, that in their writings there is not a word for the poor, for the suffering. Nor do we read anything about social reform that is not related to the desire for domination in order to obtain world power. The main objective was to acquire wealth, power and influence at all costs. To achieve this, they sought to abolish Christianity and to replace moral principles with a libertinism, masquerading as humanity and benevolence. Half a century later, they realised that to win over the masses of workers, their discourse would have to be adapted and adapted. When Weishaupt died in 1830, his Order was probably stronger than ever; but it was to change its name and present itself in public under the name of communism.

PART 3
FRENCH REVOLUTION

Official history explains the French Revolution as the inevitable clash between a feudal structure and a social reality that was at odds with it. It teaches us that the encyclopaedist writers and philosophers had unleashed an ideological storm that challenged the Church and the State and brought the old moral, political and economic ideas to the wreck. Rousseau, who in his *Discourse on the Inequality of Social Conditions* expressed his contempt for the monarchy of Louis XV, supported the grievances of the poor against the rich and attacked the privileged, proclaimed in the *Social Contract*, unlike Voltaire, who dwelt on administrative reforms, the right of nations to modify their governments. Rousseau addressed the masses and impelled them to political revolution. In 1770 he wrote: "We are approaching the state of crisis of the century of revolutions. It seems to me impossible that the monarchies of Europe will last long". It must certainly be admitted that his works and those of other thinkers influenced the development of revolutionary ideas and republican theories; but they were in no way decisive in triggering events that were planned, organised and financed abroad. In fact, Rousseau's ideas had made a large part of the nobility aware of the need for reform. The first to be convinced of the importance of implementing a reformist policy was the king, Louis XVI, who in 1774, at the age of twenty, had succeeded his grandfather Louis XV.

In any case, France was no different from other European nations. Among the general evils of the century in Europe were: poor administration; outdated and highly unjust penal codes; poor organisation of the Treasury; corruption in the collection of taxes; privileges and franchises of the clergy and nobility; unjust distribution and exploitation of land; lack of individual liberties; neglect, if not abandonment, of health and the education and instruction of the people. It cannot be denied, therefore, that profound reforms were needed in France and in all countries. However, according to the socialist politician Louis Blanc, author of a twelve-volume *History of the French Revolution*, even the socialist Babeuf, alias Gracchus, who was an enlightened man and a disciple of Weishaupt, had declared that France was no worse off than the peoples of other nations. In spite of the defects pointed out, the ancien régime of France was perhaps the best on the Continent. During the 18th century France had increased its exports tenfold, and progress in industry and agriculture was evident. In terms of communications, it was the admiration of the Continent, with a network of more than forty thousand kilometres of paved roads.

During the first two years of Louis XVI's reign, ministers such as Turgot and Malesherbes resolutely embarked on the path of reform. Turgot, who, instead of borrowing new money, managed to pay off more than 100 million of the public debt in twenty months without increasing taxes, tried to abolish the corvée, which was an abuse for the peasants, who could be forced to work for the nobles. He also planned a decentralisation plan, and wanted to implement a vast public education plan. His collaborator Malesherbes reformed the justice system by abolishing censorship, abolishing torture as a judicial test and adopting a system of health care in prisons. Unfortunately, in 1776 the adversaries of both ministers forced their departure from the government and, contrary to Turgot's wishes, France, which needed peace to restore its finances, was to take the deadly step of supporting the revolted colonies in America. Necker, a Calvinist Swiss banker, was appointed as the new finance minister, and to pay for the war he increased the public debt dreadfully. In 1781, to shore up public confidence, he published for the first time the state budgets, rigged with a surplus of ten million pounds when in fact they showed an annual deficit of seventy million. Necker was replaced, although he was reappointed finance minister on two further occasions, in 1788 and 1789. It is curious to note that Necker, despite his abysmal management, enjoyed a strange popularity: the press supported his actions and his appointments were greeted with enthusiasm by the people. His successor, Calonne, sank deeper into the abyss of debt, the interest on which came to absorb 50% of the state's revenue. The budget deficit reached 126 million, which was equivalent to 20% of the overall budget and put France on the verge of bankruptcy. Calonne then attempted a tax reform based on tax equality and the abolition of privileges that exempted the most powerful sectors from taxation. Logically, the attempt failed and the minister, having lost the protection of the monarch, emigrated to England in April 1787. By now the revolutionaries' tactics, which instead of pushing through reforms had consisted of delaying them in order to increase popular discontent, were bearing fruit: social unrest was growing and catastrophe was looming.

The revolution that led to American independence was about the achievement of property ownership by those who had worked to develop the country, who felt they owed nothing to the landed proprietors of the British Crown. The revolution was thus free of reigns of terror, of mobs led by agents, or of the atrocities associated with the French and Bolshevik revolutions; although Lord Shelburne tried, as he would later successfully do in France, to place his agents in crucial positions among the American revolutionaries. Lord Shelburne's men appeared at critical moments and presented themselves as bold patriots. According to Eustace Mullins, just as Swiss bankers influenced the French court to place the financier Necker in the Ministry of Finance, a position key to precipitating the economic depression, so Lord Shelburne played an important role in manipulating American forces during the Revolution. Most famous among these agents was Benedict Arnold, an American general who betrayed his own and spent the post-war years comfortably ensconced in England.

France and Spain played the pro-independence card for different reasons. France soon sent aid to the rebels, who in December 1774 held a congress in Philadelphia and decided to abolish taxes, pass laws, create paper money and confer command of their forces on George Washington. On 4 July 1776, in the midst of war with England, the United States of America proclaimed its independence. One of the first acts of sovereignty was to send diplomats to the major European countries. France welcomed them, but did not yet officially accept them. It was two years later, in March 1778, that Paris recognised the independence of North America on the promise of the rebels never to submit to the crown of England. The notification of this fact to Britain was tantamount to a declaration of war. Immediately naval battles began in America and in Europe between the fleets of the two countries. Charles III and his minister Floridablanca, despite the fact that the Count of Aranda, ambassador in Paris, was in favour of making war on the English, initially resisted pressure from the French Bourbons. Finally, in the hope of recovering Minorca and Gibraltar and putting an end to London's harassment of trade with the colonies, Spain, after accusing the British of having threatened its dominions in America, declared war on Britain in June 1779. The vicissitudes of the confrontation fall outside the scope of this narrative. Ultimately, the intervention of France and Spain prevented the British from quelling the revolution in their American colonies in time. By the time the Peace of Versailles was signed in September 1783, American independence was irreversible.

Benjamin Franklin, one of the fathers of the US Constitution, himself a high degree Freemason, spoke prophetic words at one of the drafting sessions of the constitutional text regarding the historic role Jews have played in the politics of the states that have embraced them. Two hundred years later they have been fully realised. Here they are, taken from the original document housed at the Franklin Institute in Philadelphia:

"There is a great danger to the United States of America. That great danger is the Jew. Gentlemen, wherever on earth Jews have settled, they have lowered the moral standard and the degree of commercial honesty, they have kept themselves apart and unassimilated, they have created a State within a State. And they have tried to economically strangle those who have opposed them, as was the case in Spain and Portugal.

For more than 1700 years they have lamented their sad fate, namely, that they were driven out of their homeland, but gentlemen, if the civilised world were to give them the property of Palestine today, they would immediately look for compelling reasons not to return there. Why? Because they are vampires and cannot live among themselves. They have to live among Christians and other people who do not belong to their race. If they are not constitutionally excluded from the United States, in less than a hundred years they will enter our country in such numbers that they will rule and destroy us. They will change our form of government, for which we Americans have shed our blood and sacrificed life, property and personal liberty. If the Jews are not excluded, in less than two hundred years our children will be working in the fields to feed the Jews, while they remain in the "Counting House" rubbing their hands with glee. I warn you, gentlemen, if you do not exclude the Jew forever, your children's children will curse you from their graves.

Their ideas are not those of the Americans, even if they have lived among us for generations. The leopard cannot change its spots. The Jews are a danger to this land, and if they are allowed in, they will endanger its institutions. They must be excluded through the Constitution"

Later, when the time comes to explain the covert coup d'état that led to the creation of the Federal Reserve in 1913, there will be an opportunity to comment on B. Franklin's warning.

The revolution is served

A threatening English pamphlet addressed to Louis XVI clearly warned him that his days as monarch were numbered and in some ways anticipated the role England would play in the coming revolution. After reproaching the French king for his intervention on behalf of the Americans and against Britain, the pamphlet concluded: "What danger is there in putting the elite of your officers in communication with men enthusiastic for liberty? How can it be that after having shed their blood in the cause of what they say is liberty, they will enforce your absolute orders? Where does this assurance come from when in America the statue of the King of Great Britain is smashed to pieces, when his name is reviled and vilified? England will be well revenged for your hostile designs when your government is examined, tried, and condemned according to the principles professed in Philadelphia, and applauded in your capital."

Having briefly outlined the background, we can now detail some of the revolutionary events that were to overthrow the Monarchy and the Ancien Régime within a few years. On 5 May 1789, the opening of the Estates General was held at Versailles in the Salon des Menus, which became known as the Salon des Trois États Généraux. The rift between the throne and the Third Estate was immediately apparent. On 17 June, on the proposal of Sieyès, the majority of the deputies set themselves up as a National Assembly. After days of wrangling between the three estates, the National Assembly proclaimed the principle of the sovereignty of the nation over the king himself.

On 11 July 1789 Necker, who had been appointed director general of finance on 25 August 1788, was dismissed for the second time; but five days later the king, under pressure from the Orleanists, was forced to put him back in charge of France's finances. In the Palais Royal of the Duke of Orleans, the nerve centre of the agitation as already mentioned, Camille Desmoulins, a lousy lawyer who stammered when he spoke and who would end up on the guillotine on 13 April 1794, perched on a chair with a pistol in his hand harangued the people on 12 July with these words: "Citizens, we must lose no time; the dismissal of Necker is the clarion call of a St. Bartholomew of patriots, and this very night the foreign battalions will come out from the Champ de Mars to slit our throats. We have but one resource left; run to arms!" The people reacted by seizing the busts of Necker and the Duke of Orleans and paraded them in triumph through the streets of the capital. This was the first act, a rehearsal for what was to happen two days later. The troops tried to break up the crowd, and violence broke out, soon encouraged by hired brigands who mistook the people for looters and terrorists. In reality, despite his good press, Necker, the financial sorcerer of those years and father of the famous Madame de Staël, whom he tried to marry off to the English Prime Minister William Pitt, had triggered inflation with his economic policies and was the instrument of Swiss and British bankers who planned to reap handsome profits from the debacle that was about to unfold. Edmund Burke went so far as to say in the House of Commons that Necker was England's best friend on the Continent.

After the proclamation intended to grant him the role of constitutional monarch, Louis XVI attempted to dissolve the Assembly by means of the troops of the Duc de Broglie. The rumour of this attempt added to the general unrest that had set in in Paris after the events of the 12th and led to the bourgeois uprising in the capital on 14 July 1789, which culminated in the famous storming of the Bastille. According to the official story, the people freed many political prisoners who were tortured in that prison; but in reality there were only seven prisoners: two madmen named Tabernier and Whyte; the Count of Solanges, a libertine convicted of various crimes; and four fraudsters named Laroche, Bechade, Pujade and La Corrége, imprisoned for counterfeiting bills of exchange. M. Gustave Bord in *The storming of the Bastille* states that "an invisible hand paid for the disorder and paid it generously". The distribution of money among the mutineers who took the Bastille is widely confirmed by numerous contemporary authors. The only disagreement lies in the amount paid to the rioters, which ranged from six to twelve francs a day. These events made it possible to transfer political power to the Assembly, which was to become the Constituent Assembly. When the Duke de la Rochefoucauld-Liancourt announced the storming of the Bastille to the King in the evening, the latter asked: "So it is a revolt? To which the Duke replied: "Sire, it is a revolution! The revolution had broken out and, as if by magic, had done so all over France at the same time, thanks to the work of the secret societies. The king realised at once that it was useless to resist, and that he could only try to control it. He then made his way on foot and unescorted to the Assembly and placed himself in its hands.

Eight days after the storming of the Bastille, on 22 July, agents of Illuminati Freemasonry, among whom Adrian Dupont is mentioned as the main instigator of the stratagem, unleashed what has gone down in history as "The Great Fear". Simultaneously in all the provinces of France, taking advantage of the famine in the country, news was spread alarming the population and inviting them to arm themselves: it was reported that groups of vagabond bandits were raping and killing women and children. Panic was also created by announcing the imminent attack by German and British troops. On the same day and at almost the same time, horsemen on horseback pretending to be the king's couriers read out a royal edict through towns and cities that read: "The king orders all castles to be burned. He wishes to keep only his own castles. The people obeyed the orders and took up arms and set about the work of destruction. Nesta Webster, who attributes this conspiracy to Freemasonry, recalls that, before being enlightened, the lodges planned a revolution for the benefit of the bourgeoisie, using the people as their instrument.

In Caen, the birthplace of the famous Charlotte Cordey, an event took place as early as 12 August that can be seen as a dire foreshadowing of the terror that was to be unleashed in France in the years to come. Stanley Loomis recounts it in his *Paris in the Terror, June 1793-July 1794*. In Caen, the formation of the Assembly had been celebrated with the erection of a wooden pyramid in the main square. A young royalist officer, Henri de Belzunce, unable to understand the extent of the events, tried to put an end to the celebrations, which caused his name to spread by word of mouth. On 11 August, Belzunce incited some of his soldiers to tear Necker's medals from around their necks. Rumours soon spread that Belzunce was planning to set fire to the city and destroy it,. As a result of this agitation, some of Belzunce's men exchanged gunfire with some of the Caen civil guard. At nightfall the young officer was summoned to appear at the town hall and Belzunce, who must have been arrogant and rather stupid, left the safety of his barracks in civilian clothes and appeared alone. As soon as he was separated from his soldiers, he was surrounded by an angry mob. Appealing to "his own safety", he was locked up in the city fortress, where he spent the night. When he left the prison the next morning, he had to pass through a mob of people armed with scythes and muskets calling for his head. Before he was torn to pieces by the mob," Loomis writes, "he decided to take his own life on the spot and tried to snatch the weapon from one of his guards, who struck him and threw him to the ground. In an instant the crowd was upon him. He was beaten to death. The mob hacked him to pieces. A man cut open his chest with a pair of scissors and extracted his still beating heart. The hideous garment was tossed into the air like a child's toy. A woman finally caught it, skewered it on a stick and screaming madly devoured it. Unspeakable atrocities were committed on the rest of his body.

Orleanist faction seeks power

During the first three years, the Enlightenment's plan was to be burnt to the ground and to make its way through the intrigues of the political factions. The Orleanist faction had caused the artificial grain shortage in the spring and summer of 1789. It also played the main role in the siege of the Bastille. On 5 October of the same year, the march on Versailles finally exposed the Duke of Orléans, who was convinced that his time had come and that the change of dynasty would come. Looking at the end of this character, there can be no doubt that he was treated in the true spirit of the Order of the Illuminati, for he was used as a mere tool, deceived, ruined and executed. Let us look at his actions in those days of October 1789, which are recorded in the declarations of the Châtelet.

First of all, the Châtelet in Paris was one of the most eminent jurisdictions in the kingdom of France under the Ancien Régime. Today, its archives are widely consulted by historians, even though it is difficult to find one's way through the series of documents housed there. The proceedings in the various chambers of the Châtelet were oral, and their jurisdiction could be civil, criminal or police. In 1789, there were calls for its demolition, as it did not enjoy a good press. A law of 24 August 1790 abolished its jurisdiction and led to the closure of the archives and the demolition of the building. On 22 January 1791, the Paris municipality decided to seal the archives of the Châtelet. Six months later, a former scribe of the civil chamber, Jean Charles Gabé, was commissioned to lift the seals and the processing of the archives could begin. The Châtelet archives entered the Soubise Palace in 1847 and together with the archives of the Parliament and other Parisian jurisdictions, they constitute the so-called judicial section of the National Archives.

The discussion on the king's right of veto provoked fierce arguments in the Assembly and violent clashes in the streets. In the Palais Royal there were threats to dismiss the royalist deputies. In addition, the famine was increasing steadily. Marat and Desmoulins demanded in their newspapers "another excess of revolution". It was in this context that a woman went through the streets beating a drum and asking for bread. Thousands of women joined her and also men armed with axes. They ransacked the arms depot of the National Guard militia and took wagons, guns and cannons and marched to Versailles, where the court was located. This was a ploy by the Orleanists. Statements from the Châtelet prove that during those days (5 and 6 October) Philippe Égalité was seen repeatedly, and when the crowd recognised him he was acclaimed with cries of "Long live Orleans" and "Long live our King Orleans". He would then retreat and appear elsewhere. His last appearance on the 5th was at about nine o'clock in the evening, when he was seen conversing in a corner with men in women's clothes and others disguised in humble garb, among whom were Mirabeau, Barnave, Duport and several deputies of the republican party. The next day, he was seen again with the same people in women's clothing. Later, he was at the top of a flight of stairs showing the assailants with his hand where they should go. He then ran down another path to stand next to the monarch, who was his cousin. When the king was led amidst insults towards Paris, Louis-Philippe d'Orléans was again seen lurking on the balcony behind some children as the procession marched by.

Two battalions of the Flanders Regiment were sent to Versallles to protect the royal family. Then the Orleanists, as good disciples of Weishaupt, put into practice his instructions on the use of women[9]. John Robison cites the declarations number 177 and number 317 of the Châtelet as the source of the information that follows. About three hundred "nymphs" from the Palais Royal, paid in escudos and gold louis by the Abbe Sieyès, were sent to meet the two battalions. Soldiers from one of the regiments informed their commanders of the attempt to break their loyalty by bribery. Mademoiselle Théroigne de Mericourt, the favourite of the moment at the Palais Royal, was one of the most active among the armed mob in Paris. Dressed as an Amazon, with all the elegance of the opera, she made more than one young man lose his head. The mob that made its way to Versailles begging bread from the king had their pockets full of coins. Orleans was seen by two gentlemen with a bag of money so heavy that it was strapped to his clothes. The Duke of Orleans himself acknowledged before his death that he had spent nearly £50,000 bribing the Regiment of French Guards.

Goya's well-known painting *Saturn devouring his children* provides the perfect picture of what happened in France as the revolution burned out and the hand of the Illuminati became more evident. One of the first illustrious victims was Mirabeau. Only human contradictions, miscalculations or misjudgements, overconfidence or self-deception can explain the actions of this character, who had behaved like a madman throughout his life, and who finally, inconsistently with his previous actions, tried to save the principles of the monarchy, which cost him his life.

---

[9] Among the papers seized by the Bavarian police from Cato (Zwack), a project for a sisterhood of women was found that could serve the Illuminati's plans. The text reads as follows: "It will be of great use and will bring us information and money, and at the same time it will do wonders to satisfy the taste of many of our most faithful members who are fond of sex. There should be two kinds of sisters, the virtuous and the vicious. They should not know each other and should be led by men, but without their knowing it. They should be given suitable books and other things to excite their passions". Another document stresses the importance of using women to achieve their goals. "There is no more powerful way of influencing men than women. They, therefore, must be the main object of our study. We must win them over with advice on their emancipation from the tyranny of public opinion. It will be a comfort to their enslaved minds to be freed from any bondage or repression. It will excite them and cause them to work for us with more enthusiasm without their knowing it; for they will only indulge their own desire for personal admiration."

Parallel to the work of the Constituent Assembly, clubs were formed to monitor the work of the deputies. It was in the clubs that calls for Mirabeau's head began to be made. According to the *Encyclopædia Britannica*, in August 1790 there were already one hundred and fifty-two in operation. The most famous was the Breton Club, where Robespierre would later dominate, led at the time by Duport, Barnave and the Lameth brothers. Its sessions took place in the Jacobins' convent, from which it took its name. The Jacobins established a network that covered the whole of France and their funds amounted to thirty million pounds. The history of the Jacobins is undoubtedly linked to that of the Illuminati: it was not for nothing that Adam Weishaupt's titles included "Patriarch of the Jacobins". The first to call for Mirabeau's head as a traitor to the revolution was Marat (Mosessohn), a Jew of Sephardic origin, whose inseparable accomplice was another Jew named Jacob Pereira. Marat in an article asked the people to erect eight hundred gibbets and to hang Mirabeau first.

Incomprehensibly, given that he was in theory allied with the Duc d'Orléans, Mirabeau tried in the Assembly, of which he became president, to moderate with his brilliant oratorical skills the deputies who wanted to deprive the king of almost all his powers. Threatening pamphlets soon multiplied. One of them, entitled "Mirabeau's great treason", read: "Beware lest the people distil gold in your viper's throat, that burning nectar, to quench forever the thirst that devours you; beware lest the people walk about with your head as they would carry Foulon's with their mouths full of hay". Mirabeau knew too much. A public trial was of no interest to the conspirators who had used him in so many circumstances. The best way to get him out of the way without a fuss was to feign a natural death, and so poisoning was chosen. On the night of 26 March 1791, he was in severe pain. The next day, despite the pleas of his friends, he attended the Assembly session for the last time. On the 28th the agony began. Every day Louis XVI sent an emissary to check on the progress of the "sick man", who asked for opium to ease the pain. Finally, amidst the atrocious suffering caused by the poison and after a night of tormenting agony, Mirabeau died on 2 April at the age of forty-one. The official version, which claims to attribute this sudden death to a sudden illness, is not credible. Pouget de Saint-André in *Les auteurs cachés de la Révolution Française (The Hidden Authors of the French Revolution)*, an extremely interesting work, reveals that Mirabeau himself believed he had been poisoned and cites the names of seven doctors who, although they had been ordered to attribute the cause of death to his excesses, concluded that he had succumbed to a mineral poison.

Mirabeau's death was a wake-up call for the royal family, who were already in contact with foreign powers. Louis XVI and Marie Antoinette tried to flee, but were arrested at Varennes. Returned to Paris, they have since been confined to the Tuileries. For his part, the Duc d'Orléans, Philippe d'Orléans, remained confident that his moment might yet come, but events were moving very quickly and his chances were soon to fade. In September 1791, the Assembly changed from Constituent to Legislative after an election in which only 10% of the electorate took part. The elected deputies were mainly from the middle classes. Brissot and the Girondins formed the last government of Louis XVI, whose share of political power was limited to the election of the prime minister and a right of veto over the decisions of the Assembly. In the upper tiers (the Mountain) sat the representatives of the clubs and the common people. Their representation was limited and their strong men (Danton, Marat, Robespierre) were outside the Assembly.

The emigration, concentrated in Koblenz and composed mainly of nobles and officers who had left the army, constituted the royalist party. Against them was one of the first decrees of the Assembly, the text of which considered the French assembled on the other side of the Rhine to be suspected of conspiracy and warned them that if they continued to assemble on the first of January 1792, they would be persecuted and punished by death. The king used his right of veto and refused to sign this decree. A few days later, he did not sanction another decree that attacked the property of the clergy and their right to worship.

After the death of Gustav III, who, as we know, was assassinated on 16 March 1792 when he was organising a coalition of foreign powers against France, several European countries threatened to intervene. Austria was the first to break off hostilities, and the Assembly declared war on 20 April 1792. The French invasion of Belgium, always unhappy under Austrian rule, took Europe by surprise, but amid the indiscipline and chaos, the first defeats soon followed. An example of the confusion and insubordination was the assassination of General Dillon, whose Dragoon unit retreated in disarray without seeing the enemy. At Lille, shouting treason, the soldiers killed their general. After the consternation created by the news of the withdrawal of the troops invading Belgium, the Jacobins became more violent by the day. Marat, from the depths of the undergrounds of intrigue, where he evaded the enquiries of the public authorities, took advantage of the suspicions of treason and demanded that the army put to death all its generals.

For the terror of the Republic

In Paris the agitation was growing, and while France mobilised battalions of volunteers and national guards, Austria-Hungary, Prussia and the kingdom of Piedmont-Sardinia formed the first coalition. Lafayette, the Freemason commander of the defeated northern army, who had known Adam Weishaupt personally and who, like Mirabeau, knew that a hidden hand was at work among the Jacobins, addressed a letter to the Assembly on 18 June 1792, from which these words come: "This faction has been the cause of all the disorders, and for this I openly accuse it! Organised as a separate empire, blindly led by a few ambitious chiefs, this sect constitutes a distinct corporation in the midst of the French people, whose powers it has usurped from its representatives and mandataries...". Two days later, a mob stormed the Tuileries palace, where the king was residing, and the king, outraged and threatened, was forced to put on the red Phrygian cap and drink a glass of wine. Mayor Petion, who had openly favoured the insurrection, succeeded in channelling it by his words and succeeded in having the palace evacuated. On the 28th, Lafayette, naively thinking he could put an end to the Jacobins, addressed the Assembly and reiterated the contents of his previous letter: "I ask the Assembly for the prompt punishment of the instigators and the destruction of a sect which invades sovereignty, which tyrannises the citizens, and whose public debates leave no doubt as to the atrocity of the projects conceived by those who lead it".

The Duke of Brunswick, Grand Master of German Freemasonry who had attended the decisive Congress of Wilhelmsbad and whose secret name among the Illuminati was Aaron, was the commander-in-chief of the armies of the Austro-Prussian coalition, the majority of whose staff was made up of military Freemasons. On 25 July 1792 he sent the Parisians the well-known manifesto of Koblenz, drawn up by Prince de Condé (Louis Joseph de Bourbon, the king's cousin). It threatened to march on Paris, introduce martial law and make a great slaughter if the royal family was harmed in any way. Two years later, repentant, Ferdinand of Brunswick was to denounce in no uncertain terms that the Illuminati had infiltrated Freemasonry in order to bring about the revolution in France and that they would be the cause of other revolutions. We now bring forward the quotation from his words, which is somewhat lengthy, but very valuable:

"...We see our edifice (Freemasonry) crumbling and covering the earth with ruins; we see destruction which our hands can no longer stop... A great sect arose which, under the pretext of procuring the good and happiness of men, worked in the darkness of conspiracy to make a victim of mankind. This sect is known to all. Its brethren are as well known as its name. It is they who have undermined the foundations of order to the point of its complete overthrow. It is because of them that the whole of humanity has been poisoned and brought to perdition for several generations. [...] The plan they laid down to break all social ties and destroy all order was manifest in all their speeches and acts. They recruited apprentices from every category and every position; they deceived the shrewdest men by alleging different intentions. [...] Their chiefs have nothing in view but the thrones of the earth, and they intend to direct the governments of nations from the nocturnality of their clubs. This is what has been done and what is still being done. We note, however, that the princes and the people are not aware in what manner and by what means they are achieving this. That is why we tell you frankly: the use of our Order has brought about all the political and moral upheavals which the world has to face today. You, who have been initiated, must unite your voices with ours to teach the princes and the people that the sectarians, the apostates from the new order, have been the authors of the present revolution and will be the authors of future ones. [...] Thus, in order to nip abuse and error in the bud, we must from this moment dissolve the whole Order...".

The Koblenz manifesto seemed designed to inflame and outrage the French, many of whom enlisted voluntarily. Mass conscriptions took place all over the country. The Assembly, under increasing pressure from the Jacobins and the mobs of "sans culottes", was forced to vote to impeach General La Fayette, who was constantly denouncing the conspiracy and the situation of anarchy in Paris, and demanding that the mayor be tried for collaborating with the insurrectionists in the storming of the Tuileries. Petion, instead of backing down, demanded the king's dismissal. The Jacobins demanded the heads of the constitutional deputies and openly stated that the Assembly could no longer be counted on to carry out the revolution. It was in this atmosphere that Danton, who had called for the dethronement of the king from the Cordeliers club, organised the second storming of the Tuileries, a veritable coup d'état which took place on 10 August 1792 and served to overthrow Louis XVI.

The commissaries of the Paris sections, perfectly organised, seized the Hôtel de Ville (Town Hall) and the leaders of the mutineers immediately constituted themselves as the Municipality. The King and his family, on the advice of Roederer and foreseeing the carnage that was to result from the fighting in the Tuileries, sought refuge in the Assembly, where about three hundred deputies, nearly all accomplices or supporters of the insurrection, had assembled in the hall of deliberations. At eleven o'clock in the morning the triumph was complete, and the armed masses, bearing prisoners and sumptuous objects taken in the storming of the palace, were led towards the Assembly, which finally invited the French people to form a national convention, that is to say, a republic. The king and his family were to be placed in the custody of the citizens. In the early morning hours of 11 August, Danton was awakened by Camille Desmoulins and Fabre d'Églantine. "You are a minister," they shouted. Drowsy and exhausted from the previous day's exertions, he looked at them in disbelief and asked, "Are you absolutely certain that I have been appointed minister?" They told him that the votes had been for him and confirmed that they were the new Minister of Justice. There was no doubt: Danton was the new hero of the hour.

The National Convention or First French Republic exercised executive power in France from 20 September 1792 to 26 October 1795 and was formed after an election in which just under 15% of the electorate participated. The Assembly could veto candidates deemed "unpatriotic", and the deputies' votes were always to be cast aloud. The forty days from 10 August to 20 September were terrible, as the terror unleashed at home was compounded by the war abroad. During this period the Assembly, which had declared itself in permanent session, declared that it approved all municipal acts. The Municipality retained the Assembly only to dictate its will to it, i.e. to legalise usurpations and to sanction, in Danton's words, "all the extraordinary measures that the people assembled in the primary assemblies". Later, at the height of his influence, he went so far as to declare: "Terror is the order of the day". The Paris Commune thus claimed absolute power: it took over the military leadership of the whole of France and indefinitely suspended the inviolability of homes and property. This insurrectionary commune,, was feverishly active, issuing about 100 decrees a day. The transfer of the royal family to the Temple Tower, the imprisonment of the editors of royalist newspapers (eleven newspapers were closed in Paris alone), the destruction of statues of kings and the creation of a "Board of Surveillance" for the capital were among its first decisions. Three men who had not known each other personally led the General Council: Danton, Robespierre and Marat. The latter, by his own admission, "had entered the Ministry through the breach in the Tuileries". Marat, whose imprisonment had been decreed many times for his bloodthirsty publications and his slander against everyone, had emerged from the sewers in which he had been hidden for three years and had arrogated to himself the leadership of the Board of Surveillance.

Marat and Danton, agents of the London Illuminati

The crypto-Jewish Marat was undoubtedly the most depraved and cruel of the foreign agents who during those days unleashed the orgy of bloodshed in Paris and throughout France. Marat was almost certainly personally acquainted with Lord Shelburne (William Petty) and Jeremy Bentham, the English masterminds who directed the revolutionary process in France from London. During the 1970s Marat had already travelled to Holland and England, where he found support among the English Freemasons. In 1772 he published there a Masonic-inspired work entitled *An Essay on the Human Soul*. His second work, *The Chains of Slavery,* was to follow in 1774. In 1777 he returned to France, but was placed under surveillance for his incendiary agitation work from *L'Ami du Peuple,* his newspaper (which was subsidised and became the *Journal de la Republique* when he was in power), so he was forced to move back to England, where he remained until 1790.

Since the role played by Lord Shelburne and Jeremy Bentham was of the first order, it is appropriate to take a little time to introduce these characters, about whom the official historians say nothing. Lord Shelburne was one of the enlightened Englishmen who attended the Wilhelmsbad congress, which he attended in the company of seven other brothers from England. Shelburne, who had been prime minister for a short time between

1782 and 1783, when William Pitt succeeded him in office until 1801, was head of the British Intelligence Service during the years of the revolution in France. According to Eustace Mullins (*The Curse of Canaan*), Lord Shelburne and his associates had paid off the numerous debts that burdened William Pitt, who in return submitted to the manoeuvres and political decisions dictated in the shadows by Shelburne and Bentham.

In a 1989 book, *Les hommes de Londres, histoire secrète de la terreur (The Men of London, secret history of terror)*, Olivier Blanc explains that William Petty (Lord Shelburne) sowed chaos in France by financing both thousands of reactionaries and Jacobins. According to this author, Marat, Danton and Choderlos de Laclos, personal secretary to the Duke of Orleans, were agents working for Lord Shelburne's secret services. As early as 1789, when Danton was practically unknown, the French ambassador in London, La Luzerne, had already denounced in no uncertain terms to the Foreign Minister, Count de Montmorin, that two individuals named Danton and Paré (Danton's secretary) were receiving money from the English government. M. Albert Mathiez (1874-1932), an authority on the French Revolution, also denounced Danton in 1916 as an agent in the service of England. In *Danton et l'or anglais (Danton and the English Gold)*, this French historian reveals that the Prussian-Swiss banker Perrégaux was allegedly in charge of paying the retribution. Mathiez quotes an official letter from the Foreign Office, a document that was part of the papers seized from Danton's house, which reads as follows: "We wish you to continue your efforts and to advance 3,000 livres to M.C.D., 12,000 to W.T. and 1,000 to de M., for the services they have rendered us by inflaming the fire and driving the Jacobins to the paroxysm of fury. [...] Help C. to discover the channels by which the money can be distributed with the greatest success".

An article by Jeffrey Steinberg in the *Executive Intelligence Review* on 15 April 1994, entitled "The Bestial British Intelligence of Shelburne and Bentham", clarifies the scope of the two men's activities and highlights their lack of ethical principles. Bentham published *An Introduction to the Principles of Morals and Legislation* in 1780, *a* work that founded the principles of British philosophical radicalism and, according to Steinberg, "catapulted him into the very centre of the then revamped British Foreign Office and British Intelligence Service, consolidated by Shelburne, a man who was then *de facto*, if not *de jure*, the Doge of Britain". In reality, intelligence operations had been in the hands of the East India Company and had since come under the control of the Secret Intelligence Service (SIS). In fact Lord Shelburne was the man of the Anglo-Dutch oligarch financiers and chaired the all-powerful three-man Secret Committee of the East India Company. Bernard Lazare, a Zionist Jew and friend of Theodor Herzl, gives in *L'Antisemitisme* the names of the Jewish financiers who supported from England the revolutionary aims of their continental colleagues: Benjamin Goldsmid, his brother Abraham Goldsmid, Moses Mocatta and Moses

Montefiore. According to Pouget de Saint-André, who cites the "Archives Nationales", two other Jewish bankers operating in Paris, Boyd and Kerr, were secret agents in the service of England.

Bentham, who rejected any difference between man and the lower beasts and had written an essay in defence of pederasty in 1785, made an impact on Shelburne, who financed him, set him up in a flat in Bowood and assigned him publishers in Switzerland and England to ensure the wide dissemination of his works in English and French. In 1787 Jeremy Bentham published a very significant pamphlet entitled *In Defence of Usury*, in which he criticised Adam Smith, who also worked for Lord Shelburne within the East India Company, for falling short in his work *The Wealth of Nations* and not being absolutely in favour of the unbridled dictatorship of money. Smith immediately acknowledged in writing that Bentham's work "was the work of a superior man".

Jeffrey Steinberg, who agrees with Olivier Blanc and Eustace Mullins in his article, writes: "Shelburne aimed to destroy France as an economic and military rival on the Continent. From the beginning the Jacobin terror was an orchestrated affair from the East India Company and British Intelligence. The bloody massacre of the French scientific elite was systematically carried out by French hands, but the guides were British". Both Mullins and Steinberg argue that the economic crisis sponsored by Necker was the precondition for provoking political chaos and insurrection, to which Shelburne contributed by setting up a radical writers' workshop, a kind of "think tank", on his Bowood estate. Steinberg writes: "the texts were prepared by Bentham, translated and transported by diplomatic pouch and other means to Paris, where the leaders of the Jacobin terror, Jean-Paul Marat and Georges Jacques Danton, delivered the ferocious speeches. Documents from the East India Company confirming payments to these Jacobin leaders are still in the archives of the British Museum". In *Les auteurs cachés de la Révolution Française (The Hidden Authors of the French Revolution)*, Pouget de Saint-André states that the Jew Étienne Clavière, Minister of Finance between 10 August 1792 and 13 June 1793, was also a London agent. Pouget de Saint-André explains that Clavière, after his imprisonment, received frequent visits from the banker Bidermann, a co-religionist who was treasurer of the Ministry of Foreign Affairs in 1792.

On 25 November 1791, Bentham, who would be rewarded with an honorary citizenship in Jacobin France, had even written a letter to the deputy of the Assembly, J. P. Garran, in which he offered to travel to Paris to take charge of the French penitentiary system. His proposal was to build detention and slave labour centres based on his famous Panopticon (predecessor of Big Brother), where detainees, thanks to a global (optical) observation system, would feel anxiously watched at all times, even in their most elementary actions, by a warden who, from a room designed with mirrors, could see everything (pan).

Knowing then who and from where orchestrated the terror, we can return to Marat, who according to his doctor, Dr. Cabanes, "suffered from a repugnant and very painful eczema which affected him from the scrotum to the peritoneum and oozed incessantly. Frequently, an excruciating headache, fever and severe pains in his arms and legs added to the torment he suffered". Marat exemplifies all the excesses better than anyone else. Having placed himself at the head of the Public Health Committee with the support of the Paris sections, he ordered the arrest of nearly four thousand people and the carnage began.

The September massacres

The massacres were perfectly planned and there is evidence of this in the documents of the Commune registers. These records were destroyed by another Commune, that of 1871; but previously they could be examined, copied and published in extract by some researchers. It has thus come to light that the assassins were hired for twenty-four pounds each. M. Granier de Cassagnac published a list of their names, addresses and professions. Stanley Loomis, in *Paris in the terror, june 1973 - july 1974,* states that many of them had already arrived in Paris at the end of July 1792 and stresses that most of them were not French. They obeyed a leader of Polish nationality called Lazowski. Let us recall here that in 1772, Jacob Frank, a protégé of Mayer Amschel Rothschild, had received money to organise paramilitary training camps in Brno, where he trained six hundred of his followers for terror. In addition to the group of foreign terrorists, the Commune had at its disposal in prisons dozens of men who had been convicted of crimes of violence, who were released days before the massacres began. Those most directly responsible for the organisation were the men who, together with Marat, were at the head of the Junta de Vigilance, namely Billaud-Varenne, Collot d'Herbois, Danton, Tallien and Panis.

Among the first victims were twenty-four priests who, on 2 September 1792, were stabbed and beaten to death by a group of two hundred hotheads. In the Carmelite convent, 150 people were massacred in an orgy of bloodshed. The executioners refused to use firearms and were happy to finish off their victims with axes, shovels and knives. A chronicler of the time, Philippe Morice, writes that the screams of pain and terror of the victims mingled with the screams of joy and pleasure of the criminals. The scene once again raises the suspicion that Jakob Frank's terrorists could have been among the murderers. The prisons of the Chatelet and of the Conciergerie were invaded by two groups of men trained to kill, who executed two hundred and twenty-five prisoners in the first place and three hundred and twenty-eight in the second, supposedly for being enemies of the people. During these massacres carried out in the prisons, the murderers made Masonic signs to their victims and pardoned those who knew how to respond. Billaud-Varenne, walking among the corpses, shouted to the criminals: "You are saving the fatherland! Continue your work, brave citizens!

Dr. John Moore, an English traveller living in Paris, wrote a fascinating diary. For him there is no doubt that the massacres were planned in cold blood by certain politicians. The pattern," he writes, "was repeated without interruption like a toxin to excite the populace". In reality, the people of Paris responded blindly to the aggression perpetrated by criminals and paid agitators from abroad. A year later, shortly before he was guillotined, Robespierre was to denounce this in no uncertain terms. Both John Moore and Stanley Loomis denounced the crimes committed in the prison of Bicêtre, where 170 inmates from the most marginalised sectors of society were imprisoned. All without exception were murdered. Among the victims were thirty-three boys between the ages of twelve and fourteen.

Madame Roland, wife of the man who weeks before had been Minister of the Interior, denounced in writing the atrocities committed in the Salpetrière prison, where prostitutes and women denounced by their husbands or their parents were locked up. If only you knew," he writes, "the terrible details. The women were brutally raped before being torn to pieces by those tigers". The most famous example that proves the truth of Madame de Roland's words is the case of Marie Louise de Savoie-Carignan, Princess de Lambelle. This middle-aged aristocrat had sought refuge in England, but out of loyalty to her friend Marie-Antoinette, she returned to Paris to be near her. The princess was captured in the Temple Tower, where she was accompanying the royal family in captivity, and taken to the prison of La Force, where the criminals, aroused to the limit by alcohol, demonstrated unheard-of ferocity and even went so far as cannibalism. Before being killed, the princess was interrogated by Hébert, who demanded: "Swear to love liberty and equality, swear to hate the king, the queen and the monarchy. Heroically the poor woman said: "I will easily take the first oath, but I cannot take the second, because it is not in my heart". Someone in the audience shouted at her to swear if she did not want to die, but she could only hide her face in her hands. Hébert then uttered the fatal phrase: "Take the lady away". Two men dragged her into the street, where there was a pile of corpses that had already been stripped. Without further ado, a sabre was swung across her neck and several pikes were thrust into her body. She was then stripped naked and left lying in the street. Shortly afterwards, her heart was ripped out, she was torn to pieces and disembowelled. Her private parts were paraded in triumph as trophies. Her head was carried in front of the windows of the Queen's cell in the Temple and held up so that Marie Antoinette could see her intimate friend. Incidentally, a Jew named Rosenthal was the commander in charge of the troops guarding the Temple and they did not prevent this macabre action. The head was then presented to the Duke of Orleans, who, attracted by the screams, rose from the table and, without flinching, saluted the murderers of the princess, who was his sister-in-law, from a balcony of the Palais Royal.

While these horrors were taking place, on 30 September 1792, the French armies that had ousted Lafayette, commanded by Dumouriez and Kellermann, managed to defeat the Prussians and Austrians in the decisive victory of Valmy. There are many doubts about the Prussians' performance, for when they could have crushed Dumuriez's vastly outnumbered army, they gave him time to receive reinforcements and supplies. For some critics Valny was "a comedy". The next day the Convention proclaimed the Republic as the sole government of France. Duke Ferdinand of Brunswick intended to open negotiations despite the defeat, but the Republic refused to listen to any proposals before the enemy troops had completely evacuated the territory. French victories were confirmed further north along the Rhine, where General Custine had also gone on the offensive and taken the cities of Speyer, Worms and Mainz. In the Alps, General Montesquieu conquered Savoy.

The Convention was composed of seven hundred and forty-nine members, of whom seventy-five had been members of the Constituent Assembly and one hundred and seventy-four of the Legislative Assembly. The Gironde formed the right side, and the Mountain, which was supported by the clubs and the Municipality, the left side. Between the two parties was the centre, called the Plain or the Orchard. Although the king was inviolable according to the accepted laws, and nothing could be done against him once he had been deposed, the Montagnards soon demanded that a trial be held. Danton said: "Since the nations threaten us, let us throw down a king's head like a gauntlet of defiance. The Convention thus set itself up as judge, although it was at the same time the accuser, and summoned the king to appear before it. Only Malesherbes dared to accept Louis XVI's dangerous defence. But, as already mentioned, the king's death had been decided in advance at the Masonic congress held in Frankfort in 1786, and the time had come for the execution. The Jacobins called for his death as a measure of public salvation. At 7 p.m. on 17 January 1793, the roll-call vote began at 7 p.m. It lasted twenty-five hours and took place amidst threats and insults in an atmosphere of extreme agitation. The words of Camille Desmoulins were: "A dead king is not a lesser man. I vote for death". Barère expressed himself in these terms: "The tree of liberty cannot grow without being watered by the blood of kings". Sieyès sentenced: "The death without sentences". Expectation was at its height when the Duke of Orléans, Philippe Egalité, took the rostrum. Everyone thought that the fact that he was a relative of the king would serve as an excuse; but he calmly said: "I am only concerned with my duty, and convinced that all those who have attacked or will in future attack the sovereignty of the people deserve death, I vote death. Finally, by three hundred and eighty-seven votes to three hundred and thirty-three, it was decided to carry out the sentence within twenty-four hours. Louis XVI asked for three days "to prepare himself to appear before God", but was refused.

On 21 January 1793, Samson, a Jewish Freemason who acted as chief executioner at the executions and who boasted of having cut off twenty-one heads in only thirty-eight minutes, guillotined the king, whose last words expressed in a firm voice in front of everyone were these: "I die innocent of the crimes of which I am accused. I forgive the authors of my death, and I wish that the blood you are about to shed may not fall on France. A young man from the National Guard picked up the bleeding head and showed it to the people. The Marseillaise began to be sung and some danced in a circle around the scaffold. Others picked up the blood seeping through the timbers of the scaffold and some drank it. It is inevitable to think again of the depraved frankists, who drank blood in their macabre rituals. It is perhaps pertinent to note here that the murderers of Tsar Nicholas II were also Jews, as will be seen, and so was the executioner who executed the Nazi leaders condemned at the shameful Nuremberg trial.

The terror continues

After the king's execution, alliances against France were again formed in Europe, and the war was resumed. Dumouriez, the hero of Valmy, who had secretly entered into negotiations with the enemy on his own, was denounced as a traitor before the Convention by Marat and Francisco de Miranda. This Venezuelan general, close to the Illuminati and considered the father of Latin American Freemasonry, was also an agent of Lord Shelburne who had risen rapidly in the French army. An atmosphere of mistrust gradually developed, which led to the inviolability of the deputies being annulled and it was decided that the Convention could proceed against any of its members. This fatal decree meant that the parties soon began to decimate each other. The imprisonment of Philippe d'Orléans, despite his vote in favour of the king's death, was the first act of internecine warfare. In an atmosphere of accusations and slander, Marat, whom the populace idolised, was denounced by a Girondin deputy, Gaudet. The Girondins succeeded in getting the Convention to vote for his arrest. The move was a mistake, as the members of the newly created Revolutionary Tribunal that was to try him were all agents of the Commune and acquitted him. Immediately, on 24 April 1793, Marat was crowned with laurels and amidst the cheers of the crowd was carried through Paris in a chair on the shoulders of four men, who carried him to the Convention amidst a shower of flowers and ribbons falling from the windows. What might have been a triumph for the Girondins was to be turned against them, for Marat then turned on them and on 2 June had twenty-nine of their deputies arrested, as well as their ministers, Clavière and Lebrun Tondu.

While enemy armies attacked on all the frontiers, insurrections broke out in different parts of the country. The situation of the Republic, surrounded by land and sea and torn apart by internal revolts, became desperate. Special mention should be made of the terrible rebellion in the Vendée, a civil war that led to one of the greatest massacres in contemporary history. In these departments of western France, so different from the rest of the country, the feudal regime was patriarchal and beneficent: the lords, of little wealth, simple and virtuous, lived with their vassals as fathers and friends; the clergy were ignorant, though pious and of simple habits. The peasants could not understand a revolution totally alien to their situation. A mass conscription of three hundred thousand men was the trigger for a general uprising of the peasantry that swept away their lords. The rebels organised themselves south of the Loire as the Catholic and Royal Army, and the war that was to unleash fierce repression began. In the proclamation of the Convention, the intention of the Jacobins was clearly expressed from the outset: "It is a question of exterminating the brigands of the Vendée in order to purge the soil of liberty of this accursed race". The problem was that the "brigands" were the entire population. Professors Reynald Secher and Pierre Chaunu (1986) agree that there was a genocidal intent in the massacres perpetrated by the Jacobins. In 1992, Michel Ragon saw a programme in the massacres and denounced the official intentions to annihilate an entire people. More and more historians now consider the extermination of at least 120,000 peasants in the Vendée to be the "First Genocide in Modern History". The survivors were deported en masse, crops razed, houses destroyed and forests burned. This fertile region remained virtually uninhabited for twenty-five years. As early as 1795, Gracchus Babeuf, the first precursor of modern communism, had already considered it appropriate to use the term "populicide" to describe the massacre.

The assassination of Marat was an unexpected event that occurred at a time when France was embroiled in internal and external wars. Charlotte Corday, a beautiful Girondine convinced that her act could save France, managed to sneak into the house of the Jacobin leader on 13 July 1793 on the pretext of updating him on the meetings of the Girondin leaders in Caen. Marat was unable to refuse the offer and ordered that she be allowed into the room where, because of the pains she was suffering from the deterioration of her skin caused by eczema, she spent much of the time with her body immersed in a tub of hot water. Marat invited her to sit on a stool and asked what he could do for her. Charlotte told him that she had come from Caen and could provide him with interesting information about the uprising there. Marat immediately took a piece of paper and, dipping his pen in ink, asked her for the names of the Girondins who were in the city. She listed them: Gaudet, Barbaroux, Pétion, Buzot? When she had finished, Marat smiled and said: "Excellent! In a few days I will have guillotined them all in Paris". Then Charlotte Corday stood up and taking a kitchen knife from her chest, with a six-inch blade, plunged it into her chest up to the hilt and pulled it out. In the course of the interrogation to which she was subjected by the police, she was asked why she had killed Marat. Her reply was: "Because he was the one who organised the September massacres". When asked what proof she had, she replied: "I cannot give you any proof. That is the opinion of the whole of France. The future will one day uncover the evidence". After the execution, on the 17th, Charlotte Corday's body was taken to a hospital, where it was autopsied and found to have died a virgin. The neoclassical painter Jacques-Louis David, as is well known, immortalised the assassination of his friend in the oil painting entitled *The Death of Marat*, signed the same year. At the funeral, organised and designed by David himself, large quantities of incense were burnt and symbolic paper pyramids were displayed all over Paris in an act of Masonic exaltation.

After Marat's demise, a new Board of Public Health, including Robespierre, Saint-Just, Collot-d'Herbois, Billaud-Varennes, Saint-André, Couthon, Hérault de Séchelles, was set up as a dictatorial power in France until July 1794. Among the measures immediately taken were the bloodthirsty repression of the Vendeans and the trial of Marie-Antoinette; but it also emerged at last that the British government was paying assassins and arsonists. Despite the fact that Lord Shelburne's agents were international and even French, the imprisonment of British subjects was ordered. On 23 August 1793, compulsory military service was decreed for all Frenchmen until the enemies were expelled from the national territory. The dictatorship of the Junta disposed of all fortunes and condemned all those who refused to arm themselves or submit to its dictates. The Convention, used to give a semblance of legality to the Junta's actions, watched in terror as prison decrees against its own members proliferated. Terror, as Danton had said, was indeed the order of the day: blood flowed on the scaffolds and nearly a hundred thousand "suspects" crowded the country's dungeons.

Among the most notable executions of those days was that of Marie Antoinette, beheaded on 16 October 1793. The verbal process that was initiated against her was signed by the mayor of Paris, Jean-Nicolas Pache, a Frenchman of Swiss origin nicknamed "Papa Pache". According to the historian Paul Thureau Dangin in *Royalistes et Republicains* (1874), reports from the Ministry of the Interior later pointed to him as one of the English agents. The discrediting of the queen in the eyes of the French people had been achieved by the campaign of the famous diamond necklace, orchestrated before the Revolution against her from London by a Jew named Ephraïm. The first pamphlets were published there by another Jew named Angelucci, who called himself W. Hatkinson. Fouquier Tinville, the public accuser, in his eagerness to present her before the revolutionary tribunal as a monstrous and ruthless woman, had the Dauphin, manipulated by his revolutionary guardians, testify against her. The poor child falsely accused his mother and aunt of having incited him to masturbate in front of them and to engage in certain sexual games. Hébert himself accused him of having sexually abused his son. Marie Antoinette, outraged, appealed in vain to the mothers present in the courtroom to defend her. Days after the queen's death, a score of Girondin leaders were accused and marched to the scaffold singing the Marseillaise.

The execution of the ill-fated Duke of Orléans, Philippe Equality, who had been Grand Master of the Grand Orient of France for twenty years, deserves special mention. He undoubtedly knew too much about the preparations for the revolution, and it was also his turn to go under the guillotine, invented by the Freemason Joseph -Ignace Guillotin. Philippe d'Orléans explained his departure from the Grand Orient of France with these words: "I no longer know who belongs to the Grand Orient. I therefore believe that the Republic should no longer allow the existence of secret societies. I want nothing to do with the Grand Orient and Masonic meetings". The Masonic lodges had already played their role and the Jacobins had begun to close them down. By 1794 only twelve lodges were functioning, those that were still useful to the Illuminati. The Duke of Orleans died in complete disillusionment on 6 November 1973. The Jew Benjamin Calmer, an agent of change and brother of the violent Isaac Calmer, was appointed commissioner for the liquidation of the assets of "Philippe Egalité".

In the provinces there were massacres carried out by mentally disturbed people who seemed to have been specially recruited for the purpose. Several authors report a certain Carrier, perhaps the most famous of these criminals. Eustace Mullins writes the following about him:

> "had an obsessive desire to torture and kill young children, as did his assistant, the hunchback DuRel, a homicidal maniac who delighted in slaughtering children by repeatedly jabbing their bodies with sharpened sticks. These two madmen herded more than five hundred young peasants of both sexes into a field outside Nantes, where, with the enthusiastic help of misfit lunatics like themselves, they bludgeoned them to death. Carrier was famous for inventing the infamous drownings on the Loire. Large rafts of victims were set afloat on the river, caused to sink and the people on board drowned. Carrier also practised the ritual known as 'republican marriages'. Men and women were stripped naked, tied in a mating position and thrown into the river.

So many victims were swallowed by the river that it was forbidden to drink from its waters. In reality, although Mullins must not have found out, for he says nothing about it, the executioners were a horde of bandits called Marat's company, who satiated themselves with rape, robbery and murder. The citizens of Nantes, accused of federalism, and the Vendeans were systematically annihilated. The number of victims of Carrier and his henchmen, who found worthy accomplices in the revolutionary junta of Nantes, amounted to about fifteen thousand. In March 1919 the Jewish-Bolshevik Chekists imitated Carrier, for after imprisoning thousands of strikers from the city of Astrakhan, they loaded them onto barges, from where they were thrown into the Volga with a stone around their necks. From 12 to 14 March 1919, between 2,000 and 4,000 workers were drowned and shot.

In Arras, Robespierre's home town, Mullins locates another notorious criminal, Joseph Lebas, a follower of Robespierre. This individual and his wife, who was a former nurse, experienced a kind of orgiastic frenzy with executions at the guillotine. Lebas first executed all the rich people who fell into his hands in order to rob them of their cellars and jewels. He then took up residence in a requisitioned house on the town square. When he could find no more rich people, he took up with some of the poor, whom he ordered to be beaten to death in front of him and his friends, who watched him with amusement from the balconies.

In Lyon, a city that had risen up against the Jacobins in Paris, two Hebertists, Collot d'Herbois and Joseph Fouché, led the massacres. Both were authors of the *Instruction de Lyon*, a text virtually unknown and silenced by socialist historiography, which is the first communist manifesto in history. On 9 October 1793 the city capitulated. The Convention decided that Lyon should be destroyed, but Couthon, who was Robespierre's right-hand man, pretended to practise a policy of moderation and indulgence, which proved impossible: the Public Health Committee overruled these intentions, ordered Couthon's return to Paris, and Collot and Fouché were sent to Lyon. During the winter of 1793-94 France's second city was subjected to one hecatomb after another. The full-scale horrors began on 4 December. Fouché, known as "le mitrailleur de Lyon" (the machine gunner of Lyon), considering the guillotine too slow, decided to shoot the detainees dead on an esplanade. The bodies of the wounded who were brought in mutilated or mangled were finished off with sables or blows with a pickaxe, hoe or axe. Many bloodied corpses were subsequently thrown into the Rhone. As early as the month of December, when the carnage was at its height, the first reports of the brutalities taking place in the city reached the capital: a Lyon deputation called by the Robespierrists appeared at the Convention. Collot d'Herbois had to return to Paris to give explanations. On 21 December he entered the Convention as the victor and, far from apologising, had his crimes approved. Since Comrade Collot did not return and remained in the capital, where the struggle between the Hebertists, Dantonists and Robespierists was to break out, Fouché was left in command in Lyon. From then on he was solely responsible for the atrocities that continued to be committed there.

Jacobin factions tear each other apart

Political hatreds soon arose among the members of the Mountain, which thus had its own right, led by Danton and Desmoulins, and its left, led by Jacques-René Hébert, Marat's successor and editor of the radical journal *Le Père Duchesne*, which advocated making terror the system of government in France. In between were Robespierre, Couthon and Saint-Just, supposedly the centre of the party. Hébert and his party, which, in addition to the two mentioned above, included the Jew Jacob Pereira, Marat's former lieutenant, Chaumette (the enlightened Anaxagoras) and Cloots (the enlightened Anacarsis), took the campaign against religion to the extreme. The Hebertists encouraged the demolition of churches, the melting down of bells, urns, monstrances and reliquaries, which were piled up in the Convention and in the Town Halls. The sculptures in the churches were mutilated. Atheism triumphed and the feasts of the goddess Reason were established, to whom the basilica of Notre-Dame de Paris was given as a temple. It is significant that those who called for rational behaviour acted as slaves to the most violent and reprehensible instincts. Chaumette, erected as the supreme pontiff of the new religion, entered the church on 10 November 1793 to institute the new cult. All the constituted bodies of the Republic occupied the magnificently decorated dais. Women dressed in white escorted the goddess, a young woman surnamed Maillard, who was barefoot and scantily clad in a white tunic. In *The World Revolution* Nesta Webster points out that the festivities of the goddess Reason were simply a consequence of Weishaupt's teaching that "reason must be the only law of man". John Robison asserts that when "corrupt women were enthroned as goddesses, the plan devised by Weishaupt in his *Eroterion* or festival in honour of the god of Love had been put into practice". The Girondin deputy Louis Sébastien Mercier, who spent a year in prison, confirms that some women danced in the church bare-breasted and adds that "in the darkness of the sacristy the desires that had been excited all day were satisfied".

At the beginning of 1794, the party of the Montagnards had destroyed all its opponents, and the sharks of which it was composed were ready to tear each other to pieces. Robespierre, after so many moratoriums and capitulations, seemed at last determined to take up the fight against the Hebertist faction. Fouché, who had the protection of Collot in the Committee of Public Health, received support for his operations; but a sixth sense made him see the danger: the rope in Paris was getting too tight and might break at any moment. Slowly he began to change his attitude and eventually stopped the criminal repression in Lyon: on 6 February 1794 he ordered a halt to the killings, and on the 18th he issued a decree prohibiting arrests. Indeed, Hébert's popularity was at an end and, frightened, he had cowardly disowned the enlightened Chaumette, atheism and communism. Danton, who seemed to have the majority support of the Convention, was disgusted.

Finally, on 13 March, Robespierre, supported by the Centre and a party of Dantonists, succeeded in arresting Hébert and, on the 18th, Chaumette. From that moment on, the events of the day began to unfold rapidly. Accused by Danton, Desmoulins and Robespierre of attempting a coup d'état, the Hébertites, about twenty in number, were executed on the Place de la Révolution on 24 March. Hébert, who had unscrupulously sent so many people to the guillotine, provoked the mockery of the populace, who howled with amusement at the fact that he shouted louder than even poor Mme. Du Barry, who had been beheaded in December. Hébert, then, behaved like a coward of the worst kind and showed his vileness before all. Among the papers seized from Jacob Pereira were ninety-six letters and hundreds of texts and articles written in English, which would constitute the evidence of the English Government's action against Pereira and his friends. Collot d'Herbois and Joseph Fouché, who was still in Lyon, had escaped the guillotine.

Four days later, the Marquis de Condorcet, a leading philosopher, mathematician, historian and political scientist, committed suicide. Condorcet, who was with the Girondins and had voted against the execution of Louis XVI, was accused and convicted of treason. He fled and remained in hiding for five months at Mme Vernet's house. On 25 March he tried to leave Paris, but was arrested and imprisoned. On the 28th, after ingesting poison, he was found dead in his cell.

On 5 April Danton, Desmoulins and their supporters were led to the guillotine. Robespierre and Saint-Just, who had relied on both of them to get rid of the Hebertists, accused them, among other things, of maintaining secret contacts with foreign powers and of being involved in the embezzlement of the East India Company, whose establishments had been closed down by a decree of the Convention[10]. In his work *Paris in the Terror*, Stanley Loomis mentions among those guillotined the Frey brothers, Junius and Emmanuel, two nephews of Jacob Frank who lived in Paris and acted as prominent Jacobin leaders. It should be remembered that Junius Frey had been one of the founders of the Asiatic Order in 1781, who flourished at the Austrian

---

[10] On 3 April 1790, the National Assembly decreed that trade beyond the Cape of Good Hope was free for all Frenchmen, thus depriving the East India Company of its monopoly. The shareholders, however, meeting in general assembly on 10 April, appointed eight commissioners charged with maintaining its activities nonetheless. The Convention accused the Company of financing counter-revolutionary actions and on 26 April 1793 decreed the precautionary closure of its establishments. A second decree made the transfer of shares subject to a high tax. Fabre d'Églantine, Danton's secretary when he was Minister of Justice, seized the opportunity to set up a lucrative business for himself. Tempted by the Company's coffers, Fabre, by falsifying documents and signatures, modified the decree ordering the liquidation of the Company and the seizure of all its assets, which amounted to more than 28 million livres. When the fraud was discovered, Robespierre and Saint-Just denounced it as a conspiracy and accused Danton of being involved.

court with the title of Baron Thomas von Schönfeld. The Frey brothers, who as good Frankists were apparently apostates from Judaism, moved within the East India Company.

François Chabot, who controlled the political police and was married to Leopoldine Frey, was also led to the scaffold. François Chabot, a former Capuchin monk, "Europe's first revolutionary", was a demagogue who appeared at the Convention in threadbare trousers, wooden clogs and a shirt open over his hairy chest, although he was capable of dressing like a dandy in certain circumstances. Chabot was a member of the all-powerful Committee of Security and had the political police under his command. The enlightened Frankist Junius Brutus Frey saw in him the presumptuous dupe who could give him access to valuable information. He therefore offered him his sister Leopoldine in marriage, whom he passed off as a sixteen-year-old virgin, even though she was twenty-one. He also offered her an annual pension of four thousand francs, house and board for five years and a dowry of two hundred thousand francs, to be paid over the same period. Such generosity undoubtedly indicates that this "revolutionary" frankist had good sources of finance and handled money in abundance. It was Chabot himself who, in order to save his own skin, gave Robespierre all the details of the plot. Rabbi Antelman confirms that all three, in addition to being Frankists, were enlightened princes working in the service of the East India Company.

After the death of Danton, France entered a brief period in its history known as the Great Terror. On 8 May, it was the turn of Antoine-Laurent de Lavoisier, considered the father of modern chemistry. The president of the court that condemned him foolishly pronounced the famous sentence : "The Republic does not need wise men". Between 12 June and 28 July no less than 1,285 people were guillotined in Paris, among them the generals Noailles, Beauharnais and Mouchy; the poets André Chenier and Jean Antoine Roucher; and even a sixteen-year-old boy. Chenier's death at the age of thirty-one interrupted a literary career of great stature, since critics consider that his mastery and sensitivity are evident in the works he bequeathed to posterity. Céline singles out Chenier as one of the best French poets. The campaign of persecution against men of talent was part of the Illuminati's plans. Weishaupt's favourite maxim, "The end justifies the means", put on the lips of the Jacobins was expressed thus: "Tout est permis a quiconque agit dans le sens de la Révolution" (Everything is permitted to anyone who acts in the sense of the revolution).

Joseph Fouché arrives in Paris

On 6 April 1794, the day after Danton's execution, Joseph Fouché arrived in Paris from Lyon. This mysterious figure, who had survived the purge that led to the guillotining of the Hebertists, was to play a decisive role in the fall of Robespierre. His political figure is one of the best-kept mysteries in history, which lends itself to all kinds of speculation. Two works of reference for understanding his actions are *Joseph Fouché: The Portrait of a Politician*, by Stefan Zweig, and *Fouché*, by Louis Madelin. A Spanish edition of the latter is available from Espasa-Calpe. Fouché, who was among the radical Hebertists and had written the *Instruction de Lyon*, which inevitably places him in the orbit of the Illuminati, remained in the shadows during the years of the Directory after getting rid of Robespierre. In 1799 he reappeared unexpectedly to be appointed Minister of Police of the Republic. After Napoleon's seizure of power he became the key man whom Bonaparte could not get rid of, however hard he tried in various ways. In 1802, with the gift of 1.2 million francs, he wanted to remove him from the scene. Fouché settled at Ferrières, a beautiful estate which in 1829 - what a coincidence - became the property of James Rothschild, who bought it from the heirs. Within a couple of years, the man who had written the first communist manifesto became one of the richest capitalists and landowners in the country. In 1804 Napoleon reappointed him minister. It soon became clear that, despite their mutual distrust, the two men needed each other. Fouché, who had been given the title of Duke of Otranto by the Emperor, was once again appointed Minister of Police during the Hundred Days; but from that post he ended up negotiating the restoration of the Bourbon monarchy. In 1815 Louis XVIII ratified him at the head of the Ministry. Stefan Zweig described him as a "born traitor, a wretched intriguer, a pure reptile, a professional transvestite, a vile soul of a brace, a deplorable immoralist". According to the author, his secret was always to "change his jacket quickly, following the direction of the wind".

Having thus presented the character, let us now consider what little is known of his actions and his confrontation with Robespierre after his arrival in Paris after nine months' absence. On 7 April, instead of appearing before the Public Health Committee to explain his actions in Lyon, which in the opinion of some members of the Committee had been too moderate, Fouché went straight to the Convention, which was tantamount to depreciating Robespierre's authority. One deputy immediately advised him to pass the report to the Public Health Committee. Among Fouché's skills was the ability to apologise or to feign humility if necessary. It was with this intention that he went the next day to the house of the carpenter Duplay, in the rue St Honoré, where Robespierre lived. The content of the interview between the two is not known, but everything indicates that Fouché was treated with the contempt in which the vanquished are treated. No doubt Robespierre must have considered that the battle against the Hebertists was already won and failed to gauge the man before him.

On 6 May 1794 Robespierre announced to the Convention that in the name of the French people the Committee of Public Health had decided to recognise the existence of God. In his speech he addressed Fouché in the harshest terms, reproduced by Stanley Loomis. "Tell us," he said, staring at

Fouché, "who has charged you with announcing to the people that God does not exist? What right have you to rob innocent people of the sceptre of reason and deliver it into the hands of crime. Only a villain who despises himself and is horrible in the eyes of others feels that nature can give him nothing better than annihilation". There is no doubt that these words constituted a public declaration of hostility. On leaving the Chamber of Sessions, Fouché's friendly deputies sought to shun him, for to many of them he was a dead man.

During the weeks that followed the announcement of God's imminent return to France, Fouché disappeared. Perhaps Robespierre may have thought that, like so many other victims who had been marked for death by him, he was hiding in fear. If so, he was wrong. Fouché began to work in the shadows, where he probably made contact with Collot d'Herbois and those Jacobins who hated Robespierre. On 6 June he was ready to respond to the accusations of 6 May, since by manoeuvring he had managed to get himself elected president of the Jacobins' Club. When he learned that Fouché had sought refuge in none other than the shrine of the revolution, the "sancta sanctorum" of the altars over which he supposedly presided, Robespierre acknowledged the coup and realised that he had underestimated him. The movement was worse than a challenge, it was a threat. Alarmed at such audacity, he decided to make two no less daring moves before snatching the presidency from the Jacobins: the first would be the celebration of the Festival of the Supreme Being, which was held on 8 June. The second was the law of 22 Pradeal (10 June), which deprived conspirators of the right of defence.

Robespierre's turn

Nesta Webster denounces a fact systematically ignored by historians. Under Robespierre's rule the Public Health Committee divided the month into three decades. In this way, Sundays and all religious holidays disappeared, which actually aggravated the sad condition of the workers, who were forced to work more than before. According to Nesta Webster, "in the time of the Monarchy, not only the day of a religious festival, but also the following one, was a holiday, and no work was done on Sunday or Monday. By replacing Sunday by the 'decades', i.e., one day in ten, and granting only half a holiday, the new masters of France added three and a half days of work for every two weeks".

Robespierre, despite the fact that after the disappearance of the men who could have overshadowed him he seemed to have all the power in his hands, was also finally guillotined. Before recounting the unexpected events that led to his execution, a few facts about this puzzling character may be of interest. First of all, it should be noted that both Count Cherep-Spiridovich, in *The Secret World Government or "The Hidden Hand"*, and the aforementioned Yüri Lina quote Louis Joseph Marchand to reveal that Robespierre was a Jew from Alsace, whose name was Ruban. Spiridovich, who was probably murdered on 22 October 1926, although, as almost always in such cases, his death was officially attributed to suicide, handled the first edition of Marchand's work (1895). Juri Lina cites the same work, republished in San Francisco in 1998 under the title *In Napoleon's Shadow*. The 791-page book is the first English edition of the complete memoirs of Louis Joseph Marchand, Napoleon's valet, friend and executor. Marchand, who died in 1876, entered the service of the emperor in 1811. The emperor immediately appreciated his intelligence and self-sacrifice and appointed him his valet. He accompanied him to the exile of St Helena, where he served as his reader, copyist and secretary. The reliability of the source is therefore extremely high, as it must be assumed that Marchand obtained the information about Robespierre's origins from Napoleon himself, who, according to various authors, had become close friends in 1793 in Toulon with Augustin, Robespierre's younger brother.

Although Kropotkin states categorically that Maximilien Robespierre, who was undoubtedly a Freemason, belonged to one of the Illuminati lodges founded by Weishaupt, there are discrepancies as to whether he had been initiated. Be that as it may, everything suggests that Robespierre, like Mirabeau before him, thought he could act on his own and failed to properly appreciate the limits imposed on his actions by the occult power. Count Cherep-Spiridovitch cites a book from 1851, *Memoires et correspondance de Mallet du Pan pour servir a l'Histoire de la Revolution Française [1794 a 1800]/ Recueillis et mis en ordre par A. Sayous* (*Memoirs and correspondence of Mallet du Pan to serve the History of the French Revolution [1794-1800] Collected and arranged by A Sayons*) and extracts from it these words of Robespierre addressed to Amar, a member of the Public Health Committee: "I have the feeling that we are being pushed by a 'Hidden Hand' above our will. Every day the Public Health Committee does what the day before it decided not to do. There is a faction whose behaviour ruins everything and whose directors we have not been able to discover".

But the words that were to cost Robespierre, who had reached the height of his power and presided over the Convention, his life were those delivered before the chamber in a speech lasting more than two hours on 26 July 1794. Resolutely he said: "I distrust all these foreigners whose faces are covered with masks of patriotism and who try to appear more republican and energetic than ourselves. [...] They are agents of foreign powers, for I know well that our enemies did not fail when they said: 'our emissaries must feign the most exacerbated patriotism' in order to be installed in our assemblies. These agents must be crushed in spite of their perfidious pretence and the masks they always adopt". At another point in the speech full of accusations against the ultra-terrorists, he added: "I dare not name them at this time and in this place. I cannot allow myself to tear away the veil that shrouds this deep mystery of iniquity. But I can state with the utmost certainty that among the perpetrators of this plot are the agents of a system of corruption and extravagance, the most powerful of all the means invented by foreigners to ruin the Republic. I refer to the impure apostles of atheism and of the immorality that is at its base". Although he did not mention names, he did make a very clear allusion to the Frey brothers, and in particular to Junius Brutus Frey, the relative of Jacob Frank: "Since the first days of the Revolution, two fiends have come to live in Paris, whose art of simulation makes them perfect instruments in the hands of the tyrants, two clever wicked men whom Austria has thrown up in our midst. One of them has added to his supposed family name the name of the founder of the liberty of Rome". The allusion to "Junius Brutus" is undeniable. Moreover, Robespierre seemed to know that the surname Frey was a false name. Throughout the speech the allusion to the Illuminati, to which Kropotkin claimed to have known and belonged, is quite clear. G. J. Renier, author of the work *Robespierre,* from which the quotations are taken, comments that if he had not made this speech he might still have been able to triumph.

Confusion and lack of rigour predominate in the texts that attempt to explain Robespierre's last days. John Goldworth Alger's *Paris in 1789 to 1794* is, among the works consulted, the one that gives the most detailed account of what happened. Much of what follows is taken from it. On 7 May Robespierre, who, as we have seen, had attacked the atheistic tendencies and the de-Christianising slogans of the Hebertists, succeeded in passing in the Convention a decree on the existence of the Supreme Being. On June 8, the aforementioned feast was celebrated in honour of the existence of this God who influenced the Universe, which evidently came to counterbalance that of the goddess Reason of the Hebertists in Notre-Dame de Paris. As president of the Convention, Robespierre presided over the proceedings. After an interminable speech and following the script of the performance, whose scenery had once again been designed by the painter David, he grabbed a torch and set fire to an effigy representing atheism. From the high place where he officiated, he looked down on 300,000 people shouting "Long live the Republic" and "Long live Robespierre"!

Two days later, on 10 June 1794, Robespierre presented to the Convention the aforementioned law of 22 Pradeal, a veritable bombshell for those who dared to conspire against the Republic, whose arrest was tantamount to death. It seemed to be the right answer for schemers like Fouché. With this tool in his hand he could expel him from the Jacobins and destroy him at the right moment. It was with this intention that he presented himself the next day at the Club to denounce his enemy. His attack was so violent that he almost succeeded in overthrowing Fouché that very evening. The latter, who was presiding as president, used his prerogative to close the debate on the grounds that it was already late. He then took advantage of the situation to make a hasty retreat and did not reappear. Robespierre went to the Club to make a speech in which he asked that Fouché be summoned to the next session so that he could be tried as the leader of a conspiracy that had to be aborted. The Jacobins applauded him with conviction and unanimously decided to expel Fouché from the Club. Fearing arrest at any moment, and no doubt well protected by people who escaped the reach of Robespierre's police, Fouché not only managed to evade capture, but also set about preparing his last move.

Some historians believe that during the second half of June there was a serious dispute within the Public Health Committee. According to this version, Robespierre is said to have demanded the heads of Tallien, Barras and Fouché, but his colleagues, fearful of his ultimate intentions, did not accede to his demand. Enraged, Robespierre did not return to the Committee and disappeared from the public scene to retire for six weeks to the home of the Duplay family, whose eldest daughter he was in love with. In the words of John Goldworth Alger, "this six weeks' absence was shameful. It undoubtedly heralded a call either to the Convention or, as some feared, to the masses, so he was summoned to the Committee on 22 July and forced to show his cards". A few weeks earlier, on 1 July, Robespierre had spoken of conspiracies against him at the Jacobins Club and had said: "If I were obliged to renounce a part of the functions entrusted to me, I would remain in my capacity as representative of the people and would maintain a war to the death against tyrants and conspirators.

On 26 July he finally appeared at the Convention and delivered the famous speech mentioned above, in which he called for an end to the terror and demanded the renewal of the committees on Public Health and General Security. The agitation was great and many wondered who Robespierre was thinking of. The Convention, moved by the eloquence of the speaker, at first passed the proposal; but some members of the Committee reacted, notably the financier Joseph Cambon, Vadier, Billaud-Varenne and Amar. Cambon accused him of having paralysed the Convention, and Billaud-Varenne demanded that the speech be printed and passed on to the committees. Panis urged him to say whether he and Joseph Fouché, who did not attend the session, were on the list of outlaws. It was decided to print the speech for distribution to the deputies, but Robespierre told the secretary that he would give it to him the next day. The Convention annulled the decrees and referred the propositions to the committees. In the evening Robespierre went to the Jacobins' club and read the speech there. When he had finished he said: "If I am to recant these truths, let hemlock be offered to me.

The next day, 9 Termidor (27 July), the Convention met at ten o'clock in the morning. The crisis was in the air and the stands had been filling up since five in the morning. According to Pouget de Saint-André, the audience in the stands was often carefully recruited and received three livres per session, although the chiefs could charge from ten to fifty livres. Maximilien Robespierre wore the same dark violet coat he had worn seven weeks earlier at the celebration of the Supreme Being. Saint-Just, began to speak to defend Robespierre's motions; but violent interruptions showed that in twenty-four hours things had changed. "Down with the tyrant" and "The blood of Danton drowns you" were among the cries heard. The convulsion increased to the point that Robespierre was not even allowed to speak. At five o'clock in the afternoon, his arrest was ordered, as well as those of Couthon, Saint-Just, Lebas and Augustin Robespierre. The session was then adjourned so that the deputies could eat.

All was not yet lost, for the detainees were taken from the prison by troops of the Commune and brought to the Town Hall, where Robespierre was surrounded by his faithful. There, in those feverish hours at where everything was decided, he may have contemplated the possibility of the triumph of the Commune or a trial before a court that would acquit him; but the days when the Convention was subject to the designs of the Junta were over. As soon as news of the release of the detainees was received, the Convention resumed debate at seven o'clock in the evening, and, although the imprudent suspension of the session had compromised its position, it declared Robespierre and his followers outlawed. The attitude of the National Guard was to be decisive. The comings and goings of their battalion chiefs and delegates were constant. The doubts as to whom they should obey were not resolved. In the sections in the capital, too, the debates went on well into the night. In addition to the Jacobins Club, eleven others remained loyal to the Commune, but thirty-nine opted for the Convention, which also declared the Commune outlawed. At about one o'clock in the morning, Barras led a column to the Town Hall, where, in brief, the following happened: Augustin Robespierre threw himself out of a window and was badly wounded. Lebas shot himself and probably offered Robespierre a second pistol. Couthon, while trying to climb down a ladder, fell and lost consciousness when he hit his head on the wall. Robespierre was found on the floor near a table with his jaw broken by a gunshot. He was not wearing a tie or shoes. His shirt and suit were stained with blood and his trousers were unbuttoned. Goldworth Alger wonders. "Had he attempted suicide or had Merda shot him? We'll never know for sure. The gendarme Merda[11] made two statements and in the second he claimed responsibility for the shooting, although a communiqué issued by the Convention reported in these terms: "Robespierre shot himself in the mouth and was shot at the same time by a gendarme. The tyrant fell down bathed in his own blood and a 'sans culotte' approached him and coldly uttered these words: 'There is a Supreme

---

[11] Charles André Merda, aged 21, was a gendarme in the "Hommes du 14 Juillet" squadron. He was later appointed second lieutenant in the 5th Fighters. He served years later in Napoleon's campaigns and was promoted to colonel in 1806. He died of wounds received in Moscow in 1812. He changed his name to Méda. He left no descendants. His grandson, Meng, adopted the name Méda in 1867.

Being'". It is possible that Merda failed, for Barras and Barère insist on the suicide attempt.

Before he was brought before a court, after an agonising night, a doctor bandaged his wound and his broken teeth were extracted. His mouth was held open with a key. Already before the judges, he repeatedly asked for writing materials, but was refused. The court considered it proven that he was an outlaw and without further delay or trial sentenced him to death. Along with him, Couthon, Saint-Just, his brother Augustin and seventeen of his followers were executed on 28 July. In the following two days seventy-three members of the Commune shared the same fate.

The death of Robespierre marked the end of an era. For more than 25 years, from 1789 to 1815, the French were the victims of a conspiracy organised by international bankers and set in motion by their agents, the most conspicuous of whom was Adam Weishaupt, founder of the Illuminati. At a session of the French Parliament on 1 July 1904, the following discussion took place and is recorded in the Journal of Sessions:

> M. de Rosanbo: "Freemasonry worked quietly but steadily to prepare for the Revolution.
> M. Junel: It is indeed something we boast of!
> M. Alexandre Zevaés: This is the highest praise you could have given.
> M. Henri Michel - It is the reason why you and your friends detest it.
> M. de Rosanbo: We are therefore in perfect agreement on the point that Freemasonry was the principal author of the Revolution, and the applause I receive from the Left, to which I am not accustomed, proves, gentlemen, that you recognise with me that it was the author of the French Revolution.
> M. Junel: "We do more than acknowledge it, we proclaim it".

What the Masonic deputies of the Third French Republic did not proclaim was that after the Wilhelmsbad Congress the European lodges of Freemasonry had been penetrated by the Illuminati.

The Revolution was followed by endless wars in Europe, the main beneficiaries of which were the same group of German, English and Dutch financiers, mostly of Jewish origin. A new order based on economic and political liberalism was then their main goal. France lost forever the dominant role it had held in the 18th century to Britain; but a new, uncrowned dynasty, as we shall see below, was to reign on the Continent throughout the 19th century: the Rothschilds.

CHAPTER III

THE ROTHSCHILDS

In the preceding pages we have already noted the central role of the Rothschilds in the historical events described above. It is now time to give them the attention they deserve. First of all, Rothschild means "red shield" in German, although this compound name has been translated as "red flag". Moses Amschel Bauer, the father of the founder of the dynasty, had already adopted a red coat of arms as his emblem (he was also the emblem of the Ashkenazi Jewish revolutionaries in Eastern Europe). The real creator of the saga was Moses' son, Mayer Amschel, who not only adopted the red coat of arms and placed it above the door of his building in Frankfurt's Judengasse, where, incidentally, the family of Jacob Schiff, Trotsky's mentor and the main financier of the Bolshevik revolution, also lived, but also changed the name Bauer to Rothschild. During the French Revolution, the red flag was seen flying at specific moments of revolutionary extremism, and since then its presence on the streets of Europe and the world has been steadily increasing. When the Judeo-Bolsheviks took it as their flag, they added the hammer and sickle, which was the emblem of the Maccabees, the protagonists of the revolt that culminated in the creation of the second Jewish state in 67 B.C..[12]

Since John Reeves published *The Rothschilds: the Financial Rulers of Nations*, the first reference work on this family of Jewish bankers, in 1887, much has been written about them. *The Rothschilds, Portrait of a Dynasty*, by Frederic Morton, an Austrian of Jewish origin, was for some time the most widely consulted work. In 1928, Count Egon Caesar Corti's two volumes, *The Rise of the House of Rothschild*, covering the period up to 1830, and *The Reign of the House of Rothschild*, covering the period from 1830 to 1871, were published in English. 1998 saw the publication of *The House of Rothschild. Money's Prophets 1798-1848* and in 1999 *The House of Rothschild. The World's Banker 1848-1999*, an authoritative biography of over a thousand pages published in two volumes. Written by Niall Ferguson, a friend of the family, it might have been the definitive work had it not been

---

[12] The Romantic poet Heinrich Heine, a close friend of the Rothschilds, recalls that in 1827 the widow of Mayer Amschel, Guttle, decorated the windows of the old house on the Judengasse with white curtains and candles to celebrate the day of the victory of Judas Maccabee and his brothers (Chanukkah).

so favourable and uncritical. Nonetheless, it is a fascinating work and an invaluable, unmissable source of information,, to which we will turn repeatedly throughout this and other chapters. More recently, in 2009, Michael Collins Piper published *The New Babylon, Those Who Reign Supreme*, a critical work denouncing the empire of this dynasty, the richest in the world, which, according to this author, is "the royal family of international Jewry". Collins Piper places them at the forefront of the international forces behind the New World Order and exposes the Rothschilds' impact on the course of history, their manipulation of finance, industry and politics in almost every state in the world, as well as their devastating influence over the media, education and other means of controlling public opinion for over two hundred years.

Mayer Amschel Bauer (1744-1812), the founder of the dynasty, was twelve years old when his father, Amschel Moses Bauer, died. Until then, *Talmudic* studies had been his priority, as he was destined by his father for the rabbinate. Soon, however, he was sent to Hannover to learn the rudiments of business in the house of Wolf Jakob Oppenheim, supposedly an associate of his father. Oppenheim's grandfather, Samuel, had been a court Jew and agent of the Emperor of Austria, and his uncle was an agent of the Bishop of Cologne. It was in Hanover that Mayer Amschel gained the experience he needed to become a court Jew himself. There he became an expert in rare coins and medals, a sphere of business in which the clients were invariably aristocratic collectors. In 1764, back in Frankfurt, he came into contact with the crown prince of Hesse-Kassel, Wilhelm, to whom he sold medals and old coins. The prince's financial advisor, Carl F. Buderus, with whom Mayer was well acquainted, played an important role in the relationship that was then established. In *The Rothschild Dynasty*, John Coleman, citing documents from the British Museum, writes: "Carl Buderus, who was equal in his ambitions and enormously tenacious, patient and secretive, had a meeting with Mayer Amschel in which there was a mental communion through which a pact of mutual assistance emerged". In 1769 Mayer Amschel had become the court Jew of Wilhelm of Hesse-Kassel. In August 1770, at the age of twenty-six, he married Guttle Schnapper, the sixteen-year-old daughter of Wolf Salomon Schnapper, himself court agent to the Prince of Saxe-Meiningen.

Guttle gave birth annually from 1771 to 1792. Of these nineteen children, ten survived. The five of interest to this story are Amschel (Anselm) Mayer (1773), Salomon Mayer (1774), Nathan Mayer (1777), Carl or Kalman (1778) and Jakob or James (1792). It was after the birth of the first son that Mayer Amschel began to enter the banking business. Soon banking became the centrepiece of his activities and he became one of the richest Jews in Frankfurt. Recall that, according to William Guy Carr, in 1773 there was a meeting of the thirteen wealthiest families in Frankfurt, who decided to finance the World Revolutionary Movement and use it to take over the wealth and resources of the planet. The Illuminati secret society, as discussed in the preceding chapter, was created in 1776 to implement the great revolutionary programme.

The French Revolution and the European war provided Mayer Amschel with new opportunities to enrich himself. As soon as hostilities began, he secured a contract to supply the Austrian army with grain and money for its operations in the Rhine region. In 1798 Mayer Amschel decided to send his third son, Nathan, to England, a decision that was to prove pivotal, for it was there, as we shall see, that the Rothschilds' supremacy in Europe and the world was forged. It was also at the end of the 18th century that Seligman Geisenheimer, a very talented accountant from Bingen who was also a polyglot, became the administrative head of the House of Rothschild. It should also be remembered that Geisenheimer and Solomon Rothschild were in 1811 prominent members of the lodge in Frankfurt, where, after the Wilhelmsbad Congress, the headquarters of Enlightened Freemasonry resided.

The treasure of the Elector of Hesse-Kassel

Rothschild scholars agree that the treasure of the Elector of Hesse-Kassel is the source of the family's fortune. Not all, however, interpret the facts in the same way. Wilhelm of Hesse-Kassel was almost the same age as Mayer Amschel and both shared an interest not only in ancient coins, but in money of all kinds. His father, Frederick II of Hesse-Kassel, who was Landgrave from 1760 to 1785, had converted to Catholicism in 1747, which had dismayed his Protestant relatives and his father-in-law, George II of England. William was taken away from his father and sent to Denmark to be trained in the principles of Protestantism. There he married Princess Caroline, daughter of the Danish monarch Frederick V. The couple resided in Denmark until 1785, when William inherited the landgraviate and one of the largest fortunes in Europe at the time. According to the *Jewish Encyclopaedia*, Mayer Amschel 'was the court agent of William IX, Landgrave of Hesse-Kassel, who on his father's death had inherited the largest private fortune in Europe, made mainly by renting troops to the British government to fight the American Revolution for independence'. Even before he succeeded his father, William was already involved in the soldier trade and had sold a regiment of some 2,000 mercenaries to fight for George III against the rebellion in the American colony. Consequently, writes Niall Ferguson, "the finances of Hesse-Kassel were more akin to those of a large bank than to those of a small state". No wonder, then, that Mayer Amschel felt a magnetic attraction to Wilhelm.

The hostilities between the French revolutionary forces and Hesse-Kassel, which had begun in the early 1790s, culminated in the bombardment of Frankfurt by Kleber's army in 1796. The walls of the Jewish quarter, which dated back to the 16th century, were destroyed, as were some of the houses in the "Judengasse", the street where Mayer Amschel had bought an entire building. The traditional ties between Hesse-Kassel and London were further strengthened and Wilhelm, as usual in exchange for money, put eight thousand soldiers on the battlefield to fight against France. John Coleman states that in some years between fifteen thousand and seventeen thousand Hessians were hired by the British government. In 1801 the Landgrave accepted the terms of the Peace of Lunéville, by which the left side of the Rhine was transferred to France. When war broke out again between France and England in 1803, the year in which William IX became Prince Elector of Hesse-Kassel and became William I, the compromise with the British was too narrow, and William was unable to join the sixteen German states that formed the Francophile Confederation of the Rhine in the summer of 1806. When the Prussian army was defeated at Jena and Auerstadt in the autumn of 1806, the Prince Elector was at Napoleon's mercy. Neither the hasty demobilisation of his troops nor his belated request to join the Confederation of the Rhine appeased Bonaparte's anger, whose openly declared aim was to "remove the House of Hesse-Kassel from the government and strike it from the list of powers in Europe".

There was no other option but flight, and Wilhelm sought refuge in the Danish territory of Holstein, first at Gottorp Castle, where his brother was governor, and then in the town of Itzehoe. On 2 November, General Lagrange installed himself in Kassel as governor general, and two days later issued a proclamation announcing that all the Elector's property was confiscated and threatening anyone who tried to hide it with a court martial.

This is the beginning of the controversy over what really happened to the Elector's treasure. According to a version no doubt inspired by the Rothschilds themselves, at the critical moment of his flight, Wilhelm hastily entrusted Mayer Amschel Rothschild, his "loyal court Jew", with the care of all his wealth. In 1827, *the German General Encyclopaedia for the Educated Classes* explained what had happened:

> "The French army was entering Frankfurt at the moment when Rothschild managed to bury the prince's treasure in a corner of the small garden of his own house, which in goods and money was worth about 40,000 thalers. He did not go into hiding, knowing that if he did, a frantic search would be launched and both his goods and the prince's treasure would be discovered and plundered. The French, like the Philistines in antiquity, pounced on Rothschild and did not leave him a single thaler of his property. In fact he was, like all the other Jews and citizens, reduced to absolute poverty, but the prince's treasure was saved".

Such altruism and selflessness, such generosity, is touching. Surely the purpose of all this was to underline the family's exceptional probity as deposit takers, willing to risk everything rather than fail and fail to pay their clients interest.

The *Jewish Encyclopaedia* reports that in 1806 the Elector fled to Denmark leaving his fortune to Mayer Rothschild and adds: "According to legend this money was hidden in wine bottles and thus escaped the pursuit of Napoleon's soldiers when they entered Frankfurt. In 1814 the money was returned intact in the same hulls, once the elector had returned to Germany". The *Encyclopaedia* itself acknowledges, however, that the reality was less romantic than the legend and had much more to do with business.

In his *The Rothschild Money Trust*, George Armstrong clarifies how the reality was indeed much less romantic. He explains that Mayer Amschel Rothschild embezzled or misappropriated the funds in his custody and spent them. Instead of putting the money in bottles of wine, he sent it to London, where his son Nathan, was already settled, and thanks to him he was able to build up his economic empire. According to Armstrong, it was with this money that Mayer Amschel's sons settled in Paris, Vienna and Naples. Nathan himself later stated that when the Prince of Hesse-Kassel gave the money to his father, there was no time to lose and that he received it unexpectedly in London.

Many years later, in 1861, the Rothschild family was still keen to clean up its image in Europe, where some of the press was full of criticism in drawings, pamphlets and writings. To this end, they commissioned the painter Moritz Daniel Oppenheim to paint two oil paintings that reflected their version of events. In the first, which depicts the moment when the Elector of Hesse-Kassel entrusts his treasure to Mayer Amschel Rothschild, Wilhelm is seen touching the left shoulder of Mayer Amschel, who, with his left hand over his heart, bows to him respectfully. Two servants carry good-sized wooden boxes out of the room, in the background of which Guttle and his daughter Henrietta appear in the background. The second painting depicts the moment when the treasure is returned. Mayer Amschel has already died. In the centre of the composition is the Elector seated in an armchair with a baton in his left hand, gesturing with his right hand to the eldest of the brothers, Amschel Mayer, who bows again and pays his respects. On the left-hand side of the painting, behind Amschel, are the other four brothers, one of whom, James, crouching, places valuable vases inside a chest of drawers. Behind the Elector is the figure of a servant who is lost walking to the right of the painting with two good-sized boxes, one in each hand.

In reality, Wilhelm's wealth was widely dispersed. Some of the most important securities, mainly bonds, were successfully smuggled by Buderus, who acted in close chumminess with Mayer Amschel. The close relations between Rothschild and Buderus von Carlshausen were reflected in a written agreement between the two. According to this document, Buderus became a secret partner of the Rothschild firm. In *The Rise of the House of Rothschild* Corti transcribes the document:

"The following confidential agreement has been signed today between the private adviser Buderus von Carlshausen and the business house of Meyer Amschel in Frankfurt: Whereas Buderus has handed over to the banking house Meyer Amschel Rothschild the capital of 20.000 gulden (Dutch guilder) 24 guilders and has promised to advise the said firm in all business matters to the best of his ability and to advance his interests as far as he deems practicable, the firm of Meyer Amschel Rothschild promises to deliver to Buderus an authentic balance of the profits made in relation to the above-mentioned capital sum of 20,000 gulden, and to allow him access to all books at any time, so that he may be satisfied with regard to his provision."

Between 1808 and 1809 Carl Friedrich Buderus von Carlshausen made risky journeys across the French lines to Itzehoe, where the Elector had been residing since the end of November 1806. During these years, the Privy Councillor to Wilhelm of Hesse-Kassel was temporarily detained on several occasions on Napoleon's orders. Buderus was undoubtedly the key man who enabled Mayer Amschel Rothschild to increasingly consolidate his position vis-à-vis Wilhelm. In any case, the French, who had managed to get hold of an inventory of the Elector's silver, would have been able to take control of a significant part of his assets had it not been for the bribe to General Lagrange, who for the modest sum of 260,000 francs consented to the disappearance of forty-two boxes containing various valuables. Soon, however, Lagrange realised that he had been bribed for an insignificant sum, given the circumstances. He then managed to intercept some of the boxes he had previously allowed to be removed and asked for more money. Fergusson explains how a second deal was struck in exchange, this time for a substantial sum. Bribery and blackmail have been and continue to be the Rothschilds' favourite means, as will be seen in the following pages.

The legacy of Mayer Amschel Rothschild

When Mayer Amschel Rothschild died on 19 September 1812, the Elector's treasury had enabled Nathan to become the banker of choice in London, and also enabled the other brothers to establish themselves in the major European capitals. The eldest, Amschel, remained in Frankfurt; Solomon ran the Vienna house; Nathan, as has been said, operated from London; Carl established himself in Naples; James was to organise the important stronghold of Paris. By September 1810 the firm of "Mayer Amschel Rothschild & Sons" had been established.

"The Old Mann", the Old Man, in the words of Solomon, laid down before his death the fundamental principles which his children and their descendants were inexcusably to observe. These precepts were strictly maintained for more than a century. He repeatedly and emphatically excluded females. Let us look at the excerpt from the will quoted by Fergusson:

> "Here and now I decree and therefore wish that my daughters and sons-in-law and their heirs have no share in the capital of the firm 'Mayer Amschel & Sons' and even less that they can or will be allowed to make a claim under any circumstances. The aforementioned firm will belong exclusively to my children and will be managed by them. Therefore neither of my daughters nor their heirs have any claim on the said firm and I could never forgive a son who, against my paternal will, would allow them to disturb my children in the peaceful possession of their business".

The most important provisions of the will include the following:

1. The eldest son of the eldest son would take the lead in running the business, unless the majority of the family members decided otherwise. During the 19th century, due to Nathan's superiority, there were some exceptions to this rule, since after Nathan's death the leadership passed to James and then to Lionel, Nathan's son.

2. The need to practice endogamy, i.e. marriage between cousins and even nephews in order to keep the family fortune intact. This rule was maintained above all by the males; but the females did not always respect it, as the possibility of advantageous marriages with other Jewish banker families was contemplated. In any case, fifty-eight marriages between cousins are recorded. Particularly noteworthy is the case of James, the youngest of the five brothers, who married in 1824 his niece Betty (1805-86), daughter of his brother Solomon, whose eldest son Anselm (1803-74) married in 1826 his cousin Charlotte (1807-59), daughter of Nathan. Nathan's first-born son, Lionel (1808-79), in turn married another cousin named Charlotte (1819-84), daughter of Carl, in 1836. Nathan's third son Nathaniel (1812-70) married another cousin also named Charlotte (1825-99), but she was the daughter of James. A daughter of Nathan's, Louise (1820-94) married her cousin Mayer Carl, Carl's heir, in 1842. And so on up to fifty-eight inbred marriages. Each marriage was accompanied by detailed legal agreements on the governance of the property of the contracting parties, the purpose of which was to prevent the five houses from splitting up and outsiders from gaining access to the immense fortune of the five brothers.

3. The obligation to stand unequivocally as members of the Jewish nation. Mayer Amschel Rothschild advocated the political reforms that were to bring about the emancipation of the Jews and the modernisation of Judaism; but as we have seen in the previous chapter, this was a necessary political ploy. Mayer Amschel, like Mosses Mendelssohn, secretly exhorted his co-religionists, and most especially his sons, to hold faithfully to Talmudic beliefs, according to which the superiority of Jews over gentiles

(goyim) is equivalent to the superiority of man over animals. In this, as in so much else, the influence of the founder of the dynasty has been profound and enduring to this day. In fact Mayer Amschel hired as tutor for his children Michael Hess, a follower and disciple of Moses Mendelssohn, who, as we know, was the leader of the Illuminati in Berlin. Today in the United States and in Europe we have multiple examples of Jews who enjoy full citizenship rights in their country of residence, but first and foremost consider themselves members of the Zionist state of Israel.

The conviction of the superiority of the Jewish race (Jewish supremacism) was absolute in Mayer Amschel. In 1813, S. J. Cohen published a memoir entitled *The Exemplary Life of the Immortal Banker Mr. Meyer Amschel Rothschild, a* kind of authorised biography. In it, Cohen recalls a significant anecdote, according to which a street urchin once shouted at him, "Jew! Mayer Amschel, very calm, approached him and offered him money on condition that he repeated what he had said. The guttersnipe took the money and with all his might shouted: "Jew, Jew! Several young men came up and started shouting as well. Rothschild listened to them with evident pleasure and said in Hebrew: "Praise be to Him who gave the laws to His people of Israel.

Of the many pieces of business advice he gave his sons, writes Niall Ferguson, one relating to dealing with politicians and non-Jewish personalities was frequently quoted by Solomon: 'Our late father taught us that if a person in a high position enters into financial association with a Jew, it belongs to the Jew' ('gehört er dem Juden'). Carl insisted on this idea in 1817: "The best thing in this world is to be in the service of the Jews".

4. The obligation to keep perpetually united in the family association. A bundle of arrows cannot be broken, but a single arrow can. Niall Fergusson quotes an 1827 article from the *Brockhaus Encyclopaedia, which* states: "Mayer Amschel obliged the five brothers to manage the whole of their business as an unbroken community of interest. This was the rule bequeathed by the dying father to his sons. Since his death, any proposal, no matter where it comes from, is the subject of collective discussion; every transaction, even if it is of minor importance, is resolved according to a plan agreed upon with their combined efforts and each of them has an equal share in the results".

Most authors agree on the unbreakable nature of the unity imposed by Mayer Amschel Rothschild on his children and converge on the idea that never has a father's last will and testament been consciously put into practice in a more profitable way. On inbred marriages, also practised by the elite of the Frankist sect, several authors point out that among Ashkenazi Jews a disease called Tay-Sachs has developed which fatally damages the brain and can lead to death. This disease is the legacy of centuries of intermarriage between individuals who share the same blood.

Nathan, commanding general

"My brother in London is the commanding general and I am his field marshal. These words of Solomon Rothschild are sufficiently explicit to demonstrate the extent to which Nathan came to dominate the family business from London. Thanks to Cromwell, as we know the agent of the Amsterdam Jews, prosperous and self-confident Jewish communities had been established in London from the 17th century onwards. These included families of Sephardic origin, such as the Montefiores and the Mocattas, and of Ashkenazi origin, such as that of the merchant Levi Barent Cohen. Also in the late 1790s Benjamin and Abraham Goldsmid, who had financed with other Jewish bankers the revolution in France, played an important role in finance.

The first document we have of Nathan's presence in London dates from 1800, a letter from him dated 29 May, although it is known that he was already in the English capital in 1798. He soon settled in Manchester, where his first occupation was related to the textile business. It did not take him long, however, to diversify his activities. In 1805 he entered into partnership with another Jewish immigrant from Frankfurt, Nehm Beer Rindskopf (son of an associate of his father's), and the two became involved in the trade in pearls, ivory, tortoise shells and other goods from the colonies of the empire. Like his father, it took Nathan little time to go from merchant to banker.

For Nathan,, who after six years in England became a British citizen, his foray into banking began in 1806, when he unexpectedly received money from the Elector. In October of that year he married Hannah Barent Cohen, the daughter of the leading London merchant Levi Barent Cohen, who in 1812 married another daughter, Judith, to Moses Montefiore, one of the leaders of the Sephardic community. With this marriage Nathan became a partner in one of the most eminent figures in London's Jewish community. Cohen encouraged his son-in-law to expand the range of goods he exported to the Continent. Thus in 1807, at the height of the Continental blockade, Nathan entered the smuggling business. Among his favourite smuggling routes were the Baltic ports and the small German island of Heligoland. Of course, the shipments could not be legally insured, so the risk involved was considerable, but so were the profits. By 1808 Nathan had earned a reputation as a smuggler and was regarded as a man who always managed to deliver the goods thanks to his contacts and foresight. In 1809, however, a large shipment to Riga was captured and only by means of bribery, as usual, could he be released. All these episodes were basically just anecdotes for Nathan, who had already decided that his main activity would be banking. He was already a banker at the beginning of 1808, although he was not yet known as such in London until 1810, when he established the firm "N. M. Rothschild and Sons. In short, Nathan used the Elector's money as if it were his own capital.

It was in the Spanish War of Independence or Peninsular War that Nathan, thanks to Wellington's financial difficulties, found one of the decisive opportunities of his career. Indeed, from the American War of Independence to the present day, as we shall see, wars have always been the Rothschilds' best business. Niall Fergusson in *The House of Rothschild* acknowledges that historians have never adequately explained how an obscure Jewish merchant who had grown rich from smuggling was able to become overnight the British government's main conduit of money to the battlefields. In 1812, the Iberian market was saturated with British government bills of exchange, and Wellington had difficulty getting Spanish merchants to accept them. To finance the Duke, bullion in the form of gold guineas had to be sent to Spain or Portugal. If this failed, Wellington had to borrow money from local bankers by selling them bills of exchange. The continental blockade made the option of large-scale gold shipments extraordinarily risky. If the second alternative was chosen, peninsular bankers demanded excessive discounts to buy the bills.

At that time the Baring Brothers were the bankers of choice for the British government, but competition was fierce and not only Nathan Rothschild was trying to emulate them, but also the brothers Benjamin and Abraham Goldsmid, as well as bankers who came to London from Germany, such as the Schröders, were vying for the war finance business and offering their services to the government. In 1810 Francis Baring had died and the leadership of the firm had passed to his son Alexander at a time when the City was in the throes of a crisis caused by the Bullion Committee's report, which recommended (against the advice of the Bank of England) an early resumption of payments in gold. The prospect of a period of limited money produced alarm and consternation, as it led to a fall in the price of government bonds. The Barings and Goldsmids found themselves with large amounts of bonds from the last loan to the government. Barings lost about £43,000 and Abraham Goldsmid committed suicide. In addition, at the same time, there was a collapse in the Amsterdam market, caused by Napoleon's annexation of the Netherlands.

Another, even more important factor contributed to Nathan's appearance on the scene. In October 1811 John Charles Herries was appointed Minister of the Treasury. Ferguson believes that Herries was Nathan's Buderus, his 'first friend' in a prominent position. Herries rose rapidly politically since he had managed to serve as a clerk in the Treasury in 1798. In 1801 he was appointed private secretary to Nicholas Vansittart, the Secretary to the Treasury. Herries had also been private secretary to Spencer Perceval when the latter was Minister of Finance from 1807-09. A former student in Leipzig, it is likely that his friendship with the Rothschilds began then. As a student, he became involved in a romantic relationship with a woman who had later married a tobacco merchant, Baron Limburger. The relationship resulted in an illegitimate child. The Limburgers later claimed that it was thanks to their recommendation that Herris had involved Nathan in the financing of Wellington's campaign. Indeed, this must have been the case, for they later claimed a 1% commission of between £30,000 and £40,000 from Nathan for the business he had done. In June 1814 the Rothschilds were still counting on Limburger's influence over Herris, which suggests, Ferguson writes, "that Limburger was blackmailing Herris into the existence of his bastard son". Clearly, leaving the Rothschilds out of the blackmail does not seem credible, but Ferguson "naively" pretends so. [13]

But the ultimate reason for Nathan's role in financing the war in the Peninsula has to do, of course, with the Elector's treasury. It was mainly thanks to the money his father had transferred to him from Frankfurt that he was able to buy £800,000 worth of gold from the East India Company. The company actually tried to sell the gold to the government, but the price was too high. While waiting for the price to come down, Nathan came along and bought it all. Here is Nathan's own succinct account of what happened: "When I had settled in London, the East India Company had £800,000 worth of gold to sell. I went to the sale and bought it all. I knew the Duke of Wellington needed it. I had bought a large quantity of his bills at a discount. The Government sent for me and told me they needed it. When they got it, they did not know how they could get it to Portugal. I took it all up and sent it to France; and that was the best business I ever did.

Let us look at these facts in a little more detail. The Government let Nathan Rothschild know that it needed the gold to finance Wellington and had to buy it from him, but by the time it did so the price had already risen. Nathan then offered his services to circumvent the continental blockade and move the gold to Portugal. What they must not have guessed was that he intended to do this through enemy territory, i.e. through France. The Rothschilds thus set out in March 1811 to smuggle the gold into French territory. This was tolerated by Napoleon himself, for James Rothschild had secretly informed Bonaparte that his brother was planning to take the gold to France and that the British were opposed to it. The French government swallowed the bait. In Paris they exchanged the gold for banknotes and then the Rothschilds moved it to Spain. In this way France facilitated the financing of the war against itself. Napoleon had accepted the advice of his Minister of the Treasury, François Nicholas Mollien, who argued that any flight of bullion from Britain was a sign of economic weakness and

---

[13] A similar case of blackmail was carried out on US President Woodrow Wilson, explained in detail by Benjamin H. Freedman in his book *The Hidden Tyranny*. The Jewish lawyer Samuel Untermayer surprised President Wilson by announcing that his client, the wife of a Princeton professor, would be willing to accept a large sum of money to keep secret the relationship they had had with Wilson when he was also a professor at Princeton. One of the purposes of the blackmail was the appointment of the Talmudist and Zionist Louis Dembitz Brandeis to the US Supreme Court. There will be an opportunity later to tell the details of this story.

consequently advantageous to France. By mid-May 1814 the British government owed Nathan £1,167,000, a figure large enough to terrify even his brother Solomon.

Checkmate at Waterloo

Despite so many good moves, the game continued and soon the occasion presented itself for a final move, a move that would allow the Rothschilds to win a game they had started in 1806, which would make them the most powerful banking family in Europe and, consequently, the leaders of international finance..

The Rothschilds had always known the importance of insider information. They therefore decided that it was necessary to intercept and control communications, which they achieved through an alliance with the house of Von Thurn und Taxis[14], who had a monopoly on mail in Europe. There is a widespread anecdote about Mayer Amschel Rothschild's first meeting with Prince Carl Anselm, head of the House of Thurn und Taxis: Rothschild was working at his desk and when the prince entered, he said to him: "Bring yourself a chair". The visitor, after a few seconds of bewilderment, remarked: "I am the Prince of Thurn und Taxis". Mayer Amschel replied: "Very well, then bring two chairs. Jokes aside, what counts is that once again there must have been some kind of bribe or secret agreement. From the pact with the Rothschilds onwards, the Thurn und Taxis watched over and examined letters and communiqués of vital importance to them at crucial historical moments.

In any case, the Rothschilds themselves had a continental network of agents and informers. They organised an espionage service covering the main European capitals and also used carrier pigeons to quickly transmit to each other news that could give them an advantage in their stock

---

[14] The Thurn a Taxis family originated in Milan, where they were known as della Torre. They invented the idea of a postal service and introduced a postal system in Tyrol at the end of the 15th century. In 1516 Emperor Maximilian I, grandfather of the future Emperor Charles V, commissioned them to organise a postal service between Vienna and Brussels. Already then, one of its members received the solemn rank of postmaster general. This was the beginning of the impressive development of the Thurn und Taxis postal system, which came to cover the whole of Europe. The headquarters were in Frankfurt. Not satisfied with the normal operation of their business, they decided to profit from the information written on the letters entrusted to them. At the end of the 18th century they began to open the correspondence and note down the contents that might be of interest. In order to keep their monopoly, the House of Thurn und Taxis offered to make the information obtained by secretly manipulating the letters available to the emperor. Mayer Amschel soon realised how important it was for a banker or merchant to have certain news and information in advance, especially in times of war. As his home town was the main post office, he easily contacted the house of Thurn und Taxis and reached a mutually satisfactory agreement.

speculations. Frederic Morton writes: "Rothschild cars sped along the roads; Rothschild boats sailed across the Channel; Rothschild agents were swift shadows along the streets. They brought money, securities, bills of exchange and news. Above all, news, the latest and most exclusive news to be vigorously processed on the stock exchange".

It was precisely a move related to the handling of information about the outcome of the Battle of Waterloo that enabled Nathan to take control of the London Stock Exchange. In 1815, the future of Europe depended on the outcome of the Battle of Waterloo. If Napoleon emerged victorious, France would be the dominant power; but if the victor was Wellington, then Britain would be able to expand its sphere of influence and control the balance of power on the Continent. As to how the events actually happened, there are several versions that differ from one another. The most fanciful even places Nathan himself on the battlefield. In *The Rothschilds: the Financial Rulers of Nations*, John Reeves claims that Nathan appeared on the battlefield and was in a position where he could see the scene of the clash between the armies. This is how his novelistic account begins: "The battle began. The dense smoke of the furious cannonading soon enveloped the whole field in a cloud; but Nathan Mayer's straining eyes were able to see from time to time the fierce charges of the French cavalry, by which the safety of the English lines was more than once endangered....". According to Reeves, certain that Bonaparte would be defeated, Nathan Rothschild spurred his horse to Brussels. There he procured a carriage which, without delay and at full speed, took him to Ostend, where he arrived exhausted on the morning of 19 July. Despite the stormy sea, he set out to cross the channel; but even the fishermen refused to attempt it. Although he offered them five hundred, six hundred, eight hundred francs, none dared. Only with an offer of two thousand francs did one accept, on condition that the money was paid to his wife before setting sail. As soon as they set sail, the wind changed and the conditions improved, which made it possible to shorten the duration of the voyage. In the evening they reached Dover. Without a moment's rest, Nathan took fast horses and continued his journey to London. The next day," Reeves continues, "he was seen leaning against his well-known pillar of the Exchange, apparently broken physically and spiritually, as if he had been overwhelmed and crushed by some dire calamity. The greatest pessimism and despondency had for days been in the City, and when Rothschild was seen it was unanimously concluded that the worst had happened....".

More credible is Frederic Morton's interpretation, who explains that the mood on the London Stock Exchange was feverish as the news was awaited. If Napoleon won, the consolidated bonds of the public debt would collapse; but if the victor was Wellington, the value of the bonds would soar. In Morton's version, Nathan Rothschild's men worked tirelessly on both sides trying to gather news. Other agents were transferring intelligence bulletins to a strategically placed post nearby, where the information was processed. At dusk on 18 June, a Rothschild representative carrying a secret report on the crucial battle jumped into a pre-arranged boat and crossed the channel. This agent was expected at dawn at Folkstone by Nathan himself, who, having examined the report, hurried to the Exchange. When he arrived, he stood as usual beside his usual column, which was already known as Rothschild Column, "without any sign of emotion, without the slightest change in his facial expressions, stony-faced". Another author, Andrew Hitchcock, in *The History Of The House Of Rothschild,* reports that the Rothschild agent who embarked and crossed the channel was one John Rothworth. Hitchcock, John Coleman and George Armstrong argue that the Rothschilds worked to finance both armies (Nathan to Wellington from England and James to Napoleon in France). According to these authors, this began their policy of financing wars on both sides.

What almost all authors agree on is what happened once Nathan reached his column. Following a pre-arranged signal, his brokers at the stock exchange began to flood the market with consolidated government bonds, hundreds of thousands of pounds worth of bonds were poured into the market and the value of the consolidated bonds began to fall and even plummet. Nathan continued to lean on his pillar with an expressionless face, without the slightest emotion. He continued to sell and sell. It did not take long for the rumour to spread on the stock exchange that Rothschild knew that Wellington had lost at Waterloo. The selling turned to panic as people rushed to dump their bonds and exchange them for gold or silver in the hope of retaining at least some of their wealth. After several hours of desperate trading, the consolidated bonds had turned into ruinous bonds. Nathan, cold as ever, leaning on his pillar, continued to emit subtle signals; but then they were somewhat different, so slightly different that only highly trained agents could detect the change. On the instructions of their boss, dozens of Rothschild agents began to buy up all the public debt at laughable prices. When news of the outcome of the Battle of Waterloo later reached London, the consolidated bonds immediately rose to even higher than their original value. Nathan Rothschild had bought control of the British economy and, according to the most enthusiastic authors, had increased his already immense fortune twenty-fold overnight, which certainly seems an exaggeration.

Niall Ferguson is one of the authors who considerably downplays the benefits of Nathan's operations at the Bourse and even minimises the importance of Waterloo. Interestingly, however, Ferguson also reports on John Rothworth and even transcribes Rothworth's own account of "an exhausting journey on foot from Mons to Genappe, walking by day in a cloud of dust under a scorching hot sun and sleeping at night on the ground under the muzzle of the guns". Ferguson also reports that a week after the day at the Bourse, someone said to Rothworth: "Nathan has made good use of the information you had about the victory at Waterloo ". Rothworth then ventured to ask Rothschild if he could participate in the purchase of government bonds "if in his opinion it might be advantageous".

Nathan Rothschild's own words clearly indicate his own perception of his power a few years later. In 1818 he negotiated a loan with Prussia. The Minister of Finance, Christian von Rother, tried to change the terms after the loan had been signed. Niall Ferguson quotes Nathan's letter to von Rother, which, by Ferguson's own admission, shows Nathan's insolence and disrespect towards Prussia and his minister:

> "My dearest friend, I have fulfilled my obligation for God, the King and the Minister of Finance von Rother, my money has been sent to you in Berlin..... It is your turn and obligation to fulfil your part, to keep your word and not to come now with new things, and everything must remain as agreed between men like us, and that is what I expect, as you can see from my money deliveries. The council there can do nothing against N. M. Rothschild, he has the money, the strength and the power. The clique has only impotence, and the King of Prussia, my Prince Hardenberg and Minister Rother should be happy and grateful to the one who sends them so much money, which increases Prussia's credit.

In 1820, aware that the Bank of England was under his power, he was even more overbearing. These are his boastful words, quoted again by Ferguson: "I care not what puppet is placed on the throne of England to rule the Empire. The man who controls the supply of money to Britain controls the British Empire, and I control the supply of money to Britain".

The Rothschilds and Napoleon

Napoleon is one of the least known of the great historical figures. Little has been written about his rise from obscurity to fame. In *The Rothschild Dynasty*, John Coleman argues that, like Disraeli, Bismarck, Trotsky, Kerensky or Lloyd George, Napoleon was originally a Rothschild man. Napoleon was extremely poor when he was introduced by the enlightened Freemason Talleyrand to the Rothschilds. It was Mayer Amschel, ever so clever and perceptive, who discovered the new talent. The Corsican's inner fire and passion impressed him and he decided to offer him money to live decently. In 1796 Napoleon married Josephine de Beauharnais, who had once paid for his uniform. A Creole lady from Martinique with an insatiable libido, Josephine was the mistress of Viscount Paul de Barras, a strongman of the Directory. According to John Coleman, Mayer Amschel Rothschild arranged or brokered this marriage with Barras, who was then in search of "a sword to wield conveniently for the conservative retreat of the Republic". It was Barras, who according to various sources was also a member of the Illuminati, who appointed

Napoleon commander-in-chief of the Italian army. It seems that while her husband was waging war against the Austrians and Piedmontese, Josephine was making love to Barras and other members of the government circle.

Napoleon was the first European leader who conceived the idea of conquering Jerusalem for the Jews and thus fulfilling the prophecy. Curiously, historians say nothing about it or about his motives, which could not have been other than to curry favour and financial support from Jewish bankers. By promising them the thrice-holy city, he adhered to the idea of an ethnically pure nation, as Hitler later did when he made a pact with the Zionists (Haavara Agreement). In 1799, the year Napoleon led the French expedition against the English in Egypt, the Paris *Monitor* of 22 May read: "Bonaparte has published a proclamation inviting all the Jews of Asia and Africa to go and settle themselves in ancient Jerusalem under the protection of his flag". A few weeks later, a second text in the *Monitor* added: "It is not only to give Jerusalem to the Jews that Bonaparte has conquered Syria. He has wider plans..."

Five years later Napoleon's perceptions of Jews and mutual relations had changed substantially. Napoleon's imperial coronation in 1804 was regarded with indifference by Mayer Amschel; but for Talmudists like the Rothschilds, the fact that the Pope was invited was not at all welcome. In 1806, after the victory of Austerlitz, Napoleon's complaints against the Jews and their terrible use of usury were reflected in a session of the Council of State. Joseph Pelet de Lozère, one of the members of the Council who attended the sessions, published in Paris in 1833 *Opinions de Napoléon sur divers sujets de politique et d'administration recueillies par un membre de son Conseil d'Etat* (*Opinions of Napoleon on various subjects of politics and administration collected by a member of his Council of State*). This is a work of great interest and can be read in full on the Internet. It contains the notes taken by Pelet de la Lozère. Chapter XX, entitled "Sur les Juifs" (On the Jews), contains the notes of the session of 30 April 1806. Here is the quotation of Bonaparte's words:

> "The French Government cannot be indifferent to the fact that a debased, degraded nation, capable of all the basenesses, has exclusive possession of the two beautiful departments of the former Alsace; the Jews must be considered as a nation and not as a sect. They are a nation within the nation. I would like to take away from them, at least for a certain time, the right to take mortgages, for it is too humiliating for the French nation to find itself at the mercy of the most wretched nation. Whole villages have been expropriated by the Jews; they have replaced feudalism, they are veritable flocks of crows. They were seen after the battles of Ulm to have come from Strasbourg to buy from the robbers what they had stolen.... It would be dangerous to let the keys of France, Strasbourg and Alsace fall into the hands of a population of spies who do not feel attached to the country."

The Jewish question was so important to the emperor that in the same year he devised a new way of dealing with it. He demanded that the Jews make a public choice between a separate nation or integration into the nation in which they resided. He summoned one hundred and twelve representatives of Judaism from France, Germany and Italy to answer a series of questions. The delegates chosen by the Jewish communities arrived in Paris to resolve the dilemma. Napoleon wanted to know simply whether they were part of the nation he ruled or whether they considered themselves part of a nation that was above all nations. The question was like an arrow shot at the principles of the Torah and Talmud, upon which the wall had been built between the Jews and other men, the gentiles. The basic issues were: did Jewish law permit intermarriage, did the Jews regard the French as foreigners or as brothers, did they regard France as their native country, did their law draw distinctions between Jewish debtors and Christian debtors, and did it make distinctions between Jewish debtors and Christian debtors? Napoleon demanded the convocation of the Great Sanhedrin so that the compromise, if reached, would have maximum legal force.

From all over Europe the traditional seventy-one members of the Sanhedrin, forty-six rabbis and twenty-one laymen, came to Paris in February 1807. It was a historic moment, for they affirmed that there was no longer a Jewish nation, that the laws of the Talmud were no longer in force, that they did not wish to live in closed communities and that they were to all intents and purposes French and nothing more. It was a short-lived illusion, for the Jews who came before Napoleon did not represent the great masses of Eastern European Khazar Jews, the Ashkenazi Jews of Russia and Poland, who would eventually cancel out the response of a Sanhedrin that at that historic moment did not represent them. It was not for nothing that the Rothschilds were Talmudists of Ashkenazi origin and held the undisputed leadership.

In 1809, a young German named Friedrich Stapps, an agent of the Illuminati according to Bonaparte himself, attempted to assassinate the Emperor in Vienna. After a conversation with the young man, Napoleon declared: "These are the effects of the German Illuminati. The new generation is taught that murder is a virtue. However, I believe that there is more to the matter than meets the eye". Stapps was executed by firing squad on 17 October. In 1810, the Emperor divorced Josephine and married Archduchess Marie-Louise. This was the point that clearly marked the beginning of the rift between Bonaparte and the Rothschilds. From then on, his former mentors began to finance a league against him and worked ceaselessly to alienate him from the Pope. Thus Napoleon ended up publicly denouncing the Jews. Here are three of his views: "One cannot improve the character of the Jews by argument. Exclusive laws must be established for them". "All their talents are concentrated in acts of rapacity. "They have a creed which blesses their thefts and misdeeds.

When Napoleon began his military invasion of Russia, the Rothschilds were already working to defeat him. William Guy Carr, author of *Pawns in the Game*, explains how Napoleon was sabotaged in the Russian campaign. Guy Carr, an intelligence officer in the Royal Canadian Navy, was well versed in how things worked at these levels. According to this author, the secret strategy used to defeat Napoleon and force his abdication was very simple. Agents were placed in key positions in the supply, communications, transport and intelligence departments of the French army. In this way, supplies were sabotaged, orders were intercepted, contradictory messages were broadcast, or transports were diverted or lost. The Russian campaign was plagued by such problems.

The Rothschilds not only enriched themselves with Napoleon's defeat at Waterloo, but also did everything in their power to bring it about. Both Count Cherep-Spiridovitch in *The Secret World Government or "The Hidden Hand"* and John Coleman in the aforementioned work reveal that Napoleon was betrayed by Soult, who was Jewish and took orders from the Rothschilds. Although Napoleon had promoted him to Marshal," writes Cherep-Spiridovitch, "made him Duke of Dalmatia and rewarded him with a millionaire's income, this Jew did not hesitate to betray his generous emperor. At Waterloo, Soult was to take and hold Genappe, an important town to protect the flank of the Emperor's army. Napoleon complained bitterly about Soult: "Soult, my second in command at Waterloo, did not help me as he should have done.... His staff, despite my orders, was not organised. Soult lost heart too easily.... Soult was of no use to me, why during the battle he did not keep order at Genappe". It should be remembered here that, interestingly, Genappe is the village where John Roothworth, Nathan Rothschild's agent, went, as noted above. John Coleman adds that the actions of Marshal Grouchy, who was supposed to arrive with reinforcements, but showed up twenty-four hours late, even though he heard the cannon fire and knew that the battle had begun, are also incomprehensible. Grouchy was publicly accused in 1846 by Georges Dairnvaell of having been bribed by the Rothschilds. In *The Rothschild Dynasty*, Coleman writes the following about Soult and Waterloo:

> ... Such is the power of the Rothschilds and the falsification of history. Had it not been for the treachery committed against him, Napoleon would have soundly defeated Blucher and Wellington. Soult served his masters well; they gave him some of the highest offices in France. That he was Bismarck's father has been suggested, but never proved. For a time Bismarck's mother was Soult's mistress as Bismarck himself confirmed: 'I was not great because of my talent or my abilities, but everyone helped me because my mother was Soult's mistress'".

Soult, who will reappear in another chapter, could be written about at length. It should be remembered that in Spain this Jew, eager for power and wealth, robbed and plundered as much as he could without any scruple. After having stolen all over Europe, specifically in Germany, Austria and Italy, he acted like a true viceroy in Seville, preparing the theft of the best paintings by Murillo and the great Sevillian masters, many of which went to swell his collections in Soultberg Castle. Soult was assisted by a Spaniard, Alejandro Mª Aguado, a Seville potentate who was a colonel on his General Staff and later a wealthy Parisian banker. Years later Aguado sold one of the finest collections of Spanish paintings. During his stay in Seville, the marshal accumulated enough paintings to send up to ten shipments to his wife. Transports full of precious objects were constantly arriving at his home, with which this thief and traitor was able to fill Soultberg and Villeneuve's mansion, his palaces in Paris. In the political caricatures that circulated throughout his life, he was often depicted surrounded by paintings and objets d'art. In one of 1834, "Les honneurs du Pantheon", he is seen hanging with other dignitaries with his neck inside a painting bearing Murillo's signature.

For more than thirty years a Napoleon scholar, Ben Weider, tried for more than thirty years to let the world know that in 1821 Bonaparte had been poisoned to death on St. Helena. Finally, on 2 June 2005, at a press conference in Illkirch-Graffenstandem, Dr. Pascal Kintz, president of the International Association of Forensic Toxicologists, confirmed Weider's thesis and proved that arsenic was found in the core of Napoleon's hair, indicating a digestive tract route and not external contamination as the magazine *Science & Vie* claimed for mysterious reasons. Dr Kintz revealed the nature of the poison used: mineral arsenic, commonly known as rat poison.

The Rothschilds reign in Europe

Until his death in 1836 Nathan led the clan from London, where, after the Waterloo coup, he continued to count on the invaluable help of Herris, thanks to whom he became increasingly close to the Secretary to the Treasury, Nicholas Vansittart. Referring to this friendship with Vansittart, Solomon wrote to James: "Nathan's relation to this gentleman of the Treasury is like that of brothers.... Our New Court gives me the impression of being like a Masonic lodge. Whoever enters becomes a Bono-mason". But if Nathan Rothschild reigned in the City, flanked by the Mocattas and Goldsmid, his four brothers were soon to begin their respective reigns on the Continent in the various European capitals from which they operated. According to Professor Werner Sombart in his *The Jews and Modern Capitalism*, "the period from 1820 onwards becomes the era of the Rothschilds, so that by the middle of the century it was generally accepted that there was only one power in Europe, and that was the Rothschilds".

For twenty-six years, from 1789 to 1815, Europe was caught up in a spiral of violence. The bloody revolution in France was followed by a succession of wars that exhausted the peoples of the old continent from Portugal to Russia. Just as the Rothschilds had enriched themselves enormously through the wars they had financed, so the Rothschilds were to profit from the economic consequences of peace. Disraeli would later explain in his novel *Coningsby*: "after the exhaustion of a twenty-five years' war, Europe needed capital to build peace.... France wanted some; Austria, more; Prussia, a little; Russia, a few millions'. Although at first their competitors tried to hold them back, the Rothschilds eventually took over all the big businesses, including railways: building railways across Europe was soon to become one of the biggest businesses, and they monopolised it.

They had a number of German nouns to refer to their rivals, such as "Schurken" (scoundrels, scoundrels), Bösewichte (rascals, wicked) and "Spitzbuben" (Thieves). Even before Waterloo they had already talked a lot about ways to put sticks in the wheels of their "evil" competitors, and that is what they did from 1818 onwards with the Barings, Labouchère and other bankers who sought to oppose them. James Rothschild aspired to be the equivalent in France of what his brother Nathan was in Britain; but the French government had negotiated a substantial loan in 1817 with Ouvrard's prestigious French bank and the Baring brothers in London. The following year, the French government needed another loan. As the bonds issued in 1817 increased in value in the Paris market and other European financial centres, it seemed certain that France would continue to rely on the services of the same banks. The Rothschilds used their vast repertoire of devices to influence the French government, but to no avail. The French, however, ignored or disregarded the cunning and ability of the Jewish bankers to speculate and manipulate money. On 5 November 1818 something unexpected happened: after a year of steady appreciation, the value of French bonds began to fall. Day after day the depreciation became more pronounced. Soon other government securities also began to devalue. At the court of Louis XVIII tension grew. Slowly observers realised that the Rothschilds had something to do with it. They had once again caused panic by secretly manipulating the stock market. During the month of October 1818 their agents, using their unlimited reserves, had bought up huge quantities of French government bonds issued by their rivals, which had caused their value to rise. Then, on 5 November, they began to flood the markets (dumping) large quantities of French debt securities. In doing so, they destabilised all the European stock markets and created panic. They were soon brought before Louis XVIII. It was in this way that France too gradually came under the control of the Rothschilds, who by the end of 1822 had also become the bankers of the Holy Alliance: "The High Treasury of the Holy Alliance".

Salomon Rothschild's relationship with Metternich, the man who made Austrian policy from 1809 to 1848, deserves special mention. Not only was he his banker, but they understood each other emotionally and intellectually. Although he came from an aristocratic family, Prince Klemens Wenzel Nepomuck Lothar von Metternick had no money. During the peace negotiations in Paris in 1815, the possibility of the first loan from the Rothschilds arose, namely with Carl and Amschel in Frankfurt. Metternich had proved to be a useful ally of the Rothschilds: he had supplied them in Paris with political information, helped them secure financial business in Austria, and sympathised with their campaign for Jewish emancipation in Frankfurt. In October 1821, accompanied by his mistress, Princess Dorothy of Lieven, he met Amschel in Frankfurt in a gesture of support for the city's Jewish community. Less than a year later he obtained a second loan, arranged six days before the brothers received the title of baron from the Austrian emperor, Franz I. This loan sealed the friendship between the brothers. This loan sealed the friendship between the Rothschilds and Metternich. In 1823, in Verona, Salomon provided him with liquidity to meet his considerable personal expenses. Two years later, James entertained him to a grandiloquent dinner in Paris. It was around this time that Metternich began to use the Rothschild mail service for important correspondence. From then on, he and Salomon exchanged information regularly: Metternich would update him on Austria's political intentions, and the banker would provide him with news he received from his brothers in Paris, London, Frankfurt and Naples. The Rothschilds often used the word "uncle" to refer to Metternich.

One of the victims of the alliance between Solomon and Metternich was the banker David Parish, whose Viennese bank "Fries & Co" was sacrificed. In 1820 Parish had been Solomon's partner on the occasion of a loan to organise a lottery which was widely criticised and described as "shameful Jewish usury". Six years later it was Parish himself who used virulent language against the Rothschilds, who had dumped him and his bank. Before committing suicide by throwing himself into the Danube, he wrote four letters: to his brother John, to the banker Geymüller, to Metternich and to Solomon himself, in which he blamed his downfall on the Rothschilds and promised to publicly discredit them. Metternich," Parish said, "has sacrificed me to the greed of a family who, for all their wealth, have no heart and care only for the money box. Parish regretted having been deceived by Solomon in the most shameful manner and "having been paid with the blackest ingratitude for services". In his letter to Metternich he complained in these terms: "The Rothschilds have understood better than I how to trap you in their sphere of interests and how to secure your special protection". In his letter to Solomon he said that the new alliance between them (the Rothschilds) and Metternich had ruined him: "Under the protection of Prince Metternich, you have succeeded in securing for yourself the exclusive control of multiple transactions in which I was legally and morally entitled to a share....". Metternich was thus the Rothschilds' key man in Austria. A silver box has recently been found in Moscow containing documents showing that Salomon kept Metternich's bank accounts and financial correspondence. The importance of this relationship clearly conditioned Austrian foreign policy. In the next chapter we will see how Salomon made his close relationship with the prince count.

Rothschild sycophants were the order of the day. According to the economist Friedrich List, they were "the pride of Israel, before whom kings and emperors humbly bowed". The *Niles Weekly Register*, the most widely circulated magazine in America, in 1835 called the Rothschilds the awe of modern banking and stated flatly that they ruled the Christian world, since no government moved without their advice. They reach out their hand with equal ease," he said, "from St. Petersburg to Vienna, from Vienna to Paris, from Paris to London, from London to Washington. Baron Rothschild, the head of the house, is the true king of Judea, the prince of the captivity, the Messiah so long awaited by this extraordinary people. He holds the keys of peace and war, of blessing and curse.... They are the agents and counsellors of the kings of Europe and the republican leaders of America. What more can they desire?"

It is beyond the scope of this chapter to go into the ways in which the various European peoples were enslaved through debt. The Rothschilds established with a number of key figures on the European political scene a network of unethical and financially driven private relationships. So much so that they were soon placed in the public eye at the centre of a web of corruption. Their image, which was also tainted by numerous cases of bribery and blackmail, deteriorated in the eyes of the general public. The jokes and caricatures of denounced him and proliferated in much of the press, which in the first third of the century had not yet been fully controlled. But what really mattered was that even before 1830 the Rothschilds had become a colossus whose resources, according to their biographer Niall Ferguson, had grown to such an extent that they were ten times greater than those of their closest competitor.

Talmudist Jews

The first chapter of this book has already explained the importance of the *Talmud* for Judaism, even greater than that of the *Torah*, and has commented on the visceral hatred that its texts exude towards Christianity. It is therefore necessary to reflect now on the implications of the fact that the world's most powerful bankers are Talmudists (it is not only the Rothschilds who are Talmudists). Mayer Amschel Rothschild was a rabbi and was educated in the principles of the *Talmud*, according to which only Jews have the right to dominate other peoples, since non-Jews are created to serve Jews. The *Talmud* teaches that plundering non-Jews and being hypocritical towards them is permitted. The consequences of following these doctrines, not only in the banking business but in any area of interpersonal relations, are obviously catastrophic. August Rohling, a professor at the University of Prague in the late 19th century and translator of the *Talmud*, states that while awaiting the coming of the Messiah, Jews live in a constant state of war with other peoples. When victory comes, all peoples will accept the Jewish religion; but Christians will not be allowed this privilege, but will be exterminated, since they belong to the devil. In this light, it is conceivable that the origins of the grand scheme of the New World Order come from the *Talmud*, and that the longed-for World Government is nothing other than the realisation of what is being called the "Jewish utopia".

The jewish Utopia is the title of a 135-page book published in 1932 by the Zionist Michael Higger, who dedicated it to the Hebrew University of Jerusalem, which represents, according to Higger, 'the symbol of Jewish utopia'. The text can be accessed as a PDF. It reviews the Zionists' entire plan for world domination. Robert H. Williams, an American nationalist writer who in World War II organised a Counterintelligence Service for the American Air Force (AAF), studied the book and paraphrased it in his *The Ultimate World Order as pictured in "The Jewish Utopia"*, published in 1957, which is also available in English on the Internet. Williams describes the book as the compendium of prophecies, philosophical teachings, plans and interpretations of the *Talmud* that underlie what he calls "the Final World Order". Higger quotes the words of the *Talmud*, according to which the "righteous" will be the Jews and those who choose to align themselves with them to serve them, while the "wicked" will be those who are perceived by the Jews as opponents of their interests. Higger points out that in the Jewish utopia "all the treasures and natural resources of the world will be in the possession of the righteous in fulfilment of Isaiah's prophecy". The accumulation of all of humanity's wealth is thus an integral part of the ancient Jewish agenda to constitute a New World Order. Some authors claim that today the Rothschilds would own half the wealth of the planet.

Mayer Amschel Rothschild therefore brought up his five children according to the principles of the *Talmud*. Already in the time of Moses Amschel Bauer, prayers and other religious rituals were observed in the family. The religiosity of the Rothschilds was immortalised by Moritz Daniel Oppenheim. This painter, who also produced the paintings described above of the handover and return of the treasure of the Elector of Hesse-Kassel, is also the author of a somewhat disturbing work entitled *The Rothschild Family at Prayer*. Niall Ferguson reproduces the painting in *The House of Rothschild. Money's Prophets*. Twelve people are depicted wrapped up to their heads in the traditional white robes of the Levites, which cover their entire bodies. The ghostly atmosphere lends the painting an enigmatic aura. Eleven of them are seated around a table on which six single-candle candles burn. Almost all of them are holding books and reading. The twelfth person, wrapped from head to toe in the large white cloak characteristic of the tribe, stands with his back to the doorway leading to another room where candles are also burning. On his deathbed Mayer Amschel read to his sons from the *Talmud* and imposed a series of obligations on them. It is therefore quite clear that, apart from business, the Rothschilds were religiously Talmudic. It is recorded that in 1820 the all-powerful Nathan Rothschild was a member of a *Torah* and *Talmudic* society in London, to which he contributed financially.

The Rothschilds in literature. Their writers: Heine and Disraeli

Books and newspapers were in the 19th century the means of propagation of ideas. As we have seen, one of the Illuminati's priorities was to select and control what to read and what not to read. Through the Reading Societies, set up by the German Union, they sought to favour those writers who favoured them and to ruin those who opposed them. In the first third of the century, the project was still in gestation and things were not yet fully in place, as not all criticism could be silenced. Ferguson, who refers to the Rothschilds as the Medicis of the 19th century, cites among their protégés several authors and also the musicians Chopin and Rossini. The Rothschilds thus had writers who worked slavishly for their "protectors". Metternich's secretary, Friedrich von Gentz, was among the first to write about the bankers in fawning terms. Gentz even sent instructions to newspapers such as the *Allgemaine Zeitung,* ordering that the Rothschilds should not be criticised.

However, some writers denounced them. One of the first who dared to criticise them in the form of novelistic fiction was Honoré de Balzac, who apart from his literary works left us the following sentence: "There are two histories: the official, deceitful one, which is taught ad usum delphini, and the real, secret one, in which the true causes of events are to be found: a shameful history". In his novel *The House of Nucingen* (1837) he portrays a roguish German banker who has made his fortune through a series of fraudulent bankruptcies and by forcing his creditors to accept depreciated paper as payment. The similarities between Nucingen and James Rothschild are too obvious to be coincidental. In another work, *The Splendours and Miseries of Courtesans* (1838-47), Balzac concludes that all wealth accumulated too rapidly is the result of legal theft. Harsher was the criticism of Georges Dairnvaell, who in his pamphlet *The Edifying and Curious History of Rothschild I, King of the Jews* (1846) insisted that Nathan, with the news of Napoleon's defeat at Waterloo, had made a huge sum of money speculating on the London Stock Exchange and also accused him of having bribed the French general Grouchy to ensure Wellington's victory. Another writer and journalist, Alphonse Toussenel, author of *The Jews, Kings of the Age: A History of Financial Feudalism* (1846), denounced in this work that France had been sold to the Jews and that the railway lines were controlled by Baron Rothschild, the King of France. Toussenel argued that the French railway network could not be in the hands of speculative capitalists.

The Jewish writer Ludwig Börne, born in Frankfurt like the Rothschilds, accused his banker friends of being the worst enemies of nations because they had lent their money to autocrats who opposed liberalism. The hypocrisy of Börne's criticism was evident when this champion of liberalism later pathetically asked: "Would it not be a great blessing for the world if all the kings were removed and the Rothschild family took their thrones". The hypocritical Börne must surely have known that the Rothschilds were simply in business when they lent money, although they did so without ever forgetting the priority of the World Revolutionary Movement, which they had set in motion through the Illuminati. As always, they financed both sides, the monarchies and liberalism, whose political ideology would enable them to trigger the revolutions in Europe.

It was quite clear to Lord Byron, who already in 1823, in the twelfth canto of his *Don Juan*, asked: "Who holds the scales of the world? Who holds sway in Parliament over royalists or liberals? Who raises up the shirtless patriots in Spain? Who causes in the old and new world pain or pleasure? Who makes charlatans of all politicians?". The answer he gave was: "The Jew Rothschild and his Christian colleague Baring". Byron seems to have been unaware that the Baring brothers were also of Jewish origin; but what is important in these lines is that Byron saw clearly that Rothschild was influencing both royalists and liberals, and that he supported revolution in Spain and insurrection in his Latin American republics. Another writer, William Tackeray, also understood perfectly well what was going on and was of the opinion that "N. M. Rothschild was playing with the new kings as little girls play with their dolls".

Two Jewish names stand out among the Rothschild stalwarts: Heinrich Heine (1797-1856), the famous German Romantic poet who, according to critics, had a decisive influence on our G. A. Bécquer, and Benjamin Disraeli (1808-1881), who served two terms as Prime Minister of Great Britain, a position from which he pursued a servile and decisive policy in the interests of the Jewish bankers. Both deserve separate attention.

Let us turn to the first. Heinrich Heine was a close friend of Karl Marx and James Rothschild. Marx said of him that he was "the most hardened of the German exiles, the most unyielding and the most intelligent". Both Heine and Börne were portrayed by Moritz Daniel Oppenheim, the painter of the Rothschild family. Heine's contact with the Rothschilds originated with his lifelong supporter, the wealthy banker Salomon Heine, known as the Rothschild of Hamburg, with whom he was already working in Hamburg in 1816. It is known that around this time Heine and his father frequented the

Masonic lodge *Zur aufgehenden Morgenröte* (*Towards the Future Red Dawn*) in Frankfurt. In 1822 in Poland he became acquainted with Hasidism, a movement of fundamentalist Talmudist Jews, and was captivated by it. Heine, who belonged to the Carbonarii, arrived in exile in Paris on 19 March 1831 and began a personal relationship with James, the youngest of the five Rothschild brothers, with whom he used to stroll the streets of the city at night, arm in arm.

Very important and significant are Heine's references to the Rothschilds and communism. The depth of his remarks suggests that he knew very well what he was talking about. In March 1841 he declared: "The Rothschilds have replaced the old aristocracy and they represent a new materialistic religion. Money is the god of our time and Rothschild is its prophet". On the leadership of revolutionary movements he wrote some most illuminating words: "No one does more for the progress of the revolution than the Rothschilds themselves... and, though it may seem even more strange, the Rothschilds, the bankers of kings, these splendid money managers, whose existence should be considered at risk if the present system of the European states should collapse, have above all in their minds the consciousness of their revolutionary mission".

But where he is most disturbing is in his predictions about communism. It does not take much insight to understand that his friendship with Marx and the Rothschilds provided him with all the information which, six years before the appearance of the *Communist Manifesto*, he unveiled in the drama *Programme*, which is not usually listed in bibliographies, but which was published in July 1842 in a Hamburg journal entitled *Französiche Zustände* (*French Positions*) and twelve years later in the book *Lutezia*. The quotation is lengthy, but worthwhile:

> "Communism, which has not yet appeared, but which will appear powerful and will be fearless and disinterested as thought... will be identified with the dictatorship of the proletariat. It will be a terrible duel. How will it end? That is known to the gods and goddesses whose future is known. Only this we know: communism, even if it is little spoken of now and lies on straw mattresses in unknown garrets, is the dark hero who has a great but passing role in modern tragedy and who is only waiting for the order to enter the scene. That is why we will never lose sight of this actor, and why we will never lose sight of the secret rehearsals with which he prepares for his stage debut. This is perhaps more important than all the information about election issues, party squabbles and cabinet intrigues.
>
> ... The war between France and Germany will be only the first act of the great drama, namely, the prologue. The second act is the European, the universal revolution, the great duel of the dispossessed with the aristocracy of property; and then there will be no talk of nation or religion, there will be only one fatherland, namely, the Earth, and only one faith,

namely, happiness on Earth. Will the religious doctrines of the past rise up in all countries in desperate resistance, and will this attempt perhaps be the third act? Will the old absolute tradition come on the scene again, but with new uniforms, new slogans and new passwords? How will this drama end? Perhaps there will be only a shepherd and a flock; a free shepherd with an iron staff, and a human flock shorn and bleating in uniform.

Savage, atrocious times are threatening us. And the prophet who wants to write this new apocalypse will have to invent completely new beasts, and so horrible that the old symbolic animals of St. John will turn out, compared to them, to be sweet little popcorn and sweethearts. The gods hide their faces out of compassion for humans and perhaps also out of fear of their own fate".

The text is not to be missed. Heinrich Heine, a Jew who is moved by Hasidic Talmudism, nephew of the banker Salomon Heine, close friend of James and Nathan Rothschild, whom he describes as "sitting as if he were on a throne and talking like a king with courtiers around him", a close friend of Karl Marx, whom he put in touch with Nathan in his London exile, is historically the first man to use the term "dictatorship of the proletariat" (Proletarienherrschaft) in public. His sources of information are obvious, so that one should not think of him as a prophet, but as someone who knew what the "gods" were preparing for mankind. He said that money was the god of our time and Rothschild its prophet. We know, then, who the gods were for him. Also significant is his allusion to "the secret trials" and to the transitory role of communism "which is only waiting for the order to enter the scene". For the rest, everything was to happen as Heine had foretold: first the Franco-Prussian war, which ends in the Paris "Commune", where James Rothschild's palaces are guarded and preserved from looting by the revolutionaries themselves; then the revolutions in Russia, Hungary, Bavaria, China and Spain, and a world in which half of humanity will bleat in a uniform way. A new apocalypse of which even the "gods" fear the consequences.

There is no doubt, then, and we shall have occasion to demonstrate this in a later chapter, that Heine's connections with the real Communist leaders were so strong and intimate that they enabled him to learn of their plan. The reasons he had for revealing it in advance are perhaps to be sought in the idiosyncrasy of the character, a man with an inordinate desire for the limelight that drove him to exhibitionism. In the State Archives in Vienna there is an Austrian secret service report on the German revolutionaries in Paris dated 28 October 1835. Count Egon Caesar Corti quotes in *The Reign of the House of Rothschild* the text referring to Heine, considered a "political chameleon and moral coward by nature". The report goes on in these bitter terms: "a liar and a man who would be disloyal to his best friend, changeable as a hen, he is totally unstable; malicious as a snake, he has all the beauty and brilliance of this being, and all its venom; without any noble or authentic instinct, he is incapable of sincere emotion. He is so vain that he would like to play a prominent part, but he has already played his part, he no longer takes it seriously, but his talent remains."

The other case of a staunch Rothschild writer and politician was Disraeli, who in 1837 published *The Wondrous Tale of Alroy*, a story whose protagonist is a Khazar who (as explained in note 2 of the first chapter) seeks to conquer Palestine in the 13th century. Benjamin Disraeli (Lord Beaconsfiled), son of Isaac Disraeli, was Prime Minister of Britain twice (1867-68 and 1874-80) and was completely subservient to the interests of the Jewish bankers who had brought him to the top. In *Coningsby* (1844), which the *Jewish Encyclopaedia* describes as an idealised portrait of the Rothschild empire, Sidonia, a character who in the novel represents both Nathan Rothschild and his son Lionel, confirms that the world is ruled by people who are hidden behind the scenes and do not appear on the public stage. Sidonia, while confessing her family's enmity towards the Russian tsars, boasts that in St Petersburg she met the Russian finance minister, Count Cancrin, the son of a Lithuanian Jew. On his European tour to negotiate loans, the interlocutors are always Jews in key positions: in Spain his interlocutor is Mendizabal, the son of a Marrano from Aragon[15]; in Paris he is received by the President of the Council of Ministers, who is also the son of a Jew. Sidonia boasts of having succeeded in placing Count Arnim, a Prussian Jew, in the Prussian cabinet. To the question whether Marshal Soult (already mentioned, who betrayed Napoleon) was a Jew, she replies that he was, and that so were other French Marshals, among whom the most famous is Massena, whose real name is Mannaseh. Sidonia states that her father (Nathan) and his brothers, thanks to loans to European states, became masters of the world's stock market.

In 1847 Disraeli published a new work, *Tancred or the New Crusade*. In one passage of the novel, Eva Besso, a character inspired by Charlotte

---

[15] Juan de Dios Álvarez Mendizábal's surname was actually Méndez, but to better hide his origin he gave himself a Basque surname. The Rothschilds met Mendizábal through Vicente Bertrand de Lys, a Madrid banker with connections to the powerful Jewish family. Mendizábal worked closely with the Rothschilds and in 1835 secured for them a £2 million loan to Portugal. Through Nathan Rothschild he speculated in debt securities and made a lot of money. In June 1835 he was appointed Minister of Finance to replace the Count of Toreno, with whom Nathan had fallen out over the confused negotiation of a loan after he had obtained the rights to exploit the Almadén mercury mines. At a family meeting, the Rothschilds decided to provoke the collapse of Spanish debt on the markets. Before launching the stock market attack, Nathan warned his friend Mendizábal of what was about to happen so that the new Minister of Finance would have time to dispose of his securities and not go bankrupt. During the period of Mendizábal, who in Europe was considered an agent of the London bankers, the public debt increased substantially. In order to raise money, he announced the suppression of the religious orders and decreed the disentailment of their assets, the so-called Desamortización de Mendizábal.

Rothschild, Carl's daughter and wife of Lionel, Nathan's first-born son, asks: "Who is the richest man in Paris?", to which Tancred replies: "The brother, I believe, of the richest man in London". Tancred then points out that they both belong to the same race and the same faith. These Rothschild-inspired novelistic characters of Disraeli's serve to explain perfectly the financial and political power of this elite of Talmudic Jews. They are therefore elements of undoubted historical value.

It is puzzling that Disraeli, who undoubtedly owed his entire political career to the influence of the Rothschilds, should have warned that secret societies controlled by Jews were behind the world revolution. In 1852, four years after the revolutionary outbreaks of 1848 and fifteen years before he became prime minister for the first time, he uttered in the House of Commons these words, quoted by Douglas Reed in *The Controversy of Zion*: "The influence of the Jews may be traced in the latest outbreak of the destructive principle in Europe. An insurrection takes place against tradition and aristocracy, against religion and property.... The natural equality of men and the abolition of property are proclaimed by secret societies which form provisional governments, and men of the Jewish race are at the head of each of them. And in his political biography *Life of Lord George Bentinck* he added: "The people of God co-operate with atheists, the most skilful accumulators of property ally themselves with Communists, the peculiar chosen race touches the hands of the scum and lower classes of Europe, and all because they wish to destroy the ungrateful Christianity which owes its name to them, and whose tyranny no one can bear any longer". Disraeli thus unequivocally confirms the thesis put forward in the previous chapter and what we have been writing.

If Heine revealed that the Rothschilds were aware of their revolutionary mission and announced in advance the coming of Communism, Disraeli alluded in precise words to a "destructive principle" intended to bring about a new order in Europe. It is very curious that two men so close to the Rothschilds, Heine and Disraeli, did not exercise discretion and give clear warning of the nature of the events that were to lead to the Bolshevik revolution and subsequently to the division of the world into two blocs.

Finally, it remains to mention a work by an anonymous author, *Hebrew Talisman*, a pamphlet published in London in 1840, four years after Nathan's death. It attributed Nathan's financial success to his possession of a magic talisman. Nathan Rothschild's power had aroused such high expectations among European Jewry that he was seen as the man predestined to re-establish the kingdom of Judah. Indeed, as early as 1830 an American newspaper suggested that, because of financial difficulties, the Sultan of Constantinople might decide to sell Jerusalem to the Rothschilds. In 1836 the French socialist Charles Fourier also suggested the same possibility in his work *La fausse industrie*. Benjamin Disraeli himself spoke in 1851 of the reinstatement of the Jews in Palestine with the help of Rothschild money.

Significantly, however, the author of *The Hebrew Talisman* concluded by accusing Nathan of preferring the advantages of assimilation in England to the difficulties and rigours of his 'sacred mission'. In fact, the mysterious author offendedly proclaimed that Nathan's sudden death had come as punishment for his decision to seek for himself a peerage and a law for the social emancipation of the Jews in England, rather than continue to strive for the recovery of Jerusalem.

Nathan's death

Count Cherep-Spiridovich, referring to Nathan's fickle social pretensions in England, formulates a very daring thesis. According to him, Nathan,, lacking any scruples, in his eagerness to accumulate more wealth and to gain titles and power in England, found that his religious creed hindered his rise in London society and was ready to apostatise. The elder brother, Anselm, was supposedly the first to learn of Nathan's intentions. In Frankfurt, where thirty-six members of the family gathered in June 1836 for the wedding of Nathan's son Lionel and Carl's eldest daughter Charlotte, the decision was taken not to tolerate the betrayal. According to Count Cherep-Spiridovich, referring to the will of Mayer Amschel Rothschild, Nathan was condemned by his brothers. Of course, there is no evidence to prove the veracity of this theory, which at first sight seems implausible.

Niall Ferguson, whose thousand-page work on the Rothschilds credits him as an inescapable source, sees Nathan's unexpected illness and death as a case study in the ineptitude of the attending physicians and the incompetence of 19th-century medicine. Ferguson writes that in early June 1836 Nathan and his wife Hannah arrived in Frankfurt from London. According to him, the marriage of their son Lionel to Charlotte was not the main reason for the meeting of the five siblings, but the most important item on the agenda was the assumption of the future relations between them, which since 1810 had not been thoroughly modified, although they had been revised periodically in order to include the heirs in the partnership. The foundations of the partnership remained basically those established by their father. The negotiations between the brothers were conducted in strict secrecy and the other members of the family were excluded from them: "They are now gathered together," Lionel informed his brother Anthony, "that is, the four of them are alone in Papa's room and we have been left out."

Nathan held all these meetings when he was ill, suffering from frequent pain due to a boil, probably an ischio-rectal abscess that was festering. The German doctors decided to perform a cut and assured Nathan that he was in no danger. The family decided to go ahead with the wedding preparations: on 13 June the ball was held and on 15 June the wedding ceremony, both of which Nathan attended. While the bride and groom left for Wilhelmsbad, where they enjoyed a one-day honeymoon, Nathan went under the surgeons' knife for the second time.

The whole month of June the family waited for his recovery, but negotiations on the partnership agreement between the five brothers were postponed, which provoked the irritation of James, who wanted to return to Paris, and the impatience of Lionel, who addressed his brothers in these terms: "Dad is getting better, but slowly". Despite this supposed improvement, the doctors continued to open and drain the wound. Finally, on 24 July, Nathan suffered a violent, life-threatening fever. Ferguson speculated that it was the beginning of septicaemia.

The next day, in a state of extreme nervous agitation, he summoned his son Lionel and ordered him to transmit to his brother Nathaniel, who had remained in London, the following instructions, which constitute his last financial operations: "He wants you to continue to sell the English securities and Treasury bills, plus £20,000 more of the Indian stocks. You must also send a report on the various shares available. I don't know if I misunderstood, but I didn't want to ask for clarification. He also said that you have to sell... the securities that the Portuguese government has given for the money they owe us, no matter what the difference of one or two per cent".

Three days later, on 28 July, Nathan died. The interest in his death in Europe was extraordinary, for Nathan Rothschild was the richest man in England "and therefore," Ferguson writes, "given Britain's economic leadership at the time, he was almost certainly the richest man in the world. Ferguson acknowledges that it was a decisive and extremely tense moment in the history of the Rothschild firm, as the leader was dying without the signing of a new partnership agreement between the brothers. "He died," wrote Solomon to Austrian Chancellor Metternich, "in full possession of his faculties, and ten minutes before his death he said, on receiving the last words of consolation customary in our religion, 'it is not necessary for me to utter so many prayers, for, believe me, according to my convictions I have committed no sin.'" Five days after his death, a carrier pigeon left Boulogne and carried the news to London in a three-word phrase: "Il est mort".

Having briefly recounted some of the most significant facts about the Rothschild dynasty's dizzying rise to power, we will now proceed with our work, bearing in mind that they and their agents are behind the major episodes in contemporary history that we are reviewing.

CHAPTER IV

THE ROTHSCHILDS AND THE DAMASCUS AFFAIR

When Ariel Toaff, son of Rome's chief rabbi Elio Toaff, published *Pasque di sangue* in Italy in February 2007, it caused a major media stir in the country. It was the first time that Jewish circles had acknowledged the veracity of ritual crimes against Christian children. The rabbis reacted furiously and the mercenaries of the press were quick to indignate and tear their hair out, to deny, to criticise the audacity, to ask for explanations. Ariel Toaff was accused of having provided Ahmadinejad with the media atomic bomb. The Islamic Anti-Defamation League filed a lawsuit against Professor Toaff and the Il Mulino publishing house. After more than a month of being subjected to all kinds of pressure, attacks and disqualifications, including from his own father, Ariel Toaff, who was even accused of anti-Semitism despite being Jewish, was forced to ask the publisher to block distribution of the book and wrote a letter publicly apologising. He also promised to submit to Jewish censorship and furthermore announced that he would give all profits from the sale of his book, once suitably expunged, to the Anti-Defamation League of fanatic Abe Foxman. At the time he provoked the scandal by writing about sufficiently proven, but always silenced, facts, Ariel Toaff was working as a professor at the Jewish university of Bar Ilan, near Tel Aviv, and was recognised as a specialist in the Jewry of the Middle Ages.

Israel Shamir, a Russian-born Jewish convert to Christianity, a staunch supporter of the Palestinian people and author of several works denouncing Zionism, was one of the few who in February 2007 dared to declare openly that what Ariel Toaff was saying was true. Shamir was quick to denounce the campaign against Toaff on his website, *Working towards Peace through Education and Information*, where he published an article entitled "Dr Toaff's Bloody Passover", explaining the ritual crimes against Christians that have been practised continuously by Jews throughout history: international researchers such as Professor Toaff have found and studied documentation of more than 150 known cases, ranging from the 12th to the 20th century.

One such crime took place in Damascus on 5 February 1840. A Capuchin friar, Father Tomaso, was murdered in the Jewish quarter of the Syrian capital and all the blood was extracted from his body to make 'matzo', an unleavened bread made on the occasion of the celebration of Passover (Pesach). Israel Shamir writes in the above-mentioned article that 'matzos' made with blood were sold in certain markets. According to Shamir, 'Jewish merchants sold them with the proper rabbinical letters of authorisation; the most prized blood was that of the 'goy katan', i.e. the gentile child'. The repercussions of Father Tomaso's murder reached a European and historical dimension. The continental press, as in 2007 in Italy, covered the case for months, and the governments of France, Great Britain, Austria and Turkey were involved in a crisis that has gone down in history as the "Damascus Affair".

The reason why this book contains a chapter on the case is to examine the decisive role played by the Rothschilds in the resolution of the case. In this way it will be possible to understand the power they already wielded over European politics at the time. In the first half of the 19th century, as we have already mentioned, the control of the press and publishing industry by the international Jewish bankers, i.e. the Illuminati, was not yet as absolute as it is today. The Jews were already very influential, but not yet all-powerful. As Shamir says in his article, "they could not treat the world as they did in 2002, after the Jenin massacre. They could not handle the US veto in the UN Security Council". It is precisely because this ability to control the media was not yet absolute that the study of what happened in 1840 takes on significant importance.

Origins of Purim and Passover

Before reviewing some famous cases of these ritual crimes and moving on to an in-depth study of the repercussions of the Damascus Affair, it is useful to enlighten the reader on the background of this barbaric tradition practised by the Jews. Purim is celebrated in March and sometimes at the end of February. The origin of this holiday is recounted in the ten chapters of the book of *Esther*, one of the later books to be incorporated into the Bible. The story tells how Xerxes, who is referred to in the Bible as Ahasuerus, had a Jewish concubine named Esther, who displaced the king's wife. Haman, who for some was the king's brother and for others an important minister, although he was probably nothing more than a figure created for the convenience of the Levites, the priestly sect that was writing the Old Testament, complained to Xerxes that the Jews had laws of their own and did not respect the laws of the kingdom as other peoples did. Then, according to *Esther's version*, Haman asked for an order allowing their destruction, to which Xerxes agreed. Letters were sent to all the provincial governors ordering that all the Jews were to be killed in one day.

Then came the intervention of Esther, who had concealed from the king that she was a Jew. The king not only cancelled the order, but ordered that Haman and his ten sons be hanged on the gallows that he himself had built for the Jew Mordechai, Esther's relative and guardian. As if that were not enough, the king gave Mordechai carte blanche to instruct the governors of the one hundred and twenty-seven provinces of the empire, which stretched from India to Ethiopia. Mordechai then ordered a massacre of seventy-five thousand of the king's subjects, men, women and children, who were supposed to be enemies of the Jews. He then ordered that the slaughter be celebrated annually thereafter, and it has been so ever since. In London, for example, Jewish bakers make cakes in the shape of human ears, which are eaten on this day, and call them "Haman's ears". In Palestine and in some regions of Russia, public processions are held, at the head of which the figure of Haman is carried, stoned, stabbed and beaten with sticks. The Jews of Monastyr (Russia) celebrated Purim in 1764 with a living Haman. This was a farmer named Adam-ko who died the next day. He had previously been drunk by the Jewish innkeeper Moscho. The case was brought to trial. The Kammetz authorities kept the documents until the Bolshevik Jews made them disappear.

Haman, Esther and Mordechai are probably imaginary characters, the product of the Levite scribes' need. Historically, there was no king named Ahasuerus. If the king was Xerxes, then he would be the father of Artaxerxes, who, as seen in the first chapter, was the king who sent Nehemiah to Jerusalem guarded by Persian soldiers to enforce the laws of racial exclusion. If the whole story is true, Artaxerxes would have favoured the Jews after seeing seventy-five thousand Persians slaughtered in his kingdom. Apart from the biblical account, there is not a single historical reference to these events, no text that could serve as a basis. Everything suggests that this is chauvinist propaganda. Regarding this biblical story, Martin Luther, of whom the *Jewish Encyclopedia*, volume VIII, p. 213, says that he linked the Jews with ritual murders, writes the following: "Oh how they love the *Book of Esther*, which is so in harmony with their thirst for blood and their hopes and desires for vengeful hatred. The sun has never shone on a people more bloodthirsty and revenge-hungry than on this one who thinks himself the Chosen People, who crave to murder the gentiles".

Passover, which is celebrated one month after Purim, is also about the salvation of the Jewish people and the genocide of another, in this case the Egyptians. It commemorates the passage of the Angel of the Exterminator through the houses of the Egyptians and the slaughter of the first-born. The Angel passes over, or leaps over, the houses of the Hebrews, hence the name Passover derives from the Hebrew word Phase or Phazahah, meaning "passage" or "leap". As we will see below by examining some prominent cases, it is on the occasion of these festivals that most ritual crimes have historically been committed.

Some background to the Damascus crime

Between the 4th and 5th centuries, St. Augustine described the Jews as 'servi regis' (servants of the king) and they received the protection of

Christian monarchs, who sought to house them in the vicinity of the royal palace or cathedral of each important city. Moreover, the Jewish quarters were often protected by walls with several gates. They thus had their own world, as Ezra and Nehemiah had ordained when they had imposed racial segregation after the return from Babylon. In addition to their particular legal and civil status, they also had their own cemeteries, which, as the *Talmud* prescribes, could not be within the walls, but outside the inhabited limits of the Christian city, preferably in the part closest to the Jewish quarters, which had their own establishments: synagogues, study centres, public baths, a hospital for the community, slaughterhouses, bread ovens and even, in the most important ones, their own prison, since the rabbis possessed legal powers over their community and could even inflict the death penalty. To understand the extent to which the rabbis wanted to maintain segregation and hold power, here is a quote from Israel Shahak's *Jewish History, Jewish Religion*: "Jewish women who cohabited with gentiles had their noses cut off by order of the rabbis, who explained that they would thus lose their beauty and their non-Jewish lovers would eventually hate them. Jews who had the gall to attack a rabbinical judge had their hands cut off. Adulterers were imprisoned after being harassed by the entire Jewish quarter. In religious disputes, those suspected of heresy had their tongues cut out".

In Christian Spain, where, according to Shahak, "the position of the Jews was the highest ever achieved in any country before the 19th century", Jews were particularly protected by specific laws enacted in the various kingdoms. Proof of this are the fueros, such as the Fuero de Castrojeriz, the Fuero de León, the Fuero de Nájera. In general, therefore, the ordinances provided for equal rights for Christians and Jews. As they had large sums of money, they became the moneylenders of the monarchs. Sometimes the authorities, as happened in Barcelona in the 11th century, commissioned them to mint coins. It was from the 14th and 15th centuries onwards that in the Christian kingdoms they were obliged to wear a sign on their clothing that distinguished them from the gentile population or, on the contrary, they were forbidden to wear certain items of clothing. This must be seen in the context of the growing atmosphere of rejection that was emerging within Christian societies.

As already mentioned, the *Talmud*, which for Jews is even more important than the *Torah*, teaches everything that can and should be done against Christians. It is in the realm of Talmudic teachings that one must look for an explanation as to why the Jews cruelly and mercilessly slaughtered Christian children for their blood. The gentile is an animal according to Jewish law and as such can be sacrificed. Only the sacrifice of a Jew would be a sin, according to Talmudic law. No wonder, therefore, that the much-lauded Maimonides, a rabid Talmudist, tried to prevent gentiles from reading the *Talmud* and declared: "If a non-believer reads the Talmud, he is worthy of death".

There are documents that allow us to study several ritual crimes committed in Europe in the 12th century, all of them at Easter time : In 1144 in Norwich (England), a twelve year old boy named William is the first known case. Other children were sacrificed throughout the century in Gloucester, Blois, Pontoise and London. In the 13th century, about twenty cases were brought to public attention. The one in Fulda (Hesse), which occurred on Christmas Day 1235, was particularly famous. Two Jews attacked five children in a mill when the miller and his wife were at mass. They drew their blood and collected it in containers they had brought for the purpose. They then set fire to the mill to erase the traces of their bestial atrocity; but the bodies of the children were brought as evidence, "corpora delicti", before the Emperor Frederick II, who was in Hagenau. The latter, who had been generously bribed, to the stupefaction of the people uttered these words: "si morti sunt, ite, sepelite eos, quia ad aliud non valent", that is, "If they are dead, go and bury them, since they are no longer of any use". Of course, the citizens of Fulda were not of the same opinion, and with the help of some crusaders present in the city, they took "justice" into their own hands and killed thirty-two Jews.

In Spain, specifically in Saragossa, the Jews had made a law for themselves, according to which anyone who kidnapped and handed over a gentile child would be exempt from payments and debts. It is in this context that on 31 August 1250, during the reign of James I and with Arnaldo de Peralta as bishop of Zaragoza, a seven-year-old boy, Domingo del Val, who sang in the choir of the Zaragoza cathedral, son of the notary Sancho del Val, was deceitfully lured by a Jew called Albayuceto, who handed him over to other co-religionists to renew in him the passion of Christ. The boy was crucified on a wall with three nails and his side was opened. After severing his head and feet, they hid his body on the banks of the Ebro. Today, the children of the city's choir have him as their protector and patron saint.

In the same 13th century, Alfonso X the Wise (1252-1284), faced with the evidence that Jews were murdering Christian children in his kingdom, as several cases of ritual crimes were judicially attested, ordered to write the following in volume 24 of *Las Partidas*, the penal code drawn up under his direction: "Since it has been legally established and proven that the Jews annually murder Christian children before their Passover feast for the mockery and humiliation of Christianity and also for the purpose of making a blood sacrifice, I order that every Jew who is found guilty of such a crime or who, even for the purpose of making a symbolic mockery of Christianity, crucifies a figure reproduced in wax representing a Christian, shall be put to death."

There is documentary evidence of a dozen ritual crimes in the course of the fourteenth century; but it is among the twenty or so known cases in the course of the fifteenth century that the most famous are to be found, among which is that committed in July 1462 in the person of the child

Andreas von Rinn, martyr of the Catholic Church, patron of children and the unborn, protector of Tyrol and of the house of Habsburg. Pope Benedict XIV, after careful personal examination of the records of the martyrdom, confirmed his cult on 17 December 1752. However, as a result of the Second Vatican Council (1962-65), under pressure from Jewish sectors, the Church declared the beatification null and void, banned his official cult and slandered those who venerated him as anti-Semites. The relics of the Tyrolean child martyr were venerated on the high altar of the Judenstein (Jews' Stone) church, built by order of Emperor Maximilian I on the site of the stone on which the child was sacrificed. In 1985 the bishop of Innsbruck, despite the opposition of the locals, banned his cult and removed his relics, which were placed in a wall in which a slab was placed with the following inscription: "Here rests the innocent child Anderl (short for Andreas), who according to tradition was murdered in the year 1462 by unknown persons. His death was unfortunately attributed for centuries to a ritual crime of Jews in transit. This then common and totally unfounded accusation led to Anderl being wrongly regarded as a martyr of the faith. The child Anderl rests here not as a martyr of the Church, but as a reminder of the many children who have fallen victim to violence and contempt for life up to the present day. We will not now go into the details of the crime of this three-year-old boy. What happened to his cult is unequivocal proof of the Vatican's capitulation and submission to the power of the Jews in the world.

Since this book is written in Spain and in Spanish, we return to the Iberian Peninsula, specifically to the town of Sepúlveda (Segovia) in 1468. There, again at Passover time, at the request of Rabbi Salomon Pecho, the Jews nailed a girl to a cross and pricked her all over her body until she bled to death. This event is documented in the *Historia de la insigne ciudad de Segovia* and in *Synopsis episcoporum Segoviensum* (p. 650). By order of Bishop Juan Arias de Ávila, the culprits were brought to Segovia, a judicial procedure was followed against them and the main perpetrators were condemned to death at the stake, some of those who had participated in the torture of the girl were hanged and a group was expelled from the city.

The most famous case of ritual crimes in the 15th century was that of the two-year-old Simon Gerber, Simon of Trent. The events took place in 1475 and there is exhaustive information about everything that happened. Engravings, carved stones, wood carvings and a painting by the prestigious Renaissance painter Gandolfino d'Asti artistically reproduce the cruel murder. The confessions of the eight main defendants, who were kept in solitary confinement and were also interrogated separately, coincide down to the smallest details.

In the first days of Holy Week, representatives of the Jewish families of Trent met in the house of the most respectable of them, named Samuel, in whose domain the synagogue and the Jewish school were also situated. They lamented the fact that the Passover matzos could not be prepared because they lacked the blood of a Christian child. Samuel then offered one hundred gold ducats for a sacrificial victim. The Jew Tobiah went out into the streets, which were deserted, for it was the time for the evening mass on Maundy Thursday. In front of his parents' house a boy of twenty-eight months, Simon Gerber, was playing. Lured by trickery, he was taken to Samuel's house and locked up until it was completely dark. The oldest of the Jews, an old man of eighty, Moses "the Elder", began the sacrifice by tearing a piece of flesh from the boy's right cheekbone with tongs. The other Jews followed suit. The flowing blood was collected in a tin tray. The right leg was similarly mutilated. The remaining parts of the body were pricked with long, thick needles in order to get all of the child's blood. Finally, he was circumcised. Finally, the executioners held little Simon, who was still in convulsions, and crucified him upside down, while the rest of the Jews pricked him again with needles and sharp instruments. The murderers shrieked: "This is what we did to Jesus, so may our enemies always achieve this end". The child, who was still breathing weakly, was finished off by crushing the bones of his skull. At this point those present began to sing a hymn of praise to Yahweh. The child's blood was distributed among the Jewish families. The Passover feast could now be prepared.

The child's body was displayed on the altar of the synagogue on Good Friday, where it was mocked and desecrated by all the Jews of Trent. After hiding it temporarily under the straw of a storehouse, it was finally thrown into a ditch that flowed near the house. In order to divert suspicion, the criminals decided to be the first to inform the Bishop of Trent of the horrible discovery of the child, who had been unsuccessfully sought by the parents and numerous inhabitants of the city. The evidence against the Jews accumulated and soon they were brought to justice. Eight were indicted and gave full details of the shameful murder. The wives of two of the accused admitted that similar crimes had been committed years before, but had not been discovered. During the trial, testimony documents were presented concerning the murder of four children in the diocese of Constance, two more in Endingen, one in Ravensburg (1430) and one in Pfullendorf (1461). The trial, conducted with the utmost rigour and meticulousness by the authorities in Trent, lasted more than three years. It was not until 7 July 1478 that the following notation was written in the documents: "causa contra judaeos finita".

The reasons for the long duration of the process deserve an explanation. Both the aforementioned article by Israel Shamir and the book by Ariel Toaff explain what happened, but our source is *Der jüdische Ritual mord. Eine historische Untersuchung (The Jewish Ritual Crime. A Historical Investigation)*, a work by Professor Hellmut Schramm published in 1941 with a wealth of quotations and documents. In 2001 R. Belser translated the text into English and the book is available online in PDF format. What happened was that the rich Jews of Italy moved heaven and earth in their quest to free the detainees. First they got Duke Sigismund of Austria to order a halt to the trial a few weeks after it had begun. Then they appealed to the Pope, who again stopped the trial on the grounds that they had to wait for the arrival of his legate. Hinderbach, the bishop of Trent who was in charge of the investigation, received a letter from Sixtus IV announcing that he should not go ahead with the proceedings against the Jews because some princes disapproved of the case altogether. At last, the papal "commissary", Bishop Baptista dei Giudici di Ventimiglia, appeared, enthusiastically recommended as a "professor of theology" and "vir doctrina ac integritate praeditus", i.e. a man of great erudition and integrity. Before arriving in Trent, Ventimiglia stopped in Venice, where he appeared in the company of three Jews, showing their influence at the papal court.

Hinderbach, the bishop of Trent, received Ventimiglia and lodged him in the outbuildings of his castle, where he soon came into contact with the spy sent by the Jews, Wolfgang. After three weeks, to prevent Hinderbach from learning of his contacts, he withdrew to Roveredo, claiming that the palace was too damp and unsuitable for his health. On 24 September 1475, Ventimiglia informed Hinderbach that "the lawyers of the Jews had come to him in order to defend their case...". These lawyers also requested the trial documents. On 1 October the Bishop of Trent complained that "by means of intrigues the Jews and bad Christians who had been bought with money and gifts were trying to win princes and prelates to their cause". Bishop Hinderbach denounced that from Roveredo "they tried to get the Doge of Venice, Mocenigo, to intervene so that the detainees would be released. The Jews," Hinderbach continued, "were trying to bribe everyone.

A so-called priest, Paul de Noravia, a Jewish spy, managed to get into the bishop's castle and for two months copied the trial documents that Hinderbach had refused to hand over. He then passed them on to the lawyers of the defendants. At the trial, Paul of Noravia admitted to having negotiated with the Jews of Novara, Modena, Brescia, Venice, Basano and Roveredo about the possibility of freeing the prisoners. He also admitted receiving money to bribe the servant of the bishop of Trent to poison him. 400 ducats had been offered to him if the plan succeeded.

In order to turn the trial on its head, a new indecency was also attempted. A citizen of Trento named Anzelin, a man free of suspicion and reputed to be incorruptible, was lured to Roveredo. There he was arrested and locked up in the Ventimiglia quarters, where he was tortured daily to get him to agree to accuse a couple from Trento (Zanesus Schweizer) of the murder of the child. Subsequently, this unfortunate man reported that the Pope's legate had subjected him to a "painful interrogation" to make him declare something of which he was completely unaware. Finally, seeing that they could get nothing from him, he was released on condition that he kept silent about the incident. Seeing the ineffectiveness of this remedy, Ventimiglia tried a last resort: using false instructions from the Pope, he illegally attempted to wrest the case from the Trent authorities so that the trial would pass into their hands. In fact his audacity was such that, under threat of excommunication, he forbade the bishop of Trent to proceed with the trial against the Jews.

In the end, Hinderbach, assisted by Germans insensitive to bribery, was victorious. At the end of October he wrote a report and sent it to the eligible princes. In it he recorded everything about the arrest of the culprits, the investigations carried out and the consistent confessions of the accused. He had the courage to refer to the investigation initiated by the papal legate, which he described as "corruptam inquisitionem". Veintimiglia had dug his own grave; his intervention had been so scandalous that the Pope had no choice but to abandon him to his fate. The populace began to demonstrate against him by singing songs of derision, in which he was branded as Caiaphas and the high priest of the Jews. To the Pope's displeasure, epigrams were published against him, as well as graphic reproductions denigrating him. Already at the end of 1477, Bishop Hinderbach, in a strong letter, addressed Sixtus IV and asked him "to put an end to the scandal and to appoint another person who is a lover of truth".

In the Vienna Hofbibliotek (Court Library) there are the trial documents written in Latin: six hundred and thirteen folios handwritten by Johann von Fatis. In addition, the Vatican bookshop has the codex from 1476-78. In the altar of St. Peter's in Trento, the sarcophagus of the child is preserved, which contains the body of the "santo bambino" in a glass urn, exceptionally well preserved. Nevertheless, the official Jewish version, which has been handed down ever since, can be found in the *Jewish Encyclopaedia*. It states that "Simon was killed by Christians who sought to blame all the evil in the world on the Jews".

We cannot let the 15th century pass without referring to the most famous of the ritual crimes perpetrated in Spain: we are referring to the case of the boy of La Guardia. Lope de Vega, the brilliant creator of the national theatre, composed a play in his memory entitled *El niño inocente de La Guardia (The Innocent Child of La Guardia)*. In the centesimoctogesimosexto volume of the Biblioteca de Autores Españoles there is a preliminary study by Marcelino Menéndez Pelayo which is of great help to us in referring to this historical event. All the known news about the terrible crime can be consulted in volume XI of the *Boletín de la Real Academia de la Historia* (1887), in which Fr. Fidel Fita published for the first time the *Proceso de Jucé Franco, judío,* quemado en Ávila el 16 de noviembre de 1491 *(Process of Jucé Franco, Jew,* burnt in Ávila on 16 November 1491).

In a lawsuit presented on Friday 17 September 1490, the bachelor Alonso de Guevara, prosecutor of the Holy Office, accused Jucé Franco, a Jew from Tembleque, the converts Alonso Franco, Lope Franco, García Franco, Juan Franco, Juan de Ocaña and Benito García, neighbours of La

Guardia, and mosén Abenamias, a Jew living in Zamora, of the nefarious crime of having crucified a Christian child on Good Friday. The statement of Jucé Franco, from which follows a fragment in Castilian Spanish of the time, will save us from adding a single word:

> "While this witness and the aforementioned.... in the cave declared by him; this witness saw how the said Christians (referring to the converts) brought with them a Christian child, who was about three or four years old; and being this witness and all the aforementioned present in the said cave, the said Christians crucified the said child on crossed sticks; And there they stretched out his arms while he was naked in leather and with his head held high, and they put a stick in his mouth, and slapped him, and beat him, and whipped him, and spat on him, and put thorny gorse on his back and on the soles of his feet, and tied his arms with twisted esparto ropes, and inflicted many other vituperations on him. And after he was thus placed on the said sticks and crucified, the said Alonso Franco opened the veins of the arms of the said boy two by two, and left him to bleed for more than half an hour; and that he took the blood in a yellow *altimia*, one of those that are made in Ocaña coarse. E que Johan Franco susodicho, while the said boy was thus placed on the said sticks, he cut the said boy's side with a knife; and that it was a knife of a span of one of these *Bohemians*. And the said Lope Franco whipped him, and the said Johan de Ocaña put the gorse on him, and the said García Franco pulled out his heart under the calf, and poured some salt into the said heart. And the said Benito García gave the boy slaps and slapped him".

The statement is much longer, but we think that what is transcribed is sufficient. Menéndez Pelayo writes that the crime of La Guardia "cannot humanly be doubted", as it is judicially proven "to the very apex". According to the distinguished polygraph, the indignation produced in Castile by this ferocious crime was universal and "must have accelerated the edict of expulsion of the Jews, given on 31 March 1492". William Thomas Walsh, in his work *Isabella of Spain* (1931), devotes almost thirty pages to his research on this ritual crime and agrees with Menéndez Pelayo in his assessment that this murder was "one of the main, if not the main factor" for the expulsion of the Jews from Spain.

As for the theatrical work, Menéndez Pelayo considers that Lope de Vega had in mind and followed quite rigorously the *Historia de la muerte y glorioso martirio del Sancto Innocente que llaman de La Guardia*, published in Madrid in 1583 by the elegant prose writer Fr Rodrigo de Yepes. For Menéndez Pelayo the crucifixion of the child on stage must have impressed the mood of the spectators. He admits, however, that the work is rough and structurally imperfect, which he attributes to the fact that Lope follows Yepes' book step by step. He also acknowledges that, as Lope de Vega is a relative of the Holy Court, he cannot avoid conveying the feeling of hatred towards the Jews.

We could continue to review the most scandalous cases of murder in the sixteenth, seventeenth and eighteenth centuries that were brought to public attention, but this would distract us from our objective, which is to study the role played by the Rothschilds in the most famous ritual crime of the nineteenth century, as well as the implications of the Damascus Affair for the revival of Jewish nationalism, i.e. Zionism.

Jewish rule in the 19th century

Those who seek to confine ritual crimes to the Middle Ages should seek an explanation for the significant increase in the number of attested cases during the 19th century. About fifty murders are recorded, which were committed during the celebration of the Purim and Passover holidays. As discussed in chapter two, emancipation and assimilation into the societies that welcomed them were supposedly the aspirations of Jewish intellectuals and their gentile friends. Legislation had thus been generated that tended to abolish the discrimination or exceptionality of the Jewish population in European states, which was considered to be medieval and linked to the Church. This legal reorganisation gave Jews the status of citizens with the same rights as other nationals. In this way an era of Jewish domination, epitomised by the Rothschild dynasty, took hold in Europe and America. The influence of the gold of the Rothschilds, and the economic and political power it conferred on them, was felt everywhere. The Jewish press was beginning to dictate public opinion, and more and more Jews were occupying key positions in government, in the judiciary and in the universities. We have also already seen what the Illuminati's plan was in this respect, and how they were gaining real power.

In the 21st century, state sovereignty no longer exists: multinational companies of all kinds, institutions such as the International Monetary Fund, the World Bank, the Bank of International Settlements, the Federal Reserve, the Bank of England, the European Central Bank, the World Trade Organisation, etc., wield absolute power and control over countries. It is well known, for example, that in the United States one cannot be president without the support of all-powerful lobbies such as the AIPAC (American Israel Public Affairs Committee), the ADL (Anti-Defamation League) and others. In *The Jewish Century* (2004), Yuri Slezkine argues that the 20th century was undoubtedly in every sense the Jewish century. However, it was in the 19th century that the foundations of this power were solidly laid. It can be said without exaggeration that the destiny of states was already increasingly determined by Jewish organisations. A decision by the Rothschilds against a state that did not comply with their designs could bankrupt it.

It is not surprising, then, that in such circumstances confidence in this increasingly evident power led to the belief that one could act without fear of punishment. Only in this way can it be explained that the number of ritual crimes carried out with incredible brazenness and apparent safety increased alarmingly. Impunity became a constant. If a court of law initiated proceedings to punish the culprits, they led to no result, when they were not nipped in the bud. As we shall see in the case of the Damascus crime, governments did not dare to confront the plague of ritual crimes because they felt at the mercy of international Jewish financiers.

The crime of Damascus

The original trial documents on the case were deposited at the Ministry of Foreign Affairs in Paris, but disappeared without trace in 1870, when the Jew and high-ranking Freemason Crémieux, a key figure in the story we are about to tell, was Minister of Justice. Nevertheless, two volumes written by Achille Laurent, entitled *Relation historique des affaires de Syrie despuis 1840 jusqu'en 1842*, are in the Bibliothèque Nationale de Paris. The second volume contains the authentic court documents. In 1843, the journal *L'Univers et l'union catholique* published an extract from the Arabic texts, which may have been preserved in a German translation made in the same year. Some official documents of the trial are also included in a work on the Damascus crime published by the Syrian Minister of Defence, Mustafa Tlass. According to information published on 27 June 2002 in issue 99 of the MEMRI (The Middle East Media Research Institute) newsletter, Tlass, one of the founding fathers of the Ba'athist regime in Syria, published a first edition in 1983, but it is in the second edition of 1986 that appendices with photocopies of official documents are added.

It all began on the evening of 15 February 1840, the feast of Purim. Tomaso, a highly esteemed Capuchin friar who had been working in Damascus since 1807 helping people (known as the doctor of vaccines, as he had initiated a smallpox vaccination programme), went to the Jewish quarter to hang a notice on the door of the synagogue regarding a charity auction to be held in the house of a deceased resident. As the sun set, his servant, Ibrahim Amara, became concerned about Father Tomaso's tardiness and decided to go in search of him. Both were seen by numerous witnesses in the Jewish quarter before disappearing.

Two days later a note like the one that Father Tomaso had hung in the synagogue appeared in the barbershop of the Jew Soliman, which raised suspicions. He was asked how the official notice had reached him. His explanation seemed so incredible and fabricated that it led one to believe that he knew something about the matter. As the missing man was a European, Sherif Pasha, the governor-general in Damascus of the viceroy of Egypt, Muhammed Ali, decided to keep him in custody and gave the French consul in Damascus, Count de Ratti-Menton, full authority to direct the preliminary investigations. It was only three months since this consul had arrived in the Syrian capital. According to the Franco-Turkish treaty of 1740, French diplomatic agents had the right to protect Catholic priests in the Ottoman Empire. There was also a specific clause in the treaty that referred to the safeguarding of Capuchin churches.

The barber denied knowing anything for several days, but when he was assured that he would not be punished and offered protection, he proposed that he go and find a number of co-religionists before whom he would confess what he knew. Rabbis Moses Salonicli and Moses Abu-el-Afieh, the three brothers David, Isaac and Aaron Harari, their uncle Joseph Harari and one Joseph Laniado were brought before him. They all denied having seen Father Tomaso. Group interrogations were unsuccessful and the decision was made to confine them in solitary confinement. The barber was again interrogated, probably whipped, and urged to confess the truth.

According to court protocols, in his partial confession the barber revealed that the seven persons mentioned above had taken Father Tomaso to David's house Harari. Half an hour after sunset, Murad-el-Fattal, David Harari's servant, had fetched him from the barber's shop. "Sacrifice this man", with these words, according to the barber Soliman, he was ordered to kill Father Tomaso, who was in the room with his hands tied. The barber said that he had refused and that Aaron Harari had then given him the note informing him of the auction to post on the barbershop door. He added that when he was arrested, David Harari told him to be careful, not to confess anything and that he would be given money.

The next person arrested was consequently David's servant Harari, Murad-el-Fattal, who revealed important details. When confronted by the head of the Jewish community in Damascus, Raphael Farhi, the servant retracted his statements. Taken back into the presence of Governor Pasha, the latter asked him why he had retracted his statement. According to the documents, he gave this explanation: "I was questioned in the presence of Raphael Farhi. I was afraid and that is why I retracted my statement, especially because of the look he gave me. Then Sherif Pasha reacted as follows: "What, you are more afraid of Raphael than of me? Murad-el-Fattal answered: "Yes, I am afraid that he will kill me. I fear Raphael more than his Excellency, because his Excellency will lash me with the whip and then dismiss me, while he, if I tell the truth, will kill me in the neighbourhood".

As enquiries indicated that it was very likely that the barber had been present at the time of the execution, Soliman was re-arrested and subjected to a harsh interrogation, probably involving some form of torture, which resulted in a detailed confession, made in the presence of several officers, a doctor and representatives of the Consulate. All confirmed the statement by signing the protocol.

In summary, the barber recounted that after being ordered to execute the capuchin, which he initially refused, the Harari brought out a knife. He himself held Father Tomaso over a large bowl on the floor and David Harari slashed his throat. Aaron finished him off with a second cut and the blood was collected in the bowl "without a drop being lost". The body was then dragged into another room, where it was stripped naked and the clothes burnt. David Harari's servant, Murad, appeared at once and was ordered, together with the barber, to quickly dismember the body. The bones were crushed on the ground with a mallet. When they had done this, they put the remains in a sack and threw them one by one into the sewers near the house of Rabbi Abu-el-Afieh. They then returned to David Harari's house, where they told the servant that they would marry him off and take care of all the expenses of the ceremony. The barber was promised money, but was also warned that he would be killed if he left his tongue. After this statement, the servant Murad was interrogated and he confirmed the barber's account in every detail.

Given the coincidence in the reports of the two witnesses, Colonel Hasez Beik proposed that an immediate inspection of David's house Harari be carried out in the presence of the French consul, a high official of the consulate and the physician Dr. Massari. In the room where the body had been dismembered, splashes of blood were discovered on the walls. Where the bones had been crushed, the floor was severely bruised. In addition, the sledgehammer was found; however, the knife was missing and could not be found.

It was then decided to search rigorously in the sewers. The workers who descended into the sewers to carry out the search found pieces of the fractured bones with flesh still attached, remains of the skull, a part of the heart and pieces of Father Tomaso's hood. All this was carefully collected and sent to the Pasha for him and the doctors to inspect. A statement by the Austrian consul, Merlato, who immediately recognised the father's black hood, as he was the only one to wear it. 2. A statement by four European doctors, Massari, Delgrasso, Raynaldi and Salina, in which they recognised that these were the remains of a human body. 3. The same statement, but made by seven Syrian doctors. 4. An informative document from the barber who used to serve Father Tomaso.

Once the remains of the father were found, there was no longer any doubt. The seven accused were again interrogated without any violence. They were warned of the serious circumstances that inevitably linked them to the crime and they did not attempt to deny anything. Subsequently, the detainees were interrogated separately. Some of their statements were quoted verbatim. Isaac Harari said: "We took the father to the house of David Harari, my brother. It was an arranged affair between us. We sacrificed him to obtain his blood, which was poured into a bottle and given to Rabbi Moses Abu-el-Afieh, specifically for religious reasons, since we needed blood for the fulfilment of our religious duties". Rabbi Moses Abu-el-Afieh, when asked about it, replied: "The Chief Rabbi of Damascus, Jacob Antebi, had a conversation with the Harari brothers and the rest of the defendants, in order to get a bottle of human blood. The Hararis promised to supply it for the price of 12,500 French francs. When I went to the Harari's house I was informed that they had obtained a man for the sacrifice. I went in and the killing had already been completed. The blood had been obtained and I was told to give it to Rabbi Jacob Antebi. I replied that they should let Moses Salonicli deliver it, but they told me that I was a sensible man and that it was better for me to take it". Moses Abu-el-Afieh added that some of the blood mixed with flour was sent to Baghdad. For his part, David Harari confirmed in another interrogation that the spiritual author of the crime was indeed the chief rabbi of Damascus, Jacob Antebi, who in the Damascus synagogue had told the seven defendants the exact plan for the execution of the father. On this plan, Isaac Harari confirmed in another interrogation that, in order to capture the capuchin, Rabbis Moses Salonicli and Moses Abu-el-Afieh had used the pretext of allowing a child to be vaccinated. The latter had invited Father Tomaso to David Harari's house and the friar had accepted the invitation without any suspicion, since he had had a close and friendly relationship with the brothers for years.

Rabbi Abu-el-Afieh converts to Islam

A surprising episode in the case was the conversion to Islam of Rabbi Moses Abu-el-Afieh. This rabbi in his forties, seeing the turn of events, fearful of losing his life, either by sentence of the court or because his co-religionists would not forgive him for having implicated the chief rabbi of Damascus, probably in order to gain the protection of the Pasha, converted to Islam on 10 May and took the name Mohammed Effendi. This was the name chosen by Shabbetay Zeví, the heretical Messiah, when in 1666 he became a Muslim in Constantinople to save his life. One of the first actions of the new "believer" was to write a report to the governor general, the beginning of which was as follows: "In obedience to your Excellency's request, I have the honour to inform you of the following circumstances of the murder of Father Tomaso. For now I know that I no longer have to fear for my life, by virtue of my faith in Almighty God and in Muhammed, his prophet, whom I thus implore and praise: thus I testify to the truth as follows...". There followed the same version of events that has already been narrated. In the report, moreover, Mohammed Effendi added that he knew nothing about what had happened to the Capuchin's servant, Ibrahim Amara, although he noted that he had suffered the same fate as Father Tomaso. In the letter he said that he had heard Isaac ask his brother David : "How are things going in this business?" David had replied: "Don't think about it any more. He too has received his share".

Mohammed Effendi not only accused Rabbi Antebi of being the mastermind of the murder, but agreed, as a loyal Muslim, to locate and translate passages in the *Talmud* that might explain the criminal behaviour of the Jews. This subject of rabbinical texts had been brought to Sherif Pasha's attention by the Christians of Damascus, who were particularly concerned and had begun to search their libraries for books showing that human sacrifice was prescribed in Judaism. An 18th century book written in Latin by Lucius Ferraris, *Prompta Bibliotecha*, drew attention to passages in the *Talmud* expressing a murderous hatred towards Christians. According to Jonathan Frankel, professor at the Hebrew University of Jerusalem and author of *The Damascus Affair*. *"Ritual Murder, Politics and the Jews in 1840*, extracts from this 18th century book were translated into French and Arabic at the initiative of Ratti-Menton and copies were distributed in and around Damascus.

Mohammed Effendi and the Chief Rabbi of Damascus were confronted days later to test the interpretation of the *Talmud*. At the end of the discussion the Pasha could not help but glancingly ask the renegade: "If a Jew gives a harmful statement against another Jew or against the Jewish people what punishment does he deserve?" The answer was, "He should be mercilessly killed. The *Talmud* does not allow him to live. This religion is built on this principle; that is why I have converted to Islam, in order to be able to speak..." Asked to comment on Mohammed Effendi's words, Chief Rabbi Jacob Antebi confirmed this and added: "We should see to it that the government kills such an individual. If not, we would kill him with our own hands at the slightest opportunity'. Having confirmed that Mohammed Effendi had told the truth, the Governor General implied that the government should act in their interests and asked again what they would do. Jacob Antebi repeated: "Depending on the circumstances, we would do everything possible to kill him; any means would be suitable for us. This teaches our faith. Mohammed Effendi had little time to, supposedly from the safe side, deepen his new religion and continue his translations of the *Talmud*, for he died shortly afterwards, according to European Jewish newspapers, as a result of the damage caused by the torture to which he had been subjected.

The murder of the servant Ibrahim Amara

What happened to Father Tomaso's servant was reported by David's servant Harari, Murad el-Fattal. Once in the Jewish quarter, Ibrahim Amara asked the Jews Aaron Stambuli, Mehir Farhi, Aslan Farhi and Isaac Picciotto, who were going out into the street, about their master. Pointing to their house, Mehir Farhi indicated that the father was with them vaccinating a child and that if he wanted to wait for him he could go and enter. Murad-el-Fattal, who was the transmission belt between the two houses and went from one to the other obeying David Harari's orders, testified that when he went a second time to Mehir Farhi's house, the lock was on. Once he had entered, he said that his master sent him to find out if the servant had been arrested. He was told that they already had him and asked if he wanted to stay or leave again. He stayed and witnessed the crime. Isaac Picciotto and Aaron Stambuli bound and gagged him and then together they threw him to the ground. In addition to the aforementioned were Murad Farhi and Joseph Farhi. A copper bowl was placed under his head and Murad Farhi stabbed him. Murad-el-Fattal confessed that he himself and Meir Farhi held his head while Aslan Farhi and Isaac Picciotto sat on him and held his legs. They held him tightly until the blood stopped flowing. Aaron Stambuli then poured the blood into a long white bottle to be given to Moses Abu-el-Afieh. This version was later confirmed by the young Aslan Farhi. It should be noted that Aslan's father, Raphael Farhi, was one of the most distinguished members of the Jewish community in Damascus.

After the murders of both victims, the participants gathered at the house of David Harari to drink and talk until dawn, according to the statement of the same servant, who filled the pipes of the "distinguished and wealthy Jews". The massacres were discussed in detail and experiences were exchanged. In particular, the time spent was discussed, as it could be valuable for future cases.

Sherif Pasha, accompanied by senior officers and Consul Ratti-Menton, went to the Jewish quarter, in accordance with the court summons, and all the facts could be verified on the spot. A drainpipe in the neighbourhood was opened and the victim's liver, bones and a belt were found. Doctors Massari and Raynaldi declared that the remains belonged to a human being. The only one of the detainees who denied the facts was Meir Farhi. Confronted by the young Aslan Farhi and the servant Murad-el-Fattal, who repeated the story of the horrible crime in detail, Farhi began to shout: "You are crazy, you have lost your minds". He then tried to attack them in a fit of rage and impotence. In any case, he was unable to offer any alibi and continued to be detained.

Several of those accused of involvement in the murder of Ibrahim Amara, however, managed to flee and, in hiding, elude arrest. By the end of April 1840, a little more than two and a half months after the crimes, the trial could be considered completed. Sixteen Jews had participated in the double murder, ten of whom were sentenced to death. The people of Damascus awaited the execution of the bloodthirsty men.

Executioners become victims

As soon as news of what was happening in Damascus reached Europe, the machinery was set in motion to turn the criminals into innocent victims and those who sought justice into ruthless executioners driven by hatred of the Jews. A smear and smear campaign was immediately orchestrated against the French consul, who was isolated and lost the support of his European colleagues. All the consuls in the area were, as we shall see, instructed by their governments to stop supporting the actions of the Count of Ratti-Menton. The reference work to learn all the ins and outs of the negotiations and manoeuvres carried out is the aforementioned work by Jonathan Frankel, *The Damascus Affair "Ritual Murder". Politics and the Jews in 1840*. Unfortunately, this professor at the Hebrew University of Jerusalem exculpates his Damascus brethren of the crime and does so with the hypocrisy and chutzpah that Jews adopt when they lie and know it (Chutzpah). Despite this, the work is well documented and is of great value for the number of texts reproduced in it.

Already in the same month of February the first letters arrived in Europe that alerted European Jews. The wealthy Dutch merchant of Ashkenazi origin, Rabbi Abraham Zevi Hirsch Lehren, who in 1817 had assumed in Amsterdam the leadership of a pro-Zionist organisation called "Officers of the Land of Israel", was the first to contact the Rothschilds. On 18 March he wrote two letters, one addressed to the Dutch Foreign Minister, Baron V. Van Soelen; the second, written in French, was to James Rothschild. To the latter he described the plight of the Jews of Damascus. Here is an extract: "The Jews will never be free from persecution until our Messiah comes, for which time we look forward with resolution; but the good God... has always given us eminent men with sufficient influence to alleviate their misfortunes. And in our times He has given us the renowned Rothschild family, who have the power to save their persecuted brethren.... Here is the opportunity for you to show yourself as the guardian angel of the oppressed and to open for yourself the gates of Paradise....".

A week later, the rabbi wrote, dramatising the situation: "the lives of many thousands of our co-religionists are in danger". Hirsch Lehren asked James Rothschild for a reply. It so happened, however, that at the time James was in London attending the wedding of his grandson Anthony (1810-1876), Nathan's second son, to Louise Montefiore (1821-1910), granddaughter of Moses Montefiore. Apparently, therefore, no action was taken in Paris until the end of March. It was Montefiore, accompanied by Isaac Adolphe Crémieux, who was to become the Rothschilds' top representative in managing the Damascus Affair crisis. It was Albert Cohn, the family's children's guardian for Jewish affairs, who was instructed to contact the lawyer Crémieux to prepare a series of articles to counter reports in the hostile press accusing the Jews of Damascus. Cremieux had been one of James Rothschild's most trusted men for years: in August 1834, on a trip related to the exploitation of the Almaden mines, he had gone to Madrid with Lionel, Nathan's heir, to negotiate with the Spanish Minister of Finance, the Asturian Count of Toreno. James then considered Toreno an "enemy" and tried to bribe him.

It was also to the Rothschild family that the Jewish leaders of Constantinople appealed for help: Samuel de N. Trèves, I. Camondo and Salomon Fua wrote letters to the Rothschilds in London, Naples, Vienna and possibly also to those in Paris and Frankfurt. The Rothschilds were well known throughout the Middle East, as they were involved in Jewish affairs and collaborated with Rabbi Hirsch Lehren in supporting Ashkenazi Jews in Palestine. In short, the Rothschilds had by 1840 acquired mythical status among Jewry throughout the world.

Before proceeding further, it is necessary to explain very briefly the hierarchical structure and political situation in the area. The ultimate authority with regard to the events in Damascus was the Viceroy of Egypt, Muhammed Ali (1769-1849), who had incorporated Syria into his domain and in 1838 had announced his desire to become independent from the Ottoman Sultan, then Abdulmecit I, and to turn Egypt into a hereditary kingdom. This had provoked a Turkish-Egyptian war, triggered by a treaty between the British and the Ottomans that Egypt refused to accept. In 1839 the Turkish army was defeated at Nisibis. In the face of Egypt's growing power, Britain, Russia and Prussia supported the Ottoman cause, with only France backing Egypt. The European consuls in Alexandria thus had the upper hand over the consuls in Damascus, and were also able to meet directly with the viceroy. The French consul general in Alexandria was Adrien-Louis Cochelet, an experienced diplomat who had served Napoleon and held representative posts in Brazil, Mexico, Portugal and Moldavia. He had served in Egypt since 1837. On the other hand, the Austrian consul general to Muhammed Ali was Anton Joseph Laurin. According to Hellmut Schramm, Laurin was a crypto-Jew who, like Adam Weishaupt, had been trained among the Jesuits at a centre in Slovenia. Finally, it is worth noting that the highest authority to whom both the consuls in Damascus and Alexandria reported were the ambassadors, who resided in Constantinople.

On 27 March, Laurin sent to his immediate superior, Baron Von Stürmer, the Austrian ambassador to Constantinople, the first report by Merlato, who, as we have seen, had initially shared the views of his colleague Ratti-Menton. Von Stürmer rejected the report and did not accept religious motives to justify the crime. The accused," he wrote, "are the richest and most prominent Jews in Damascus". Laurin passed on the instructions to Merlato and urged him not to accept the accusations from now on. It is very likely that Solomon Rothschild and his good friend Prince Metternich had already had some talks in Vienna on the matter. It has already been mentioned in the previous chapter that the Rothschilds had made huge loans to the Austrian government and had the business of building railway lines throughout the empire in their hands. Salomon Rothschild was the banker to the leading aristocratic families, including Metternich's own. Melanie Zichy-Farrari, Metternich's third wife, had close relations with Salomon's sisters-in-law, Betty in Paris and Adelheid in Naples.

Jonathan Frankel reveals that Laurin, who had previously served in various consular posts in the kingdom of the Two Sicilies, enjoyed a personal friendship with none other than Carl Rothschild, with whom he shared an interest in ancient coins, jewellery and other objects. While in Egypt, where he had a reputation as an archaeologist, he had made some purchases for Karl, who rewarded him by sending him Neapolitan wines, pasta and other supplies. In case it is not clear that he was a Rothschild man, Frankel adds that, as Consul General in Alexandria, Laurin worked in close cooperation with Rabbi Hirsch Lehren and had sent consular officials to Palestine to obtain compensation for Ashkenazi Jews settled there.

The French consul soon realised that he was being left on his own, but he remained incorruptible, even though bribery attempts even reached his consulate. Ratti-Menton denounced that the Jews had offered one of his officers, Beaudin, 150,000 piastres, and had even suggested to him to increase the sum if he could get his brothers exonerated of the ritual crime. After this failed attempt at corruption, the Jewish negotiators tried to gain access to the French consul through another consulate. This time 500,000 piastres were offered. These attempts were publicly denounced by the Ausburg *Allgemeine Zeitung,* which, although slowly yielding to pressure, in the first few months showed sufficient independence to publish these words:

> "The trial against the Jews is not over and the criminals have not yet been punished; but that Father Tomaso was murdered by the Jews for religious reasons has been clearly demonstrated. The review of several file folders to which we had access leaves no room for doubt. The French consul in Damascus, Count de Ratti-Menton, has shown the greatest possible activity in the search for the truth.... The Jews there have shown that they surpass all others in fanaticism. Having previously been constantly used as businessmen by the Pasha because of their wealth, they possess great influence, and the Christians there are terrified. Although every year in Damascus Christian children suddenly disappeared without a trace, although the Jews were always under suspicion because of this, no one dared to accuse them, indeed no one dared to attempt a trial on a well-founded suspicion, so great was the influence their money gave them with the corrupt Turkish authorities. Now, moreover, there has been no shortage of offers of money. The secretary of the French consul was offered a large sum to try to change the consul's attitude to the case...".

Soon the European press controlled by Jewish capital circulated the most terrible stories of torture. Here is a selection from the "official report", edited and distributed on 13 May by the Anglican missionary George Wildon Pieritz, a disguised Jew, member of the "London Society for Promoting Christianity Amongst the Jews", which was the first Christian organisation to raise the banner of Jewish protection. The title of the report reads:

Statement of Mr. G.W. Pieritz, a Jewish Convert, a Jewish *Convert. Pieritz, a Jewish Convert, and assistant missionary at Jerusalem, respecting the persecution of the Jews at Damascus: the result of a personal inquiry on the spot. (Report of Mr. G.W. Pieritz, a Jewish convert, and assistant missionary at Jerusalem, respecting the persecution of the Jews at Damascus: the result of a personal inquiry on the spot. Pieritz, Jewish convert, and assistant missionary at Jerusalem, respecting the persecution of the Jews at Damascus: the result of a personal inquiry on the spot).* According to Pieritz, the "unfortunate prisoners" together with their children had been immersed in freezing water and then slowly roasted. Their eyes had been squeezed out of their sockets by machines and hot irons had been inserted into their bodies. The "victims", pinched day and night, had had to stand for three whole days, and burning candles had tickled their crooked noses. Hundreds of Jewish children had been thrown into prisons where they were dropping like flies, etc. etc. etc.. Hellmut Schrammm reveals that G. W. Pieritz was a Jew who studied to become a rabbi and then converted to Christianity. This rabbi went to Damascus, where he arrived on 30 March, "in consideration of the Christian mission which obliged him to defend human rights in places of despotism". There he contacted British Consul Nathaniel Werry, who offered to introduce him to Ratti-Menton and Sherif Pasha, but he refused. On 6 April Pieritz left Damascus for Beirut. In an illuminating dispatch to his superior John Bidwell dated 24 April 1840, Werry refers to Pieritz as a Jewish convert who had different views on what had happened and who planned to publish an extremely violent pamphlet against Ratti-Menton and Sherif Pasha. Thanks to a quote from Jonatahn Frankel, we have the text. Werry, who shared the official version, wrote: "he comically shares his displeasure with me, pretending that I was the French consul's adviser.... Mr Pieritz is angry with me because he has not been able to convince me of his views, when he is totally ignorant of the evidence and relies only on the information of his brothers here. He, who I am convinced in his conscience and in his heart is still a Jew, rejects any information and is determined to exculpate the Jews and blame the Christian and Muslim population. We shall see what he publishes. I think the case is substantially correct".

On the basis that the criminals were innocent victims whose self-incriminating statements had been obtained through the most atrocious torture, the campaign was unleashed with the aim of pressuring and confusing public opinion with the ultimate goal of securing a pardon for the Jews detained in Damascus. International Jewry mobilised simultaneously. In the synagogues, rabbis howled or threatened, as appropriate. The most heated speeches were made in Marseilles, in Smyrna, in Munich, in Magdeburg, in Leipzig, where Rabbi Isaac Levin Auerbach, with tears in his eyes, appealed to Zion, to Jerusalem and to the honour of his religion. In Vienna, in St. Stephen's Cathedral on Ascension Day, Dr. Emmanuel Veith, a Jewish convert and dean of the cathedral, known for his brilliant oratory in the pulpit, said the following at the end of his sermon in front of thousands of devout Christians: "You all know, my dear parishioners, and if perhaps someone does not know it, he can know it now, that I was born a Jew and converted to Christianity. I have given comfort and hope to all Christians in my ministry. And therefore I swear here, in the name of the Trinity, that the lie spread by diabolical cunning that the Jews in the celebration of their Passover make use of Christian blood is a malicious and blasphemous slander, and nothing of it is said in the Old Testament or in the writings of the *Talmud*, which I know perfectly well and have carefully researched. This is the truth. God help me.

Where, however, the need to change opinion was most pressing was in France. In February, reports from Damascus were received by Marshal Soult, the Jew who had betrayed Napoleon at Waterloo, who was then Foreign Minister. On 1 March Soult was replaced by Adolphe Thiers, who in addition to the Presidency of the Council took over the foreign portfolio. He had to deal with the consequences of the Damascus Affair. In France, as we shall see, the role played by Crémieux, the Rothschilds' man, was decisive. The text that brought about the turnaround was a long eight-page letter published on 8 April in two Paris newspapers, the *Gazette des Tribunaux* and the *Journal des Débats*. Jonathan Frankel claims that it "caused a sensation and brought about a radical transformation in the treatment of ritual crime in the French press". In it Crémieux began by explaining the case clumsily, followed by the rosary of tortures, and ended by calling on the press and the French to protect the Jews with appeals of this kind: "French Christians, we are your fellow citizens, your friends, your brothers! You have given the world an example of the purest and most delicate tolerance; be a shield for us, just as you have been our protectors! But above all, let the French press take up the sacred question of truth and civilisation with the noble zeal which glory has conferred upon it. It is a beautiful role which suits it well and which it plays so magnanimously!"

Palmerston receives and instructs

The role of the press will deserve more attention later, but it is pertinent to note first how the Rothschilds and other Jewish bankers asked the governments of their respective countries to put pressure on the Egyptian and Turkish authorities in order to free the criminals.

In London on 21 April, the Council of Representatives of British Jews met, which included the most prominent figures of the Jewish financial elite in Britain. Baron Lionel de Rothschild, Sir Moses Montefiore, Isaac and Francis Goldsmid, David Salomons and Louis Cohen attended this decisive meeting. Adolphe Crémieux travelled from Paris to attend the session, and was thanked in a resolution for writing the above-mentioned letter "in the cause of truth and humanity". Other resolutions were adopted with a view to publication. These described ritual crime as "a strictly medieval phenomenon which had long since disappeared". It was decided to demand that the governments of England, Austria and France intercede in Constantinople and Alexandria in order to put an end to the atrocities against the Jews. A summary of the meeting entitled *Persecution of the Jews in the East* was printed. A delegation was appointed to meet with the Foreign Office Secretary, Lord Palmerston, and a committee was appointed to circulate the decisions taken at the Council to the press, which were to be published in no less than thirty-one daily and weekly newspapers.

On 30 April, Lord Palmerston received representatives of the Council. Its President Joseph G. Henriques had previously provided the Minister with a dossier containing documents from the Middle East and the Council's resolutions. The delegation was led by Lionel Rothschild, Goldsmid, Salomons and Montefiore. Palmerston was determined even to intervene by force if persuasive measures failed: his idea was to get Muhammed Ali to return the territories of Syria, Lebanon and Palestine to the Sultan of Constantinople. Palmerston was determined to act on behalf of the Jews of the Middle East and had no trouble assuring members of the delegation that he would send the most suitable dispatches to both Colonel Hodges in Alexandria and Lord Ponsonby in Constantinople. He expressed his 'surprise that the calumny which had been invented should have been given so much credence' and promised that 'all the influence of the British Government would be exerted to put an end to the atrocities'. This meeting of the Council of British Jews with Palmerston received immediate public attention both in England and on the Continent. This contrasted with the situation in Austria, where Solomon Rothschild's close friendship with Metternich kept the negotiations in the strictly private sphere.

Henry John Temple, 3rd Viscount Palmerston (1784-1865), known as Lord Palmerston, served in government from 1807 until his death. In addition to holding the Foreign Office at the time, a post he held from 1830, he was Prime Minister twice, the first time between 1855-1858 and the second between 1859-1865. Before moving on to his administration, it is interesting to know what Monsignor George F. Dillon wrote about him in 1884, nineteen years after his death, in his work *The War of Antichrist with the Church and Christian Civilization*, published in Edinburgh. According to Monsignor Dillon, Palmerston was not only Grand Master of Freemasonry, but went on to become a patriarch of the Illuminati and thus coordinated secret societies all over the world. Dillon claims that he was the successor of Nubius[16] and links him to the atheists' plans against

---

[16] Nubius was the pseudonym of the head of the Haute Vente, a secret society which had in the terrible sect of the Carbonarii its executing arm. The Carbonari had Giuseppe Mazzini, Adam Weishaupt's successor, as their undisputed leader, and thus both were part of the Illuminati. One of Nubius' most trusted men was a Jew known as Piccolo Tigre, who travelled under the guise of a jeweller and itinerant banker. A letter written in

Christianity. When Nubius died in 1837, Mazzini, who is suspected to have been in charge of his demise, took up permanent residence in London. It was perhaps in these years that Palmerston may have been chosen to carry out the plans of the Illuminati, which included the formation of a German empire in the centre of Europe from the union of the small German states and the union of Italy. London, where Jews had two lodges in which Christians were not allowed to enter, thus became the seat of the revolution. Karl Marx settled in the city in 1849 and did not leave it until his death. In 1846, two years before the revolutions of 1848 broke out all over Europe at the same time, Palmerston again became a minister in the Foreign Office.

Knowing, then, who Lord Palmerston was and whom he served, it is hardly surprising that he played a decisive role in the case of the Jews of the Middle East. On 5 May 1840 he sent two dispatches to Hodges and Ponsonby, clearly warning them that the interests of the Jewish community in the Levant were in danger and ordering them to do all in their power to avoid "the most serious persecutions". Hodges in particular was asked to make it clear to Muhammed Ali that the "enormous barbarities" perpetrated in Damascus reflected a disgraceful image of his administration, which had astonished Europeans, who could not expect "atrocities such as those which have been committed" to be permitted under his rule. The level of brazenness in the demand to Muhammed Ali was unconscionable. The text ended: 'His Majesty's Government has no doubt that Muhammed Ali will not only immediately make the fullest reparation to the unfortunate Jews, but will also remove and punish those officials who have so blatantly abused their powers'.

However, the first dispatches from Nathaniel Werry arrived on Palmerston's desk shortly afterwards. They were those in which the British Consul in Damascus expressed his total conviction in the guilt of the Jews, explained the ritual motivations of the *Talmud* and justified the actions of Ratti-Menton and Governor Sheriff Pasha. The minister's indignation can easily be imagined. On 21 May he hastened to send Werry a consignment of documents relating to the case and warned him in the most imperious tone with these words: "I have to inform you that I have read with absolute

---

1822 by Piccolo Tigre giving instructions from the Alta Venta to the Carbonari lodges of Piedmont is transcribed in full by Monsignor Dillon. It stresses the need to debase and deprave human beings and once again reveals the criminal aims already revealed by Robison and Abbé Barruel. Another letter cited by various researchers is the one addressed by Vindex, another pseudonym, to Nubius, dated 9 August 1838 in Castellmare. It is a document which expresses the aim of destroying Catholicism and shows absolute contempt for human life by advocating murder. According to the historian Jacques Crétineau-Joly, the mysterious disappearance of Nubius could be explained by the fact that he was murdered by poisoning. The use of pseudonyms, it has already been said, was used by the Illuminatti to hide their identity. Weishaupt, as is known, was Spartacus, Baron Knigge was Philo, and so on. Who Nubius was has not been ascertained. According to Monsignor Dillon, an Italian nobleman was hiding behind Nubius.

surprise your report relating the atrocities... committed on the Jews of Damascus, and I have observed that.... either it shows that you are completely uninformed as to what is going on in the city in which you live, or it shows on your part a complete lack of the principles and feelings which should distinguish a British officer". He went on to repeat that Mohammed Ali would have to compensate the Jews and dismiss the officers responsible.

Metternich, under Salomon Rothschild

As noted above, it was in Austria that the alarm first spread about what was happening in Damascus, thanks to the close relations between Salomon Rothschild and Metternich. The two worked in perfect harmony to help the "defenceless Jews". Professor Frankel confirms that "one solicited and the other granted personal favours, all with complete discretion and due respect". Metternich thus not only discussed the case with Solomon, but was willing to go to any lengths to satisfy the banker's demands.

Among these demands was surely that of controlling the press, as is shown by the *Österreichischer Beobachter*. On 11 April 1840, this newspaper, the most important in the country, devoted its front page and a few pages inside to a lurid account of the murder of Father Tomaso by the rabbis and elders of the Jewish community in Damascus. The consternation of Prince Metternich and his friend Rothschild is easy to imagine. The former's intervention was immediate and had a fulminating effect. In the next day's edition, 12 April, the treatment of the news changed radically. Again on the front page, though this time in a terse way, it was reported that, according to official reports from Beirut concerning the murder, "there was no proof that the crime had taken place; it had not been established who were to blame for the disappearance... and the doctors and surgeons had declared that the bones found in the sewers of the Jewish quarter were already old and, moreover, were those of animals". It then went on to lament the onslaught to which the Jews of Damascus were being subjected. According to Professor Frankel, whose work reports on this episode, the sudden change in the editorial line of the newspaper was the subject of ironic comment in some German newspapers, as it made it clear that the Austrian government was not prepared to tolerate accusations against the Jews.

The dispatches Metternich sent on 10 April were also undoubtedly the result of meetings with Solomon. In his letter to Laurin, Metternich reminded him that there were a number of Jews in Syria who enjoyed Austrian protection, including the consul general in Aleppo[17], and demanded that he

---

[17] It so happens that Isaac Picciotto, accused of the murder of the servant Ibrahim Amara, in addition to belonging to one of the most influential families in the area, had a relative, his uncle Elias Picciotto, who held the post of Austrian consul general in Aleppo, so the Damascus crime constituted a direct threat against the family of an Austrian diplomat.

take steps to prevent the matter from burdening them. It also asked him to urge Muhammed Ali "without interfering with the course of justice, to control the cruel and stupid steps taken by the subordinate officers". A significant passage from Metternich's dispatch to Laurin quoted by Professor Frankel follows:

"The accusation that Christians are deliberately killed on the occasion of an alleged bloody Easter is absurd by its very nature and the ways the governor of Damascus has chosen to prove this unnatural crime are completely inappropriate; no wonder the real culprits have not been discovered.... The Egyptian authorities are obliged to ensure prompt and strict justice. Abuse of power, persecutions and maltreatment of innocent people might, however, become known in Europe and would undoubtedly be in open contradiction to what is expected of the viceroy."

These words show that Metternich considered it a good tactic to pressure and threaten Muhammed Ali with the loss of his carefully cultivated reputation, which presented him to Europe as the champion of civilisation against barbarism. In his reply sent on 5 May, Laurin expressed his delight that his views were fully shared in Vienna.

On 7 May, Solomon received a letter from his brother James, who urged him from Paris to ask Metternich for help in orchestrating a press campaign. Since Laurin, the Austrian diplomat, had sent him letters, James Rothschild asked his brother to get permission from the Austrian government to publish extracts from these letters in the French press. Metternich, who was unaware that Laurin, otherwise a friend of Carl Rothschild, had himself sent letters to James, did not like the initiative of his consul in Alexandria, and on 27 May sent him a dispatch in which, in addition to approving his "vigorous action in the pursuit of justice", he regretted that he had been "allowed to enter into direct correspondence with the House of Rothschild in Paris" and reminded him that "disputes between consuls in Damascus were matters for the imperial government".

Laurin was obviously stunned by the rebuke, but he did not shrink from it. The fact that Laurin had sent letters to James Rothschild had a certain logic to it, since James was the Austrian Consul in the French capital and in a sense an Austrian agent. Laurin immediately replied that he had written to the Rothschild in Paris because Isaac Picciotto had been threatened with imminent execution and Cochelet, the French consul general in Alexandria, had refused to help him. To avoid this disgrace," he wrote to Metternich, "I

Austria was already in the habit in those years of appointing Jews to consular positions. For this reason Isaac Picciotto was transferred from the prison of the French consulate to that of the Austrian consul, from where between 17 and 27 March, always accompanied by an Austrian officer, he appeared four or five times before Sherif Pasha for interrogation.

felt obliged to seek help from someone who, as a co-religionist, would be personally interested.

James Rothschild fails to beat Thiers

As Laurin had well understood, only the French government could bring about a rapid solution to the Damascus affair. Adolphe Thiers was, as has been said, the prime minister and was also at the head of the Foreign Ministry. Moreover, France was the country which fifty years earlier had emancipated the Jews and which, after the revolution of 1830, which elevated Louis-Philippe d'Orléans, the "citizen king", to the throne, had reinforced the principle of Jewish equality. Moreover, Thiers had obligatory relations with James Rothschild, since from his early days as Prime Minister he had been negotiating with the Rothschild bank for the financing of the railway lines that were to connect France with Brussels and Le Havre.

Nevertheless, Thiers did not initially bow to the demands and pressure. He claimed that he needed more time to examine the reports from the Middle East and offered no further explanation. The pro-government press also adopted a position of silence, and Crémieux's demands were not even answered. On 17 April Thiers had responded to Ratti-Menton's first report from Damascus. It was this dispatch that was the only one he sent personally to his consul. In it Thiers wrote that the report seemed to be written under the effect of impressions that were still very recent, so that he could not form an opinion on "a matter so serious and still shrouded in obscurity". He told the consul that he was impatiently awaiting further reports that would enable him to dispel this obscurity. Thiers, however, did not reproach Ratti-Menton for advocating the execution of the accused, but praised his determination, which he considered "based on reasons of both wisdom and humanity". In the dispatch, the consul was asked to strive to prevent such an unfortunate affair from degenerating into "a pretext for attacking the Jews".

This text, whose tone differs greatly from those used by Palmerston and Metternich, indicated the path Thiers intended to follow with regard to the case. He intended to control it and limit the damage, but without disavowing the Count of Ratti-Menton. As for the accusation of ritual crime, Thiers tended to attribute the murder to a handful of religious fanatics. Nevertheless, he decided to send a consular official to Damascus to prepare a report on the murder of Father Tomaso. It soon became known to the press that the man appointed to the task was the Count de Meloizes, a twenty-six-year-old diplomat serving in Alexandria as vice-consul under Cochelet. The protocols that de Meloizes was supposed to draw up on the case were supposed to confirm or question what Consul Ratti-Menton had done.

Naturally, the Rothschilds expected nothing from Meloizes' future report, as this letter from James Rothschild to his brother Solomon, written on 7 May, shows:

"Unfortunately, the steps I have taken have not had the desired results, since the regime is inactive. The fact is that, considering the praiseworthy conduct of the Austrian Consul, the Consul will not be adequately reprimanded on this side. The matter is too far away and does not attract enough attention. All that I have been able to get is published today in the *Moniteur* in a few words. The vice-consul in Alexandria will examine the conduct of the consul in Damascus. This, however, is only an evasive measure, since the vice-consul is a subordinate of the consul and it is not to be expected that the latter will be reprimanded for his conduct. In these circumstances, the only thing left to do is to ask for help from an element that is omnipotent here, namely the press".

In a subsequent letter, sent the following week, James Rothschild was even more pessimistic. In it he regretted that Thiers had allowed a ministerial evening paper, the *Messager*, to publish a report that the French Prime Minister had personally told the banker "that the case was based on truth, that it was best to disregard the matter, that the Jews in the Middle Ages were fanatical enough to have required Christian blood for their Passover, that the Jews in the East still held such superstitions, etc.". In other words, whatever the Rothschilds said or thought, Thiers sincerely believed that his diplomats in the Middle East were telling him the truth, and he had communicated this to James Rothschild.

Christian boy goes missing in Rhodes

Just as the campaign to discredit the Ratti-Menton consul was beginning to take shape, another alleged ritual crime took place in Rhodes. The fact that the investigation was aborted does not, however, allow us to state categorically, as in the case of Father Tomaso, that the perpetrators were Jews, although the chances are extremely high that they were. Here are the known facts.

Several weeks after the murder of Father Tomaso, at Passover time a twelve-year-old Greek boy from the northern town of Trianda disappeared without a trace. The mother reported the disappearance to the Turkish governor of the island, Yusuf Pasha, who began investigations. Two witnesses reported that on the day of his disappearance they had seen him talking to the head of the Jewish community, Stamboli, and that he had entered the Jew's house. Stamboli was brought before the authorities and in tears declared that he knew nothing. He tried to present an alibi, but was unsuccessful. As a result of the investigation, it also emerged that three

Jewish strangers had been seen on their way to Trianda. The police managed to locate them and they were brought before the governor, who interrogated them in the presence of several foreign consuls. They too declared that they knew nothing. The Rabbi of Rhodes, Jacob Israel, explained that neither the Jewish laws nor the religious books said anything about these crimes of which the Christians accused them. "We are absolutely incapable of such a crime. We would not deserve to be children of God if by our conduct we could cause the slightest trouble to the Government..." Here he was interrupted by one of the consuls, who ordered him to finish, for "they did not want to hear apparent justifications or long explanations, but where they could find the child." The rabbi also assured him that he knew nothing.

On the orders of Yusuf Pasha, a military unit cordoned off the Jewish quarter of Rhodes in order to draw up a list of the Jews present and search their houses. The measure provoked great lamentation. Several foreign consuls, a civil judge and representatives of the Islamic population were assigned to make a decision. Nevertheless, the governor refused to lift the cordon until the child had been found.

Meanwhile, Jewish agents on the island rushed to London to report the "calumnies and cruelties" to which the Jews of Rhodes were being subjected. Orders soon arrived from Lord Palmerston in Constantinople, urging "protection of the afflicted Jews". Pressure on Yusuf Pasha to lift the siege of the neighbourhood had an effect; but the governor kept the suspects in solitary confinement and interrogations continued in the presence of several consuls. Major contradictions soon emerged, which only increased suspicions that these Jews were involved in the child's disappearance.

The Chief Rabbi of Constantinople was then negotiating with the Turkish government and managed to have both the child's mother and the three Greek citizens who held the charges brought to Constantinople along with a large delegation of Jews from the island. Fourteen days after the group's departure, orders came from the Turkish capital instructing Governor Yusuf Pasha to release the prisoners[18]. Although both the mother of the missing child and the three plaintiffs had maintained their position vis-à-vis the Turkish authorities, the High Court of Justice in Constantinople announced shortly afterwards in a public statement the "innocence of the Rhodesian Jews". The Jews were "totally acquitted of the accusation of

---

[18] Jonathan Frankel comments in *The Damascus Affair* that since 1830 the Rothschilds had been in contact with the Sultan about the possibility of a loan, a project that was supported by Metternich himself, Lord Ponsonby and George Samuel, a grandson of Moses Montefiori who represented the bankers' interests in Constantinople. The Turkish regime had serious financing problems and urgently needed money, but the loan was not forthcoming because the Ottoman government did not offer the adequate guarantees demanded by the Rothschilds. It was even rumoured that the island of Crete (then in the possession of Viceroy Muhammed Ali) had been offered in the negotiations. Perhaps this helps to understand the attitude of the Turkish authorities towards the Rhodes crime.

kidnapping and murder of a child, and as compensation they were entitled to some aid.... Those who had unlawfully accused them were to pay compensation...".

The child's mother was sent back to Rhodes and was not even left with the possibility of further investigation. In contrast to what was happening in Damascus, the judicial investigations in Rhodes could be abruptly aborted, and by 20 July the alleged perpetrators of the Christian boy's disappearance had been cleared. Yusuf Pasha was subsequently formally demoted and replaced by a governor close to the Jews. In any case, the population did not forget: protests and unrest over the resolution of the case were widespread and Jews, according to the correspondent of the *Orient* newspaper, were not allowed to venture outside the city gates.

Thiers resists

Paris, London and Alexandria were the places where, in June and July, various events took place that in one way or another were to determine the outcome of the case. In Paris there were parliamentary debates which showed Adolphe Thiers' willingness to resist pressure and support the French consuls in Damascus and Alexandria. On 2 June, Benoît Fould, a prominent Jewish banker and member of the Chamber of Deputies, lashed out harshly against Ratti-Menton. His words are worth quoting:

> "Gentlemen, this is a question which concerns not only the national honour of France, but the whole of humanity. Two million people are today under the yoke of persecution.... The consul's duty was to find out what had happened to the religious.... But, faced with murder, he chose to accuse not an individual, not a family, but an entire nation no less.... What we are dealing with is a religious persecution under the pretext that a religious has disappeared. The French consul incited torture... despite the fact that the French nation represents an example not only of equality before the law, but also of religious equality".

As can be seen, as early as 1840, the figures were being inflated and the persecution of millions of people was being referred to, when in fact only a group of criminals was being accused. Benoît Fould told the deputies that all the consuls were united in their opposition to Ratti-Menton and vehemently criticised the decision taken by Thiers to send de Meloizes, the young vice-consul, to investigate the matter on behalf of the government. "I think a senior diplomat should have been moved when the fate of two million people is at stake," he said, again dramatising the two million figure. Fould did not resist the temptation to refer the House to the speech (quoted above) of Johann Emmanuel Veith, the Jewish convert and Habsburg preacher, who in Vienna Cathedral had sworn by Christ that the accusations against the Jews of Damascus were false and absurd.

In his reply to the banker, Thiers appealed to the need to look at the matter objectively and told MEPs that he had secret information that he did not want to reveal. The debate took on an unintended virulence and Thiers retorted:

> "Although I have read all the interrogatories and am therefore familiar with the documents, I would consider it objectionable for me to express my opinion on the innocence or guilt of the accused at this rostrum. Whatever my opinion may be, it is my duty not to express it here. I only want to do one thing... and that is to vindicate the actions of a diplomat who has behaved as an officer doing his duty should... In contrast to the wish expressed here that we should be fair to the Jews of the East, we must be allowed to be fair to French diplomats who find themselves in a difficult position".

Thiers had the last word in the debate and appealed to patriotism. He defended the consul by describing the harassment to which he was being subjected by the rest of the European players. Aware that the crisis was taking on unexpected proportions and that there was a danger that France would be isolated, he gradually raised the tone of his speech. He deplored the fact that some Members of Parliament claimed to have knowledge of the case without having the information and reproached them for being more concerned about Jews in Damascus than about French representatives who were being unjustly attacked. To those who were protesting on behalf of Jews, he said he was protesting on behalf of a French agent who had done his duty "with honour and loyalty". Thiers ended his speech with the following remarks addressed to European Jews:

> "...They (the Jews) have risen up all over Europe and have devoted themselves to this matter with an enthusiasm that does them deep honour. And, if I may say so, they are more powerful in the world than they pretend to be. They are at this very moment presenting their claims in all the chancelleries of Europe. And they are doing so with extraordinary vigour and with a passion that is hard to imagine. It takes courage for a minister to defend his agents who are under attack? Gentlemen, you should know, I repeat, that the Jews are now pressing in all the chancelleries and our consul has only the support of the French Ministry of Foreign Affairs".

In light of these naïve words: "they are more powerful in the world than they pretend to be", it is clear that Thiers did not properly appreciate the significance of the facts and was unaware of the real intentions of those who were using European countries against his government.

A month later, on 10 July, the debate took place in the Senate. New documents confirming the official version had been sent to Paris, and the head of government had further strengthened his support for Ratti-Menton's action. I must report," said Thiers, "that, having read the protocols of the case that have been sent to me, I find nothing to reproach our consul. Moreover, Thiers told the senators that Cochelet, whom he described as one of France's most valuable and prestigious diplomats, fully supported the consul in Damascus. Thiers certainly had months to change his position and, like Palmerston and Metternich, could have overruled his subordinates in the East, but he did not. Such was his conviction that the Jews of Damascus were the murderers of Father Tomaso that he candidly told James Rothschild and Crémieux privately. Crémieux noted in his diary that the minister had told him to his face without mercy: "They are guilty. They wanted the blood of a priest. You do not know the extent of the fanaticism of the Jews of the East. This is not the first case of such a crime".

While in Britain and Austria the press was almost completely controlled, in France Catholic publications and others close to the government maintained their positions. Thus, the *Journal des Débats*, after the parliamentary session of 2 June, asked to wait for the definitive results of the investigation before pronouncing one way or the other. A Catholic newspaper labelled Bonapartist, *Commerce*, publicly accused James de Rothschild of interfering in French diplomatic affairs. The *Univers*, for its part, defended Ratti-Menton unequivocally and praised Thiers' courage in protecting him, despite attacks from the Jews and the chancelleries of Europe. The legitimist newspaper *Quotidienne* insisted after the parliamentary debate that Ratti-Menton's cause was "the cause of justice, the cause of France". It also echoed persistent rumours accusing Jews of having tried to bribe the French consul. The *Quotidienne* also attacked James de Rothschild, accusing him of arrogance and of spending large sums of money in support of the accused. We must warn Mr. Rothschild," the paper said, "that by his incredible persistence he not only fails to justify his co-religionists in Damascus, but in fact compromises himself and perhaps also his co-religionists in France. Be careful. We do not know if he can buy a certain number of high officials, but we are sure that he cannot buy public opinion". Another Catholic newspaper, the *Gazette de Languedoc*, reproduced verbatim on 12 June the *Quotidienne*'s warning to James de Rothschild.

The *Leipziger Allgemeine Zeitung*, a Protestant newspaper, also published a report by its Paris correspondent on the debate in the Chamber of Deputies. The article reported on the confrontation between the European consuls and reported that there had been a rejection in France of James de Rothschild, who was seen as the instigator of a Jewish league against the Thiers government. The text emphasised the fact that, despite their emancipation, French Jews were incapable of subordinating their ethnic and religious interests to the national interest of their adopted country, and had taken a stand against their government, to which they had declared war. The German newspaper correspondent also reported on the sums of money that French Jews were using to buy the political position of various newspapers, and also on attempts to bribe even German correspondents in France to write in favour of their cause.

Already in July, on the 4th to be precise, the *Gazette de Languedoc* insisted on the existence of an uninterrupted chain of murders connecting Jewish ritual crimes from the Middle Ages to the present day. In that edition the French newspaper detailed at some length the crime of Hagenau, which took place in the 13th century, about which we have given succinct information in the first pages of this chapter. As will be recalled, the German Emperor Frederick II was bribed at the time and the bloodthirsty men escaped unpunished. For the *Gazette* there was an exact analogy with the murder of Father Tomaso.

The mission to the East

Much more favourable was the situation in London, where the power of the Jewish financial elite was almost absolute since the creation of the Bank of England and the East India Company. It was there that a mission was organised to travel from Marseilles to Alexandria and Damascus in order to secure the release of all those accused in the murders of the Capuchin friar and his servant.

The events can begin to be recounted from the beginning of June, when Adolphe Crémieux wrote to Lionel Rothschild to tell him that what had happened in the Chamber of Deputies debate was not exactly "wonderful for our poor Jews in Damascus". Crémieux confirmed in the letter his immediate departure for London. Nathaniel Rothschild, Nat, Lionel's younger brother who was in Paris at the time, perhaps preparing to marry his cousin Charlotte, the eldest daughter of his uncle James, also wrote to his brothers on 3 June to announce Crémieux's journey. It is precisely in another letter from Nathaniel to Lionel written on the 4th that news of the preparations for the journey to the East is given. In it, Nat asks his brother to start organising a large subscription to pay the expenses of Crémieux's journey to the East. He suggests that he start with a donation of £1000 and confesses that he is curious to know how much Isaac Goldsmid will contribute.

Crémieux arrived in London on 8 June and soon learned that Sir Moses Montefiore, an incorrigible fool with a penchant for pomposity and self-promotion, who was also related to the Rothschilds, was the person chosen to accompany him on his trip to Alexandria. The fact that in 1839 Montefiore had spent the months of May and June in Palestine had probably played a part in his choice. He therefore knew the viceroy of Egypt personally, since he had returned to Europe via Alexandria, where he had met Muhammed Ali on 13 July. The announcement was made on the 15th at the meeting of the assembly of the Council of British Jews. The Council decided that Lionel Rothschild himself should receive the contributions and called a public meeting in the Great Synagogue, known as Duke's Place, for this purpose.

The meeting at the Great Synagogue took place on the 23rd and was an impressive demonstration of the unity of London's Jews. The meeting was chaired by Moses Montefiore himself, who was the chairman of the London Committee of the Deputation of British Jews. The highest representative of the French Jews was Adolphe Crémieux, and representing the German Jews was Rabbi Löwe. Mentions of gratitude were first expressed to Colonel Hodges, His Majesty's Consul in Alexandria; to Prince Metternich, His Highness; to Merlato, Austrian Consul in Damascus; to Laurin, Austrian Consul General in Alexandria, and to James Rothschild. The assembly then decided to send Crémieux and Montefiore to Syria on behalf of the Israelites. Prime Minister Thiers was accused by one of the speakers of "lacking humanity before the forum of civilised Europe". Montefiore confirmed that he would travel with Crémieux and said they would "go to defend the requirements of humanity, which was being offended in their persecuted and afflicted brethren. We are going," he added, "to bring light on the dark chaos of diabolical deeds, to uncover the conspiracy and shame the conspirators... moreover, we want to try to instil in the governments of the East progressive principles of legislation and the administration of justice.

A day earlier, on 22 June, there had been a meeting of the House of Commons attended by Lord Palmerston. At this meeting Sir Robert Peel, who in a personal letter had assured Nathaniel that he would "make Thiers a little more cautious in the instructions he sent to the East", took the floor to refer to the abusive persecution to which the Jews of Damascus were subjected. He told the chamber of the accounts of cruelty and torture that Merlato and Pieritz had circulated, and called for England's intervention: "the Jews of England, as well as those of other nations, would have confidence that England's intervention would lead to the discovery of the truth". Palmerston replied that the subject he had brought before the House had long since merited the attention of the Government, "which would lose no time in taking appropriate action".

Another of the large meetings that took place in London was announced in three columns in the *Times*. The headline was: "Persecution of the Jews in Damascus: Great Meeting at the Mansion House". The meeting took place on 3 July, when the Crémieux and Montefiore entourage was already in Paris. It was attended by some two hundred important Christian personalities, including bankers, merchants, scholars and financial experts from the City of London. The Mayor of the City of London was also present.

The purpose of the meeting was "to show fervent sympathy with regard to the terrible oppression of the Jews". Although it was a meeting of gentiles, the Rothschilds, the Goldsmids and other prominent Jewish financiers and businessmen were present in the room.

These "Christians", whose vested interests must surely be linked to the economic power of the Jewish financial elite, vied with each other in championing the cause of the poor Jews of Damascus, whose suffering, said one speaker, "will serve to improve the situation of Jews everywhere". The torrent of hypocritical verbiage that flowed through the meeting was greeted with sustained applause. Of course Reverend Pieritz's report was read out again. About Lionel Rothschild, it was said that he was a benefactor of London and that his name would be linked to that of the city as long as it existed. An Anglican minister, B. Noel, in his eagerness to exculpate the accused, said: "would it not be logical to suppose that Father Tomaso was murdered by his servant, anxious to escape with some of his money? Samuel Capper, another speaker, expressed his satisfaction at seeing men like Lord Palmerston and Sir Robert Peel championing this great cause, and said that "England had never proved herself so ready to deliver suffering humanity from cruelty, persecution and torture".

Muhammed Ali and the consuls in Alexandria

In Alexandria, meanwhile, the French Consul Cochelet and the Austrian Consul Laurin were fighting a hard battle with Muhammed Ali, who feared that the pardon of the indicted Jews might lead to a revolt in Syria and hoped that in the event of a conflict with Constantinople and its European allies, France would come to his aid. So much so that Colonel Hodges, who appeared twice before the viceroy, on 28 May and 18 June, to deliver Palmerston's messages, left the palace on both occasions without hope that the case could be easily resolved. On the second occasion Muhammed Ali declared to Hodges that he would not make any decision until he knew the official report being prepared by the French vice-consul, Maxime des Meloizes, who was in Damascus. We know that neither the Rothschilds nor Palmerston nor Metternich expected anything good from this report.

Cochelet, in order to counter Laurin's campaign and to familiarise Europeans living in Alexandria with the protocols of the Damascus trial, had a lengthy document published in Arabic by Sibli Ayub, translated by Jean Baptiste Beaudin, the consulate interpreter, and annotated by Ratti-Menton. It gave in detail the statements and confrontations of the accused, as well as the forensic evidence produced by the medical experts. The impact of the text was considerable, as even the consuls of Prussia, von Wagner, and Russia, Count Medem, who were Laurin's allies, informed their superiors that the protocols were being widely read and that public opinion considered the Jews guilty. Hodges wrote to Palmerston in July to inform him that even

Count Medem had told him personally that he "feared it was the Jews who had murdered Father Tomaso".

For his part, Laurin, well informed by Merlato of events in Damascus, continued his pressure on Muhammed Ali and had succeeded in getting the viceroy to order Sherif Pasha to substantially improve the conditions of the detainees. In a letter dated 15 July, he wrote to Metternich to inform him that the viceroy in his last interview had told him that: "the investigation had proved that the Jews were guilty, but in order not to hurt the feelings of his co-religionists, particularly those in Europe, he was prepared to throw a veil over the nature of their crime, so that he would try to present personal revenge rather than the procurement of Christian blood as the motive for the murder". Another of Laurin's achievements in his interviews with Muhammed Ali was his consent for the defendants' European friends to send two lawyers to Damascus. Laurin wrote to his friend Carl Rothschild and the men chosen were Isaac Loria and a Mr. Ventura, who by mid-July were already in the city trying to interfere with the French vice-consul's work. Finding that among the Christian community there was no one willing to testify on behalf of the detainees, these lawyers devoted their efforts to seeking out prominent Muslims who would testify in the sense they were interested in. They were soon accused of bribery attempts and, inevitably, a collision between them and the French consular team soon followed.

By the end of July, despite all kinds of pressure, Maxime des Meloizes, the vice-consul appointed by Thiers, had produced a five-hundred-page report that was sent to Paris. It contained the interrogations he had conducted with the prisoners, as well as interviews with their families and other enquiries. Unsurprisingly, the conclusion was that the Jewish detainees were the murderers of Father Tomaso. However, the background battle in the shadows was beginning to take its toll on both Sherif Pasha and Muhammed Ali himself, who was under pressure from all but France to order a retrial, which, if held at all, could be conducted by European jurists or, perhaps, by the Egyptian authorities. When Crémieux and Montefiore's trip to London was arranged, it was assumed that Muhammed Ali had agreed to reopen the case and would allow a new investigation. Moreover, to make it clear to Muhammed Ali that other things were at stake besides the Jewish case, on 15 July Turkey, England, Austria, Prussia and Russia signed a treaty directed against Egypt. Ponsoby in Constantinople and Hodges in Alexandria received letters from Lord Palmerston in early August explaining the meaning of the treaty.

Crémieux, Montefiore and Muhammed Ali

Before leaving Marseille, Crémieux had several meetings with Thiers in order to obtain some kind of governmental accreditation, but did not obtain it. He did not even bring a letter of introduction to the French consul general in Egypt. By contrast, Montefiore travelled with the backing of the Foreign Office and carried letters from Palmerston to the British consuls in Alexandria, Damascus and Beirut.

On 4 August Crémieux, Montefiore and the members of the large party travelling with them arrived in Alexandria. They settled in two hotels, which they occupied almost exclusively, while waiting to leave for Damascus. On 5 August Colonel Hodges introduced Montefiore, who was in uniform, to Muhammed Ali. Crémieux did not attend, as he had not yet contacted Cochelet. Montefiore, clearly seeking a review of the case, formally asked the viceroy for permission to interview witnesses and collect evidence on behalf of the Jewish prisoners. Crémieux made the same request days later. In the text, read aloud by Montefiore in English, the pretence of flattery to the viceroy was evident. Here are a few brief snippets reproduced by Professor Frankel: "The eyes of all Europe are upon Your Highness and.... by granting him our prayers the whole civilised world will be pleased..... The great man, who already has such a glorious name, must have a great love for justice. There can be no greater way to pay homage to the genius of Your Highness... than this mission sent by the Israelites all over the world to ask for justice". Muhammed Ali promised to respond in a few days.

It soon became clear that Montefiore and Crémieux were competing with each other for credit. As a result, the two developed different strategies. Montefiore relied on Samuel Briggs, a Briton who managed banking business for the Rothschilds in Alexandria and had amassed a huge personal fortune. Briggs had been to Syria and had personally asked Sherif Pasha to reopen the investigation.

For his part, Crémieux held tense talks with Cochelet. The Jewish leader presented two demands as non-negotiable. The first demanded that the Egyptian authorities proclaim that the accusation of ritual crime was false and defamatory; the second, that the accused be released after their innocence had been declared. In return, a review of the case would be waived for the time being. Cochelet, following what was now the official line, seemed willing to accept the first of the conditions, but refused to consider the second. Seeing that he would get nothing from the consul, Crémieux decided to play his trump cards with Antoine Clot and Gaetani, two renowned doctors who were constantly treating the ageing Muhammed Ali. He asked both of them to help him convince him. Jonathan Frankel reveals that, before leaving Egypt, Crémieux paid each of them ten thousand francs for their services in interceding for the Jews of Damascus with the viceroy, which indicates that they were, to put it bluntly, bribed.

On 16 August Rifaat Bey, the Ottoman Sultan's envoy, landed in Alexandria to present Muhammed Ali with the ultimatum signed on 15 July in London by Turkey and four European powers, according to which he had to evacuate within ten days most of the territories in Syria and Lebanon and renounce his hereditary claims to Palestine if he did not want to lose all his possessions except Egypt. The viceroy was also warned that he and his heirs would lose even Egypt if he did not accept the conditions demanded by the deadline. Muhammed Ali rejected the treaty and told Rifaat Bey that France was ready to come to his aid and had more than once offered to intervene. On the same day, 16 August, Thiers' envoy, Count Walewski, had also arrived in Alexandria. Two days later, he informed the French president that the viceroy of Egypt had formally requested France's diplomatic intervention, i.e. "the protection and mediation of France".

On 17 August Montefiore and Crémieux were received in audience by Muhammed Ali, who apologised for taking so long to respond to Montefiore's request. He admitted that he had not given it much thought, as he had a lot of other things on his plate. Brigss, who was present, asked the viceroy to consider that "the two men were representing not only France and England, but the entire Jewish population of the world". Muhammed Ali was adamant, however, and would not agree to a further investigation. He merely assured that the prisoners in Damascus were being well treated.

When it became clear that reopening the case was not feasible, Montefiore proposed to present Muhammed Ali with a plea asking him to sign a decree announcing the innocence of the prisoners and their release. It was also intended that the viceroy would proclaim his disbelief that the Israelites had committed a ritual religious crime. Crémieux was sceptical, but the document was still delivered to the palace on the 22nd. Muhammed Ali flatly refused the request. On 25 August Montefiore wrote a letter to London recounting the tension of the moment in the face of the possibility of war breaking out after the ten-day deadline. Here," he said, "we await an order to embark. As far as we know, the viceroy is unwilling to yield. The English admiral (Robert Stopford) is already here sailing with his fleet through the harbour in company with Austrian warships.... On all sides we see preparations for war...".

On the 26th Muhammed Ali summoned the Turkish envoy, who was accompanied by the consuls general of the four European Allied powers, and informed him of his decision to reject the ultimatum. On the same day, the British fleet operating off the Lebanese coast intercepted several Egyptian ships carrying supplies for the army in Syria. When this news reached Paris, rumours of a European war became widespread in the press and stock market values plummeted alarmingly.

But just when the die seemed to have been cast, the Egyptian viceroy unexpectedly reversed his approach. On 27 August, in the course of a long meeting with his advisers, he announced that he was ready to give up his claims to Syria. The next day he informed Rifaat Bey and the consuls of the Allied powers that he accepted the terms of the second Utimatum, which guaranteed him hereditary rule of Egypt and dispossessed him of the remaining territories. However, he reserved the right to make a "humble supplication" to the Sultan, asking him, in an act of the utmost generosity, to allow him control of Syria and Crete for as long as he lived. Muhammed Ali asked Rifaat Bey to leave at once for Constantinople; but the consuls intervened to point out that mere words were not enough and that only the evacuation of the Egyptian army from Syria could stop the war.

Cochelet was dismayed to learn that Muhammed Ali had taken such an important decision without prior consultation. Such was his indignation that when he was asked to come to the palace, he initially refused. In a dispatch to Thiers on 30 August, he regretted the Egyptian viceroy's action, as he felt that France should have been warned of the change of policy. Cochelet reported that on presenting himself to Muhammed Ali he found him depressed, with a weak and broken voice. According to Cochelet he had suffered a minor operation for boils. "I can only explain this great concession as the result of a weakening of his morale and the fear of a bitter struggle in which he fears defeat". In the end it was Thiers' envoy Walewski, and not Rifaat Bey, who on 30 August sailed for Constantinople with the request for a settlement. Along with the plea, Walewski carried the warning that, if his offer was rejected, the Egyptian army was ready to invade Anatolia.

Let us now return to the subject matter of this paper to see how Muhammed Ali's concessions to European Jewish leaders came about. From the diaries of Crémieux and Montefiore, later edited by Rabbi Löwe, it is known that Adolphe Crémieux and his wife Amélie Crémieux left Alexandria for Cairo at seven o'clock on the morning of Friday the 28th. An hour later, as they were about to board a barge to cross the Nile, they saw a carriage approaching at full speed. In it were Clot and Gaetani, Muhammed Ali's doctors, who related that at dawn they had been working to remove a boil from the buttocks of the viceroy, with whom they had discussed the Jews of Damascus. The doctors had argued that with the international crisis at its height the voice of six million Jews on behalf of the viceroy of Egypt could be of vital importance. During the conversation Muhammed Ali had suddenly announced: "I will release the prisoners and allow the fugitives to return. I will go to and give the appropriate orders. Crémieux and his retinue immediately returned to Alexandria.

Hebrew University of Jerusalem professor Jonathan Frankel believes that with this decision Muhammed Ali intended to begin to distance himself from France and to secure as far as possible an understanding with the other European powers. The confrontation between the consuls in Alexandria had shown that the Damascus Affair was a determining factor in the dispute between the great powers. The release of the prisoners was obviously a gesture to the Anglo-Austrian alliance," Frankel said, "whose ships plied the waters of the port of Alexandria.

At two o'clock in the afternoon of the same day on the 28th Montefiore went to the palace and managed to gain access to the viceroy, who confirmed that what the doctors had told Crémieux was true. In the evening it was Crémieux who came to the palace to thank Muhammed Ali on behalf of "six million Jews scattered all over the world". Among the kindnesses he extended to him was this: "Kebler said to Bonaparte: 'You are as great as the world. You, Sir, are at this moment as great as Napoleon.

On Saturday 29th copies of the official documents in favour of the Damascus prisoners and the fugitives were collected by members of the Jewish delegation. They soon found in the document a term they did not like. The decree contained the word "pardon", which connoted the sense of guilt. It was Crémieux again who went to meet the viceroy to explain that the Jewish embassy felt the need to protest publicly unless the word in question was replaced. The discussion between the two went on for more than an hour, until Muhammed Ali agreed to replace it with the expression "set free".

Before leaving Alexandria, Montefiore and Crémieux co-signed a letter of thanks addressed to the viceroy of Egypt, although it was actually written with European public opinion in mind, which was to be read in newspapers on the Continent. The letter stated:

> "His Highness has shown to the world that he rejects with contempt the defamatory slanders which our enemies wished to cast upon the Jewish religion... upon the odious principle of the shedding of human blood to mix it with unleavened bread, an accusation which would make our old and pure religion barbarous and bloodthirsty. The act that Your Highness has performed will take its place in history alongside the two decrees signed by Suleiman II and Amurath (al Murad), who nobly cleared the Jewish religion of the same accusation... Christian princes and even popes have done the same thing".

Freedom for Father Tomaso's murderers

On 6 September, the order to release the murderers of Father Tomaso and his servant Ibrahim Amara arrived in Damascus. The edict signed by Muhammed Ali stated that Messieurs Moses Montefiore and Adolphe Crémieux had presented their petitions and hopes to him. It continues as follows:

> "They were sent to Us by the whole population of the Mosaic religion in Europe and implored Us to decree the release of their co-religionists who have been arrested and to secure the peace of those who, in consequence of the investigations which have followed the disappearance (!) of Father Tomaso and his servant Ibrahim, have fled. And since, being so numerous among the population, we consider it inadvisable to refuse their request, we order that all Jews who are imprisoned be released. As for those who have left their homes, I order that they be guaranteed the utmost security so that they may return. Every one of them will go again to his trade or business and as before will be able to carry out his customary work. I

order that they shall feel completely secure from any refusal (of this order). This is Our will.

The Count of Ratti-Menton was stunned by the unexpected turn of events and expressed his bitterness in a series of private letters he wrote to his colleague des Meloizes. It is difficult," he wrote on 6 September, "to describe the impression... that has been made on the Christian and Muslim population. All day long Christians and many Muslims have been coming to the consulate to find out what could have motivated this action which is incomprehensible to them". A few days later, he reported on the big celebration that took place in the Jewish quarter, in which "Father Tomaso and I took part in the form of wimps". Ratti-Menton regretted in another letter of 12 September that Sherif Pasha had not been able to avoid the celebrations, where it had been shouted "Long live Austria! Long live France! Hurray for the Ottomans! Down with the Cross!"

Years later, one of the most learned men on the *Talmud* and on the Jewish world in general, the former Rabbi Simon Drach, who eventually converted to Christianity, wrote the following: "The murderers of Father Tomaso, convicted of their crime, have nevertheless escaped conviction thanks to the efforts of Jews of all nations. In this case money played the most important role.... Justice has not been done.

The truth, however, is proclaimed today on the epitaph of a humble tomb in the church of the Holy Land, but which until 1866 was in the cemetery of the Capuchin convent in Damascus. The text, written in Italian and Arabic, reads: "Qui riposano le ossa del P. Tomaso da Sardegna, Misionario Apostólico Capuchino, assassinato dagli ebrei il giorno 5 di febbraio dell'anno 1840" (Here lie the bones of Fr Tomaso da Sardegna, Capuchin apostolic missionary, killed by the Jews on 5 February 1840).

After the impunity of Father Tomaso's crime, those areas of the East became the El Dorado for numerous bloodthirsty murderers. Three years later, other ritual crimes of several children were reported in Corfu, a new murder in Rhodes and other cases in seven different places. Across Europe, the increase in crimes took on alarming proportions. There is no definitive list, but researchers have documented fifty-nine cases which between 1800 and 1933 came to court. It is an established fact that between 1840 and 1888, murders and complaints skyrocketed. The wealth of books, pamphlets and articles for and against is considerable. One of the most publicised crimes was that of Tisza-Eszlár (Hungary) in 1882. There is a novel, *Blood Libel at Tiszaeszlar*, by Andrew Handler, and a film, *The Raftsmen*, made in Hungary in 1990.

As for Jewish ritual crimes in the United States, Eustace Mullins denounces them in *Mullin's New History of the Jews*, published in 1968 by The International Institute of Jewish Studies. In it he attributes the death of Charles Lindbergh's son, a twenty-month-old baby girl abducted and murdered in March 1932, to Jewish criminals and ritual practices. Arnold Leese, too, in *Jewish Ritual Murder*, provides details of the Jewish plot surrounding the case of Colonel Lindbergh's son. Mullins reveals that Chicago is the American city where most cases of ritual crimes take place and claims that the city is one of the centres that supplies blood to Jewish communities all over the world. The chief of police even admitted that three hundred children went missing in the city every month. In October 1955, brothers John and Anton Schuessler, aged thirteen and eleven, and their friend Bobby Peterson, aged fourteen, were abducted and murdered in Chicago. In December 1956, also in Chicago, sisters Barbara and Patricia Grimes met the same fate. These murders could not be prevented from becoming public knowledge. *The Daily News* published an evening edition with the news that Bobby Peterson's body was pierced in the same places where Christ had been wounded on the cross. The edition was immediately withdrawn from the newsstand. Although, as usual, the official police version attributed the deaths to sex crimes, none of the bodies showed any signs of rape or sexual assault. On the contrary, they all had ligature marks on their wrists and ankles and had suffered cuts, punctures and punctures: the young men had slowly bled to death.

Nationalism and Proto-Zionism

Although during the 18th century, spurred on by messianic predictions, many Kabbalists had made pilgrimages to Palestine, by the early 19th century there were only about 5,000 Jews there. In 1812 the first colony of Ashkenazi Jews belonging to the Hasidist movement had been established in Hebron, whose main protector was Rabbi Hirsch Lehren, who, as we know, since 1817 had led the pro-Zionist organisation Officers of the Land of Israel in Amsterdam. Ten years before the crisis triggered by the Damascus Affair, the American weekly *Niles Wekly Register* suggested that the Ottoman Sultan was considering selling Jerusalem to the Rothschilds, whose power and influence would enable them to reunite their nation in Judea. According to this publication, the territory was of little value to the sultan, "but in the hands of the Jews, led by men like the Rothschilds, what might it not become in a short period of time?" In 1836 Rabbi Zeví Hirsch Kalisher appealed to Amschel Rothschild to buy all of Palestine, a prerequisite for the Redemption of the Jewish people. If this was not possible, the rabbi asked the banker to buy at least the city of Jerusalem with all its surroundings. In 1839 Kalisher also wrote to Moses Montefiore, who, as we know, travelled to Palestine for the first time that year. He asked him to lease Muhammed Ali a large area of land for a period of fifty years, in order to settle thousands of Jewish families there. When Montefiore was received by the viceroy on 13 July, the Jewish chief presented him with the ambitious plan. The proposal was to lease one or two hundred villages that would be free of taxes or contributions. The lease would be paid annually in money in Alexandria. Montefiore wrote in his diary that, if the concession was obtained, he would set up a company to cultivate the land and encourage his brothers from all over Europe to return to Palestine. Weeks and months passed, but there was no reply from Egypt. By the summer of 1840, however, Montefiore's plan to transfer Jews to Palestine on a large scale had become public knowledge, and reports were published of industrial projects in various parts of Judea in which only Jewish workers would be employed.

Historically, Jews have used conversion to other religions to work within them for their racial and religious interests. This was the case with the Marranos in Spain, many of whom came to hold important positions within the Church. We already know that Shabbetay Zeví, the 17th century Jewish Messiah, had no problem adopting Islam to save his life and later downplayed the value of his conversion. Jakob Frank also converted to Islam and Christianity successively in order, in his words, to bring about the destruction of Christianity from within, like "soldiers storming a city by passing through its sewers". Indeed, numerous works today denounce the systematic penetration of Jewish agents into the Catholic and Vatican hierarchy. These include Viscount Leon de Poncins' *Judaism and the Vatican*, Peirs Compton's *The Broken Cross* and Bill Cooper's *Behold a Pale Horse*. A recently discussed example of what we have been writing about is that of the bishop of St. Stephen's Cathedral in Vienna, Johann Emmanuel Veith, a Jewish convert who brazenly swore by Christ from the pulpit that the murderers of Father Tomaso were innocent. The Doenmes, the equivalent of the Spanish Marranos in the Muslim world, were Jews who converted to Islam and, while outwardly behaving like Muslims, remained faithful to their religion. We know that Mustafa Kemal Ataturk and the Young Turks who ended the Islamic state in Turkey in 1923 were Doenmes. All this is relevant now because a Christian organisation was also founded in London in 1809, the aforementioned "London Society for Promoting Christianity Amongst the Jews", which worked with real fervour for the cause of the return of the Jews to Palestine.

If we agree that Zionism is a movement that seeks the reunification of a scattered people in a territory supposedly promised by a God who has chosen them out of all others, we must consider that the London Society was a pro-Zionist organisation. It was swarming with numerous Jewish converts to Christianity, such as the ineffable missionary George Wildon Pieritz, author of the pamphlet *Statement of Mr. G.W. Pieritz, a Jewish Convert, a Jewish Convert. Pieritz, a Jewish Convert, and assistant missionary at Jerusalem, respecting the persecution of the Jews at Damascus: the result of a personal inquiry on the spot.* The main purpose of these "Christians" was to take advantage of their new status to work advantageously for the cause of Jewish nationalism. After all, most of them considered themselves members of the Jewish nation. Among the leading figures of the London

Society was the theologian Alexander McCaul, who claimed that the conversion of the Jews to Christianity and their return to Palestine was a single goal. In a letter to the Society's executive committee in 1839, he decided that in all branches established in the Mediterranean and Poland, missionaries should devote at least two hours a day to the study of the *Talmud*. McCaul undoubtedly considered that to be a good Christian the most appropriate thing to do was to read the most anti-Christian book in existence, which preaches a fierce hatred of Christ and breathes a pathological thirst for vengeance against Christianity.

One of the most prominent figures in the London Society was Lord Ashley, 7th Earl of Shaftesbury, who in 1835 had been appointed vice-president of the Society. Ashley had an intimate relationship with the Secretary of the Foreign Office, Lord Palmerston, as his mother-in-law, Lady Emily Cowper, was Palmerston's mistress until 1839, when she became his wife. Through these influences, the London Society secured the appointment of the British vice-consul in Jerusalem. It was Ashley who ensured that the vice-consul's area of responsibility was the ancient boundaries of what he called "the ancient kingdom of David and the twelve tribes". The person chosen for the post in 1838 was W. T. Young, who at the same time became a member of the Society's General Committee. An entry in Ashley's diary reveals the rapport between him and Palmerston:

> "Farewell this morning to Young, who has just been appointed His Majesty's Vice-Consul in Jerusalem.... What a wonderful event! The ancient city of God's people is about to regain a place among the nations, and England is the first of the kingdoms of the Gentiles to cease trampling it under foot..... God has put it into my heart to devise a plan in His honour, has given me the influence to influence Palmerston, and has provided the right man for the situation.

Lord Ashley regarded the historical period of Cromwell and Charles II as a gift from "the Providence that never sleeps". For him, the fact that England had then given protection to the Jews had been the beginning of its prosperity and commercial dominance. This Zionist avant la lettre published a memorandum in the *Times*, signed "in the name of many who hope for the re-establishment of Israel", which was sent privately to all the heads of the Protestant states of Europe and North America. It referred to the Church of Rome as "the great Babylon about to sink into the abyss of unfathomable doom... when her time comes (and it is very near!)". Appealing to the spirit of the Persian King Cyrus, Protestant governments were called upon to act to restore the people of Israel to their inheritance. Lord Palmerston himself presented the document to Queen Victoria.

All this Zionist fervour only increased during 1840 and in subsequent years. Lady Palmerston herself, commenting on the outbreak of Jewish nationalism that had occurred as a result of the Damascus Affair, said: "the fanatical and religious elements... in this country... are absolutely determined that Jerusalem and all Palestine shall be reserved for the return of the Jews; this is their only desire". The main argument was that in order to prevent future repetition of cases like that of the "poor Jews of Damascus and Rhodes", return to Palestine was necessary. Moses Hess devoted an entire chapter of his famous book *Rome and Jerusalem* to the impact the Damascus ritual crime episode had on him. In it he argued that the way in which Jews had been persecuted, even in Europe, marked a new departure in Jewish life. This book by Hess and Hirsch Kalischer's *Drishal Zion* (*The Search for Zion*), both published in 1862, constitute the first expositions of modern Jewish nationalism.

According to Eustace Mullins, in 1811, Zeví Hirsch Kalisher (1795-1874) was only sixteen years old when he frequented the Masonic lodge in Frankfurt, which was the headquarters of Enlightened Freemasonry. His friendship with Amschel Rothschild thus dates back to those years. There he also met Solomon Rothschild and Sigismund Geisenheimer, the administrative head of the House of Rothschild, both of whom attended the sessions. In *Drishal Zion* this Ashkenazi rabbi called for the reconstruction of Eretz Israel. His plan envisaged the creation of settlements, which would be protected by security forces, as is currently the case, for today the centre of Hebron, which is inaccessible to the 130,000 Palestinians living in the city, is occupied by some 500 settlers who enjoy the protection of the army. Rabbi Kalisher announced in his work that the beginning of the Redemption would be under the auspices of the peoples of the world and that the settlement of Jews in their land would precede the coming of the Messiah. The publication of this work caused a great stir in the Jewish world and was cited by Moses Hess, who a few months later was to publish *Rome and Jerusalem*, the great work of Proto-Zionism.

Meyer Waxman, translator in 1918 of Moses' work Hess (1812-1875) into English, refers to *Rome and Jerusalem* as a book ahead of its time. Hess is for him a prophet and considers the work "the herald of nationalism and the trumpet of Zionism". We do not want to linger now, for other topics require our interest. We shall see only a few of the ideas which this nationalist fanatic expounds in his work. Hess, who was friends with Marx and Engels during the gestation years of the *Communist Manifesto* and participated enthusiastically in the revolutionary movement, as will be seen in the next chapter, envisages a starring role for the future Jewish state. The Zionist state, he foresees, "seated on the road to India and China, will be the mediator between Asia and Europe". According to him, 'the purpose of all creation will only be fulfilled with the establishment of the messianic kingdom and the coming of the Messiah'. Hess quotes Isaiah to distinguish two types of nations: "those doomed to eternal death and Israel, whose destiny is to be resurrected". Having used the French revolution to obtain equality and emancipation, Hess warns that Jews who have emancipated and integrated and "deny the existence of a Jewish nationality, are not only deserters in the religious sense, but traitors to their people, their race and even their family..., for the Jewish religion is above all patriotism". On the subject of apostasy, discussed above, he says: "In reality Judaism as a nationality has a natural basis which is not lost by mere conversion to another faith or another religion. A Jew belongs to his race and consequently to Judaism, even though his ancestors may have been apostates. The converted Jew is still a Jew...". Here is a significant passage in which, in his nationalist delirium, Hess believed it feasible that Jewish bankers could enforce the creation of a Zionist superstate by means of money: "What European power today would object to the plan that the Jews, united through a Congress, should buy their ancient homeland? Who would object if the Jews threw a few handfuls of gold at decrepit old Turkey and said: 'Give me back my home and use this money to consolidate other parts of your tottering empire'? There would be no objection to the realisation of such a plan, and Judea would be allowed to extend its boundaries from Suez to the port of Smyrna, including the whole area of the western mountain range of Lebanon". In another particularly remarkable passage Hess insists on the claim to Turkey and acknowledges the role of the Jews in the French revolution and in the revolutionary movement in general. Addressing the Jewish people, he writes: "The time has come for you to reclaim by way of compensation or by other means your ancient homeland from Turkey, which has devastated it for years. You have contributed sufficiently to the cause of civilisation and have helped Europe on the road to progress, to make revolutions and to make them successfully".

It is regrettable to note how this Zionist insinuates that they were motivated by philanthropy in triggering for their own benefit revolutionary processes in which millions of Europeans lost their lives and property. But perhaps even more outrageous is the cynicism with which he attributes a supremacist role to Judaism, and the contempt with which he refers to other cultures and religions, especially knowing the crimes of Zionism and the ruin that the creation of Israel has meant for all the peoples of the Middle East. Still addressing the Jewish people, he goes on to say: "You will become the moral reference of the East. You have written the Book of Books. Become, then, the educator of the savage Arab hordes and of the African peoples. Leave the old wisdom of the East, the revelations of the Zend, the Vedas, as well as the more modern Koran, group them around your Bible". To conclude this brief review of *Rome and Jerusalem*, let us see how Moses Hess conceived the steps to be taken for the creation of the State. First of all, the Jewish princes, i.e. the Rothschilds, Montefiore and others, should organise a Society for the colonisation of Palestine, whose programme would include the following activities: 1. 2. Jews from all parts of the world, especially from Russia, Poland and Germany, should be settled in Palestine, where they would receive loans and be assisted by agricultural technicians employed by the Company. 3. A police force should be established to protect the settlers from possible Bedouin attacks and to maintain order in general. 4. Under the auspices of the Company, schools would be opened for Jewish youth, in which all sciences and, of course, the nationalist ideology would be taught. Hess finally specified that this "did not mean a total immigration of Jews to Palestine, since even after the establishment of the Jewish state, the majority of Jews living at the time in the civilised West would remain there".

To conclude this section, it may be of interest to know that, as soon as Syria and Palestine were again under the rule of the Sultan of Constantinople, Lord Ashley's London Society, evidently with the approval of Palmerston and the support of the Archbishop of Canterbury, rushed forward with a project to build an Anglican church in the Holy Land, which was carried out with unusual speed. The church, which the London Society began to build on Mount Zion, became the seat of an Anglican bishop in 1841. The post went to Michael Salomon Alexander, who, as might be expected, had had a traditional Jewish upbringing before converting to Christianity. Captain Valmont, who commanded the *Euphrate*, a French warship operating off the Lebanese coast, reported to Cochelet on 9 November of the same year that the English priest spoke freely about the promise to re-establish the kingdom of Israel in the Holy Land.

James Rothschild and the fall of Thiers

All that remains to be seen now is the political repercussions of the Damascus Affair, which led to the downfall of Adolphe Thiers and was a serious diplomatic humiliation for France. According to Niall Ferguson, the resolution of the affair was a personal triumph for James Rothschild and marked one of the high points of the banker's political power. Ferguson argues that the crisis presented James with the ideal opportunity to undermine the Prime Minister, who had never been a great admirer. Nathaniel Rothschild at the height of the crisis expressed the view that defenestration of Thiers, whom he considered "the most arrogant of upstarts", would then be almost impossible and "in fact dangerous as well as unwise". The question was therefore to what extent the Rothschilds were capable of hastening his downfall.

The key was the impact of the crisis on the price of public revenues. On 3 August 1840 there was a dramatic fall in the price of government bonds. It was only the beginning of a prolonged decline that persisted until October, driven by fears about events in the East. The key to the Rothschilds' position is again to be found in a comment by Nat, which is quoted by N. Ferguson: "Thank God, the house had hardly any rent". This means that on 2 August, the day before the collapse of the French government bonds, the French Rothschilds, who undoubtedly had inside information from the London and Vienna houses, had covered themselves in advance and disposed of them.

Thiers defended himself as best he could, and on 12 October fired a volley at James Rothschild and his manoeuvres through the pro-government newspaper *Constitutionnel*. Here is the text extracted from Niall Ferguson's work:

> "According to *The Times*, Mr de Rothschild is a financier and does not want war. Nothing could be easier to understand. Monsieur de Rothschild is an Austrian subject and the Austrian consul in Paris, and as such has little concern for the honour and interest of France. That too is understandable. But what, tell me, have you to do, Mr. de Rothschild, a man of the Stock Exchange, Mr. de Rothschild, agent of Metternich, with our Chamber of Deputies and our majority? By what right and by what authority does the King of Finance interfere in our affairs? Is he the judge of our honour, and should his pecuniary interests take precedence over our national interest? We speak of pecuniary interests, but, very surprisingly, if highly reliable reports are to be believed, the Jewish banker does not only bring against our cabinet financial claims... It seems that he also wants to satisfy his wounded vanity. Mr. de Rothschild has promised his co-religionists the dismissal of our consul-general in Damascus because of the position he defended at the trial of the Jews in that city. Thanks to the firmness of the President of the Council [Thiers], these insistent demands of the all-powerful banker were resisted, and Mr. Ratti-Menton was kept on. Hence the irritation of the all-powerful banker and the fervour with which he devotes himself to intrigues that have nothing to do with his business."

James Rothschild must have been little perturbed by this attack. In reality it was nothing more than the right to complain, for eight days later Thiers resigned. By 29 October 1840 a new government had been formed, headed once again by one of the Rothschilds' most loyal supporters, the traitor of Waterloo, the indefatigable Marshal Jean-de-Dieu Soult, Duke of Dalmatia, who had taken office for the third time and was to remain in office until 19 September 1847. Nathaniel Rothschild was pleased to say that the stock exchange had the utmost confidence in the new government.

The consequences of the crisis in the East showed that international tension benefited the Rothschilds. The fall of Thiers led almost immediately to new business. Soult's government hastened to negotiate with the Rothschild house a new loan for the construction of a system of fortifications around Paris. A loan of 150 million francs was granted in October 1841, demonstrating James Rothschild's undisputed dominance of French finance. Further loans were granted in 1842 and 1844. International tension also led to increased spending on armaments in the German states. "If France continues to arm itself, so must Germany", reasoned Amschel Rothschild. This meant new business for the Rothschilds.

Incidentally, it may interest the reader to know what happened to the incorruptible Count de Ratti-Menton. In the summer of 1841 he was ordered to report to Paris. Although the Catholic community in Damascus insisted on his return to the consulate, his return never took place. The government headed by the Jew Soult, so closely linked to Rothschild interests, must have felt that a diplomat who had shown so little compassion towards poor innocent Jews deserved a special posting: in 1842 Ratti-Menton was appointed to the post of consul in Canton.

CHAPTER V

"OUR GOOD MASONS, BLINDFOLDED"

Ever since the Illuminati penetrated Freemasonry in order to make use of it and, hidden within it, functioned as a secret society within a secret society, Freemasons all over the world have played the role assigned to them by the directors of the MRM (World Revolutionary Movement). Let us recall the words of Rabbi Antelman: "When the Illuminati and the Frankists infiltrated the Freemasons, it did not mean that they harboured any feelings of love for Freemasonry. On the contrary, they hated it and only wanted its cover as a means of spreading their revolutionary doctrine and providing a place to meet without arousing suspicion".

As the 19th century progressed, the control of Freemasonry became so irreversible that in 1861 the ineffable Adolphe Isaac Crémieux, 33rd degree Mason and Grand Master of the Grand Orient of France, founder in 1860 of the Universal Israelite Alliance, proclaimed the following on page 651 of *the Israelite Archives,* the organ of the Alliance: "In place of the Popes and Caesars, a new kingdom, a new Jerusalem, is going to arise. And our good Masons, blindfolded, help the Jews in the 'Great Work' of building that new Temple of Solomon, that new Caesarian-Papist Kingdom of the Kabbalists!" These words of Crémieux seemed to us ideal to head this chapter, in which we will see how the good Masons, blindfolded, acted in the various historical episodes of the century at the orders of the occult power that instrumentalised them.

In principle, according to its statutes, Freemasonry was to be a secret association with philanthropic, humanitarian and progressive aims, whose aim was to change Christian civilisation into a world based on rationalist atheism. Having been imbued with the ideas of the Bavarian Enlightenment, the Freemasons, together with the Jews, began to work tirelessly for the triumph of the universal revolution. It is an established fact that in the various countries the majority of high-ranking Freemasons are Jews. On August 3, 1866, Rabbi Isaac M. Wise published in the newspaper *The Israelite,* edited by himself in the United States, the following words: "Freemasonry is a Jewish institution, whose history, degrees, costs and enlightenments are Jewish from beginning to end.

Albert Pike, indefatigable scholar of the Kabbalah and the occult, 33rd degree Freemason, world leader of Freemasonry who declared himself a priest of Lucifer, an inescapable character to whom we will devote separate attention in this chapter, writes the following in *Morals and Dogma,* his seminal work: "All genuinely dogmatic religions derive from the Kabbalah and lead back to it. Everything that is scientific and great in the religious dreams of such enlightened ones as Jacob Böhme, Swedenborg, St. Martin and the like has been borrowed from the Cabala. All Masonic associations owe their secrets and symbols to it".

Those who seek to question the Jewish control of Freemasonry argue that initially there were no Jews among the Masons and that they only appeared in the late 18th century. While this may be relatively true, it is undeniable that from the 19th century onwards Freemasonry became a form of Kabbalistic Judaism for the consumption of more or less selected gentiles. We have seen that there was a very well worked out plan in favour of Judaism. We have also seen how the admission of Jews into the lodges came about, and the importance of the Wilhelmsbad Congress, where the ideas of their emancipation triumphed. It matters little, then, whether or not there were Jews in the lodges in the beginning. We know how they achieved penetration, and in this chapter we shall continue to show the results, about which there can be no doubt: the good Crémieux Masons were the spearhead of the World Revolutionary Movement financed by the Rothschilds and other Jewish bankers. The facts and assertions about the control of international Judaism in Freemasonry are evident.

Kabbalah, the mystical heresy of Shabbetaism and Frankism

The Kabbalah is a part of the *Talmud,* but specialised, mystical, occult and secret in nature. The Kabbalistic tradition comes not only from Jewish sources, but from a great variety of pre-existing esoteric traditions: Indo-Iranian, Assyrian, Egyptian, Persian, Babylonian and Canaanite. For the Kabbalists the whole world is a "corpus symbolicum", hence so is the Kabbalah, to which all Masonic associations owe their secrets and symbols. At this point, it is necessary to delay our historical study to comment on the Kabbalah in a concise manner, in order to understand its importance in secret societies, in Freemasonry and in the Jewish neo-Messianic movement, considered heretical by many orthodox rabbis, which had its origin in Shabbetay Zeví and was continued by the Frankists and the Illuminati. In *The Great Trends in Jewish Mysticism,* Gershom Scholem, whose works on the subject are indispensable, gives an overview of Kabbalah from its origins to 19th century Hasidism, which he calls the latter stage, since there was an earlier Hasidist movement in medieval Germany. We turn to him, then, for a glimpse into the understanding of the Kabbalah by Albert Pike, who declared Lucifer to be God, and other Satanists such as Jacob Frank. It has already been said in chapter two that the Frankists, whose perversion and duplicity knew no bounds, believed that by sinning and violating the *Torah,* cosmic redemption (ticun) could be achieved.

Before its crystallisation into medieval Kabbalah, Jewish mysticism spanned a period of about a thousand years from the first century B.C. to the tenth century A.D., which Scholem calls "Merkabah mysticism" and relates to Jewish Gnosticism. The most notable documents of this movement were written in the 5th and 6th centuries. We know from the study of the Spanish mystics, St. John of the Cross and St. Teresa, that the ultimate ecstasy of mystical experience consisted in the vision of God and the union of the soul with the Beloved. In the Jewish mysticism of those centuries, however, this ultimate delirium or rapture consisted in the vision of the chariot as the throne of God (the Merkaba). The visionaries knew the hosts of heavenly angels and saw the Great Majesty, His throne and palace. "The most ancient Jewish mysticism is the mysticism of the throne. It is not the absorbed contemplation of the true nature of God," writes G. Scholem, "but the perception of his appearance on the throne, described by Ezekiel, as well as the knowledge of the mysteries of the heavenly throne-world". The sphere of the throne - the Merkaba - has its "dwellings" and its "palaces". It seems that it was even customary to place scribes or stenographers on either side of the visionary, who transcribed his ecstatic description of the throne and its occupants. On quite a few occasions the mysticism of the Merkaba degenerated into pure and simple magic.

In the second century there was already a current of heretical Jewish mystics who broke with rabbinical Judaism. The ideas of this school or group were mixed with those of Gnosticism. During the second century the boundary between Jewish Gnostics and Christian Gnostics was very thin. Most scholars of early Christianity today subscribe to the thesis of the German scholar Walter Bauer (*Orthodoxy and Heresy in Ancient Christianity*) that Christianity in Alexandria was originally Gnostic in character. He deduces this from the fact that the first Christians who are known to have been Christians in that city at the time of Hadrian were Gnostic teachers. Gnostic Christians were also considered heretics by the orthodox current. Thus in Alexandria, the capital of the Jewish diaspora, groups of Jewish and Christian Gnostics lived together and exchanged ideas.

In *The Pluriformity of Early Christianity* Gerard P. Luttikhuizen devotes a chapter to explaining the central idea about the origin of evil held by the Gnostic Christians of the second century. They believed that material reality was not created by the superior divinity, "Deus absconditus", but by a second-order divinity, the creator god or demiurge, whom they considered an adversary (the word "Satan" is of Hebrew origin and means adversary) of the superior God and an enemy of mankind. It is inappropriate to spend more time than is strictly necessary on the development of this subject. We will therefore only say that it is in the *Apocryphal of John*, the "Bible of the Gnostics", a book composed in the middle of the 2nd century and discovered in 1945 among the Nag Hammadi documents, that all the concepts are developed. The manuscript had already disappeared by the 4th century, as the theologians and leaders of the proto-orthodox church considered it to be a heretical book. The first part of the writing deals with the superior God, his thoughts or qualities, called "Aeons", conceived as purely abstract divine beings, and ends with the tragic events that gave rise to the first demonic figure, who turns out to be the creator of the material world. The second part is devoted to the creation of man and the history of the first generations. In the *Apocryphon of John,* writes Luttikhuizen, "the three levels of reality are described, namely the pure, spiritual world of the perfect God, the middle astral level of the planetary powers and the material realm of the sublunar world. These three levels would also be present in man: the spirit of the human being (the "Pneuma") is in relation to divinity, the soul to the astral and planetary world, and the body to the materiality of the sublunar world.

Gershom Scholem, referring to the stream of Jewish mystics who deviate from rabbinic teachings, warns against the danger of introducing the dualistic view of the Christian Gnostics, for whom the God of Israel, the God of the Old Testament, would not be the true, pure, spiritual and superior God, but the demiurge responsible for the appearance of a material and imperfect world. Many scholars who have dealt with this question even consider that the mythological gnosis of the *Apocrypha of John* arose in a Jewish context. According to these scholars, the disqualification of the biblical God by Jewish Gnostics would have its origin in disenchantment and frustration. Scholem also acknowledges that certain Jewish Gnostic groups who sought to remain faithful to the religious community of rabbinic Judaism kept these ideas alive. He also admits that speculation about the eons and other technical terms of Gnosticism became part of the lexical baggage of the early Kabbalists, since they are preserved in the oldest Kabbalistic text, 'the obscure and enigmatic book *Bahir*', published in Provence in the 12th century, which is itself based on an older book of Eastern origin, *Raza rabba* (*The Great Mystery*).

Following Scholem, we will outline very schematically the main milestones in the history of Kabbalism until we come immediately to Shabbettay Zeví and Jacob Frank, for what concerns us is to connect with the heresy of Shabbetaism and, from there, with the elite of international Jewish bankers who, as we already know, used Frankists and illuminati to implement the World Revolutionary Movement.

The first famous Kabbalist was Abraham ben Shemuel Abulafia, born in Saragossa in 1240, who referred to his school of practical mysticism as "Prophetic Kabbalah". He lived underground and his ecstatic experience consisted of a meditation technique reserved for a select few. The Kabbalists who followed this mystic decided not to publish his writings, as his mystical revelation conflicted with the revelation of Mount Sinai and thus with rabbinic orthodoxy. Scholem reveals that "in the year 1280, inspired by his own mission, he undertook a risky and inexplicable task: he went to Rome to appear before the Pope and argue with him on behalf of all Jews. It seems that at that time he harboured messianic ideas". The interview never took place: while Abulafia was already in Rome, Nicolas III died suddenly. The central idea of his mystical theory was to "untie" the knots that bind the soul, to overcome the barriers that separate it from the cosmic lifestream. He also developed a theory of the mystical contemplation of the letters and their configurations as constituent parts of the name of God and expounded a discipline which he called "the science of the combination of letters" ("Hojmat ha-tseruf"). The mysticism of numbers and the numerical value of words - "guematria" - were of paramount importance. Numerology became an essential element of the kabbalists. "The doctrine of the combinations of Abulafia," says Scholem, "came to be regarded by later generations not only as the key to the mysteries of the Divine, but also as an initiation into the exercise of magical powers."

Undoubtedly the greatest of the books of Kabbalistic literature is the "Sefer ha-Zohar" or *Book of Splendour,* written somewhere in Castile after 1275. Scholem considers that 'its place in the history of Kabbalah can be measured by the fact that it is the only book of post-Muddhist rabbinic literature that became a canonical text and that for several centuries it was on the same level as the Bible and the Talmud'. The authorship of the Zohar has finally been attributed to the Spanish kabbalist Moshe de Leon. A number of ideas in the *Book of Splendour* owe their development to the Gnostic school. The concept of "left emanation" appears, that is, and we quote Scholem, "an ordered hierarchy of the forces of evil, of the kingdom of Satan which, like the kingdom of light, is organised in ten spheres or stages. The Zohar agrees with Talmudic teachings in considering the souls of non-Jews or gentiles as emanating from the kingdom of demons. The ten 'holy' sefirot (spheres or regions) have their counterpart in the ten 'impure' sefirot. The latter differ from the former in that each has a very personal character. Each has a name of its own, whereas the divine 'sefirot' represent only abstract qualities such as wisdom, intelligence, and grace. The Zohar alludes to the "Deus absconditus" as "En-sof", the "Infinite". It possesses no qualities or attributes. However, to the extent that this hidden God acts in the universe, He also possesses attributes that represent certain aspects of the divine nature. There are ten fundamental attributes of God which constitute at the same time ten stages through which the divine life comes and goes. The hidden God - "En-sof" - manifests Himself to the kabbalists under ten different aspects, which in turn comprise an infinite variety of shades and degrees. Each degree has its own symbolic name. The sum total constitutes a very complex symbolic structure which the kabbalists apply to the interpretation of the Bible. The "Sefer ha-Zohar" is a very difficult text that was explored in depth by Yitshak Luria, who could spend months meditating on a verse until he found its hidden meaning.

The third inexcusable Kabbalist, then, is Yitshak Luria, born in 1534 in Jerusalem, where his father, an Ashkenazi Jew from central Europe, had emigrated after marrying a Sephardic woman. Safed, a small town in the upper Galilee, had become the centre of a new Kabbalistic movement, and it was from there that Luria's peculiar doctrines and the new Kabbalah spread. In Safed he coincided with Moshe ben Ya'acob Cordovero, whom Scholem considers the most important theorist of Jewish mysticism. Cordovero dealt with the intrinsic conflict between theistic and pantheistic tendencies in the mystical theology of the Kabbalah, which had already appeared in the Zohar. His ideas on the subject are summed up in the following formula: "God is all reality, but not all reality is God".

Luria, who died at the age of 38 in 1572, had no literary faculties and left no written legacy. Scholem says of him that "he was a visionary who did not differentiate between organic and inorganic life, but insisted that souls were present everywhere and that it was possible to communicate with them". Three important theosophical ideas, largely reminiscent of the Gnostic myths of antiquity, stand out in his system, which was made known to his disciples. The first is the theory of "tsimtsum", according to Scholem, "one of the most astonishing and far-reaching concepts ever formulated in the history of the Kabbalah", which originally means "concentration" or "contraction", but which in Kabbalistic language is better translated as "withdrawal" or "withdrawal". In short, it means that the existence of the universe is made possible by a process of God's contraction. To quote Professor Scholem's explanatory passage: "According to Luria, God was forced to make room for the world by abandoning, as it were, a zone of Himself, of His interiority, a kind of mystical primordial space from which He withdrew in order to return to the world in the act of creation and revelation. The first act of the 'En-sof', the infinite Being, is therefore not a step outwards, but a step inwards, a movement of retraction, of withdrawal into itself, of withdrawal into itself. Instead of emanation, we have the opposite: contraction".

The Gnostics believed that the demiurge who had created the world did not succeed in completely covering the divine light in man. Luria also spoke of a vestige or residue of divine light - "reshimu" - remaining in the primordial space created by the "tsimtsum" even after the withdrawal of the "En-sof". Luria used the simile of the residue of oil or wine left in a bottle whose contents have been emptied. In the work we have been discussing, Professor Scholem recognises that this idea of 'reshimu' has many elements in common with the Gnostic system of Basilides which flourished around the year 125. Basilides speaks of the relationship of the Son to the Holy Spirit or Pneuma and says that when the Pneuma became empty and separated from the Son, the Son retained the aroma which permeates everything in the upper and lower world, including amorphous matter and our own existence. Basilides also used a simile of a bowl in which the delicate fragrance of a most sweet-smelling ointment lingers even though the bowl has been carefully emptied.

Luria's other two basic ideas are the doctrine of "shebirat hakelim" or "Breaking of the Vessels" and that of "tikkun", meaning "amendment" or "reparation". We will focus only on the latter, since Shabbetaics and Frankists, as we saw in chapter two, wielded this concept to justify redemption through sin. "The mysteries of the 'ticun' constitute - in Scholem's opinion - one of the main themes of Luria's theosophical system and represent the greatest achievement ever made by anthropomorphic thought in the history of Jewish mysticism". In the process of "ticun", the scattered lights of God would be reintegrated into their rightful place. These are clearly purely spiritual processes, which again resemble the myths of gnosis. The conflict posed by Gnosticism is latent in this doctrine of Luria's and, in trying to explain it, Professor Scholem asks himself a question that alludes to the dualism of the Gnostics: "Is the 'En-sof' the personal God, the God of Israel, or is the 'En-sof' the 'Deus absconditus', the impersonal substance? For Luria the coming of the Messiah is but the consummation of the ongoing process of Restoration, of the "ticun". The true essence of the redemption," says Scholem in a very significant passage, "is mystical, and its historical and national aspects are but secondary symptoms which constitute a visible symbol of its consummation. The redemption of Israel concludes the redemption of all things, for does not redemption mean that everything is in its rightful place, that the stain of original sin has been erased? The 'world of the ticun' is thus the world of messianic action. The coming of the Messiah means that this world of the 'ticun' has received its final form". The Lurianic Kabbalah became the mystical theology of Judaism in the 17th century. In its most popular aspects it taught a doctrine of Judaism that did not renounce its messianic pathos. The doctrine of the 'ticun'," Scholem concludes, "elevated every Jew, in a hitherto unheard-of way, to the role of protagonist in the great process of restitution. It seems that Luria himself believed that the end was near and nourished the hope that the year 1575 would be the year of redemption". Unfortunately, in line with Zohar and Talmudic teachings, Luria also proclaimed the absolute superiority of the soul of Jews over that of non-Jews.

A brief biographical sketch of Shabbettay Zeví has already been given in note 6 of chapter two. Since we have now come to the mystical heresy of Shabbetaism, we refer the reader to a re-reading of that heresy and will now devote space to explaining its doctrine, but not before noting that Professor Scholem notes that Shabbetay, who left no writings or phrases worthy of mention, was a physically ill man with a manic-depressive character. Scholem considers that without his prophet, Nathan of Gaza (1644-1680), he would never have come to anything. Nathan of Gaza, who admits in some texts that the temptations to which Shabbetay was exposed in his states of depression were demonic and erotic in character, explained in a letter dated 1667, recently discovered in a Shabbetaic notebook preserved in the library of Columbia University in New York, how he knew that Shabbetay was the Messiah. Here is part of the text:

"...This same year, my strength having been stimulated by visions of angels and blessed souls, I undertook a long fast in the week following the feast of Purim. Having shut myself in a completely isolated room, in purity and holiness, and having finished morning prayer amidst many tears, the spirit appeared to me, my hair stood on end, my knees trembled, and I saw the Merkaba. I had visions of God all day and all night, and true prophecy was granted to me as to any other prophet, when the voice spoke to me and began with these words: 'Thus speaks the Lord!' and my heart perceived with absolute clarity to whom my prophecy was addressed (i.e. to Shabbetay Zeví), and until that day I had never had such an important vision, but it remained hidden in my heart until the Redeemer Himself was revealed to me in Gaza and proclaimed Himself the Messiah; only then did the angel allow me to reveal what I had seen."

It now remains to be clarified how Shabbetay Zeví proclaimed himself Messiah in Gaza. A certain Shemuel Gandor wrote a letter to Shabbetay, who was in Egypt, in which he told him of an enlightened one who in Gaza revealed to all the secret root of his soul and the particular "tikkun" it needed. Shabbetay then travelled to Gaza to see Nathan in order to find a "ticun" and peace for his soul. It was in this way that Nathan, who apparently in another hallucination had seen the figure of Shabbetay Zeví, convinced him, after wandering together for several weeks in the holy places of Palestine, to proclaim himself the Messiah. One might laugh if the repercussions were not as tragic as we shall see.

Philologist, historian and theologian, Gershom Scholem, considered the world's foremost authority on Jewish mysticism, extensively paraphrases texts by Nathan of Gaza and Shabbetaists such as Abraham Miguel Cardozo, the school's main propagandist. According to Scholem, Nathan of Gaza, in his eagerness to make an apology for the mental state of Shabbetay Zeví, made use of the very ancient Gnostic myth of the Ophites or Naassenes about the destiny of the Redeemer's soul, although he constructed it from Kabbalistic ideas, since this myth was already to be found in the doctrines of the Zohar and Luria. It is the mystical symbolism of the serpent. We reproduce Professor Scholem's disturbing paraphrase verbatim:

"After the Rupture of the Vessels, when some sparks of the divine light, which radiates the 'En-sof' in order to create forms and shapes in primordial space, fell into the abyss, the soul of the Messiah, which was part of that original divine light, also fell. From the beginning of Creation, this soul dwelt in the depths of the great abyss, held in the prison of its 'chelipot', the realm of darkness. In the depths of the abyss, along with this absolutely holy soul, dwell the 'serpents' that torment and attempt to seduce it. These 'serpents' receive the 'holy serpent' who is the Messiah, for does not the Hebrew word serpent - 'nachash' - have the same numerical value as the word 'Mashiah' - Messiah? Only to the extent that the process of the 'ticun' of the whole world results in the separation of good and evil in the depth of primordial space will the soul of the Messiah be liberated from its bondage."

The fact that Shabbetay Zeví publicly renounced his Jewish faith and committed apostasy in front of the sultan and his court should have ended his halo; but it did not. Again Nathan of Gaza came to the rescue of the Messiah he had created, explaining that by this act Shabbetay had saved all the Jews who believed in him. From this moment on, a conflict with the dogmas of rabbinical Judaism began that was to continue for centuries to come. Professor Scholem, for whom Shabbetaism represents the first serious revolt in Judaism since the Middle Ages, considers that until Shabbetay's apostasy, Lurianic Kabbalism placed greater emphasis on the spiritual nature of the Redemption than on its historical and political aspects, since, as Scholem explains, "it placed the regeneration of the inner life far above the regeneration of the nation as a political entity. At the same time, he expressed the conviction that the former was the essential precondition for the latter. Moral progress was to bring about the liberation of the people from their exile". However, the religious movement that developed as a consequence of the apostasy of the new Messiah, Scholem goes on to argue, "drove a wedge between the two spheres of the drama of Redemption: the inner sphere of the soul and the sphere of history. Inner and outer experience, the inner and outer aspects of 'Gehulah', Redemption and Salvation, were suddenly and dramatically split." Large groups of Shabbetaists who, following the example of their Messiah, saw Marranism as the way to salvation twice organised mass apostasies. In 1683 the sect of the Doenmé was formed in Salonica: this was the name given by the Turks to the apostate Jews who apparently converted to Islam (we refer the reader to note 7 in chapter two).

The mystical heresy of Shabbetaism was instrumental in creating the moral and intellectual atmosphere that was conducive to the reform movements that emerged in the late 18th and early 19th centuries. In 1776, the same year as the creation of the Illuminati, Moses Mendelsshon, who was one of the leaders of Adam Weishaupt's sect, founded the Haskala. In 1807 Israel Jacobson was the driving force behind the Reform Movement. The number of rabbis, many of them very influential, who adhered to the new sectarian mysticism gradually increased. According to Professor Scholem, "in no book of Jewish history can one find any reference to this extremely important relationship between the mystical heretics and these rationalist and Reform movements". In the course of the 18th century the sect established itself in many German cities, but above all in Bohemia and Moravia, where the most influential Jews, as well as rabbis, manufacturers and merchants, were secret adherents. Decisive in the spread of Shabbetaism was the emergence of Frankism, the sect of the followers of Jacob Frank.

The rise of the Frankist movement, the second phase of Shabbetaism which saw its consolidation as a doctrine, was undoubtedly of extraordinary gravity for the moral credibility of Judaism. For many Marranos the apostasies of Shabbetay Zeví and Jacob Frank could be seen as the religious glorification of the very act they had committed. Scholem warns: "the doctrine that the Messiah, by the very nature of his mission, could be drawn into the inevitable tragedy of apostasy was ideal for providing an emotional outlet for the tormented conscience of the Marranos". The new messianic freedom subverted the old order and contradicted traditional values. Abraham Perez, a disciple of Nathan in Salonika, in a tract written in 1668 already openly declared that those who remained faithful in the new world to the rabbinic tradition, that is, to the real and existing Judaism in the "Galut" (exile), were to be considered sinners. The full quotation of a paragraph by Professor Scholem will help to understand the magnitude of the subversion:

"The consequences of these religious ideas were absolutely nihilistic, especially that of the conception of a voluntary Marranism under the motto: We all have to descend into the realm of evil in order to overcome it from within. Under various theoretical approaches, the apostles of nihilism preached the doctrine of the existence of spheres in which it is no longer possible to carry on the process of 'ticun' by pious acts; Evil must be fought with evil. This gradually leads us to a position which, as the history of religion shows, happens by tragic necessity in every crisis of the religious spirit. I refer to the baleful and at the same time fascinating doctrine of the holiness of sin. This doctrine reflects in a remarkable way the combination of two very different elements: the world of moral decay, and another, more primitive one, which is the region of the soul in which long dormant forces are capable of a sudden resurrection. That both elements participated in the religious nihilism of Shabbetaism, which in the eighteenth century proved so dangerous to Judaism's most precious asset, its moral substance, finds no better proof than the tragic history of its last phase: the Frankist movement."

Jacob Frank (1726-1791) was born in Korolowka, in the eastern part of the Polish province of Galicia. The son of a rabbi and follower of Shabbetay Zeví, he was initiated in Smyrna into the mysteries of the Kabbalah by a certain rabbi named Issakhar. On one occasion Frank asked his teacher why Shabbetay Zeví had to die. Issakhar replied, "Shabbetay Zeví came to enjoy everything, including the bitterness of death." Then he asked again, "Why then did he not enjoy the sweetness of power?". On the advice of this kabbalist, Frank travelled to Salonika, where he arrived in 1753. There he became acquainted with the teachings of the Doenmes and decided to proclaim himself Messiah. He went to the main synagogue in the city and announced that he was the reincarnation of Shabbetay Zeví. Frank, who had married a woman named Hanna, claimed that he had had a vision in which Shabbetay Zeví asked him to continue his work; but the Jews of Thessaloniki did not follow his story and irritably reviled him. Then, according to him, he had a new vision and decided to return to Poland, although he did so alone, for he left his wife in Nicopol (Bulgaria), where his daughter Eva, who would later succeed him at the head of the sect, was born. It was in his native Korolowka that his halo was forged with the proclamation of the doctrine of salvation through sin, a new materialistic and hedonistic religion that sought the end of traditional rabbinical law. The pleasures of sex were characteristic of the sect: married women, for example, indulged in all sorts of excesses with other men in the presence of their husbands; incestuous relations were common practice; a woman named Hanna, the daughter of a rabbi, a kind of Frankist priestess, recited whole passages from the *Zohar* while enjoying the raptures of coitus. In 1756 the Frankists were excommunicated by the orthodox rabbis and tried to cross over to Turkey, but were rejected, probably due to pressure from the rabbis themselves. Frank, who had Turkish nationality, managed to enter and once there, following the example of Shabbety Zeví, he and a group of disciples became Muslims. Years later, before the court of the Warsaw Inquisition, he justified his behaviour on the grounds that he needed to keep up appearances. The new followers of Muhammad obtained safe conduct from the sultan and returned to Poland, where, under the protection of the Polish king, they decided to convert to Catholicism.

In 1759, in Lemberg, the capital of eastern Galicia, twelve hundred Jews, followers of the sinister prophet Jacob Frank, were baptised en masse in the Catholic cathedral. This was three years after the synod of the Polish Jewish community had pronounced anathema on the Frankists.[19] Let us

---

[19] To take revenge on the orthodox rabbis who persecuted them, Jakob Frank even dared to denounce to Catholic priests that Jews committed ritual crimes with Christian children and used their blood to celebrate the Purim festival. Gershom Scholem himself in his work *Le messianisme juif* quotes the historian Meir Balaban, who in turn reports a conversation that took place in 1759 in Lvov between Rabbi Chaim Rappaport and the Frankist Eliezer Jezierzany, who said to the former: "Chaim, we have given you blood for blood. You pretended to legalise the shedding of our blood and now you have been given blood for blood". Judah David Eisenstein, Otzar Yisroel, in an encyclopaedia (*Hebrew Publishing*) written in Hebrew within the scope of the *Jewish Encyclopaedia*, revealed in 1917 a case that perfectly illustrates the extent of the hatred between the orthodox rabbis and the Frankists. Otzar Yisroel recounts that in the small "shtetl" (small Jewish town in Yiddish) of Villovich, the Frankists took revenge on the town's rabbi by dressing and characterising one of his wives as the rabbi's wife. The disguise was so perfect that she had the courage to go before a Catholic priest to accuse her husband of having sacrificed a Christian child for the Jewish Passover. According to Yisroel the consequences of the incident were dire, as the rabbi and several members of his congregation were tried and sentenced to death.

recall that Jacob Frank himself was baptised in Warsaw Cathedral and that his godfather was King Augustus III. (These facts have already been reported in the section "Frankists and Illuminati" in Chapter Two).) The members of both groups continued to call themselves "maaminin", a common term used by the Shabbetaists to refer to themselves, meaning believers in the mission of Shabbetay Zeví. Evidently these conversions were only extrinsic.

Although nihilistic doctrines are not usually proclaimed publicly, and if they are written down they are presented with many reservations, the gospel that Jacob Frank preached to his disciples is contained in *The Words of the Lord*, a work with more than two thousand dogmatic sayings. This, according to Scholem, "unique document" was preserved because of the enthusiasm and devotion of his followers, who considered their teacher "the incarnation of God". The most fanatical disciples indulged in indescribable rituals in which they sought to achieve the ultimate moral degradation of the human personality: "he who plunged into the most extreme depths was most likely to see the light". According to the *Talmud*, "the son of David will only come in an age either completely guilty or absolutely innocent." From this epigram the Shabbetaist Frankists formulated a maxim: "since we cannot all be saints, let us all be sinners."

In conclusion, we will give the floor again to Professor Scholem in order to understand through his conclusions what was the solution proposed by the Shabbetaists to the mystery of God. It was a new form of Gnostic dualism of the hidden God and the God who created the world:

"The Shabbetaists distinguish between the hidden God, whom they call the 'First Cause', and the revealed God, who is the 'God of Israel'. The existence of a first cause is, in their view, self-evident to every rational being, and its knowledge forms an essential part of our consciousness. No creature capable of employing intelligence can fail to perceive the necessity of a First Cause of existence. But the knowledge we receive through our reasoning has no religious significance. Religion is not concerned with the First Cause at all; its essence lies in the revelation of something which the mind alone cannot apprehend. The First Cause has nothing to do with the world or with creation; it does not exercise providence or retribution. It is the God of the philosophers, the God of Aristotle whom, according to Cardozo, even Nimrod himself, Pharaoh and the pagans worshipped. The God of religion, on the other hand, is the God of Sinai. The Torah, the documentary proof of revelation, says nothing about the hidden root of all being, about which we know nothing except that it exists, and which is never revealed to anyone anywhere. Revelation alone has the right to speak, and does so, of that 'God of Israel' (Elohé Israel), who is the creator of all, but at the same time is Himself the First Effect of the First Cause. While the ancient Gnostics despised the God of Israel, the Shabbethites despised the unknown God. According to them, the error committed by Israel in exile consists in having confused the First Cause with the First Effect, the God of Reason with the God of Revelation".

It is clear from this passage of Scholem's that for the Shabbetaist and Frankist sectarians the God of Israel was not the "First Cause", the "Deus absconditus", but the demiurge alluded to by the Gnostics, the adversary ("Satan") of the superior God, the enemy of humanity who would have created the world. At the beginning of the 19th century, the children of Frankist families in Prague, who were educated in the spirit of the sect, continued to make pilgrimages to Offenbach, where in 1786, after his alliance with Weishaupt, Jacob Frank had taken up residence in the castle of the Duke of Isenburg, a Freemason who belonged to the Order of the Illuminati. He lived there until his death in 1791.

From enlightenment to communism

The alliance of the Illuminati and the Frankists, the role they played in the French Revolution, their use of Freemasonry, as well as the instrumentalisation of these sects by an elite of Jewish bankers was sufficiently established in chapter two. It is now time to take up and reinforce the ideas put forward in order to show how these same driving forces of the World Revolutionary Movement set communism in motion.

The first thing to consider is that the Frankist elite, which like the Rothschilds practised inbreeding and intermarriage, was perfectly organised in the 19th century. It included powerful Jewish bankers such as Isaac Daniel von Itzig, whose family supplied Prussia with silver to mint coins. This Berlin magnate was a prominent leader of the Asiatic Order, which was dominated by Shabbetaist conceptions and practised Frankist rites. David Friedländer, his son-in-law, was also a Frankist brother in the lodge. Both had belonged to the Haskala movement, Moses Mendelssohn's decisive reform circle[20], and both were co-founders of the Jewish Free School in

---

[20] Orthodox Rabbi Marvin S. Antelman refers in the second volume of *To Eliminate the Opiate* to a little known document in Hebrew, a letter to Christoph Friedrich Nicolai, a famous Masonic bookseller who belonged to the Illuminati, which was located in the Schiff (the banker who financed the Bolsheviks) collection of the New York Public Library. It lists the leader of the Illuminati, Moses Mendelssohn, as a high priest of the reformist Gnostic rabbinate. In this document there is a record of the ordination line of the high priests of the new neo-Messianic creed, which is as follows: Shabbetay Zevi (1626-1676), Nathan of Gaza (1643-1680), Solomon Ayllon (1655-1728), Nechemiah Chiyon (1655-1729), Judah Leib Prossnitz (1670-1730), Jonathan Eibeschutz (1690-1764) and Moses Mendelssohn (1729-1786). Orthodox rabbis such as Antelman consider these Reform priests of a neo-Platonic Gnosticism that seeks to destroy the traditional Jewish clergy. David Philippson in *The Reform Movement in Judaism* reports of a meeting in Berlin in 1845, at which the Reform rabbis, having usurped the authority of the Orthodox, imparted blessings to the congregation.

Berlin, which in 1796 changed its name to the "Oriental Printing Office", with its own influential press that enabled it to become an effective instrument of cultural reform in the service of the Illuminati. Moses Dobrushka himself, a cousin of Jakob Frank and one of the founders of the Order, married Elke Joss, the granddaughter and adopted daughter of his uncle, the Frankist banker Joachim von Popper, who before adopting this noble name was called Jaim Breznitz. One of his sisters, Franceska Dobrushka, was related to the Hönigs. Israel Hönig succeeded in gaining a tobacco monopoly in Austria. His business partner, Aaron Moses, had ten children, all of whom were baptised in 1796. Another powerful Frankist, Bernhard Gabriel Eskeles, had married the daughter of Rabbi Samson Wertheimer, who at the beginning of the 18th century was considered one of the richest Jews in Europe. Their son Bernhard von Eskeles, whose birth cost his mother her life, was a banker and court Jew in Vienna. He married Cecilia Itzig, daughter of the ubiquitous Daniel Itzig. Bernhard von Eskeles entered into a partnership with another Frankish banker, his brother-in-law Nathan Arnstein. Thus was born the Arnstein and Eskeles banking house, which played a prominent role in the Congress of Vienna. We could follow the links in an endless chain, but that seems sufficient.

In *Le messianisme juif*, Professor Scholem reports that around 1820 the Frankists, as the Illuminati had done, went underground and kept their activity hidden inside the Masonic organisations. According to Scholem, their emissaries went from town to town and from house to house to try to collect all the secret writings in order to control them. One should not think, however, that their intellectual and economic position weakened, for exactly the opposite was the case. The centre of their activity shifted from Frankfurt-Offenbach to Prague and later to Warsaw. Today they are part of the international group organised around the cult of the "All-Seeing Eye". This does not prevent them from being dominant in the United States, for example, in the Anti-Defamation League, the American Jewish Congress and Jewish lawyers' groups.

We are now in a position to understand that from Shabbetaism, the Kabbalistic movement that revolutionised the traditional conceptions of Orthodox Judaism, an elite of wealthy Jews, at the head of which the Rothschild dynasty was consolidated, understood in the course of the 18th century that in order to gain total control of the countries and societies into which they had entered, in addition to the economic domination traditionally exercised through usury, it was necessary to gain ideological, political, social and cultural control. To do this, it was necessary to break out of the ghetto that the rabbis had self-imposed on themselves since the Levites forbade mixed marriages on pain of death and locked themselves behind the walls of Jerusalem. Jacob Frank had explained to his disciples that baptism would be the beginning of the end of the Church, that apostasy was necessary to destroy the enemy from within and that the true Jewish faith had to be kept secret. Consequently, various movements and organisations were created, ostensibly promoting ideas of emancipation, reform, assimilation and social integration. At the same time, using men like Jacob Frank and Adam Weishaupt (others were to follow), it was decided to create subversive sects that were to use Freemasonry and make use of it to impose the World Revolutionary Movement.

The Bavarian Order of Illuminati entered the United States when the revolution that led to the country's independence was already underway and had no significant influence on it. However, before the thirteen colonies established the Republic and the Constitution was adopted, fifteen Illuminati lodges were already established in the young country. Columbia Lodge was founded in New York in 1785 and Clinton Roosevelt was one of its most prominent leaders. In 1786 the Virginia Lodge was founded, whose leader was Thomas Jefferson, a fervent Illuminatus who, when the Order was discovered in Bavaria, defended Weishaupt and called him an "enthusiastic philanthropist ". When Weishaupt died in 1830, the foundations of communism were already well established in Europe, as will be seen, and were also taking root in America.

In 1829, the Scottish-born Frances ("Fanny") Wright gave a series of lectures at Tammany Hall, a Masonic lodge in Virginia, organised by American Illuminati in which she advocated Weishaupt's full programme. Attendees were informed that the Illuminati intended to unite nihilists, atheist groups and other subversive organisations into a communist-intended organisation, the strength of which was to be used to foment future revolutions. To raise funds for the new enterprise, a committee was appointed, including Charles Dana, Horace Greeley and Clinton Roosevelt, the family ancestor of the future Franklin Delano Roosevelt. Nominated in 1836 by the Democratic Party and emboldened by success, in 1841, twelve years after the famous Tammany Hall session and seven years before Karl Marx, Clinton Roosevelt published in New York *The Science of Government, Founded on Natural Law, a* book that plagiarised Weishaupt's teachings and once again proposed the communist programme of the Illuminati.

Dr. Emanuel M. Josephson, an American physicist and historian of Jewish origin, in *Roosevelts' Communist Manifesto* (1955) considers Adam Weishaupt the father of communism, since Clinton Roosevelt's proposals and those put forward by Marx seven years later do nothing more than reproduce Weishaupt's ideas. In Roosevelt's case, the doctrine is slightly adapted to the American scenario. Weishaupt demanded that all arts, sciences and religions be abolished and proposed that they be replaced by the only true science based on "natural law". Among the proposals of Clinton Roosevelt, who set himself up as a defender of the working class, was to destroy the Constitution, which he compared to "a sinking ship", in order to establish the dictatorship he called the "new social order". Weishaupt had ordained that the superiors of the Order should be regarded as the most perfect and intelligent men and should not be allowed to doubt their infallibility. Clinton Roosevelt proposed himself as one of these infallibles and declared his contempt for God: "There is no God of justice to rightly order things on earth; if there were a God, he is a vengeful and wicked being who created us out of misfortune".

Karl Marx and Moses Hess, Frankist-Shabbetaist Jews

Universities, institutes and educational centres in general present Karl Marx as one of the most important intellectuals of the 19th century. Students, unable to discover that Marxism is a prestigious ideology that has nothing prestigious about it, helplessly accept the doctrines of the international left, which continues to regard Marx as an untouchable holy man. So let us now provide some little known information about this "good mason" of the 31st degree, Frankist and enlightened, at the service of international bankers who protected him. In the second volume of *To Eliminate the Opiate*, Rabbi Antelman uncovers unknown aspects of Marx that are very significant. Like his 18th and 19th century colleagues, this orthodox rabbi fiercely denounces the Shabbetaic-Frankist-Enlightenment conspiracy as a heresy that has subverted Judaism.

Karl Marx's (1818-1883) father, Heinrich, was the son of the chief rabbi of Trier, Meir Levi, whose father-in-law, Moses Lwow, had himself been chief rabbi of the same city. It was therefore the father, Heinrich Levi, who overnight changed his surname to Marx. What happened was that, after the death of his grandfather, Karl Marx's father was tempted or, perhaps better, bribed by Shabbetaic groups, who encouraged his appointment as a judge, prompted his conversion to Christianity out of love for the cause, and - in the words of Rabbi Antelman - "initiated him into Satanic Shabbetaist illuminism". Thus Karl Marx, whose Christianity was only the consequence of a social manoeuvre, came to be at the service of the conspiracy. So was his sister Louise, who married Jan Carel Juta. The couple moved to South Africa, where Jan Carel was very influential among the judges in Cape Town. Their son, Harry Herbert Juta, served the conspiracy as attorney general to Prime Minister Cecil J. Rhodes, the great gold and diamond magnate who in his third will bequeathed everything to Lord Rothschild, Natty de Rothschild. Rhodes and Rothschild were the driving forces behind Fabian socialism and the secret society known as "Round Table". Harry Herbert Juta's daughter married Sir Courtney Forbes, who served the interests of the English enlightened internationalists as British secretary for Mexico, Spain and later ambassador to Peru.[21]

---

[21] Rabbi Antelman's source for this data is the book *The Unbroken Chain: Biographical Sketches and Genealogy of Illustrious Jewish Families from the 15th-20th Century*,

Marx was given the name Moses Mordechai Levi at birth. It was at the age of six that he was baptised and became Karl Heinrich. He attended a Jesuit school that had been restructured into a secular school, but at the same time attended a Talmudic school. Already Karl Marx's youthful poems are disturbing: they are full of threats, hatred and violence, which shows that he remained faithful to the principles of the Frankist sect, whose members, as we know, passed for Christians, but inwardly remained Jews. In *Oulanem*, a little-known tragedy written in verse by Marx in 1839, Satanism and the Frankist idea of salvation at through sin is very evident. In this play all the characters are aware of their degradation, of their own corruption, which they flaunt and even celebrate with full conviction.

In 1841, at the age of 23, he met his mentor, Moritz Moses Hess, whose work *Rome and Jerusalem*, as seen in the previous chapter, is considered a precursor of Zionism. Professor Nachum Glatzer claims that Hess divined the intellectual potential of the young Marx and introduced him to the doctrine of communism. Like Marx, Moses Hess was also a Frankist-Shabbetaist. His membership of the sect goes back to his great-grandfather, David T. Hess, who was promoted to Chief Rabbi of Mannheim as soon as the Shabbetaists gained a foothold in the city thanks to their economic power. According to Rabbi Antelman, the rise of the Shabbetaist-Frankish connection throughout Europe was facilitated by the adherence of wealthy followers, among whom he mentions "some Rothschilds". Precisely Moses Hess himself declared that the brutal struggle to impose socialist power should be waged under the red banner of the Rothschild family. No doubt it may seem incredible that Hess, who proclaimed that private property should be abolished, should appeal to the richest family in the world to lead the revolution of the proletariat, but so it is: the facts are incontestable. This Zionist leader knew perfectly well, as did Heine, Marx himself, Trotsky and so many others, that the struggle of the proletariat was in reality the use of this social class by the leaders of the MRM to impose their programme of global domination. In his *Red Catechism for the German People* Moses Hess writes: "The red flag symbolises the permanent revolution until the complete victory of the working class in all civilised countries.... The socialist revolution is my religion..... Since the dawn of history we Jews have propagated the belief in a messianic world epoch". For Hess the social revolution was something akin to a final judgement that was to bring them "the Sabbath of History". In *Rome and Jerusalem* (1862), in which he directly appealed to the Rothschilds to buy Palestine, Hess's priorities underwent a fundamental change: "the racial struggle is the main thing, the class struggle is secondary". This is the unambiguous expression of the new messianism: the objective of the Jews must be the establishment of the

---

written by Neil Rosenstein and published in New York in 1976. The book has been republished, although this first edition is still accessible. We cite it in the bibliography for readers who may be interested in pursuing this line further.

messianic state in Palestine "to prepare mankind for the revelation of the divine essence". Moses Hess had founded the *Rheinische Zeitung* in 1841 and a year later made Marx its editor.

Marx, Heine and Hess in Paris

Before turning to the gestation of the Communist Manifesto and the revolutions of 1848, we will go back a few years to follow in Marx's footsteps in Paris. In 1819 a cousin of Moses Hess, the Frankist rabbi Leopold Zunz, whose Jewish name was Yom-Tob Lippman, in collaboration with other German Jews belonging to rabbinical families, had founded the association "Verein für Kultur und Wissenchaft der Juden" (Union for the Culture and Science of the Jews). In 1823, under the auspices of the Union and edited by Leopold Zunz himself, the journal *Zeitschrifft für die Wissenschaft des Judentums* (*Journal for the Science of Judaism*) appeared[22]. Gershom Scholem in *Le messianisme juif* places Leopold Zunz in Prague in 1835, where he was a preacher for the city's Shabbetaist-Frankists. Forced to resign by the orthodox rabbis, another communist and Frankist leader named Michael J. Sachs took his place and carried out the same mission. Leopold Zunz later founded a school in Berlin, the "Hochschule für die Wissenschaft des Judentums" (School for the Science of Judaism), where prominent leaders of the movement, such as Rabbi Abraham Geiger, who was very close to James Rothschild, taught. The programme of Zunz's association was partly a continuation of the work of Moses Mendelssohn, but at the same time it already outlined that of the future Universal Israelite Alliance, which was to be founded in 1861 by our old acquaintance Adolphe Crémieux. The main idea of the leaders of the Union for the Culture and Science of the Jews was the announcement of a new messianism, that of the heretical sect of Shabbetaism: the rabbis had made a mistake in expecting a human Messiah, they had misunderstood the old rabbinical texts. It was the Jewish people themselves, and not one or other of their children, who,

---

[22] Flavien Brenier, from whose texts in the *Revue de Paris* of 1928, signed under the pseudonym Salluste, some of the information comes, in an article written to refute a reply by Rabbi Liber, reports that in 1824 the Union for the Culture and Science of the Jews announced its dissolution. The aforementioned rabbi attributes this to funding problems, a reason that seems absurd considering the financial support the Reform movement had. Flavien Brenier points to the real cause, which was none other than the danger of being subjected to persecution by the Prussian police, who, alarmed by its propaganda, were suspicious of its teachings aimed at "civilising the Jews" and foresaw the dangers of the "reform of Judaism". Prussia therefore decided to keep a close eye on the Union for the Culture and Science of the Jews. Flavien Brenier or Salluste doubts that it would disappear and recalls that anyone who studies secret societies knows that the first measure of an association of conspirators that feels persecuted is to proclaim that it has ceased to exist. The fact that its leaders continued to meet and that the orientation of its political activities continued under other forms of association proves him right.

realising their ethnic superiority, were to conquer the world and bring it under the yoke of the chosen race.

Although he converted to Christianity in 1825, among the leaders and enthusiastic supporters of the Union was the romantic poet Heinrich Heine. Recall that Heine knew so much about the plans of the directors of the MRM that six years in advance he was able to announce that after some rehearsals communism was awaiting the order to enter the scene. He also announced that one day there would be a global government: "there will be only one fatherland, namely the Earth"; and he was the first to use the expression "dictatorship of the proletariat". It is clear that his information came from a source located in the heights of the conspiracy. If we remember that his friendship with James Rothschild was so close that they even walked arm in arm, this source can be none other than the Rothschild family itself. It should come as no surprise, then, that this "romantic" poet and salon revolutionary, whom James Rothschild enriched by advising him on how to invest in the stock market, had this to say:

"No one does more to further the revolution than the Rothschilds themselves... and, though it may seem even stranger, these Rothschilds, the bankers of kings, these magnificent possessors of money, whose existence might be most seriously endangered by the collapse of the European system of states, have, nevertheless, in their minds a perfect consciousness of their revolutionary mission. I see in Rothschild," he continues, "one of the greatest revolutionaries that modern democracy has ever established. Rothschild... by raising the system of State bonds to supreme power, thus mobilising property and revenue, and at the same time endowing money with the ancient privileges of land, destroyed the predominance of land. Thus he created a new aristocracy."

When he refused to accept the censorship of the *Rheinische Zeitung* intended by the Berlin authorities because of the mass agitation promoted by the newspaper, Karl Marx expatriated and landed in Paris in 1844. There Heinrich Heine was waiting for him, who, twenty years his senior, immediately saw what he could gain from the young Marx and put him in touch with Arnold Ruge, a German refugee who in 1840 had founded an important journal, *Annales Franco-Germanes*, whose contributors included Bakunin, who signed under the pseudonym of Jules Elysard. This Arnold Ruge was the head of "Young Germany", a section of "Young Europe" founded by Giuseppe Mazzini in 1834, which brought together the most prominent elements of Carbonariism and Freemasonry. Four years after the death of Adam Weishaupt, Mazzini, the Italian revolutionary leader about whom we shall write later, had been appointed by the Illuminati as director of the revolutionary programme, a position in which he remained until his death in 1872. It is significant that Heine, a lecturer at the Union for the

Culture and Science of the Jews, referred to this association as the "Young Palestine"[23].

The young revolutionaries Heine was introducing to Ruge, exiles from Germany who arrived in Paris eager to write for the revolution, were all Jews and the sons or close relatives of rabbis. Among them was also Friedrich Engels, who was younger than Marx and also came from a rabbinical family in Barmen; and Ferdinand Lassalle, grandson of a Breslau rabbi, a haughty, insolent, smartly dressed young man, of whom Heine wrote that "he was one of these tough gladiators who marched fiercely to the supreme combat". Arnold Ruge soon realised that his publication was getting out of hand, as it defended ideas he did not share. The editorial board of the journal and the committee of correspondence with the secret sections in Germany were filled with young Jews in complete solidarity with Marx. Ruge thus lost control of the publication to Marx and his team of young intellectuals, which is why he chose to resign and leave France. Marx also managed to replace Ruge as head of the secret committees of Young Germany without the substitution becoming public knowledge.

The presence in Paris of Moses Hess in 1844 together with Marx, Heine and Engels is mentioned by various authors. Jüri Lina states in *Under the sign of the scorpion* that Hess had connections with the Illuminati and that it was he who introduced Marx and Engels to Freemasonry: both were 31st degree Freemasons. Rabbi Antelman and Jüri Lina agree that it was Hess who connected Marx with the men behind the "Bund", i.e. the Illuminati. Antelman argues that it is through Moses Hess that the connection between Shabbethism, Illuminism and Communism can best be understood: "his life is the master key to unlocking and understanding the extent of the Illuminati-Communist conspiracy". The works that Antelman uses and on which he relies for his strong assertions are those of E. Silberner (1910-1985) and Theodore Zlocisti (1873-1943). The latter, a pioneer among Zionists in Germany, settled in Palestine after World War I and in 1921 published in German the most comprehensive study of Hess, *Moses Hess, der Vorkämpfer des Sozialismus und Zionismus* (*Moses Hess: The Champion of Socialism and Zionism*).[24]

---

[23] The nationalist or Zionist connotation is obvious: it was not for nothing that Moses Hess and Heine were close friends. On the other hand, the political meaning is clear, for all the revolutionary committees that were formed in Europe were called thus: the "Young Italy", the "Young Switzerland" or, later, the "Young Turks".

[24] Jüri Lina also cites this work. In addition, Zlocisti compiled Hess's correspondence, which did not see the light of day during his lifetime, but was published in Hebrew by G. Kressel in 1947 under the title *Moshe Hess Ub'nai Doro* (*Moses Hess and His Contemporaries*). Edmund Silberner, a Pole by birth and a professor at prestigious European and American universities, published several books on Hess while living in Israel, the most valuable of which is the one published in Hebrew in 1955, entitled *El socialismo en Europa occidental y el problema judío, 1800-1918* (*Socialism in Western*

The League of the Righteous and the *Communist Manifesto*

A meeting took place at the Socialist lodge in Brussels on 5 July 1843. There, the Masonic leader Joseph Marie Ragon submitted for consideration the draft for the revolutionary plan of action that was later to be embodied in the Communist Manifesto. The proposal was sent to the highest Masonic authority in the country, The Supreme Council of Belgium, which unanimously accepted Ragon's anarchist programme "equivalent to the Masonic doctrine concerning the social question which the world, which is united to the Grand Orient, should endeavour to put into practice by every conceivable means". On 17 November 1845 Marx and Engels joined this lodge in Brussels, the city in which they were living after their expulsion from France, which, despite Heine's attempts to prevent it, had come about at the demand of the Prussian government, which had been watching Marx closely since the closure of the *Rhine Gazette*. In 1847 both Marx and Engels became members of the League of the Righteous ("Bund der Gerechten"), one of the clandestine branches of the Illuminati, where, curiously enough, the Jew Jacob Venedey, whom we shall meet again when examining the *Protocols of the Elders of Zion*, played an important role.

Communism was already well designed by the time of Weishaupt's death. The occult masterminds who wanted to establish it had in 1836 led to the founding of the "Bund" in Paris, which was run by revolutionary socialist Jews. When, on 12 May 1939, the "Societé de Saisons", a secret organisation led by the socialist Freemason Louis Auguste Blanqui[25], called for a coup to seize power in France, the League of the Righteous, led by Joseph Moll and Karl Christian Schapper, two Jewish Freemasons, joined the attempt. A provisional government was even formed and military commanders were enlisted to lead the fighting, but the plan failed. The centre of gravity of the organisation then shifted from Paris to London, the Mecca where conspirators of all kinds have always made their pilgrimage and found refuge. It was there that the members of the League of the Righteous took refuge. In London, this German secret society gradually became international. No wonder, then, that it was in the English capital that the text

---

Europe and the Jewish problem, 1800-1918). In 1966 he also brought to press in German an extensive biography of nearly seven hundred pages, *Moses Hess: Geschichte seines Lebens* (*Moses Hess: History of his Life*). Some of these works are now available in English for the interested reader.

[25] Louis Auguste Blanqui, in collaboration with the Carbonari, had earlier founded another organisation known as the Families, in which each Family consisted of twelve members. In 1836 he was discovered, but it took him less than a year to found the "Society of the Seasons. Paul H. Koch, in his *Illuminati The Secrets of the sect most feared by the Catholic Church*, explains how it worked. The basic unit was the Week, composed of six members and led by a seventh. The sevenths of four Weeks met and formed a Month. Three Months had a Station as head and organiser. Four Stations were under a revolutionary chief, who, according to Koch, was appointed by the Illuminati.

calling on the workers to establish the so-called dictatorship of the proletariat finally appeared. The League of the Righteous, "der Bund", behind which were the most prominent Illuminati in Germany, soon spread to Belgium, Poland and other countries on the Continent. Karl Marx was hired by this organisation to draft the Communist Manifesto.

Paul H. Koch states categorically in *Illuminati* that the cheques with which Marx was rewarded for the production of his famous works, written on behalf of the League, were paid by the Rothschilds and points out that the original writings proving this are kept in the document collections of the British Museum. It was again Moses Hess who in November 1847 proposed transforming the League of the Righteous into a communist party. Before the end of the year Marx and Engels reorganised the League, which became the League of Communists. Finally, on 21 February 1848, the *Communist Manifesto* was published in London. Although it added basically nothing new to the texts of Adam Weishaupt and Clinton Roosevelt, the text would come to be regarded as one of the most influential political documents in history. The proletariat, the most disadvantaged class of society, conveniently manipulated, was henceforth to be used by the agents of the "money aristocracy", finance capital, to dispossess the landed aristocracy and the industrial bourgeoisie of their wealth in order to seize international power and ultimately impose a New World Order.

When the thirteen banking families decided to implement the plan to take control of all countries using the MRM, they started from a fundamental premise: the end justifies the means. The *Communist Manifesto* clearly states that force must be used to conquer the world: "We can only achieve our aims by overthrowing the established order through violence". At the same time as the expression "dictatorship of the proletariat" was used, an appeal was made to freedom to justify the class struggle and to seize property. Through propaganda, the workers began to be exhorted not to shy away from civil war in order to achieve their aims. The quotation from a text by Lenin makes this quite clear. In a letter of 17 October 1914 to Alexander Shlyapnikov Lenin wrote: "The lesser evil in the immediate sphere would be the defeat of Tsarism in the war [...] The whole essence of our work is to direct ourselves towards the transformation of the war into a civil war." Four years later, in 1918, another of Trotsky's words in the *Protocols of the Fourth Session of the Central Executive Committee* insists on the same idea: "Our party is in favour of civil war. Civil war is the struggle for bread..... Long live civil war!

Marx was simply a pawn used by those operating behind the scenes to draft a programme that did not belong to him. For twenty years after the publication of the text his name did not even appear in connection with the *Communist Manifesto*. If anything was missing from Weishaupt's plans, it was the lack of an instrument capable of accelerating the implementation of his plans for world domination and the destruction of the traditional structures of society: family, property, inheritance, fatherland, religion. In theory, the plan he devised to control opinion and spread new ideas through the press and book publishing was well conceived and was progressively implemented with enormous success. However, what was missing was the ultimate idea that would both deceive and delude the masses: communism and the dictatorship of the proletariat. A letter sent to Karl Marx in 1848 by Rabbi Baruch Levy dispels any doubts. The text, published by the *Revue de Paris* on 1 June 1928, as well as by the Dutch historian Herman de Vries de Heekelingen in the French edition of his work *Israël. Son passé. Son avenir (Israel. Its past. Its future)*, and also by the Swedish professor Einar Alberg in various publications, reads as follows:

> "The Jewish people will collectively be their Messiah. Their kingdom over the universe will be obtained by the unification of the other human races, the abolition of frontiers and monarchies, which are the bulwarks of particularism, and the establishment of a universal republic which will everywhere recognise the rights of citizenship to the Jews. In this new organisation of humanity, the children of Israel, now scattered in every corner of the earth, all of the same race and of the same traditional background, without, however, forming a distinct nationality, will everywhere, without opposition, become the ruling class; especially if they succeed in bringing the working masses under their exclusive control. The governments of the constituent nations of the future universal republic will fall, without effort, into the hands of the Israelites, thanks to the victory of the proletariat. Private property can then be abolished by the rulers of the Jewish race, who will everywhere administer the public funds. Thus will be realised the promise of the Talmud, according to which, when the time of the Messiah comes, the Jews will possess the property of all the peoples of the earth."

The revolutions of 1848

The haste and eagerness with which the revolutions were unleashed despite the slim prospects of success are incomprehensible. Only hidden interests can explain the urgency of those who launched the attempts when conditions were not ripe and failure was foreseeable. It is unreasonable to think that those who passed for experts in political and economic sociology were so wrong in their foresight. Perhaps the explanation is that in the end it mattered little to use and sacrifice the masses of manipulated workers, cannon fodder. The revolutions were predestined to fail and perhaps what was really intended was a rehearsal for the future. If we compare 1848 with 1917, for example, we see how the Bolsheviks, apart from the fact that they were financed by international Jewish bankers, managed to impose the revolution in Russia because there was no consolidated middle class, no well-established bourgeoisie. There they were able to use and deceive the peasantry, as will be seen in due course, in order, together with the workers of the big cities, to carry out a genocidal revolution which at the same time constitutes the greatest robbery in history, an unprecedented plundering of private property. But in the France and Europe of 1848, this was impossible and it is unlikely that it was not known. The French peasantry, for example, conservative by nature, tightly clinging to their property, did not even want to hear about communal ownership of the land they cultivated and did not join the urban proletariat in 1848. He was therefore treated with the utmost contempt by Marx. The petty bourgeoisie, considered the people when it allies itself with the proletariat, is the object of harsh reproaches when it clings to its humble shops and trades. The restrictive use of the word "people" comes precisely from the failure of that revolution. It was from then on that socialists and communists considered only the industrial proletariat as the people.

In 1844 Benjamin Disraeli wrote: "There is no more vulgar error than to believe that revolutions are produced for economic reasons. They come, no doubt, very frequently to precipitate a catastrophe". Official history, however, justifies the revolutions of 1848 by arguing that they were due to economic and social circumstances. Marxist historians frequently reproduce the theses and analyses of Marx and Engels, which allude to international causes. In the essay *The Class Struggles in France (1848 to 1850)*, Marx states that "two world economic events accelerated the outbreak of general discontent and caused unrest to ripen into revolt". The first was the potato blight and crop failures of 1845 and 1846. The second was the general crisis of trade and industry in England, "which led to the bankruptcies of the great colonial merchants in London, closely followed by those of the agricultural banks and the closures of factories in the industrial districts of England. The repercussions of this crisis on the Continent had not yet subsided," he adds, "when the February revolt broke out. Marx offers in the above work his irony-laden view of the events in France and expresses his unbounded contempt for everything that opposes the dictatorship of the working class. His interpretation of the events helps, however, to understand why it was then impossible to change the tricolour flag for the red flag, as was supposedly intended.

The reasons put forward by Marxist historiography to explain the spontaneous eruption of the workers on the streets of the various European cities are not credible. The official historians do not explain how the workers were able to agree to act at the same time and in a coordinated way all over Europe. The answer is that in 1848 the revolution broke out again because it was organised by the Masonic societies, whose socialist and communist leaders took the lead. In Paris alone there were about six hundred secret societies. To prepare for the outbreak in a convenient way, previously, as happened in 1789 and as was to happen in 1917, the tactics were repeated again and again, took advantage of a poor harvest in 1846 to organise a famine. Jüri Lina, in *Under the sign of the scorpion*, gives the name of a

Jewish merchant named Ephrasi, who, acting as an agent of James Rothschild, bought up massive stocks of grain. Over the next few years prices tripled and groceries became scarce in the stores. People went hungry. In addition, there was certainly growing unease in Europe about wage adjustment and lack of work. Moreover, in France, ministerial corruption was being denounced and demands were being made for electoral reform that would grant universal suffrage. The bourgeoisie, many of whose leaders were Freemasons, despite the fact that it was becoming a conservative class, viewed the demands of the workers with sympathy; but theirs had been the revolution of 1789 and it was clear that half a century later it could not be used a second time, especially if it was intended to parade behind the red flag to implement the programme of the *Communist Manifesto*. It was therefore the turn of the new social class, the proletariat, which the professional agitators and charlatans had been preparing.

As had already happened in 1789, a great Masonic congress was held in May 1847 in Strasbourg. The international organisation of Freemasonry was to be used once again. It was in the lodges that the "good Masons" drew up the plans that were to trigger the revolutions. The congress in Alsace was attended by important Jewish leaders who played their leadership role as agents of the Illuminati. Some of the future ministers of the Provisional Government that was formed in France in February 1848 were present, including Adolphe Isaac Crémieux, famously James Rothschild's most trusted confidant, a 33rd degree Mason and Grand Master of the Scottish Rite, who was Minister of Justice; the banker Michel Goudchaux, another Jew and close friend of James Rothschild, who was Minister of Finance. Other prominent French Freemasons involved in the revolution and present in Strasbourg were Simon and Louis Blanc, Léon Gambetta, a Jew who was an adopted son of Crémieux, Alphonse Lamartine, who was to become Foreign Minister, Alexandre Ledru-Rollin and Marc Caussidière, who was Prefect of Police in Paris in February 1848.

The kingdoms of the future Italy were chosen to trigger the wave of conflict. On 12 January 1848, the first revolutionary movement took place in Sicily, which had independence pretensions. Interestingly, the Sicilian people enjoyed extraordinary privileges, unique in Europe, as taxes were very low and there was no compulsory military service. Travel books by adventurers of the time record that life, property and the streets of Palermo and Sicily in general were as safe as those of northern European cities. On 8 February it was the turn of Piedmont. In Tuscany the revolt began on 17 February. Two illuminati, Giuseppe Mazzini and Adriano Lemmi, were the coordinators. Another Freemason, Giuseppe Garibaldi, a Grand Master who would later become world famous, was also involved in the planning of the Italian revolutions. We will now turn to Mazzini and Lemmi, whose role in Freemasonry and in the revolutionary movement deserves a separate mention.

It is not possible to dwell on all the scenarios, but we will dwell as briefly as possible on France, for it was there that Marx, Engels, Hess, Heine and other exiled German Jews had made Paris one of the centres of the conspiracy. The revolution of July 1830 had placed the bourgeoisie in power, personified in the new king, Louis-Philippe d'Orléans. Although in reality, as Marx himself acknowledged, it was the bankers, the money aristocracy, who dominated the period up to 1848, personified in James Rothschild, in whom Heinrich Heine saw "one of the greatest revolutionaries that modern democracy has established". Let us recall the words of James's poet friend and protégé: "No one does more to further the revolution than the Rothschilds themselves, the bankers of kings, those magnificent possessors of money."

In *The Class Struggles in France*, Marx obviously cannot express himself with the impudence of his friend Heine, but he understands that he must keep up appearances and decorum, and he does so. He explains perfectly well how the power of money, of banking, of the stock exchange is pernicious for the whole of society, he alludes to the "kings of the stock exchange", but at no time does he dare to point the finger at the Jews, let alone criticise the man who was on everyone's lips: James Rothschild. He mentions him only once in a brief fragment of the text that is introductory and descriptive of the situation: "The industrial bourgeoisie saw its interests in danger, the petty bourgeoisie was morally indignant; the popular imagination was in revolt. Paris was flooded with libels: 'the dynasty of the Rothschilds', 'the usurers, the kings of the age', etc., in which the domination of the financial aristocracy was denounced and anathematized, with more or less ingenuity". Only once does he refer to Crémieux, the Minister of Justice in the provisional government, and he does so with the utmost respect: while he is handing out epithets of value or pejorative epithets left, right and centre, he refers to him as "Mr Crémieux".

It took only two days in Paris to overthrow the Guizot government and bring about the resignation of Louis-Philippe d'Orléans. After the first signs of what was coming, the king replaced Guizot with Barrot and decreed a state of siege. On 23 February, barricades were erected in the streets. The insurrection spread rapidly and the National Guard sided with the insurgents. A clash on the Boulevard de las Capuchinas, where workers marching behind the red flag clashed with the troops, served as a trigger to accelerate the initial triumph of the revolutionaries: someone fired a rifle and the soldiers responded with a barrage that left dozens of workers dead and wounded in the street. During the night of 23-24 February, the secret societies gave instructions for the following day.

Karl Marx was in Paris: he had managed to enter France from England and took part in organising the revolts at the insurgents' headquarters. Pierre-Joseph Proudhon and Louis Blanc were also among the leaders. At dawn, chaos reigned in the city, armouries were stormed and groups of angry insurgents opened fire on the windows of the Tuileries. Some of the municipal guards were killed and by mid-morning the troops were no longer resisting. At 1 p.m. the royal family left the country and the Republic was proclaimed. The provisional government that was soon formed included the various parties that considered themselves victors after the abdication of the king. The distribution of power among those who had overthrown the July monarchy revealed the diversity of interests. The bourgeois parties were in the majority and only two representatives of the proletariat became members of the provisional government: Louis Blanc and the worker Albert. Marx would later say that the workers' struggle had served to conquer the bourgeois Republic.

Incredibly, on the very same 24th James Rothschild, as Niall Ferguson reveals in *The House of Rothschilds Money's Prophets 1798-1848,* visited the newly appointed finance minister, who was none other than his banker friend Michel Goudchaux, to ask that the new regime take over the interest on maturing Greek debt bonds, which had been guaranteed by the previous regime and which he would normally have paid. Sarcastically Ferguson adds: "There was a quid pro quo. The next day it was announced that Rothschild was to make an ostentatious donation of 50,000 francs to defray the expenses of those wounded in the street fighting, and that he intended 'to offer his co-operation to so good and honest a revolution'."

Shortly after the formation of the Government, three hundred Freemasons bearing the flags of the various representative rites of French Freemasonry marched to the Hotel de Ville. There they offered their banners to the Provisional Government of the Republic and proclaimed aloud the part they had played in the glorious revolution. Lamartine pronounced the following words, which were received with enthusiasm: "It is from the depths of your lodges that have emanated the ideas, first in darkness, then in gloom, and now in broad daylight, which have been the foundations of the revolutions of 1789, 1830 and 1848". Fourteen days later a new deputation of the Grand Orient, adorned with its jewels and Masonic scarves, reappeared at the Hotel de Ville. They were received by Grand Master Adolphe Isaac Crémieux, who addressed them in a speech that ended with these words: "The Republic exists in Freemasonry. If the Republic does what the Freemasons have done, it will favour the luminous promise of union with all men, in all parts of the globe, and on all sides of our triangle".

However, it soon became clear that the union of unequals was not going to be so easy. Louis Auguste Blanqui, the socialist leader and Freemason who had been imprisoned after the attempted coup d'état of 1839, was already free in 1848. On 17 March Blanqui led a demonstration calling for the postponement of elections for the National Assembly and for the National Guard, whose chiefs were elected. A month later, on 16 April, the struggle between the factions continued. What happened on that day varies according to the source. For Marx, it was a trap by the bourgeoisie for the proletariat; for non-Marxist authors it was a mistake by the socialist leaders who intended to overthrow the Provisional Government through the workers and proclaim a communist government. Ultimately what happened was that a rupture was staged between the workers and the soldiers, from whose ranks cries of "Down with the communists! Down with Blanqui! Down with Louis Blanc!" spread throughout Paris.

Universal suffrage showed that the French did not support the socialist and communist revolutionaries. The bourgeois parties dominated the Constituent Assembly which met on 4 May. Marx comments on the new situation: "It is not the Republic which the proletariat of Paris imposed on the Provisional Government; it is not the Republic with social institutions; it is not the dream of those who fought on the barricades". On 15 May the riots resumed and a mob invaded the Assembly. Louis Blanc himself tried to control the situation and from the table told the crowd that "the people had violated their own sovereignty". Then there were cries of "we want Blanqui", who made his entrance on the shoulders of the workers. Blanqui demanded that France declare war on Europe in order to liberate Poland, whose revolt had been suppressed on 5 May by Prussian troops. Another revolutionary, Huber, shouted that the Assembly "was dissolved in the name of the people."

Once order was restored, the new government was formed after the elections, and its first measures triggered the final crisis. From 22 to 25 June, barricades were again erected. The instigators succeeded in ensuring that the insurrection was followed by a crowd which, without excluding common criminals, included the Paris proletariat, sections of the petty bourgeoisie and even disgruntled legitimists. On the 26th, the troops commanded by Generals Cavaignac and Lamoricière left in the streets the bodies of more than ten thousand people, pawns sacrificed in the strategy of hidden characters who had played with them the strange game of 1848. Some socialist leaders were arrested and the arrests amounted to twenty-five thousand. Secret societies were severely persecuted and even the freedom of the press was suppressed. The revolution thus ended in complete defeat.

Among those who did not show their faces and remained scheming in the councils was Karl Marx, who, according to Salluste (Flavien Brenier) in *Les origines secrètes du bolchevisme Henri Heine et Karl Marx*, took part in the Paris revolution and was arrested in the course of the repression. Karl Marx," writes Salluste, "was to be shot or at least deported. Heinrich Heine intervenes and declares that he guarantees his innocence, and gets him thrown out of the court martial: who would have doubted the sincerity of the gentle poet? Karl Marx was merely interned in the Morbihan department. A few weeks later, armed with false documents, he escaped to England. Brenier wonders through what organisation Marx kept in touch with the conspirators, who supplied him with false documents to cross borders when he needed to escape, and how he prepared his raids on the Continent. His answer is that he made use of a carbonari organisation which he himself headed. The carbonari, illegal throughout Europe, operated in small groups that were recruited with great secrecy: "They existed side by side," Salluste explains, "and they ignored him. They only contacted the organisation through one member, the group leader, appointed from above and not elected by his fellow members. A Supreme Committee maintained contact with the group leaders through liaison officers. No outside propaganda, which could attract the attention of the police. The immediate end proposed to the members could be an attack on a notable enemy of the revolution, so assassinations were frequent".

As early as July 1848, Lionel Rothschild travelled from London to join his uncle James. When he arrived in Paris, he found him locked up with Goudchaux, who was still Finance Minister in the government that had emerged from the May elections, and with whom he was negotiating the conversion of the 3% interest on 1847 bonds into 5% interest, thus "turning a loss of 25 million francs," Ferguson explains in the book, "into a gain of 11 million francs. The fact that Goudchaux was a Jew merely fed the extreme suspicion of a conspiracy to prop up Rothschild". We do not know whether Marx is alluding to the same operation that Ferguson unveils when he writes in *The Class Struggles in France*: "to remove the suspicion that it was unwilling or unable to honour the obligations bequeathed by the monarchy, to awaken faith in bourgeois morality and in the solvency of the Republic, the Government resorted to a bluff as unworthy as it was puerile: that of paying the State's creditors interest at 5%, 4.5% and 4% before the legal maturity". Be that as it may, it is clear that the Minister of Finance was one of the men brought into the government by James Rothschild. It was also Goudchaux who was responsible for burying the nationalisation of the railways, one of the Rothschilds' big businesses in Europe, which had originally been planned by the Provisional Government.

There is a very significant text addressed to James Rothschild published in August. It is an editorial in the radical newspaper *Tocsin des Travailleurs* (*Workers' alarm bell*) which was supposedly intended as a call to the banker to put his financial power at the service of the Republic. The content invites the suspicion that, perhaps, as happened in 2008 in the crisis triggered by the bankruptcy of Lehman Brothers, what was intended was to divest itself of competitors, to provoke their bankruptcy, in order to further monopolise and concentrate power. Here is the text:

> "You are a marvel, sir. In spite of your legal majority, Louis Philippe has fallen, Guizot has disappeared, the methods of constitutional and parliamentary monarchy have fallen by the wayside; you, however, remain impassive!... Where are Arago and Lamartine? They are finished, but you have survived. The princes of banking have gone into liquidation and their offices are closed. The great chiefs of industry and of the railway companies are tottering. Stockholders, merchants, manufacturers and bankers have been ruined en masse, big men and little men are alike

overwhelmed; you alone among all these ruins remain unaffected. Though your house felt the first violence of the shock in Paris, though the effects of the revolution pursued you from Naples to Vienna and Berlin, you remain unmoved by a movement that has affected the whole of Europe. Wealth vanishes, glory is humbled and dominion is broken, but the Jew, the monarch of our time, has remained on his throne, But this is not all. You could have escaped from this country where, in biblical language, the mountains skipped like lambs. You remain, announcing that your power is independent of the old dynasties and you boldly extend your hand to the young republics. Undaunted you stick to France.... You are more than a statesman, you are the symbol of credit. Is it not time that the bank, that powerful instrument of the middle classes, should help to fulfil the destiny of the people? Without becoming a minister, you stand simply as the greatest businessman of our time. Your work may be more extensive, your fame - and you are not indifferent to fame - may be even more glorious. After getting the crown of money you will reach your apotheosis. Doesn't this appeal to you? Be confident that it would be commendable if one day the French Republic were to offer you a place in the pantheon!"

Thank goodness it was a newspaper of the radical left!

There is no room to dwell on other "spontaneous revolutions". We will only add that on the first of March the insurrection took place in Baden. The banker Ludwig Bamberger (1823-1899), a Jew and Freemason, editor of the *Mainzer Zeitung* newspaper, was the champion of the revolt in Germany. Once order was restored, he was sentenced to death, but managed to escape to Switzerland with other subversives and later arrived in London. Years later,, the revolutionary banker was already a director of the Bischoffheim & Goldschmidt bank, and in 1870 he was one of the founders of the Reichsbank. Other German Freemasons who led the revolts were the Jewish Johann Jacoby, who was at the forefront of the actions in Berlin, Joseph Fickler, Friedrich Franz Karl Hecker, Robert Blum and Georg Herwegh (1817-1875). The latter had a passionate affair between 1849 and 1850 with Natalie Herzen, wife of Alexander Herzen, to whom we will devote the following section.[26]

---

[26] The German poet and revolutionary Georg Herwegh, the subject of a poem by Heinrich Heine, with the consent of his wife Emma, had an intense and tormented relationship with Natalie Herzen, a disciple of George Sand and wife of the Russian revolutionary Alexander Herzen. The Herzens and the Herweghs were friends. After the defeat of Herwegh's battalion of revolutionaries in Baden Baden, Herwegh arrived in Paris and the two couples made plans to live in a commune of four. Herzen found a house in Nice and the two families moved there in the mid-1850s. Herzen did not know that his wife had been committing adultery with Herwegh for six months. When he learned of the betrayal in 1851, he was furious, but wasn't a central point of the revolutionaries a break with traditional values, including family, inheritance and religion? The affair became a scandal in European socialist circles, and the German Arnold Ruge even wrote the drama *The*

In Heildelberg and Prague, too, the lodges organised conspiracies. On 13 March it was Vienna's turn. There the main promoters of the rebellion were Adolf Fischhof and Joseph Goldmark, two Jewish doctors identified with Moses Mendelssohn's rationalist Haskala movement, which advocated the emancipation of Jews and their "assimilation" into European societies. Two days later the revolution began in Hungary, again organised by two Freemasons of Jewish origin: Mahmud Pascha led the mutiny in Budapest and Lájos Kossuth acted in the provinces. Like the two previous ones, they moved within the Haskala. On 14 March Mazzini declared a republic in the Papal States. On 18 March, the five hundred and thirty-fourth anniversary of the death of the Grand Master of the Templars, Jacques de Molay, burned at the stake in 1314, rebellions broke out in Milan, Stockholm and Berlin at the same time. The riots in Stockholm were among the most violent in the city in living memory. Estonian author Jüri Lina cites Bunny Ragnerstam's book, *Arbetare i rörelse* (*Workers in Action*), as the source of his information. It explains that the Communist Association in Stockholm, founded in 1847, organised the revolts in connection with the Communist League. The leading figure was a Jewish writer, Christoffer Kahnberg, who wrote the proclamations that appeared all over the city. In Venice, the Jewish lawyer Daniele Manin, a descendant of the old Medina family, who had been arrested and imprisoned in January, was freed by Mazzini's revolutionaries, who proclaimed him president of the Republic in August 1848, a position he held for a year. The Venetian government was made up almost exclusively of Freemasons, including the Jews Leon Pincherle, who was Minister of Agriculture, and Isaac Pesaro Maurogonato, Minister of Commerce. This was followed by Munich, Dresden, Bohemia.... In the following months, a second wave of revolts took place in half of Europe. It all happened, according to the history books, spontaneously.

James Rothschild and Alexander Herzen

Before leaving 1848 for good, it is interesting to note the friendship of James Rothschild and the Russian revolutionary Alexander Herzen, one of the fathers of Russian socialism, the author of the phrase "land and liberty", for this relationship is prime evidence of the Rothschilds' involvement in the revolutionary movements in Russia and of their leadership of the MRM. Herzen, born in Moscow in 1812, was the illegitimate son of a Russian aristocrat and a German Jewish convert to Protestantism, Luise Hagg, who had a decisive influence on him. Herzen was therefore Jewish, since among Jews it is the mother and not the father who

---

New World, based on these events. "I belong to the revolution to which Mazzini and his disciples belong," Herzen wrote to his anarchist friend Proudhon in an attempt to justify his "bourgeois attitude".

determines racial affiliation. At the age of twenty he was already an agitator at Moscow University, for which he was arrested and sentenced to several months in prison. Despite this, in 1839 he worked in St. Petersburg as secretary to Count Stróganov, a general who was aide-de-camp to the emperor, and later became Regency Councillor in Novgorod, a post from which he resigned to go and live in Moscow, where, under the pseudonym "Iskander" (Arabic translation of Alexander), he had revolutionary works of a subversive nature clandestinely printed in 1841.

Again it is Marvin S. Antelman who in the second volume of *To Eliminate the Opiate* puts us on the track. "Project Iskander," writes the rabbi, "is the name given by the Illuminati to the overthrow of Russia. The name symbolises their overthrow for an ultimate purpose: world government. Iskander is the Arabic term for Alexander the Great. It is written in the Koran that Iskander enclosed the savage tribes of Gog and Magog behind iron walls (hence the term iron curtain)." Alexander Herzen was the ideologue and one of the leaders of the "Narodnicks", an intellectual and radical class of revolutionary socialists who sought to use the peasantry to overthrow the Tsarist monarchy. They are regarded as the intelligentsia that provided the bridge between Marxist communism and the Bolsheviks. It follows that Alexander Herzen was an agent of the Illuminati, a man who, like Heinrich Heine, knew what the future plans were. His relationship with the Rothschilds, with Marx, Proudhom, Bakunin and other revolutionaries reinforces the validity of the assessment.

After his father's death in 1846, he inherited a considerable fortune and travelled abroad, never to return to Russia. Berlin was the first point of contact with the conspirators. There he met Leopold Zunz, who, as we have already seen, played a very influential role in the Jewish intelligentsia. Zunz made him a potential communist, and they probably had occasion to consider together the doctrine of neo-Messianism. In 1847 Herzen arrived in Paris, from where he went on to Italy for a short stay. In May 1848, when the revolution was at its height, he returned to the French capital. He took part in the June days alongside Marx and Proudhon, whom he helped financially with 24,000 francs so that he could maintain the publication of his newspaper, *Voix du People* (*Voice of the People*), in which he wrote furious articles.

Contact with the Rothschilds had already occurred in 1847, before his trip to Italy, as Niall Ferguson reveals that they did him favours with small banking services when he was in Italy and helped him invest some 10,000 roubles when he began to sell his Russian properties. Herzen himself explains that he asked James Rothschild to exchange bonds from a Moscow savings bank and, on his advice, bought American and French shares and a house in Amsterdam Street near the Havre Hotel. James Rothschild's involvement with the Russian revolutionary reached its zenith when the Moscow government tried to prevent Herzen from taking any more money out of the country by mortgaging his mother's property in Komostra. James accepted in advance an invoice signed by Herzen for the value of the property to be mortgaged. When the Russian authorities refused to authorise the mortgage, an irate James Rothschild was ready to take action against the bank and demanded an explanation from the Minister of Finance. The Russian ambassador, Count Kiselev, then intervened and warned the banker that he could not trust his new client. James then wrote a harsh letter to Gasser, his agent in St Petersburg, threatening the Russian government with legal action and the use of the press. In his autobiography *My Past and Thoughts,* Herzen confirms the sending of the letter:

"When half an hour later I was ascending the stairs of the Winter Palace of Finance in the Rue Lafitte (he means Rothschild's palace), the rival of Nicholas (he means the Tsar) was coming down.... His Majesty, smiling gently, and majestically extending his august hand said: 'The letter has been signed and sent. You will see how they will change their minds. I will teach them to play with me'..... I felt inclined to kneel down and offer an oath of allegiance together with my gratitude, but I merely said: 'If you are quite sure of this, let me open an account, even if it is only for half the total amount'. His Majesty the Emperor replied: 'With pleasure' and went on his way towards the Rue Lafitte. I bowed."

Six weeks later the money was paid. Undoubtedly, in an attempt to dissuade Rothschild, Ambassador Kiselev must have informed him of Alexander Herzen's revolutionary background. One cannot therefore entertain the innocent notion that James Rothschild was unaware of the Russian aristocrat's true character. He knew very well the reasons why he was prepared to play the card of his co-religionist. Herzen boasts of having maintained an unbeatable relationship with the banker ever since. I was for him," he later wrote, "the battlefield on which he had beaten Nicholas I". In 1850 Louis Napoleon's regime expelled Rothschild's revolutionary friend from France, but James continued to look after his investments in America and other bonds[27]. The 1851 balance sheet of the Rothschild house in Paris shows him owing 50,000 francs. Herzen settled in London, where else, and there he regained contact with Marx and other French and German refugees. Herzen arrived in the British capital, of course, with the relevant recommendations to Rothschild House in London, where Lionel Rothschild assumed command of his account.

---

[27] There is a recent work by Derek Offord, published in the "Academic Electronic Journal in Slavic Studies" of the University of Toronto, entitled *Alexander Herzen and James Rothschild.* It gives a full and detailed account of the amounts of money that the French Rothschild handled. The study provides an insight into the various countries where investments in bonds and annuities were made for Herzen's benefit.

Further evidence of Alexander Herzen's relationship with the Shabbetaics and the revolutionary movement set in motion by the Illuminati is found in a letter he wrote to Moses Hess on 3 March 1850, which is reproduced in *To Eliminate the Opiate,* taken from the above-mentioned book by Theodore Zlocisti, *Moses Hess and His Contemporaries.* In it he asks Hess to give him a copy of a pamphlet he had written to Georg Herwegh, the revolutionary poet who was then having an affair with his wife Natalie without his knowledge. Herzen asks Hess if he intends to travel to London, asks for the address and suggests that he can write to him by addressing his letter to the attention of the Rothschild brothers in Paris. He confesses to Hess that he does not even think about money and offers him financial help if he needs it. This document also confirms once again that London was the city of refuge. In return for maintaining immunity on its territory, the British government allowed fugitives from all over Europe to roam freely in England.

In London Herzen met Marx again. In their discussions it soon became clear that they did not share views as to which nation was to be conquered first. Marx still had France in mind and intended to use Freemasonry to spread the revolution throughout Europe; but Herzen did not believe that France was the right soil for social revolution. Nor did he believe that Germany was. Both countries were in his opinion too conservative and even feudal. Russia, on the other hand, seemed to him to be the ideal starting point for a movement that was to shake up and transform the world, since it had the most backward peasantry in Europe. Herzen therefore founded a Russian-language revolutionary printing press in London in 1851, which he used to publish two journals, the *North Star* and the *Russian Voice, as* well as numerous subversive pamphlets. These magazines were smuggled into Russia and distributed. A text entitled *A Socialist Evening,* published shortly before the creation of the International Workingmen's Association in a Vienna newspaper and reproduced on 23 June 1871 in the *Gazette de France,* gives an insight into Alexander Herzen's life in London. It recounts the atmosphere of a meeting of revolutionaries in the elegant country house he owned in the London suburb of Putney. Servants aside, it describes the foyer covered with oriental tapestries and decorated with exotic flowers, from which a marble staircase, also decorated with tapestries, led up to the first floor. There, a "maître d'" in white gloves and white tie ushered the guests into a salon full of ladies and gentlemen, including Louis Blanc, Ledru Rollin, Edgar Quinet and Karl Marx, who is described as drinking beer and arguing vehemently with a group of Germans whom he assured that the revolutionary avalanche was to set out from London and roll over France.

Giuseppe Mazzini, Albert Pike and Adriano Lemmi

Numerous sources agree that Giuseppe Mazzini (1805-1872), the Italian revolutionary leader who has gone down in history as a great patriot, "apostle of Italian unity", was elected by the Bavarian Order of the Enlightened to head the revolutionary programme, a position in which he remained until his death. Des Griffin, Paul H. Koch, William Guy and others propose 1834 as the date of his appointment. Mazzini, who would have reached the 33rd degree of Italian Freemasonry while at the University of Genoa, was also Jewish according to Jüri Lina, but no other author confirms this. His name is repeatedly linked to all the revolutionary events, and his collaboration with Albert Pike, whose correspondence is cited by various researchers, is an inescapable episode.

Mazzini encouraged Italian Freemasons to join the organisation of the Carbonari, a society that was very popular in the Italian and French countryside. Just as classical Freemasonry was born in the builders' guilds, so Carbonari or Forest Masonry was born in the forests of the Jura among the workers who made charcoal from the felling of trees. Initially the lodges of the Carbonarii consisted of ten members who were initially called the Jurassic Forests and later became the Sales. Their rites and ceremonies took place inside the forests. The pledge of secrecy about the Brotherhood was made with a dagger held against the chest and oaths were sworn with a clenched and raised fist. From the beginning of the 19th century, Freemasons and Illuminati infiltrated the Carbonari until they became an Illuminati-controlled organisation. It was in 1815 that Adam Weishaupt decided to revive and reorganise it, realising that he could use this secret society to assassinate those who opposed internationalism. Already during the years of terror in France the Illuminati had made use of Jacob Frank's terrorists, trained in Brno. The Grand Secret Consistory met in 1820 and as a result of this meeting the Carbonari became part of the Grand Orient. Since then its members committed most of the political assassinations. The Mafia is actually one of its offshoots. According to some authors, the word Mafia is an acronym for Mazzini Autorizza Furti Incendi Avvelenamenti (Mazzini authorises robberies, fires and poisonings). Mazzini was initiated into Carbonariism and Grand Orient Freemasonry in 1827.

The central lodge of the cabonari was the Alta Venta, with whose leader, who used the pseudonym Nubius, Mazzini came into conflict. As a result of the confrontation Mazzini allegedly succeeded in poisoning him in 1837 and thus usurped power and control of the Alta Venta from him (see note 16 in the previous chapter). From then on Mazzini moved to London, where he took up residence and definitively assumed the leadership of the revolutionary movement. There he established direct contact with Lord Palmerston, who, as we know, was Grand Master of the Scottish Rite of Freemasonry and Patriarch of the Illuminati. After having been a key player in the Rothschilds' strategy in the Damascus Affair in 1840, Palmerston went into opposition in 1841; but between 1846 and 1851 he was again Foreign Secretary. From this post he unashamedly favoured the 1848 revolts on the Continent. In fact, all the national movements that made up Young Europe were coordinated by the British Secret Service. It is understandable that all the revolutionary Freemasons ended up in misty exile in London.

The unification of Italy was of interest to the Illuminati and so the Carbonari became an instrument for creating a federated republic, for which a triangular flag bearing the Illuminati's seal was envisaged. In 1832 Mazzini had formed a political group which he called Young Italy and in 1834 he also founded Young Switzerland, where he was living in exile. It has already been said that Mazzini was imitated throughout Europe. With the support of Lord Palmerston's diplomacy and the British Secret Intelligence Service (SIS), revolutionary committees were set up on the model of Young Italy. This led to the federation of these committees in Berne under the name of Young Europe. After the failure of the 1848 revolutions, Mazzini, who had left his residence in London to take part in the revolts, took refuge in the English capital again at. There he met many of the fugitives who had been involved in the various plots: the Hungarian Lájos Kossuth, Ledru-Rollin, Herzen and, of course, Karl Marx, with whom Mazzini was at times closely associated. It was Mazzini himself who noted that Marx's "heart burned more for hatred of men than for love".

Alongside Mazzini, a second character, Albert Pike, appears. The relationship between the two is noteworthy. Major Guy Carr in *Satan, Prince of this World, a* posthumous work published by his son, states that Mazzini, following instructions given to him by Weishaupt before his death, travelled to America to synchronise the Illuminati conspiracy. The 1845 founding of Young America is often attributed to Mazzini, but it is certain that the author of the manifesto was Edwin de Leon, a member of a Portuguese slave-trading Marrano family who belonged to the Jewish Masonic lodge B'nai B'rith. De Leon acted on the instructions of August Belmont, a Prussian-born Jew who was the highest representative of the Rothschilds in the United States. Further information about B'nai B'rith, Edwin de Leon and August Belmont is given below. In *Four Reich of the Rich* Des Griffin also considers that Albert Pike and Mazzini made contact to co-ordinate the European Masons with the American Masons. When exactly the relationship was established is not known. Edith Starr Miller, Lady Queenborough, about whose sudden death in Paris at the age of 45 there are serious suspicions of murder, reports in *Occult Theocracy* (1933) a certain contact that would have taken place some years before 1870, perhaps in 1866. This classic work is available online in PDF format.

Before American independence, fifteen Illuminati lodges operated in the United States, but between 1830 and 1840 Freemasonry fell into disrepute because of the assassination of Captain William Morgan and almost ceased to exist. This captain had attained a high degree and enjoyed a certain authority in Freemasonry, but after discovering in his New York lodge, Lodge 433 in Batavia, some of the secrets of the Illuminati, he decided to defect. Not content to turn away from the conspiracy, he felt it was his duty to inform other Masons and the general public of the hidden aims of the cult that had penetrated Freemasonry. He travelled throughout the country and visited numerous lodges. In 1826 he signed a contract with a publisher, Colonel David C. Miller, and published *Freemasonry Exposed*. In a work published in 1958 by William J. Whalen, *Christianity and American Freemasonry*, an explanation of what happened is given in figures. If Whalen's figures are correct, there were about fifty thousand Freemasons in the United States, and after the publication of Captain Morgan's book some forty-five thousand left Freemasonry. Nearly two thousand lodges closed their doors and the remainder cancelled their activities. In New York State alone there were thirty thousand Masons and after the publication of the book the number was reduced to three hundred.

Richard Howard, an enlightened Englishman, was sent to America to execute Morgan as a traitor. Warned that he was to be killed, William Morgan tried to escape and made his way to Canada, but Howard and his henchmen caught him at the border and killed him near Niagara Falls. His body was found a month after his death in the waters of a lake, where he had been thrown tied up and loaded with large stones. In *Pawns in the Game*, Major Guy adds that his investigation led him to learn that one Avery Allyn had made a brief affidavit in New York City, in which he claimed to have heard Richard Howard's report at a meeting of the Knights Templar at St. Johns'Hall in New York, in which he explained how he had "executed" Morgan. Allyn also told how Howard's shipment back to England had been arranged. Richard Carlile in his *Manual of Freemasonry* gives a very detailed account of the events, which differs in some respects from the one we have given here, but does not alter the essentials.

William Morgan paid with his life for daring to describe the secret rituals of the Illuminati and Satanist Masons, but his sacrifice paid off and soon an Anti-Masonic Party was formed, which for some years was led by a Pennsylvania congressman, Thaddeus Stevens. In 1832, in his address to the delegates to the national convention of the Anti-Masonic Party, Stevens denounced Masons as having taken by intrigue the most important political offices in the nation and defined Freemasonry as "a criminal institution sworn to secrecy which endangers the continuance of the Government of the Republic." This congressman tried to suppress Freemasonry and wanted to investigate the satanism of the Order. He even succeeded in getting an anti-Masonic governor elected in Pennsylvania. Soon, however, the Anti-Masonic Party was infiltrated and Stevens' initial vigour gradually waned until he gave up the fight. There is a possibility that he was the subject of blackmail, as in 1824 he was suspected of killing a black servant girl in

Gettysburg whom he had impregnated, and the matter was never aired in the press. Almost thirty years later, Thaddeus Stevens was competing with Abraham Lincoln in the Republican Party and advocated a provocative and aggressive policy towards the South, i.e. he was pushing for civil war.

Soon the fire of the stake was to burn with renewed energy. The Jew Moses Holbrook was during the first half of the 19th century Grand Commander of the Supreme Council of Charleston, which was one of the two organic divisions of the Ancient and Accepted Scottish Rite in the United States. He and his private secretary, the poet Henry Wadsworth Longfellow, two avowed Satanists, adopted the cabalistic rites of Satanic initiation that in Europe had been adopted by Grand Orient Masonry in France and Italy, whose Masters were Crémieux and Mazzini.

It must have been about 1830 at Harward College or as early as 1833 in Arkansas, where he had his home in Little Rock, that Albert Pike came in contact with Masons who were members of the Illuminati, men who had connections with Moses Holbrook, Clinton Roosevelt, Charles Dana, Horace Greeley. In 1837 he was already close friends with Gallatin Mackey, who was the secretary of the Supreme Council of Charleston, and had known Longfellow. In *Satan Prince of this World*, Major Guy Carr states the following: "there is evidence that after 1840 the thirteen-room house which Pike owned in Little Rock was used as the secret headquarters of those who constituted the Synagogue of Satan, and that within its walls occultism was practiced, and satanic rituals based on the Cabala were performed, just as Moses Mendelssohn did when before 1784 he conducted initiations for high degrees of Weishaupt's Illuminati in Frankfort"[28]. Among these Little Rock rituals was the celebration of the Black Mass, in which the officiant represents Satan and a young priestess symbolises Eve. The seduction and possession of Eve takes place before the devotees. The second part of the ceremony perpetuates Christ's defeat of Satan. Pike proposed to Moses Holbrook "to revise and modernise the ceremony so that it would not appear so Talmudic." Holbrook died in 1844 and Pike subsequently completed the reform by himself. The new ceremony was called the "Adonaicidal Mass". Adonai is the name Masons give to the Christian God. It is well known that Albert Pike owned a very famous statue of Baphomet (Satan), which a Jewish Mason named Isaac Long had brought in 1801 to Charleston, a city situated exactly on the 33rd parallel of latitude.

With Holbrook dead, Albert Pike became the new Grand Commander of the Supreme Council of Charleston in 1859 and gradually established himself as the true head of the Scottish Rite. Pike (1809-1891), like Mazzini in Italy, has gone down in American history as a patriot. A statue was erected in his honour in Washington. Pike served during the Civil War as a general

---

[28] When Albert Pike moved out of the Little Rock house, it was taken over by John Gould Fletcher, who also practised occultism and spiritualism. Gould Fletcher won the Pulitzer Prize for poetry. Among his poems, one is entitled *The Ghosts of an Old House*.

on the side of the Confederacy, whose government commissioned him to enter into negotiations with the savage tribes to raise an army of Indian warriors. Appointed governor of Indian Territory, he got Comanches, Osages, Cherokee Chickasaws, Creeks, Chocaws and Miamis to agree to fight under his command. Terror characterised the actions of Pike's army of Indians, who, following their customs, horribly mutilated enemy soldiers on the battlefield. Confederate President Jefferson Davis, faced with protests and accusations, chose to disband General Pike's Indian troops. After the Civil War ended, he was tried and sentenced for his responsibility for the atrocities committed. After the assassination of Abraham Lincoln, Masonic pressure on President Andrew Johnson, himself a Mason, had immediate effect and Pike was pardoned on 22 April 1866. The next day he visited President Johnson, who within Freemasonry was subordinate to his authority. In the White House itself, dressed in their ceremonial robes, there was a meeting of the members of the Supreme Council of Charleston, whose Grand Commander was Pike.

Albert Pike's curriculum vitae prominently features the creation of the Ku Klux Klan. In the spring of 1867, eight months after Lincoln's assassination, at the Maxwel House Hotel in Nashville, Pike, who had been one of the driving forces behind the Civil War, as will be seen below, held a meeting with a group of Confederate generals to form the Order of the Knights of the Ku Klux Klan, which was a Scottish Rite project. He himself is believed to have drafted the military rules and rituals, their signs and passwords. At a later meeting also in Nashville, General Nathan Bedford Forrest was chosen as Imperial Wizard of the Klan and Pike was given the title of Grand Dragon of the Realm. Most of the funding was provided by the Jewish lodge B'nai B'rith, about which more in the next section.

While the bloody civil war was raging in the United States, in Europe Mazzini was manoeuvring in St. Martins Hall, where on 28 September 1864 the First International was founded. Mazzini was given a welcoming reception and his secretary, a Polish Jew named Wolf, was his representative on the International Committee set up to prepare the statutes to be adopted the following year in Belgium at an international congress. At the first meeting of this Committee, Wolf brought up the statutes of Mazzini's Workers' Association and proposed them as the basis for the new association. Karl Marx, who had deliberately kept himself to himself and contented himself with the position of secretary in charge of correspondence with Germany, manoeuvred the Committee into rejecting this proposal. A year later, in 1865, Lord Palmerston died. He had been Prime Minister of Great Britain since 12 June 1959, and was both Grand Master of the Scottish Rite and Patriarch of the Illuminati. It was probably at this time, after Palmerston's death, that Mazzini conceived the project of a Supreme Rite.

On 22 January 1870 Mazzini wrote Pike a letter in which he proposed that the international federations should continue as they were with their systems, their central authorities and their organisation, but then added: "We must create a super rite which will remain unknown, into which we shall introduce those Masons of high degree whom we shall select.... By means of this supreme rite we shall govern Freemasonry, which will become the greatest centre of international power, the most powerful because its direction will be unknown". Mazzini dreamed of international control through Freemasonry. Absolute control by the Freemasons had been one of Adam Weishaupt's aims at Wilhelmsbad. On 20 September 1870, the day on which the troops commanded by the Freemason general Raffaele Cadorna entered Rome and the King of Piedmont, Victor Emmanuel, became King of Italy, Albert Pike and Giuseppe Mazzini reached agreement to form the New and Reformed Palladium Rite. They then divided their powers: Pike, as Sovereign Pontiff of Universal Freemasonry, became the highest dogmatic authority. Mazzini, who implicitly recognised Pike's supreme authority, retained executive authority as Head of Political Action. Albert Pike then simultaneously held the offices of Grand Master of the Central Directory in Washington, Grand Commander of the Supreme Council of Charleston, and Sovereign Pontiff of Universal Freemasonry, thus becoming also the visible leader of the Illuminati.

Charleston thus became the headquarters or holy city of Palladianism. The New and Reformed Palladian Rite is a Luciferian rite which teaches that divinity is dual. Lucifer is God and so is Adonai, the difference being that Lucifer is the God of light and goodness, while Adonai, the divinity of the Christians, is the God of darkness and evil. In fact, the dualism of the Gnostics explained at the beginning of the chapter was taken up again. For the Christian Gnostics the unseen God was the creator of the universe, while this world was the work of the demiurge, Satan, whom they identified with the God of Israel or of the Bible. Now Palladism, influenced by Gnostic and Kabbalistic doctrines, reversed the terms somewhat. Precisely, the Shabbetaist and Frankist kabbalists insisted that a distinction must be made between the First Cause and the God of Israel. The former would be the God of rational philosophy and the latter the God of religion. Once again we turn to the undisputed authority of Gershom Scholem, who in *Le messianisme juif* attempts to explain the mystical heresy of Shabbetaism and confirms that the Shabbetaist and Frankist sectarians believed that "the Jewish people had mistakenly identified the impersonal First Cause with the personal God of the Bible, which was a spiritual disaster, for which Saadia Gaon, Maimonides and the other philosophers were responsible. It is - Scholem adds - a typically Gnostic scheme, but in reverse: the good God is not the 'Deus absconditus'. This is the God of the philosophers and could not be the object of a cult. The good God is the God of Israel, who created the World and who gave the Torah to Israel". Scholem, for whom Jacob Frank is "a terrifying and truly satanic figure", sees these doctrines as "the radical collapse of the traditional Jewish universe."

Pike published his famous *Morals and Dogma of the Ancient and Accepted Scottish Rite of Freemansonry* in 1871. In it he readily acknowledges that the blue degrees - the first three: Apprentice, Fellow and Master - are meant to mislead the newcomer to Freemasonry with false interpretations. "Freemasonry," says Pike, "like all religions, all mysteries, hermeticism and alchemy, hides secrets from all but the Wise Initiates or Elect, and employs false explanations and interpretations of its symbols to deceive those who deserve to be deceived, and to hide from them the truth, called Light, and to separate them from it."

Mazzini, who had spent the last ten years of his life in London in a flat in Fulham Road, died on 11 March 1872. William Guy quotes a text found after his death, addressed to a doctor named Breidenstine, with whom he had close relations: "We form an association of brothers in all parts of the globe. We wish to break all yokes. But there is still one that cannot be seen, that can hardly be felt, but which weighs on us. Where does it come from? Where is it? No one knows, or at least no one says. This society is secret even to us, the veterans of secret societies". These words invite one to think that Mazzini knew that they were in fact being used by occult forces beyond them.

One of the most valuable works with first-hand information on the facts we have been discussing is *Souvenirs d'un trenta-troisième: Adriano Lemmi, chef suprème des franc-maçons*, by Domenico Margiotta, a 33rd degree mason who renounced the satanic path traced by Albert Pike and Mazzini. This book explains how 33rd degree Scottish Rite Masons were carefully selected for initiation into the Palladian Rite. Those who became members could recruit others, hence its international ramifications. This Supreme Rite was organised in triangles: the Palladian Councils. Pike organised a Supervisory Council in Rome, whose head was Mazzini until his death and then his successor, Adriano Lemmi; another in Berlin, which he called the Supreme Dogmatic Directory; and the third was based in Charleston.

On July 14, 1889, Albert Pike masterfully addressed the twenty-three Supreme Councils of world Freemasonry in order to explain the dogma of the Palladian Rite. Here are some of these instructions: "To you, Sovereign Instructors of the 33rd Degree, we say that you are to repeat to the brethren of the 32nd, 31st and 30th Degrees that the Masonic religion should be, for all of us initiated in the higher degrees, maintained in the purity of the Luciferian doctrine [...] Yes, Lucifer is God, and unfortunately Adonai is also God. By the eternal law there is no light without shadow, no beauty without ugliness, no white without black". Further on it becomes clear that Pike knows the Gnostics and is also an expert Kabbalist, for in his doctrine some of Yitshak Luria's fundamental concepts discussed above are identifiable, namely that of "tsimtsum", meaning "withdrawal" or "contraction". Here is a passage: "The Universe is balanced by two forces that maintain equilibrium: the force of attraction and the force of contraction. These two forces exist in physics, in philosophy and in religion. And the scientific reality of divine dualism is demonstrated by the phenomenon of polarity and by the universal law of sympathy and antipathy. Hence the intelligent disciples of Zoroaster, and after them the Gnostics, the Manichaeans and the Templars have admitted the system of two divine principles eternally struggling."

One of the most complex points of Palladism is the difference, which only Pike must understand, between Satan and Lucifer. In the instructions to the Sovereign Instructors Pike says the following on this subject: "The doctrine of Satanism is a heresy; and the pure and true philosophical doctrine is the belief in Lucifer, who is equal to Adonai; but Lucifer, God of light and God of goodness, fights for humanity against Adonai, the God of darkness and evil. Adriano Lemmi himself, whom Pike accepted as Mazzini's successor without being the saint of his devotion, did not seem to understand the difference between Satan and Lucifer very well either. Lemmi had asked his brother mason Giosuè Carducci to compose a hymn to Satan. The result was the *Hymn to Satan* (1865), which was sung on Lemmi's orders at Palladian Rite banquets, a fact that must have displeased Pike.

As for Albert Pike's absolute control over universal Freemasonry, it must be said that there were exceptions. In 1874 he signed an agreement with Armand Levi, who represented the Jewish lodge B'nai B'rith in America, Germany and England. Under this pact, Pike granted Levi authority for that lodge to organise Jewish Freemasons in these countries into a secret federation, called the Sovereign Patriarchal Council. The international headquarters were set up in a building on Valentinskamp Street in Hamburg. The head of this secret federation earned hundreds of thousands of dollars in dues annually. In the next section we will expand on the importance of this exclusively Jewish lodge.

The third figure is Adriano Lemmi (1822-1906). Born of Catholic parents, he met a Polish rabbi in Constantinople in 1845 who convinced him to convert to Judaism and taught him the *Talmud*. Another rabbi, Abraham Maggioro, introduced him to the mysteries of the Kabbalah and initiated him into magic and the occult. It was an English Freemason who recruited him into Freemasonry in 1848. In 1849 he met the Hungarian revolutionary Lájos Kossuth, who had taken refuge in Constantinople. Kossuth and Lemmi became friends and travelled together to the United States in 1851, but the same year Lemmi returned to Europe to join Mazzini's Young Italy, whom he met in London. From then on Lemmi joined the Carbonari and took part in the sect's political assassinations in Italy, which were ordered by Mazzini.

Freemasonry was an instrument of Lord Palmerston and the Rothschilds in provoking the Crimean War (1853-1856), from which the Rothschilds profited greatly through the debts incurred by the states involved in the conflict. The House of Rothschild supported the belligerent countries:

they underwrote the British war loan of £16 million and participated extensively in the large loan of 75 million francs. They also participated in the granting of a loan to Turkey guaranteed by France and England. In addition, investors in England lost faith in government bonds because of the war and the Rothschilds were able to buy them cheaply. Apart from making a business out of a catastrophic war that impoverished Europe and helped consolidate liberalism, the Rothschilds aimed once again to weaken the Tsars' Russia, which had helped quell the revolts of 1848. Nearly a million human beings between civilians (750,000) and combatants lost their lives. Mazzini and Kossuth worked hard to encourage the outbreak of the conflict. Lemmi, thanks to his contacts with both of them, obtained contracts for Italian ambulances that he sent to the Crimea from Genoa and took advantage of these contracts to enrich himself, since apart from pocketing part of the money, he paid with forged cheques and then fled to Malta. This was his first great robbery," writes Lady Queenborough in *Occult Theocracy,* "but the flight did not prevent a Swiss judge from convicting him and his two associates of non-appearance and non-payment.

In January 1855 Mazzini and Felix Pyat, president of a group known as the Revolutionary Communists, met in London to plan the assassination of Duke Charles III of Parma. Mazzini sent a passport to Malta for Lemmi under the name of Lewis Broom. Lemmi left the island immediately and went to Parma. There he arranged a secret meeting at Castel-Guelfo on 25 March, where Antonio Carra was selected to commit the assassination. Two days later Charles III was stabbed while walking through the streets of Parma. The criminal managed to escape. The circumstances of the event are known because Lemmi himself boasted of the role he had played. Mazzini, who unabashedly declared: "we aspire to corrupt in order to govern", was very proud of Lemmi, whom he called a "little Jew", for, he said, he was worth ten men. So much so that on 12 June Lemmi was in Rome with a new passport in the name of Ulrick Putsch. There he failed this time in an assassination attempt on Cardinal Antonelli, Pius IX's secretary of state and right-hand man, who had also been targeted for assassination in 1853, but the papal police succeeded in neutralising the plan. We could go on recounting the assassinations and plots in which this nefarious and nefarious character was involved, almost always on the orders of Mazzini and Kossuth; but we think that what has been said is enough to give the reader an idea of this Satanist.

By the time of Mazzini's death in 1872, Lemmi had been able to amass a fortune and own extensive estates and other properties. A 33rd degree Mason and head of the Rome Supervisory Council of the Palladian Rite, he tried to control the lodges of the Grand Orient of Italy as Mazzini had done, but the rivalry for supremacy of the Scottish Rite was very strong. Lemmi knew that his secret title as head of Palladism gave him a certain supremacy and he decided to approach the Sovereign Pontiff in Charleston.

He explained to Albert Pike the danger that existed in Italian Freemasonry because of dissension. Specifically, he referred to the opposition of Timothy Riboli, Grand Master of the Council of Italy in Turin. In the end, Pike opted to buy out Riboli and offered him an indemnity of 30,000 francs, which was accepted. The money was taken from the Order's central fund. In the Supreme Administrative Directory in Berlin, the payment of this amount was recorded in the 1887 balance sheet as extraordinary expenses in the following terms, quoted by Lady Queenborough: "Suppression of the Supreme Council of Italy with headquarters in Turin. Extraordinary indemnity allowed to F.-. T. R. on the proposal of F.-. A. L. and approved by the secret committee of February 28th, 30,000 francs."

On 21 November 1888 Adriano Lemmi, one of whose obsessions was the destruction of the Church and the de-Christianisation of Italy, wrote again to Pike in these terms: "Help us in our struggle against the Vatican, for your authority is supreme. With your encouragement all the lodges of Europe and America will rally to our cause". It was in these same years that this criminal, using swindle and other illicit means, seized control of the tobacco monopoly in Italy. The affair reached Parliament, but the intimidated MPs voted in favour of the sect in order to cover up the scandal. Although several parliamentarians and a newspaper tried to prevent impunity, the affair was eventually buried in oblivion.

After the death of Albert Pike in 1891, Lemmi manoeuvred to try to attain supreme Masonic power, the international organisation of which consisted of seventy-seven triangular provinces. To this end, he relied on the Executive Directory in Rome, where his agents, virtually all of whom were Jews, worked to secure for him the support of the powerful Jewish lodges, grouped in the federation of the Sovereign Patriarchal Council of Hamburg. *Occult Theocracy* maintains the thesis that the Jewish lodges did indeed support Lemmi. What in fact happened," says Lady Queenborough, "was a plot by the Sovereign Patriarchal Council against the Supreme Dogmatic Directory of Charleston. Hamburg won in the end and secret Jewish control of the mighty machine of international Freemasonry was assured." Lemmi, who had inherited from Mazzini the headship of Political Action, then sought to move the Supreme Dogmatic Directory from Charleston to Rome on the pretext that it would be better able to fight the Vatican. In the end, after a hard struggle and through shady manoeuvres, the transfer was achieved. Adriano Lemmi died in 1896.

B'nai B'rith and the Universal Israelite Alliance

The Independent Order B'nai B'rith (Sons of the Covenant) was founded in October 1843 in New York by a group of twelve Jewish Freemasons of German origin: Isaac Rosenburg, Reuben Rodacher, Henry Jones, William Renau, Isaac Dittenhöfer, Jonas Hecht, Valentine Koon,

Hirsh Heineman, Henry Kling, Michael Schwab, Samuel Schäfer and Henry Anspacher, but who was behind it once again was the ubiquitous Lord Palmerston, creator of several cults from his position as Grand Master of the Scottish Rite. Edward E. Grusd in his *B'nai B'rith. The story of the covenant* makes it clear that in reality the real mastermind behind the rapid growth of the Order was Baruch Rothschild, who was related to Mayer Amschel Rothschild, the founder of the dynasty in the 18th century. Baruch Rothschild was sent to the United States shortly after the founding of the Order to purge the membership of B'nai B'rith, because, according to him, "not all members were sufficiently educated and the mental capacities were too different". In other words, not just any Jew, for it was a lodge for Jews only, could belong to the Order.

In 1885 Julius Bien, president of the Order in New York, inaugurated the first German Grand Lodge of the I.O.B.B. (International Order of B'nai B'rith). The supremacy of B'nai B'rith in the Jewish world is so great that Zionism and the Jewish World Agency, created in October 1928, depend on its international guidelines. When the Bolshevik revolution broke out, the Grand Master of B'nai B'rith for Russia was named Sliozberg. He was one of the international Jewish leaders advising Alexander Kerensky, whose real name was Aaron Kirbiz, a 32nd degree Scottish Rite Mason. As will be explained in a later chapter, this Menshevik leader, following the orders of B'nai B'rith, eventually surrendered power to the Bolsheviks and went into a golden exile.

Today B'nai B'rith, whose parent cult is the Scottish Rite of Freemasonry, is the largest Jewish organisation in the world. It is both the largest Masonic Order and undoubtedly controls and directs international Freemasonry in the pursuit of its objectives. According to the *Encyclopaedia Judaica*, at the end of the last century it had more than half a million male members in more than 1,700 lodges in 43 countries. The women's lodges of B'nai B'rith numbered six hundred, with over two hundred thousand women members. Of these lodges, seventy are established in Europe. According to Aron Monus in his book *Verschwörung: das Reich von Nietzsche* (*Conspiracy: Nietzsche's Empire*), published in Vienna in 1995, the Order's primary purpose is to secure the power of the Jews over the rest of humanity. Its budget was around 13 million dollars at the end of the 1960s. The secret service of B'nai B'rith is the ADL (Anti-Defamation League), founded in October 1913. One of the ADL's enforcement arms is the JDL (Jewish Defense League), a Zionist terror organisation founded in 1968 by Rabbi Mehir Kahane. In fact the FBI (Federal Bureau of Investigation) has referred to it on several occasions as a criminal terrorist group.

It seems that B'nai B'rith managed to establish itself in Spain even before the death of General Franco, who received the Grand Master Label Katz. The Order's headquarters were established in Madrid, Barcelona, Ceuta, Melilla and Las Palmas; but it was expressly forbidden to promote the founding of mixed Jewish and Christian lodges. In 1979, King Juan Carlos I also received David Blumberg, the new Grand Master of the Order. Until his death, the head of B'nai B'rith in Spain was the businessman Max Mazin, an executive member of the CEOE.

The Order of B'nai B'rith is the executive body of the Universal Israelite Alliance, a Jewish Masonic Grand Lodge founded in 1860 by Adolphe Crémieux, Rabbi Elie-Aristide Astruc, Isidor Cahen, Jules Carvallo, Narcisse Leven and others. The motto of this organisation is "All Israelites are comrades". Two well-known figures were among the initiators of the Alliance, Rabbi Hirsch Kalisher and Moses Hess, authors of the most important works of Proto-Zionism. The main objective of this organisation with its clearly Zionist ideology was political, since the Universal Israelite Alliance was intended to be a kind of representative government for all Jews. After James Rothschild's death in 1868, his sons contributed some 500,000 francs annually to the Alliance. Sixty years after its founding, on 6 September 1920, the London daily *The Morning Post* reproduced the manifesto addressed to all the Jews of the world, in which the aims of the Alliance were openly declared. Let us look at the most significant concepts:

"The union we desire will not be a French, English, Irish or German union, but a Jewish union, a universal union! Other peoples and races are divided into nationalities. All the important faiths are represented in the world by nations, that is, they are embodied in governments specially interested in them and officially authorised to represent them and to speak on their behalf. Only our faith alone lacks this important advantage; it is neither represented by a State nor by a society, nor does it occupy a clearly defined territory.... Under no circumstances will a Jew befriend a Christian or a Moslem; not before the time comes when Judaism, the only true religion, will shine over the whole world. Disseminated among other nations, we wish first of all to be and to remain Jews immutably. Our nationality is the religion of our fathers and we do not recognise any other nationality. We live in foreign lands and cannot concern ourselves with the ambitions of countries completely foreign to us.... The Jewish Magisterium must embrace the whole earth! No matter what the destination, though scattered over the whole earth, you must always consider yourselves members of a chosen race. If you recognise that the faith of your forefathers is your only patriotism, if you recognise this, regardless of the nationalities you have adopted, you always and everywhere form one nation. If you are convinced of this, O Jews of the universe, then come, answer our call and give your consent..... Our cause is great and sacred and its success is guaranteed.... Catholicism, our eternal enemy, lies in the dust mortally wounded in the head. The net which we Jews are casting over the globe is daily widening and expanding..... The time is at hand when Jerusalem will become the house of prayer for all nations and all peoples and the banner of Jewish deity will be unfurled and hoisted in the farthest lands.... Let us avail ourselves of ourselves in all circumstances. Our power is immense. Learn to use this power for our cause... What are you afraid of? The day is not far distant when all the riches and treasures of the world will be the property of the children of Israel."

This extensive quotation is crystal clear and of great value, for it shows that the Jews never really thought of taking advantage of the emancipation they so much demanded, never thought of leaving the ghetto to integrate into the societies that welcomed them, to live and assimilate with other human beings. Acceptance of the nationality of the countries in which they lived was only apparent. The equal rights they claimed were to be used to accumulate power around the world and to work for the cause of national Judaism. The quotation makes it clear that already in 1860 the Jews were ready to realise the Jewish utopia, i.e. their will to dominate all nations, to destroy their enemies, to impose themselves as the chosen race and to monopolise all power in the world.

The same weight that Albert Pike had in the United States and Giuseppe Mazzini in Italy was held by Adolphe Isaac Crémieux in France. Crémieux, Grand Master of the Order of the Rite of Memphis-Mizrain and Grand Master of the Grand Orient of France, was President of the Central Committee of the Alliance in two periods: between 1863-1867 and then between 1868-1880. Viscount Léon de Poncins considered the Universal Israelite Alliance to be a sort of Masonic senate with international influence, since it had all the organisations of Martinist, Frankist and Zionist Freemasons under its authority. *The Israelite Archives*, the organ of the Alliance, published in March 1864 the statement of one of its members, Levy Bing, calling for the establishment of an international Jewish court. Surely he must have had in mind something similar to the current International Court in The Hague, this parody of a court, utterly discredited for its partiality, since it only judges and condemns those who oppose the global powers. In his work *Freemasonry and Judaism Secret Powers Behind Revolution* (1929), Léon de Poncins reproduces Bing's text: "Is it not natural, necessary and much more important to see soon another court, a supreme court, invested with the power to judge great public contests, disputes between nations, giving a final verdict, and whose word would be the law? And this word is the word of God, spoken by his wise children, the Hebrews, to which all nations shall bow with respect."

Crémieux set an example of universal justice in 1870, when, as president of the Central Committee of the Universal Israelite Alliance, he combined this position with that of French Minister of Justice. On 24 October 1870, he signed a decree granting French naturalisation to the Jews of Algeria, but denying it to Muslims. Moreover, the decree placed the Municipal Councils and the General Councils, i.e. the power, in the hands of the Algerian Jews. Logically, Minister Crémieux's justice served to seriously deteriorate relations between the two communities. During the Algerian war of independence, the decree had disastrous effects, and once the conflict was over, most Algerian Jews emigrated to the metropolis.

B'nai B'rith and Freemasonry, instruments of England and Jewish banking in the American Civil War

The widespread thesis that the American Civil War was basically about ending slavery is now discredited. It is absurd to believe that a war that left more than two million dead and wounded was fought for democratic and moral reasons. It is quite another thing to use the pretext of the abolition of slavery as a pretext for unleashing it. There is a work by the American revisionist historian David L. Hoggan, *The Myth of the 'New History': Technics and Tactics of the New Mythologists of American History*, which reviews the theses of the more or less official historiography on the causes of the war. None of them consider the role played by Freemasonry, an instrument in the service of Lord Palmerston and international Jewish banking, whose interest was the division of the country into two states. However, Paul Goldstein, author of *B'nai B'rith, British Weapon Against America*, an illuminating essay published in December 1978 in the monthly magazine *The Campaigner,* and Eustace Mullins, a cursed intellectual, watched by the FBI for thirty-two years, expelled from the "staff" of the Library of Congress for political reasons,[29] argue that Freemasonry was a determining element in the prefabricated agitation that eventually provoked the war. In any case, before relying on these sources, we will draw very briefly from Hoggan's work the views of some historians that we believe to be accurate.

Undoubtedly, the greatest disaster for a nation is civil war. Thus the first thesis worthy of consideration is that of Allan Nevins, who in his *Ordeal of the Union* argues that the American Civil War "was not an unstoppable conflict, but an unnecessary war". Another generally accepted consideration is that the United States, despite significant industrial progress following the removal of Britain's mercantilist controls, remained a predominantly agrarian country. Many historians argue that the Civil War was tantamount to a second industrial revolution. It was precisely this issue of an

---

[29] In 1955, Guido Roeder brought out an edition of *The Federal Reserve Conspiracy* by Eustace Mullins in Oberammergau, Germany. The book was confiscated and the entire edition of 10,000 copies was burned on the orders of Dr. Otto John, director of West German Intelligence, who days later defected to East Germany. The burning of the book was upheld on 21 April 1961 by Judge Israel Katz of the Bavarian Supreme Court. The US government refused to intervene because the American High Commissioner to Germany, James B. Conant (president of the University of Bavaria), had been a member of the German government. Conant (president of Harvard University from 1933 to 1953), had approved the initial order to burn the book.

industrialised North and an agricultural South that gave rise to the crisis of 1832, known as the Nullification Crisis, which Richard Hofstadter argues was instrumental in the outbreak of war. In what Hoggan considers a sensational article published in the *American Historical Review* in 1938, Hofstadter argued that a high tariff imposed by the federal government that only benefited the northern states infuriated the southern states and was a major cause of the war. In short, what happened was the following: Northern industry needed protection from European competition. The aim was to make the South a "captive" market in which the North could place its products. To this end, European imports were heavily taxed. This tariff, for example, increased the cost of British textiles and benefited clothing producers in the northern states. At the same time, it reduced British demand for raw cotton, the mainstay of the southern economy. In 1832, the State of South Carolina repealed the protectionist tariff and declared the federal law unconstitutional.

Other historians argue that the South would have abolished slavery in less than ten years, since by 1861 it was practically bankrupt: the suppression of the slave trade and its enshrinement in international law, the high price of blacks and the low percentage of profit from their use made it unfeasible to maintain. Historian James G. Randall points to Stephen Douglas of the Democratic Party as the politician most interested in avoiding civil war. His debates with the Republican Lincoln had become nationally famous in the late 1950s, and Douglas had defeated him in his senatorial campaign. Randall believes that only Douglas had the political formula for reconciliation that could have prevented civil war. When all indications were that he would be the Democratic Party's nominee for the 1860 election, the fiasco occurred in Charleston: at the Democratic National Convention, John C. Breckinridge, who was then vice-president of the country, denied Stephen Douglas the loyalty he demanded and thus prevented party unity. On 6 November 1860 Lincoln received 1,865,908 votes; Douglas, 1,380,202; Breckindridge, 848,019. It follows that the split vote among the Democrats prevented the peace candidate from winning.

Having outlined these facts, we can now present some circumstances that official history overlooks. Let us begin by looking at this character, John C. Breckindrige. The first thing to say about him is that he was the Masonic vice-president of the Masonic President James Buchanan, who had become President in January 1857. Buchanan had appointed for the office of Attorney General the Pennsylvania Mason, Edwin M. Stanton, and as Secretary of the Treasury, Howell Cobb, another Georgia Mason, who in March 1860 was raised to the 33rd degree by Albert Pike. For the post of Secretary of War, President Buchanan chose John B. Floyd, yes, also a Mason, specifically from St. John's Lodge in Richmond, Virginia. Two weeks before the 1860 presidential election, Floyd secretly agreed to send ten thousand Federal Government rifles to South Carolina Governor William

Gist. Lincoln having already been elected, Floyd completed his treachery on 20 December by ordering the shipment from the Allegheny (Pittsburgh) arsenal of one hundred and thirteen heavy guns and thirty-two smaller ones to the unfinished forts at Ship Island (Mississippi) and Galveston (Texas), where they could be used by the secessionists. But let us return to Breckindrige, the Democratic candidate of those who wanted war. Breckindrige was no ordinary Freemason: he belonged to the Knights of Golden Circle, an order of B'nai B'rith, and on 28 March 1860 he received the 33rd degree of the Scottish Rite from Albert Pike. When the war broke out, Confederate Masonic President Jefferson Davis appointed him his Secretary of War.

On the subject of slavery, we must begin by explaining that the great tragedy of the slaves, the inhumane treatment and the great loss of human life occurred in what historians call the "Middle Passage", i.e. the transatlantic transport of blacks. Academic studies put the number of victims of the cruelty of the slave traders, who were the first masters of the Africans, at between seven and ten million. The official historiography, supported and reinforced by the Jewish propagandists of the Hollywood film industry, says nothing about the real culprits of these deaths, which are once again attributed to European and American Christians. The reality is that the real perpetrators of the genocide were mainly Jews, since they controlled the slave trade from the time of the Roman Empire.

Prestigious historians of Jewish origin acknowledge that for two thousand years the slave trade and slave trade has been dominated by Jews. Marc Lee Raphael, for example, in *Jews and Judaism in the United States: A Documentary History* (1983) acknowledges the predominant role of Jewish merchants in the slave trade. In fact," he writes, "in all the American, French, British, or Dutch colonies, Jewish merchants often dominated". Prominent names include Isaac da Costa of Charleston; David Franks of Philadelphia; Aaron Lopez of Neewport; and the aforementioned Edwin de Leon, whose family of Portuguese Marranos was involved in the slave trade from the early 16th century. This family eventually settled in Charleston and during the Civil War were traitors in the service of B'nai B'rith and British interests. Edwin de Leon, the author of the Young America pamphlet, whose points included collaboration with Young Europe, which was being promoted by the British Secret Service, was part of a commission sent to London by Judah Benjamin, one of the heads of B'nai B'rith, to meet with Lord Palmerston. Among the members of this commission, whose purpose was to raise funds for the Confederation, was George Sanders, an August Belmont man and former employee of the Bank of England. Members of these families, such as Isaac da Costa and Mendes Lopez, were part of a group of merchants who, as "select Jews", operated within the networks of the Secret Intelligence Service of B'nai B'rith. Historians have found documents that show that these families almost entirely controlled the slave trade: the fact that no auctions were held on Jewish holidays is further evidence of this. Another Jewish author, Arnold Wizniter, in his book *Os judeus no Brasil colonial* recognises that 'because of the lack of competitors the Jewish buyers who appeared at the auctions were able to buy slaves at low prices. The *Jewish Encyclopaedia* also admits that in ancient Rome "the slave trade constituted the major means of livelihood for the Jews. If we recall that the *Talmud* teaches that the soul of non-Jews is equivalent to the soul of animals, it is understandable that the Jewish religion approves of slavery as long as the slave is not another Jew.

In reality, once landed in America, the worst was over for black Africans. This is not to say that they were not subject to occasional abuse and ill-treatment, but on the whole their life was relatively acceptable. A correspondent for the *Morning Herald* in London, Samuel Phillips Day, wrote:

> "On Sunday, June 8, 1861, in Asheville, Kentucky, I was walking with some friends; judge my surprise, reader, when I found the whole negro population strolling through the streets, some of them driving carriages! They were dressed so gayly and so elegantly, and looked so happy and contented, that I was obliged to exclaim, "Surely these people are not slaves!" The reply was, "Of course they are." Some of the women wore lace shawls and gold watches and (but for the colour) looked like London duchesses going to the ball. The men were also well-dressed. I reflected for a moment on the condition of the British workers and the London seamstresses.... The contrast was too painful to be mortified.... Like a flash of lightning it flashed through my mind that slavery was not so wicked after all, and that it had a good side and a bad side."

Be that as it may, the abolitionists' campaign against slavery was used as a way of stirring up the mood and preparing for the war of secession between the North and the South. In 1851, *Uncle Tom's Cabin*, one of the most important best sellers of the 19th century, was published. This work by Harriet Beecher Stowe, the first by this previously unknown writer, was the subject of an unprecedented and incessant promotional campaign. It should be remembered that Weishaupt considered it essential to mould people's thoughts to his interests through books and publications in general. To this end, the Enlightenment soon set up the "Deutsche Union" (German Union), which was intended to bring together writers, publishers and booksellers to serve them. It seems clear that *Uncle Tom's Cabin* was the work chosen to create a state of opinion. Even today in the United States, a black man who makes a comment deemed inappropriate on the basis of his racial circumstances is still called an "Uncle Tom".

Abolitionists, secessionists, the Young America movement and Masonic organisations such as the Knights of the Golden Circle, supervised and directed by the B'nai B'rith lodge, working in collusion with the British

Secret Intelligence Service (SIS), were the tools used to prepare for the civil war. B'nai B'rith, in order to be able to direct and indoctrinate Jews migrating to the United States from Europe, organised a web of associations called "Hebrew Benevolent and Hebrew Orphan Aid Societies". To this end, he made use of funding from the Seligmans[30], Baltimore and New York bankers, and the oligarchy of slave merchant families mentioned above, who were also part of the Dutch West India Company, whose main trade was in slaves and gold. The first of these "philanthropic" societies was founded in Charleston by Mendes Lopez in 1784. Attached to these organisations were the inevitable Hebrew Literary Societies. Judah Benjamin, a key figure, since he probably gave the order to assassinate President Lincoln, was recruited to the cause in 1827 in the Charleston Society. To get an exact idea of who was behind these societies, whose real purpose was to select and indoctrinate political and religious leaders among the Jews of America, it is sufficient to note that in 1801 the Grand Council of the Princes of Jerusalem of the Supreme Council of the Knights Commanders of the House of Solomon's Temple of the Ancient and Accepted Order of the Scottish Rite of Freemasonry granted an official charter to the merchants of Charleston and South Carolina - Isaac da Costa, Israel de Lieben, Isaac Held, Moses Levi, John Mitchell, and Frederick Dalacho - members of the Dutch West India Company, for having established in America the foothold of the Hebrew Aid and Benevolent Societies.

Young America also played an active role in the abolitionist movement. One of its leaders, William Lloyd Garrison, who was later to write the introduction to the authoritative biography of Mazzini, acted as a firebrand from the pages of his radical newspaper *The Liberator,* which was distributed in the southern states. Garrison was also one of the founders of the American Anti-Slavery Society. As part of the abolitionist movement's strategy, he made several trips to London and lectured with Mazzini. One of Garrison's excesses was the public burning of a copy of the Constitution, which was in his opinion "a pact with death and hell." Exactly as the Russian revolutionaries did, as will be seen in due course, the abolitionists worked to prevent the gradual peaceful emancipation of the slaves, which had received the majority approval of the plantation owners. Millions of dollars were invested in promoting rebellions and precipitating events.

One of the most famous attempts to provoke an uprising was that of John Brown. According to Wikipedia and the usual myopic, supposedly left-wing and progressive writers, Brown was a defender of freedom, a martyr, a hero. In reality, he was a homicidal maniac, a terrorist funded by a group that

---

[30] The Seligmans are a family of Jewish bankers originally from Germany who, like Nathan Rothschild when he came to England, were originally in the textile business. In partnership with the Rothschilds, they moved into banking and in 1857 placed bonds on the Frankfurt Stock Exchange in the US market. As early as 1879, the Seligmans and the Rothschilds took over the entire $150,000,000 US government bond issue.

has gone down in history as "The Secret Six". Very few sources mention that Brown was linked to various secret societies such as the Oddfelows, the Sons of Temperance, and that he belonged to Hudson's Masonic Lodge No. 68 and Young America. On 24 May 1856, Brown began a string of slaughter of slaveholders that left nearly 200 dead in half a year of attacks. Finding that the desired revolt was not achieved, the Secret Six planned a larger-scale action: the storming of Harper's Ferry arsenal in Virginia to arm the blacks and provoke an uprising. The attack took place on 16 October 1859, but failed. Brown was hanged on 2 December. Ralph Waldo Emerson, the ideological leader of Brown and the Transcendentalism movement, elevated him to the altars: "He has made the gallows as glorious as the cross". There is no space to introduce John Brown's godfathers. The richest of "The Secret Six" was Gerrit Smith, son of an associate of John Jacob Astor, of the East India Company (linked to the opium trade and to the British Secret Service). His mother was a Livingston, related to two Masonic leaders, Edward (Grand Master) and Robert Livingston. Smith, with a million acres of land, was one of the largest landowners in New York State. Gerrit Smith had gifted land to John Brown and spent close to eight million dollars, a huge sum for the time, to finance it. It takes a great deal of naivety to view all the turmoil that preceded the Civil War with idealism.

Samuel Morse, the inventor of the telegraph and the code that bears his name, was also a counter-intelligence officer. There is a text of his entitled *The Present Attempt to Dissolve the American Union, a British Aristocratic Plot*, which makes clear what was going on: "If we glance at the attitude of England towards the United States," writes Morse, "we see that there are two parties, neither of them friendly to us as a nation; one, that of the cotton interests, on the Southern side; and the other, that of the abolitionist cliques, on the Northern side. Thus England balances deftly between these two parties..... She may aid the one, the other, or both, to prevent conciliation, as best serves England's political purposes-the permanent division of America." With this delation written in 1860, Samuel Morse summarised his discoveries concerning the vast British espionage network operating in his country, the centre and key instrument of which was B'nai B'rith. In the same text Morse quoted for his readers the words of the 7th Earl of Shaftesbury, Lord Ashley (a fiery Zionist whom we have introduced in the previous chapter). To Dr. Cheever, one of the directors of the plot in London, Shaftesbury declared: "I like all English statesmen sincerely desire the break-up of the American Union". Morse, in derisive rejoinder, writes: "True words, sir, you have typified with great accuracy and brevity the goings-on of the British aristocratic mentality for many years."

Eight years before the war, in June 1853, the directors of the conspiracy, Lord Palmerston, the Earl of Shaftesbury and Lord Russell summoned Belmont[31], Sanders and Buchanan to London for a series of meetings with Mazzini, Garibaldi and Orsini of Young Italy; Kossuth of Young Hungary; Herzen of Young Russia; and others who made up Young Europe. As a spearhead for the break-up of the Union, the secret order of the "Knights of the Golden Circle" was created in Cincinnati, Ohio, in 1854, which immediately absorbed the operational structures of Young America. Castles were opened in Ohio, Indiana, Illinois, along the Mississippi River and the Gulf of Mexico. Mason John Quitman opened a Knights of the Golden Circle castle in Mississippi; Albert Pike did the same in New Orleans. Among those recruited was Masonic General P. T. Beauregard, brother-in-law of John Slidell, a Louisiana secessionist leader and close associate of Judah Benjamin. Beauregard is mentioned because he is credited with starting the Civil War with the surprise attack on Fort Sumter in 1861. What was salvageable of the Knights of the Golden Circle after the Civil War was integrated by Albert Pike into the KKK. There is little doubt that the leaders of the Knights were the Masters of the Scottish Rite of Freemasonry and the Independent Order B'nai B'rith, viz: Benjamin Peixoto, President of B'nai B'rith; Albert Pike, Sovereign Pontiff of Universal Freemasonry, worshipper of Lucifer and creator of the Palladian Rite; August Belmont, the Rothschilds' personal agent in the United States; Judah Benjamin, who worked in close collaboration with Belmont and was Secretary of State in the Confederate Government, thereby assuming control of the Confederate espionage service.

---

[31] August Belmont, whose Jewish surname was Schönberg, entered the Rothschild house in Frankfurt as an apprentice at the age of fifteen. He learned and progressed so quickly that in 1837 it was decided to send him to New York, where he established himself under the name of August Belmont & Company at 78 Wall Street. His political career soon made him one of the leaders of the Democratic Party. In 1848, the year of the revolutions in Europe and also of the Mexican-American War, Belmont was one of the bankers who financed the war. The Rothschilds also had another man in Mexico, Lionel Davidson, who for several years received the mercury that the Rothschilds sent him from the Almaden mines to refine Mexican silver. Before being visited at the end of the year by James Rothschild's eldest son Alphonse, sent to New York to meet his agent, Belmont shipped large consignments of silver to the London house. Alphonse saw at first hand the extent to which August Belmont had become an indispensable man, whose social position and political influence made him a valuable agent who commanded all resources. In 1849 Belmont announced his engagement to Caroline Perry, daughter of Commodore Matthew Galbraith Perry, one of America's finest families. Belmont was in charge of business on the Atlantic coast of the country, while on the Pacific coast the agent was Benjamin Davidson, sent there after the news that gold had been found in California. Another agent named May immediately travelled to San Francisco to assist him. According to James Rothschild, May was "a nice fellow, a clever Jew from Frankfurt". After the Civil War, Belmont remained in the limelight. In 1877, for example, he negotiated with Treasury Secretary John Sherman for a loan of $50,000,000 in gold coins, which enabled the adoption of the gold standard in 1879.

The outbreak of the war was preceded by a series of chain secessions that occurred immediately after Abraham Lincoln's election, before he was sworn into office. On 20 December 1860, the State of South Carolina, where the headquarters of Masonry's southern jurisdiction were located, was the first to secede from the Union. On the same day Mississippi followed in its footsteps, and the man responsible for secession was John A. Quitman, a native of New York, who had long before moved to that State and by marriage had become related to a wealthy Southern family. Quitman was commissioned to form a Scottish Rite organisation in Mississippi. A Boston Masonic magazine reported on 1 February 1848 that Brother John Quitman, then a general in the U.S. Army, had been invested as Sovereign Grand Inspector General of the 33rd degree, which meant that all lodges in the South were under his authority. Quitman was among the most prominent leaders of the secessionist movement. On 22 December the next state to leave the Union was Florida, a breakaway led by David Levy Yulee, a member of Hayward Lodge No. 7. The State of Alabama seceded on 24 December. On 2 January 1861, Georgia's secession was also managed by two Masons, Howell Cobb, Secretary of the Treasury under former President Buchanan, and Robert Toombs, who became the first Secretary of State of the Confederacy. After the war, both received the honorary 33rd degree. On 7 January it was Louisiana's turn, led, of course, by two Masons, John Slidell, also from New York, and Pierre Soule. Both were also awarded the honorary 33rd degree at the end of the war. Texas seceded from the Union on 1 February. Governor Sam Houston, though a Mason himself, opposed secession; but pressured by thousands of Gold Circle paramilitaries, he could not prevent it. Houston insisted that the act was illegal and on 16 March refused to pledge allegiance to the Confederacy, for which he was removed from office and deposed.

Finally, on 12 April 1861, Masonic General Pierre T. Beauregard, a Knight of the Golden Circle, as mentioned above, was ordered to attack Fort Sumter in South Carolina, one of the few federally held forts in Confederate territory, which surrendered on the 14th. Eustace Mullins is highly critical of President Abraham Lincoln's actions and suggests that he used the incident to trigger the war. According to Mullins, Secretary of State William Seward favoured the peaceful cession of the fort to the State of South Carolina and even held unauthorised meetings with the Confederates. President Lincoln, however, was unwilling to compromise and reacted by mobilising 75,000 volunteers for 90 days, but the war was to last four years.

One of the most overlooked, if not underestimated, historical facts by Anglophile historians is the role played by Russia for the territorial integrity of the United States. We will now briefly explain how the alliance between Tsar Alexander II and President Lincoln prevented British and French intervention in the Civil War. The great architect of the alliance was the American ambassador in St. Petersburg, Cassius Clay, who, like Samuel

Morse, was convinced that the dismemberment of the United States was the cornerstone of the new world order based on economic liberalism and Rothschild monetarism, which the money aristocracy wanted to impose through Britain and France. The break-up of the Russian empire was undoubtedly one of the major aims of the World Revolutionary Movement and the Rothschilds; but in 1861 Russia remained a formidable enemy. In order to split the Union and encourage the Balkanisation of the country, Lord Palmerston, Prime Minister, and Lord Russell, Minister of the Foreign Office, were prepared to help the Confederates; but also, in order to weaken Russia's chances of intervention, six weeks after the outbreak of the American Civil War they promoted an uprising in Poland.

As early as 1812, during what Americans consider their second war of independence, Alexander I had already addressed Britain, demanding that it sign an honourable peace with the United States as soon as possible and forget its claims to territorial expansion. Almost half a century later, Russia was prepared to do more than pay lip service to prevent the partition of the United States. Alexander II and his foreign minister, Prince Gorchakov, were pushing ahead with an ambitious programme of railway construction, which until 1857 had been built and operated by the state. An American team led by Major Whistler supervised work on the St. Petersburg-Moscow line. There were also plans to nationalise credit. Another step not usually aired in official historiography was the emancipation of the serfs: an imperial decree of 19 February 1861 freed some 23 million souls. Many peasants, however, were dissatisfied with the measure despite the fact that, among other options, it was intended to enable them to become landlords. It was in this context that President Lincoln appointed Cassius Clay as ambassador to Russia.

Cassius Clay brought with him to Russia many copies of Henry Charles Carey's (1793-1879) *Principles of Political Economy,* a treatise that was to dominate American economic thought for years to come, and gave them as gifts to Alexander II, Gorchakov, Prince Dolgoruky, the Minister of the Navy, Grand Duke Constantine and numerous high officials and industrialists. In contrast to the ideas of the physiocrats, Adam Smith and David Ricardo, Russia and the United States preferred to apply the ideas of this prestigious American economist for the development of their economies. He also rejected the ideas of Thomas Malthus, as he was convinced that the growth of production would allow the population to increase. Henry Carey believed that England wanted to use free trade to turn weaker countries into mere producers of materials for British factories. He therefore advocated that young countries like his own should apply protectionist measures, which could only be abolished when their own industry was in a position to compete on equal terms. He also advocated the abolition of the gold standard and proposed issuing money to provide for the population in times of economic contraction. Constantin George, in an article entitled *The U.S.-Russian Entente that Saved the Union,* published in *The Campaigner* magazine in July 1978, explains that Cassius Clay was hyperactive in spreading Henry Carey's principles of political economy. The ambassador delivered lectures in Russia's major cities "which were greeted with thunderous applause by heads of industry, merchants and government officials." Clay's speeches on the need for industrialisation and Carey's political ideas were widely reported in the Russian press.

On July 25, 1861, Clay, in a letter to Lincoln reproduced in the above-mentioned article, expressed himself in these terms: "I perceived at a glance what was the sentiment of England. They meant our ruin. They are jealous of our power. They care neither for the North nor for the South. They hate both. And later Cassius Clay informed the President of Russia's predisposition in relation to a possible Anglo-French intervention in the war: "All the Russian newspapers are with us. In Russia we have a friend. The time is coming when it will be a powerful friend to us. The decision for the emancipation of the serfs is the beginning of a new era of strength. Russia has immense, fertile and untapped lands, with iron and other minerals." The Russian authorities demanded only a guarantee, a certainty, before they would commit themselves completely. They wanted assurance that Lincoln would stand firm to the end in the fight to preserve the Union. In one of Clay's first interviews with Alexander II, the Tsar asked the ambassador what Lincoln's attitude would be in the event of British intervention. In the alluded-to article in *The Campaigner*, Constantin George, citing as a source the "Diplomatic Correspondence of the United States in the Archives of the Department of State", reproduces a letter from Clay to President Lincoln in which Ambassador Clay's commitment in his reply to the Tsar's question appears: "I told the Emperor that it did not matter to us what England did, that her interference would only tend to bring us closer together". In another letter to Cassius Clay, President Lincoln asked, "Please convey our gratitude to the Emperor and assure H.M. that the whole nation appreciates this new manifestation of friendship. Of all the communications we have received from European governments, yours is the most loyal." Lincoln then asked Clay to ask the Russian authorities for permission to give maximum publicity to Foreign Minister Gorchakov's letter, which contained Russia's offer of aid. Permission was granted.

British Fifth Column agents infiltrating Lincoln's government soon began to press for Clay's replacement. In the spring of 1862 William Seward, who months earlier had favoured ceding Fort Sumter to the Confederacy to supposedly avoid war, persuaded the President to make a double change: on the one hand Secretary of War Simon Cameron was replaced by the Masonic Edwin Stanton, an unfortunate choice by Lincoln, as Stanton was to be one of the traitors implicated in his subsequent assassination; on the other, Cameron was proposed for the post of ambassador to St. Petersburg. Cassius Clay, bitter and disappointed by the manoeuvre, begged Lincoln to allow his nephew, who was working with him as an assistant, to be his replacement;

but despite protests, Cameron showed up in St. Petersburg in June 1862. In Russia, too, British agents took advantage of Clay's absence to undermine Gorchakov's policies. Nevertheless, Clay fought doggedly to thwart the dirty tricks that sabotaged all his work and were intended, he claimed, to cut off communication with the Russian government during the most critical phase of the war. As soon as he arrived in Washington, he submitted a report to the President on the European situation, which warned: "Governments throughout Europe are disposed to interfere in American affairs and to recognise the independence of the Confederate States". Seward and Clay fought bitterly, but Clay finally prevailed, and in the spring of 1863 he regained his ambassadorial post in St. Petersburg.

During the months of Clay's absence, Alexander II's support did not weaken, although the autumn of 1862 saw a critical moment when Britain and France came within a hair's breadth of intervention in favour of the Confederacy. The pressure on Russia from both countries to abandon its position reached extreme levels. Proof that the timing was extremely delicate is provided by President Lincoln's personal letter to Minister Gorchakov to be delivered to the Tsar. The text of the reply, drafted by the foreign minister on Alexander II's instructions, is reproduced by Constantin George in *The Campaigner*. The letter is taken from the documents published in 1930 by the historian Benjamin Platt Thomas under the title *Russian-American Relations 1815-1867*. An excerpt is reproduced here for your interest:

> "You know that the United States Government has few friends among the powers. England rejoices at what happens to them. She longs and prays for their overthrow. France is less active in her hostility; her interests would be less affected by the result; but she is not unwilling to see it. She is no friend of his. Her situation is worsening by the hour. The chances of preserving the Union are becoming more and more desperate. Nothing can be done to stop this dreadful war? Hopes of reunification are dwindling, and I wish to impress upon your Government that secession, which I fear may happen, will be regarded by Russia as one of the greatest misfortunes. Only Russia has been on your side from the very beginning, and will continue to be. We are very, very concerned that some measures should be taken - which would have to be exercised in due course - which can prevent the split that now seems inevitable. One split will be followed by another, you will be fragmented into pieces."

In October 1862 Louis Napoleon offered to mediate and proposed a six-month armistice, which could be extended if necessary. Among other things, it was intended that Lincoln would end the war and lift the naval blockade of the Confederacy. The idea had probably originated in England, as a month earlier Lord Palmerston had suggested to his Foreign Secretary, John Russell, that he offer mediation to the Union Government. Lord Russell's reply clearly shows the true intentions behind the armistice proposal: "I agree with you," he said, "that the time has come to offer mediation to the Government of the United States with a view to recognising the independence of the Confederacy. Moreover, I agree that, if it ends in failure, we should on our part recognise the Southern States as an independent State."[32] Clearly, such recognition would have been a declaration of war. The British were thus engaged in a crucial debate about their intervention. Doubts about Russia's position were dispelled by the receipt of a telegram from St Petersburg by the British ambassador, Lord Napier, warning that Russia rejected the French proposal. Tsar Alexander II personally clarified his position in the following words: "I will consider the recognition of the independence of the Confederate States by Great Britain and France as a 'casus belli' and in order to make the governments of France and Great Britain understand that it is not a mere threat, I will send a Pacific fleet to San Francisco and an Atlantic fleet to New York".

On 13 July 1863 one of the wildest riots in living memory broke out in New York. The riots had been conveniently prepared by an intensive press campaign; but the material organisers of the riots were the "Knights of the Golden Circle", i.e. Freemasonry. Their most prominent leader was Jacob Thompson. A month earlier, on 10 June, a meeting had taken place in Springfield, where a revolutionary plan had been drawn up. It was decided that New York would take the lead and other states would follow and assume independence. Fifty thousand people took to the streets in New York in protest at Lincoln's announcement to draft more troops for the war. The uprising was stoked by the mayor himself, Ferdinand Wood, who headed a corrupt council and had gone so far as to propose that the city become independent of the country. Wood whipped the masses into a frenzy. The riots were extremely violent. Murders, lynchings, looting and arson went on for five days and the city was razed to the ground. The hatred of the masses was concentrated on blacks, employed as labourers in the ports, taverns and other establishments in the city. Even an asylum for coloured orphans was robbed and burned. By the time the troops managed to stop the violence on 17 July, more than 100 people had lost their lives. The following weeks saw an exodus of blacks that greatly reduced New York's population.

Also in mid-July of the same year, while the two Russian fleets were already sailing on both oceans, the British-orchestrated uprising in Poland was being put down. Two months earlier, in May, the French foreign minister, Édouard Drouyn de Lhuys, had hypocritically invited Lincoln to join the ultimatum that Austria, France and Britain had sent to Russia in favour of Polish independence. Despite evidence of the failure of their strategies, Britain and France again threatened Russia on the "Polish question". Also in the summer of 1863, Palmerston and Russell were still

---

[32] The quotation comes from an extensive six-volume work, *Abraham Lincoln: A History* (New York, Century, 1890), which is one of the many documentary sources exhibited by Constantine George in the interesting thirty-page essay under discussion.

deliberating whether to intervene against the Union. It was in this context that on 24 September the two Russian fleets arrived simultaneously in the United States. The admirals commanding them, Lessovsky in the Atlantic and Popov in the Pacific, had sealed orders that they were to be opened only under certain circumstances. In short, the sealed envelopes stated that if the European powers intervened in the war, the fleets were to be placed under the command of President Lincoln.

The arrival of the ships prompted a number of welcoming events, including a parade of Russian sailors on Broadway on 17 October, escorted by a US Army honour guard, who were cheered and applauded by the crowds lining both sides of the avenues. There were no US naval forces on the Pacific coast, so the Russian fleet became the Union's war fleet, although it could only become involved in the event of intervention by a third power. The Russian fleets remained in American waters for seven months, until April 1864. Only then, when the danger of war with the European powers had passed, were they ordered to return.

One inescapable question is the financing of the war. To get an accurate picture of the situation, it should be borne in mind that in the 19th century the Rothschilds' power became omnipotent, as they held half the world's wealth. However, as their dominance grew, they chose to hide in the background. As a result, their name appears on only a small fraction of the companies and credit institutions they control. In 1861, also began the economic war, for when Lincoln needed money to meet the costs of the conflict, international lenders, behind which were the Rothschilds, offered loans at unacceptable interest rates of 24% and 36%. The explanation for the demand for such high interest rates can only be one: the financial powers of Europe had gambled on the partition of the country. Lincoln declined the offer and turned to an old friend, Colonel Dick Taylor, for a solution. Taylor advised him to have Congress pass an act authorising the issuance of Treasury notes, which could be used to pay soldiers and meet other expenses. When asked by Lincoln if the people would accept the notes, Taylor replied: "The people, or whoever they may be, will have no choice in the matter if you give them legal value. They will have the full recognition of the Government and will be as good as money".

The Treasury notes were printed with green ink on the back and were therefore known as "greenbacks". Lincoln printed $449,338,902 in these Treasury notes, interest-free money that was legally used to pay all public and private debts. With them he paid soldiers, civilian employees and bought war supplies. In 1865 in an editorial article the *Times* of London wrote: "If this evil financial policy, which has its origins in America, takes hold and is confirmed, then that Government will begin to print its own currency without cost. It will pay off all its debts and be left with none. It will have all the money it needs to continue doing its business. It will become prosperous without precedent in the history of the world. That Government must be destroyed or he will destroy all the monarchies of the globe." There is only one fundamental error in these words: what would be destroyed would be the power of the usurious bankers who enslave with debt all the peoples and governments of the world. Hitler too stood up to international banking with a system like that of Lincoln. In National Socialist Germany, too, Treasury bonds were issued, free from the slavery of interest, which brought the country out of ruin, as we shall see in the chapter on the Second World War.

The ideas of Henry Carey, the great American economist who proposed abolishing the gold standard and issuing money to help the population in certain circumstances, were being applied to some extent with the greenbacks. If we consider that taxpayers were no longer paying high interest rates, that public enterprises could be financed without usury, that the maintenance of government stability was assured and that Treasury policy was at the service of the Administration, it is clear that money was no longer the master but at the service of the people and the nation. Having found that the system devised by Colonel Taylor worked, Lincoln went so far as to consider adopting this emergency measure permanently and declared : "We have given to the people of this republic the greatest blessing they have ever had - their own paper money to pay their debts".

Although the war was drawing to a close, B'nai B'rith lodges in the southern states continued to be used as sanctuaries and centres for the espionage operations led by Judah Benjamin. Thus, as early as 17 December 1862, General Ulysses Grant had issued an order for the arrest for espionage of all Jews from Tennessee to Mississippi. Simon Wolf was the defence counsel for numerous B'nai B'rith officers and other Jews who were indicted and put on trial; but Grant ordered that Wolf also be arrested as a spy. Wolf's release was obtained through Lincoln's Secretary of War, the traitor Edwin Stanton. A few years later Wolf became president of B'nai B'rith. Among the spies infiltrating the Northern States working under Judah Benjamin was John Wilkes Booth, the Mason chosen to assassinate the President.

On 4 March 1865 Lincoln was inaugurated for his second term as President of the United States. The re-election was a relative surprise, since international bankers had been working against him since the creation of the greenbacks. A circular ("Hazzard Circular") from the Bank of England, controlled by Lionel Rothschild, issued in 1862 and printed by Senator Pettigrew, clearly stated that Treasury notes should not be accepted for certain payments or in international transactions:

> "Slavery will probably be abolished by the war power. On this I (Rothchild?) and my European friends agree, because slavery is the possession of labour and carries with it the care of the workers, whereas the European plan, led by England, is that capital will control labour by controlling wages. This can be done through the control of money. The huge debt arising from the war, which the capitalists have to face, has to be used as a means of controlling the volume of money. To accomplish

this the bonds must have a banking base. We now expect the Treasury Secretary to make these recommendations to Congress. The "greenback", as it is called, should not be allowed to circulate as money any longer, because we cannot control it. But we can control the bonds and through them the bank issues."

In this way, the bankers succeeded in getting Congress to vote in 1862 an Exception Clause, according to which greenbacks could not be used to pay taxes, duties or import duties. As early as 1863, the bankers succeeded in getting Congress to repeal the Greenbacks Act, which was replaced by the National Banking Act, introduced in Congress on the initiative of Salomon Chase, an agent of the Rothschilds who was Secretary of the Treasury until 1864. Under this act, private banks handled interest-bearing money. After the passage of the Act, greenbacks were withdrawn from circulation as soon as they entered the Treasury. Lincoln then stated: "I have two great enemies, the army of the South in front of me and the bankers at my back. Of the two, the bankers are my worst enemy". The president was forced to reserve the right of veto until after the war, which ended on 9 April 1865. It is unlikely that Lincoln would have been able to stand up to the bankers had he not been assassinated. In any case, his diagnosis and his forecasts were very pessimistic. Before his re-election he had declared: "The money power is a parasite on the nation in time of peace, and conspires against it in time of war.... I see in the near term a crisis approaching which makes me uneasy and makes me tremble for the future of the nation: corporations have been enthroned, an era of corruption in high places will follow. The money power will attempt to prolong its reign... until wealth is accumulated by a few hands and the Republic is destroyed."

On 14 April, a few days after the end of the war, the actor John Wilkes Booth, a Jewish Freemason who belonged to the Knights of the Golden Circle, shot President Lincoln in the back while he was attending a performance at Ford's Theatre in Washington. He then jumped from the box onto the stage and before fleeing shouted, "This is how tyrants die. The South has been avenged. The real leaders of the conspiracy, such as Judah Benjamin, who would have given the order for the execution, went unpunished, for only the wretches of the day were executed. The involvement of the aforementioned Edwin Stanton is widely acknowledged. This traitor removed Lincoln from personal custody when he went to the theatre, and after the assassination he distributed photos of the assassin's brother to the press, which bought time for John Wilkes Booth, whom Stanton himself had helped to escape by clearing a way out of Washington. In addition, Stanton forbade General Grant, who was due to attend the function, to accompany the president.

Nevertheless, a police operation was launched to try to capture those suspected of involvement in the plot. Albert Pike, who was also accused of the killings when he commanded his Indian troop, took refuge for a time in British-ruled Canada, where he met Jacob Thompson, a leader of the Knights who had provoked revolts and riots against blacks in northern cities. Pike was allowed to return to the United States, where he was arrested. We already know that he was immediately pardoned by the Masonic President Andrew Johnson. Judah Benjamin, who had established his main base for espionage services in Montreal, Canada, escaped to England. There he met other exiled Masons such as Robert Toombs, a 33rd degree Mason, and James Bulloch, an agent who had acted as August Belmont's liaison to England and had been the principal arms dealer for the Confederacy. John Slidell remained permanently in France. John Surrat, a secret Confederate agent, whose mother was arrested and hanged on charges of aiding and abetting Lincoln's assassination, left for Italy. Surrat was discovered and had to return for trial, but was acquitted, although he publicly admitted that he had planned with Booth to kidnap Lincoln before the assassination.

After the Civil War, the Rothschild agent, August Belmont (Schönberg), imposed his leadership on Jewish finance between London and New York. Joseph Seligman became part of the banking syndicate of the Rothschilds and J. P. Morgan. In April 1866 Congress passed the Contraction Act, which allowed the Treasury to withdraw greenbacks from circulation. The next steps were aimed at establishing the gold standard, a metal owned mainly by the Rothschilds. It is they who set the price of gold on a daily basis from the City of London. In order to achieve their purpose, they created instability and panic by contracting credit and provoking a depression (a tactic they have been applying time and again). Through the press, always in their hands, they spread the belief that the lack of the gold standard was the cause of the hardship. At the same time they used the Law of Contraction to reduce the volume of money in circulation, which in ten years decreased by 70%. In 1872 the Bank of England sent Ernest Seyd to the United States, who set about bribing congressmen to support his plan to demonetise silver. Seyd personally drafted the bill that became the "Coinage Act", which stopped the minting of silver coins. Ernest Seyd himself explained: "I went to America in the winter of 1872-73 authorised to secure, if I could, the enactment of a law demonetising silver. It was in the interests of those whom I represented - the Governors of the Bank of England - that this should be achieved. In 1873 the only coins being minted were gold."

Predictably, with the dominance and influence of British agents in the White House, the entente with Russia that had allowed Lincoln to avoid British and French intervention declined. A year after Lincoln's assassination, on 16 April 1866, an individual shot at the Tsar in St. Petersburg. A man managed to knock the terrorist's gun away and Alexander II was saved. Shortly afterwards Cassius Clay met the Tsar and congratulated him on having escaped death "so soon after the assassination of Lincoln". The Tsar replied: "I trust that with the help of Providence our mutual calamities will strengthen our friendly relations and make them permanent". Powerful enemies had an interest in Alexander II's wish not being fulfilled. In the following years four more attempts were made to assassinate the Tsar. Finally, on 13 March 1881, the very day that Alexander II had signed the Constitution consolidating far-reaching reforms for the Russian people, a commando under the command of a Jewish revolutionary and narodnik, Vera Nikolayevna Figner, succeeded in killing Alexander II. Figner, who in 1879 had attended the Congress of Land and Freedom (Zemlia i Volia), the Narodnik organisation founded by Alexander Herzen, was a member of the Executive Committee of "Narodnaya Volia" (People's Will). Figner was also a leader of its military wing, in the organisation of which she had played a leading role. Already in 1880 Vera Figner had attempted to kill the Tsar in Odessa. In the end, a Narodnaya Volia commando of three terrorists succeeded. Figner, who after the assassination was the only member of the Narodnaya Volia Executive Committee to remain in Russia, was not captured until 1883. Sergey Degayev, an infiltrated police mole, denounced her. She was sentenced to death, but the sentence was commuted to life imprisonment in Siberia. Dr. Joseph Kastein, a prominent Jewish historian, wrote that Jewish involvement in the murder was "natural".

From the above it can be concluded that the American Civil War did not break out, as is claimed, to end slavery, but was prepared in advance by certain European financial powers, the Rothschilds and their associates, who, relying on France and Great Britain, whose Prime Minister Lord Palmerston was Grand Master of the Scottish Rite of Freemasonry and Patriarch of the Illuminati, intended to divide the United States into two federations, two zones of influence. Some authors refer to an alleged conversation in 1857 between Benjamin Disraeli, Lionel Rothschild and James Rothschild, who were meeting in London for the wedding of Lionel's daughter Leonora to his cousin Alphonse, James's first-born son. Disraeli reportedly suggested informally that, once the break had been achieved, the English Rothschilds could dominate in the north and the French in the south: "Divide et impera". The Jewish lodge B'nai B'rith and the "good Masons", some of whom were traitors who held key positions in one or the other government, acted as determining elements employed in the service of the conspiracy. From within the lodges, with complete impunity, all sorts of stratagems were set in motion, including, of course, terrorist activities, the purpose of which was to inflame tempers and eventually provoke war.

Bismarck, the Franco-Prussian War and the Rothschilds

The revolutionary six-year period is perhaps the most picturesque period in Spain's contemporary history. It had a bit of everything. It began with the revolution, known as the Glorious Revolution, led by a handful of military and political Freemasons. It was followed by the Provisional

Government with the Regency of Serrano, who was a Freemason. The period was characterised by the desperate search for a king for Spain and the promulgation of the Constitution of 1869. Amadeo I of Savoy finally arrived, a high degree Freemason who in two years had to deal with three presidents, six cabinets and an assassination attempt. He resigned. Then came the first federal Republic, which enjoyed four presidents in eleven months. Then came the Pavia coup d'état. The history of the six-year period continued with the unitary Republic until December 1874, when Martinez Campos's dictatorship was overthrown, bringing back the Bourbons. All this was accompanied by three civil wars: the third Carlist war, the cantonal insurrection and the war in Cuba. Let's see who gives the most.

The offer of the Spanish throne to various candidates became a European issue and was the pretext that lit the fuse for the Franco-Prussian war. The first candidate was the Duke of Montpansier, brother-in-law of Isabella II, who was convinced that he would be the new king of Spain; however, Napoleon III was opposed to him, he had practically vetoed it, and General Prim made this known to him. Antoine d'Orléans, Duke of Montpansier, was the son of Louis-Philippe d'Orléans. The second candidate was Prince Leopold of Hohenzollern-Sigmaringen. His candidacy had been suggested by Otto von Bismarck himself to Eusebio Salazar y Marredo, who, in an article in a German newspaper, proposed the candidacy of Leopold, who spoke perfect Spanish and was married to a daughter of the King of Portugal. Salazar offered to mediate and Prim accepted, on condition that everything was done with extreme caution. Salazar soon informed Prim that Prince Leopold would agree if his father, Prince Karl Anton, and the King of Prussia gave his permission. The Prussian king, Wilhelm I, was the most reluctant, but Eugene Salazar was assisted by Bismarck himself in trying to convince the king. There was an exchange of correspondence between Prim and Bismarck, mediated by Lothar Bucher. Everything was being done with due discretion and nothing was suspected in Paris.

Let us see from this point on how things went from the Spanish side. On 26 June 1870 Salazar went to Madrid to meet the President of the Government. Unfortunately Prim, a high degree Freemason whose lodge name was Washington, was not in the capital that day: accompanied by Milans del Bosch he was hunting ducks in Daimiel. Salazar then decided to meet the Minister of the Interior, Práxedes Mateo Sagasta, another 33rd degree Mason and Grand Master of the Grand Orient of Spain. Upon hearing Salazar, Minister Sagasta took him to the President of the Cortes, Manuel Ruiz Zorrilla, who was also a Freemason and Grand Master of the Grand Orient of Spain. "Prince Leopold King of Spain? And you say that the arrangements are so far advanced?" asked an astonished Ruiz Zorrilla. The next step was a demonstration of the utmost stupidity of this politician, who supposedly must have had a sense of State and understood the value of discretion in a matter that affected the whole of Europe: Ruiz Zorrilla had no better idea than to tell a journalist friend, José Ignacio Escobar, editor of *La Época*, who, of course, had no time to publish the news, which immediately spread throughout Europe.

General Prim, indignant, called a meeting of the government and finally reported on his secret dealings in Prussia. The ambassador in Paris, Olózaga, was ordered by telegraph to speak to the French emperor. At the same time, convinced that he could not turn back, Prim sent Rear-Admiral Polo de Bernabé to Prussia to convey to Prince Leopold the Spanish government's intention to support his candidacy in the Cortes. From this moment on, war began in the European chancelleries. Napoleon III sent an agent to the Freemason general Francisco Serrano, who held the Regency, urging him to disavow Prim, who accepted the request. Serrano immediately commissioned a nephew of his, Colonel of the General Staff José López Domínguez, to travel to Prussia and try to dissuade Prince Leopold from accepting the Spanish Crown. In turn, the ambassador in Paris, Olózaga, dispatched the Romanian diplomat Stratz, a personal friend well regarded among the Prussians, to the Prussian court.

The issue as seen from France and Prussia took on other connotations. First of all, it should be mentioned that the penetration of the French economy and French capital in Spain was considerable during the 1960s. A group of banks grouped in the "Banque de Paris" had become an unforeseen competition for the Rothschilds and Spain was one of the stages of the struggle. The Banque de Paris had presented its credentials to the Spanish government for a large-scale credit operation. Moreover, Adrian Delahante, a director of the Bank of Paris who was on the board of directors of the Madrid-Zaragoza-Alicante railway line, coveted the profits from the exploitation of the Almaden mercury mines and the Rio Tinto copper mines. It is not surprising, then, that the French government was unwilling to accept the candidacy of a Prussian prince to the Spanish throne, especially if, as we have seen, it was being promoted by Bismarck himself.

Bismarck's real aim in supporting Prince Leopold was to provoke a reaction from France that would trigger the war that would enable him to unite Prussia and the southern German states. The greatest difficulty lay in convincing Leopold's father, Karl Anton, and King Wilhelm I to stand up to France. Leopold had initially declined the offer on 22 April 1870, but Bismarck had been manoeuvring in the shadows until he changed his mind. It was in this context that, as a result of Ruiz Zorrilla's indiscretion, the whole thing came to light and events were precipitated. The French ambassador in Berlin, Benedetti, following instructions from his foreign minister, the Duke of Gramont, demanded that the King of Prussia disavow Prince Leopold's candidacy for the Spanish crown and that he undertake in writing not to present it again. Leopold of Hohenzollern-Sigmaringen refused to recant in view of the disgrace that the rectification meant for his person. It seems that his father then said to him: "You madman! You are a madman! Your throne is not in Madrid, but in the madhouse...". Thus pressurised by his own father and requested by King Wilhelm I, the prince resigned once again.

On 12 June Karl Anton declared that his son would not be a candidate, and the King of Prussia acknowledged to Benedetti that this was "good news that saves us all from difficulties". On the same day the king assured Ambassador Benedetti that he personally approved of Leopold's withdrawal "in the same sense and to the same degree as he had given his approval", i.e. "completely and unreservedly". Bismarck had been out of the game and all seemed settled when on July 13, 1870, he received the famous telegram from Ems, which contained the essential point of the meeting between Ambassador Benedetti and Wilhelm I, according to which the King of Prussia was to give the assurance that he would "never in the future give his consent to a Hohenzollern candidacy." In Bismarck's rewriting of the telegram for the press, it was reported that the king could not assume such a definite statement; but he further implied that the demand had been offensive to him. Bismarck thus sought to offend Gramont and to use the telegram which he himself had doctored to unleash a campaign of anti-French propaganda aimed at domestic and international opinion.

A week earlier, on 6 July, in the midst of diplomatic negotiations, the French government had unwisely adopted an inflammatory declaration drawn up by the Foreign Minister, Alfred Agénor, Duke of Gramont, and read out in Parliament, in which, in violent language, it demanded an absolute veto by the king of the Hohenzollern candidacy and threatened a declaration of war if Leopold accepted. It was clear that after the conversation between King Wilhelm and Ambassador Benedetti on the 12th, Leopold's candidacy had been withdrawn. There was no reason to insist on such a textual and concrete statement as was demanded in the Ems telegram. Obviously, Gramont and those familiar with the many flourishes of diplomatic language knew that this was an unnecessary, reckless provocation, as was a letter demanding that the King of Prussia apologise to Napoleon. Instead of resting in relief after William I's conciliatory words to the French ambassador, the Duke of Gramont used the Ems telegram as a "casus belli" and on 14 July mobilisation took place. On 15 July 1870 France declared war on Prussia.

Before going on, a few lines may help you to get to know this character. Antoine Alfred Agénor, Duke of Gramont, was appointed Minister of Foreign Affairs two months before the outbreak of war, on 15 May. His friendship with the Parisian Rothschilds is well known. James Rothschild, the last of Mayer Amschel's five surviving sons, had died in 1868. The head of the Paris house was since then Alphonse, who after hearing of the appointment declared: "We shall be delighted with the appointment from any point of view, because it is necessary to have at the head of this Ministry a man of experience, who is intelligent enough not to pretend to gain fame for himself by brilliant genius". Well, we don't know whether or not pushing for war can be considered genius, but we do know from Niall Ferguson that later, in 1878, the Duke of Agénor's son became related to the Rothschilds by marrying Margaretha Rothschild, daughter of Mayer Carl Rothschild, head of the House in Germany. Curiously, history was to repeat itself sixty-nine years later, in 1939, when the man who worked hardest to bring about the outbreak of World War II, Lord Halifax, Minister of the Foreign Office, related his heir son to a granddaughter of the British Rothschilds.

With or without the Ems telegram, with or without the succession question in Spain, it is likely that France and Germany would have ended up at loggerheads; but the fact remains that the candidacy for the Spanish throne was used by both sides as a reason for going to war. On the other hand, the fact that France started hostilities was decisive, as it determined Britain's non-intervention. The first clashes took place on 4 August, and the first French defeats at Wörth and Forbach came on 6 August. The battles of Borny, Rézonville and Gravelotte followed between the 14th and 18th. As a result of these defeats, Marshal Bazaine retreated as far as Metz, where he was blockaded. Faced with these events, Napoleon III and Marshal Mac-Mahon took command of the French army at Chalons. Between 1 and 2 September, the Battle of Sedan was fought, which decided the outcome of the war. Faced with the scale of the slaughter, Napoleon III ordered the raising of the white flag and surrendered with the entire army to the Prussian General Helmuth von Moltke. It has been said that the Krupp guns, which were breech-loaded while the French guns were muzzle-loaded, were decisive in the Prussian victory. That may be so; but two years earlier they had not been so in Spain: on 28 September 1868, at the famous Battle of Alcolea Bridge, the government troops of the Marquis of Novaliches had modern Krupp guns at their disposal and were nevertheless defeated by the rebels under the command of the Duke de la Torre.

As soon as the news of the disaster at Sedan and the capture of the emperor reached Paris, the agitation increased. On 4 September, thousands of people took to the streets, and soon shouts of Long live the Republic, long live the Prussians! The military governor of Paris, General Trochu, remained inactive, and Gambetta was later to reward him by appointing him head of the Provisional Government. The crowd moved towards the Parliament, where Gambetta took the rostrum and proclaimed the decline of the empire and the advent of the Third Republic. Finally, the demonstrations moved on to the City Hall, the place of the revolutionary tradition, where, after singing the Marseillaise, the deputies of Paris staged the coup d'état and proclaimed the Third Republic once again. Between cheers and jeers, the Freemason Jules Ferry proposed: "The deputies of Paris to the Government! In fact, the list had already been drawn up the night before. Among these fathers of the fatherland who had led the marches and formed the Government of National Defence, Republican Freemasons predominated as usual. We will mention only the most prominent Brothers: the indefatigable Adolphe Crémieux, the

Grand Master of the Scottish Rite, who ceded the limelight to his adopted son, a corrupt Jew and Freemason named Leon Gambetta who was Minister of the Interior and War; Emmanuel Arago, who in 1878 would attain the post of Grand Orator of the Supreme Council of France; Jules Favre, a Freemason who in addition to the vice-presidency assumed the portfolio of Foreign Affairs; Jules Simon, Minister of Public Instruction, who called on the officials in his department to fight until the Republic was proclaimed in Berlin; Eugène Pelletan, who joined Freemasonry in 1864 in the lodge "l'Avenir", where he attained the degree of Venerable before joining the Council of the Grand Orient of France.

While in Paris the Republican leaders were rushing to organise the defence of the country, Bismarck and his army were approaching the capital. On their way they reached Ferrières, where the Iron Chancellor established his headquarters. It should be remembered that the chateau at Ferrières originally belonged to Joseph Fouché and in 1829 had been bought by James Rothschild. Significantly, Ferrières, an estate of 3,000 hectares of fields and woods, was the place chosen by Bismarck to settle with his General Staff for the duration of the siege of Paris. Moreover, it was at Ferrières that the complicated financial negotiations between France and Prussia, whose bankers were all Jewish, were to take place, and from which the Rothschilds were to emerge as the winners. Should one think, as Niall Ferguson suggests, that this is just irony?

The first to arrive at Ferrières on 14 September were Generals von Eupling and Gordon. By the 19th the King of Prussia, Wilhelm I, arrived, accompanied by Bismarck; Moltke, Chief of the General Staff; Roon, Minister of War; and about three thousand generals and army chiefs. Niall Ferguson recounts the arrival in these words: "For some of these uninvited guests at least, Ferrières was a revelation. With its dreamy exteriors and exotic interiors, it seemed like 'a fairy tale, magnificent', despite the fact that it was the creation of a Jew - of the king of the Jews ('Jüdenkönig'), as Roon called it, tempering his admiration with disdain. The initials JR - James Rothschild - that adorned walls and ceilings were translated as 'Judeorum Rex' with rueful humour." On 21 September Bismarck himself wrote the following to his wife: "I am sitting here under a picture of old Rothschild and his family... negotiators of all kinds cling to the coat tails of my jacket like Jews around a market vendor." Days later, when asked if he was willing to negotiate peace terms with a republican regime, Bismarck replied sarcastically that he would recognise "not only the Republic, but also, if necessary, the Gambetta dynasty... in fact, any dynasty, be it Bleichröder or Rothschild." So much so that Bismarck later granted Gerson Bleichröder a title of nobility, making him the first Jewish nobleman in Prussia. His father, Samuel Bleichröder, had founded the bank in 1803 and acted as a subsidiary of the House of Rothschild in Berlin, so close was their relationship. In *The Reign of the House of Rothschild* Egon Caesar Corti writes that Gerson

Bleichröder had long dreamed of founding a large Prussian bank in partnership with the Rothschilds and eventually created the Rothschild Group with them.

A little known fact is that Otto von Bismnarck's mother, Luise Wilhelmine Mencken, was of Jewish origin. John Coleman in *The Rothschild Dynasty* claims that he himself found her background. According to Coleman, Haim Solomon, one of General George Washington's financiers, to whom he donated his entire fortune so that he could start the revolution, was an ancestor of Bismarck's mother. Coleman cites a newspaper, *The Jewish Tribune of New York*, which on 9 January 1925 confirmed in an article that Luise Mencken was a descendant of Haim Solomon. Similarly, John Reeves states in *The Rothschilds: the Financials Rulers of Nations* that Bismarck was half-Jewish and suggests that he was a man close to the Rothschilds. Benjamin Disraeli's novel *Coningsby* and *Lord Beaconsfield's Letters* note that the Rothschilds had already taken notice of Bismarck as a young man in his early twenties and that by 1844 he was under their influence. If the latter is true, Bismarck would have been a co-opted politician.

Be that as it may, Otto von Bismarck's personal glory in going down in history as the statesman who put all the pieces of the Second German Reich together is personal and non-transferable. After his victory over France, in 1871 he not only achieved the union of Prussia with the southern German states, but also annexed Alsace-Lorraine, the two former provinces which for more than two centuries had maintained the German language and customs. It was this intended annexation that delayed the signing of the armistice until 28 February 1871, as the French republicans were unwilling to cede territory. However, Mayer Carl Rothschild, as soon as the first French defeats occurred, was quick to inform his uncle Lionel and his cousins in London on 15 August of the mood on the Frankfurt Stock Exchange: "I dare say that France will lose her two old German provinces, a considerable part of her fleet and will have to pay a great deal of money besides".

The Republican government thought that a moderating intervention by Britain would prevent any territorial cession. Consequently, no sooner had the Council of Government and National Defence been formed than Jules Favre declared that they were not prepared to cede an inch of territory. On 17 September the British Ambassador to France, Lord Lyons, after a personal interview with the Iron Chancellor, advanced the German position to Gustave Rothschild, Alphonse's brother: Bismarck had told him in advance that he did not need money and that what he wanted was Metz and Strasbourg. Lyons warned Gustave that if his request was refused, he would cut off communications and enter Paris. A day later, on 18 September, the first meeting between the French foreign minister and Bismarck took place. Favre offered Bismarck five billion francs if France would retain the disputed territories; but "old B" ("old B", as the Rothschilds familiarly referred to Bismarck) was blunt: "We will talk about money later, first we want to determine and secure the German frontier".

It was Jules Favre himself who called for the arming of the National Guard. Gambetta ordered that two hundred and eighty-three battalions be recruited mainly from among the working class, which was suffering from very high unemployment. By the end of September Paris already had a proletarian army, a quarter of which were Communists and anarchists registered with the International. Since the guards elected their leaders, many of the elected commanders were revolutionaries. On 14 October Favre, who had received expressions of solidarity from Spanish Republicans, in a desperate attempt to get help from a European country sent Emile Keratry to Madrid. Keratry, prefect of police in Paris, left the capital by balloon, as there was no other way to circumvent the siege imposed by the Germans on 19 September. On 19 October 1870, he was received by Prim at the Buenavista Palace. The first thing the Frenchman tried to do was to convince General Prim to proclaim himself president of the Republic. Then, in exchange for an army of 80,000 men capable of going on campaign within ten days, to be maintained by France, Keratry offered 50 million francs and the ships Spain needed to suppress the Cuban insurrection. Prim not only refused the offer, but told him: "There will be no republic in Spain as long as I live".

If we bear in mind that putting an end to the monarchies and the power of the Church is the main objective of Freemasonry, we cannot understand the attitude of Prim, who, moreover, was called Washington in his lodge. It is clear that the ideas of the Illuminati did not influence this Catalan general, who was assassinated two months later. Keratry left the meeting enraged and ready to take reprisals against Spain. The orders he gave to the sub-prefect of police in Bayonne and to the commissioner general, who were waiting for him across the border, are recorded in Don Carlos' diary. To both he ordered the following in a loud voice: "Official and complete protection for the Carlists, broad powers for them to make policy, to gather people, arms and battalions. In the event that Don Carlos should go to the frontier, he was to be given every consideration and all the honours due to his high rank"..

In view of the Republican government's intention to hold out despite the siege of Paris, King Wilhelm I decided on 5 October to leave Ferrières and return to Prussia. Before leaving, he had personally ordered that the French Rothschild estates were not to be searched and that neither the wines in the cellars nor the game birds were to be touched. Bergman, who was in charge of the estate, confirms that before leaving, the king handed over 2,000 francs for the service staff. He also demanded a written declaration that nothing was missing from the palace at the time of his departure and left seventy-five men in charge of the protection of the premises. Only blankets and mattresses were requisitioned for the wounded convalescing in nearby hospitals.

The defeat that the Masonic Republicans who seized power in Paris after the coup d'état of 4 September wanted to ignore became increasingly evident. Hopes of a counterattack were finally dashed when, on 27 October, Bazaine, with an army of 113,000 soldiers, capitulated at Metz, where he had held out under siege since 19 August. In view of the irreversible victory, William I was proclaimed Emperor in the Hall of Mirrors at Versailles on 18 January 1871. Ten days later, also at Versailles, Jules Favre obtained a three-week armistice from Bismarck so that a National Assembly could be elected to negotiate peace. Among the conditions imposed by Chancellor Bismarck was the disarmament of the Paris garrison, with the exception of twelve thousand soldiers for the maintenance of order and twenty thousand municipal guards. Jules Favre begged Bismarck not to disarm the 190,000 National Guards, and "old B", whose intelligence service necessarily had information of what was being prepared, agreed.

On 8 February 1871, legislative elections were held in France and the Republicans were clearly defeated. For an Assembly of 675 deputies, the Radical Republicans won 38 seats and the Moderate Republicans 112, while the Orleanists won 214 seats and the Legitimists 182. The Liberals won 72 seats and the Bonapartists 20. As in 1848, the results once again demonstrated the conservatism of French society, ignored time and again by those who sought to impose themselves through violence. This was demonstrated by the Paris Commune, which provoked a new civil war, almost exclusively confined to the capital, in which some thirty thousand Frenchmen lost their lives. The new Assembly chose Adolphe Thiers as head of government. In addition to postponing the discussion on the final form the state would take, as the monarchists dominated the Parliament, Thiers led the negotiations with Germany until 1873. One of the first decisions of the Assembly meeting in Bordeaux was to abolish the salaries of the National Guards, except for the indigent. It was hoped that this would reduce their numbers, but only a few thousand workers returned to their workshops. The revolutionary elements remained in their battalions with or without pay. If the intention was to leave the guardsmen without pay, Favre's request to Bismarck not to disarm them is, if not suspicious, then quite incomprehensible.

Before turning to the events that took place in Paris during the two months of the Commune, it is worth noting a few financial facts. The first thing to note is that the House of Rothschild, with offices in the main European capitals, emerged stronger from the crisis. The banks on both sides that ran into difficulties were those that lacked liquidity. While the French market collapsed and the German market rallied, the London Stock Exchange remained unscathed. Mayer Carl Rothschild, who headed the Frankfurt House and was of course invited by Wilhelm I to his imperial proclamation at Versailles, did not miss the opportunity to make the most of the war. To strengthen the capacity of his management, Mayer Carl asked his cousin Lionel of London, to whose sister Louise, his cousin, he was married, to transfer substantial sums of money to him, which were used to demonstrate the extent to which the Frankfurt Rothschilds could be useful to the German government. The government of Napoleon III considered it advisable for the Banque de France to suspend convertibility into gold, in order to prevent attempts at capital outflows. From the beginning of the conflict, French capital began to flow to England. The French Rothschilds revealed as early as 4 August, the day of the first skirmishes on the battle front, that they were not prepared to take any risks, as they tried to pass two million francs in silver to Belgium to exchange for gold. The police seized the money, convinced that it was being smuggled illegally. This information comes from Niall Ferguson in *The House of Rothschild. The World's Banker 1849-1999*. According to Ferguson, the shipment was made on behalf of the government; but this claim does not seem credible, since if the operation had been legal the police should have been warned. On 12 August the Bank effectively suspended the gold conversion, which was followed by a moratorium on bills of exchange. Alphonse Rothschild himself comments in a letter that a high-ranking military officer asked them to send a portion of their financial securities to the London headquarters for safekeeping, and adds: "Such a suggestion on his part, as you can imagine, has aroused our suspicions, and we plan to follow his example". After these words it is even more difficult to believe that the shipment to Belgium of two million francs in silver was on behalf of the Government.

As for the negotiations for the payment of compensation, they began as soon as Thiers was invested with authority. Alphonse, who alluded to Thiers with the euphemism "our friend", knew that Thiers' relations with his father had not been good. As we know, James had forced his downfall in 1840 when they clashed over Thiers' attitude in the Damascus Affair. Alphonse once remarked that "he was the small president of a great Republic". But pragmatism prevailed because Thiers realised that the political situation was subordinate to financial issues. After the election result, Alphonse travelled to London on 21 February 1871 to plot strategy at New Court with his cousin Lionel, who after James' death had become the undisputed leader of the family. It was then that they decided that the financial operations would revolve around the London House. On the 22nd Alphonse was asked by Thiers to return to France. Talks had begun at Versailles, and Bismarck had initially asked for compensation of 6 billion francs, a figure that had been described by the French negotiators as exorbitant. In addition, a payment procedure was being sought in which the German bankers Bleichröder and Henckel would be instrumental. Favre put it this way: "They wanted to carry out a colossal operation with our millions". On the 25th Alphonse presented himself at Versailles as the representative of the Rothschilds of London and Paris. The next day Thiers and Favre agreed to the figure of 5 billion gold francs which France would pay to

Germany at 5% interest; but it was further agreed that the Rothschilds, namely the House of London, and not the German bankers, would control and manage the financial operations of the indemnity. Once again it was demonstrated that wars and revolutions in Europe caused losses and even the ruin of certain banking institutions, yet the Rothschilds, apart from profiting from them, appeared to be the key to guaranteeing international stability. The head of Crédit Lyonnais, Mazerat, lamented that the French joint-stock banks had been practically squeezed out. The quote comes from Ferguson:

> "In all the affairs contracted since the war, the House of Rothschild and, under its aegis, the high banking group have played an almost exclusive part.... It was the Rothschilds and their friends, with the backing of the Bank of France, who advanced 200 million francs needed by the city of Paris to pay its war contribution (demanded by Bismarck). It was the same group that reserved the 2 billion loan and it was only as a favour that, at the last minute, the credit establishments were allowed to obtain a paltry 20 million commission which the Rothschild consortium had also secured for themselves.... Now the next loan for the city of Paris is announced on the same terms...".

The Paris Commune, Marx and Bakunin

The Franco-Prussian war showed that the internationalist ideologues, agents of the bankers who financed the MRM, had not succeeded in eliminating patriotism in the workers. The German workers stood with their compatriots and looked with pride on Bismarck's victories. But even Marx and Engels did not believe in fraternal union between the proletarians of different countries. While the French workers in 1870 appealed to the Germans, the correspondence between Max and Engels (*Der Briefwechsel zwischen Marx und Engels*) shows that Marx himself wished for the victory of the Prussians. "The French," he wrote on 20 July 1870, "need a thrashing ('Die Franzosen brauchen Prügel'). If the Prussians win, the centralisation of state power will be useful for the centralisation of the German workers. Moreover, the German preponderance will shift the centre of gravity of the workers' movement from France to Germany; and it is enough to compare the workers' movement in the two countries to understand... that the German worker is superior to the French, whether one considers the theoretical order or the organisation. The preponderance of the German proletariat over the French, in the theatre of the world, will become at the same time the preponderance of our theory over that of Proudhon". These words show that Marx did not believe in what he preached. In fact the French branch of the International in London denounced him as an agent of Bismarck. Marx wrote again to Engels on 3 August telling him that he was accused of having received £10,000 from Bismarck. True or not, it is undeniable that Marx and

Engels applauded the German victories and in the name of the General Council of the International tried to convince the French proletariat not to fight the invaders. For many internationalists their position was shameful. Quite different was the attitude of Bakunin, who was in Locarno and borrowed money to answer the call of the revolutionary socialists in Lyons. Marx remained a refugee in London and, surprised by the speed of the French military defeat, was unable to react. While the Blanquists and the republicans living in Paris organised themselves in one night, Marx was initially overwhelmed by events.

Nevertheless, within half a year he had time to draw up a strategy and was able to establish the necessary mechanisms for contacting his supporters in Paris through liaison. Hardly had the principle of agreement been reached in Versailles when the events that led to the famous Paris Commune, one of the revolutionary episodes most mythologised by the communist and socialist left, began. It was a new revolutionary rehearsal that ignored the election results and tried to impose a political option that had barely obtained any representation. On 1 March, under the pretext that the Prussians were to enter the city, the Vigilance Committee ordered the National Guards to invade the artillery parks. Two hundred and seventy-seven cannons were taken away and taken up the hill of Montmartre. The National Assembly, meeting in Bordeaux, had just ratified the terms of a disastrous peace. On 6 March the Comité de Surveillance met in the Paris premises of the Internationale and, under the pretext that the Bordeaux National Assembly, dominated by the royalists, intended to overthrow the Republic, issued a proclamation announcing a Republican Federation of National Guards and provisionally assumed all powers. Hence the name federates given to the communist insurgents. The composition of the Central Committee was dominated by members of the International. On 11 March, a manifesto of this Central Committee addressed to the National Guardsmen invited them to "remain united for the salvation of the Republic, to oppose any attempt at disarmament, to oppose the surrender of the guns, to oppose force to force".

In Bordeaux, the National Assembly, faced with the turn of events in Paris, decided to hold its sessions in Versailles. Thiers then tried to disarm the National Guard and recover the Montmatre guns, but the result was the arrest of Clément-Thomas, the old general of the National Guard, and General Lecomte. On 18 March 1871, both were shot on a fence in the rue des Rossiers after a mock trial. They were the first victims of the fratricidal struggle that was to follow. The tricolour flag was lowered at Paris City Hall and the Rothschilds' red flag, the flag of the social revolution, was raised. The military governor of Paris, Joseph Vinoy, and General Ducrot were in favour of immediately establishing order by a coup de force before the revolutionaries could organise the defence; but Thiers, who hoped to avoid bloodshed by negotiation, ordered the evacuation of the capital: all loyalist troops and civil servants were concentrated in Versailles. A municipal election held on March 26th in the Paris town halls under bayonet pressure gave a pretended legitimacy to the Commune Government, in whose General Council Marx placed a dozen of his representatives in the International.

Marxist historiography has taken over the internet and it is difficult to find a version critical of the revolutionaries, who are presented as patriots, martyrs and champions of freedom. Marx, who had asked the French proletariat not to fight against the invaders, in March sarcastically encouraged civil war and now, yes, wanted the workers to fight against their compatriots, class enemies. If one examines, for example, the massacre on the Place de Vendôme, the difference is abysmal depending on which version one reads. For non-Marxist historians, a demonstration of unarmed National Guardsmen and civilians, including women and children, marching against disorder behind the tricolour flag was met with a volley that left some thirty dead. According to Max, "... under the cowardly cloak of a peaceful demonstration, these bands, secretly equipped with the weapons of thugs, put themselves in marching order, mistreated and disarmed the National Guard patrols they met in their path, and on reaching the Place Vendôme, to shouts of 'Down with the Central Committee! Down with the murderers! Long live the National Assembly!' attempted to break through the cordon of guard posts and take by surprise the headquarters of the National Guard." Apparently, the result of the elections was of no importance. Marx had only words of contempt for those who opposed his pretended dictatorship of the proletariat. Prince Kropotkin writes that Max gave orders to his agents through the General Council of the International and pretended to direct the insurrection from London, where he received the reports which he demanded to be sent to him daily.

Yet it was absurd to want to control events from abroad when on the ground Bakunin's anarchists and other enlightened Freemasons were in direct contact with daily events. On 26 April, for example, a Masonic commission that came to congratulate the Commune was greeted with the slogan "Long live the Universal Republic", the battle cry of illuminism coined by Cloots (Anacarsis). One of the speakers from the delegation of Freemasons, Brother Thirifocque, declared that "the Commune was the greatest revolution the world could contemplate, that it was a new temple of Solomon which the Freemasons were obliged to defend". On May 1st, in imitation of the 1789 revolution, the Commune created a Public Health Committee and wanted to adopt the old revolutionary calendar. Louis Énault in *Paris brulé par la Comunne* writes that some fifty thousand foreigners and seventeen thousand criminals released from prison took part in the events. As had happened in 1792-93, there was desecration of churches, smashing of images and paintings, theft of relics and instruments of worship. As usual, pulpits were used as tribunes for blasphemy. When the cause was seen to be lost, during the so-called Bloody Week, looting, murder and arson were continuous and systematic. On 27 May, a general massacre of prisoners, including sixty-six gendarmes, was carried out. A few days earlier, on 24 May, the Archbishop of Paris, Mgr Georges Darboy, and four other priests had already been shot in the Roquette prison. Before his death, the archbishop reproached his murderers for using the word freedom: "Do not utter the word freedom, which belongs exclusively to those of us who die for freedom and for the faith". The elderly parish priest of the Madeleine and Abbé Deguerry were also murdered in cold blood. Landmark buildings in the capital: the Tuileries Palace, the Palace of Justice, the Palace of the Legion of Honour, the Ministry of Finance, the Town Hall, some twenty palaces, as well as numerous houses in the rue Royal, rue Bac and rue de Lille were burnt to the ground. The Public Assistance Office and the granaries where oil, grain and wine were stored were also burned.

Yet, despite all this maelstrom, amidst more than six hundred barricades scattered throughout the city, the sumptuous houses of the Parisian Rothschilds miraculously remained intact. The mansion on rue Saint-Florentin, for example, was protected night and day by a picket of guards charged with chasing away all the greedy. The patrols continued for two months, until the barricade two steps away from the building was demolished by the Versailles troops. It is very significant to note that the protection of the Jewish banker's property ordered by the communists was never disallowed. None of the French Rothschilds' possessions suffered the slightest damage, and certainly not Ferrières, where the invaders stayed for a year. When in August 1871 the last Prussian soldiers, though perhaps it would be better to say Prussian guests, left the estate, Lionel's brother Anthony visited Ferrières to see what the Prussians had done. A letter from Anthony states that "there is not the slightest damage either to the house or the park or the trees, there are just as many pheasants in the park as before, nothing broken in the gardens.... I think it's wonderful that nothing has been stolen". His cousin Gustavus, James's second son, when he visited the palace days later, acknowledged the same: "The estate is in as good a condition as it would have been possible to expect."

Like the Parisian revolutionaries, Marx always left the Rothschilds untouched. Marx refers to big financiers, to the moneylenders, to stock speculation; but not a word about the Jewish bankers as the main financiers, let alone a direct criticism of the Rothschilds as the greatest capitalists of all time. Marx's dishonesty is evident. It should not be forgotten that he was a Frankist Jew and, as Jacob Frank had prescribed, lying and falsehood constituted basic rules of conduct. By contrast, Werner Sombart in *The Jews and Modern Capitalism* refers to the Rothschilds as the world's leading loan sharks, as the kings of the railways. Sombart sees the Rothschilds as exercising absolute power in Europe from 1820 onwards.

On 10 May 1871, the French government signed the Treaty of Frankfurt, which put an end to the Franco-Prussian war. It was agreed that by right of war and because the population of Alsace-Lorraine was predominantly German, these provinces would become part of the German Empire. In exchange, 100,000 prisoners of war were released, who contributed to the repression of the Paris Commune, which was bloodily crushed. The final toll was nearly thirty thousand dead, including many revolutionary guardsmen, some of whom were shot on the spot on the orders of a number of exalted officers. However, in the opinion of those in favour of merciless repression, there was too much clemency, since of the two hundred and seventy condemned to death in the courts martial, only twenty-six were executed. However, on 14 March 1872, the new French Republic passed a law providing for penalties for those who belonged to the International, forcing many into exile and the usual refuge in London and Switzerland.

One of the most serious consequences for the International after the defeat of the Commune was the confrontation and definitive rupture between Bakunin and Marx. Marx, as he had done after the revolution of 1848 with *The Class Struggles in France,* hastened to publish in London a Manifesto of the General Council of the International Workingmen's Association, entitled *The Civil War in France.* This pamphlet appeared in June 1871. With it he wanted to regain the prestige he had lost in the eyes of the workers by his statements in favour of the Germans. However, he could not prevent his authority from being challenged: the revolt against the Marxist autocracy of the International, "the Marxist synagogue" as Bakunin called it, began immediately. Many did not forget his declared sympathies for the Germans. It was in Switzerland that Bakunin, who had abhorred communism in 1869 because he considered it "a denial of freedom", led an organised offensive.

In order to better understand the antagonism between Marx and Bakunin, it is useful to give a brief outline of the leader of anarchism before proceeding. Mikhail Bakunin (1814-1876) was born in Russia into a family of landowners. At his father's wish, he entered the military academy, but in 1836 he dropped out when he was an officer in the imperial guard. In a confession to Tsar Nicholas I, he told him: "I fell in love, I got entangled, I went astray". In 1840 he went abroad to study at the University of Berlin. At the age of 27, he decided to join the Carbonari centres, where he endeavoured to put the doctrines of Mazzini and Young Europe into practice. In 1842 he settled in Dresden, one of the main centres of Young Germany, and joined this organisation. He then met Arnold Ruge, who offered him to contribute to the *Franco-German Annals,* where, as mentioned above, Bakunin wrote under the pseudonym Jules Elysard. The Saxon police began to monitor his activities, and Bakunin fled to Paris in 1843, where he stood out among the Russian and Polish émigrés as the most active agent of carbonarism. He had no godparents, like Karl Marx, and unlike Alexander Herzen, who thanks to James Rothschild was able to get his fortune out of Russia, Bakunin could not count on money from his country, since the Russian government, which ordered his immediate return, withdrew the permission to travel abroad that it had granted him in 1841. For a living, Bakunin contributed to *Réforme*, an extreme left-wing newspaper founded by the Freemason Ferdinad Flocon, one of the leaders of French carbonnarism. It was at this time that he met Karl Marx, who, like him, was a member of the editorial staff of the *Franco-German Annales*. From the outset there was no cordiality between them, quite the contrary. In early 1848 Marx even threatened him if he persisted in opposing his politics. In March 1848 he took part in the revolutionary events in Prague,. Arrested in Dresden in 1850, he was sentenced to death in May, but was eventually commuted to life imprisonment. Recalled by Austria because of his involvement in the Prague uprisings, he was extradited. In May 1851 Bakunin was court-martialled and again sentenced to death. A new appeal, this time from the Russian government, saved him from execution. Back in St. Petersburg, he was tried and sentenced to death for the third time in September 1851. The death penalty was officially abolished in Russia and capital executions were very rare, so the Tsar commuted the sentence to hard labour. He spent ten years in Siberia, until Alezander Herzen managed to organise his escape from London. It was in this way that Bakunin arrived in England in 1862. This was the time when Marx was working in the English capital to lay the foundations of the International.

Although their relations, it has already been said, were unfriendly or unfriendly, Marx could not prevent Bakunin from joining the International. Soon, however, he tried to get rid of him. Marx spread the rumour that Bakunin was an agent of the Tsarist police, to whom he passed information about the international revolutionary movement. Bakunin discovered the source of the turmoil around him and ascertained that it was German Jews affiliated to the International, followers of Marx, who were attacking him. In 1869 he wrote a study on the German Jews, *Polemic against the Jews*, which can be found in volume V of the *Collected Works*. In it, while acknowledging that he "exposed himself to enormous dangers", he said: "the sect of the Jews, much more formidable than that of the Jesuits, Catholics and Protestants, constitutes today a real power in Europe. It reigns despotically in commerce, in the banks, and has invaded three quarters of German journalism, and a very considerable portion of the journalism of other nations, and woe betide anyone who commits the clumsiness of displeasing them!" Bakunin knew that Jewish bankers financed Marx, which is why he claimed that he and his comrades "had one foot in the bank and one foot in the socialist movement."

After the Franco-Prussian war and the failure of the Commune, Bakunin led the movement of the discontented against Marx, who was reminded of his Germanophile statements, while holding him responsible for the leadership of the insurrection and calling for an end to his personal power. In a manifesto addressed to all the national branches of the Association, they proposed that the International should be a federation of autonomous groups which would freely establish their doctrine, instead of receiving it from the hands of an infallible prophet. Marx realised that the

Association could get out of hand and replaced the Congress which was to be held in 1871 with a simple conference, which was held in London from 13-23 September. Instead of weakening Marx's position, this conference increased the powers of the General Council, controlled by him, which would henceforth have the power of admission to and exclusion from the International. Against this resolution, the Spanish delegate Anselmo Lorenzo and others protested vigorously.

Only two months later Bakunin organised a protest conference in Sonvillier (Switzerland), from which the Jura Federation of the International was born. In addition, all national branches were asked to join. Positive responses were immediately forthcoming. The first was sent by Kropotkin from Russia. Then followed those from Spain, Belgium, Holland, which adhered in their entirety. The French and Italian sections also accepted Bakunin's theses in the majority. Only the English and German-speaking countries remained loyal to Karl Marx, who, enraged, did not hesitate to counterattack with infamous procedures. His son-in-law, Paul Lafargue, after failing in his attempt to organise a new Spanish branch to replace the one that had defected, published a list of the names of the Spanish leaders of the International and handed it over to the police. The same thing happened in France, where a delegate of Marx, Dentraygues, unable to bring the Midi sections back to orthodoxy, denounced them to Thiers' police. On 14 December 1872, Engels recognised that the party was lost in France, Belgium, Spain and Italy. In September 1873 a congress in Geneva brought together delegates from seven federations from Spain, Italy, France, Jura, Holland, England and Belgium, who responded to Bakunin's call.

Having seen the consequences of the Franco-Prussian war and analysed its political and social repercussions, it is clear that the power of the Rothschilds was once again decisive in all respects. John Atkinson Hobson in *Imperialism: A Study* asks the question: "Can anyone seriously suppose that a great war can be undertaken by any European state, or that any great loan can be subscribed to a state if the house of Rothschild and its connections object?" The same author answers his question with a bold and extremely critical statement, "There is not a war or a revolution, an anarchist murder or any other social commotion, which does not generate a profit to these men; they are harpies who sip their profits from any sudden disturbance of the public credit."

CHAPTER VI

PROTOCOLS OF THE ELDERS OF ZION, THE MASTER PLAN OF THE WORLD GOVERNMENT

"We will transform the universities and reorganise them according to our plans. The presidents of the universities and their professors will be specially prepared by means of action programmes, secret and well studied". This fragment of the *Protocols* reminds us once again of the importance that, as early as the enlightenment, education was accorded in shaping the thinking of individuals and society. The control of education and educational establishments, of book publishing, of the press, is as much an obsession in the Illuminati programme as it is in the *Protocols*. However, despite the almost absolute domination of ideas exercised through the media and books in general, it can be said that attempts to discredit the document that has gone down in history as the *Protocols of the Learned Elders of Zion* have partly failed. This chapter, in addition to tracing the history of this text that accurately reflects the current state of the world and humanity, presents contributions from researchers who have studied the *Protocols*, the latest of whom is Peter Myers, an Australian professor who, with commendable tenacity, has endeavoured to demonstrate their authenticity and to refute the repeated arguments of those who have claimed that they are forgeries.

In reality, the *Protocols* do nothing more than concretise in detail the plan that had been hinted at since Adam Weishaupt in texts and statements by various Talmudist and Zionist or Proto-Zionist leaders throughout the 19th century. The idea that the end justifies the means, for example, is basic to both enlightenment and the *Protocols*. Weishaupt wrote. "Consecrate yourselves to the art of counterfeiting, to conceal and disguise yourselves when observing others.... The good of the Order justifies slander, poisoning, murder, perjury, treachery, rebellion, in a word, all that the prejudice of men regards as crimes". In the *Protocols* he expresses himself in much the same way: "He who aspires to dominate must make use of cunning and hypocrisy. We must not shrink from bribery, deceit and perfidy if they help us in the triumph of our cause. The end justifies the means. In drawing up our plans, we must look not so much to what is good and moral, but to what is profitable and necessary".

We have seen that Rabbi Baruch Levy wrote to Marx that "the children of Israel.... will everywhere, without opposition, become the ruling class..." Adolphe Crémieux, in the founding manifesto of the Universal Israelite Alliance addressed to all the Jews of the world, insisted on the same idea: "The day is not far distant when all the riches and treasures of the world will be the property of the children of Israel." In the 18th century Weishaupt had expressed it in these words, "It is necessary to establish a universal regime of domination, a form of government which will embrace the whole world." Consequently, the text of the *Protocols* once again points to the unrenounceable goal of a world government. In a reduced format, the European Union (where countries have lost sovereignty and are subject to fines or sanctions and to the suffocating speculation of the markets, where international Jewish banking wields omnipotent power) could be an example of what is wanted at the global level: "In place of the present governments, we will place a monster, which would be called the Supergovernment administration. Its power, like enormous pincers, will extend everywhere and it will have at its disposal such an organisation that it will be almost impossible not to extend its dominion over all nations." The continuity of the same line of thought is evident. With the appearance of the *Protocols of the Learned Elders of Zion*, the plan of World Government exercised by the Jews and their acolytes was laid down unmitigated for posterity. So disturbing and disturbing was the mass dissemination of the text in the early 20th century that the Bolshevik leaders, almost all of whom were Jews, after the seizure of power in Russia, condemned to death anyone who had a copy of the *Protocols* in their homes. Alexander Kerensky had earlier ordered the search of bookshops in Moscow and St. Petersburg in order to confiscate any copies found.

Biarritz, the strange novel by the spy Hermann Goedsche

Before focusing on the *Protocols,* mention should be made of a text that precedes them and which has been the subject of various controversies. Umberto Eco even published a novel on the subject in 2010. The text we are referring to is *Biarritz* (1868), a novel of almost two thousand pages published in four volumes under the pseudonym of Sir John Retcliffe, behind which Hermann Goedsche was hiding. Goedsche, who died in 1878, worked as a spy for the Prussian secret police, who occasionally commissioned him to follow and monitor political figures. Under the pseudonym Retcliffe he published numerous narrative works of historical content in which he combined fact and fiction with great skill and talent. His works, written in German, have not been translated into English and only some of them can be read in English. Currently, the four volumes of *Biarritz* can still be found in German. In one of the chapters of the novel, "The Jewish Cemetery in Prague and the Council of the Representatives of the Twelve Tribes of Israel"[33], we find the text that interests us, since it is a summary of the *Protocols of the Elders of Zion.*

Retcliffe recounts a meeting in the Jewish cemetery in Prague at which Rabbi Reichhorn, referred to as 'the director of the meeting', gives the floor to the attendees, who one after the other deliver prophetic speeches over the tomb of Simeon ben-Judah, the great teacher of the Kabbalah. This meeting, called the "Kabbalistic Sanhedrin"[34], attended by thirteen people dressed in the ritual white robes of the Levites, is held only once every century, as the rabbi himself confirms at the beginning of his speech: "Every hundred years, we, the sages of Israel, are accustomed to meet to review our progress towards the world domination which Jehovah has promised us, and our conquests over our enemy, Christendom". The speech alludes to the previous Sanhedrin and reviews the achievements since then: "This year, united at the tomb of our reverend Simeon ben-Judah, we can proudly state that the past century has brought us very close to our goal and that this goal will be reached very soon". Then each of the attendees, coming from Amsterdam, Toledo, Worms, Budapest, Krakow, London, New York, Prague, Rome, Lisbon, Paris and Constantinople, took the floor. In the Prague cemetery, in addition to the tomb of Simeon ben-Judah, there is also the tomb of Rabbi Judah Löw, another renowned Kabbalist who in the 16th century created the "Golem", the famous monster that has been repeatedly depicted in literature and film. Both graves are today objects of veneration by Jewish tourists, thanks to the fact that the Nazis, despite propaganda to the contrary, respected Jewish cemeteries in the occupied countries.

---

[33] In 2010 Umberto Eco published *The Cemetery in Prague*, yet another of his best-selling novels. In it the author, who increasingly resembles one of those intellectuals Weishaupt wanted to win over to the cause, works to discredit the *Protocols*. In the book everyone conspires to defame the Jews. The French secret service, the Russians, the Vatican, the Jesuits, the Freemasons vie for political power and all try to blame the Jews, who, of course, are the only ones who are not accused of anything and do not conspire against anyone. Echo treats them as if they were saints. Now, when one of them dares to criticise his fellow Jews, they are Jews who hate themselves because they are Jews (the same accusation that the Zionists hurl against those who dare to denounce their crimes). In reality, this professor shows his feather duster with this novel and discredits himself.

[34] The meetings of the Sanhedrin are known only to the highest Jewish leaders in the world. It is thought that since 1491 they would have taken place every ninety years. The calculation takes into account the mystical value of numbers ("guematria"). It follows a mathematical relationship and chronology that matches the sum of the numbers of each year of the Sanhedrin's celebration with the Kabbalistic number '6', which is sacred to them. According to these calculations, the years of meeting would have been 1581, because $1+5+8+1=15$, and $5+1=6$. The third meeting would have taken place in 1671. The fourth, in 1761. If this logic is true, Retcliffe wrote about the fifth Sanhedrin, held in 1851. The sixth would have been held in 1941, and in 2031 the seventh should be held, for $2+0+3+1=6$.

As to whether the meeting at the Prague cemetery described in *Biarritz* actually existed, this can certainly be questioned, and the fact that it is reported in a novel suggests that the author may have used this ploy to reveal his knowledge. The fact that it is reported in a novel suggests that the author may have used this ploy to reveal his knowledge, but it cannot be denied that Hermann Goedsche, alias John Retcliffe, surprisingly announced in 1868, through the speeches of those attending the Prague cemetery meeting, a series of events that were subsequently put into practice. It is likely that this Prussian spy was very well informed about the activities of Jewish organisations and their relations with Freemasonry. Goedsche probably had at his disposal the texts pronounced by Crémieux at the founding of the Universal Israelite Alliance, which announced Zionism and blatantly revealed the intentions of Jewish world domination. It is also possible that Goedsche was also familiar with the *Dialogues in the Infernos between Machiavelli and Montesquieu*, a text published by Maurice Joly in 1864, which, as we shall see in more detail below, is cited as a source for the *Protocols*. Another text that the spy Goedsche may have known is a famous speech delivered by a rabbi of the Simferopol synagogue, a document known as *A Rabbi's Discourse on the Goyim,* which in the middle of the 19th century was circulating among the Jewish leaders of Russia. Years later, in 1900 to be precise, the Simferopol rabbi's speech was published in the form of a denunciation by the Austrian MP Wenzel Brenowsky under the title *The Jewish Claws*. In any case, John Retcliffe's text is real, it exists in *Biarritz*. The following are some of the ideas that Retcliffe put into the mouths of the rabbis at the Prague cemetery almost a century and a half ago:

1. "Let us try to replace the circulation of gold by paper money; our coffers will hoard the gold and we will regulate the value of the paper, which will make us masters in all positions." 2. "Already the leading banks, the exchange houses of the whole world, the credits of the governments are in our hands." 3. "The other great power is the press. By endlessly repeating certain ideas, the press finally succeeds in getting them accepted as realities. The theatre does us a similar service. All over the world, the press and the theatre obey our orders". 4. "By ceaselessly praising democracy, we will divide Christians into political parties, we will destroy the unity of nations, we will sow discord everywhere. Reduced to impotence, they will bow before the law of our bench." 5. 5. "We shall force Christians into wars by exploiting their pride and stupidity. They will slaughter each other and clear the way for our people." 6. 6. "We have among us many orators capable of exciting and persuading the masses. We shall spread them among the people to announce changes that would ensure the happiness of the human race. By money and flattery we shall win over the proletariat, who will themselves annihilate Christian capitalism. We will promise the workers wages they have never dared to dream of, but at the same time we will raise the price

of what is needed, so that our profits will be even greater." 7. "In this way we shall prepare revolutions which the Christians will make themselves and from which we shall reap the fruit." 8. "By our mockery and our attacks we shall make their priests ridiculous and odious, and their religion as odious and ridiculous as their clergy. We shall be the masters of their souls..." 9. 9. "But above all, let us monopolise education. In this way we shall propagate ideas that are not useful and form the brains of the children as it suits us." 10. "Let us not hinder the marriage of our men to Christian women, for then we shall enter into the most reserved circles. If our daughters marry 'goyim', this will be no less useful to us, for the children of Jewish mothers are ours..."

The *Protocols* arrive in Russia and are being published worldwide.

Among the most frequently cited books on the history of the *Protocols* and their connection to Zionism is *Waters Flowing Eastward*, by Leslie Fry, the pseudonym of Paquita Louise de Shishmareff, an American citizen who married an Imperial Russian naval officer named Feodor Ivanovich Shishmareff, an aristocrat murdered by the Bolsheviks during the revolution, in 1906 in St. Petersburg. Paquita de Shishmareff, following her husband's instructions, left the country in time with her two children and the family fortune. In her book Leslie Fry explains that the person who introduced the text to Russia was Justine Glinka, the daughter of a general who worked for the Russian Intelligence Service. It was this young woman who established contact in Paris with the Jew Joseph Schorst, alias Schapiro, who was a member of the Mizraim Masonic Lodge, a Jewish lodge whose complicated rites were based on the Mysteries of Memphis and Eleusis.

Perhaps in the late 19th century the use of women as agents was not as common as it is today: today they are commonplace in intelligence services. The Mossad, for example, used a female agent to kidnap Mordechai Vanunu, a Jewish nuclear technician of Moroccan origin who in 1986 revealed to the British newspaper *The Sunday Times* that Israel had a nuclear programme[35]. It is impossible to know with certainty what means Justine

---

[35] A Mossad agent, Cheryl Bentov, codenamed "Cindy", posed as an American tourist and lured Vanunu with her charms. After having sex with him in London, on 30 September 1986, she persuaded him to travel together to Rome, where she was to continue her European holiday. Once in the Italian capital, Cindy drove her victim to a hotel. There she gave him a sleeping pill and he was abducted by the Mossad. Vanunu was put on a ship that sailed to Israel, where he was secretly tried and sentenced to 18 years in prison for treason and espionage. In 2004, after serving his sentence, he tried to leave Israel, but was not allowed to do so. He is still forcibly detained there today, without freedom of movement. On 5 February 2004 Shabtai Shavit, former head of the Mossad, told Reuters that in 1986 the option of killing Vanunu was considered, but dismissed, as "Jews don't behave like that towards other Jews." Joseph Schorst, however, was not so lucky.

Glinka used to get Schorst to offer to take a copy of the *Protocols* out of the lodge. Leslie Fry reports that he bribed him with two and a half thousand francs, then a fortune, which was sent to him from St. Petersburg. Joseph Schorst soon realised that his life was in danger because of his treachery and fled to Egypt, where, according to French police records, he was eventually murdered.

Justine Glinka sent a French copy of the document to General Orgevsky in St. Petersburg, enclosing a Russian translation. Orgevsky, General Cherevin's secretary, handed both texts to his superior, who was Minister of the Interior. However, instead of sending the document to the Tsar, he decided to file it away. According to Leslie Fry, Cherevin "had obligations to rich Jews". In 1896 Cherevin died and wanted Tsar Nicolas II to receive a copy of his memoirs, which contained the *Protocols*. In the meantime, certain books about life at the Russian court appeared in Paris which displeased Nicholas II. They were published under the pseudonym of Count Vassilii, behind which another woman, Juliette Adams, was hiding; but they were maliciously attributed to Justine Glinka, who when she returned to Russia fell into disgrace and was removed to her estate in Orel. There, the young woman gave a copy of the *Protocols* to Alexis Sukhotin, marshal of the nobility of that district, who showed the document to two of his friends, Stepanov and Nilus. The former had it printed in 1897 and in the same year it was circulated privately. In an affidavit Philip Petrovich Stepanov explains his decision to print the text as follows:

"In 1895, my neighbour in the district of Toula, Marshal (retired) Alexis Sukhotin, gave me a handwritten copy of the *Protocols of the Elders of Zion.* He told me that a lady friend of his, whose name he did not mention, while residing in Paris, had found them in the house of a friend, a Jew. Before leaving Paris, she had secretly translated them and had brought a copy to Russia and given it to Sukhotin. I first mimeographed the translation, but seeing that it was difficult to read, I decided to print it without mentioning the date, the town or the name of the printer. I was helped in this by Arcadii Ippolitovich Kelepovskii, who at that time was head of the household of Grand Duke Sergius. He gave the document to the printer. This was in 1897. Sergei Nilus inserted these Protocols into his work and added his own commentary."

Professor Sergei Nilus published in 1902 *The Kingdom of Satan on Earth. Notes of an Orthodox Believer,* in which he quoted excerpts from the document bought by Justine Glinka. In 1903 Pavel Khrushchevan, editor of the newspaper *Znamya (The Banner),* published passages and quotations from the document in his newspaper. Khrushchevan suffered an attempt on his life and thereafter decided to go armed for protection and even hired a personal cook to prevent any attempt at poisoning. In 1905 Sergei Nilus published the full text of the *Protocols* in Tsárkoye-Seló under the title *The*

Great in the Small in Tsárkoye-Seló. A friend of Nilus, George Butmi, a lieutenant in the Imperial Guard, had also published the text in 1901, and had reportedly taken it out of the country. A copy was deposited in the British Museum under the entry stamp of 10 August 1906, number 3926, d. 17. It is a black leather-bound copy of the Antichrist, consisting of 417 pages, in which, in Appendix XII, the 24 Protocols appear. As early as 1907, G. Butmi published his fourth edition of the *Protocols* in Russian in St. Petersburg. In January 1917 Nilus had prepared his second edition, but before he could publish it, the March revolution took place and Kerensky, i.e., the Jewish 32nd degree Mason Aaron Kirbiz, ordered the edition to be destroyed.

In 1924 Professor Nilus was arrested, imprisoned and tortured by the Kiev cheka. Although he was released for a few months, he was arrested a second time and taken to the Moscow cheka, which imprisoned him again. In 1926 he was confined in Vladimir, a district located a hundred kilometres east of the Russian capital. He died there in 1929. Some copies of his second edition were saved and sent to other countries, where editions were published. In Germany Gottfried zur Beek, pseudonym of Ludwig Müller von Hausen, published the text in 1919. In England a translation by Victor E. Marsden was published in 1920 by a society called *The Britons*. In France Monsignor Jouin, a prelate of His Holiness and an expert in Masonic-Jewish affairs, published the *Protocols* in *the Revue Internationale des Societés Secrètes*. Urbain Gohier did the same in *La Vieille France*. In the United States, also in 1920, the Protocols were published in Boston by Small, Maynard & Co. in 1921. In 1921 Beckwith Co. published them in New York. Subsequent editions appeared in Italian, Arabic and Japanese.

The Anti-Defamation League of B'nai B'rith was quick to insert denunciatory writings throughout the United States. One of its members, Louis Marshall, personally "persuaded" George Haven Putnam, of the New York publishing house Putman & Son, to desist from publishing the Protocols. Putnam had reproduced in book form a series of eighteen articles published by the journalist Howell Arthur Gwynne, editor of the *Morning Post* in London, entitled *The Cause of World Unrest*, with the cover advertising the forthcoming edition of *The Protocols of the Elders of Zion*. On October 131920 Louis Marshall wrote a letter to G. H. Putnam expressing his desire for a new edition of The Protocols of the Learned Elders of Zion. Putnam in which he expressed his indignation at the publication of Gwynne's articles and alluded to the text of the *Protocols* as the work of a gang of conspirators: "The slightest knowledge of history," he said, "and the most elementary analytical ability or even the slightest notion of what the Jew is and has been in history would be sufficient to trample this book and the false *Protocols*, on which it is based, as the most formidable libels in history." Marshall appealed to patriotism and urged Putnam to refrain from going ahead with the edition. In the reply, dated 15 October, the publisher disagreed with Mr Marshall, pointed out that his publishing house published books of all persuasions, and reminded him that "it would be impossible to carry on the business of publishing books of opinion, whether the ideas relate to subjects of the present or to matters of the past, if the publisher were to assume the views of one author or another." The letter ended with an allusion to freedom of speech and with the offer of the publisher's services for any rejoinder he might wish to make, whether from his own pen or any other personality of his choice. On 29 October Louis Marshall wrote again to reject the publisher's "theories". In a very harsh and uncompromising letter he referred to the many publishers who had sensibly refused to publish the *Protocols*, and warned him that if he needed to replicate in the future he would have no need at all to rely on his company. On 1 November Putnam wrote to Marshall to announce that he was giving up publishing the book. Putnam acknowledged in writing to one of the parties interested in the edition that he had come under so much pressure that he had not only had to abandon publication of the *Protocols*, but was also forced to withdraw unsold copies of *World Unrest*. It seems that the threats he received included bankruptcy. In fact, the publishers who did not back down and published the document ran into financial difficulties within a year or two.

Henry Ford face-off: *The Dearborn Independent*

1920 was the year that marked the beginning of a historically unprecedented offensive to discredit a document and try to prevent its publication: no effort was spared to achieve this aim. The pressure on publishers was already beginning to bear fruit and the ADL was intimidating advertisers with its denunciations when one of the most famous episodes in the struggle against international Judaism took place in the United States. The protagonist was Henry Ford. This time it was not a publicist who could be easily intimidated, but the famous automobile magnate, a traditionalist and conservative patriot who had the courage to stand up to them. Against all odds, Ford dared to massively disseminate the text of the *Protocols* in the pages of his weekly newspaper, *The Dearborn Independent*. It came as an unexpected surprise to those who aspired to take complete control of the press. Ford's personal secretary, Ernest G. Liebold, bought the weekly in 1918. On 11 January 1919, the first issue appeared under the editorship of Henry Ford, who decided to publish *The Protocols of the Elders of Zion* from March 1920. The paper, whose title was *Chronicler of the Neglected Truth*, reached a circulation of nearly 800,000 copies in 1925 and, despite all kinds of attacks, survived until December 1927. Hypocrisy-laden accusations against Ford's attitude, such as "persecutions without a Christian spirit", "attack on the spiritual fusion of the races" and other such slogans preceded claims of "anti-Semitism" by the ADL and San Francisco Jewish lawyer Aaron Sapiro. The Anti-Defamation League organised a coalition of Jewish organisations, which continually used the Detroit press to slam Ford.

Woodrow Wilson himself, a president totally dominated by a group of Jewish agents who had forced America's entry into the world war, joined in the accusations of anti-Semitism before leaving office. A boycott was also organised against Ford's products, and under pressure from everyone, including his own family, he was forced to close the paper in December 1927.

Ford, who denounced the group of Jews surrounding W. Wilson and associated them with the financiers who had fomented the war, did not write personally for his paper, but on his behalf William J. Cameron, a well-known journalist hired to edit *The Dearborn Independent.* It was Cameron who in 1920 brought Henry Ford into contact with Paquita de Shismareff, who had just arrived in the United States after a brief stay in England and Canada. She herself personally gave the industrialist a copy of the *Protocols* that she had brought from St. Petersburg. Other sources, however, claim that it was Boris Brasol, author of *The World at the Crossroads*, who gave Ford the *Protocols* in English translation. One way or another, Ford had first-hand information about the crimes being committed in Russia by Judeo-Bolsheviks financed by American and European Jewish bankers. The material published in the newspaper was collected in 1920 in a book signed by Henry Ford himself, entitled *The International Jew, which* was promptly translated into other languages, including Spanish. Theodor Fritsch translated it into German and it was so widely read in Germany, where the brilliant industrialist's views were fully shared, that by 1922 there had been twenty-two editions of Fritsch's translation.

Henry Ford, "a self-made man", a hard worker with an iron will, had founded the Ford Motor Company in 1903, which by 1908 was able to produce twenty-five units per day of the famous Model T. By 1913 he had started up the assembly line and was able to produce a car in ninety-three minutes. In 1913 he had started up the assembly line and succeeded in producing a car in ninety-three minutes. The line demanded machine-like behaviour from the workers, which was exhausting. Ford, aware of the effort required, hired a thousand men for every hundred jobs and doubled the wages of his employees, thus establishing the five-dollar day, a fact that met with public approval. Henry Ford soon realised that his enemies could wrest control of the company from him by buying up shares. So in 1919 he bought the shares of all the shareholders at very high prices. He, his wife and his son Edsel thus became sole owners, able to do whatever they wanted with the Ford Motor Company. Naturally, his opponents did not like the move and likened him to a dictator. It was then that he set up the largest industrial complex on the planet, the "Rouge Plant", which employed up to 100,000 workers and had a hospital, a fire brigade, an internal police force and around 5,000 maintenance staff. It was at "the Rouge" that *The Dearborn Independent* was located. Henry Ford then became the man of the hour and, consequently, the *New York World* newspaper decided to interview him in

February 1921. Inevitably, the reporter asked him about his campaign to publicise *the Protocols,* to which he replied: "The only comment I will say about them is that they fit in entirely with what is going on". In other words, what was said in the *Protocols* was almost entirely true in 1921. Can anyone who has read the text deny that the world today is as it was intended to be in the late 19th century document, regardless of who wrote it?

The automobile as a means of locomotion within everyone's reach was the idea Ford had conceived, which is why he wanted to build good, strong and durable cars, capable of adapting to the muddy roads of the time. Luxury and ostentation were not part of his initial approach. In an effort to make it easier for people to buy his cars, he adopted a franchise system that allowed him to have a dealership in every city in the United States and in major cities around the world. However, competition from General Motors, which soon fell into the hands of financial institutions as its founders, unlike Ford, soon lost control of their company, made the famous Model T obsolete. The market was not satisfied with utility alone, with cars affordable by the majority, but demanded style, luxury. So the Ford Motor Company revived the old Model A, the first car of 1903, and successfully remanufactured it. Edsel Ford was in charge of the ornamental aspects and Henry Ford continued to oversee everything concerning the mechanics. Ford's response to the 1929 crisis caused by speculators was to raise the wages of his workers and reduce the price of his cars.

When the 1932 presidential election was held, Ford endorsed the Republican Herbert Hoover, a candidate he considered "a man of heart, honest and hard-working, who has been facing the enemy for three years and knows the tactics of the forces of destruction". Although he had been forced to abandon his campaign of denunciation in 1927, Henry Ford continued to take clear aim at the international Jewish financiers, whose candidate, Franklin Delano Roosevelt, won the election. Keeping the unions out of the Ford Motor Company was another of Henry Ford's aspirations; but in May 1937 union leaders Richard Frankenstein and Walter Reuther began an offensive that culminated in a strike in 1941. Ford, who was asked by his wife Clara to give in, eventually lost the battle. Despite these years of struggle against the unions, when a stroke took his life in 1947, seven million workers across the country paid their respects to Henry Ford.

On the authorship of *the Protocols*

Much has been written about the possible author(s) of the *Protocols of the Elders of Zion.* We will begin by outlining what Leslie Fry writes in *Waters Flowing Eastward.* In her opinion, what is said in the twenty-four Protocols had already been said in one way or another by scholars, philosophers or statesmen. What is really important to her is the extraordinary shrewdness with which the practical application of the plan was suited to existing conditions. Leslie Fry thinks she sees the announcement of the revolution in Russia in the last paragraph of protocol number thirteen: "To show that we have enslaved all the gentile governments in Europe, we shall manifest our power by subjecting one of them to a reign of terror, violence and crime." Certainly, if one takes into account what happened in Russia from 1917 onwards and considers that these words were written some twenty years earlier, one can think two things: either that the author was a visionary or that he had inside information about what the World Revolutionary Movement was planning to do.

L. Fry's thesis is that the author of the text was Asher Ginsberg, whose name as a writer was Ahad-Ha'am. Ginsberg, born in 1856 in Skvira, Kiev province, was a member of a Hasidic family. He received a rabbinical education and married the daughter of a prominent rabbi named Menachem Mendel. In 1878 Ginsberg was living in Odessa. Between 1882 and 1884 he visited Berlin, Breslau and Vienna, where he met Charles Netter, one of the founders of the Universal Israelite Alliance, who introduced him to the organisation. These were the years when Leon Pinsker and Moses Lilienblum led the "Hoeveve Zion" (Lovers of Zion) movement, which in the 1980s encouraged a return to Palestine. The movement's programme was contained in the pamphlet *Self-Emancipation,* which Pinsker published anonymously in German on 1 January 1882: "We will not accept any emancipation granted by others; we will emancipate ourselves", it was arrogantly stated. In 1884 Ginsberg, who also demanded a Jewish state in Palestine, returned to Odessa and in 1889 formed a secret organisation, "B'nai Moshe " (Sons of Moses), whose meetings were held in his house on Yamskaya Street. The best known members of the group were Ben Avigdor, Jacob Einsenstaat, Louis Epstein and Zalman Epstein. Leslie Fry claims that Ginsberg, who was called 'king of the Jews' in the city, read the *Protocols* to these co-religionists, from which she infers that they must have been written between 1880-1890. Russian Colonel Prinzeff also testified under oath in Riga that he had seen the *Protocols* and that they circulated among the Jews of Odessa.

Leslie Fry's allegations about the reading of the document in Odessa were also supported by William Cameron, Henry Ford's secretary. He claimed that the Jewish Herman Bernstein, Detroit editor of the Free Press, admitted to him that he had personally read the Hebrew-language *Protocols* in Odessa. The ADL accused Cameron of having lied and he proposed to settle the matter in court, but B'nai B'rith did not accept the challenge. If all these statements are true, it would prove that the text was circulated in the city of Odessa at meetings of prominent Jews. At the first Zionist congress, held in Basel in 1897, the text of the *Protocols* was part of the congressional documents. Leslie Fry attributes to Ginsberg a prominent leadership role within the Zionist movement, since, according to her, the greats of Zionism - Chaim Weizmann, Nahum Sokolov, Jabotinsky and others - would initially have been disciples of Asher Ginsberg, who in one of his writings said: 'Even if we succeed in establishing a Jewish state in Palestine, how can this achievement satisfy us? Have we really suffered so much for centuries to be satisfied merely with the foundation of a small state? It seems clear that if Ginsberg was aiming for world supremacy, Palestine would obviously be a lesser goal.

America's entry into the war of 1914-18, the British occupation of Palestine and the famous *Balfour Declaration* in 1917 were obvious achievements of Zionist agents during the conflagration years. As early as 1903 Max Nordau, co-founder with Theodor Herzl of the World Zionist Organisation, had declared that the Zionist ambition of Palestine would be achieved through the coming world war. In the *Protocols* it is stated that "universal war" would be the answer to any attempt to resist the plan. Not for nothing were the Bolshevik revolutionary leaders Jewish, almost none of them Russian. These Jewish communists had nipped in the bud the publication of the *Protocols* in Russia and applied the death penalty to those who had copies of the edited books. The tactics used in the seizure of power had been in many respects identical to those recommended in the *Protocols*. This led to a revival of interest, after the war, in the dissemination and study of the plan for world domination set out in the document.

Between 1919 and 1921, the battle to influence public opinion was fought mainly in England and the United States. Howell Arthur Gwynne, editor since 1911 of *The Morning Post*, published in 1920 in the paper eighteen articles on the *Protocols*, which later, as mentioned above, were the basis for the book *The Cause of World Unrest*. In the same year, Victor E. Marsden, the same newspaper's correspondent in Russia during the years of the revolution, published his translation of the text in "The Britons Publishing Society". The fact that Marsden, who was married to a Russian and was arrested and imprisoned by the Mensheviks, was well versed in the Russian language makes this edition one of the most cited. To these publications must be added the American ones, already mentioned above. Nothing could be more contrary to the spirit of the *Protocols* than this continued dissemination of the document, for the Protocols state the following about the control of information: "Not a single announcement will reach the public without our control. Even now we are already achieving this, since all news is received by a few agencies in whose offices it is concentrated from all over the world. These agencies will be completely ours and will publish only what we send them. This, which is now a reality, had not yet been fully achieved at the time in question: newspapers like *The Times, The Morning Post, The Spectator, The Dearborn Independent* were not yet under the absolute power of the conspirators, though they were not about to become so.

The battle for control of *The Times* will be discussed below, as it was the newspaper used to launch the campaign that attributed the drafting of the

Protocols to the Tsarist secret police, the "Ojrana". However, on May 8, 1921, *The Times*, then the most prestigious newspaper in the world, owned by Lord Northcliffe (Alfred Harmsworth), still published these words: "What do these Protocols mean? Are they genuine? Have such plans really been drawn up by a group of criminals and are they being carried out? Are they a forgery? But how then can this prophetic gift which foresees all this in advance be explained? Have we fought all these years to destroy the world power of Germany only to find ourselves now confronted by a far more dangerous enemy? Have we saved ourselves through great efforts from the 'pax Germanica' only to fall victim to the 'pax Judaica'...? If the *Protocols* were written by the sages of Zion, then whatever has been attempted and done against the Jews is justified, necessary and urgent." A few months later the paper's editorial line began to change.

Specifically, on 16, 17 and 18 August of the same year, *The Times* published a series of articles entitled "The Truth about the Protocols", which asserted categorically that the *Protocols* were nothing but a crude fraud by a plagiarist who had paraphrased a book (first published in Geneva in 1864 and then in Brussels in 1865) entitled *Dialogue in Hell between Machiavelli and Montesquieu*, authored by Maurice Joly. The newspaper published excerpts from both books in parallel columns and drew comparisons between the texts. *The Times*, dissociating itself from the Jewish press, boasted of its impartiality and claimed that it had uncovered the fraud in truth. Finally, it proclaimed that incontrovertible evidence had been established and called for the 'legend' of the Protocols to end soon and forever.

Proof that a battle for control of the paper was raging in those August days is provided by another article, also published on 17 August 1921, which insisted that what had happened in Russia had been announced in the *Protocols*. Here is an excerpt: "These documents attracted only a little attention before the Revolution of 1917 in Russia. The astonishing collapse of a great state due to the onslaught of the Bolsheviks and the presence of countless Jews among them has caused many people to seek reasonable explanations for the catastrophe. The Protocols provided this explanation, particularly the tactics of the Bolsheviks in many respects followed identically the recommendations of the Protocols."

Most astonishing, however, is the story *The Times* invented to explain how it had come to discover the forgery. It was said in a report that a correspondent of the paper in Constantinople, Philip Graves, happened to meet a Russian, referred to as Mr X, a mysterious character who gave the paper's representative the text by Joly that had led to the discovery of the plagiarism. This gentleman, Mr X, had obtained the copy of the *Dialogue in Hell between Machiavelli and Montesquieu* directly from an officer of the "Ojrana", the Russian secret police. The correspondent added in his chronicle that the forgery had been concocted for the purpose of influencing the conservative Russian court against the Jews. Specifically, it was intended to try to make the "imaginary Jewish danger" plausible. Predictably, the publication was greeted with enthusiasm among Jews: on 18 July 1921, coinciding with the third instalment of the report, Zionist leader Israel Zangwill published a letter of thanks in the same newspaper, beginning with these words: "Sir, your correspondent in Constantinople has done the whole world a service by identifying the source of the Protocols...".

Leslie Fry laments in *Waters Flowing Eastward* that instead of correctly quoting the title of Joly's book, which at the time had been published anonymously, *The Times* alluded to the *Geneva Dialogues* to refer to the book in question. The writer ironised the lack of rigour and seriousness of the English newspaper and revealed the existence of a second work, *Machiavelli, Montesquieu and Rousseau,* written by Jacob Venedey and published in 1850 in Berlin by the publisher Franz Dunnicker. This book was the source from which Maurice Joly had drawn his *Dialogue in Hell between Machiavelli and Montesquieu.* It follows, and is universally accepted, that the author(s) of the *Protocols of the Elders of Zion* had drawn on earlier, existing texts in the drafting of the document.

Let us now see who Maurice Joly and Jacob Venedey really were. Let us start with the latter. Perhaps the reader remembers that Jacob Venedey has already been mentioned in the previous chapter. Specifically, he played a leading role in the League of the Righteous ("Bund der Gerechten"), the clandestine branch of the Illuminati that hired Karl Marx to write the *Communist Manifesto.* Venedey was Jewish. Born in Cologne in May 1805, he was expelled from Germany for his revolutionary activities and in 1833 settled in Paris. The French police kept him under surveillance, but thanks to his friendship with Crémieux and Arago, he was not expelled from France. Venedey was a personal friend of Marx and worked with him in Brussels, where Moses Hess proposed in 1847 the transformation of the League of the Righteous into the League of Communist Workers. After the 1848 revolution in Paris, he went to Germany, where he was a member of the revolutionary committee. Jacob Venedey was a member of Freemasonry and also belonged to the Carbonarii. He was later among the founders of the Universal Israelite Alliance, whose founding manifesto considered Catholicism the eternal enemy and proclaimed that the Jews, "a chosen race whose cause was great and sacred... were casting a net over the globe".

As for Maurice Joly, Gottfried zur Beek in the preface to his edition of the *Protocols* reveals that he is a Jew whose name was Moses Joel when he was circumcised. In 1935, a portrait of Maurice Joly in Masonic dress uniform was kept in a London club. At the Berne trial, which will be discussed below, the Jewish origin of the author of the *Dialogues in Hell between Machiavelli and Montesquieu* was confirmed; however, it was clarified that his Jewish name was Joseph Levy and that the name Joly had been made up from four letters of his name. This clarification caused a sensation in the courtroom where the trial was held. Considering, as we have seen with the Frankists, how easy it was for some Jews to change their names, these concealments of identity should no longer be surprising. Whether he was Joel, Levy or Joly, what is interesting to know is that this character was strongly influenced by Adolphe Isaac Crémieux, which means that he must also be placed in the orbit of the Universal Israelite Alliance. It was his hatred of the Emperor Napoleon III, fuelled by Crémieux himself, that led him to publish the *Dialogues* anonymously. Joly first declared himself a socialist and later became a communist. In 1865 he was arrested and, accused of inciting hatred and contempt for the government, spent two years in prison. On his release from prison, with the help of Crémieux, Jules Favre, Arago and others, he founded the newspaper *Le Palais*. In 1878 he committed suicide, and the funeral was attended by Crémieux and his adopted son, the famous Léon Gambetta, who gave a post mortem speech.

The conclusions seem clear. All the texts which, according to *The Times*, were used as sources for the *Protocols of the Elders of Zion* were written by Jewish revolutionaries who also moved in the orbit of Karl Marx and communism, and in the orbit of Adolphe Crémieux and the Universal Israelite Alliance, a Jewish organisation which had declared that it aspired to "all the riches and treasures of the world to be the property of the children of Israel". Rabbi Baruch Levy had also written in his letter to Marx that the time would come when "the promise of the Talmud, according to which, when the time of the Messiah comes, the Jews will possess the property of all the peoples of the earth" would be realised. It is generally accepted that many passages of the *Protocols* are found in the *Dialogues in Hell between Machiavelli and Montesquieu*. It must therefore be admitted that the author of the *Protocols* would have drawn on or plagiarised in part from the texts of a Jew, Joly, who in turn had plagiarised from another Jew, Venedey. In other words, the Jewish author of the document took advantage of texts previously written by other Jews in which the same ideas were expressed.

Lord Northcliffe also stands up: control of *The Times*

On 27 August 1921, ten days after *The Times* sought to shelve the *Protocols* affair, another "uncontrolled" newspaper, *The Spectator*, published an article by Lord Sydenham, then a respected authority, calling again for an investigation. For Sydenham the most striking feature of the paper was a strange kind of knowledge that had enabled a series of prophecies to be made and fulfilled. This was one of the last occasions on which major newspapers took a stand against the all-powerful Zionist Jews: the proprietor of *The Times*, Lord Northcliffe, was sidelined on the grounds that he was going mad. *The Morning Post* was subjected to a campaign of reproach and slander that prompted the owner to sell the paper. Henry Ford, as we know, was forced in 1927 to publicly apologise and cease publication of *The Dearborn Independent*.

Douglas Reed, author of *The Controversy of Zion*, is a first-hand source for how Lord Northcliffe was removed. In 1922 Douglas Reed worked for the famous English newspaper and was Lord Northcliffe's secretary. We will therefore follow his version of events from now on. Alfred Charles William Harmsworth, Lord Northcliffe (Dublin 1865 - London 1922) was known as the "Napoleon of the Press" because, in addition to being the main owner of *The Times* from 1908, *he* also owned the *Daily Mail*, which at the turn of the century had a circulation of one million copies, the Sunday paper *The Observer*, the *Daily Mirror* and other smaller newspapers. Northcliffe once gave a definition of news that should be taught in information science faculties: "News is what someone somewhere is trying to suppress, the rest is just propaganda". This is exactly what happened with the news that Robert Wilton, *The Times* correspondent in Russia, sent to the paper after the revolution: someone was suppressing it[36]. Northcliffe, though a powerful newspaper magnate, was a man of integrity who had taken a stand against what was happening in Russia and in May 1920 had had an article on the *Protocols* printed in *The Times* calling for an impartial investigation: "Are we to dismiss the whole thing without investigation and allow such a book as this to go unchecked?"

In January 1922 Lord Northcliffe travelled to Palestine in the company of the journalist J. M. N. Jeffries, who later published *Palestine: The Reality*, a now classic book of the period. Lord Northcliffe, who travelled in the company of the editor of the *Manchester Guardian*, gained an accurate picture of the situation on the ground and, unlike other newspapers, wrote a series of articles from there independently: "In my opinion we have, without sufficient reflection, secured Palestine as a home for the Jews, despite the fact that seven hundred thousand Muslim Arabs live here and own the land..... The Jews seemed to be under the impression that the whole of England was devoted to the cause of Zionism, in fact enthusiastic; and I told them that this is not so, and to beware of committing our people to the secret importation of arms to fight the seven hundred

---

[36] Carrol Quigley, the author of the famous *Tragedy and Hope*, in his book *The Anglo-American Establishment* gives more insight into what was going on behind the scenes to control the famous newspaper. Quigley reveals that the Milner Group, to which the Astors belonged, had controlled the paper since 1912. Alfred Milner and Cecil Rhodes had already founded the Round Table, which was to become the most influential of the secret societies throughout the 20th century. Three organisations that are offshoots of the Round Table now constitute the major centres of power and decision-making: the RIIA (Royal Institute of International Affairs), organised in London in 1919; the CFR (Council of Foreign Relations), organised in New York in 1921; and the IPR (Institute of Pacific Relations), organised in 1925. Although they did not own *The Times*, the Milner Group had a decisive influence on the paper from 1912 to 1919. According to Quigley, it was only during the three years that Lord Northcliffe tried to take control, from 1919 to 1922, that the Milner Group was unable to exert its dominance over the London paper.

thousand Arabs..... There will be trouble in Palestine... the people here dare not tell the Jews the truth. They have had a little from me."

Either Lord Northcliffe was a man of very strong principles or he had no idea exactly who he was standing up to. To use his newspapers, which communicated with millions of people, to tell the truth about the Palestine affair and to demand an investigation into the origin of the *Protocols* was a challenge. With his attitude he became a dangerous man, an opponent of unscrupulous conspirators for whom the end justifies the means. The person chosen to remove Lord Northcliffe from *The Times* was Henry Wickham Steed, who had been appointed in 1919 as head of the International department and editor of the paper by Lord Northcliffe himself, who was the main shareholder of the paper, but not the sole owner. Thus, while all the papers he owned published his articles on Palestine, *The Times* refused to do so. Wickham Steed refused to visit Palestine when Lord Northcliffe asked him to do so, nor would he write against Zionist interests, even though he had received a telegram from the majority owner asking for an editorial article denouncing the attitude of Lord Balfour, the Foreign Office Minister, towards Zionism.[37]

On 26 February 1922 Lord Northcliffe left Palestine in anger at Wickham Steed's refusal to follow his instructions. On 2 March 1922, at a conference at the publishing house, he was extremely critical of the publisher's failure to comply. Lord Northcliffe wanted Wickham Steed to resign and could not understand how, after publicly reprimanding him, he could continue in his post. Instead of resigning, the controversial editor decided to consult a lawyer to find out under what circumstances a dismissal could be considered unlawful. To this end, on 7 March he consulted Lord Northcliffe's own legal adviser, who suddenly told Wickham Steed that Lord Northcliffe was "abnormal", "unfit for business", and that judging by his appearance he was "unlikely to live long". His advice to the editor was that he should continue in his post. Wickham Steed travelled a few days later to Pau in France to see Lord Northcliffe. The editor decided on 31 March that Northcliffe was indeed "abnormal" and informed one of the editors of *The Times* that "he was going mad". In other words, it was the editor whom Lord Northcliffe wanted to replace who suggested his insanity.

On 3 May 1922, Douglas Reed reports, Lord Northcliffe attended a farewell luncheon for the editor of one of his newspapers and "was in fine form". A few days later, on 11 May, he made "an excellent and effective speech" to the Empire Press Union and "many people who had thought him 'abnormal' thought they had been mistaken". A few days later he telegraphed instructions to the managing editor of *The Times* to arrange for Wickham Steed's resignation. The managing editor saw nothing "abnormal" in the

---

[37] As Douglas Reed points out in *The Controversy of Zion*, all this is recounted "with surprising candour" in *The Times' Official History* (1952).

instructions received and had "not the slightest concern regarding Northcliffe's health". Another director who also saw him on 24 May "considered Lord Northcliffe's life to be at the same risk as his own" and noted "nothing unusual in Northcliffe's manners and appearance".

On 8 June 1922 Lord Northcliffe asked Wickham Steed from Boulogne to meet him in Paris. They met on 11 June and Northcliffe announced to the editor that he would personally take over the editorship of *The Times*. The next day, 12 June, they all left by train for Evian-les-Bains. Somewhere along the way, Wickham Steed secretly brought a doctor onto the train. On arrival in Switzerland, "a brilliant French neurologist" (anonymous) was called in, who certified in the afternoon that Lord Northcliffe was insane. Wickham Steed immediately cabled instructions to the newspaper to ignore and not to publish anything sent by Lord Northcliffe. On 13 June Wickham Steed left and they were never seen again. On 18 June Lord Northcliffe returned to London, but was removed from all control and even prevented from communicating with his companies. His telephones at *The Times* were cut off. The manager even posted policemen at the door to prevent him from gaining access to the newspaper's offices. On 14 August 1922 Lord Northcliffe died, presumably of ulcerative endocarditis. In his will he had written that he wanted each of his six thousand employees to receive three months' salary. According to a pathetic Wikipedia account, Lord Northcliffe died of exhaustion in London at the age of 57.

In *The Controversy of Zion* Douglas Reed reports that the account we have excerpted came to light in 1952, thirty years after Lord Northcliffe's death, and that he took it from an official publication such as the *Official History* of *The Times*. This master of journalism adds that no one, except a small circle of close associates, had the slightest idea of what had happened in 1922. Reed believes that there is no historical precedent for concealing information about the displacement and disappearance of such a wealthy and powerful man in such mysterious circumstances. Reed's testimony is particularly valuable, given that he worked at the newspaper and Lord Northcliffe called him from Boulogne in the early days of June when he was preparing to dismiss Wickham Steed. Reed says that the attitude and conduct he observed in Northcliffe was as he had been told by those who had been working with him; but he adds: "Lord Northcliffee was convinced that his life was in danger and several times said so; specifically, he said that he had been poisoned". Reed, who remained at the paper for sixteen years, says that on his return to London he spoke to Northcliffe's brother, Lord Rothermere, and George Sutton, a senior associate, both of whom wanted his opinion.

All that remains is to find out who took over *The Times*. On 22 July 1922, the Oslo *National Tidscrift* reported that a certain Jewish banker had bought *The Times* of London. Today it is known that after the death of Lord Northcliffe the paper was bought in 1922 by the Astors. Fritz Springmeier in his *Bloodlines of the Illuminati* provides a wealth of information about this family of Jewish lineage, whose origins have remained hidden. John Jacob Astor (1763-1848), the first Astor on record, was born in Waldorf, Germany. By 1784 he was in the United States, where he was Master of Dutch Lodge Number 8 in New York. President Jefferson, an illuminati who considered Weishaupt a benefactor of humanity, and Gallatin Mackey, the illuminati Satanist Mason who was secretary of the Supreme Council of Charleston, were his connections. Dr. John Coleman in *The Committee of 300* reveals that he made an enormous fortune in the Chinese opium trade, which enabled him to purchase large tracts of land in Manhattan. Since then, according to Coleman, Manhattan real estate has been in the hands of members of the Committee of 300. John Jacob Astor was part of a committee that selected the families of select Americans who were allowed to participate in the lucrative opium business. Coleman also links him to the East India Company and, consequently, to the British Intelligence Service. It should be remembered, as mentioned in chapter two, that British intelligence operations had been in the hands of the East India Company until Lord Shelburne, who chaired the East India Company's Secret Committee and was the man of the Anglo-Dutch oligarch financiers, organised the SIS (Secret Intelligence Service). Astor became a banker and took a large part of the shares of the Bank of the United States created by Alexander Hamilton. According to Springmeier, the tendency to secrecy is characteristic of the Astors, a family that moves in the orbit of the Warburgs and Morgans, the Jewish bankers at the origin of the US Federal Reserve cartel. We could go on, but we think this is enough for the reader to understand who were the conspirators Lord Northcliffe had the courage to stand up to. *The Times* was bought by John Jacob Astor V.

The Berne Trials

The effort to bury the *Protocols* and to promote their oblivion led international Jewry to denounce in 1933 Silvio Schnell, the Swiss editor of the text; Georg Haller, editor of the National Socialist newspaper *Eidgenossen*; Juris Johann Konrad Mayer, the newspaper's legal adviser; Walter Äbersold, a member of the National Front; and Theodor Fischer. The lawsuit was brought by two organisations of the Swiss Jewish community, the Swiss Israelite Communal League, represented at the trial by Dr. Matti, and the Jewish Worship Community of Bern, represented by Georges Brunschvig, both of whom requested a ban on the publication of the paper. The defendants' lawyers were Ursprung and Ruef. The true intentions of the trial were clarified by the chief rabbi of Stockholm, Marcus Ehrenpreis, one of the prosecution witnesses, who even allowed himself to cry during the trial. According to Ehrenpreis, who had been secretary of the committee chaired by Theodor Herzl in Basel, this was not a trial against Schnell and his colleagues, but the trial of all Israelis in the world against all their detractors. Sixteen million Israelites," he said, "are looking at Berne". The preliminary trial began on 16 November 1933, but the trial was delayed for almost a year, as the defendants sought to dismiss the judge, who in the first instance was Walter Meyer, a Swiss Marxist judge who handed down his sentence in May 1935. The defendants' defence appealed to a higher court, and a second judgement was handed down on 1 November 1937.

A commentary on the events will give the reader an idea of how the trial unfolded before the court of first instance. Silvio Schnell was a National Socialist and had distributed copies of the German edition of the *Protocols* at a meeting of Swiss nationalists. The prosecution relied on an article of the law of the canton of Bern which referred to "immoral literature" and "instigation by means of the press". The fact that the defendants were members of the National Front, a Swiss National Socialist party, made the Nazis an interested party in the trial, which, after a postponement in 1933, began on 29 October 1934. Judge Walter Meyer allowed a large number of witnesses to appear in support of the plaintiffs; by contrast, he accepted the presence of only one witness for the defendants, Dr. Zander.

The plaintiffs decided to call first a supposedly prestigious witness, none other than Chaim Weizmann, a supporter of Asher Ginsburg, one of the greats of Zionism, the architect of the *Balfour Declaration*, who in 1948 was to become Israel's first president. Weizmann, who of course denied that they intended world domination, declared: "These Protocols surely come from a sick fantasy... something from another planet." Armand Alexander du Chayla, the next to testify, was no longer an embellished witness. The lawyers for the prosecution handed the judge articles on the *Protocols* that Du Chayla had published in 1921, on 12 and 13 May and on 1, 2 and 3 June, in the newspaper *Dernières Nouvelles*. Du Chayla, who passed for a Russian Orthodox Christian of French citizenship, said that he had been in Russia in 1909 and had met Sergei Nilus, whom he referred to as a paranoid whose thoughts focused on the coming of the Antichrist. Du Chayla stated that Nilus had given him to read the *Protocols* in the French language. He added that he remembered that the manuscript had a faint blue ink stain on the first page and that Nilus had told him it was the original.

This blue inkblot ruse forces us to introduce a character we had planned to avoid, as she deserves no credibility whatsoever. This is Princess Radziwill, an adventuress who at the turn of the century tried to hunt down the billionaire Cecil Rhodes in South Africa. Catherine Radziwill asked him to marry her, but Rhodes turned her down and she took revenge by accusing him of loan fraud. This scheming woman was interviewed by Isaac Landman in the New York newspaper *American Hebrew* on 11 March 1921. She had separated from Prince Wilhelm Radziwill and in 1914 she had remarried an engineer named Kolb, from whom she also separated shortly afterwards. At the time of the interview she already bore the surname Dunvin, which was that of her third husband. Radziwill/Kolb/Dunvin said that the protocols were drawn up after the Japanese war (1904-1905). She said that she was living in Paris in 1905 when she was visited one day by a certain Golowinsky, a secret policeman who knew her, who revealed to her that the head of the Russian Foreign Police, Pyotr Ratschovsky, had commissioned her to write a false Jewish conspiracy plot. Radziwill said that Golowinsky had shown him a manuscript recently written by himself and a renegade Jew named Manassevich Manuilov, which had a large blue ink stain on the first page. Du Chayla pretended in his statement to the Berne court that he had seen precisely the same original manuscript at Nilus' house in 1909. These anecdotal, invented details, contrivances concocted by delusional minds, are nothing but falsehoods, hoaxes designed to try to fool the gullible into believing these impossible curiosities. Lesly Fry relates that Princess Catherine Radziwill later contradicts herself, for, whether by distraction or unwittingly, she herself states that General Cherevin gave her his memoirs when he died in 1896, which included the *Protocols*. On the other hand, the reputation of Radziwill, the daughter of a Jew who ran a betting parlour in Monaco, as revealed in Berne, is blacker than bitumen. We could go on for pages about the lies, forgeries of documents and other impostures that adorn the CV of this compulsive liar and swindler.

The judge asked the witness whether he thought that Nilus believed the *Protocols* to be genuine, to which Alexander du Chayla replied: "I had the impression that Nilus himself doubted the authenticity of *the Protocols*". This witness then opined that the text had been distributed in Russia for the purpose of influencing the Tsar to adopt a reactionary, anti-Jewish position. The judge's next question was whether Nilus had himself forged the *Protocols*. The answer was that this was impossible, for, although he could not guarantee his mental health, Nilus was an honest man, but obsessed with the idea that the Freemasons and the Jews were in cahoots to destroy Russia and the Christian world. Finally, this witness testified that Nilus insisted that he had indirectly received the *Protocols* from the policeman Ratchkovsky, who held a high position in the official hierarchy.

The next witnesses were Sergei Svatikov and Vladimir Burtsev, who were responsible for making the court swallow the story about Princess Catherina Radziwill. The defendants' lawyer, Ruef, managed to prove the following: 1. Catherina Radziwill never had a residence in Paris. 2. Burtsev had made the mistake of stating that Ratchovsky had never been in the French capital in the years 1904-1905. 3. The famous Princess Radziwill was the daughter of a Jew named Blanc. These defence achievements were presented to public opinion by the newspaper *Die Front* in a report published on 4 May 1935.

Waters Flowing Eastward reports other articles by Alexander du Chayla which he probably did not care to mention at the trial. One appeared in the *Tribune Juive* in Paris on 14 May 1921, and another on 13 June in the violently communist *New York Call*. Neither of these two media seems appropriate for a supposedly orthodox Christian. In fact Nilus mentions Alexander du Chayla in one of his books and says he took him for a devotee of the Russian Orthodox Church. Leslie Fry reproduces a text by Tatiana Fermor dated 9 June 1921 in Paris. This woman personally knew the personage, whom she refers to as Count du Chayla. She met him in a monastery near Moguileff, where she spent her summer holidays, and was introduced to him by the abbot, Archimandrite Arsene. Du Chayla told her that he was studying Russian and the Orthodox religion, of which he declared himself a devotee. According to Tatiana Fermor, he sought to demonstrate an even greater Orthodox zeal than the Patriarch himself, which even led him to remove two beautiful Renaissance sculptures of angels from the monastery chapel, as he found them too Catholic. Fermor relates that Count du Chayla expressed to him the hatred he felt for the Jews and went so far as to say that "a good pogrom was needed in Russia." Du Chayla recommended that Tatiana Fermor read the books of Drumont, author of the book *Jewish France*, in order for her to understand the extent to which the Jews had conquered France. In short, Fermor explains that the ecclesiastical career of this witness for the plaintiffs in Berne was meteoric, a fact that allowed him to become close friends with bishops renowned for their strict orthodoxy and to frequent the famous salon of Countess Ignatieff. His social ascent led him to become involved in politics, to the point of becoming a supporter of Count Bobrinsky, leader of the Panslavic Party. He even led violent racial campaigns against Poles and Finns. At the outbreak of war, Alexander du Chayla was a student at the Petrograd Academy of Theology and was appointed head of a field hospital organised by Bishop Pitirim. Tatiana Fermor's account concludes: "I then lost track of him until after the revolution, when I heard that he acted as an agent provocateur inciting the Cossacks against the White Army. In 1919 du Chayla was tried by a court martial and convicted of seditious activities in favour of the Soviets. The sentence was published in Crimean newspapers". In other words, Alexander du Chaila, one of the star witnesses at the Berne trial, was an infiltrated agent of the Communists, one of many operating in Russia before the revolution.

In November 1934, the procession of witnesses for the plaintiffs came to an end, as only one had been allowed for the defence. The judge had decided to appoint experts who were to consider four questions: Are the *Protocols of the Elders of Zion* a forgery? Are they plagiarism? If so, what is their source, and do the *Protocols* fall under the term "Schundliteratur" (junk literature)? Arthur Baumbarten was the plaintiffs' expert. Carl Alber Loosli, supposedly neutral, acted as the court's expert. Colonel Ulrich Fleischhauer was the defendants' expert. The fact that this expert had not had time to prepare his report forced the defence to ask for an adjournment of the case. The judge granted six months and set the reopening of the trial for 29 April 1935.

Lawsuits against the witnesses were filed by the defendants' lawyers, but on 4 January 1935 they were dismissed. On 17 March a new suit was filed against a few witnesses. On 26 April 1935, the *Jewish Daily Post* announced that the start of the trial scheduled for the 29th had been postponed, as Silvio Schnell, one of the defendants, had sued ten witnesses for false testimony. The news of the postponement turned out to be false and the trial started on the scheduled date, but the announcement caused people who had planned to travel to Bern to attend the trial to postpone their trip. It should be noted that the courtroom was packed with Jewish sympathisers from all over Europe and the defendants' lawyer had asked the judge for 30 passes so that his supporters could attend. On 28 April, the same newspaper had already passed sentence in advance: "That the book is an insolent forgery goes without saying. It is not a question of proving or disproving the allegations. The matter is settled. What matters now is that this refutation be given the widest possible publicity.... The judgment should be widely publicised."

As soon as the trial was resumed, the defendants insisted on demanding legal action against the witnesses who had made untruthful statements. The judge reported that the criminal complaints against the witnesses had been dismissed for lack of foundation, but made an exception: the witness Vladimir Burtsev, a Russian journalist, was to be prosecuted because he had claimed in court that General Globitchoff had told him that the *Protocols* were a forgery, which proved to be a lie, since the General himself, who was still alive, vehemently denied having made the statements attributed to him by Burtsev. This information appeared in *Die Front*, but was not mentioned in any other media.

When the court resumed its sessions, secret documents came to light which the Soviet Government had made available to Loosli, the court's expert. Naturally, the defendants' expert, Fleischhauer, asked for permission to review these documents; but he was only allowed to glance at them. This glance was enough for him to realise that some of the documents might have been forged, leading him to believe that they might contain false or erroneous information. Fleischhauer insisted that he wanted to examine them calmly, but the Court replied that it would only authorise him to do so if he gave his word of honour that he would not divulge their contents, which he refused to do. The plaintiffs' lawyers tried to establish the thesis that Fleischhauer was an inappropriate expert because he was a known anti-Semite and had preconceived opinions about the case. It follows from this accusation that only they could have preconceived opinions. Unfortunately, one of the preconceived ideas that Fleischhauer expressed before the court was the view that the only solution to the Jewish problem was the end of their dispersion and the attainment of their own state. In fact, Hitler and the German Zionist leaders had already signed the Haavara Agreement ("Haavara Agreement") on 25 August 1933, a collaboration agreement whereby about 100,000

German Jews voluntarily travelled to Palestine with all their property. We will return to this shameful pact in a later chapter.

The plaintiff's expert, Arthur Baumgarten, began by claiming that the *Protocols* were a historical invention and put forward the hackneyed thesis that they had been forged and plagiarised to bias the Tsar against the Jews. He noted that they had been composed between 1890-1900. He even compared some paragraphs with Joly's text and also mentioned the possibility that Goedsche's book was used. He stated emphatically that they were totally opposed to the spirit of Judaism. He denied, of course, that Jews had ever conspired. He also denied that Jews had anything to do with the Bolshevik revolution. Undeterred, with immeasurable cynicism, he also denied that there was any connection between Freemasonry and the Jews: "the Jews have nothing to do with the Freemasons and they do not rule the world". Baumgarten expressed his conviction that the *Protocols* had undoubtedly contributed to the Aryan nations' distrust and horror of the Jews. This last assertion is evidently true. "If the Protocols were authentic," he said, "and there were a Jewish world conspiracy, then one would have to accept that the whole story is only a farce, and the historians, stupid victims, because behind the scenes were the bearded sages of Zion, who pulled the strings of emperors, kings, generals, popes, poets and philosophers." These are his words.

Fleischhauer, to the dismay of the plaintiffs and their sympathisers, replied with a presentation that lasted five days: he spoke for twenty-three hours. Among the arguments in favour of the authenticity of *the Protocols, he* noted that the text presented the Police as connected with Freemasonry, which would not have been said if the document had been produced as a political weapon to influence the Tsar. He presented evidence about the true identity of Maurice Joly, a Jewish Freemason whose real name was Joseph Levy. He came down hard on the witness Alexander du Chayla and exposed some of the lies and inaccuracies of the complainants' witnesses. He spent some time identifying those who had written against the *Protocols*. He alluded to Leslie Fry's revelations about Asher Ginsberg. Naturally, he did not leave some of Baumgarten's denials unanswered: he explained Jewish interconnections with Freemasonry and described Masonic ceremonies as stemming from Kabbalistic rituals. He exposed the deep connection of Judaism with the Revolutionary Movement and with Bolshevism. He accused the Jews of being behind the French Revolution and, above all, of having prepared the revolution in Russia. He even denounced Sir Philip Sassoon, a member of the famous banking family related to the Rothschilds, as an opium dealer. The intervention of Fleischhauer, who was insulted and attempted to be assaulted as he left the court building, had an enormous impact on the non-Jewish press throughout Europe. On 9 May, as recorded, the judge alluded to the attacks on Flesichhauer and apologised to him for the gross violation of Swiss hospitality.

The last expert to speak was Loosli[38], the man in court, who began his speech by announcing that the Hammer publishing house in Germany was preparing a new edition of the *Protocols* and was going to use Fleischhauer's report as an introduction. In his attempt to refute Fleischhauer, who had claimed that the Jew and Freemason Kerensky had removed the *Protocols* from Russian bookshops, Loosli went so far as to deny that Kerensky was a Jew and linked him to a family of priests. In his attempt to refute an assertion by Fleischhauer, he also denied that Freemasonry and the Jewish lodge B'nai B'rith had anything in common. One of the surprises of his speech was the exhibition of a baptismal certificate of Maurice Joly dated 1829. It is not clear what he wanted to prove with it: it has already been seen that Shabbateists and Frankists did not cease to feel Jewish because they converted to Islam or were baptised. Referring to the report of the defendants' expert, he said that it was "nothing more than an anti-Semitic propaganda pamphlet which should never have been admitted before a court of law." Loosli then launched into a furious attack on National Socialism and Germany. "If there is a world conspiracy, it is headed by the German National Socialists," he said, "and it threatens us all." The nationalist newspaper *Die Front* expressed surprise on 8 May that a supposedly neutral expert had directed such virulent attacks against Germany and asked "Can this attitude be compatible with impartiality?"

In his final intervention, Ruef, one of the defence lawyers, asked how the defendants could be found guilty of selling a forgery when they were precisely trying to establish the authenticity of the text. Relevantly, Ruef observed that the judge would not have appointed three experts if the forgery had been proven before the trial. On the intervention of this lawyer, *Die Front* reported on 14 May 1935 that Ruef had again complained that defence witnesses had not been accepted and that witnesses who had given false testimony had been refused prosecution. In this connection, it should be noted that Burtsev, the only declarant who was to be prosecuted for lying, was acquitted due to a formal defect, since the minutes of the statements had not been signed as required.

Finally, a verdict was rendered. Since the plaintiffs had not provided evidence that a forgery had been committed, this fundamental point was never mentioned by the judge, who nevertheless ruled in their favour because

---

[38] One fact carried out by this neutral court expert will help the reader to understand the extent of Loosli's servility. Since it had been proved that the alleged forgery of *the Protocols* could not have been made in Paris in 1905, this expert, in his eagerness to make the Radziwill report credible and to support a witness who had lied, falsified in his written report in October 1934 the date of the year 1905 and transformed it into 1895. When seven months later Fleischhauer publicly denounced him in court and recalled that Princess Radziwill had said that their alleged meeting in Paris took place after the Russo-Japanese war, Loosli tried to make believe that it was a typing error. None of this fazed the supposedly impartial Judge Meyer.

the defendants had failed to prove that the *Protocols* were genuine. From the logic behind this verdict, one would think that all writings whose author cannot be identified or located, for example many texts of the Pentateuch, are forgeries. This reasoning runs counter to the universally accepted principle of historical criticism, according to which, when a document is discovered, it must be regarded as authentic until its falsity has been proven. Moreover, if the aim was to establish authenticity and not forgery, it is hard to understand why more than thirty-five defence witnesses were refused to appear. As for the defendants, Silvio Schnell, a 23-year-old, was sentenced to a fine of 20 francs and Theordor Fischer to a fine of 50 francs. Except in Germany, the Jewish victory was triumphantly announced by the press all over the world, a press which, as they had declared at the trial, they did not control. A member of the Jewish Information Bureau said that in a political trial the echo was everything and the sentence nothing.

An appeal was lodged with the Bern Court of Appeal, which on 1 November 1937 rejected the verdict of Judge Walter Meyer. In conclusion, let us look at some passages from the judgment of this high court (the quotations in quotation marks are taken from the German text of the trial published by M. de Vries de Heekelingen). The Court of Appeal considered that, despite what was prescribed by law, the reports of certain testimonies were drawn up by private informants of the Jewish plaintiffs: "The proceedings, as they were conducted by the court of first instance, were not in conformity with the usual practice and the law.... The manner in which the reports were prepared contradicted the binding prescriptions of the law". The Court of Appeal found that the witness statements had not been read to the defendants and had not been signed, as prescribed; it also found that the defence witnesses had not been called and that the judge had accepted from the plaintiffs translations of documents from Russia, the authenticity of which had not been sufficiently verified. A very interesting point concerns the appointment of the experts, in particular that of the third expert, C.A. Loosli, whose choice was strongly criticised by the Court of Appeal. This Court deplored "the lack of impartiality of Loosli, who in 1937, a little more than a year after the first trial, had already published "a pamphlet entitled *Die Schlimmen Juden* (*The Bad Jews*), in which he described the *Protocols* as a malevolent fabrication and disdainfully disqualified them in a purely polemical and unscientific manner".

The Jewish Chronicle of 5 November 1937 wrote that the Court of Appeal had declared that the *Protocols* were a forgery and should be considered junk literature. It further stated that the Court had concluded that the falsity of the *Protocols* had been proved. In fact, the Court acquitted the defendants and ordered the Jewish organisations to pay the costs of the proceedings. As for the literary value of the text, the Court found that it was indeed "sloppy literature and rubbish from an aesthetic and literary point of view", on which one can only agree. On who was the author of this literary rubbish and on the question of the authenticity of the document, the Court of Appeal declared itself incompetent.

Peter Myers upholds the authenticity of the *Protocols*

We do not want to conclude these pages without a brief reference to the Australian professor Peter Myers, a scholar of vast historical knowledge. Myers has been publicly debating the authenticity of *the Protocols of the Elders of Zion* for twenty years on the internet with anyone who wants to challenge him on his arguments for its authenticity. He maintains that they are a genuine document and has since written hundreds of pages rebutting the major authors who have published works claiming them to be forgeries. With his reasoning he challenges the theses of three well-known Zionists, Israel Zangwill (1864-1926), Herman Bernstein (1876-1935) and Norman Cohn (1915-2007). The latter published *Warrant For Genocide* in 1970, in which he claims that without the *Protocols* there would have been no Auschwitz, i.e. he blames the book for the alleged genocide committed in the famous Polish labour camp. Cohn also wrote the introduction to the 1971 edition of Hermann Bernstein's *The Truth about "The Protocols of Zion": A Complete Exposure*, a book first published in 1935. In response to Cohn's book, Professor Myer published in 1994 his text *Hiding Behind Auschwitz*, a document updated twice, in April 2001 and March 2004, in which he considers that the 20th century could not be understood without the existence of the *Protocols*.

Norman Cohn reveals in his book that a few months before her assassination in Ekaterinburg, Empress Alexandra received a copy of the Nilus edition of the *Protocols* from a friend, Zinaida Sergeyevna Tolstaya. A week after the assassination, the dismembered and cremated remains of the Russian imperial family were discovered at the bottom of a mine shaft. During the investigation, three books that the empress had carried with her to her sad end were found: the Russian Bible, *War and Peace* and *The Great in the Small*, the Nilus edition. The logical question Myers asks Cohn is this: "If the *Protocols* were a forgery made by the Tsar's Secret Police, why would the Tsarina have kept a copy in her own room, one of the three books she kept until her death? If it was a forgery, it would have been of no value to her".

Herman Bernstein also insists on similar information. Bernstein writes that Nicholas II himself was deeply interested in the *Protocols* and adds that during his research he discovered a copy of Butmi's 1906 edition in the Tsar's private library, which had been acquired years earlier by the Library of Congress in Washington. Cohn, relying on the testimony of Vladimir Burtsev at the Bern trial, writes in *Warrant For Genocide* that Interior Minister Stolypin had convinced the tsar that the *Protocols* were a forgery. Myers shrewdly warns: "If the Tsar was convinced of the forgery, why did he have a copy of the *Protocols*, copy of a worthless document, forged by his own Police? Does this make any sense?"

As for the fact that the *Protocols* contain passages analogous to those in Maurice Joly's *Dialogues in Hell between Montesquieu and Machiavelli*, Myers considers that this does not necessarily prove that they are false. In a September 2002 paper, updated in 2012, Professor Myers shows that he has worked intensively on comparing the two books. Joly's book, written during the reign of Emperor Napoleon III of France and directed against him, portrays Napoleon III as a Machiavellian, a trickster who dupes people; whereas in the *Protocols*, the Machiavellians are the revolutionaries, who create confusion, chaos, aspire to totalitarian control and a reign of terror. In his opinion, the word "hell" alludes to the spirit of the world, and the book presents a discussion between the ghosts of Machiavelli and Montesquieu. Myers reveals that the analogies in the *Dialogues* make up 16.45% of the *Protocols*, which, although a substantial percentage, constitutes only one-sixth of the total. However, he points out that even in the supposedly identical fragments there are important differences in meaning. Myers reproaches Norman Cohn for not having examined the similar paragraphs between Joly's book and those of Jacob Venedey, *Machiavelli, Montesquieu and Rousseau*, since the passages from the *Protocols* that cites as copied or plagiarised from the *Dialogues* are at the same time plagiarised from the book published in 1850 by Venedey, the Jewish Freemason member of the League of the Just who collaborated with Karl Marx. Another thing Myers notices is that Cohn especially omits in his work the extensive coverage of the world financial system in the *Protocols*, a subject about which very little is said in the *Dialogues*.

In another paper also published in September 2002 and revised in July 2008, Peter Myers touches on the issue of World Government, which is central to the *Protocols*. His study focuses on the attempts to establish it at the Versailles Peace Conference of 1919, where Jews predominated in several delegations, notably the US delegation. Proposals for a world government were presented under the guise of slogans such as "unifying mankind", "preventing future wars" and the like. Jacob Schiff (1847-1920), the leading banker who financed the Revolution in Russia, and Bernard Baruch (1870-1965), whom Henry Ford called "Judah's proconsul in America", were the main promoters of the idea. At the Versailles Conference Bernard Baruch was President Wilson's personal adviser on economic matters. Jacob Schiff[39] tried hard to get the Bolsheviks, who were still trying to spread their revolution in Europe and consolidate power in Russia, where they were exercising criminal repression, to be recognised and to send a

---

[39] In the book *Jacob H. Schiff: His Life and Letters* (1928), Cyrus Adler presents texts taken from Jacob Schiff's letters in which he confesses his obsession with overthrowing the Russian government of the Tsars. The banker admits that he lent money to Japan for political purposes to wage war in 1904-1905.

delegation to Paris. It should not be forgotten that by the end of March Hungary was already Bolshevik and Austria, Czechoslovakia, Poland and Germany were in danger. The fact that a Jewish banker and Zionist was the ultimate advocate of totalitarian communism is clear evidence of the nature of the world conspiracy. Had Schiff succeeded in his claims, the establishment of the World Government would probably have been more feasible. Another key agent working for a totalitarian world government and for the immediate recognition of the Communists was Colonel Edward Mandell House, the alter ego of Woodrow Wilson. These three characters will be the focus of attention in the next chapter.

In the document cited, Myers comments on a work by Herman Bernstein published in New York in 1924, *Celebrities of Our Time: Interviews*, dedicated to Colonel Mandell House, the World Government's defence lawyer. In it, Bernstein talks to various leading figures of the time: Alexander Kerensky, Leon Trotsky, Robert Cecil, Walter Rathenau, Chaim Weizmann. During the interview, the latter explains in what terms he expressed himself to the British government with regard to its claim to Palestine. The quote shows how powerful the Zionists knew they were: "The Jews will get Palestine, whether you want it or not. There is no power on earth that can stop the Jews from getting Palestine. You gentlemen can make it easy for them or you can make it hard for them, but you cannot stop them".

The third Zionist to whom Peter Myers turns his attention in relation to the *Protocols* and the aspirations for dominance expressed in them is Israel Zangwill, a Fabian socialist and supporter of World Government whose arguments were taken up by Herman Bernstein. In a 1911 article entitled *The Problem of the Jewish Race* Zangwill expressed himself in these terms: "Where the soul of the Jewish race is best seen is in the Bible, steeped from the first page of the Old Testament to the last page of the New with the aspiration for a just social order and with the unification of mankind, of which the Jewish race will be the means and the missionary". Zangwill, who presented the League of Nations as created by Jewish inspiration, was a fervent Zionist who sought to ridicule those who denounced the Conspiracy. Professor Myers reviews *Israel Zangwill's Speeches, Articles and Letters* (London 1937), in which he pays tribute to Lord Rothschild, recipient of the *Balfour Declaration*; Baron Edmond de Rothschild, for his aid and investment in Palestine; and Jacob Schiff, for his role in financing the Bolshevik Revolution, which "in all probability brought freedom to six million Jews." In a 1921 text, *The Voice of Jerusalem*, Zangwill insists on the Zionist state for the "peculiar people"; but at the same time, while denying the authenticity of the *Protocols*, he reiterates, relying on biblical texts, his aspirations for a world government, which he presents seasoned and camouflaged with a cloying, hypocritical philanthropism through the following syntagms: "Universal brotherhood." "Invisible King". "League of Nations aiming at world unity'. "The mission of Israel". "Unification of mankind". Professor Myers warns that those who deny Jewish leadership in the Bolshevik Revolution also deny the authenticity of *the Protocols*. Israel Zangwill is one of these: he covers up that the Bolshevik leaders were Jews; yet he claims at the same time that the Revolution brought freedom to six million Jews and expresses his conviction that "the United States of Russia would be more congruent to world peace than a swarm of conflicting nationalities."

David Ben Gurion, Prime Minister of Israel, once declared: "Who cares what the Goyim say, what matters is what the Jews do". This phrase is found almost exactly in the *Protocols*. Two ministers in Sharon's government, Uri Landau and Ivet Lieberman, called for a thousand Palestinian goyim to be killed for every Jewish victim. The *Protocols* state: "Each Jewish victim in the eyes of God is worth a thousand goyim". Why do Zionist leaders repeat what they claim was written by two policemen? In short, Peter Myers considers the Jewish claim that the *Protocols* were written by two members of the Russian Secret Police to be absurd, since the entire prophetic programme presented in the document is now a reality. In other words, how could two police officers write a text announcing a complete change of the world, the destruction of two empires, the accumulation of gold in the hands of Jewish bankers, the absolute subjugation of nations through credit, the control of the teaching of history and of educational content in general, the complete domination of the media?

On the 24 *Protocols*

In the *Protocols* it says: "The administrators whom we shall choose from among the people, strictly on the basis of their ability to serve obediently, will not be persons qualified in the art of government, and will therefore easily become pawns in our game in the hands of men of knowledge and talent who will be their advisers, specialists bred and educated from infancy to direct the affairs of the whole world." Douglas Reed asks his readers to judge whether this is not exactly what has been happening on an ongoing basis. If we judge, as Reed intends, what is happening in Europe and the world, we see how co-opted politicians, theoretically "democratically" elected pawns, are merely carrying out orders, governing with their backs turned to the people who elected them, following the instructions of an invisible power. On the other hand, the existence of a servile and subservient attitude of the world's "rulers" towards Zionism, which, in addition to committing all kinds of crimes with impunity since the creation of its usurper state, imposes war after war in the Middle East, is manifest.

Since it is beyond the scope of this work to dwell at length on this chapter, we will conclude by quoting and commenting briefly on a few fragments of interest. The first *Protocol* insists on an "invincible power because it is invisible, and will continue to be so until it has acquired a degree of potency that no force and no cunning can undermine it". This invisible power has been confirmed several times by powerful Jews who have known it. Benjamin Disraeli in his novel *Coningsby* puts into the mouth of Sidonia, a character representing Lionel Rothschild, a phrase quoted many times: "The world is governed by characters very different from those imagined by those who are not behind the scenes". While this quote is revealing, even more so in this regard is that of Walter Rathenau, a German businessman of Jewish origin who was Foreign Minister of the Weimar Republic. Rathenau felt himself to be German and denigrated Jews who did not want to integrate. Specifically, he referred to them as "a gang of extravagantly dressed foreigners who make a band apart". On 24 June 1922 Rathenau, about whom we will write more in due course, was assassinated. Years earlier, on 24 December 1912, in *The Wiener Freie Presse* he had had the courage to denounce the invisible power: "Three hundred men, each of whom knows the others, govern the destiny of Europe and they choose their successors from among those around them." This power is referred to today as "the markets" or "the speculators", who enslave countries because there are no national banks and states are at the mercy of the hidden power to finance themselves.

"When we have made our great coup d'état, we shall say to the peoples: Everything is going very badly for you; you are all exhausted with suffering. We shall abolish the cause of all your torments, namely, nationalities, frontiers and the diversity of currencies". World Government has been attempted after each of the world wars. It has been noted above who the Jewish leaders were who called for it at Versailles. After the Second World War and with the world divided into two blocs, both controlled by the hidden or invisible power, an attempt was made, as will be seen below, to get Stalin to accept a world government based on a monopoly of nuclear violence. Today, globalisation is being taken on board by the masses: the idea of a global world has already penetrated people's thinking. Everything indicates that after a new world war, with the peoples "exhausted by suffering", a third attempt will be made at world government, which will abolish borders, nations and currencies.

On foreign borrowing by states, an excerpt from the *Protocols* illustrates the current situation in Greece, Portugal, Ireland, Spain, Italy and other countries of the European Union and the world: "A foreign loan is an issue of bonds or debentures by a government with the obligation to pay certain interest on the capital lent to it. If the loan is at five per cent, at the end of twenty years the state will have uselessly paid interest at twice the rate.... Under the system of universal taxation, governments will extract from the unfortunate taxpayers their last pennies to pay interest to foreign capitalists, from whom they have borrowed the money, instead of obtaining within the country those sums of which they had need without paying interest, which are like a perpetual tribute..... To pay the interest, they are obliged to resort to new borrowing which increases the principal debt instead of amortising it. When the credit is exhausted, they find themselves in the necessity of creating new taxes, not to pay off the loan, but to pay the interest on it...". This is exactly what is happening in Europe, where countries have no sovereignty and have given up issuing currency because they have no state banks. Both in the past, in the case of National Socialist Germany, and in the present, in the cases of Iraq and Libya, when nations have wanted to act sovereignly to free themselves from the usury that has always been imposed by the Jewish moneylenders, they have been destroyed in the name of freedom and democracy.

"Literature and journalism are two of the most important factors for education; that is why our government will become the owner of most of the newspapers; as for the others, we will buy them by means of subsidies. In this way we shall acquire enormous influence. But as the public must not even suspect such a state of affairs, our newspapers will be of the most opposite opinions, which will secure our confidence and attract to us our adversaries; and thanks to this cunning, we shall be able to form the lists of our enemies." The creation of dissent or prefabricated and controlled criticism is a fundamental idea that constitutes one of the best strategies for deceiving the naïve. This function, initially thought of in the *Protocols* for literature and journalism, is also carried out today through other media that appear to be uncompromising in their criticism. Examples are non-governmental organisations that pass for independent, such as "Human Rights Watch", financed by the Jewish tycoon George Soros, or the prestigious Amnesty International, which is penetrated by Zionist Jews and run by representatives of the US State Department. Theatre groups, intellectuals, comedians and prestigious actors also contribute, sometimes unconsciously, to this strategy of dissent produced in the shadows by the powers-that-be.

In a letter to Thériot, Voltaire defines in a few words one of the methods most valued ideologically by the *Wise Men* in the drafting of the *Protocols*: "It is necessary to lie like a devil! Not timidly, not for a while, but fearlessly and always". In this sense, the falsification of history is one of the greatest achievements among the stated aims. Most history textbooks used in schools lie or are inaccurate. In Europe, where politicians and the press pay lip service to freedom of speech, revisionist historians and researchers are imprisoned for thought crimes. The persecution, sometimes to the point of murder, of those who seek the truth and denounce the impostures of history is unequivocal proof of the importance attached to the concealment of truth and reality. The text of the *Protocols* is very clear in this respect: "We shall replace the study of the classics and of ancient history - which contains more bad examples than good - by the study of the problems of the present hour and of the future. We shall erase from human memory all the facts of the past centuries whose memory is unfavourable to us; we shall allow to remain only those where the errors of the governments of the Goyim are revealed. At the head of our programme of education we shall place the study of practical life, of the compulsory social order.... This programme will be worked out according to a special plan for each profession and must never degenerate into a system of general instruction. This question is of the greatest importance". Once again, these ideas are the harsh reality. In every educational establishment in the world, Jews are taught that they are the eternal victims of history. Anyone who disagrees is an anti-Semite. Since 1789 revolutions and their crimes are the effect of the decomposition of the previous regime. As far as the teaching-learning process is concerned, there are no more learned and educated people: knowledge has become so compartmentalised that the training of students is geared to the "study of practical life". A "general education" that would enable people to question reality must be made impossible. In short, it is a question of destroying freedom of thought: "Knowing that it is through ideas and theories that people are led, and that they are instilled in them by teaching.... We will know how to absorb and grasp for our own benefit the last vestiges of independence of human thought, which we have been directing for centuries in the way that is favourable to us".

This exercise of quoting the fragment and checking its compliance could be done with the twenty-four *Protocols*, but this is not a monographic work. The desire to continue reviewing the main chapters of contemporary history prevents us from delaying any further. The interested reader can read the *Protocols of the Learned Elders of Zion* and will find that a text that is over a hundred years old accurately reflects the world we are living in. Since we are about to begin the study of the First World War and the Bolshevik Revolution, let us conclude with this last quotation: "We will present ourselves as the liberators of the workers, proposing to them to join our socialist, anarchist and communist armies - which we will always support, under the pretext of our pretended principle of fraternal solidarity - for such armies constitute our social Freemasonry.... Whereas we have a great interest in seeing our workers hungry and weak, because deprivation enslaves them to our will and, in their weakness, they will find neither vigour nor energy to resist us..... We manoeuvre the masses and use their hands to crush those who hinder us".

CHAPTER VII

ZIONISM AND WORLD WAR I

BANKERS AND REVOLUTIONS (2)

PART 1
JEWISH BANKERS AND THEIR AGENTS
ACHIEVE THEIR GOALS

At the beginning of the 20th century a major offensive by the international Jewish bankers, led by the Rothschilds, achieved two goals central to their global strategy: control of the mines of South Africa and dominance over the booming US economy. It was only the prelude to a grand operation aimed at world super-government. Shortly thereafter, between 1914 and 1945, humanity experienced an era of blood and fire on a scale previously unknown. The crimes committed during these thirty-one years are unparalleled in history. In this and the next chapter, which will be devoted to the build-up to World War II, the real culprits of the genocide carried out against the peoples of Europe and the whole world will be exposed. In other words, it will present the sinister characters who, following the project of global domination denounced in this work, manoeuvred unscrupulously behind the scenes in order to provoke both wars and establish the dictatorship of communism halfway around the world by means of terror.

The outbreak of the First World War was preceded by two very significant events, both in the United States: the accession of the Freemason Thomas Woodrow Wilson to the White House and the creation of the Federal Reserve cartel. Before going into these matters, however, a brief preamble is inescapable to outline how in the early 20th century, using the military might of the British Empire, the international Jewish bankers, namely the Rothschilds and the Oppenheimers, gained control of the largest known reserves of gold and diamonds, which had been discovered in the South African goldfields.

The Boers, Cecil Rhodes, Nathaniel Rothschild and the Round Table

When the British annexed the Transvaal to the UK in 1877, the Dutch farmers, the Boers, also known as Afrikaners, did not accept it and started a revolt in protest. This led to the first war, which began on 16 December 1880 and ended with a peace treaty signed on 23 March 1881, granting the Boers self-government of the Transvaal. In 1887, gold prospectors found the world's largest lode on the Witwatersrand, a 100-kilometre mountain range south of Pretoria. Transvaal President Paul Kruger prophetically announced that the find would be the cause of a bloodbath. In 1895 Cecil Rhodes attempted an armed raid, known as the Jameson Raid, to seize control of the territory and the mines, but the coup failed. It was then that planning began for military intervention, called for by the governor of the British colony of Cape[40], Sir Alfred Milner, and by mine owners Alfred Beit, Barney Barnato and Lionel Philips. On 12 October 1899, war was declared. Milner, Rhodes and company thought it would be a military walkover, but it lasted until 31 May 1902. The British, who mobilised 450,000 troops to take on some 80,000 Boers, soon lost their phlegm and showed the world their true colours. In 1901 they adopted a scorched-earth policy and confiscated cattle, poisoned wells, burned farms and crops and displaced some 154,000 men, women and children, who were massively interned in thirty-three huge concentration camps, where starvation and disease were used as weapons of mass destruction to subdue the enemy. A similar number of black Africans were also interned. According to a post-war report, some 22,000 Afrikaner children under the age of sixteen died in the infamous camps, to which must be added as many indigenous children. After this very brief summary of the facts, to find out what was going on behind the scenes, let us now turn to sources whose wealth of information runs parallel to the canonical version of history.

On more than one occasion from these lines we will turn to Dr. Carroll Quigley, professor of history at Georgetown University, who also taught at Princeton and Harward. Quigley, an insider who boasted of his membership of the power elite, decided to write a book on the secret structure of world power when he felt that the conspiracy could now be unravelled, since its

---

[40] In 1805 the British occupied Cape Town, which was in the hands of Dutch settlers, the Boers. Ten years later, the Congress of Vienna handed the territory over to them. From then on, the Boers lived under English administration, but as more and more English settlers arrived, they were forced to emigrate inland. Ten thousand families made the "great Trek" (emigration) in 1837. The trekkers crossed the Vaal and Orange rivers and created the republics of Transvaal and Orange, whose existence was recognised by the British between 1852 and 1854. The new lands were soon found to hold enormous diamond and gold wealth, which led Britain to proclaim sovereignty over the Transvaal in 1877.

triumph was irreversible. Thus, in 1966, published *Tragedy and Hope,* a work of more than 1,300 pages, which is a source cited repeatedly by almost all scholars of untold occult history. Quigley considers John Ruskin's arrival at Oxford University in 1870 as Professor of Fine Arts to be an earthquake, as he outlined in his initial lecture the basis of a project of global domination for the good of mankind by the British Empire, whose elite was to take control of the means of production and distribution in order to rule the masses of the world. Ruskin's biographer Kenneth Clark says in *Ruskin Today* that the bedside book Ruskin read every day (which had also been an essential source for Weishaupt, Marx, Engels, Proudhon and Saint-Simon) was Plato's *Republic.* As is well known, Plato wanted a ruling elite, kept in power by a powerful army, and a society subordinated to its authority. He advocated the use of force necessary to eliminate any existing power or social structure, so that the new rulers could design their project unimpeded. In the *Republic,* as in communism, the elimination of marriage and the family was envisaged. Women were to belong to all men and vice versa. The children resulting from this promiscuity would be left in the care of the government as soon as they were weaned. Plato wanted equality of men and women, both for war and for work. Reproduction would be selective and controlled by the government. John Ruskin, a Freemason whose ideas were pure enlightenment and who according to his biographer would have approved of communism but not National Socialism, was the ideological mentor of Cecil Rhodes (1853-1902), who attended this inaugural address and preserved the text until his death.

Cecil Rhodes, initiated into Freemasonry at Oxford, attained the degree of Master on 17 April 1877. Subsequently, he joined Lodge No. 30 of the Oxford Scottish Rite, called Prince Rose Cross. Rhodes was associated in South Africa with Alfred Beit, a Jewish Freemason of German origin, and Barney Barnato, another London-born Jew of Portuguese origin whose real name was Barnet Isaacs. Barnato had arrived in South Africa in 1873 and had amassed an enormous fortune in diamonds and gold. It is an established fact that Rhodes became an agent of the Rothschilds in London. The origins of the relationship of Nathaniel Rothschild, Natty, with Cecil Rhodes go back to 1882, when the banker sent Albert Gansl to Kimberley, the main diamond mining centre, in order to get a first-hand view. Within months Gansl issued a report to Nathaniel in which he said that a host of small companies, about a hundred in number, were competing in mining and ruining each other. Soon, therefore, plans were afoot in London to merge them. Thus it was that Cecil Rhodes became the man chosen by Lord Rothschild to carry out the plans that led to the creation in 1888 of De Beers Consolidated Mines Ltd., through which today the Rothschilds and the Oppenheimer's control 90% of the world diamond market.

As for the Witwatersrand gold mines, Cecil Rhodes raided the territory of the Matebelé king, Lobengula, in order to enter the Transvaal, whose border is the Limpopo River, from the north. By deception he got Lobengula to sign a treaty granting Britain a large territory, on which Rhodes founded the colony of Rhodesia (now the republics of Zimbabwe and Zambia). In January 1888 he wrote a long letter to Natty asking for his support. He told him that he had obtained a concession from King Lobengula to develop the "unlimited gold deposits" on the other side of the Limpopo River. So convinced was he that he had the support of Lord Rothschild, at whose London headquarters he had his bank account, that in June 1888 he amended his will to name Nathaniel Rothschild trustee of all his property, except for 2,000 shares in the De Beers company, which he left to his brothers and sisters. Niall Ferguson reveals that in a letter attached to the will Rhodes told Natty that this money was to be used to found what his biographer called "a society of the elect for the good of the empire". This is an allusion to the "Round Table". Clearly, Cecil Rhodes saw in Nathaniel Rothschild the man capable of realising his vision of a global British empire. At the end of the same year, Rhodes repeated his request for Lord Rothschild's support in a new letter, in which he explained that once the territories of the King of the Matebelé were under control, the rest was easy, for it was "a simple system of villages with a separate chief in each and independent of each other".

Rhodes became Prime Minister of the Cape between 1890 and 1896 and influenced the political parties with money, since his immense personal fortune had, according to C. Quigley, "annual receipts of at least a million pounds sterling". He then pushed from power for the colonisation of Rhodesia, where English settlers ("uitlanders") began to arrive from 1890 onwards. His next step was to try to persuade the Boers, whose leader was Paul Kruger, to accept reconciliation in order to create a greater South Africa under British colonial rule, but he was unsuccessful. Cecil Rhodes was determined to undertake a plan of expansion and encirclement that was incompatible with the existence of the two Boer republics. The result was the aforementioned Jameson Raid fiasco in December 1895, which resulted in Rhodes' resignation as prime minister.

The project of a greater South Africa was naturally welcomed by the Rothschilds. To begin his expansion into Matebelé territory, Rhodes set up the new Central Search Association, which was formed through Rhodes' union with the Bechuanaland Exploration Company, which had been established by Lord Gifford and George Cawston, as well as the Portuguese Government. Natty soon became a majority shareholder and when in 1890 the company became the United Concessions Company, Lord Rothschild increased his shareholding. As early as 1889, Nathaniel Rothschild had been a founding shareholder of the British South Africa Company, also set up by Cecil Rhodes. In a January 1992 letter quoted by Niall Ferguson in *The House of Rothschild. The World's Banker 1844-1999*, the commitment of "New Cort" (the London Rothschilds) to Rhodes is expressed by Natty in the following terms: "Our first and foremost wish in relation to things in South Africa is that you will remain at the head of affairs in this colony and that you will be able to carry forward the great imperial policy which has been your life's dream. I think you will do us justice by admitting that we have always loyally supported you in carrying out this policy, and you may rest assured that we shall continue to do so."

In order to support their agent, the Rothschilds tried to persuade the Portuguese government to cede Delagoa Bay, the main port on the Mozambique coast, which was the strategic key to the future of the Transvaal. During the negotiations Natty proposed to buy this part of the Mozambican coast, but the Portuguese resisted the pressure. Rhodes tried to negotiate on his own with the Portuguese government envoy, Luiz de Soveral, but Soveral reiterated that there was nothing to be done. In his expansionist delirium Rhodes regretted in a letter of 1893 that Natty did not take a more aggressive stance and even demanded it: "I thought you would do your best, as you have for several years thought correctly that Delagoa is key to our position in South Africa..... I am afraid we are going to buy Delagoa Bay. We want it and we are prepared to pay for it". Convinced as he was of the power of Rothschild money, Rhodes could not accept that Portugal had no intention of selling.

The arrival in South Africa in 1897 of another of Lord Rothschild's protégés, Alfred Milner, as high commissioner to the government, was a key factor in the choice of war. The atrocities committed in the concentration camps were directed by this sinister character, who should go down in history as a war criminal. Milner proposed in 1898 to gain control of the Boer republics by war. Lord Rothschild had a close relationship with Milner and wrote to congratulate him warmly "on having firmly established His Majesty's dominions in South Africa". However, the first defeats of the British expeditionary force were not long in coming, and the supposed military ride eventually cost the lives of 22,000 British soldiers. Anti-imperialist writers, the most prominent of whom was John Atkinson Hobson, publicly denounced the war as being fought in the interests of certain financiers who coveted the gold and diamond fields. Concerned by these criticisms, Natty wrote to Rhodes and warned him: "Be careful in your comments on the war and in your dealings with the military authorities. The tension in this country is now very high. There is a tendency on both sides of Parliament to blame the capitalists and those with interests in the mines in South Africa for everything that is happening. It would be very unfortunate to add fuel to the fire...".

Regarding the Round Table, Carroll Quigley says the following in an oft-quoted paragraph:

"There is, and has been for a generation, an Anglophile network which operates to make the radical right believe in communist action. In fact this network, which we could identify as the Round Table groups, is not averse to co-operating with communists or any other group, and they frequently do so. I know about the operations of this network because I have studied them for twenty years, and I was able, for two years in the early 1960s, to examine their secret papers and recordings. I have no aversion to it or to most of its purposes, and I have spent much of my life close to it and to many of its instruments. I have objected, both in the past and recently, to some of its procedures. But in general my main difference of opinion is her desire to remain hidden. I think her role in history is significant enough to be known."

Cecil Rhodes wrote seven wills. The last one establishes the Rhodes Scholarships to study at Oxford, whose beneficiaries include Henry Kissinger, Bill Clinton and General Wesley Clark, among others. Of the seven, the best known is the so-called Testament of the Secret Society. In 1891 Rhodes himself and his closest associate William T. Stead founded Table Mountain. On 24 July 1902, four months after Rhodes' death, several members of his entourage presented the "Pilgrims Society". Finally, in 1909, Alfred Milner, Rhodes' successor and also a 33rd degree Mason who held the title of Grand Warden of the United Grand Lodge of England, founded the Round Table, whose members included Lord Rothschild, Lord Balfour, Lord Esher, Sir Harry Johnston and other select English initiated Scottish Rite Masons. Lord Alfred Milner, whose role in financing the Bolshevik revolution will be discussed later, became the Rothschilds' man after the demise of Cecil Rhodes. According to Dr. John Coleman, the Round Table, the all-encompassing instrument of the Committee of 300, now consists of a labyrinth of companies, institutions, banks, elite educational establishments and various other associations, whose purpose is to control fiscal and monetary policies in the countries where it operates. The Round Table has spawned a network of globalist bodies that wield power at the international level today: Royal Institute of International Affairs (RIIA), Council of Foreign Relations (CFR), Bildelberg Group, World Trade Organisation (WTO), Trilateral Commission, World Economic Forum (Davos Group), Tavistock Institute of Human Relations and others.

To conclude this introductory preamble to the chapter, it only remains to add that more than a hundred years after the South African gold and diamond wars, the Rothschilds are the masters of the gold market and can therefore manipulate its price according to their interests. It is in an office of N. M. Rothschild & Sons in the City of London that the price of gold on the world markets is fixed daily. On the other hand, the Oppenheimer family dominates the international diamond market. The current head of the family is Nicholas Oppenheimer, who succeeded his father, Sir Harry Oppenheimer, in 2000 and maintains offices in South Africa.

Woodrow Wilson and his entourage of Zionist conspirators

"Some of the most renowned men in America, in the field of commerce and industry, are afraid of somebody, they are afraid of something. They know that there is a power somewhere, so organised, so imperceptible, so watchful, so interwoven, so persuasive, that they had better speak softly when they condemn it". These words of President Woodrow Wilson about the existence of a hidden power in no way excuse his multiple capitulations, but serve only to discredit him further, for, knowing full well that he was in the hands of agents of that organised power and knowing who, why and how they were using it, he submitted time and again.

After the initially failed attempt by the international Jewish bankers to establish a central bank in the United States, i.e. the Federal Reserve System, Democrat Woodrow Wilson was the man chosen for the Presidency by the Zionist conspirators, since President William Howard Taft and the Republicans had opposed the bill which had been introduced in the Senate by Nelson Aldrich, a J. P. Morgan man, whose daughter Abby was married to John D. Rockefeller. Since Taft was very popular and it seemed impossible that he would lose the election, the old scheme of splitting the Republican vote was used. To this end, Teddy Roosevelt, who had already served as Republican president from 1901 to 1909, volunteered to sabotage his own party and run against Taft at the head of a newly created Progressive Party. Even before the election, central bank promoters had launched an operation to create a climate favourable to the Federal Reserve idea among the public. Two J. P. Morgan agents, Frank Munsey and George Perkins, provided the money and directed Roosevelt's election operation. Wilson's principal financiers, meanwhile, were the Rockefellers, one of whose agents, Cleveland H. Dodge of the National City Bank, channelled the funds and controlled the campaign. Other Jewish financiers who supported Wilson with money were Jacob Schiff, Henry Morgenthau and Bernard Baruch. The latter, who contributed $50,000, was to become the key man during the coming war and was subsequently the advisor to every president up to Eisenhower. The fact that Morgan was supporting Roosevelt's campaign did not prevent him from also contributing money to Wilson's candidacy. The idea was to give enough support to Roosevelt so that the split Republican vote would allow the Democratic candidate to beat them both. The strategy worked and Wilson was elected 28th President of the United States.

To ensure that President Wilson would have the right advisors, the bankers who put him in power surrounded him with their own agents, the most famous of whom was Colonel Edward Mandell House (he never served in the army and the position he held was only honorary). Mandell House was the son of a wealthy British planter who had represented the Rothschild interests in cotton purchases in the southern states during the Civil War. The surname Mandell was not paternal, but was given to Edward by his father to honour a Jewish merchant from Houston who was a close family friend. This man, whom Woodrow Wilson said was "my other self", became the virtual president, as the real president was a puppet in his hands. House was the main promoter of the central bank project and the income tax. Professor Charles Seymour, who edited *The Intimate Papers of Colonel House* (1926), asserts that Mandell House, who acknowledges in his diaries his passion for the secret exercise of power, was the "invisible guardian angel" of the Federal Reserve Act. He was the intermediary between the White House and the financiers. His constant contact throughout 1913 with Paul Warburg, the main architect of the Act, is perfectly documented by House himself in his private papers. His biographer, George Sylvester Viereck, states that "the Schiffs, the Warburgs, the Rockefellers, the Morgans, and the Kahns had faith in House".

The year Woodrow Wilson, secretly handpicked by the conspirators, was elected president, a novel was published by Mandell House, who found time between December 1911 and January 1912 to write *Philip Dru: Administrator* in six weeks, a book that was published anonymously. It is a brash, bewildering work in which the most influential presidential advisor in American history, the alter ego of the president of the quintessential capitalist country, describes how to establish "socialism as Karl Marx had dreamed it". The hero, Philip Dru, a young West Point graduate influenced by Karl Marx, is elected leader of a mass movement by acclamation. House describes Dru as a messianic figure who arrives in Washington and, having seized power in a totalitarian fashion, begins to reshape society. He issues a decree that any attempt to restore constitutional order will be considered seditious and punishable by death. Having proclaimed himself "Administrator of the Republic", his (and President Wilson's) greatest achievement is the introduction of "a graduated income tax which excludes no income at all". Marx, too, in the *Communist Manifesto* called for "a heavy progressive income tax". Likewise in the *Protocols* "a progressive tax on property" is called for. Professor Seymur points out that the House/Wilson/Dru ideology was "social democracy in the style of Louis Blanc and the revolutionaries of 1848", i.e. revolutionary Marxism. The unusual word "Administrator" is a clear allusion to the *Protocols*, where reference is made to "the Administrators we shall choose". The action of the novel spans a time period from 1920 to 1935. In fact the subtitle is *A Story of Tomorrow, 1920-1935*.

Chapter XIV, entitled "The Making of a President", deserves a brief commentary, as it faithfully reflects what happened to Wilson and thus turns the novel into a historical document. In that chapter, a senator named Selwyn prepares to lead the nation with an iron fist without it being known. It seems clear that Selwin is a transcript of Mandell House. So much so that the author could not resist the temptation to give a hint of his identity and has Selwyn invite the man he has chosen to be his puppet-president to dine with him at Mandell House. The novel describes "a wicked plan" hatched with John

Thor, "the high priest of finance", whereby a "compact organisation", using "the most infamous kind of deception in relation to its true intentions and opinions", is to "choose its creature for the Presidency". Selwyn finally selects one Rockland "recently elected Governor of a Midwestern State" (Wilson), who after the election, drunk with power and with the praises of sycophants, acts once or twice on his own without first consulting Selwyn. After being bitterly warned, he henceforth "made no further attempts at independence". This passage in the novel coincides with House's private diary, in which he recalls his relationship with Wilson during the campaign. It reports that House reviewed the candidate's speeches and ordered him to pay no attention to any other advice. Admitting the indiscretions, Wilson promised "never to act independently again in the future". In Chapter XV, entitled "The Exultant Conspirators", Selwyn is introduced informing Thor of Rockland's attempt to escape from his servitude: "When he told him how Rockland had made an attempt at freedom and how he had led him back, ashamed of his defeat, they laughed merrily".

Woodrow Wilson had left Princeton, where he had been Chancellor since 1902, to become Governor of New Jersey. Before an audience of electors, Zionist Rabbi Stephen Wise demonstrated in 1910 an astonishing foreknowledge of the future: "On Tuesday," said Wise, "Mr. Woodrow Wilson will be elected Governor of your State. He will not complete his term in office as governor. In November, 1912, he will be elected President of the United States. He will be inaugurated as President a second time." Further investigation revealed that the source of Rabbi Wise's mysterious knowledge had been Colonel House. Years later, in his autobiography *Challenging Years*, Stephen Wise referred to Mandell House as "unofficial Secretary of State". There can be little doubt that at Princeton Wilson had been closely observed in secret; but in 1910 neither Stephen Wise nor Edward Mandell House, who was introduced to Wilson on 24 November 1911, had yet met him personally. In any case, as early as December 1911, on the campaign trail, Wilson delivered a speech on Jewish rights which confirms that he was being conveniently indoctrinated into obedience to Zionism. "I am not here," he said, "to express our sympathy with our fellow Jews, but to bring out our sense of identity with them. This is not their cause; it is the cause of America." Before Wilson took office as president, Mandell House drew up in collaboration with Bernard Baruch, another key figure in the conspiracy, a list of future ministers.

In his book *The International Jew*, Henry Ford devotes a chapter to Bernard Baruch, whom he describes as "Judah's proconsul in America". Ford charges that Baruch knew as early as 1915 that the United States would enter the world war two years later. In 1915, when the country's neutrality was sacred to public opinion, an Advisory Commission was set up and eventually chaired by Bernard Baruch. In 1915 Baruch proposed to Wilson the creation of the National Defence Committee and a War Industries Board.

Paradoxically, Wilson's main promise during the 1916 campaign for re-election was to keep the country out of the war. Years later, in oversight sessions of the House of Representatives, Congressman Jefferis asked what Baruch's powers had been in these bodies. His reply was this: "I took the responsibility, and it was I who then decided ultimately what the Army and Navy should receive; what was to be given to the railways, or to the Allies; whether locomotives were to be given to General Allenby in Palestine or used in Russia or France." Baruch recorded that thirty-five branches of industry were under his control: "I decided, in short. By virtue of my position, I belonged to all the Boards, it being my task to inspect them." In other words, during the war the decision on industries, on raw materials and their prices; on purchases and sales; on the movement of capital..., was in the hands of this personage.

The first chapter of this book introduced Benjamin H. Freedman, a Jewish billionaire who was present at the Versailles Conference and who defected from Judaism to Christianity in 1945. We turn to him again for a first-hand account of an episode that demonstrates the extent to which the conspirators had President Wilson in their grip. In *The Hidden Tyranny* Freedman explains that after his first election in 1912 the president was visited at the White House by Samuel Untermayer, a prominent Jewish lawyer from New York who had contributed generously to the campaign that installed Wilson as president. Untermayer was later to go down in history for his famous speech, published in full in *The New York Times* on 7 August 1933, in which he called on all the Jews of the world to "holy war" against Germany and an "international boycott of German goods". The reason for the visit could not have been more unpleasant. Untermayer had been hired by a woman who accused Wilson of having broken a marriage vow. The lawyer informed the president that his client was willing to accept $40,000 to drop the suit. Untermayer's client was the former wife of a Princeton University professor, a colleague of Woodrow Wilson's during his years as a professor and chancellor at Princeton University. The lawyer showed a packet of letters written by Wilson, who acknowledged their authorship after examining them, in which the illicit relationship was perfectly demonstrated. During Wilson's years as governor of New Jersey, his former mistress had divorced and married a second time.

Wilson considered it fortunate that his former love had gone to Samuel Untermayer, for if he had consulted a Republican lawyer, the situation would have been even more embarrassing for him. The president then informed the lawyer that he did not have the money. Untermayer suggested that he think carefully about the matter and promised to return to discuss it. After a few days, President Wilson reiterated that he could not meet the blackmail because he did not have such a large sum. It was then that the lawyer Untermayer offered a solution to the problem: he would pay the amount requested by the former mistress out of his own pocket on one condition: Wilson had to promise that when the first vacancy on the US Supreme Court arose, he would appoint the person he recommended to the post. Samuel Untermayer had an enormous personal fortune, as the New York law firm of which he was the senior partner was among the largest in the country. The President readily accepted the generous offer and thanked Untermayer for what he was doing.

The day soon came when a new member of the Supreme Court had to be appointed, and Untermayer proposed Louis Dembitz Brandeis, a Jewish Zionist and Talmudist, for the vacancy. Never before had a Talmudist made it to the highest judicial institution in the land. Benjamin Freedman notes that "in 1914 Justice Brandeis became the most prominent and politically influential Zionist in America. Brandeis was in a unique position to serve Talmudic Jews in and outside America. The facts soon proved this assessment to be true, as President Wilson and Justice Brandeis became unusually close friends. The judge, who was naturally not unaware that he had obtained the office through his friend Untermayer, even heard Wilson's own account of the circumstances of his appointment.

Both Gershom Scholem and Rabbi Antelman provide information about Louis D. Brandeis' Frankist ancestors. Justice Brandeis' grandfather, called Dembitz, and his grandfather's brother, Gottlieb Wehle, were first Shabbetaists and later Frankists. Judge Brandeis' wife also came from a Frankist family: she was the granddaughter of Gottlieb Wehle. We already know that the frankists married among themselves. In any case, in Louis Brandeis, Frankism had become radical Zionism. In 1907 Jacob Schiff, the banker who financed the communist revolution in Russia, declared that "one could not be both a true American and an honest supporter of Zionism." Brandeis, for his part, argued that "to be good Americans, we must be better Jews, and to be better Jews we must become Zionists."

The creation of the Federal Reserve System

The history of the creation of the Federal Reserve is well known, but perhaps the general public is unaware of how Eustace Mullins, the author we have been quoting throughout this book, was the first to undertake research. There are many works on the Fed today, but the first book on the subject appeared in 1952 thanks to two disciples of Ezra Pound, John Kasper and David Horton, who financed with their own money the publication of *Mullins on the Federal Reserve*, later published as *The Secrets of the Federal Reserve*. Mullins himself says in the foreword that it was Ezra Pound, a political prisoner in a hospital for the insane, who commissioned and directed the work. Pound, perhaps the most important American poet of the 20th century, publicly denounced from the microphones of Radio Rome that international Jewish bankers were the instigators of World War II. Perhaps there will be an opportunity to expand on his story later. For now it is enough to know that, accused of treason and anti-Semitism by the authorities, Pound was locked up without trial in a mental hospital. Eustace Mullins, also the author of *This Difficult Individual, Ezra Pound*, visited him regularly during his thirteen years in St. Elizabeth's Hospital. Mullins explains that one day in 1949 Pound asked him if had ever heard of the Federal Reserve System. When he replied in the negative, the poet asked him if he could do some research at the Library of Congress and offered him ten dollars a week for a few weeks to begin his work. The first enquiries revealed that Ezra Pound's suspicions about the existence of a secret plan were true. Thus came the commission: "You must work on it as a detective story". Mullins recounts in the foreword how the work was done: "I researched four hours a day at the Library of Congress and went to St. Elizabeth's Hospital in the afternoon. Pound and I would go over the previous day's notes. I would have dinner with George Stimpson at Scholl's Cafeteria and he would supervise my material. I would return to my room to type up the corrected notes. Stimpson and Pound made many suggestions guiding me in a field in which I had no previous experience."

What happened in Germany when Eustace Mullins' work, published by Guido Röder under the title *The Federal Reserve Conspiracy*, was published in 1955, has been discussed in note 29 of chapter five. As will be recalled, Otto John, a communist spy who held the post of Director of Intelligence in West Germany, before moving to East Germany, confiscated and burned the ten thousand copies of the edition of the book denouncing the international bankers. Earlier we have seen how Edward Mandell House, agent of the bankers who created the Federal Reserve System and transmission belt between them and President Wilson, wrote the book, *Philip Dru: Administrator*, in which he aspired to "socialism as dreamt of by Karl Marx". The paradoxes are overcome antitheses; however, it is extremely difficult to understand these paradoxes, i.e. how can one be both a supporter of communism and a supporter of capitalism? In the following pages we will continue to explore this question.

The story of the creation of the Federal Reserve begins on the night of 22 November 1910 at the Hoboken railway station in New Jersey, where a group of reporters saw a number of financiers boarding a train with a sealed carriage with armoured shutters that departed for an unknown destination. Senator Nelson Aldrich, an insider who chaired the National Monetary Commission, created in 1908 after the panic of 1907,[41] headed the entourage

---

[41] The panic of 1907, like all panics, was a provoked panic, which occurred because the large reserve banks in New York refused to provide money to their depository banks in the rest of the country, which at the same time needed liquidity to pay their depositors. John Pierpont Morgan was one of the banksters most involved in the operation, as he caused the failure of his rival, Knickerbocker Trust Co, which dragged down more than 200 banks. The crisis, which had been announced a few months earlier by Morgan himself in a lecture to the New York Chamber of Commerce, where he called for the creation of

which, in addition to his secretary, included Frank Vanderlip, president of Rockefeller's National City Bank of New York; Henry P. Davison, a partner and personal emissary of J. P. Morgan, who was the most influential of all. P. Morgan, who was the most important American agent of the English Rothschilds; Charles D. Norton, president of the Morgan-dominated First National Bank of New York; Benjamin Strong, known as J. P. Morgan's lieutenant; Paul Warburg, Kuhn's partner, Loeb; and A. Piat Andrew, assistant secretary of the Treasury. Only later did it emerge that the destination was Jekyll Island, a thousand miles south in Georgia, owned by an exclusive group of millionaires who had bought it as a winter retreat. The secrecy of the meeting was evident, as Jekyll's usual servants had been replaced by others brought in from Europe for the occasion. In addition, the members of the meeting had decided to use only first names in their conversations and to dispense with the use of surnames.

This group, representing the most powerful men in the world, stayed at the Jekyll Island club for nine days. Their aim was to enlighten a law that would protect the private banks that planned to take over the nation's currency issuance. Let us remember once again Mayer Amschel Rothschild's famous phrase: "Give me control over a nation's currency and I care not who makes its laws". If this law could be passed, the right to print money without limit, to control its supply and price, and to lend it at interest, even to the government itself, would be in the hands of the Federal Reserve cartel (in 2013 the US national debt was $16 trillion, 40% of which is interest payable to the Fed). The most technical man, the real mastermind behind the plan to establish this central bank was Paul Warburg, who hailed from Frankfurt am Main, the home town of the founder of the Rothschild dynasty. The Warburgs began as early as 1814 doing work for the Rothschilds in Hamburg; but it was not until 1830 that close transactions and relations between them were established on a regular basis.

Paul Warburg had arrived in the United States in 1902 with his brother Felix, while his brother Max, who in 1917 would become Trotsky's financier, had remained in Germany. Paul married Nina Loeb, daughter of Salomon Loeb of Kuhn, Loeb & Co. Felix married Frieda Schiff, daughter of Jacob Schiff, who also financed Trotsky in particular and the Bolsheviks in general. In the 18th century the Schiffs and the Rothschilds had shared the famous "Judengasse" (Jewish Passage) house in Frankfurt. It is thought that it was with Rothschild money that Schiff bought Kuhn's company, Loeb. Since 1907 Paul Warburg had devoted part of his time to writing and lecturing on the need for banking reform. Nelson Aldrich had worked

---

a central bank, was due to a lack of money in circulation and an inadequate method of increasing the supply of currency. There was therefore a widespread demand for changes in the system so that there would be an adequate volume of money to meet the needs of commerce. Congress then appointed a committee, which was called the Monetary Commission.

alongside him. It was Aldrich who, arguing that the public already associated his name with monetary reform, insisted that his name should be associated with the law. Thus the Jekyll Island meeting produced the Monetary Commission report and the Aldrich Act. However, linking this name to the legal standard was counterproductive, as his patronage was too closely linked to Morgan and the interests of international bankers. Warburg wanted to avoid any allusion to "Central Bank" and had proposed that the law be called the "Federal Reserve System", which was the name that would eventually prevail when the Aldrich Act failed.

As soon as the participants in Jekyll's work returned to New York, a national propaganda campaign in favour of the "Aldrich Plan" was launched in the spring of 1911. The universities of Princeton, Harvard and Chicago, the latter endowed with millions of dollars by John D. Rockefeller, were the places from which the strategy that gave rise to the "National Citizens' League for the Promotion of a Sound Banking System" was developed. The Aldrich Plan was presented to Congress as the result of three years of work and study by the National Monetary Commission; but, despite propaganda campaigns and press support, it met with strong opposition led by William Jennings Bryan and Charles Lindbergh senior, father of the famous aviator who flew solo across the Atlantic on a non-stop flight from New York to Paris. In addition, President William Howard Taft was unwilling to sign the Aldrich Act. On 15 December 1911, Congressman Charles Lindbergh denounced the Aldrich Plan as "Wall Street's plan, simply a scheme in the interests of the Trust". Also in the Senate, Robert M. LaFollete publicly denounced that a fifty-man "trust" controlled the United States.

Congress tried to appease popular sentiment against the Aldrich Act by creating a committee to investigate the control of money and credit. The Pujo Committee, headed by Congressman Arsene Pujo, was formed in 1912. The hearings lasted five months and produced six thousand pages and four volumes of statements from the bankers who paraded before the Committee; but nothing clear came out of these sessions, as the financiers insisted only that they always operated in the public interest. Samuel Untermayer was appointed special counsel to the Pujo Committee and his work was more obstructive than helpful. When Jacob Schiff came forward to testify, Untermayer's questioning allowed him to talk and talk without clarifying the operations of Kuhn, Loeb & Co, which Senator Robert L. Owen had identified as representing the European Rothschilds in the United States. Before the provoked panic of 1907, Jacob Schiff had made the following statement at the New York Chamber of Commerce: "If we have no central bank which will sufficiently supervise the funds of credit, this country will know the most severe and profound crisis in its history". Eustace Mullins considers that the Pujo Committee ended up being a farce.

In the end, the Aldrich Act was presented under the name of the Federal Reserve Act, which had been proposed by Paul Warburg at the Jekyll

Island meetings. With the strategy described above, in November 1912 the elections were finally held that were to unravel the situation. With Wilson in office, the process was led by Mandell House, who shamelessly behaved throughout 1913 as an agent of Paul Warburg. In *Mullins on the Federal Reserve*, taken from House's own private papers, the meetings between the bankers and their man in the White House are dated. Here are some of the "colonel's" accounts of his interviews with the bankers:

> "March 13, 1913. Warburg and I had a private discussion about money reform.
> March 27, 1913. Mr. J. P. Morgan Jr. and Mr. Denny, of his firm, came promptly at five o'clock. McAdoo came almost ten minutes later. Morgan had already prepared a money plan. I suggested typing it up, so it would not look prearranged, and he sent it to Wilson today.
> July 23, 1913. I tried to show Major Quincey (of Boston) the stupidity of the Eastern bankers in adopting a contrary attitude to the money project....
> 13 October 1913. Paul Warburg was my first visitor today. He came to discuss the money project...
> 17 November 1913. Paul Warburg telephoned about his trip to Washington. Then he and Mr Jacob Schiff came for a few minutes. Warburg bore the brunt of the conversation. He had a new suggestion regarding the grouping of the banks... in connection with the Federal Reserve Board."

Thus, December 1913 approached. *The New York Times*, whose owner, Adolph Simon Ochs, was a Zionist Jew of German origin, devoted an editorial article to extolling the excellencies of the new system: "New York will be on a firmer footing of financial growth and we shall soon see it the money centre of the world". Finally, on Monday 22 December, the same newspaper announced the imminent passage of the money bill and alluded to the "unprecedented speed" with which both Houses had agreed. As a matter of parliamentary courtesy, it was a tradition not to vote on important legislative bills during Christmas week, but this custom was broken in order to get the Federal Reserve Act passed on the 22nd. To this end, the Parliamentary Conference Committee met between 1:30 and 4:30 in the morning, while the parliamentarians were asleep, and the bill was voted on the following day, despite the fact that many members of Congress had already left for their Christmas holidays and those who remained had barely had time to study it and learn about its content.

The New York Times devoted only one sentence to Congressman Lindbergh's critical speech. Eustace Mullins offers a significant quote from his speech in Congress: "This bill creates the most gigantic Trust in the land. When the President signs this bill, the invisible government through the Money Power will be legalised. The people may not know it immediately, but the day of reckoning is only a few years away. The trusts will soon realise that they have gone too far even for their own good. The people must make a declaration of independence to free themselves from Monetary Power. This they can do by taking control of Congress. Wall Street could not swindle us if you Senators and Representatives do not make a sham of Congress...". The director of the strategy to pass the Act at Christmas time had once again been Paul Warburg, who, ensconced in an office in the Capitol building, was constantly receiving congressmen and senators to give them instructions. The result of the vote in Congress was 298 votes in favour of the Act and 60 against. In the Senate, 43 senators voted in favour and 25 voted against. On 23 December 1913 Wilson signed the Federal Reserve Act. On 24 December Jacob Schiff, the most prominent representative of the Rothschild banking syndicate, wrote to Edward Mandell House in these terms: "My dear Colonel House: I wish to say a word to you for the quiet, but undoubtedly effective, work you have done in the interest of money legislation and to congratulate you on the measure. With my good wishes, yours faithfully, Jacob Schiff."

Article 1, section 8, paragraph 5 of the US Constitution expressly charges Congress with the "power to coin money and regulate the value thereof". The Federal Reserve Act was a direct assault on the sovereignty of Congress, i.e. the American people. In 1935 the US Supreme Court ruled that Congress cannot constitutionally delegate its power to another group or body. Congressmen, therefore, in passing the Federal Reserve Act violated the Constitution they were sworn to preserve. Dr. Quigley explains perfectly in *Tragedy and Hope* the extent of the operation perpetrated by the international Jewish bankers and their agents. According to him, what they intended was to use the power of Britain and the United States to force most countries to operate "through central banks free from political control, with all matters relating to international finance agreed by agreement of these central banks without any interference from governments." Caroll Quigley argues that the true dimensions of the whole scheme can be fully appreciated when it is realised that the far-reaching aim of these banking dynasties was: "... nothing less than to create a world system of financial control in private hands, capable of dominating the political system of each country and the economy of the world as a whole. This system was to be controlled by the world's central banks, which were to act in concert, through secret agreements reached during private meetings and conferences. The apex of the system was to be the Bank for International Settlements in Basel, Switzerland, a private bank owned and controlled by the central banks of the world, which were at the same time private corporations". About this Bank for International Settlements (BIS), a long review could be given. Its existence is unknown to most mortals. Founded in 1930, it is a hermetic and inviolable entity that does not answer to any political power. The BIS is at the pinnacle of power: it is the central bank of its member central banks.

In an appearance before the Banking and Money Committee in 1913 Paul Warbug stated that one of the objectives of the Federal Reserve Act was the "mobilisation of credit". The world war began seven months after the passage of the Act, and the first task of the Federal Reserve System was to finance it. The European countries involved in the conflict ended up owing $14 trillion to the Reserve Banks. It is estimated that the international financial elite earned $208 trillion from the war. Henry Ford notes in *The International Jew* that 73 per cent of the new millionaires in New York who emerged as a result of the war were Jewish, which is not surprising considering that it was Bernard Baruch who held in his hands the life or death of industries and control over "priorities" in the movement of capital.

Fifty years later, on 4 June 1963, Kennedy issued Presidential Order EO 11110, which gave the President the authority to issue currency. He then ordered the US Treasury to print $4 billion in banknotes to replace those of the Federal Reserve. His intention was to take back the power that had been illegally usurped from Congress. He intended to gradually replace the dollars issued by the Federal Reserve with the new currency. A few months after the plan was put into effect, President Kennedy was assassinated in Dallas. As soon as Lyndon B. Johnson took office, Kennedy's presidential order was rescinded and the old power of the cartel was restored. The assassination was undoubtedly a very serious warning to any other president who might conceive of such a plan in the future.

PART 2
ZIONISM AND WORLD WAR I

The four years of World War I saw unprecedented carnage in Europe, followed by a decade of chaos, misery and oppression. Habsburg, Romanov and Hohenzollern, three powerful European Christian dynasties, disappeared in one fell swoop as a result of the war. While this was important and significant for the future of Europe, the triumph of the Bolshevik Revolution was an even more momentous event. The fall of Russia into the hands of agents of the international Jewish bankers and the installation in power, with the acquiescence of the United States and Britain, of a criminal and totalitarian ideology, was to mark humanity throughout the 20th century. This was the spectacular result that the Illuminati had longed for since Adam Weishaupt had launched his conspiracy against all the religions and governments of Europe. Then there was the Young Turk Revolution, which gave birth to modern Turkey after the dissolution of the Ottoman Empire. Kemal Ataturk and the Young Turks were not only Freemasons but also "Doenmes", i.e. crypto-Jews who had apparently converted to Islam, although they continued to practise their Jewish religion. They were responsible for the genocide of 1.5 million Armenian Orthodox Christians in 1915-16. All these events make the First World War one of the most decisive episodes in history. It gave rise to communism and Zionism, two terrifying heads of the same monster that had been patiently conceiving them throughout the 19th century.

The atmosphere in Europe became increasingly poisoned after the Young Turks ousted Sultan Abdul Hamid II from power. The Italo-Turkish war that began in Libya in 1911 was followed between 1912 and 1913 by wars in the Balkans: the first pitted the Ottoman Empire against a Balkan league comprising Montenegro, Bulgaria, Greece and Serbia; in the second, the coalition partners fought each other. Russia and the Austro-Hungarian Empire, whose interests overlapped, had been left on the sidelines, but it was clear that those who wanted to provoke an explosion had the most propitious scenario in the area. Moreover, in 1872, a German engineer, Wilhelm von Pressel, had designed the "Orient Express" project, which the British frowned upon because it would jeopardise their old imperial line: Gibraltar, Malta, Port Said, Suez, Aden, Ceylon, Hong Kong. If Germany or any other nation wished to trade with Eastern countries, or just to enter or leave the Mediterranean with its ships, it had to have permission from the British, who could close the Mare Nostrum thanks to their control of the Suez Canal and the fortress of Gibraltar. In 1888 Germany had obtained permission from the Turks and intended to link Berlin and Baghdad via a railway line to the Persian Gulf, where it was planned to build a port that would take the Germans to the Indian Ocean.

Against this backdrop, journalists and pamphleteers all over Europe in the service of the financial groups were preparing public opinion for the coming war. The powerful *Neue Freie Press*, controlled by the Rothschilds, sworn enemies of the Czars, was stirring up Germans and Austro-Hungarians against Russia, which was accused of being responsible for the wars on the Balkan peninsula. On the other hand, the Jewish organisations Poale Zion and the Bund were promoting anti-Tsar hatred in southern Russia and Poland with their propaganda. To complete the picture, it should be remembered that the head of German espionage during the war was the Jew Max Warburg, brother of Paul Warburg, and that the German chancellor between 1909 and 1917 was Theobald von Bethmann-Hollweg, another Jew with ties to the Rothschilds from Frankfort am Main, the city where anti-Russian sentiment had always been generated. Bethmann-Hollweg was unable or unwilling to oppose the German Jewish financiers who wanted to dismember the Russian empire. Bismarck, who considered the integrity of the Russian empire indispensable to Germany's prosperity, had been very different in this respect. Publicly he had expressed it thus: "The maintenance of monarchical governments in St. Petersburg is for us Germans a necessity which coincides with the maintenance of our own regime.... If the monarchies do not understand the necessity of holding out together in the interests of political and social order, I fear that the international revolutionary and social problems which will have to be faced will be very dangerous...." Bismarck was well aware of the depth of the revolutionary movement, which is why he had even advocated the need for a "Dreikaiserbund" (league of the three emperors).

If we consider who were the main beneficiaries of the catastrophe, we have to agree that, once again, those who got the richest were the usual bankers and moneylenders, who financed both sides. These same bankers, through the use of the Judeo-Bolsheviks, perpetrated an unprecedented robbery in Russia, the greatest plunder in history. In the following pages we will provide data and arguments in favour of this thesis, without neglecting the ideological aspects used to manipulate, manage and mercilessly use the great masses, sacrificed to the interests of hidden characters.

The Good Masons and the Sarajevo assassination

When on 28 June 1914 Archduke Franz Ferdinand of Austria, heir to the Austro-Hungarian Empire, and his wife were assassinated in Sarajevo, those who encouraged the crime knew that they had created the trigger that was to ignite World War I. On 15 September 1912, Mgr Jouin, editor of the *Revue Internationale des Sociétés Secrètes*, announced two years in advance that the Archduke had been condemned to death by the Freemasons. Monsignor Jouin predicted that perhaps one day the following words about the Austrian heir, uttered by a Swiss high-ranking Freemason, would be clarified: "He is an extraordinary man; it is a pity he is condemned, he will die before he reaches the throne". Count Ottokar von Czernin, the Austro-Hungarian foreign minister between 1916-1918, in his work *Im Welt Kriege* (In *the World War*) reveals that the archduke himself knew he was going to die: "The archduke knew perfectly well that the danger of an attack was imminent. A year before the war he confessed to me that Freemasonry had decided on his death. He also told me the city where such a decision had been taken and mentioned the names of several Hungarian and Austrian politicians who probably knew about it".

It can be said that the fate of the Archduke was known throughout Europe. Everything suggests that the criminals were used by conspirators who wanted war at all costs. In *Under the Sign of the Scorpion*, the Estonian Jüri Lina quotes Yuri Begunov, whose works have not been translated. This Russian author reveals that in the spring of 1914 Trotsky travelled to Vienna as a member of the Grand Lodge of France in order to meet with a brother Mason named V. Gacinovic to discuss plans for the assassination of Franz Ferdinand of Austria. According to Begunov, Radek and Zinoviev, two other Jewish communist leaders and Freemasons, were aware of what was being hatched. Another tip-off that the Archduke was to be killed came on 11 July 1914 with the appearance of a document in *John Bull*, a newspaper owned by Horatio Bottomley, a British financier, politician and journalist who in 1888 had founded the *Financial Times*. In his paper Bottomley published a text obtained from the Serbian Consulate in London and dated 14 April 1914. The document was written in Ladino, the language spoken by Sephardic Jews. It offered £2,000 for the 'elimination' of the Archduke. Professor Robert William Seton-Watson in *German, Slav, and Magyar: A Study in the Origins of the Great War* refers to this text published in *John Bull* and clarifies for the layman that Ladino was a dialect of Spanish spoken by the Jews of Salonika. Seton-Watson adds that the man who tried to sell the document to various London newspapers, until it was finally accepted by Horatio Bottomley, was a Jew connected with the Committee for Union and Progress, which depended on the Jewish lodges of Salonika, which were under the control of the Grand Orient of Italy, which in turn depended on the Grand Orient of France. There is a record of a transfer of 700,000 francs from Paris to Rome through the Grand Orient by the Universal Israelite Alliance. This money may have financed the Sarajevo assassination.

The facts are well known. The Archduke arrived on an official visit to Sarajevo, a city in Bosnia-Herzegovina close to the Serbian border. He and his wife were in the back seats of a motor car. Seated in front of them was General Potiorek, while Count Harrach was next to the driver. The car was moving slowly in the direction of the town hall. Blending in among the population were Cabrinovic, Princip and Grabez, the three most determined fanatics among the eight assassins armed with bombs and pistols. On the Cumurja Bridge, Cabrinovic threw a bomb that hit the car and exploded on the ground. The occupants of the car behind him and several people were injured. The Archduke's car stopped to check on the wounded, but the programme was not suspended and the motorcade continued on its way to the Town Hall. After the reception, the couple went to the hospital to visit the wounded. On the journey, Count Harrach, in order to protect his Highness, stood on the step on the left-hand side of the vehicle. At the corner of Franz Joseph Street, the car stopped right in front of one of the assassins, the young Jew Gavrilo Princip, who fired at the Archduke from close range with an automatic pistol until the magazine was empty. Archduchess Sophie, trying to protect him, stepped in in an instinctive reaction and fell badly wounded on her husband's shoulders. Count Harrach heard Franz Ferdinand say tenderly: "Sophie, Sophie, don't die, live for the sake of our children". The archduke continued to sit holding his wife while a little blood appeared on his lips. "It is nothing, it is nothing," he said several times in a weak voice to Count Harrach before he fell unconscious. The governor's palace was reached and both bodies were carried to a bed on the first floor, but the doctors who arrived in haste found them already dead. The tragedy had only just begun: in the years to come, millions of people would also die a violent death under bullets as a result of those first shots.

In *Freemasonry and Judaism. The Secret Powers behind the Revolution*, Viscount Léon de Poncins reproduces extracts from the interrogation to which the criminals were subjected during the trial, held in October of the same year. The trial of the members of the "Black Hand", as the secret society was called, went unnoticed because of the turmoil of the war and the self-interested silence of the press. One of the assassins, Cabrinovic, declared nonchalantly to the judges of the military court that "in Freemasonry it is permitted to kill". Cabrinovic alluded in his statement to a Masonic leader named Casimirovic, who came and went, who was allegedly the man who was in contact with the alleged leadership coordinating the assassination, the courier who passed on orders to those who had volunteered to carry out the assassination. Cabrinovic also referred to a certain Ciganovic, who had told him that two years ago, and this fully confirms Monsignor Jouin's revelation, that Freemasonry had condemned the heir to the Austrian throne to death, but that they had not found people willing to carry out the sentence. There is one interesting fact in the statement that allows us to assume that Casimirovic was in contact with Jewish leaders and that he himself could be one. Cabrinovic told the judge that when Ciganovic handed him the automatic pistol and ammunition, he had remarked that Casimirovic came from Budapest, where he had been in contact with certain circles. It is known that in those years ninety percent of Hungarian Freemasons were Jewish. The incorporation documents of the Grand Symbolic Lodge of Budapest in 1905 bear the calendar date of the Jewish era, i.e. 5885. The passwords and the text of the oaths taken by the members of the lodge were written in the Hebrew language. The names of the members of this lodge also prove the Jewish origin of the Hungarian Freemasons. [42]

Another passage reproduced by Léon de Poncins contains a brief dialogue between the president of the tribunal and the young Gavrilo Princip, the perpetrator of the shooting. The quotation will allow the reader to appreciate the tone of the interrogation.

"The President: Did you talk about Freemasonry with Ciganovic?
Princip (insolently): Why do you ask this?
The Chairman: I am asking because I need to know. Did you talk to him about it or not?
Princip.- Yes, Ciganovic told me that he was a Freemason.
When did the president tell you this?
Principality: He told me when I asked him about the means to carry out the assassination. He added that he would speak to a certain person and that he would receive the necessary means. On another occasion he told me that the heir to the throne had been condemned to death in a Masonic lodge.
The President: And you are also a Freemason?
Principle: Why this question? I will not answer (after a short silence) No. (after a short silence) No.
The President: Is Cabrinovic a Freemason?
Princip.- I don't know. Perhaps he is. He once told me that he was going to join a lodge".

Three of the defendants sentenced to death were hanged on 2 February 1915. Princip, Cabrinovic and Grabez, being under the age of twenty, were sentenced to twenty years' imprisonment. The last two died in prison.

Responsibilities for the outbreak of war, a work of Freemasonry

This paragraph would be unnecessary without Article 231 of the Treaty of Versailles, which forced Germany to admit that it had been solely responsible for the war. This article states exactly: "The Allies and

---

[42] After the end of Bela Kuhn's regime in Hungary, known as the "Red Terror", the authorities banned Freemasonry. In 1921, Mgr Jouin published *Le péril judéo-maçonnique, a* five-volume work containing the secret papers found in the Budapest lodges. The volume on Freemasonry in Hungary is divided into three parts. The first, entitled *The Crimes of Freemasonry*, written by Adorjan Barcsay, contains a large number of documents from the lodges dissolved in 1920. The second part, written by Joseph Palatinus, is entitled *The Secrets of the Provincial Lodge.* It explains how the secret Masonic work of destruction in Hungary led to the October revolution of 1918 and communism in 1919. The third part contains a list of the members of the Hungarian Masonic lodges, which shows that ninety percent of Hungarian Masons were Jews.

Associated Governments affirm and Germany accepts the responsibility of Germany and her Allies for causing all the loss and damage which the Allies and Associated Governments and their citizens have suffered as a result of the war which was imposed upon them by Germany and her Allies". On 16 June 1919 there was an amplifying note to the article, repeating that all responsibility lay with Germany, which was accused of having planned and initiated the war. It said that Germany and "her people" were responsible for the deeds of her government. It thus added to the alleged guilt of the war a moral condemnation and humiliation of an entire people. This note was an ultimatum that forced Germany to sign the Treaty of 28 June 1919, which, in addition to placing sole responsibility on Germany, imposed disarmament and the payment of devastating reparations. Those who blamed the German people evidently did not share the maxim of Sir Patrick Hastings, for whom "war is a creation of individuals, not of nations".

Germany rushed in 1919 to publish a white paper with official documents. The other countries also brought out their own documents in so-called colour books. The Austrian government published the red book; the French brought out the yellow book; the English the blue book; the Bolsheviks the orange book. Historians were thus able to begin reviewing documents and researching the facts and attitudes of the belligerent countries. It was then that a school of revisionist historians was born in the United States who questioned the version of the winners of the war. Its main representative was Professor Harry Elmer Barnes. We will now look at various works published by representatives of revisionism in order to provide the reader with data and information that will enable him to form an idea of who was responsible for the outbreak of the First World War.

Among the first texts is *New Light on the Origins of the World War, the* three famous articles cited by all revisionists, published in 1921 by Professor Sidney B. Fay in the *American International Review*. This researcher, whose arguments had a considerable impact, rejected the guilt of Germany that the victors had imposed on the world. In 1924, historical revisionism received a new impetus with the publication of *Current History* by Harry Elmer Barnes, who from then on was at the forefront of the revisionist movement. In *In Quest of Truth and Justice*, a book published in 1928 that has since become a classic, Professor Barnes referred to an alleged role of the Serbian intelligence services in the conspiracy. His accusation was then supported by the startling revelations made in 1923 by Stanoje Stanojevic in the book *Die Ermordung des Erzherzogs Franz Ferdinand (The Assassination of Archduke Franz Ferdinand)*, in which Dragutin Dimitrievich, a colonel in the intelligence service, and Milan Tsiganovitch, one of his subordinates, were implicated in the plot. In 1918 Dmitrievich was assassinated in Salonika, a relevant fact which suggests that he knew too much. Harry E. Barnes also cites *The Blood of the Slavs, a* work published ten years after the crime by Ljuba Jovanovitch, Speaker of the Serbian

Parliament and Minister of Education in 1914. According to Jovanovitch, the Serbian government was informed of the plot by Prime Minister Nikola Pashitch three weeks before the assassination attempt. Despite this, nothing was done to try to stop the terrorists and Austria was not adequately warned. In other words, the "casus belli" could have been avoided by the Serbian government. Of course, without a reason for war, the war-makers would have had to fabricate another triggering event.

For readers who read only in Spanish, there is an interesting work published by Espasa-Calpe in 1955, *Odio incondicional. Culpabilidad de guerra alemana y el futuro de Europa (Unconditional Hatred: German War Guilt and the Future of Europe)*, authored by English Captain Russell Grenfell. This military man shares Professor Barnes's thesis that the countries most likely to start the war were Serbia, France and Russia, as all three had territorial claims: France had been yearning since 1871 for a revenge that would allow it to recover Alsace and Lorraine; Russia aspired to control the Black Sea straits. Serbia wanted to expand its territory in Bosnia. Grenfell thus points to two names as the main instigators or those responsible for the disaster: Sazonov, the Russian foreign minister, and Poincaré, who in 1912 had combined the post of prime minister with that of foreign minister and had been president of the Republic since January 1913. Poincaré had pledged support for Russia under any circumstances, whether Russia was attacked or attacked. This attitude would be incontrovertible proof that Poincaré and the supporters of the war in Paris envisaged the possibility of regaining Alsace-Lorraine through a revanchist war, as they were convinced that France and Russia would defeat the Central Powers. Grenfell divides the countries that participated in the war into two groups: those that wanted to make gains and those that wanted to hold on to what they had. In the first group he places Serbia, France and Russia; in the second, Germany, Austria-Hungary and Britain.

Having presented these arguments, let us now look chronologically at the most significant events of July 1914. On 5 and 6 July Germany allegedly offered a "blank cheque" to Austria-Hungary if it were to take any action against Serbia. The Austrian ambassador in Berlin, László Szögyény, sent a telegram to his foreign minister, Leopold Berchtold, informing him that Kaiser Wilhelm II on the 5th and Chancellor Bethmann-Hollweg on the 6th had promised unconditional aid. On this point, Professor Fay points out in the famous articles cited above that on 26 July Germany cancelled its blank cheque and cooperated with Britain to contain Austria in order to avoid general co-flagration.

On 7 July the Austro-Hungarian government held a council of ministers to consider whether to take military action against Serbia or opt for diplomacy. Minister Berchtold, confident of German backing, favoured the first option. The Hungarian Prime Minister, Count Stephen Tisza, opposed it. In the end it was agreed that a series of unacceptable demands should be presented to Serbia, which would justify a war between Austria and Serbia. Sixteen days passed before these demands were presented to Serbia. On 13 July, telegrams arrived in Vienna from Sarajevo. Friedrich von Wiesner, the investigator the government had sent to the city, believed there was evidence of Serbian complicity in the assassination, but had no proof that the Serbian government was or could be involved.

On 15 July President Raymond Poincaré and René Viviani, who was both head of government and foreign minister, travelled to Russia. They arrived in St Petersburg on the 20th and spent three days in talks with the Russian Foreign Minister, Sergei Sazov, who, according to various sources, was a Freemason. Although there are no official records of these consultations, it is believed that France also offered Russia a blank cheque if it supported Serbia against Austria-Hungary. Both Maurice Paléologue, another Freemason who served as French ambassador to Russia, and Alexander Izvolski, the Russian ambassador to France who was present in St. Petersburg, reportedly strongly supported their respective countries' solidarity with Serbia. The Austro-Hungarian ambassador to Russia, Count Szapáry, who was also a Freemason, was informed by Poincaré and Sazov of their countries' support for Serbia. If it is true that war is a creation of individuals and not of nations, as Sir Patrick Hastings said, Poincaré would be one of the individuals who worked hardest for the war, and various documents confirm this. In Ambassador Paléologue's memoirs, it is admitted that Poincaré was active in encouraging and strengthening the pro-war camp while in St. Petersburg. Baron Schilling of the Russian Foreign Ministry also refers in his diary to the grandiloquent speeches made by Poincaré, which, as Paléologue informed the Russians, were to be taken as binding diplomatic documents. Another interesting piece of information comes from the *British War Origins Papers*, which record that on the 22nd Poincaré vetoed a proposal by the Foreign Office Secretary, Sir Edward Grey, for direct talks between Vienna and St. Petersburg. Alfred Fabre-Luce, the renowned French writer and journalist, wrote that after Poincaré's visit to St. Petersburg there was little chance of avoiding war.

At 6 p.m. on 23 July, after Poincaré had already left Russia, the two-day ultimatum that had been slowly brewing in Vienna was delivered to the Serbian government by the Austrian diplomat Baron Giesl. It demanded a response by 6 p.m. on the evening of the 25th. During the morning of the 24th, the terms of the ultimatum became known to the other European powers. There were attempts to extend the deadline and offers of mediation, but there were also Russian statements of support for Serbia. Eyewitnesses report that when Zazov learned of the ultimatum, he became angry and called for immediate Russian mobilisation.

On the evening of 25 July, influenced by Russia, Serbia mobilised. Before the deadline expired there was a response rejecting the essential points of the ultimatum. Austria hardened its position. France and Britain took some precautionary military measures, but did nothing to try to contain Russia. In the afternoon, Zazov confirmed to the British ambassador in St. Petersburg, the High Mason George Buchanan, that since France "had placed herself unreservedly on Russia's side," they were prepared to "assume all the risks of war." The French Ambassador Paléologue noted in his diary that day that he went to the Warsaw station to see off Izvolski, who was returning to his post in Paris after attending talks with Poincaré. The two exchanged hasty impressions and agreed on the essential point: "This time it's war. One disturbing fact remains to be added: on that same 25th Sir Edward Grey, the British Foreign Secretary, told the Russians that Austria's ultimatum to Serbia would justify Russian mobilisation and added that Germany would not mobilise if Russia mobilised against Austria alone.

On the 27th Austria began its mobilisation against Serbia, Germany perceived that the position taken by Russia was leading to a European war. It changed its political position and asked Vienna in vain to negotiate with Serbia. Izvolski, the Russian ambassador in Paris, again insisted that war was inevitable. Surprise again came that day from Britain. Foreign Office Minister Grey informed St. Petersburg that the continued concentration of the British fleet was to be taken as an obvious sign of intervention, which, however one looked at it, was a way of encouraging military action.. Professor Barnes states emphatically that Zazov felt he could count on Britain.

On the 28th Austria declared war on Serbia. Kaiser Wilhelm II proposed that the Austrians should stop in Belgrade, and Chancellor Bethmann-Hollweg asked Edward Grey for support, who agreed that the war should be limited and not spread. In Russia, Zazov again staged an uncontrolled bout of anger that was only mitigated after the decision was taken to proceed with general mobilisation, which had to be endorsed by the Tsar's signature. Zazov himself admitted that after learning of the Austrian declaration of war he thought only of preparing for war. Nicholas II and Wilhelm II exchanged personal telegrams that verified that events were leading to a European conflict. News of the British position is again available that day in a lengthy private letter from Arthur Nicolson, Under-Secretary for Foreign Affairs, to Ambassador Buchanan. The letter is recorded in the *British Papers*. It reveals the customary duplicity of British policy, as Nicolson announced Britain's intervention to his colleague.

On the 29th Nicholas II signed the order for general mobilisation; but a counter-order was issued in the evening due to a plea from Wilhelm II. A partial mobilisation of 1,100,000 troops was decided instead, but this order was never carried out. From the 29th, pacifist anti-war demonstrations were strictly forbidden in France. Poincaré, however, refused to order mobilisation before Germany had done so, in order to avoid France's being singled out as the driving force behind the war. On the evening of the 30th Nicholas II was finally persuaded to order general mobilisation in Russia. A few words from the Tsar show that he was aware that this meant a general conflict was inevitable: "Remember," he told Sazov, "it is a question of sending thousands and thousands to their deaths.

On the morning of the 31st it became known in Berlin that the general mobilisation in Russia was under way. At noon the government proclaimed "danger of war", which was a preliminary to mobilisation, and in the afternoon it sent ultimatums to Russia and France. It demanded that the former suspend the mobilisation and the latter that it remain neutral in the event of a German-Russian war. On the same day, Jean Jaurés, a socialist who represented pacifism within his party, was assassinated in Paris. The French left's opposition to the war vanished with the death of this influential politician.

From this point on, events unfolded very quickly. On 1 August, Germany declared war on Russia without having received any reply to its ultimatum. Paris and Berlin respectively ordered the mobilisation of their armies: France did so at half past three in the afternoon and Germany an hour and a half later. On 2 August Germany asked for Belgium's benevolent neutrality and in the evening occupied Luxembourg to secure the railway lines. On 3 August France responded to the ultimatum with evasions and Belgium refused the German request. Germany began the invasion of Belgium. On 4 August Britain sent an ultimatum to Germany to stop the invasion of Belgium. Berlin refused and London declared war on Germany. The local war between Austria-Hungary and Serbia had turned into a European war that would become a world war.

In *In Quest of Truth and Justice* Harry Elmer Barnes points to the existence of secret agreements between France and Britain that Sir Edward Grey had frequently denied in the House of Commons. He believes that both Germany and Austria were counting on British neutrality. According to him, they correctly believed that France and Russia would not have gone to war without the guarantee of London's backing. Professor Barnes reminds us that it should not be forgotten that there were powerful hidden forces in British politics that supported the war party. In his opinion, if England had pressed Russia as Germany pressed Austria or declared neutrality, it is unlikely that conflict would have broken out in Europe. Prominent among the voices calling for British neutrality on 1 August was that of the London *Daily News* editorialist A. G. Gardiner, who in an editorial article entitled "Why England Must Not Fight" warned that the greatest calamity in history was looming over Europe. "At this moment," wrote Gardiner, "our fate is being sealed by hands we do not know, by motives foreign to our interests, by influences we would surely reject if we knew them." As for the warmongering propaganda of certain newspapers, Gardiner asked, "Who is paving the way for this stupendous catastrophe?" We have already seen in the previous chapter who considered the control of the press to be a fundamental objective.

The fact that we have noted that Zazov, Buchanan, Paléologue, and perhaps also Izvolski, were Freemasons invites comment. As will be seen below, all the members of the Provisional Government that emerged after the February 1917 coup d'état that forced the Tsar to abdicate were Freemasons. It was a transitional executive which immediately handed over power to the Jewish-Bolsheviks, whose main leaders - Lenin, Trotsky, Plekhanov, Radek, Zinoviev, Bukharin, Kamenev, etc. - were also Freemasons. Until December 1906, when M. M. Kovalevsky opened the Lodge *North Star* under the jurisdiction of the Grand Orient of France, there were no Masonic lodges in Russia; nevertheless, by 1915 there were already half a hundred operating, supervised by the Supreme Council of Russia, whose three secretaries were Nekrasov, Tereshchenko and the Jew Kerensky, an agent of B'nai B'rith.

The leaders of the Russian Supreme Council met no less than twice a month in St. Petersburg and Moscow. According to Andrei Priahin in an article published on the website of the Grand Lodge of British Columbia and Yukon, the British Ambassador Buchanan and the French Ambassador Paléologue were among those who attended these meetings of the Supreme Council, which were held in private homes. Moreover, in *Architects of Deception* (2004), a book available in PDF, Jüri Lina confirms that in 1915 Buchanan was frequently visited by the Russian foreign minister, Zazov, Alexander Goutchkov, leader of the Octubrists, and Mikhail Rodzyanko, president of the Duma. All were Freemasons and plotted to overthrow the Tsar. According to Lina, British Ambassador Buchanan met in St. Petersburg in January 1917 with a large number of Freemasons, including General Nikolai Ruzky, to prepare the coup d'état that was to take place on 22 February, although it finally took place on the 23rd. It has recently come to light that the date was postponed by one day to coincide with the Jewish holiday of Purim. On 24 March 1917, the Jewish newspaper *Jevreyskaya Nedelya* (*Jewish Week*) published an article about the February Revolution with a significant title: "It Happened on Purim Day". And there are even more surprises, in *Trnov Venac Rusije - Tajna Istorija Masontsva* (*The Russian Crown of Thorns: The Secret History of Freemasonry*), a book published in Moscow in 1996 and reported by Jüri Lina, of which there is no English translation, the Russian author Oleg Platonov reveals that in late February 1917 a delegation of local Zionists visited Ambassador Buchanan to thank him for his contribution to the destruction of the Monarchy in Russia. It will be seen later that Buchanan and the infamous Alfred Milner also financed the Bolsheviks.

On the early years of the war

In 1899 Ivan Bloch, a Polish writer and banker, had estimated that the cost of a war between the major continental powers would amount to £4 million per day. Bloch was convinced that these costs and the ever-increasing destructive capacity of armaments made a full-scale war virtually "impossible". He was obviously wrong. He was not, however, John Atkinson Hobson, who, let us remember, had asserted with absolute certainty that "a great war could not be waged by any European state if the house of Rothschild and its connections were opposed to it". This idea is not Hobson's, for it had already been expressed by Guttle Rothschild, the wife of Mayer Amschel, when she once declared, "There will be no war, my sons will not provide the money." Disraeli put it another way after the Polish crisis of 1863: "Peace has been preserved not by politicians, but by capitalists." In more recent times, French President Chirac quoted a Rothschild who would have said, "There will be no war because the Rothschilds don't want it." In 1914 they did want it, of course, and the loan business started immediately: Britain promptly agreed to a £1.7 billion loan to France through the Rothschilds. According to Niall Ferguson, during the war France borrowed £610 million from British banks, to which must be added a further £738 million from US Federal Reserve banks. Britain itself borrowed £936 million from the Federal Reserve. As Ferguson confirms, "As soon became apparent, the key to the financing of the war, at very high interest rates, was not in London or Paris, but in New York".

If we look at the theatre of war operations, we must begin by saying that one of Germany's advantages was its mobilisation system, which was much more efficient and faster than that of its adversaries. To take advantage of this, she had to strike at once, and she did. His plan was to defeat France as soon as possible and to deal with Russia second. The German General Staff, confident that the Russian mobilisation would be slow and that Austria-Hungary would attack the Russians with 37 divisions, decided to defend its eastern frontiers with only 13 divisions, while sending 83 against France. For his part, Poincaré was confident that this time the French army would reach Berlin. Within days the French plan was in tatters: on 24 August almost 1.5 million German troops burst into France, and by 2 September they had reached the Marne River and were seventy kilometres from Paris.

France was saved by Grand Duke Nicholas, who, without waiting for the end of the concentration of Russian troops and against national interests, ordered an immediate offensive against East Prussia. This forced the German General Staff to withdraw two corps of its army and a cavalry division from France and transport them to the eastern front. The French general Cherfils in his work *La Guerre de la Délivrance* has this to say about Grand Duke Nicolas: "He conceived the operations as an intervention of relief, distraction and relief for the French front. He was, as a generalissimo, more of an ally than a Russian. He sacrificed the interests of Russia for those of France. He had a truly anti-national strategy". It was an offensive that brought heavy losses and a tragic outcome for Russia, but the sacrifice saved Paris. Marshal

Foch himself later said: "If France has not been wiped off the map of Europe, we owe it above all to Russia".

While hundreds of thousands of men were losing their lives on the battlefields, the conspirators who had been waiting for the war knew that the time had come when the political situation would be favourable for the achievement of their aims. Therefore, the strategy for Palestine to be handed over to international Zionism was still being devised in the offices of the conspirators. One of the most active figures was Chaim Weizmann, the leader of the Zionist movement who in 1910 had been granted British citizenship. Weizmann visited in 1914 the editor of the *Manchester Guardian*, Charles Prestwich Scott, who was pleased to learn that the visitor was "a Jew who hated Russia". As has been seen, Russia was at the time saving the French and British with its offensive in the east. Scott proposed to Weizmann to share a breakfast with Mr. Lloyd George, who was the Chancellor of the Exchequer. The meeting took place in early December and a fourth person, Herbert Samuel, a Jewish leader who between 1920-25 was to serve as High Commissioner of the British Mandate of Palestine, shared the table. Of Lloyd George, Weizmann wrote that he had found him 'extraordinarily frivolous' about the war in Europe; but 'encouraging and favourable towards Zionism'. Lloyd George proposed an interview with Lord Balfour.

The meeting took place on 14 December 1914. Balfour casually asked Weizmann if he could do anything concrete for him. At the time, Zionist headquarters were still in Berlin, and although it was becoming increasingly clear that Britain was being backed, many Zionists were convinced that Germany would win the war. The answer was: "Not while the guns are roaring, when the military situation becomes clearer, I will come back again". It was at this meeting, and gratuitously, that Lord Balfour said to him: "When the guns stop firing, perhaps you can get your Jerusalem". In any case, the British Zionists had little doubt that it was through England that they were going to achieve the usurpation of Palestine. On 28 January 1915 Prime Minister Asquith wrote in his diary: "I have just received from Herbert Samuel a memorandum entitled 'The Future of Palestine'... He thinks we should transplant into this territory three or four million European Jews." Asquith, who was not a Zionist, confessed in the diary that he did not share these views at all.

In early 1915 the Germans were preparing another major offensive on the Franco-British front, but the advance of Russian troops in the Carpathians again forced the Teutonic General Staff to reconsider its plans. After a meeting in Lille, it was decided to move the best troops to the eastern front, where the number of German divisions was increased from forty to seventy-seven. General Cherfils also refers to this moment in the war with further words of gratitude: "... the Russian armies have saved us from disaster. Their daring offensive in the Carpathians, in the middle of winter, caused Austria to sweat in agony..... Thanks to her, Grand Duke Nicholas has saved us by sacrificing himself. We can never find enough words of gratitude for our heroic Russian allies". From this point on, the war on the Western Front became a war of positions that allowed the French and British to build up their forces and armaments while hundreds of thousands of Germans lost their lives in the East. In addition, on 26 April 1915, a conference was held in London at which Italy decided to participate in the war in exchange for important territorial concessions. The secret London treaty would be revealed two years later, on 28 February 1917, by the Bolshevik newspaper *Izvestia*.

But it was not only on the battlefields that the war was being fought; on the seas, especially in the Atlantic, other operations were taking place: economic blockades. Germany was blockading Russia, but at the same time it was suffering from the blockade imposed by Britain. It is difficult to understand how Russia, as an ally of the world's leading naval power, could suffer from the blockade of its exports, which before the war had been carried out through the Bosphorus Strait. The reason was the loss of Anglo-Russian influence in Turkey. Instead of supporting its ally's efforts to maintain its position in the straits, Britain had incomprehensibly obstructed it. David Louis Hoggan makes clear in *The Myth of the New History* that "alliances between nations do not always mean genuine friendship, and Britain was in fact more hostile than friendly towards Russia during the period when the two nations were allies". By contrast, the United States, without having entered the war, behaved as the best of allies with France and, above all, with England: without sending hundreds of millions of dollars worth of all kinds of goods during the early years of the conflict, the French and English would have had to accept the peace offered to them by Germany in 1916. The fact that the Germans had at their disposal the heavy industry of Belgium and the French industry located in the Lille district had deprived France of important resources, and England alone could not make up for these shortages.

America Goes to War (1938), a now classic work by Charles Callan Tansill, explains in detail all about the economic blockade and submarine warfare in the Atlantic. In 1909 came the London Declaration, which sought to codify international maritime law and addressed neutrality issues. When hostilities began in 1914, the Declaration had not been ratified, but it was understood in the United States that belligerent countries would recognise it in their dealings with neutral countries. No sooner had the war begun, on 20 August 1914, than the British government adopted blockade measures that harmed American trade with Europe, prompting William Jennings Bryan, the US Secretary of State, to prepare a note of protest on 26 September. Colonel Mandell House immediately raised objections with President Wilson. The conspirators' agent said that Bryan's note, which purported to vigorously defend the rights of the United States, was "extremely undiplomatic". On 24 October, Foreign Office Secretary Sir Edward Grey was informed that the United States was withdrawing its "suggestion that the Declaration of London should be adopted as a temporary code of naval warfare to be observed by belligerents and neutrals during the present war".

This concession was soon seized upon and on 2 November 1914 there was a British declaration that "the North Sea was henceforth to be regarded as a military area or war zone". This meant that Britain gave itself the right to fix the extent of foreign trade through the North Sea. In response to this measure, Germany proclaimed on 4 February 1915 that it would establish a submarine war zone around the British Isles. This zone was established by order of the Kaiser on 22 February. Until then there had been no mention of submarine warfare in international law. In fact, British naval submarines attacked German and neutral trade in the Baltic Sea during the war, so the United States voluntarily refrained from sending merchant ships to the Baltic area. They did not do the same, however, in the case of the German-imposed zone. In other words, the Americans were willing to accept British infringements, but not German ones. On 20 February, however, Secretary of State Bryan sent identical notes protesting the infringements to Britain and Germany. The Germans replied that they would gladly desist if the British would lift the blockade that was intended to starve them out. Predictably, the British refused to give up their best weapon.

The first incident, which was very serious considering the number of casualties, soon followed. *The Lusitania*, a British Navy auxiliary cruiser used as a passenger and cargo ship, was sunk on 7 May 1915 by a German torpedo off the coast of Ireland. The ship sank in eighteen minutes and twelve hundred people lost their lives. Of the one hundred and ninety-seven American citizens on board, one hundred and twenty-eight died. In addition to the passengers, the *Lusitania* was carrying a cargo of six million pounds of ammunition, four thousand two hundred boxes of metal cartridges and twelve hundred boxes of shrapnel, making the liner a floating bomb. The Wilson government had refused to accept this fact, despite the fact that before the ship sailed, representatives of the German government in the United States, aware of the *Lusitania*'s cargo, had published several notices in all the New York newspapers. They denounced that munitions were on board, reminded that Germany and Britain were at war, and warned citizens of other nationalities "very seriously" not to cross the Atlantic on board the *Lusitania,* as they were in danger of being targeted by their U-boats. On the same day, 1 May, while embarkation was taking place, the warnings were repeated verbally to the passengers.

Colonel Mandell House and Winston Churchill, then First Lord of the Admiralty, were convinced that if the Germans sank a ship with Americans on board, the United States would enter the war against Germany. In 1955 Emrys Hughes in *Winston Churchill: British Bulldog* revealed this information: "More incomprehensible are the following facts. When the *Lusitania* sailed from New York, the usual captain had suddenly been replaced by Captain William Thomas Turner (decorated by Churchill after the disaster). When the ship reached the danger zone, he ignored strict sailing orders. Formal orders Turner had received in New York instructed him to avoid the extremely dangerous area where the ship was sunk, to increase speed in the danger zone, and to zigzag through the waters in order to increase the difficulty of being hit by a torpedo. All these orders were violated. Not only were these rules ignored, but the *Lusitania* even reduced her speed as she approached the Irish coast, and Churchill ordered the withdrawal of the military vessel *Juno*, which was escorting her.

A tide of propaganda flooded the country after the sinking of the *Lusitania,* the outraged American press spoke of an innocent passenger ship viciously torpedoed by the Kaiser's treacherous U-boats, and the Germans were portrayed as bloodthirsty monsters. The campaign to provoke US intervention in the European war then began. Simultaneously, Secretary of State Bryan, who had tried to enlist Wilson's support for a ban on American citizens travelling on ships like the *Lusitania,* lost faith in the president. On 8 June 1915, William Jennings Bryan resigned in protest at the contradictions in Woodrow Wilson's foreign policy. The Secretary of State could not accept scrupulous accounting for Germany while British violations of international maritime law were tolerated, justified and condoned. After leaving office, Bryan became involved in the "Keep Us Out of War" movement and led a campaign against the international bankers who planned to crucify the American people on a cross of gold.

The year 1916 began with a military conference to plan Entente military operations. It was decided that the Russians would begin an offensive in mid-June and the Western Allies a fortnight later, but once again the German General Staff went ahead and the Battle of Verdun, one of the most terrible of the war, began in February, forcing all available French forces into the fray. The battle lasted ten months and resulted in 300,000 dead and half a million wounded. The Austrians, too, attacked the Italians as soon as spring began and put them in a critical situation that threatened Venice. Russia was again called in, and in May it attacked the Austrians on the Polish Galician front, forcing them to withdraw divisions from the Italian front. Despite the serious economic situation at home, Russia was even able to launch the planned offensive in the summer of that year. General Brusiloff conducted a brilliant campaign in which he captured half a million Austro-German prisoners and practically reconquered Galicia. However, the inability of Russia's allies on the western front and the need for long-range guns, which they could only receive from France and England, made it impossible for the Russians to achieve greater success.

Precisely in order to improve the capacity of the Russian armies, in June 1916 the British Prime Minister, Herbert Henry Asquith, sent Lord Kitchener to St. Petersburg, who had publicly lamented Britain's inability to deliver promised arms and ammunition to Russia. The circle of English politicians and businessmen associated with Zionism had been widening as the war progressed, but neither Kitchener nor Asquith was part of it. If there was a military man of prestige in England, with immense authority and great popularity, it was Lord Kitchener. It was Kitchener himself who proposed the mission to Russia to Asquith, the fundamental aims of which were to meet the arms needs of his ally, to assist in its reorganisation and to establish close relations in a spirit of sincere friendship between the two empires. Boris Brasol, in *The World at the Cross Roads* (1921) adds: "It was understood that Lord Kitchener would put a definite end to the ambiguous policy of Sir George Buchanan, the British Ambassador to Russia. It was obviously dishonest on the part of the British Government to meddle and take sides in matters of Russian internal politics. Whatever the sympathies of some British leaders, it was inexcusable to give support to radical elements in the Duma (as Buchanan did) in order to hinder the policy of Russian unity." In St. Petersburg, therefore, Lord Kitchener's arrival was eagerly awaited, and it was thought that after his interview with the Tsar the intrigues of Buchanan, the shady Masonic ambassador working for the conspirators, would be paralysed, and the Government would obtain the moral support it so urgently needed. Unfortunately for Russia, Lord Kitchener mysteriously disappeared. Various authors believe that he was the man who could have sustained Russia. For both the world revolution and the pretensions of Zionism, Lord Kitchener was a formidable obstacle.

Lord Kitchener met his death on 5 June 1916, shortly after leaving Scapa Flow on board the cruiser H. M. S. Hampshire, which sank off the coast of Scotland. A number of circumstances lead one to suspect that he was simply killed. Strangely, Lloyd George, who in 1915 had been appointed Minister of Munitions and was due to embark with Lord Kitchener, decided to stay ashore at the last moment. After the "accident", Lloyd George was appointed Secretary of State for War. Another surprising development was the authorisation for the escort of H. M. S. Hampshire to return to base, allegedly because the cruiser could not maintain speed in rough seas. The British Government announced that the ship had foundered because it had been torpedoed by a German U-boat or hit by a mine.

Commander W. Guy Carr, the author quoted several times in this book, is adamant that this is a lie. Guy Carr, a marine expert who served as a submarine navigation officer during World War I and as a naval control officer during World War II, undertook a thorough personal investigation and in 1932 published a book of his findings, *Hell's Angels of the Deep*. Commander Carr considers it proven that the H. M. S. Hampshire sank either because of sabotage or because of an error by the navigating officer; although he finds it hard to believe that a professional with proven skill and experience could make such a grave error of judgement. I believe," he says, "that a saboteur probably forced or tampered with the steering compass magnets. Gyro compasses (gyro compasses) were not then standard equipment and even ships that had them found the Sperry models (a type of gyro compass) unreliable, as I know from my own experience." That the official version was a falsehood was corroborated by General Ludendorff, Chief of the German General Staff, who studied the circumstances surrounding the loss of H. M. S. S. Hampshire and Lord Kitchener. "No action by German naval units, whether submarines or minelayers," Ludendorff asserted, "had anything to do with the sinking of the ship." Douglas Reed in 1916 was a young soldier and recounts the following: "I remember that the soldiers on the Western Front, when they heard the news, felt as if they had lost a great battle. Their intuition was truer than they could have imagined."

On 29 December 1916 an important conference was held, attended by all the chiefs of staff of the Russian armies. To counter the superiority of the German artillery, it was decided to form new artillery brigades, especially heavy artillery, which had to be on the front lines by May of next year. The Russian generals were preparing an offensive with a colossal force of seven million men, which was to be final if combined with a simultaneous offensive on the Western front. The Russian generals did not count on the fact that the seeds of future revolution sown by Mensheviks and Bolsheviks could eventually germinate: for the first time since the beginning of the war revolutionary pamphlets had appeared on the front in the spring of 1916. The tsarina was slandered in connection with the sinister influence of Rasputin, the tsar was accused of weakness, the soldiers were told that, while they were fighting, the nobles were taking advantage of their absence to take their land. Gradually, the propaganda became more aggressive: pacifist slogans were constantly being spread, soldiers were asked to disobey their officers, they were told that their real enemy was the imperial government, supported by the nobility and the bourgeoisie.

Zionism is definitely betting on Britain and betraying Germany

At the beginning of the war, the American financier Roger Bacon admitted that no more than fifty thousand Americans in the United States were in favour of entering the war on behalf of France and England against Germany. In 1916, fifty-four percent of Americans were of Germanic origin. When independence was proclaimed, a single vote prevented German from being considered the official language of the Republic. For the first 100 years, German was the only language heard in some parts of the country. A poll conducted that same year asked Americans, "If we had to go to war, would you choose to side with Germany or England?" An overwhelming majority responded that they would prefer to support Germany. Considering that the British had been the great enemies of the country's independence, this was entirely logical. Among the Talmudic Jews, too, there were many supporters of Germany. The Emancipation Edict of 1822 had guaranteed civil rights to German Jews. Germany had been the only country in Europe to remove restrictions. Another fact to consider was Wilhelm II's continued collaboration with the World Zionist Organisation. The Kaiser had personally arranged a meeting between Theodor Herzl, the visionary who had published *The Jewish State* in 1896, and the Ottoman Sultan. Bleichröder & Company, Jewish Talmudists from Berlin, had for generations been the private bankers of the imperial family. The Warburgs of Hamburg, who were also Talmudists, collaborated with the German government, and Max Warburg controlled the secret services. The Zionist movement was not unaware of these circumstances, which is why during the first year of the war it even considered using Germany to achieve its aims. It was only when the decision to go for Britain was confirmed that the cards were laid on the table and Zionist headquarters were moved from Berlin to London, although the Provisional Zionist Emergency Committee was established in New York, headed by Judge L. D. Brandeis.

The World Zionist Organisation's betrayal of Germany was consummated at the end of 1916. Earlier in the year French troops had suffered mutinies which Petain had severely suppressed, and the Italians had been decimated by the Austro-Hungarians. As 1916 progressed, Britain was facing supply difficulties because of the German submarine campaign. By autumn, U-boat operations were at their peak and food and ammunition stocks were running low, putting Britain in desperate straits. The French Army again mutinied in Italy, whose troops had again been defeated near Venice, and was negotiating a separate peace. In general, the belligerent countries were experiencing serious problems, and the suffering of the European population was increasing. The fronts were deadlocked and no military solution was in sight. Germany had submitted several proposals to Britain to stop the war, and the latest, presented in October 1916, was under serious consideration by the British War Cabinet. It was at this point that a Zionist delegation led by Chaim Weizmann and Nathan Sokolov offered the British a secret 'gentlemen's' agreement. The Zionists promised that through their influence they would bring the United States into the war alongside Britain and France. The price Britain had to pay was to occupy Palestine and then allow the Jews to found the state of Israel there. Although a new formal peace proposal was submitted by Germany on 12 December, the agreement was not reached until the end of 1916. This required the dismissal of Prime Minister H. H. Asquith, who was replaced by David Lloyd George, and the placing at the head of the Foreign Office of Arthur James Balfour, Lord Balfour, who was to go down in history for the famous *Balfour Declaration.*

The main obstacle to the deal was Prime Minister Asquith. The Zionists needed to get him out of the way in order to put in place co-opted politicians, necessary tools to do a job that could only be done from power. Just as the carnage was about to stop and peace was about to be achieved, the press informed the masses that Prime Minister Asquith was incompetent to win the war. In November 1916, Lloyd George, who since Lord Kitchener's death had been Secretary of State for War, advised Mr. Asquith to cede to him the chairmanship of the War Cabinet. Both were Liberals, but were part of a coalition government. Lloyd George made the suggestion to Asquith after securing the support of the Conservative leaders, so in effect it was an ultimatum. Lloyd George also demanded that the Conservative Lord Balfour be removed as First Lord of the Admiralty. Predictably, Asquith, the Liberal Prime Minister, indignantly refused to hand over the chairmanship of the War Cabinet and dismiss Lord Balfour. The next step in the strategy was taken by Balfour himself, who unexpectedly tendered his resignation to Prime Minister Asquith. The latter promptly sent him a copy of his own letter in which he had refused to dismiss him. Lord Balfour, though he had retired from the scene with a bad cold, found the strength to write another letter insisting on his resignation, as Lloyd George had requested. The next tactical manoeuvre was the resignation of Lloyd George himself. Prime Minister Asquith was being left on his own. On 6 December the party leaders announced after a meeting that they were prepared to support a government headed by Lord Balfour. Lord Balfour declined the offer, but gladly offered to be part of a government led by Lloyd George. On 7 December David Lloyd George began his term as Prime Minister and Arthur James Balfour was appointed Minister Secretary of the Foreign Office. Thus the two men who had met two years earlier with Weizmann and expressed their support for Zionism became the most important figures in the British government.

Lloyd George's first decision was taken even before he was confirmed in office. It was of great importance to inform the many American Jewish Talmudists of the existence of the secret pact, for whom it was not easy to believe that Britain had promised something it did not have (Palestine) as compensation for getting America into the war. In order to dispel any doubts, on the same day that Asquith resigned, 5 December, Lloyd George rushed Josiah Wedgewood, a renowned parliamentarian, to New York, travelling with documentary evidence confirming the London agreement. Wedgewood arrived in New York on 23 December and was met on the dock by Colonel Edward Mandell House, the agent who had acted as President Wilson's adviser since 1912. During his stay in the city, Josiah Wedgewood lived in Mandell House's flat on 54th Street. Colonel House had already arranged the meetings Mr. Wedgewood was to hold to explain the secret pact. Benjamin Freedman, who knew Mandell House personally, explains in *The Hidden Tyranny* that on Sunday afternoon, December 25, at the old Savoy Hotel on 59th Street and Fifth Avenue in New York, Wedgewood addressed fifty-one Jewish Talmudists to present them with certain evidence to clear up all their doubts. On behalf of Prime Minister Lloyd George, Josiah Wedgewood gave them assurances of the promise to hand over Palestine to International Zionism after the defeat of Germany, as compensation for the introduction of the United States into the war.

At the same time, a second far-reaching decision was taken in London: Lloyd George expressed his willingness to launch a campaign in Palestine as soon as possible in order to seize the territory from the Turks. This was a clear danger, since the security of the Western Front was at stake. The person who dared to raise the issue was Sir William Robertson, a military man of Lord Kitchener's style, a general who had received the support of Prime Minister Asquith when in September 1916 he was already in trouble with the Secretary of State for War. Lloyd George had then tried to get rid of Robertson by sending him to Russia to ask the Russians for maximum effort; but he had refused. In texts to Sir Douglas Haig, Robertson wrote that Lloyd George's attempt to move him to Russia was "the Kitchener dodge" - an excuse "to become top dog" so that he could "have his wicked way". Sir William Robertson opposed the sending of troops to Palestine on the grounds that the proposal was dangerous and could jeopardise victory in the war.

As soon as the new War Cabinet was formed, the General Staff was asked to examine the possibility of extending operations to Palestine. It was concluded that a campaign would require three additional divisions, which could only be drawn from the Western Front. The military's report took up Sir William Robertson's thesis and warned that the project was problematic and also seriously damaged expectations of success in France. These conclusions were disappointing to ministers who wanted to occupy Palestine at once. In February 1917 the War Cabinet urged the Chiefs of Staff to contemplate the possibility of an autumn campaign in Palestine. In the meantime, numerous Zionists were being introduced into the government, and new "administrators" were given key posts in the Ministry of Defence. Secret codes and cable communication facilities were made available to Talmudic Jews so that they could communicate to their co-religionists around the world the secret agreement they had reached with the British Government. General Smuts, a military man in South Africa whom the Zionists regarded as their most valuable friend, was ordered to travel to England. Thanks to a successful press campaign, when he arrived in London on 17 March, he received an enthusiastic welcome. Prime Minister Lloyd George introduced him to the War Cabinet as "one of the most brilliant generals of the war". In fact, General Smuts had conducted a small colonial campaign in South Africa. On 17 April this general submitted recommendations in which he regretted that British forces were engaged in France, but favoured a campaign in Palestine. By this time in Russia the February coup d'état had taken place and Germany could begin to move troops to the Western Front.

The War Cabinet ordered the military commander in Egypt, General Murray, to attack in the direction of Jerusalem. Murray claimed that his forces were insufficient and was dismissed. The command was then offered to General Smuts, who was cautious and before taking the risk had a conversation with Sir William Robertson. Robertson made him aware of the enormous possibilities of military failure, and Smuts finally did not accept Lloyd George's offer. It was undoubtedly a great disappointment, but the commitment to Zionism compelled the occupation of Palestine, and in September 1917 Lloyd George decided that: "the troops required for a major campaign in Palestine could be taken from the Western Front during the winter of 1917-18 and, their work in Palestine completed, they would be back in France in time for the commencement of the spring campaign".

In short, after Smuts' frustrating response, one of Robertson's subordinate generals, Sir Henry Wilson, finally agreed with Lloyd George's approach and even opined that the supposed German attack might never happen. Then General Edmund Allenby, commander-in-chief of the Egyptian expeditionary force, made an advance movement into Palestine and found that Turkish resistance was less than expected. With evidence that the conquest of Jerusalem was only a matter of time, on 2 November 1917 came the *Balfour Declaration*, a document drafted by a Jew who concealed his origin, Leopold Amery, Assistant Secretary to the War Cabinet. Lord Balfour addressed it to Sir Walter Lionel Rothschild, President of the Jewish communities in Britain. The *Balfour Declaration* was to become one of the most important texts in history because of its far-reaching and enduring effects. It committed Britain to the whole world to do everything in its power to make the creation of a Jewish state in Palestine a reality. There will be an opportunity to examine the text of the Declaration in another chapter. Eleven days later, on 13 November, Allenby won a decisive victory against the German General Erich von Falkenhayn, who commanded the Ottoman forces. On 9 December 1917, Allenby's troops entered Jerusalem, but much of Palestine remained to be conquered. Proof that the British soldiers knew they were waging this war for Zionism is the song they sang, the chorus of which repeated: "And they gave the Holy City to the Zionist Committee".

On 7 March 1918, orders were issued for "a decisive campaign" to conquer all the territory of Palestine. General Smuts was sent to Jerusalem with precise orders for General Allenby. On 21 March the long-awaited attack on the Western European front took place. The Germans knew that before more men and material could reach the front from the United States, they had to attempt an offensive that would give them the final victory. The "decisive campaign" in Palestine was immediately suspended and as many troops as possible were rushed back to the French front. The British army suffered one of the greatest defeats in its history: 175,000 soldiers were taken prisoner. The British refer to this battle as "The Great March Retreat". Although the German offensive marked the biggest territorial advance since 1914, on 15 July, near the River Marne, the Germans were stopped in what became known as the Second Battle of the Marne. With the unstoppable intervention of the American colossus, any chance of victory for Germany vanished.

Zionists do their part: Wilson declares war on Germany

Long before the secret London agreement, it was clear to those scheming in the shadows behind the scenes that the United States' entry into the war was to be encouraged. The sinking of the *Lusitania* at in May 1915 had been provoked for this purpose. One of the people who was most active in this regard was Colonel House. Yet it was he who came up with the slogan for Wilson's 1916 campaign: "He kept us out of the war". A slogan that suggested that it was the president's will to keep his fellow citizens out of war. Even Rabbi Stephen Wise, who in *Challenging Years* (1949) acknowledged that House "was the official link between the Zionist movement and the Wilson administration", preached against the war during the campaign, even though he longed for it as much as anyone. To top it all off, Justice Brandeis, who had pledged his life to Zionism, was the President's adviser on the Jewish question. The web of Zionist collusion in which President Wilson was entangled now, as we can see, spanned both sides of the Atlantic and both governments were caught up in it. In case it was not clear to Wilson, before he was even sworn into office in February 1917, Rabbi Wise let him know that he had changed his mind and that he was "convinced that the time had come for the American people to understand that it was our destiny to take part in the struggle". On 12 February 1917, Mandell House wrote in his diary, "We are moving towards war as rapidly as I had hoped."

In addition to the *Lusitania* episode, another sinking, that of the *Sussex*, was used as an excuse to ask Congress to declare war. *The Sussex,* a cross-Channel steamer, was torpedoed on 24 March 1916 by a German U-boat that mistook it for a mine-laying vessel. Although fifty people, none of whom were Americans, lost their lives in the incident, the ship did not sink and was towed to the port of Boulogne. Interestingly, among the victims were Enrique Granados, the famous Spanish composer and pianist, and his wife, who drowned. President Wilson informed Congress that the ferry had been sunk by a German U-boat and that the North American citizens on board had been killed. The danger of war between Germany and the United States then increased considerably, prompting Kaiser Wilhelm II, in a desperate attempt to avert conflict, to make a pledge on 4 May 1916 that has gone down in history as the Sussex Pledge. President Wilson empowered his ambassador James W. Gerard to convey to the Kaiser that in exchange for Germany's abandonment of submarine warfare, the American president would work for a compromise peace if elected in November 1916. In other words, the Germans were to renounce retaliation against the British blockade in the hope that Wilson would help them achieve a compromise peace that they had proposed earlier that year. The Sussex Pledge was thus a deal whereby Germany agreed to change its policy of unrestricted submarine warfare and to end the sinking of non-military ships. The merchant ships would only be inspected and sunk if they were carrying contraband, and only after the lives of passengers and crew had been secured.

By December 1916 it was clear that Wilson was not going to keep his side of the bargain, as the various peace offers Germany had been making went unanswered. So the Germans, after a conference on 8 February 1917, decided to resume submarine warfare on 11 February. Chancellor Bethmann-Hollweg expressed his conviction that the United States would have the excuse to enter the war; but Hindenburg naively believed that he could force Britain to accept peace before the Americans intervened in Europe against the exhausted German troops. On 27 March President Wilson asked Mandell House "whether he should ask Congress to declare war or whether he should say that a state of war exists". The declaration of the existence of a state of war was only the preliminary step. On 2 April 1917 Woodrow Wilson addressed both houses in joint session, and following the opinion of Louis D. Brandeis, the Justice Samuel Untermayer had placed at the head of the Supreme Court, the President alluded to the sinking of the *Sussex* as a reason for declaring war. "The world must be made safe for democracy" was one of Wilson's best-known phrases that day. Senator Norris retorted on the 4th that war was "war upon the command of gold". Senator LaFollete said something that no one could deny: "Germany has been patient with us". Senator Warren Harding, who was to succeed Woodrow Wilson as President, denounced the "war for democracy" slogan. In one of his most disturbing speeches, President Wilson implicitly threatened to overthrow the German government through revolutionary action, opening the gates of central Europe to Bolshevism. On 6 April, at President Wilson's request, Congress declared war on Germany. The Zionists thus fulfilled the promise of the secret London agreement.

A propaganda campaign designed by James T. Shotwell, whose mentors were Fabian socialists, and George Creel, a socialist who proved to be an unscrupulous propagandist, was immediately set in motion. Wilson chose him to direct American wartime propaganda, which began that same April. The two worked together in the war of ideas aimed at manipulating American thinking. On 14 April 1917 Creel accepted the chairmanship of the Committee on Public Information. He was soon confronted by men like Robert Lansing, Mark Sullivan and others, who were appalled by the ruthless dishonesty of Creel's methods. Creel claimed that, by telling bigger lies and better ones, he was simply trying to "disabuse" the American public of the effects of German propaganda.

The account of the astounding rubbish created by Creel's propaganda can be found in *Opponents of War, 1917-1919,* published in 1957 by H. C. Peterson and G. C. Fite. These authors insist that right up to the last moment American public opinion was against the war. William Jennings Bryan, the Secretary of State who had resigned in disagreement with Wilson's foreign policy, campaigned against the war to great public acclaim. The propaganda campaign reached its peak in 1918. These authors denounce what they call "America's Reign of Terror," as there were waves of arrests, burning of German books, beatings and many murders. A widespread practice was to tar and feather those who protested against the war. Elihu Root, a Wall Street lawyer who had won the Nobel Peace Prize in 1912, insisted that those who opposed the war should be executed. This idea of ruthlessly eliminating opponents was a constant during the continuing years of the Jewish-Bolshevik terror. An American Protective League was organised to silence opponents. It was common to force foreigners to kiss the American flag. During 1918, Creel organised an army of one hundred and fifty thousand "four-minute men", so called because they sprang up everywhere and within minutes spread their message of hatred.

In another work published in 1939, *Words that Won the War: The Story of the Committee on Public Information,* the authors, James R. Mock and Cedric Larson, present George Creel as America's first propaganda minister. This work analyses several anti-German propaganda films, most notably *The Kaiser: the Beast of Berlin, which* depicts German soldiers snatching a child from its mother's arms and violently throwing it to the ground while laughing mercilessly at the woman. The Kaiser is presented as an avant-la-lettre Hitler. If in Charles Chaplin's film Hitler plays with the ball of the world, here a King Kong-like Kaiser takes the ball of the world in his hands and squeezes it. Creel and his group anticipated the lies that would be repeated against Germany in World War II: they even claimed to have proof that Germany wanted to turn the United States into a colony and deport non-Germans to a reservation in southern New Mexico.

The Landman document

A Zionist Jew named Samuel Landman, who in 1912 was honorary secretary of the Zionist Council of the United Kingdom and was editor of *The* Zionist between 1913-1914, published in March 1936 under the auspices of the Zionist Organisation a work entitled *Great Britain, The Jews and Palestine,* which fully confirms the facts we have been narrating. It is a Jewish document and therefore has the relevance of official texts. Léon de Poncins reproduced a significant fragment in his work *State Secrets.* Because of its importance, we dedicate this section to the quotation of the document, taken from the above-mentioned work:

"Since the Balfour Declaration originated in the War Office, was consummated in the Foreign Office, and is being implemented in the Colonial Office, and since some of those responsible for it have left this world or have retired after their migrations from one Ministry to another, there is necessarily some confusion or misunderstanding as to its raison d'être and the importance of the parties principally concerned. It would seem timely, therefore, to summarise briefly the circumstances, the inside story and the events that finally led to the British Mandate for Palestine.

Those who witnessed the birth of the Balfour Declaration were numerically few in number. This makes it important to highlight properly the services of one who, thanks mainly to his modesty, has hitherto remained in the shadows. His services, however, should occupy an appropriate place in the front rank alongside those far-sighted Englishmen whose services are widely known, among whom must be included the late Sir Mark Sykes, the Right Honourable W. Ormsby Gore, the Hon. Sir Ronald Graham, General Sir George Macdonagh, and Mr. G. H. Fitzmaurice.

In the early years of the war the Zionist leaders, Dr. Weizmann and Mr. Sokolov, especially through the late Mr. C. P. Scott of the *Manchester Guardian* and Sir Herbert Samuel, made strenuous efforts to get the Cabinet to support the cause of Zionism.

These efforts were, however, unsuccessful. In fact, Sir Herbert Samuel has publicly stated that he took no part in the initiation of the negotiations which led to the Balfour Declaration. (*England and Palestine*, a lecture delivered by Sir Herbert Samuel and published by the Jewish Historical Society, February 1936). The real initiator of the negotiations was Mr. James A. Malcoln and what follows is a brief account of the circumstances in which the negotiations took place.

During the critical days of 1916 and the imminent defection from Russia, the Jews, as a whole, were against the Czarist regime and were hopeful that Germany, if victorious, would hand over Palestine to them under certain circumstances. Several attempts had been made to bring America into the war on the side of the Allies through the influence of powerful Jewish opinion, and they had failed. Mr. James A. Malcolm, who was already aware of Germany's pre-war efforts to secure a foothold in Palestine through Zionist Jews and of the failed Anglo-French efforts in Washington and New York; and knew that Mr. Woodrow Wilson, for good and sufficient reason, always attached the greatest possible importance to the advice of a prominent Zionist (Justice Brandeis of the United States Supreme Court); and had a close relationship with Mr. Greenberg, editor of the Jewish Chronicle, and a close relationship with Mr. Wilson. Greenberg, editor of the *Jewish Chronicle* (London); and he knew that several important Zionist leaders had come to London from the Continent because of the imminence of the expected events; and he appreciated and understood the depth and strength of Jewish national aspirations, he spontaneously took the initiative in convincing first Sir Mark Sykes, Under-Secretary to the War Office, and then M. Georges Picot, of the Embassy of the United States. Georges Picot, of the French Embassy in London, and M. Gout, of the French Foreign Ministry (Eastern Section), that the best and perhaps the only way (which proved true) of getting the American President to enter the war was to secure the co-operation of the Zionist Jews by promising them Palestine, and thus to capture and mobilise the hitherto unsuspected and powerful forces of the Zionist Jews in America and throughout the world in favour of the Allies on the basis of a quid pro quo arrangement. Thus, as will be seen, the Zionists having done their part and having helped enormously to involve America, the Balfour Declaration of 1917, the public confirmation of the secret gentlemen's agreement of 1916, was necessarily made with the prior knowledge, consent and/or approval of the Arabs and of the British, American, French and other Allied governments, and was not merely a voluntary, altruistic and romantic gesture on the part of Britain, as some people suppose out of pardonable ignorance or would like to interpret or misinterpret out of unforgivable ill-will.

Sir Mark Sykes was Under-Secretary to the War Cabinet specially concerned with Near Eastern affairs, and, although he was then scarcely familiar with the Zionist movement and unaware of the existence of its leaders, he had the talent to respond to the reasoning anticipated by Mr. Malcolm and to the strength and importance of this movement of Jewry, despite the fact that many Jewish millionaires in international or semi-assimilated Europe and America were either openly or tacitly opposed to the Zionist movement or remained timidly indifferent. Messrs Picot and Gout were equally receptive.

An interesting account of the negotiations conducted in London and Paris and the subsequent developments has already appeared in the Jewish press, and need not be repeated here in detail, except to recall that immediately after the gentlemen's agreement between Sir Mark Sykes, authorised by the War Cabinet, and the Zionist leaders, the latter received from the War Office, the Foreign Office, and the British embassies, legations, etc., facilities for telegraphing and communicating the good news to their friends and organisations in America and elsewhere, and the change in official and public opinion, as reflected in the American press, in favour of joining with them, facilities for telegraphing and communicating the good news to their friends and organisations in America and elsewhere, and the change in official and public opinion, as reflected in the American press, in favour of joining the Allies in the war was as gratifying as it was surprisingly rapid.

The Balfour Declaration, in the words of Professor H. M. V. Temperley, was a definitive agreement between the British Government and Jewry (*History of the Peace Conference in Paris*, vol. 6, p.173). The main reward brought by the Jews (then represented by the leaders of the Zionist Organisation), was their help in persuading President Wilson to help the Allies. In addition, the Balfour Declaration, then officially interpreted by Lord Robert Cecil as 'Judea for the Jews' in the same sense as 'Arabia for the Arabs', conveyed an excitement throughout the world. The first Sykes-Picot agreement of 1916, according to which northern Palestine was to be separated and included in Syria (French sphere), was subsequently modified at the behest of the Zionist leaders (by the Franco-

British Treaty of December 1920) so that the Jewish national state would comprise all of Palestine, in accordance with the promise they had previously received for their services from the British, Allied and American governments, and to give full effect to the Balfour Declaration, the terms of which had been established and known to all Allies and belligerent partners, including the Arabs, before it was made public.

In Germany, the value of the Allied pact, to all appearances, was duly and carefully noted. In his *Through Thirty Years* Mr. Wickham Steed, in a chapter in which he assesses the importance of Zionist support in America and elsewhere for the Allied cause, says that General Ludendorff would have said after the war: 'The Balfour Declaration was the cleverest thing done by the Allies in a propagandistic sense and I wish I had thought of it first'. (Vol. 2, p. 392). Incidentally, this was said by Ludendorff to Sir Alfred Mond (later Lord Melchett) shortly after the war. The fact that it was Jewish intervention that brought the United States into the war on the side of the Allies has since exasperated the German mind and has contributed greatly to the prominence which anti-Semitism occupies in the Nazi programme".

(S. Landman: *Great Britain, the Jews and Palestine*, pp. 3-6)

The international press and official historiography have been permanently silent on this crucially important document, which remains virtually unknown. The text leaves no doubt about the role that the Jews themselves claim for themselves in the outcome of the First World War. One cannot understand the evolution of the 20th century, with its two world wars, the one that followed in 1939 being the second part of the same universal tragedy, without a proper assessment of what the creation of the State of Israel has cost. As for the Landman document, it should be borne in mind that it was published in March 1936 in a context that was unfavourable to Britain,. The situation in Palestine was explosive. The situation in Palestine was explosive and the British went so far as to stop illegal immigration of international Jews because of doubts in London. This was actually a warning: "You forget," reads another passage, "that you did not give us Palestine as an unsolicited gift (Balfour Declaration). It was given to us as the result of a secret pact concluded between ourselves. We scrupulously respected our part in bringing America to your side in the war. We ask you for your part to fulfil your obligations. You are aware of our power in the United States, be careful not to incur the hostility of Israel. Otherwise you will be faced with serious international difficulties."

Such brazenness seems unbelievable. Only from a firm conviction of the irreversibility of one's own power can such a compromising and reckless document be published, with paragraphs that clearly threaten the British Empire itself, under whose protectorate the Zionists were sheltered in Palestine.

Lord Milner and his mission in Russia

Having studied the events in England and the United States, it now remains to see how the catastrophe in Russia was being prepared. For this purpose we will go back to the summer of 1916, for it was then that a secret dossier arrived in Russia from one of its agents in New York. The report, the existence of which has been confirmed by various sources, gave news of a meeting of the Russian Revolutionary Party of America held on February 14 on the East Side of New York, attended by sixty-two delegates, fifty of whom were revolutionary veterans who had left Russia after the revolution of 1905. It was noted that a high percentage of the delegates were Jewish. In an excerpt from the report, reproduced by Boris Brasol in *The World at the Cross Roads*, the agent writes: ".... The discussions at the first meeting were entirely devoted to finding ways and means of starting a great revolution in Russia, since the most favourable moment was approaching. It was said that secret reports from Russia had been received which described the situation as very favourable, for all preparations for an immediate outbreak were ready. The only problem was that of financing, but when the subject came up, some members assured the assembly that this should not be a cause for concern, since abundant funds, if necessary, would be provided by persons sympathetic to the liberation movement of the Russian people. The name of Jacob Schiff was repeatedly mentioned".

In fact, reports of the source of the revolutionary movement's funding had been reaching the Russian government since the 1905 revolution. Surely the generosity shown by Russia to its allies during the war, acknowledged on several occasions by French military officers, was intended to find solid support in Britain and France. Events showed, however, that Britain's attitude towards its Russian ally could not have been more unfaithful, as its ambassador Buchanan worked for the overthrow of the Tsar. After Lord Kitchener's baffling demise and the advent of Lloyd George as prime minister, things only got worse. Nevertheless, Russian troops had been reorganised and the generals on the General Staff, convinced of the army's capabilities, were preparing thoroughly for the spring offensive that had been designed with the Allies.

Shortly before the coup d'état of February/March 1917, the London Government sent Lord Milner as High Commissioner to St. Petersburg. Milner, a 33rd degree Freemason, an agent of the Rothschilds who had precipitated the Boer War, and a founding member of the Round Table, was a leading agent of the conspirators. Far from feeling supported, there was a conviction in Russia that the High Commissioner, instead of showing solidarity and support, instead of curbing the harmful activity of the Masonic ambassador, had conveyed the Lloyd George Government's support for Buchanan's destabilising policy. Alfred Milner's mission to Russia, which was not even interested in the Russian army's arms needs, also aroused suspicion in London, as an interpellation in the House of Commons showed. The Foreign Office minister, Lord Balfour, in reply to the Dillon MP, replied that 'Lord Milner during his recent visit to Russia did not seek to interfere directly or indirectly in the internal affairs of Russia'.

Back in London, Lord Milner, who months later would become one of the financiers of the Bolshevik Revolution, produced a report on Russia's armaments needs, which served as a pretext for the British Treasury to reduce allocations for arms supplies to Russia. For its part, the Admiralty frequently refused to provide ships of sufficient tonnage for the transport of heavy armaments and other war materials. In short, Lloyd George's government contributed to fuelling internal tensions and turned its back on its Russian ally for good: instead of cooperating with it, it boycotted it. So much so that, according to Princess Olga Paley in *Souvenirs de Russie 1916-1919*, Prime Minister Lloyd George, on receiving the news of the coup that deposed the Tsar, declared: "one of the aims of the war has been achieved". For readers who find the above source unreliable, we have the words of the British ambassador, published on 21 March 1917 in *Russkoie Slovo*. A few days after the fall of the Tsar, Buchanan openly declared to journalists: "The autocratic and reactionary regime has never inspired us with sympathy. That is why the advent of the Provisional Government is enthusiastically acclaimed throughout Britain". The facts proved right those who had warned at the beginning of the war that the British would fight to the last drop of Russian blood.

PART 3
BANKERS AND REVOLUTIONS (2)
THE BOLSHEVIK-JEWISH REVOLUTION

The idea that history is a permanent conspiracy against the truth is especially true of Russia, a country that suffered during the 19th century from the declared enmity of the Rothschilds. This hostility was in reality a covert declaration of war against the country that had led the Holy Alliance at the Congress of Vienna in 1815. The Holy Alliance put Christian tradition and values before the secularism and progress supposedly brought by liberalism, a political, economic and social ideology that throughout the 19th century international bankers succeeded in imposing on nations, today subjected to disastrous neoliberal globalism.

We have already seen how Alexander Herzen, the revolutionary who plotted against Russia from London, enjoyed the protection and friendship of James Rothschild. Before the revolution, newspapers in Europe and America controlled by Russia's enemies hammered public opinion for decades with the idea that the Russian government was a machine of oppression. According to the press, the tsars were monsters intent on keeping their people in slavery. Since then, the idea of an anti-progressive, reactionary, autocratic and authoritarian regime has been repeated ad nauseam by propagandists of the revolution and by liberal democracies. Today, as if the communists had brought freedom, democracy and welfare to the Russian people, it is still taught in academic centres all over the world that the tsars were the worst despots in Europe and therefore the communist revolution was justified. Exactly the same strategy that was put into practice after the French Revolution.

Thus, the social upheavals brought about by the World Revolutionary Movement (WRM), launched by the Bavarian Enlightenment with the financing of Mayer Amschel Rothschild and other bankers, are always looked upon favourably and indulgently, since they are seen as an improvement on what went before. Before narrating some of the most significant events of the revolution, we will introduce the reader to some realities of Tsarist Russia that the conspiracy of lies pretends to ignore. Arsene de Goulévitch, whose work *Tsarisme et Révolution* is one of our sources, rightly says that "the history of a nation is generally told by its friends, but that of Russia has been written above all by its enemies".

If we look at Russia today, we can see that, after more than seventy years of atheistic communism that sought to wipe out Christianity in Russia, after a long period in which several generations were educated outside of any religious teaching, a large part of the Russian people have returned to their secular Christian tradition. The Church today once again occupies an important role in Russian society. This fact, which is surprising, can be explained by the traditional role of the Orthodox Church in Russia, a symbol of patriotism and confused with the nation and the state. This did not, however, prevent the tsars from granting their Muslim subjects the same rights as Christians. During the World War, Russian army corps were commanded by Muslim generals.

As for the Jews, it should be remembered that during the 19th century half of the world's Jewish population lived in Russia. These Russian Jews were not Semites, they were Ashkenazi descendants of the Khazars. Talmudist rabbis educated them in the ghettos in a visceral hatred of Christianity, making them unassimilable and practising inbreeding. This population was subject to various restrictions, one of which was the obligation to settle in a large area bordering Central Europe, corresponding to what is now Lithuania, Belarus, Poland, Moldova and Ukraine. In this huge Zone of Residence, Jews dominated economic life during the 19th century. Jewish banks based in Warsaw, Vilna and Odessa were among the main commercial lending agencies of the Russian Empire.

A. L. Patkin in *The Origins of the Russian-Jewish Labour Movement* (1947) explains that in 1856 Baron Joseph Günzburg and a delegation of Jewish notables presented a memorandum to Alexander II, humbly asking him to "separate the wheat from the chaff", i.e. to distinguish between the lower classes and the more dignified and educated Jews, in order to obtain some privileges for the latter. Thanks to the tsar's permissiveness, between 1860 and 1870 the first generation of Russian Jewish intellectuals, whose mother tongue was Yiddish, immersed themselves in Russian cultural life. Most of them had no qualms about adopting Orthodox Christianity in order to gain easier access to important positions and university careers. These Jews gained access to high positions in the Tsarist bureaucracy, entering it as judges, lawyers, professors. Some even made it into the Senate. Patkin writes that Jewish capitalists entered the field of Russian industrial development and soon attained important positions of great influence. The non-admission of Jews into state service thus did not affect this elite. Thus, a good number of qualified Jews were allowed to live outside the settlement area, which had been created in 1791 by Catherine the Great. Jews could, however, participate in the Duma elections and were also eligible. That said, let us look at some of the realities of Tsarist Russia by sector.

Social and political organisation of Tsarist Russia

The first thing to note is that before the revolution freedom of the press, assembly and association existed in Russia to an even greater extent than in some Western countries. The idea that the administration of the empire was corrupt and parasitic is not true at all. The number of civil servants in Russia was much lower than in most other countries: in 1906 there were just under three hundred and fifty thousand civil servants, while in France, for example, the number of people registered in the state budget was half a million. These figures for the civil service are particularly significant when one considers the spectacular population growth that Russia experienced in the course of the 19th century, from 36 million inhabitants in 1800 to 135 million in 1900. The trend continued into the 20th century, with the population reaching around 175 million in 1914.

In the provinces or departments, following the imperial decree of 19 February 1861, which freed some 23 million peasants, emancipated by Alexander II, the liberating tsar, as the Russian people called him, it was necessary to create a series of local institutions unique to all classes of the population. In 1864, the imperial government took advantage of this necessary reorganisation to expand the functions and role of local administration and created district governments, the "zemstvos", whose powers turned them into small self-governments. Their powers covered all matters relating to public instruction, assistance, provisioning, road construction and maintenance, social hygiene and the fight against epidemics, prison inspection, etc. All of this required considerable expenditure. All this required considerable expenditure, which is why the "zemstvos" were authorised to levy local taxes on the population. The results of their activity included free medical care. Arsene de Goulévitch draws on the opinions of French scholars to proudly point out that the "zemstvos" had under the imperial regime "a grandiose organisation of social medicine such as existed nowhere else". One of the animators of this medical organisation was Dr. Fréderic Erismann, a professor at Moscow University of Swiss nationality. De Goulévitch writes in *Tsarisme et Révolution* that in 1897 he visited Professor Erismann in Zurich, where he was attending a congress on the protection of workers. He acknowledged to him that "the medical organisation set up by the Zemstvos was the greatest success of the time in the sphere of social medicine, since it provided free medical care, open to all, and had a profoundly educational character".

At the same time as the administrative reform of 1864, the country was equipped with a new judicial apparatus which functioned perfectly. Justice was swift, fair and accessible to all. Judges were irremovable and independent. The system of election of magistrates, considered revolutionary in many countries, allowed justices of the peace to be appointed in district assemblies or in municipal "dumas" (consistories). An appeal against the sentence of a justice of the peace could be made to the local assembly of justices of the peace. The Russian penal code did not include the death penalty, which distinguished it from all European countries. When the death penalty was applied in Russia, it was applied exceptionally by courts martial or extraordinary tribunals. The abolition of corporal punishment in Russia predated even the judicial reform of 1864. The communists killed more people in a single day than the tsarist justice system did in the whole of the

19th century. Stéphane Courtois in *The Crimes of Communism* provides concrete figures in this regard. According to Courtois, one hundred and ninety-one people were sentenced to death in Russia between 1825 and 1905. Courtois, who describes the Tsar's justice system as "true justice", writes: "Prisoners and convicts benefited from prison regulations and the regime of confinement or even deportation was relatively mild. The deportees could go to their families, read and write as they pleased, hunt, fish and meet their fellow sufferers in their leisure time. Both Lenin and Stalin could personally verify the accuracy of these words.

Education was a priority concern of Nicholas II. Primary education was equal and free for all. An 1862 project aimed to provide Russia with compulsory general education, but it had to be abandoned at the time due to a lack of sufficient resources for its implementation. Nicholas II took up his grandfather's idea and from 1908 launched a new plan for compulsory education within his empire, an unprecedented project for the education of the masses of the people. A census was ordered to study the needs and it was found that thirteen and a half million children were of school age, so that two hundred and fifty thousand schools were needed. Since the existing primary schools numbered seventy thousand, one hundred and eighty thousand more were needed. Up to 1914, ten thousand schools were opened annually in Russia. If the war and the revolution had not interrupted the process, compulsory primary education would have been a fact in ten years. Nevertheless, a survey conducted by the communists in 1920 showed that eighty-six percent of children between the ages of twelve and sixteen could read and write. In terms of the development of women's education, Russia was the most advanced country in Europe in terms of the number of women in school in the 19th century.

Agriculture before and after the Revolution

The use and subsequent destruction of the peasantry by the Soviets is one of the most significant points of what happened in Russia. Revolutionary propaganda spread the idea that the poverty of the "mujik" (peasants) was due to the fact that most of the arable land belonged to the big landowners. The following is a brief summary of the main data provided by Boris Brasol in *The Balance Sheet of Sovietism* and by Arsene de Goulévitch, which basically coincide. The study of these authors is based on the land of European Russia, as all cultivated land in Siberia belonged to the peasants. According to an agricultural survey of 1916, of 71,709,693 deciatins sown (the Russian deciatine is equivalent to just over one hectare) that year in European Russia, only one tenth belonged to the capitalist landowners, the rest being divided into small plots and in the possession of the peasants.

To appreciate the transfer of land from landowners to peasants, one has to start from 1861, the year in which Alexander II, the liberating Tsar, emancipated nearly 23 million souls. It should be remembered that while Russia was peacefully liberating the peasants, the United States was plunged into civil war under the pretext of abolishing slavery. In 1861 the area of land allocated to peasants in the forty-four governments of European Russia amounted to 113.7 million deciatins, in 1916 small farmers already owned 188 million deciatins. This extremely rapid development leading to the total democratisation of land ownership in Russia was determined by the measures taken by the tsarist governments to ensure the welfare of the peasantry. Under the terms of the 1861 emancipation law, the former serfs were granted personal freedom and the landlords were dispossessed for the benefit of the peasantry of 35 million deciatins, representing about a third of all land and more than half of the arable land they owned, which, from a legal point of view, was an expropriation. The State, for its part, divested itself of 80 million deciatines belonging to it and exploited by peasants who were not subject to servitude, but who were tied to the crown lands. These were also freed. The peasants were emancipated and provided with sufficient land for their subsistence.

Since between 1861 and 1916 new tenths of the arable land in European Russia passed into the hands of the peasants, the state founded the "Peasants' Bank" in 1882 to support and encourage the democratisation of land. This institution was intended to facilitate access to land for small farmers in increasing proportions. Its main operations consisted in buying rentier-type land and reselling it to peasants on extremely advantageous terms. The loans he arranged with the peasants often amounted to ninety per cent of the purchase price. Their duration was, almost without exception, fifty years. The interest retained by the bank was so low that several times its operations resulted in deficits which were covered by the Treasury. Two figures will serve to show the progression of the loans granted by the Peasants' Bank. In 1901 it granted loans worth 222,001,000 gold roubles. In 1912 the figure rose to 1,167,994,000. The Danish economist Wieth Knudsen referred to this bank as "the largest real estate lending institution in the whole universe". De Goulévitch wryly notes that "it could also be said to have been the most social, if not the most socialist, bank in the world."

In addition, the government distributed all the arable land in Siberia to the peasants. Russia's march to the Pacific began in the late 16th century, but was accelerated and expanded in the reign of Nicholas II. In 1831 the government organised an organised migration; but despite state encouragement, the colonisation of Siberia proceeded very slowly. At the time of the liberation of the serfs, the Russian population in Siberia was no more than three million. With the impetus of the construction of the Trans-Siberian Railway, which began in 1891, colonisation began to increase rapidly. The Trans-Siberian Railway Committee was particularly supportive of emigration, organising health centres and canteens for the distribution of food to emigrants. In 1906 construction of the railway line was completed, and from 1907 onwards between 400,000 and 600,000 people a year set out for Siberia. State aid to the settlers rose from five million roubles in 1906 to eleven million roubles in 1907, reaching an average of thirty million roubles a year. The settlers were transported free of charge by the government and received subsidies of between 100 and 400 roubles per family. Each family received on average a forty-deciatine plot of land.

Later we will devote some space to Stolypin, a statesman of great stature who, as usual, was assassinated. His reforms brought about an enormous boost in agriculture. During the ten years before the war, the production of agricultural machinery quadrupled and its importation also increased. The number of agricultural societies rose from 447 in 1902 to 4,685 at the end of 1913. The rise of agricultural cooperatives was unprecedented: in 1902 there were 2,000, ten years later there were 22,000 cooperatives. All this led to Russia becoming the largest producer and exporter of grain in the world. We will spare you the statistics showing the growth in annual production and export figures for rye, wheat, barley, oats and other cereals. Apart from cereals, pre-revolutionary Russia ranked first in the world in the production of potatoes and fodder plants. It was also the world's third largest producer of tobacco. It also produced an abundance of vegetables and various fruits. Despite the propaganda of the revolutionaries to win over the peasantry, the peasants were never interested in taking action against the Tsar and refused to rebel against him because they did not believe he was an instrument of oppression.

We cannot end this section without recalling that famines were a constant feature of the communist era and without denouncing one of the greatest crimes against humanity that nobody remembers because it does not touch. In contrast to the consideration shown by the tsars towards the peasants, the cruelty and absolute disregard for their lives shown by the Soviets is in stark contrast. After the fall of Tsarism, famine reigned permanently because Bolshevism, as is well known, completely ruined the peasantry. The ferocious collectivisation carried out in 1929-30 was the coup de grâce for the Russian rural economy. As early as 1921, the communist regime's disastrous agricultural policy led to a famine in the Volga region of southern Ukraine, the so-called "breadbasket of Europe", and in the Crimea, which, according to some sources, claimed between four and five million victims. But the worst for Ukrainians came in 1930, when the Ukrainian peasantry's land and all their belongings were confiscated by the state: "deskulakisation". Farmers were forced to join collective farms, and those who objected were arrested and deported. While Western markets were supplied with Ukrainian wheat confiscated from its producers, the peasants were blamed for the lack of bread and strict rationing in the cities.

A hitherto unknown genocide by starvation, "Holodomor", Ukrainian for "to starve to death", then took place before the eyes of an impassive world. The idea of "liquidating the kulaks as a class" (farmers who owned land and hired labourers) came from the Jew Lazar Kaganovich, who was not only a communist but also a Zionist who had been a member of "Poale Zion", an organisation in which thousands of Bolsheviks were active. His assistant in organising the famine was Yam Yakovlev, another Jew whose real name was Epstein. The NKVD requisitioned all grain, potatoes, beets, cabbage, which was stored salted, and all foodstuffs. In the winter of 1932-33 supplies ran out in the Ukraine. A huge cordon was set up and no one was allowed to leave the country. Vigilante platoons forbade starving peasants to enter the towns: they were prevented from boarding trains, and many died in the stations or on the tracks. The fields were guarded by the NKVD and those who tried to forage in them were shot. The agents received 200 grams of bread for each corpse they delivered. Numerous dying people were buried alive: "the earth was moving," eyewitnesses to the burials later testified. In the spring of 1933, the death toll was as high as 25,000 people a day, so it is not surprising that the streets of the cities were littered with corpses. Between six and seven million people were exterminated by starvation. Finally, after a thunderous silence, in March 2008 the Ukrainian Parliament and nineteen governments of other countries acknowledged that the actions of the Soviet government were a planned genocide. On 23 October of the same year the European Parliament adopted a resolution deeming the 'Holodomor' a crime against humanity. In June 2009 the Ukrainian Security Service published a list with the names of Soviet officials, most of whom were Jews, who were denounced in connection with the Holodomor. Ukrainian lawyer Aleksander Feldman, leader of the Ukrainian Jewish Committee, said it was a farce to publicise the case, since all the organisers of the Great Famine were dead. In the next chapter there will be an opportunity to expand on this largely unknown genocide.

Industry before the Revolution

The role played by the state as a promoter of industrial development in Russia was of great importance. Again, although it does not fit the image of ruthless monsters, one must begin by recognising that both Alexander III and Nicholas II showed great concern for the conditions of the workers, a concern that was shared by most Russian industrialists. Alexander III decreed a series of workers' laws and instituted the corps of labour inspectors, charged with monitoring factories, defending the interests of the workers and preventing their exploitation by the bosses. For his part, Emperor Nicholas II introduced new labour legislation, which can be considered among the most advanced of the time. This was acknowledged by W. H. Taft, President of the United States, in a public address in 1912: "Your Emperor has created a more perfect labour legislation than any that democratic countries can boast of".

The Tsarist empire was the world's leading producer of platinum, and before the revolution 95 per cent of platinum came from Russia. It was also the world's leading producer of manganese, a mineral needed for steelmaking. Before the war, Russia produced 56% of the world's manganese. Oil production, though a recent creation, developed to such an extent that by 1897 Russia had become the world's leading oil producer. However, in 1905, as a result of the insurrectionary movement that shook Russia, production suffered a severe crisis. In Baku, revolutionaries set fire to wells, committed numerous acts of sabotage and succeeded in provoking a civil war between Tatars and Armenians. Three-fifths of the oil fields were destroyed and all activity was halted. In addition, work on unaffected installations was temporarily suspended. From 1906 until the revolution, production resumed in earnest thanks to the discovery of new fields in Baku and Grozny. In 1913, the extremely rich Novo-Grozny deposit was discovered east of this Caucasus city, and on the eve of the revolution it was ready to be exploited. Twelve years after the revolution, the Russian oil industry was unable to exploit its potential and its production lagged behind twelfth place. Among precious metals, gold was also abundant and the Tsarist empire ranked fourth in the world, after the Transvaal, the United States and Australia. Silver mining was also developing very rapidly at the beginning of the 20th century. To conclude this quick look at mineral resources, it can be added that Russia ranked fifth in copper and asphalt production. Hard coal mining also developed enormously as the railway network spread throughout the empire from the second half of the 19th century onwards.

Of all Russian industries, textiles was both the oldest and the most important. The weaving mills employed almost a million workers and, encouraged by the government, supported a whole series of institutions such as schools, infirmaries, hospitals, kindergartens, workers' quarters, libraries, nursing homes, and so on. These enterprises became in reality small towns. It should be noted that almost all the capital involved in this industry was Russian. Within the textile industry, the cotton industry was in first place, so that Russia held the third position in the procurement of raw cotton, after the United States and Great Britain. The wool industry was the second most important, but it did not meet the needs of the domestic market. Russia had become the world's leading producer of flax by 1913, and its flax industry progressed rapidly, yet it consumed only 20 per cent of the total amount produced in the country, which before the war accounted for 80 per cent of the world's flax crop. Czarist Russia supplied four-fifths of the flax used in Europe. Silk, hemp and jute completed the list of the most important materials used in the textile industry.

Transport in Tsarist Russia

The first railway line in Russia was opened in 1837 by Russian engineers. Until 1857 the railways were built and operated by the state, but from that date until 1881 they were run by private companies whose creation was financially supported by the state. In *The Jewish Century, an* apologia which, as announced in the *Protocols,* demonstrates the absolute dominance of the Jews in all areas of the modern world, Yuri Slezkine reveals that a handful of Jewish bankers based in Russia amassed immense fortunes through the railway business. In addition to taking advantage of the budgetary largesse of the War Ministry, these bankers were supported by the Jewish financiers who monopolised the railway business in Europe, above all the Rothschild clan, but also the Pereira, Bleichröder, and Gomperz families. These consortiums of Jewish financiers and builders built the Warsaw-Vienna, Moscow-Smolensk and Moscow-Brest lines, among others. The Polyakov brothers: Samuel, Yakov and Lazar were one of the most influential Jewish financial clans. Samuel Polyakov built, financed and managed a number of private networks and became "the king of the railways". For this reason, 93% of the Russian railway network belonged to these companies, which competed with each other.

Faced with the chaotic tariff situation in the country, the state agreed for a period of ten years not to grant any more concessions. However, not only did it build most of the new lines, but it also rescued privately-owned companies. Thus, in 1889, tariffs were unified and in 1890, 29% of the network belonged to the State. From 1891 to 1901, the rescue policy continued and the construction of new lines remained in state hands. As a result, by 1901, private companies held only 30.4% of the network, which was mainly European lines, since the state took over mainly the Asian railway network. It should be remembered that the Trans-Siberian line, begun on 19 May 1891 and completed on 1 January 1906, which was a construction speed record, is the longest in the world. It crosses 28 rivers, passes over five major bridges and through 40 tunnels.

Another fact to bear in mind is that Russia imported neither locomotives nor wagons, as there were highly organised and well-equipped mechanical engineering companies in the industrial centres which were able to meet all the needs of the Russian network without any problems and were even able to export. The operating ratio of the Russian railways was the lowest in the world, and their trains were among the most comfortable in the world. Arsene de Goulévitch states categorically that, "from a qualitative point of view, in the domain of the railway industry, Russia enjoyed a superiority over all other countries". As far as the accident rate was concerned, Russia was among the countries that suffered few railway accidents, but with the arrival of the Soviets, all records in this respect were broken. The *Wall Street Journal* of 15 June 1926 reported on the chaotic state of the Russian railways, a situation that continued to worsen. A report in the Soviet press itself acknowledged that accidents had increased by 50%. Perhaps the cause of the chaos and mismanagement was the massacre of Russian engineers by the communists. Half of those who survived fled abroad.

As far as inland waterway navigation is concerned, we can only say that at the end of the 19th century Russia possessed the largest fleet in the world. The consequences of the Soviet authorities' actions were even more disastrous than in the case of the railway network. Numerous barges were destroyed to feed the heating system, and within a few years two thirds of the river fleet was destroyed without compensation.

Finance in Tsarist Russia

The Rothschilds' enmity towards the Tsars was due not only to the position they had taken in defence of Christianity, but also to their inability to exert their financial control over the Russian empire. Only in 1862, for the first time in forty years, had they succeeded in getting Alexander II to sign a loan of any significance with them. James Rothschild had tried on numerous occasions to secure his position in St Petersburg, but had failed. Shortly before his death in 1868, he failed for the last time, as he tried unsuccessfully to negotiate a large deal with Russian Finance Minister Michael von Reutern, who only offered him a stake in the privatisation of the Moscow to Odessa railway line. The Rothschilds, who had taken over the railway business throughout Europe, failed to control the Russian railway bond market.

Relations worsened after the assassination in 1881 of Alexander II. His successor Alexander III, after evidence of the involvement of Jewish revolutionaries in the assassination and convinced that their "pernicious activity" had to be guarded against, enacted a series of laws imposing new restrictions on them. The Rothschilds declared themselves "dismayed" and began to discuss what practical measures could be taken "on behalf of our unfortunate co-religionists". In a letter to his London cousins, Alphonse de Rothschild, James's heir, referred to Alexander III's intolerance and compared him to Louis XIV and Philip II of Spain. The truth was that the Rothschilds were trying by all means to establish a solid foothold in Russia. The arrival in 1892 of Sergei Witte at the Ministry of Finance made things somewhat easier for them. The German ambassador in Paris, Count Münster, commented on the opening of negotiations for a loan with the House of Paris as follows: ".... That the wife of the new Minister of Finance, Witte, whom the Russian ladies here have described to me as a very clever and very intriguing Jewess, is of great help in reaching agreements with Jewish bankers seems to me quite probable." The Rothschilds' private allusions to the Jewish origins of Witte's wife lend credibility to this interpretation, according to N. Ferguson. It is the same author who reveals that the

Rothschilds, who in 1891 had initiated a rapprochement with Baron Gunzberg[43], a Jew who owned the Lena gold mines in Russia, welcomed Witte's announcement to put Russia on the gold standard, as it coincided with their global gold mining interests. The Gunzberg family had made their fortune in the vodka business and then moved into banking and mining.

During the 19th century, the Russian state hardly needed to borrow at all because it made an effort to meet its extraordinary expenses out of its ordinary revenues, which was one of the reasons why it did not need Rothschild money. Some authors argue that perhaps if it had borrowed more, especially in the second half of the 19th century, it might have been able to bring its enormous natural wealth to the fore more quickly. The fact is that in almost a century and a half, from 1769, when Catherine the Great closed the first loan, until 1914, the imperial government borrowed a total of 15 billion roubles, both at home and abroad, 40% of which was repaid in the same period. In 1914, therefore, the public debt amounted to 8.825 billion roubles. A large part of this debt was in Russia, since out of 398 million roubles of interest, only 172 million roubles had been paid abroad. As has already been mentioned, among the main expenses that forced the state to resort to credit from the second half of the 19th century were the advances made to the peasants after the abolition of serfdom so that they could buy back the land that had been expropriated from the landowners. Secondly, there were the expenses for the construction and rescue of the railways. In third place came the costs of the war against Japan in 1905, which was imposed on Russia from outside, as will be seen below.

In 1903, two years before the Russo-Japanese war, Russian finances were in an excellent situation, since the difference between income (2,032 million roubles) and expenditure (1,883 million roubles) had produced a positive balance of 149 million roubles, which, together with the balance of previous years, gave the Treasury an availability of 331 million roubles. De Goulévitch gives comparative figures for 1908 on the debt per capita in different European countries: in France it was 288 roubles, in Italy 189, in the Netherlands 178, in Belgium 172, in Great Britain 169.5, in Germany 135.5, in Russia only 58.7 roubles per capita. De Goulévitch adds that it must be borne in mind that the railways in France and Great Britain belonged to private companies. If we deduct from the Russian debt the funds earmarked for the construction and rescue of Russian railways, the debt per capita would

---

[43] A letter sent from St. Petersburg by the American Ambassador Francis to the Secretary of State, published by Antony C. Sutton in Wall Street and the Bolshevik Revolution, reveals that there were powerful Jews in Russia who did not share Communist views. Sutton in *Wall Street and the Bolshevik Revolution*, makes it clear that there were powerful Jews in Russia who did not share communist views. Among them were the baron Alexander Gunzsberg, and the bankers Boris Kamenka and Henry Sliosberg, who wanted a liberal republic in Russia, but not Bolshevik dictatorship.

be reduced by a third. This debt is therefore insignificant compared to that of European countries.

Another source of wealth coveted by the international Jewish bankers was Russian gold. Of all the state banks, Tsarist Russia had the largest gold reserves in the world. Another interesting economic fact that shows that Russian finances were in good health is the number of savings banks, which grew from about 4,500 in 1900 to about 8,500 in 1914. The holders of savings books, who were mainly workers, cooperative members and small shopkeepers, increased from three and a half million to nine and a half million. In 15 years, the total deposits in these savings institutions rose from 680 million roubles to 2,236 million roubles. In terms of the tax burden on European citizens, in 1912 the Russians ranked last among the leading European states.

We conclude this hasty summary of the reality of the Russia of the Tsars by recalling that fifteen years after the revolution, Russia had been subjected to a despoilment unprecedented in history, and that the Russian masses of the people were subjected to appalling misery and the worst slavery.

The 1905 revolution

Since 1776, when the Jewish bankers decided to finance the Illuminati, the World Revolutionary Movement has been in the final stages, and at the beginning of the 20th century the great coup that had been laboriously plotted for decades was being prepared. Despite the divergences and contradictions that arose among the leading agents of the MRM, the time had finally come to put into practice the communist dictatorship of the proletariat, announced so long in advance by Heine. If the First International split after the Franco-Prussian war between the followers of Marx and those of Bakunin, in the Second International (1889-1916), made up of the Labour and Socialist parties, there were ideological disagreements from the outset between the internationalists and those who leaned towards the interests of the nation-state. Stalin's purges, as will be seen, were the latest example of the clash between these two tendencies. It was the Second International, also called the Social Democratic International, which adopted May Day, the date on which Adam Weishaupt founded the Bavarian Order of the Enlightened Ones, as International Labour Day.

The birth of the Russian Social Democratic Party was decisively influenced by the General Jewish Workers' Union of Russia and Poland, the "Bund", an organisation set up in 1897 whose Central Committee had an official organ, *Die Arbeiterstimme* (*The Voice of the Workers*). The first congress of the Russian Social Democratic Party, attended by only nine delegates, was held in Minsk on 1 March 1898. It produced the *Manifesto of the Russian Social-Democratic Workers' Party*, which laid down the guidelines for action, including the overthrow of the Tsar. In December 1900 the first issue of *Iskra* (*The Spark*) was published in Leipzig, a newspaper which brought together a number of Russian Social-Democrats who had been living abroad since 1900, the so-called "Iskrovtsi", including Lenin, Martov (Zederbaum) Plekhanov and Starovier (Potrésov). Lenin's Jewish wife, the Krupskaya, acted as secretary of the editorial board. A Jewish multimillionaire and Freemason from Odessa, Alexander Parvus (actually Israel Helphand), in addition to contributing some articles, provided Lenin with financial support for the publication, which was smuggled into Russia. Another of *Iskra*'s financiers was Savva Morozov, a wealthy Jewish industrialist who also helped with his fortune to foment the uprising of the fleet during the Russo-Japanese war. Among the Jewish contributors to the paper were Trotsky, Axelrod and Rosa Luxemburg.

In 1902 Lenin published a pamphlet entitled *What is to be done?* in which he advocated the unreserved use of any means to suppress the bourgeoisie and the government. From 1903 onwards, in addition to the numerous strikes, the workers began to be inculcated with the necessity of an armed conflict, for which the army was needed. Propaganda among the military had already begun, and a league of revolutionary officers had been in existence since December 1902. In June 1903 a general party congress was convened in Brussels, which was moved to London in August because of a ban by the Belgian government. Of the sixty delegates in attendance, only four were or had been workers. The majority were Jewish intellectuals, thirteen of whom belonged to the editorial staff of *Iskra*. In addition to these "Iskrists", the groups which had formed the party in 1898 were represented: the Jewish "Bund", the Georgian Social-Democrats and the Polish Social-Democrats of Rosa Luxemburg. The speech delivered by Plekhanov leaves no doubt as to the anti-democratic and totalitarian character of the ideas of the Russian Social-Democrats. His words recall those of the Jacobins: "Tout est permis a quiconque agit dans le sens de la Révolution" (Everything is permitted to those who act in the sense of the Revolution), i.e. "the end justifies the means", as Adam Weishaupt declared. Let us read an extract from Plekhanov's text:

> "The triumph of the revolution, that is the supreme law! Consequently, if for the triumph of the revolution it were necessary to eliminate this or that democratic principle, it would be criminal not to do so. It is possible that we may find it necessary to speak out against universal suffrage. The revolutionary proletariat will obviously be able to limit the political rights of the bourgeois classes on the principle: 'salus revolutionis suprema lex'. The same principle must guide us in the matter of the duration of parliaments. If, for example, in a burst of revolutionary enthusiasm the people had elected a good parliament, we should apply ourselves to making it last, but if, on the contrary, the elections were bad for us, our mission should be to dissolve it, not after two years, but in two weeks."

The London Congress gave birth to an alleged split among party members as a result of disagreements between Lenin and Martov over the composition of the Central Committee. Martov and twenty other delegates were left in the minority ("menchistvo"), hence the name for Mensheviks (minority). Lenin thus led the majority ("bolchinstvo"), i.e. the Bolsheviks (majority). Both, however, agreed on the need to take advantage of the Russo-Japanese war to overthrow the Tsarist regime. The famous Bolshevik Revolution was a long-planned work that required three acts, the first of which took place in 1905.

It is a fact acknowledged by sources of different persuasions that the illuminati Jacob Schiff, one of the most prominent financiers of the Rothschild banking syndicate, financed the war that enabled Japan to defeat the Russian empire and served as the trigger for the first attempt to overthrow the Romanovs. While the money flowed freely to the Japanese, European banks, in the hands of the usual Jewish financiers, closed credit to Russia. According to the *Encyclopaedia Judaica,* Schiff's loan amounted to $200 million. Apart from weakening Russia through war, the Jewish bankers sought its economic suffocation. At the same time, through their control of the international press, they maintained a relentless campaign blaming the Tsar for all the problems of the Russian people. In 1905 Jacob Schiff was awarded a medal, the Second Order of the Treasury of Japan, by the Mikado (Emperor of Japan) in recognition of his decisive role in financing the war against Russia, which began in February 1904 and ended on 5 September 1905 with the Treaty of Portsmouth. Among those present at the signing of the Treaty was Jacob Schiff, who presented a series of demands concerning Russian Jews to Count Witte, whose wife was the Jewess Matilda Khotimskaya.

War had broken out on the night of 8 February 1904, when the Japanese torpedoed the Russian ships anchored in Port Arthur by surprise and without a declaration of war. The fall of this port into the hands of the Japanese on 2 January 1905 was the signal for the beginning of the provocations of the revolutionaries, who were following the orders of Trotsky and Parvus. During the year 1905, with the country plunged into an imposed war, fourteen thousand strikes were organised in Russia by Jewish agitators who intended to take advantage of the defeat. The first action, organised by Parvus and another Jewish comrade, Pyotr (Pinhas) Rutenberg, took place on 22 January ("Bloody Sunday"). Igor Bunich in *Zoloto Partii* (*The Gold of the Party*) (1992), a source quoted assiduously by J. Lina, reveals that these two Freemasons, when a demonstration led by Pope Gapon was heading towards the Winter Palace demanding better wages, ordered several terrorists to shoot at the guards from trees in order to provoke them. Georgi Gapon was actually an agent of the Ojrana (Tsarist police) and was eventually killed by Pinhas Rutenberg. [44]With the disintegration of the USSR, works by researchers who have gained access to secret Communist Party documents have been published and the truth of what happened has emerged. The propaganda of the Revolutionary Socialists put the number of victims of "Bloody Sunday" in the thousands, but in reality the dead numbered about one hundred and fifty and the wounded about two hundred. Dismayed at the news, the Tsar granted a subsidy for the collective of families with dead or wounded and received a revolutionary delegation in a fraternal manner.

This provoked episode marked the beginning of actions intended to overthrow the Tsarist regime. On 17 February two Jewish terrorists, Ivan Kalyalev and Roza Brilliant, Savinkov's lover, assassinated the governor of Moscow, Grand Duke Serguei Romanov, who was the uncle of Tsar Nicholas II. Days after the assassination, the Grand Duke's widow, Grand Duchess Elisabeth Fedorovna, visited Kalyalev in prison: she tried to persuade him to repent in order to save his soul, but the terrorist refused. Meanwhile, the social democrats began to develop their strategies to take advantage of the growing discontent. In the midst of the war, Bolsheviks and Mensheviks prepared simultaneous uprisings on all ships of the Black Sea fleet, which were to take place in July 1905, during the manoeuvres of the Russian fleet. The premature uprising of the crew of the battleship Potemkin on 14 June led to the discovery of the treacherous plan, which ultimately failed.[45]

When on 6 August 1905 Nicholas II, influenced by Count Witte and other liberal circles, published a manifesto for the convocation of the Duma,

---

[44] The murky relationship of the pope Gapon with Pyotr (Pinhas) Rutenberg is explained in a few lines of a Wikipedia article, according to which Rutenberg participated in the demonstration and saved Gapon's life. The two fled Russia together and marched to Paris, where they met Russian émigrés, among them Plekhanov, Lenin and Kropotkin. Before the end of 1905 they returned to Russia, where Gapon admitted that he had contacts with the police and set out to recruit Rutenberg on the grounds that dual loyalty also served the cause of the workers. Rutenberg told Yevno Azef and Boris Savinkov, the Social-Democratic leaders, who demanded that the pope be executed. On 26 March 1906 Gapon was found hanged in a house near St. Petersburg, where he had met with three revolutionary socialists and Rutenberg himself. The party of the Socialist Revolutionaries denied responsibility for the murder and claimed that Rutenberg had himself killed Gapon for personal reasons.

[45] Not all Russians accepted with resignation the treachery and terrorist activities of the Jews, many of them orchestrated by various Zionist and socialist organisations and parties, such as the Zionist Socialist Workers Party, the Kahal (Jewish local government), the Bund and Poalei Zion, the latter party contributing thousands of terrorists to the struggle to overthrow the Tsar. Between 18 and 20 October, violent pogroms took place in Russia, the battle cry of which was "let's wipe out the Jews". Numerous Jewish shops, where prices were exorbitant, were raided and set on fire, and nearly 800 people were killed. According to a clearly exaggerated official report by Soviet Zionists, between 1905 and 1907 four thousand Jews were killed in the anti-Jewish pogroms.

the Bolsheviks announced that they would boycott it. The Mensheviks, however, decided to participate with the intention of making it a revolutionary chamber. The *Iskra* Social-Democrats organised the strike of the Moscow typographers on 19 September 1905, which immediately took on a markedly revolutionary character. On 7 October the railway strike broke out, which was the signal for the beginning of a general strike throughout Russia. On the streets there were demonstrations with red flags and banners calling for a republic. On 13 October, following the model described by *Iskra* in its 101st issue, the first "workers' delegates' soviet" met in St. Petersburg. Its first chairman was the Jew Peter Khrustalyev, who passed for Georgi Nosar. His closest collaborators were Parvus and Trotsky (Bronstein). After Nosar was arrested in November, he was quickly replaced by Trotsky, who was then a Menshevik. This Soviet met as if it were a parliament and elected an executive committee, which edited the *Izvestia* (news) *of the Soviet of Workers' Deputies*. Juri Lina cites the names of some of the delegates to the Soviet: Grever, Edilken, Goldberg, Simanovsky, Feif, Matzelev and Bruser, who claimed to represent the Russian working class, but in reality, according to the Estonian author, they were neither peasants nor workers, but Jewish conspirators and Freemasons.

On 17 October, the same day that the imperial decree that was to make Russia a constitutional monarchy appeared, the liberal Freemasons Alexander Guchkov, Mikhail Rodzyanko and other brothers founded the Octubrist Party, which was supposedly intended to maintain the monarchical order under a democratic constitution. Meanwhile Lenin, who was living in Geneva, Vera Zasulich and other revolutionaries entered Russia. This St. Petersburg Soviet openly prepared the insurrection by means of publications, thousands of proclamations and the delivery of arms to the workers. The three Jewish agents who led the revolt were Leon Deutsch, Alexander Parvus and Leon Trotsky. On 2 December they issued a call to the people urging them not to pay taxes, to withdraw their deposits from the savings banks and to arm themselves for the final assault to establish a social and democratic republic. The government then ordered the arrest of 49 members of the St. Petersburg Soviet, including Parvus and Trotsky. Both were sentenced to exile in Siberia. The former managed to escape before reaching his destination and Trotsky did so in February 1907.

At the same time, another Soviet of workers' delegates had been formed in Moscow, which, after learning of the events in St. Petersburg, decided to go over to armed insurrection. Rifles, revolvers and bombs were distributed among the workers in numerous districts of the city, and on 8 December the revolt began. Following traditional patterns, barricades were erected and attempts were made to occupy strategic places: stations, telegraphs and other sensitive buildings. In view of the turn of events, the government ordered the troops to act energetically, and the revolution was put down within a few days. The defeat of the Moscow insurgents decided the fate of the 1905 coup d'état. By the time Rosa Luxemburg arrived in Russia at the end of December to take part in the events, the insurrection was already over. The Social-Democratic Party was not going to forget the lesson. Numerous Bolshevik and Menshevik leaders, convinced that the method followed had been the right one, fled abroad and devoted special attention to the creation of cells to prepare the next attempt. Lenin himself declared in a paper published after the Bolshevik victory that without the insurrection of 1905 the triumph of 1917 would not have been possible.

In 1906 the Russian Social-Democrats held a congress in Stockholm at which they focused their attention on developing propaganda for the peasants, who were to be convinced that their conditions would be immediately improved by the confiscation of land. Through this interest in the agrarian question, the social democrats drew closer to the Socialist Revolutionary Party, whose doctrine converged with that of Alexander Herzen's old "narodniks". Under Lenin's impetus, numerous terrorist organisations sprang up in Russia whose murderers did not distinguish between the victims, for they could assassinate both high-ranking officials and the humblest representatives of the administration. Arsene de Goulévitch gives an account of the number of victims in Russia from the beginning of the insurrection in 1905 to 1908. According to him, by the beginning of 1906, 12,000 people had lost their lives to the bullets and bombs of the revolutionaries. The terrorist acts committed in the empire during the following three years yield these figures: 4,742 attacks in 1906 claimed the lives of 738 civil servants and 640 private individuals. In addition, 948 civil servants and 777 private individuals were wounded. In the course of 1907 there were 12,102 attacks, killing 1,231 civil servants and injuring 1,284. The number of private individuals killed by terrorists was 1,768 and 1,768 injured, and 1,734 injured. The number of attacks perpetrated in 1908 was 9,424. A further 1,349 private individuals were killed and 1,348 wounded. Only from 1909 onwards, as a result of Stolypin's crackdown, did the number of terrorist attacks decrease.

In addition to the financing of the banker Jacob Schiff, between 1905 and 1910 the Bolsheviks found other means of obtaining money, among them organised groups of bandits. A former Russian Social-Democrat, M. G. Alexinsky, who was a member of the Bolshevik faction, explains that this faction was led by a central committee within which there was another small committee whose existence was unknown not only to the Tsarist police, but also to the party members themselves. On this secret committee were Lenin, the Jew Leonid Krasin (Goldgelb), a stockbroker who worked under the name of "Comrade Nikitich", and a third person especially involved in finance, not revealed by Alexinsky, whom he calls "X". In *Wall Street and the Bolshevik Revolution* Anthony Sutton links Krasin to the Jewish banker Olof Aschberg, with whom he was associated, and confirms that kept his Bolshevik membership secret until the October revolution. According to

Sutton, Comrade Nikitich passed for the director of Siemens-Schukert in St. Petersburg until 1917 when he emerged as a Bolshevik leader.

This "little trinity" organised armed robberies. On 27 October 1905, in the very centre of St. Petersburg, at the entrance to the Kazan Cathedral, four Jews stopped a Treasury wagon and stole 270,000 dollars. They were arrested, but were able to hand over the cash box to a woman who immediately vanished without a trace. On 8 November another group of Jewish revolutionaries robbed a Treasury car near Ragow in Poland and disappeared with $850,000. In addition to emptying post office and station cash registers, the most notorious robberies were of branches of banks not controlled by their Jewish friends on Wall Street. The most famous were the looting of the Helsinki State Bank in 1906 and that of the Tiflis branch of the State Bank in 1907, where 340,000 roubles were stolen. The protagonists in the latter were Maksim Litvinov, another Jew who was to become USSR foreign minister in the 1930s, and Stalin himself, who planned the robbery. The explosion of the dynamite bomb used to carry out the robbery killed around 30 people. The improvised devices used in the robberies were made in a laboratory designed by Leonid Krasin, who was an accomplished engineer. When Krasin travelled to London in 1920 as Trade Commissioner, Lord Curzon, Secretary of State at the Foreign Office, refused to see him and shake his hand. He only agreed to do so after a scolding from Lloyd George, who reprimanded him with these words: "Curzon! Curzon! Be a gentleman!

In *The World at the Cross Roads* Boris Brasol reproduces a secret report submitted on 3 January 1906 to Emperor Nicholas II by Russian Foreign Minister Count Lamsdorf. This report, the full text of which was also published by the *American Hebrew and Jewish Messenger* in its issue of 13 July 1918, shows that the Russian intelligence service knew almost immediately that the 1905 revolution had been orchestrated abroad. Since the information contained in the document is relevant, a lengthy quotation follows:

"The events which took place in Russia during 1905, and which reached their climax at the beginning of last October,... are clearly international in character. The decisive indications justifying this conclusion come from the circumstance that the revolutionaries are in possession of large quantities of arms which are imported from abroad, and of very considerable financial means, for there is no doubt that the leaders of the revolution have already spent on the movement against our government, which includes the organisation of all kinds of strikes, large sums of money. However, it must be recognised that this support given to the revolutionary movement by sending arms and money from abroad can hardly be attributed to foreign governments and it must be inferred that it is international capitalist organisations that are interested in supporting our revolutionary movement. It must be faced that the Russian revolutionary movement has the obvious character of a movement of the heterogeneous nationalities of Russia, which one after another, Armenians and Georgians, Latvians and Estonians, Finns, Poles and others, are rising up against the imperial government..... If we add to this, as has been proved beyond any doubt, that a very considerable part within these movements is played by Jews, who individually, as ringleaders in various organisations, and in their own Jewish Bund (League) in the Western provinces, have always presented themselves as the most belligerent element in the revolution, we can rightly declare that the above-mentioned foreign support for the Russian revolutionary movement comes from Jewish capitalist circles. In this connection the following coincidences of fact must not be ignored, which lead to further conclusions, namely, that the revolutionary movement is not only supported, but also to a large extent directed from abroad. On the one hand, the strike broke out with particular violence and spread throughout Russia not before and not after October, that is, at the very moment when our Government was trying to obtain an important foreign loan without the participation of the Rothschilds and just in time to prevent the realisation of this financial operation. The panic caused among the buyers and owners of Russian loans brought additional advantages to the Jewish bankers and capitalists who openly and with foreknowledge speculated on the fall of Russian bonds..... Moreover, certain very significant facts, mentioned even in the press, confirm the obvious connection of the Russian revolutionary movement with foreign Jewish organisations. Thus, for example, the above-mentioned importation of arms, which according to our agents was carried out from Europe through England, can be properly appreciated if it is considered that already in June 1905 a special Anglo-Jewish committee of capitalists was openly set up in England for the purpose of collecting money for arming violent groups of Russian Jews, and that the famous anti-Russian Jewish publicist Lucien Wolf was the chairman of this committee. On the other hand, another committee of Jewish capitalists was formed in England under the leadership of Lord Rothschild, who raised considerable contributions in England, France and Germany for the alleged purpose of aiding Russian Jews suffering from pogroms. And finally, Jews in America raised money to help the victims of pogroms and to arm Jewish youth."

According to information in the London *Jewish Chronicle*, the contribution of international Jewry to the Russian revolutionary movement in 1905 amounted to £874,341. America's own ambassador to Russia during the Russo-Japanese War, George von Lengerke Meyer, in a letter written on 30 December 1905 to his Secretary of State, Elihu Root, reported that "the Jews had undoubtedly fed the brains and energy of the revolution throughout Russia". Various Jewish sources proudly claimed that the revolution had been their doing. *The Maccabean* of London, for example, published an article in November 1905 entitled *A Jewish Revolution,* in which it proclaimed that Jews were the ultimate revolutionaries in the empire.

Another article by journalist and writer William Eleroy Curtis, published on 14 December 1906 in *the National Geographic Society*, not only singled out the 'Bund' as the first revolutionary agency, but also denounced the ongoing murders by Jewish terrorists: 'Wherever a fierce deed is committed it is always carried out by a Jew and there is hardly a single individual of this race who is loyal to the Empire.... Wherever you read about a murder or a bomb explosion, you will read in the newspaper reports that the perpetrator was a Jew." In that article, entitled "The Revenge of the Jews", Eleroy Curtis unveils the names of various individuals of this race at the head of revolutionary activities. Thus, for example, a Jew named Krustaleff organised a strike of prison officers from prison, where he spent only three weeks. Another Jew named Maxim was the organiser of the revolution in the Baltic provinces. A Polish Jew, Gerschunin, is identified as a skilled terrorist leader who was behind the assassination of Interior Minister Dmitry Spyagin in 1902. Sentenced to death in 1904, Gerschunin was pardoned by the Tsar and his sentence was commuted to life imprisonment in silver mines on the Mongolian border. This terrorist escaped and was in San Francisco in 1906. Gerschunin's right-hand man, Yevno Azef, the son of a Jewish tailor, was involved in numerous assassination attempts, including that of Vyacheslav Plevhe, the Minister of the Interior, who was assassinated on 28 June 1904.

The 1905 revolution led to the revival of Freemasonry in Russia, and the consequences of this were of decisive importance within a few years. On 17 October 1905, Tsar Nicholas II announced a series of constitutional freedoms that were to allow "good Masons" to gradually appear on the scene. Until 1906 there were no Masonic lodges in Russia, although they did exist in Poland and Lithuania. It was in December 1906 that M. M. Kovalevsky opened the *North Star* Lodge in St. Petersburg. The opening ceremony was attended by V. Maklakov, a representative of the Constitutional Democratic Party, a liberal-leaning organisation whose members were called "kadetes" (abbreviation of the name of the K-D party in Russian) and which stood to the left of the Octubrists. The *North Star*, which was under the jurisdiction of the Grand Orient of France, was the first permanent Masonic lodge in Russia and the first lodge of the Kadetes. In fact, the history of Russian Freemasonry in the 20th century had begun in Paris at the end of the 19th century, when several Scottish Rite lodges began to accept Russian emigrants. The aforementioned Maksim Kovalevsky, who was a member of the Parisian lodge *Les Vrais Amis Fideles* and formed *Cosmos* Lodge No. 288 in Paris in 1887, is considered the founding father of Russian Freemasonry. On 14 November 1901, Kovalevsky opened the "Ecole de Hautes Etudes" in the French capital, which, under the patronage and tutelage of *Cosmos* Lodge, became a reception and assistance centre for Russian emigrants between 1901 and 1906. During these years, the *Mount Sinai* Lodge No. 6 was formed, which was also made up of Russians and worked the Scottish Rite.

From 1907 to 1909 the Masonic lodges in Russia were under French jurisdiction, but in 1910 they became independent and were no longer subject to the Grand Orient of France. Recording of proceedings or sessions was forbidden and orders were issued orally. All lodges were strictly supervised by the Supreme Council of the Peoples of Russia, formed in 1913. It has already been stated above that this Supreme Council had as its secretaries Nekrasov, Kerensky and Tereshchenko. The latter, whom the Rothschilds in London considered "a friend of the Jews", was to become in 1917 the future Finance Minister of the Provisional Government. In 1915, the number of lodges under the Supreme Council of Russia was around fifty. However, the *North Star* lodge maintained its oath of loyalty to the Grand Orient of France and its Supreme Council. Inspired by their French brethren, the Russian Freemasons made every effort to gain a foothold in the higher echelons of the State, especially in diplomatic and military circles. They soon gained an important presence in the Council of State and, through the Octubrists and Kadets, in the Duma (Parliament). Clearly, their main aim was to change the monarchical government into a liberal republic. By the time of the February 1917 revolution, a network of Masonic lodges covered the whole of Russia. Kropotkin, the father of the Russian anarchist movement, declared that the revolutionary movement considered its relationship with Freemasonry to be a good and useful one, which is nothing new: Hess, Marx, Lenin, Trotsky and so many other Jewish leaders were Freemasons. Adolphe Crémieux had already announced in the *Israelite Archives* that "good Masons, blindfolded, help the Jews in the Great Work".

Stolypin and land reform

Pyotr Stolypin was an outstanding statesman, precisely the kind of statesman Russia needed to defuse the international conspiracy that its enemies had been devising for decades. Absolutely convinced of the results of his policy, he declared in 1908 to a French journalist : "Give me ten years of peace and creative work and you will not recognise our country". Unfortunately, he had only half the time he wanted to complete an agrarian reform that would have left the Judeo-Bolshevik agents working tirelessly to provoke revolution with no arguments. In September 1911, a Jewish terrorist named Dimitri (Mordechai) Bogrov assassinated Prime Minister Stolypin in Kiev.

After the emancipation of the serfs by Alexander II, a new system was initially put into operation, which was called a commune (in Russian "mir"). These communes were peasant communities whose land was owned and tilled in common. Each peasant family was given a plot of land to cultivate according to its size. The families paid a share to the "mir" and retained the rest as profit. The affairs of the commune were administered by the peasants themselves, who were controlled by a mayor elected by the heads of families.

The "mir" was responsible to the government for the payment of taxes. In principle, therefore, they had not dared to replace the system of serfdom with that of individual ownership. Without intending to do so, the foundations of a future communism had been laid, since it was not envisaged that intelligent and enterprising peasants would be able to develop the entrepreneurial instinct. Predictably, the revolutionaries took advantage of the unrest generated by the Russo-Japanese war to introduce revolutionary cells into the communes. The Russian defeats in the Japanese seas were the signal for the revolts throughout the country. It fell to the peasants, as in 1789, to set fire to the manorial domains. The Volga provinces were razed to the ground and disorder gripped the Russian countryside.

In 1902 Stolypin was appointed governor of the Belarusian province of Grodno, where he launched a programme of economic and social reforms. In February 1903 the Tsar entrusted him with the government of Saratov Province, where he faced peasant uprisings that set fire to the landlords' estates. Alexandra Stolypin, daughter of the late statesman, recounts in *L'homme du dernier tsar. Stolypine* tells how her father, as soon as order had been restored, wanted to visit the still smouldering regions to try to calm things down and to personally meet the demands of the peasants. Again and again he met people of good will, peasants who expressed to him their desire to obtain "the blue paper, with the imperial arms", i.e. a title deed granting them a small plot of land for themselves and their families, a piece of land that they could love and cultivate with all their souls. Stolypin understood that a new horizon had to be shown to the majority class of Russian farmers.

Stolypin, who suffered eleven attempts on his life, received one day at his home in Saratov a cruel letter from the revolutionary committee, condemning his youngest son, then still a baby, to death by poisoning. The event terrified the whole family and forced a strict food control. In 1905 Stolypin became Minister of the Interior and cracked down on the terrorists who were plaguing the country. It has already been said that in the three revolutionary years about 12,000 people were killed. Among these measures was the application of martial law for those who committed murder. Some six hundred terrorists were sentenced to death and executed in 1906. Another 2,300 terrorists were tried and sentenced to death between 1907-08. About 35,000 revolutionaries then left the country and the situation was more or less under control, allowing Russia to finally recover. Since 1906, Nicholas II had placed all his confidence in Stolypin and appointed him prime minister. After his nomination, his house in St. Petersburg was the target of a terrible bomb attack that killed thirty-three people and injured thirty-two others. Two terrorists disguised as policemen detonated a bomb in the room where people were waiting to be received in audience. Among the wounded were his son Arkadi, who was three years old and was wounded in the head, and Natalia, the eldest daughter, aged fourteen, who was crippled for life.

When considering the dates of historical events, it should be borne in mind that in Tsarist Russia the Julian calendar was in force until 1918, which was thirteen days behind the Gregorian calendar. One of the first measures related to land reform, adopted by the government in a decree ("ukase") issued on 3/16 November 1905, was the abolition of the arrears of payments due to the peasants for the purchases of land they had received in 1861, which meant a reduction in the state coffers of about 80 million roubles. These lands were thus freed of all debts, and there were no obstacles to the farmers' departure from the commune. Stolypin's agrarian reform decree of 9/22 November 1906 gave every head of a family, a member of a commune, the right to take private ownership of the land he had worked. He also obtained the right to ask the commune to exchange these lands, which were often small plots in different locations, for a single equivalent plot. This was intended to bring about the gradual abolition of the "mir" or commune. This historic decree became a law passed by the Duma on 14/27 June 1910.

In order for the reader to understand why it took almost four years for the decree to become law, we will briefly sequence its parliamentary procedure. Following the imperial decree that made Russia a constitutional monarchy in October 1905, the Tsar promulgated the Russian Constitution in 1906. The Duma was the lower house of parliament and the State Council the upper house. The Constitution gave the Tsar the power to dissolve the Duma and call new elections. The Constitutional Democratic Party (kadetes), with 179 seats, won the most votes in the first Duma elections. Eight parties were represented, including the Menshevik Social Democrats, which won only 18 deputies. From the beginning, tensions between the government and parliament were evident, as most of the seats were held by people who had undermined the regime underhandedly and saw parliament as a means to continue the revolt. Their primary interest was not to enact laws or pass a budget that would allow the country to recover from the war, but to continually question. In view of the intentions of the parties and the impotence of his collaborators, Nicholas II dissolved Parliament in June 1906, ten weeks after it was formed. Most of the deputies met in Vyborg (Finland) and issued a declaration calling on the country not to pay taxes, to refuse to perform military service and not to obey the authorities. It was in this context that the tsar placed his trust in Stolypin, who then became prime minister. In addition to calling new elections, Stolypin carried out his land reform.

In March 1907 the Second Duma was formed, in which the revolutionaries announced that they would not take part in the debates and that they would fight the government with the "eloquence of silence". It soon became clear, however, that it was the deputies of these parties who did most of the talking. When Stolypin presented the reform programme drawn up by the Council of Ministers to the chamber, there was a violent clash between the parties, with shouting and threats flooding the parliament. In his second speech, Stolypin insisted that the government wanted to find a basis of agreement to work with the parliament and called on everyone to abandon the language of hatred and anger. The government," Stolypin said, "must choose between two methods: either to stand aside and leave the way open for revolution, forgetting that power must be the guardian of the culture and integrity of the Russian people, or to act with strength and wisdom and uphold what has been entrusted to it. By adopting the second solution, the Government will fatally bring accusations upon itself. The revolution cannot be stifled without sometimes causing harm to private interests." Stolypin warned that his Government would respond with strength to those who sought to paralyse the Government's action and discredit it.

On 10/23 May 1907 Stolypin presented his agrarian reform to the Duma in order to pass into law the decree of 9/22 November 1906. He analysed the opposition's agrarian programme, which called for the pure and simple nationalisation of all land and its distribution to farmers. The Prime Minister outlined the moral and economic consequences and gave the figures that made the proposal unfeasible; but there was no will to understand in Parliament, which pronounced itself against Stolypin's agrarian reform. In parallel with the debates, the police discovered that Social Democratic (Menshevik) deputies in the Duma were holding secret meetings with soldiers stationed in St. Petersburg, which coincided with uprisings in Cronstadt and Sveaborg. At the same time, the tide of revolution was flooding back into Poland and the Caucasus. On 1/14 June the Prime Minister took to the rostrum to announce that fifty-five Social Democratic deputies were being prosecuted on charges of plotting against the Tsar and the government. Stolypin asked Parliament to strip the defendants of their parliamentary immunity so that the judicial investigation could begin, since otherwise he could not answer for the security of the state. The Duma rejected the request, and on 3/16 June 1907 an imperial decree dissolved the Second Parliament. Among the complaints and reproaches contained in the decree of dissolution, one could read: "The Duma has been unwilling to study the bills submitted by the Government. It has either always postponed the debates or rejected them. It has even disapproved laws punishing the praise of crime and revolt among the troops. The deliberate slowness in examining the budget has led to the imbalance of the Treasury, whose duty it is to respond to the needs of the country. The decree then alluded to the abuse of the right of interpellation and finally to the conspiracy within Parliament itself.

In the meantime, land reform was developing intensively and changing the living conditions of millions of Russian peasants. A series of measures were taken to induce landowners to sell their property to the state. A special agency set up by the government, the Agrarian Bank, bought at low prices the land which the landowners wanted to transfer to it, to which was added land belonging to the Crown. The members of the communes were free to leave them and buy a plot of land on credit. In order to help enterprising farmers to set up a private estate, the law provided that they would only pay to the Bank the sums they had at their disposal, the Treasury helping to pay the difference. The results of the land reform were phenomenal and ushered in a new era for Russia. At the beginning of the world conflagration Russia was in the midst of agrarian transformation: in January 1915 the number of heads of households who had left the "mir" and become individual landowners exceeded three million. A year later, despite the fact that the country was at war, more than five and a half million farmers had taken steps to leave the communes, in some of which it was the case that all members had opted to become landlords. The rural population unreservedly supported Stolypin's reform.

The work of property reorganisation was a gigantic effort for which twelve thousand surveyors were called upon and cost the treasury more than one hundred million roubles. In order to organise individual properties, it was necessary to prepare partition plans and draw up individual certificates. In short, it was necessary to carry out a series of operations that would have been impossible without the initiative and financial efforts of the state. In addition to facilitating the conversion of collective rural property into individual properties, the Imperial Government provided the peasants with material aid aimed at increasing the yield of their land. The disbursement of the State Administration and local administrations ("zemstvos") for this purpose had been insignificant until 1906; but in 1913 it reached 25 million roubles from the State, to which must be added another 12 million from the zemstvos. About 5,000 state agronomists were engaged in helping small farmers to improve their methods of cultivation. By 1900 these agronomists numbered only a few hundred. The number of agricultural schools rose from about nine thousand in 1907 to eighteen thousand in 1913. On the eve of the war more than three hundred thousand peasants were attending courses in agricultural practice.

In November 1907, after new elections, the third Duma was formed. In his speech presenting his government programme, Stolypin announced that, once the revolts had been quelled, the government intended to serve the people and put them in a position to benefit from the important reforms made for them. Here is a brief quotation from his words: "To give the people initiative and independence, to endow them with local institutions, to give them a part of the task and responsibility of government, the part they can carry on their shoulders, to create at last a powerful agricultural class, which will be in permanent contact with the authorities of the country: this is the aim of our efforts". Finally, this third Parliament approved Stolypin's agrarian reform by a majority: on 14/27 June 1910, the decree of 9/22 November 1906 finally became law.

Stolypin's reforms had a twofold aim: on the one hand to increase agricultural production and boost economic life in general, on the other to create a peasant petty bourgeoisie (kulaks) which was to serve as a solid basis for the social structuring of the country. Our main aim," he told a French journalist, "is to strengthen the farming people. In them lies the whole strength of the country. If the roots of the country are healthy and robust, believe me, the words of the Russian government will have a new force in Europe and in the world." All this was viewed with horror from outside, where the revolutionary committees recognised in their resolutions that the continuation of the agrarian reform was a serious setback for the revolution they were still preparing, since they were left without their main propaganda weapon, whose slogan was: "take the land". Lenin and company knew that the Russian peasants could become, as in fact they did, the worst enemies of the soviets.

In the summer of 1910 Stolypin, accompanied by the Minister of Agriculture, made a trip to Western Siberia and the Volga provinces. The two travelled hundreds of kilometres by carriage to study the possibilities of colonising Asiatic Russia. In three hundred years of Russian rule,, Siberia had barely reached a population of four and a half million, yet between 1895 and 1910 more than three million new immigrants had settled there, one million of whom between 1907-1909. On his return, Stolypin presented a report setting out his views on the rational exploitation of Siberia. His first conclusion was that the land should be distributed to the aborigines and settlers, but not for exploitation, as had hitherto been the case, but for ownership. According to him, only the right of ownership would give stability to the rural economy and facilitate the rational distribution of land. Once again, the social aspect was given special attention, and in his report, the Prime Minister envisaged the creation of agricultural schools capable of preparing the necessary specialists to help and direct the settlers.

Stolypin was unable to see the results of his work. His death became a priority target for the revolutionaries, and they soon succeeded in carrying out an attempt on his life. On September 1/14, 1911, the Emperor, the court and high dignitaries of the country were in Kiev, where various events were scheduled to celebrate the 50th anniversary of the liberation of the serfs. A monument to the liberating Tsar Alexander II was unveiled, and the festivities included a performance of *The Tale of Tsar Saltan,* an opera by Rimsky Korsakov based on a poem of the same name by Pushkin. Reports from the secret police hinted at the possibility that a dangerous terrorist from abroad might be in the city. The false information came from a young policeman named Bogrov, who had been infiltrated into the secret service a few years earlier. The police chiefs, inexplicably, attached great importance and credibility to the revelations of this new agent and, even though they knew he was carrying a revolver, authorised him to enter the theatre.

Alexandra Stolypin, whose story follows, says that her father had asked in the morning whether the much-talked-about terrorist had finally been arrested. Back in the theatre, the Prime Minister watched the show from the front row of the stalls. The opera was divided into four acts, so between the second and third acts, many spectators left the theatre. The imperial family box was also deserted. Stolypin was leaning on the balustrade separating the orchestra from the hall, talking to people who came to greet him. No one paid any attention to a young man approaching from the corridor of seats. Dimitri Bogrov, the supposed police officer, in reality a Jewish terrorist who was a member of the "Bund", fired two shots, one of which fatally wounded the Prime Minister in the chest, who, seeing that his white waistcoat was becoming covered in blood, left his hat and gloves on the balustrade before collapsing in his armchair. Nicolas II rushed into the box and Stolypin, perhaps fearing for his life, waved him away, but the Tsar remained petrified, mute. Then Stolypin, holding his wounded right hand with his left, managed to sanctify himself, and before he lost consciousness he said in a weak but firm voice to those around him: "Let the emperor know that I am happy to die for him and for Russia".

The assassin tried to leave the room, taking advantage of the initial stupor, but an officer managed to block his way. Several enraged people immediately rushed at him. From a box someone jumped straight at Bogrov and knocked him to the ground. A cool-blooded officer managed to prevent the lynching by pushing him into a room. The chief of police, absent at the time of the attack, came running in with his face unhinged and looked at the young man with a bloodied face and torn clothes. As he grabbed him by the shoulders and shook him angrily, he shouted, "It's Bogrov who betrayed us, the scoundrel!" During the trial it could not be ascertained who had ordered the crime on the Jewish fanatic, but the historian O. Soloviev notes that Dmitri (Mordechai) Bogrov was a close associate of Kerensky, who after the murder immediately fled. The terrorist was sentenced to death by an extraordinary court and was hanged wearing a tailcoat, as on the day of the attack.

Pyotr Stolypin struggled for four days between life and death. According to his daughter, in his delirium he still struggled to talk about state affairs while a secretary tried to take down his last intelligible words. He spoke of land reform and above all of the countries bordering the empire, one of the problems he intended to tackle after the Kiev celebrations. He expired on 5/18 September. "I want to be buried in the place where I will have been killed". These words in Stolypin's will, written several years before the assassination attempt, are evidence of the stature, nobility and willingness to serve of a man who found encouragement in the tragic feeling of life[46]. A few days before the assassination attempt, Stolypin had

---

[46] In *L'homme du dernier Tsar*, Alexandra Stolypin reproduces other words of her father's which show his deep Christian faith, despite the tragic feeling of life to which we have alluded in the text. They deserve to be known: "Every morning when I wake up, I say my prayers. I consider the day that begins as if it were the last of my life and I prepare to do my duty, with my eyes already set on eternity. When dusk comes, I thank God for having

accompanied the emperor on a visit to Lavra, the most revered Orthodox Christian monastery in Kiev. There he had remarked to the Tsar: "It must be nice here to sleep the eternal sleep". By the emperor's decision, Stolypin was buried in Lavra a few days after his death. A year later, a monument to Stolypin was unveiled in Kiev. On one side of the stone was inscribed: "Russia to Stolypin". On another were engraved the last words of one of the Prime Minister's most moving speeches to the second parliament, the one that rejected his land reform: "They want great upheavals; we, we want Great Russia".

Many of Stolypin's reforms were carried out after his death. In 1912 an industrial protection law for workers came into force, which provided compensation for workers in the event of illness or accident. This compensation consisted of two-thirds or even three-quarters of the usual wage. The new labour code for workers also provided for the legalisation of strikes of an economic nature. The increase of public schools was another positive consequence of the policies designed by the most impressive politician of imperial Russia. In order to develop these social policies, Stolypin had planned to raise money for the treasury through higher taxes on alcohol and higher taxes on real estate. Another proposal submitted to the Tsar was the establishment of a higher school for civil servants. Finally, the laws of religious tolerance and freedom of conscience, which removed restrictions on believers who did not profess Orthodox Christianity, should be mentioned.

Nevertheless, eight years after his murder in Kiev, the hatred of the Jewish revolutionaries for Stolypin persisted to such an extent that it even claimed the life of another of his daughters, Olga, who was cowardly murdered in public, in cold blood, in 1919. The story is told in Alexandra Stolypin's book. A few days before her death, Olga herself explained on her deathbed how she had received the bullet wounds that ended her life. During one of the agonising nights that preceded the end of her life, Olga Stolypin related to her sister Alexandra that after she had been arrested by a group of Bolsheviks, a Jew in uniform came forward and said, "I am a Jew:

- "Hand that woman over to me, comrades. You know I have a score to settle with Stolypin."

- "Take it," said the other, "but don't forget that the regiment leaves in an hour."

- "Oh, I'll be finished in less time," said the soldier, laughing.

Reproduced dialogue between the Bolsheviks. The first-person account continues: "He took his rifle and loaded it. I looked everywhere for help, but everyone avoided my gaze. The Jew rested the barrel of his rifle on my chest and fired. I felt a strong jolt that made me fall. With a kick with his

---

granted me one more day. I proceed in this way because I believe that the end of my life is near, with which I will have to pay for my ideas. Sometimes I clearly feel that the day is near when my murderer will finally achieve his purpose".

boot, the man rolled me to a corner of the room. I didn't move, pretending I was dead. But he came at me again and fired a second time. I lost consciousness.

Alexandra Stolypin, whose particular epic would merit a few lines, spent the night awake at the bedside of her dying sister, who, after finishing her dreadful tale, closed her eyes and fainted from emotion and exhaustion. A few days later she died.

February/March 1917: second revolutionary act and coup d'état

When the Russian General Staff was convinced of the chances of winning the war and seven million soldiers were preparing to launch the spring offensive agreed with France and England, the revolution of February/March 1917, also known as the 'Kerensky revolution', took place, triggering the coup d'état that forced the abdication of the tsar and put a government of Freemasons headed by Prince Lvov into power. In his memoirs Pavel Milyukov reveals that on 13 August 1915 a meeting was held in Pavel Ryabushinsky's flat, where a preliminary list of the future Provisional Government was drawn up, in which only the Jewish lawyer Kerensky was missing. Very recently, in the aforementioned article on the website of the Grand Lodge of British Columbia and Yukon, Andrei Priahin confirms the information and confirms that in 1916 the Freemasons had agreed on the list of ministers of the government that was to take power after the fall of the Tsar. According to this Freemason, the agreement was reached in the flat of Yekaterina Kuskova, but the list was slightly altered in the same year in the flat of Prince Lvov and in the suite of the "Frantsiya" hotel in St. Petersburg. Priahin confirms that all the members of the Provisional Government that took power in Russia in March 1917 were Freemason brothers. So too, although Priahin does not acknowledge it, was Pavel Milyukov, whose connection with Freemasonry and with Jacob himself Schiff leaves no room for doubt.

Andrei Priahin writes that Alexander Kerensky (1881-1970) "had been specially trained for his future position". He adds that some of the members of the Supreme Council also managed to participate in the Bolshevik government and notes that Tereshchenko (temporarily) and Nekrasov (permanently) cooperated in the trade organisations of the USSR. All this is also confirmed by Boris Nikolayevsky in *The Russian Freemasons and the Russian Revolution* (1990), a work published in Russian in Moscow and cited as a source by J. Lina. There is therefore no doubt that the "good Masons" were part of the conspiracy that brought communism to Russia. Let us recall that among the Freemasons who did not cease to work for the overthrow of the Tsar was Woodrow Wilson, elevated to the presidency of the United States, as we know, by international Jewish banking, Zionism and

Freemasonry. It has already been mentioned above that the start of the revolution on 23 February/March 8 was timed to coincide with Purim, the annual Jewish holiday celebrating the extermination of seventy-five thousand Persians, according to the Old Testament.

Alongside the defeatist propaganda of the Judeo-Bolsheviks, who were constantly stirring up the masses against the war and accusing the Tsar and his generals of wanting to exterminate the entire Russian people, the slogan of the Freemasons was "For democracy, against Tsarism! It is evident that the violent and disloyal speeches of the liberal Freemasons in Parliament, such as those delivered at the end of 1916 by the aforementioned Milyukov, were of great help and were perfectly exploited by the revolutionary parties, which, taking advantage of difficulties in the supply of St. Petersburg, intensified the agitation during the month of February. Difficulties in the transport system due to snowstorms caused shortages in the city, and in some districts queues began to form outside bakeries. At the same time, many of the city's factories had to close due to a lack of materials. Both factors combined and conveniently exploited were of great importance. St. Petersburg, the city with the largest Jewish population in the country outside the settlement areas, had been during the war years the main centre of armaments production in Russia and consequently had the largest industrial population in the country. With the closure of the factories, idle workers began to appear in large numbers on the streets of the capital, which became increasingly crowded. On 21 February and 6 March, the government, trying to anticipate the problems, introduced Cossack units into the city. The atmosphere became increasingly tense, and many shop owners began to board up shop windows and windowsills. In factories that were still operating, workers were being urged to strike. The tsar was not in the city, as he was at the front with the troops.

On 23 February/8 March about ninety thousand workers walked off the job, citing supply difficulties, and a general strike was declared, which took effect the next day. In addition to the Purim holiday, the international holiday of the women's proletariat was celebrated and a crowd of women took to the streets in protest against the shortage of bread. Veteran agitators of the 1905 revolution took charge of organising demonstrations in the working-class districts, marching behind red flags and sometimes singing the Marseillaise. At the corner of Nevsky Street and the Catherine Canal the mounted police dispersed the crowd with the help of the Cossacks without casualties; but the next day, early in the morning, these same parts of the capital were crowded by a more enraged mob which stretched as far as the St. Nicholas station. The cars could not move. The Cossack cavalry received orders to disperse the demonstrations on Nevsky Street and repeatedly charged the masses. Some people were trampled by horses. The Cossacks, however, used only the flat parts of their sabres and never used their firearms, which emboldened the crowd. On the outskirts of there were clashes between the workers and the police. A bomb was thrown on a detachment of gendarmes and several policemen were killed. Three hundred thousand people were involved in the strikes and demonstrations, a figure which may seem very high, but in reality it can be said that, from the beginning to the end, the organised revolts achieved their goal with surprisingly few people, considering that there were 180 million people in the Russian Empire at that time.

On 25 February/10 March a committee of workers' delegates was formed which became the sole leadership of the movement. According to Arsene de Goulévitch, the main organiser was the Social-Democrat Yuri Steklov (Nakhamkis), a 32nd degree Freemason and son-in-law of Kerensky who was in reality an agent of Germany who had been conveniently paid off at the beginning of hostilities. De Goulévitch points out that this character posed for tactical reasons as an internationalist close to the Mensheviks, but later openly aligned himself with the Bolsheviks. Once the council of workers' delegates had been set up, almost all the factories ceased production. However, the supply difficulties had already been remedied in the bakeries, where supplies had returned to normal after the receipt of supplementary rations of bread. In the afternoon large crowds gathered around St. Nicholas station. In *Behind Communism* Frank L. Briton reproduces the account of the American photographer Donald Thompson, an eyewitness to the events:

"About two o'clock a man richly clad in furs arrived in the square in a sledge and ordered the driver to pass through the crowd, which was already very upset, though it seemed willing to make way for him. The man was impatient and perhaps cold and began to reason. All Russians feel the need to argue. Well, he misjudged the crowd, and he also misread the situation in St. Petersburg. I was a hundred and fifty feet from the scene. He was pulled from the sledge and beaten. He took refuge in a tramway station, where he was chased by the workers. One of them took a small iron bar and chopped off his head. This seemed to give the masses a taste for blood. I was immediately dragged along with the crowd which surged down Nevsky Street and began to smash shop windows and create general disorder. Many of the men carried red flags and sticks. Most of the shops on Nevsky Street are protected by heavy iron shutters. Those without were smashed. At this time I observed ambulances coming and going in the side streets, there were usually three or four people lying in each."

Disorder became widespread. The decisive moment came when the mob, well armed and organised, moved angrily towards the various police barracks, whose officers barricaded themselves inside the buildings in a last desperate attempt to resist. Almost all were massacred and their bodies dragged through the streets. The few policemen who surrendered in the hope of saving their lives were killed. The prisons were then emptied. Among the released prison population were the worst criminals. Police archives were burned. Control of St. Petersburg thus passed into the hands of the angry masses and chaos ensued in the city. The life of any well-dressed person was in danger if he dared to appear in public. It can be said that on 26 February/11 March the military government of St. Petersburg, in the hands of General Sergei Khabalov, had lost control. From the suburbs the workers flocked en masse to the city centre. The massacres of policemen who still resisted the detachments of armed men continued, and it can be said that the police force was practically annihilated. The riots, reinforced by the ravages of the newly freed criminals, who roamed free, became widespread.

Alexander Netchvolodow, a general in the Imperial Army and author of several works, gives in *L'empereur Nicolas II et les juifs* the testimony of a soldier who took part in the coup d'état. This soldier, a simple fellow who worked as a carpenter before joining the military service, after a month's leave returned to his detachment at the front, where in the presence of the officers he declared to the general that on 26 February a group of young men, perhaps students, were enrolling soldiers in the streets and stations of Rostov to take them to Petrograd to fight "for freedom of the press and for freedom, so that everyone would become a citizen and have all his rights". To the question whether they had received money he replied, "Certainly, Mr. General, at the Rostov station we were given fifty roubles, and in Petrograd, at the State Duma, we were given still fifty roubles more." According to this account, on 28 February they arrived before nightfall at the St. Petersburg station, where Alexandr Guchkov, one of the Masons in the conspiracy who was Minister of Defence in the first cabinet of the Provisional Government, was waiting for them. After making a speech, Guchkov gave the order for them to be handed weapons that had been transported to the station in trucks. I was given a rifle," the soldier declared, "which I had to return on my way back, but those who received revolvers kept them. They were nice, big revolvers." Asked where they spent the night, he said that the first night he had spent in a barracks and the following nights at random with his comrades in private houses, but that they had been well received everywhere and well fed. Asked if he had had to fight, he replied that he had not had the opportunity, although he admitted that some of them had fired on police officers in the city. The soldier said that in the Duma, where the new government was about to be formed, there were many people and everyone could make a speech, since there was freedom of speech and freedom of the press. Finally, he was asked why he had returned to the front. The man pointed out that those who were not from Petrograd had nothing more to do there, since they had run out of money.

Instead of showing solidarity with the government and denouncing that thousands of policemen were being killed by organised and well-armed revolutionaries, the Duma elements supporting the revolution managed to get the following catastrophic message sent to the Tsar, who was on his way by train to St. Petersburg: "The situation is serious. The government is paralysed. The situation, as regards transport, food supplies and fuel, has reached a point of complete disorganisation. Discontent is growing among the police. Uncontrolled gunfire erupts in the streets. Different sections of the troops are firing at each other. Immediate confidence must be placed in a person who has the backing of the country with the creation of a new government." Unfortunately, the tsar's reaction was inadequate, not in keeping with the reality of the situation. It is certain that he did not even have an idea of what was really going on. In an out-of-tune decision, Nicholas II ordered the dissolution of the Parliament, the majority of which would have been loyal to the Tsar if a vote had been taken.

It should be borne in mind, however, that this Duma, which was the fourth, had been elected in 1912 and its five-year term of office had been extended until after the Easter holidays. On 27 February/12 March the Duma, already dissolved by the emperor, was meeting in an unofficial session to examine the situation. Most of the parliamentarians were baffled, and it was the influential Masonic deputies who took control. Milyukov himself, leader of the Kadets, later wrote: "The success or failure of the revolutionary movement depended on the participation or abstention of the Duma". The evidence is clear: the role of the Duma was decisive for the leaders of the rebellion. The Speaker of the House, the Freemason Mikhail Rodzyanko of the Octubrist Party, sent a new message to the Tsar: "The situation is worsening. Important measures must be taken immediately. Tomorrow it will be too late. The last hour has struck and the fate of the fatherland and the dynasty is being decided". It remains to be seen whether the emperor ever read this text, which went unanswered.

On the same day the two governmental organs were formed which were to run Russia for eight months until the October revolution. While the Duma rushed to form a provisional committee, consisting of twelve members and headed by Prince Lvov, the council of workers' and soldiers' delegates organised itself definitively and formed the St. Petersburg Soviet, dominated by the Mensheviks and Bolsheviks of the Social-Democratic Workers' Party of Russia and seconded by the Socialist Revolutionary Party. Its chairman was initially Cheidze, leader of the Social Democrats in the Duma, and the vice-chairman was the Bolshevik Skobelev, but the key man was the famous Kerensky, who was part of the Provisional Government and played the key role of connecting agent between these two bodies that had emerged from the revolution.

The group of Freemasons who had set up the Provisional Committee soon became the Provisional Government, which ruled with the permission and tolerance of the St. Petersburg Soviet, which played the role of watchful guardian of the government's actions and gradually ceded power to the Bolshevik faction which was to take the lead months later in the third and final act of the revolution. As in the first act of 1905, the Soviet was at first composed of the leaders of the cells operating in the factories, but this time the soldiers' delegates also took part in it. One hundred and fifty members attended the first meetings, but on successive days the number increased to a thousand delegates. From the very day of its formation, 27 February/12 March, the Soviet published its organ *Izvestia*, which had already functioned in 1905. In the first issue a clearly Bolshevik and internationalist ideological manifesto appeared as a supplement. Here is a significant paragraph: "The most urgent work of the Provisional Government consists in agreeing directly with the proletariat of the belligerent countries for the revolutionary struggle of the peoples of all countries against their oppressors and exploiters, the imperialist governments and their capitalist cliques, and for the immediate cessation of the bloody slaughter imposed by them on the enslaved peoples". These words are sarcasm when one considers that the bankers who enriched themselves by the world war are the same bankers who financed the revolution in Russia, and that the Russo-Japanese war was defrayed and imposed on Russia by Jacob Schiff, the same Jewish banker who financed Trotsky.

The role of the British was also significant, especially Lord Milner, who financed the revolution with more than 21 million roubles, and the Masonic ambassador Buchanan, a tireless conspirator from the Embassy. St. Petersburg was full of British agents lodged in private homes, handing out money to the soldiers and inciting them to mutiny. In the early morning of the same day, 27 February - 12 March, a sergeant of the Volynski regiment shot a commander, and from this event began a rebellion of the soldiers, who killed their officers. The killing of army officers was a constant. By eleven o'clock in the morning, eleven regiments had joined the revolt, and horrible crimes were committed in all of them. According to Jüri Lina, sixty soldiers were killed in Kronstadt alone, among them Admiral von Wiren, who had both arms cut off and was dragged through the streets alive until the revolutionaries took pity on him and killed him. Lina, citing Stasnislav Govorukhin's documentary *The Russia We Lost*, Govorukhin, reports that in Vyborg, officers were thrown off a bridge onto rocks and elsewhere bayoneted or beaten to death. At half past eleven the same morning the garrison of the Peter and Paul Fortress in St. Petersburg surrendered and joined the revolution. Two days later, on 1/14 March, the St. Petersburg Soviet issued "Prikaz" No. 1 (order) which meant the destruction of any discipline in the army. The revolution had triumphed and henceforth the instructions of the Soviet were accepted without question by the Provisional Government. On 3/16 March, Tsar Nicholas II, whose train never reached St. Petersburg, abdicated.

As soon as he heard of the events in St. Petersburg, he sent a telegraph dispatch to General Khabalov ordering him to put an end to the disturbances in the capital, which were "inadmissible in this painful wartime. The general in turn telegraphed the emperor and acknowledged that he had been unable to maintain order in the city. Following news of the military rebellion of 27/12, Nicholas II granted dictatorial powers to Prime Minister Nikolai Golitzyn, who was arrested before he could exercise them. At the same time he ordered General Ivanov with a battalion of Knights of the Cross of St. George to take a train to St. Petersburg, where he was to replace General Khabalov and assume military command of the city. At the same time, three additional battalions, stationed in Finland in anticipation of a German invasion, were ordered to be sent to St. Petersburg and placed under the command of the new military governor of the capital. But the revolutionaries had prepared the coup well, and the railway personnel had been conveniently infiltrated. The railway network in the vicinity of the capital had been in the hands of the insurgents since 27 February, and rail access to the city was under their control. In addition, in the north, near the Finnish border, the tracks were immediately dismantled, which prevented the troops travelling from there. General Ivanov, for his part, did not manage to approach the vicinity of St. Petersburg until 1/14 March. By then the situation seemed irreversible and the Tsar himself ordered him not to take any action. In fact, Nicholas II himself had decided on 27/12 to go to Tsarskoye Seló, the residence of the imperial family in St. Petersburg, where he never arrived, as his train was stopped by order of the new masters of the railway network.

The Provisional Committee then addressed the General Chief of the General Staff, Mikhail Alexeyev, and notified him that the revolution, which held St. Petersburg, Cronstadt and the Baltic Fleet, was spreading throughout the country, and that resistance to the revolutionary movement would only lead to civil war, fatal while at war with an external enemy. The "good Masons" also added that the movement was above all directed against Nicholas II, who should abdicate in the interests of the country and the dynasty itself. General Alexeyev, who shortly afterwards bitterly regretted his error of judgement, allowed himself to be convinced by these arguments and passed on to the various military commanders information similar to that announced to him from the capital. The idea that the only possible solution to save Russia and the dynasty was abdication eventually prevailed, and Alexeyev asked his colleagues to address a plea to the Tsar to this effect. Nicholas II, convinced that his generals were acting out of patriotism and love for the monarchy and trying to avoid the predicted civil war, abdicated on 2/15 March, on his own behalf and on behalf of his haemophiliac son, in favour of his brother Grand Duke Michael.

The latter was in the capital and was warned by the Masons of the Provisional Committee that they were not in a position to vouch for his life. Finally, at Kerensky's particular insistence, Grand Duke Michael refused to accept the throne and handed over power to the Committee, although it was understood that his resignation was valid until such time as the Constituent Assembly decided on the form of government. General Alexeyev had only a short time to understand the true extent of the events unfolding, and on March 3/16 he confessed: "I shall never forgive myself for having believed in the sincerity of certain people, for having accepted their advice, and for having sent the telegram concerning the Emperor's abdication to the chiefs of the Armed Forces". Nicholas II wrote a farewell message to the army, but it never reached the military, as it was intercepted by the Provisional Government, which forbade its publication for fear that it might provoke a patriotic movement.

Zionism's support for the February/March revolution has been ignored, but it was very significant. The Petrograd Zionist Assembly was quick to issue a resolution which read: 'Russian Jewry is called upon to support the Provisional Government in every possible way, for enthusiastic work, for national organisation and consolidation for the benefit of the prosperity of Jewish national life in Russia and the national and political revival of the Jewish nation in Palestine'. George Kennan[47] reports on a rally held on 23 March 1917 at Carnegie Hall, where thousands of Marxists, socialists and anarchists gathered to celebrate the abdication of Nicholas II. There, publicly reported that through the Society of Friends of Russian Freedom, funded by Jacob Schiff, the revolutionary gospel had been spread among Russian officers and soldiers held in Japanese prison camps during the 1904-1905 war. The next day, 24 March, *The New York Times* published a telegram from Jacob Schiff to the attendees in which he regretted not being able to attend the event and described the February coup and the Tsar's resignation as the event "for which they had waited and for which they had fought long years".

In April 1917 the Russian Zionist movement was powerfully reinforced by a public statement by Jacob Schiff, who had decided to unreservedly join the Zionists. The statement said that Schiff, "fearing Jewish assimilation as a result of civil equality for Jews in Russia, believed that Palestine could become the centre for spreading the ideals of Jewish culture throughout the world". All the falsehood and hypocrisy of the financiers of the revolution is revealed in these words. In other words, while calling for equal rights, they feared racial assimilation. At the beginning of May the Zionists staged a big rally at the Petrograd Stock Exchange, during which the Zionist anthem was played repeatedly. At the end of May, an All-Russian Zionist Conference was held at the Petrograd Conservatory, where the main Zionist goals were outlined: cultural revival of the Jewish nation,

---

[47] George F. Kennan, an information officer in the US State Department, considered an expert on communist-related issues, who held the post of Chargé d'Affaires in Moscow, sent the famous "long telegram" to the State Department in 1946. In this 8,000-word telegram, signed Mr. X, he concluded that the main element of US policy towards the Soviet Union should be "patient and continued vigilant restraint" towards the expansionist tendencies of Russian communism. The "long telegram" was published in 1947 by the prestigious journal *Foreign Affairs*.

increased emigration to Palestine and mobilisation of Jewish capital for the financing of Jewish settlers.

The fact that the revolution of February/March 1917 is also known as the "Kerensky revolution" indicates the decisive role played by this character. Kerensky's mother was a Jew surnamed Adler (Nadezhda) who was married twice. Her first husband was a Jew with the surname Kürbis. She remarried to Fyodor Kerensky, a teacher who adopted little Aaron Kürbis. In *Wall Street and the Bolshevik Revolution*, Anthony C. Sutton cites Freemason Richard Crane, advisor to US Secretary of State Robert Lansing, as one of the men who supported Kerensky from the United States. Kerensky had also initially received support from Jewish banker Grigori Berenson, who in 1930 emerged as a committed Zionist. The Austrian politician and scientist Karl Steinhauser reveals in *EG - Die Super-UdSSR von Morgen* that the British ambassador in St. Petersburg, the Freemason George Buchanan, was the contact between Kerensky and London, Paris and Washington, which confirms once again the miserable and treacherous role of the British ambassador with an allied country. Buchanan on 21 March told journalists of *Russkoie Slovo*: "The autocratic and reactionary regime has never inspired us with sympathy.... That is why the advent of the Provisional Government is enthusiastically acclaimed all over Britain.[48]

The Freemason Andrei Priahin, as we know, revealed that Kerensky "had been specially trained for his future post". Alexander Kerensky (Aaron Kürbis), in addition to being deputy chairman of the St. Petersburg Soviet, held three posts in the Provisional Government, each more important than the last: first as Minister of Justice, from which he invited Trotsky and Lenin to return to Russia, and from which he appointed Pyotr (Pinhas) Rutenberg, the Jewish, Freemason and Zionist terrorist who had organised the "Bloody Sunday" with Alexander Parvus, as Chief of Police. Rutenberg was one of the founders of the Jewish Legion, which fought alongside the British during the war. Kerensky's second post was that of Minister of War, a position in which he succeeded Guchkov. Finally, following the resignation of Prince Lvov on 7/20 July, he was appointed Prime Minister, a post he held when he finally ceded power to the Bolsheviks. According to historian Sergei Yemelyanov, Kerensky, who during the three years preceding the coup

---

[48] In a speech to the Anglo-Russian Society, reproduced in part by the same newspaper *Russkoie Slovo* on 12 April 1917, Ambassador Buchanan insists on publicly expressing his duplicity. The last time," he said, "that I had the honour of addressing the members of the Anglo-Russian Society was precisely on the eve of the session of the Duma at which my honourable friend Milyukov made his famous speech in which he drove the first nail into the coffin of the old regime. I said then that we must not only come to a victorious end, but that the final victory must be achieved over the enemy within our own camp. Today I can congratulate the Russian people on having got rid of such an enemy so quickly. Certainly, it takes a great deal of cynicism to speak of the "enemy within one's own camp" when one has conspired from the embassy against a country that was behaving in the war as a loyal friend and ally.

devoted himself exclusively to the defence of revolutionary terrorists, was a 33rd degree Freemason.

All the members of the Provisional Government were Freemasons. Among the most prominent, apart from Kerensky himself, were Nikolai Nekrasov, Minister of Communications; Pavel Milyukov, Foreign Minister and leader of the Kadets; and Mikhail Tereshchenko, Minister of Finance. The latter was a young Ukrainian-born millionaire who invested money in the revolutionary movement. His good relationship with the Rothschilds of "New Court" (London) is commented on by Niall Ferguson, who writes that Tereshchenko proved to be a good friend of the Jews. His appointment as finance minister was widely celebrated by the Rothschilds, who soon saw their optimism justified. The new minister had no time to write to London to offer the Rothschilds to underwrite a loan of one million roubles, issued by the Kerensky government to keep Russia in the war.

As for Foreign Minister Milyukov, on 19 March he received a telegram from the banker Jacob Schiff, who now pretended to be a friend of Russia and put it in these terms: "Permit me, as irreconcilable enemy of the tyrannical autocracy which mercilessly persecuted our co-religionists, to congratulate through you the Russian people on the action you have just so brilliantly accomplished, and to wish your comrades in the new government and yourself complete success in the great task you have so patriotically undertaken." In his reply, Milyukov showed solidarity with the Jewish banker who had launched Japan against his country, and, besides reiterating old Masonic and Illuminist ideas, addressed him as if he represented the United States: "We are united with you in common hatred and antipathy for the old regime, now overthrown, let me be equally united with you for the realisation of new ideas of equality, liberty and concord among peoples, participating in the universal struggle against the Dark Ages, militarism and autocratic power proceeding from divine right. Please accept our thanks for your congratulations, which enable us to determine the change brought about by a beneficial coup d'état in the reciprocal relations between our two countries".

In *No One Dares Call It a Conspiracy*, Gary Allen refers to document no. 861.00/5339 from the State Department archives, which records the plans of various Jewish leaders to overthrow the Tsar. Among the names that appear are once again Jacob Schiff, so influential within the Masonic organisation B'nai B'rith, and his colleagues Felix Warburg, Otto Kahn, Isaac Seligman, Mortimer Schiff and others. All of them Jewish bankers. Also the *Encyclopedia of Jewish Knowledge* acknowledges in its article "Schiff" (New York, 1938) that Alexander Kerensky, the man who had been trained specifically for his mission, received a million dollars from Jacob Schiff.

As early as April, Kerensky's Provisional Government issued an order by telegraph for the release without individual investigation of all Jews suspected of espionage who had gone into exile. Some of them resided in occupied territories, but others could return safely. Many deportees asked for permission to live in the cities of the European part of Russia. Immediately there was an influx of Jews to Petrograd, where in 1917 their numbers increased to 50,000, and to Moscow, where they reached 60,000. Numerous Jewish émigrés from New York returned to Russia. Many who lived in Britain also declared their readiness to return to take up the struggle for the new social and democratic Russia. From London alone, some 10,000 expressed their willingness to travel. The Provisional Government initially decided to hold the Emperor and the Imperial family in Tsarskoye Selo, but in August the ineffable Kerensky decided to move them all to Tobolsk in Siberia. Once Nicholas II was overthrown, the Masonic government dispensed with the national anthem *God Save the Tsar*, which coincidentally had been composed by Prince Lvov and written by the poet Vasily Zhukovsky. In its place was adopted a hymn pleasing to Freemasonry and Jewry, entitled *The Glorious Lord in Zion*.

Leon Trotsky (Leiba Bronstein)

Next to Marx and Lenin, Trotsky ranks third in the saints' calendar of the world left. Trotsky has gone down in history as a myth, whose popularity and prestige remain intact. Propaganda has always presented him as a gigantic personality. The media, encyclopaedias and books in general continue to regard him as a progressive and revolutionary intellectual who devoted his life to the struggle for the cause of the proletariat. From now on we shall see that the truth is quite different: Trotsky was an agent of international banking, an unscrupulous cynic who married the daughter of a banker close to the great Jewish banking families.

Leiba Bronstein was the name he was given when he was born in Yanova, a village in Khertson province, Ukraine, on 25 October 1879. His father, David Bronstein, was a wealthy landowner who owned virtually all the land in the village. At the age of seven he attended a Jewish school taught in Hebrew and began to study the *Talmud*. At seventeen, a Czech Jew, Franz Schwigowsky, introduced him to a secret society, the Workers' League, whose members were arrested in 1898. The young Bronstein, who had already joined Freemasonry in 1897, spent two years incarcerated in an Odessa prison, where he devoted himself to studying the history of secret societies and delving deeper into Freemasonry. In fact, in the initiation to the 33rd degree it is stated that "Freemasonry is nothing more and nothing less than revolution in action; continuous conspiracy." From Odessa he was exiled to Siberia, from where he escaped in 1902 to Vienna. There he met Victor Adler, a Jewish revolutionary and Freemason who published the newspaper *Arbeiter Zeitung*. Shortly afterwards he went to London, where, unknown to us, he came into contact with another high-ranking Jewish

Freemason and enlightened man named Israel Helphand, although he called himself Alexander Parvus. It was Parvus who turned Leiba Bronstein into Leon Trotsky in late 1902. Trotsky, as mentioned above, returned to Russia in 1905 in the company of Alexander Parvus to organise the revolution. In addition to organising and chairing the "workers' delegates' soviet", Trotsky edited with Parvus the newspaper *Nachalo* (*The Principle*). Igor Bunich, author of the book *Zoloto Partii* (*The Gold of the Party*) (St. Petersburg, 1992), claims that Parvus was the main organiser of the 1905 revolution and that he received £2 million from the Japanese to plan the seizure of power in Russia.

Jüri Lina states in *Under the Sign of the Scorpion* that Trotsky, with the help of Alexander Parvus, came to the conclusion that the purpose of Freemasonry was to eliminate national states and cultures in order to establish Jewish world domination. Trotsky, writes Lina, "thus became a convinced internationalist, who was taught by Parvus that the Jewish people were their own collective Messiah, that they would achieve dominion over other peoples through the mixing of races and the elimination of national boundaries, and that an international republic was to be created, in which the Jews would be the leading element, since no one else would be able to understand and control the masses". It was Parvus who instilled in Trotsky the idea of "permanent revolution".

The writer Maxim Gorky, whose agent Parvus was in Europe, complained that Parvus had stolen one hundred and thirty thousand gold-marks from him and called him a miser and a swindler. Alexander Parvus, born in 1867, was about twelve years older than Trotsky. He had worked for several years in various banks in Germany and Switzerland and was also a skilled publicist. Parvus knew Russian history and was convinced that if the nobility and the intelligentsia were eliminated, the country would be defenceless and could easily be thrown into the flames of revolution. Parvus and Trotsky, as mentioned above, led the 1905 revolution and were both condemned to exile in Siberia. Trotsky did not manage to flee until February 1907, but Parvus did so at once and made his way to Constantinople, where he served as an adviser to the Young Turks (Jewish converts to Islam, as we know). At this time he established contacts with German diplomats, who were to be of great use to him later on, and managed to accumulate a lot of money through his activity as a mediator in the German-Turkish trade. However, it was during the Balkan War (1912-13) that he made a fortune that made him a multimillionaire. His commercial transactions covered a wide range of goods. His coal business alone earned him nearly 30 million Danish kroner in gold. For a time, this Illuminati agent was also a collaborator of Rosa Luxemburg, with whom he appears in numerous photographs. A leading epigone of Adam Weishaupt, indecent and cynical if ever there was one, but at the same time fiendishly cunning and intelligent, while preaching the permanent revolution that was to put an end to private property, Israel Helphand, alias Parvus, led a fabulous lifestyle that included no shortage of orgiastic parties. To get an idea of his wealth, suffice it to say that when he died in 1924 he owned, among other real estate, three houses in Copenhagen, a castle in Switzerland and a palace with thirty-two rooms on an island in Lake Wannsee in Berlin, which is now a museum open to the public.

After escaping from Siberia, Trotsky managed to return to Vienna, where he is known to have met with the Zionist leader Chaim Weizmann. Both Trotsky and Lenin received financial support from Parvus and were even invited to live with him in Munich for a short time. It was in this Munich home of Parvus that Lenin and Rosa Luxemburg met. After having been a war correspondent in the Balkans in 1912, a job provided by Parvus, Trotsky lived in France, where he founded with his co-religionist Julius Martov (Julius Zederbaum) the Russian-language newspaper *Nashe Slovo*. It has been said above that the author Yuri Begunov claims that in the spring of 1914 Trotsky, sent by the Grand Lodge of France, was in Vienna, where he had a meeting with the Freemason brother V. Gacinovic for the purpose of a meeting with him. Gacinovic in order to coordinate the attack on the heir of Austria-Hungary.

Under surveillance by the French police after his participation in the Zimmerwald Conference in September 1915, Trotsky was arrested in Paris because of his inflammatory articles. The Gallic authorities suspended publication of the paper and Trotsky was deported to Spain. In *Wall Street and the Bolshevik Revolution* Anthony Sutton writes that he was "kindly escorted to the Spanish border." A few days later, the internationalist was arrested by the police in Madrid and housed in a "first-class cell", which cost one and a half pesetas a day. It seems clear that "orders" were received for his release, since he was taken to Cadiz, perhaps for the purpose of embarking him. If so, this first option was reconsidered, as the port of Barcelona was finally chosen, where Trotsky was reunited with his family and a group of collaborators and sailed aboard the transatlantic liner *Montserrat* for New York.

On 13 January 1917 Trotsky's group, which included Moses Uritsky, Grigori Chudnovsky and other of his Jewish collaborators who would later play a prominent role in the October revolution, landed in New York. Trotsky made early contact with the B'nai B'rith lodge, of which he became a member. He undoubtedly attained a high degree within the Misraim-Memphis rite, as he belonged to the Shriners Lodge, which only allows entry to Masons who have attained the 32nd degree. Franklin Delano Roosevelt, Alexander Kerensky and Bela Kun, to cite significant examples, were among the select membership of this lodge. In his autobiography *My Life* Trotsky claims that his only profession in New York was that of a socialist revolutionary, which is to say that he lived by his articles in *Novy Mir, the* New York newspaper of the Russian socialists which had been founded by two Jewish comrades, Weinstein and Brailovsky. Two other Jews, Nikolai Bukharin (Dolgolevsky) and V. Volodarsky (Moses Goldstein) worked in the editorial office. The only funds Trotsky admits to having received in 1916 and 1917 are $310, money which, he said, "I distributed among five emigrants returning to Russia." However, the impoverished revolutionary Communist leader is known to have driven around New York in a chauffeur-driven limousine, probably made available to him by one of his banker friends. In addition, the $310 had paid in advance three months' rent for an excellent flat where he lived with his wife, Natalia Sedova, and their two sons, Leon and Sergei.[49]

Natalia Sedova was the daughter of a Jewish banker named Givotvosky. The first reference to the fact that Trotsky was married to a banker's daughter appears in the work *L'empereur Nicolas II et les juifs* 1924). In it Alexander Netchvolodow cites a document, located much later by Anthony Sutton in the State Department's Decimal Files (861.00/5339), which is dated 13 November 1918 and entitled *Bolshevism and Judaism*. The text is a report stating that international Jewish banking is behind the revolutionary events in Russia and cites as involved the leaders of Kuhn, Loeb and Co. banking: Jacob Schiff, Felix Warburg, Otto Kahn, Mortimer Schiff, Jerome H. Hanauer. Two more names of Jewish bankers are added: Guggenheim and Max Breitung. In the second point it is stated: "The Jew Max Warburg also financed Trotsky and company, who were also financed by the Westphalian-Roman syndicate, as well as by another Jew, Olof Aschberg, of the Nya Banken in Stockholm, and also by Givotovsky, a Jew whose daughter is married to Trotsky. In this way relations were established between Jewish billionaires and proletarian Jews."

Anthony Sutton comments on Trotsky's kinship with the Jewish banker and refers to Abram Givatovzo in these terms: "Another Bolshevik banker in Stockholm was Abram Givatovzo, brother-in-law of Trotsky and Lev Kamenev. A State Department report reaffirms that while Givatovzo pretended to be very anti-Bolshevik, he had in fact received through couriers large sums of money from the Bolsheviks to finance revolutionary operations. Givatovzo was part of a syndicate that included Denisov of the former Bank of Siberia, Kamenka of the Don Azov Bank, and Davidov of the Bank of Foreign Trade. This syndicate sold shares in the former Bank of Siberia to the British Government." We see, then, that the inbred practices practised by the Frankists of Jacob Frank were still in full force among the Jewish revolutionaries. It is evident that in Trotsky's case, as in so many others, propaganda has sought to keep secret his marriage to a banker's

---

[49] In 1902 Trotsky had met in Paris Natalia Sedova, his second wife, who was a few years younger than his legal wife, Sokolovskaya, which was completely ignored. In his autobiography Trotsky devotes scarcely a line to commenting on the affair. However, Sokolovskaya bore the communist leader two daughters whom he neglected.

daughter, which is totally inconvenient for the halo of the myth in the eyes of the working class.

The true identity of the Sedova, who was at Trotsky's side in the 1905 revolution, is also revealed by two other authors: the Spaniard Mauricio Carlavilla and the Estonian Jüri Lina. The latter writes: "Natalia Sedovaya-Trotskaya was in fact the daughter of a Zionist banker, Ivan Givotovsky (Abram Givatovzo), who helped finance the Bolsheviks' seizure of power, first in Russia and then in Stockholm, via Nya Banken (a Swedish bank run by the Jewish Aschberg family). This was another reason why Freemason Leon Trotsky always protected the international interests of wealthy Jews. Ivan Givotvosky had close connections with the Warburgs and the Schiffs." For his part Mauricio Carlavilla[50] in *Sinfonía en rojo mayor* puts in Christian

---

[50] About Mauricio Carlavilla and *Sinfonía en rojo mayor* a clarification is very necessary, which will inevitably be a little lengthy, for which we apologise in advance. Julián Mauricio Carlavilla (1896-1982), a policeman, writer and publisher, demonstrated through his works a profound knowledge of communism. As a policeman he carried out infiltration work and it is likely that throughout his police career he obtained information from foreign secret services. He remains virtually unknown, but his tireless work as a writer and publicist deserves recognition. Carlavilla initially published his works under the pseudonym Maurico Karl, although on rare occasions he also used the pseudonym Julien d'Arleville. His works were henceforth to become sources of information, especially those dealing with various aspects of the Second World War. We mention here in advance *Pearl Harbour, Roosevelt's betrayal* (1954) and, above all, his edition of *Sidney Warburg* in Spanish, a very valuable and little-known book, published in 1933 in Holland under the title *De Geldbronnen wan het Nationaal Socialisme,* the translation of which appeared in Spain in 1955 published by NOS under the title *El dinero de Hitler (Hitler's Money)*. Mauricio Carlavilla published his own books and others he considered of interest in the NOS publishing house, which he himself had founded and which was based in his own house.

As for *Sinfonía en rojo mayor*, the first thing to say is that it is a highly cited work on the Internet. The work takes the form of a novelised memoir, those of Dr José Landowski, whose main characters are mostly historical figures. Not knowing at all who Mauricio Carlavilla was, those who mention the work accept the authorship of the narrator, Dr. Landowski, a doctor in the service of the N.K.V.D., and give the work a documentary value that it does not really possess. In my opinion, Landowski is a creation of Carlavilla. The text that is repeatedly quoted on the Internet is the alleged interrogation of Trotskyist leader Christian G. Rakovsky, one of the main defendants in the Trial of Twenty-One, where he was sentenced to twenty years in prison, although he was eventually shot in 1941 together with Maria Spiridonova and Olga Kameneva, Kamenev's wife and Trotsky's sister, in the presence of Dr. Landowsky, on 26 January 1938. The interrogator is a Stalinist agent, Gabriel G. Kuzmin, to whom Rakovsky reveals information of great historical and political value.

The explanation of how and why the confusion arises is simple. For the reader to better understand Carlavilla's literary game, I reproduce below the WARNING at the beginning of the book: "This is the painful translation of some notebooks found on the corpse of Dr. Landowsky, on an island in front of Leningrad, by the Spanish volunteer A. I. He brought them to us. I. He brought them to us. Their reconstruction was slow, laborious, given the state of the manuscripts. It took years. Even longer we hesitated to publish them. So

Rakovsky's mouth these words: "Sedova is the daughter of Givotovsky, linked to the Warburg bankers, partners and relatives of Jacob Schiff, a group that financed Japan and, through Trotsky, at the same time financed the 1905 revolution. This is the reason why Trotsky, in one fell swoop, rose to the top of the revolutionary ladder. And there you have the key to his real personality."

As soon as the news of the coup d'état and the fall of the Czar reached the United States, preparations were rushed to send Trotsky to Russia to lead the third and final act in the tragedy of the Russian people. Edward Mandell House, the Communist and Zionist illuminati, took it upon himself to request President Wilson, the puppet in the hands of the conspirators, to order the issuance of an American passport for the revolutionary. The passport was accompanied by a Russian entry permit and a British travel visa. In *Woodrow Wilson: Disciple of Revolution* (1938) Jennings C. Wise writes that "historians must never forget that Wilson made it possible for Trotsky to enter Russia on an American passport." On 27 March 1917 Trotsky, his family and two hundred and seventy-five other people, including Wall Street brokers, American Jewish Communists and international terrorists, boarded the *Kristianiafjord*. On 3 April the ship called at Halifax, Nova Scotia, and Canadian border police ordered Trotsky, his wife and two children, as well as five other alleged Russian socialists, Nikita Mukhin, Leiba Fishelev, Konstantin Romanenko, Grigori Chusnovsky and Gerson Melichansky, to disembark. All were arrested as they were considered German agents. In the Canadian archives, Trotsky is listed as a German prisoner of war. Two of his closest comrades, Volodarsky (Goldstein) and Uritsky, remained on board. A few days before the arrest, on 29 March, the Canadians had received a telegram from London stating that Leiba Bronstein, who was in possession of $10,000, and his comrades were going to Russia to start a revolution against the Government. The Canadian secret service was convinced that

---

marvellous and incredible were his revelations of the end that we would never have decided to publish these memoirs if the actual men and facts did not give them full authenticity. Before these memoirs saw the light of day, we have prepared ourselves for trial and controversy. We personally vouch for the absolute truth of its capital facts. We will see if anyone is able to refute them with evidence or reason. The translator, Mauricio Carlavilla". In other words, the text, which in some editions exceeds six hundred pages, would be the memoirs of a doctor who, when he died, carried them with him in handwritten notebooks. A careful reading of *Sinfonía en rojo mayor* reveals that it is in fact a work written, not translated, by Carlavilla himself, in which, in addition to his own erudition and assessment of the events recounted, he demonstrates his exclusive knowledge. Carlavilla uses a novelistic plot to reveal everything he knows, which is a lot, about what was going on in the USSR before the Second World War. In other words, and we return to the quotation from the text, long before J. Lina and A. Sutton, Carlavilla had information about who Natalia Sedova, Trotsky's second wife, was, and he reveals it through C. Rakovsky, who, during a very long interrogation attended by José Landowski, the supposed first-person narrator of *Sinfonía en rojo mayor*, reveals all the information that Carlavilla knows and intends to divulge.

Trotsky, who spoke German better than Russian, was an agent acting on the orders of the German Government.

The misunderstanding lasted about two weeks, during which time all sorts of pressures were brought to bear to get Trotsky released. Despite the fact that Russia would sign peace with the Central Empires if the Bolsheviks ended the Provisional Government, which was "supposedly" against British interests, Lord Melchett and Sir. Herbert Samuel, members of the Grand Lodge of England, run by Zionist Jews, intervened with the Lloyd George Government. At the same time the British Embassy in Washington received a request from the State Department not only to order the Canadian authorities to release the detainee, but also to assist him in any way necessary. Subsequently, the ubiquitous Bernard Baruch, answering questions from a US Senate Committee, admitted that it was under his responsibility that Trotsky had been released twice. Pressure, then, finally brought about the counter-order. The Canadian authorities were instructed to inform the press that Trotsky was an American citizen travelling on a passport and that his release had been requested by the State Department in Washington. Thus Leon Trotsky and his party were able to continue their journey and on 4 May 1917, via Sweden and Finland, they arrived in Petrograd to lead the revolution. Thousands of extremist Yiddish-speaking Jews among them were massing in the capital. To this influx of revolutionaries who had left Russia during the Stolypin years must be added the influx of tens of thousands of prisoners from Siberia, who had been released by the Provisional Government.

Lenin

Until recently it had been said that Lenin, whose real name was Vladimir Ilych Ulyanov, was the only non-Jew of the twenty-five men who assumed the leadership of Russia. It was also accepted that he was born on 22 April 1870 in Simbirsk. Both of these are now disputed and are certainly false. Since the fall of communism, various research studies on Lenin have been carried out, the results of which are presented by Jüri Lina in *Under the Sign of the Scorpion*. The following is a very brief summary.

As for his birth, it is known that both Lenin and Stalin changed the dates and that the official biographies of both were manipulated for propaganda purposes. It is not in our interest to dwell on this question now and we prefer to provide information about their origins. It seems that their grandparents both ended up in institutions for the mentally ill. Lenin's father, Ilya Ulyanov, a Kalmuck, was a school inspector, and his mother, Maria, whose maiden name was Blank, came from a noble family and was the daughter of a wealthy landowner. Maria Blank's father, Israel, was born in 1802 in Starokonstantinovo, Volnya province. Israel Blank and his brother Abel wanted to study at the St. Petersburg Medical Academy, and to gain admission they were baptised in the Russian Orthodox Church. Israel took the name Alexander and Abel took the name Dimitri. Both graduated in 1824. Alexander became a military doctor and pioneered the study of spas in Russia.

The writer Marietta Shanginyan discovered Lenin's Jewish roots in 1930, but was unable to reveal what was considered a state secret. Only in 1990 was it possible to publish this information. Until then, the Blank family had been presented as "Germans". Maria's maternal grandfather Blank, the notary Johan-Gottlieb Grosschopf, came from a German merchant family. Maria Blank's paternal grandparents were Jewish, which makes Maria Blank, who spoke Yiddish, German and Swedish, at least half-Jewish, as only her father was Jewish. However, some researchers have suggested that the Grosschopf family was Jewish. If so, Lenin would be Jewish, for, as far as we know, Jews consider anyone born of a Jewish mother to be Jewish. Another recent revelation in Russia concerns Lenin's paternal grandfather, Nikolai Ulyanov, who had four children with his own daughter Alexandra Ulyanova, who passed herself off as Anna Smirnova to the authorities. Lenin's father, Ilya, was to be the fourth child, born when Nicolai Ulyanov was already sixty-seven years old. Ilya Ulyanov married the Jewish Maria Blank, and German was spoken in the family, a language Lenin knew better than Russian. Soviet propaganda, in order to strengthen the myth, claimed that his parents consciously educated Lenin to be the Messiah who would lead the proletariat. In a 1989 poll, seventy percent of respondents believed Lenin to be the greatest personality in history.

Yuri Slezkine in *The Jewish Century* (2004) confirms that Lenin was Jewish. Slezkine writes that it was Lenin's sister Anna who in 1924 told Kamenev, who said: "I had always suspected it". Bukharin reportedly commented, "And what do we care about your opinion? The real question is: what are we going to do?" Slezkine adds, "What they were going to do, or rather what the party, through the Lenin Institute, was going to do, was to decide that this information 'should not be made public' and to decree that it should be 'kept secret'." In 1932 Anna Ilinitchna, arguing that the discovery constituted decisive scientific proof of "the exceptional abilities of the Semitic tribe", asked Stalin to reconsider the decision. According to the author, Stalin ordered her to "maintain absolute silence".

As for his relations with Freemasonry, Lenin was already a Freemason in 1890. According to Karl Steinhauser, he belonged to the *Art et Travail* lodge in Switzerland and France. Oleg Platonov claims that Lenin was a 31st degree Freemason (Grand Commander Inquisitor Inspector). Not only Trotsky and Lenin were Masons: various Masonic scholars who have researched B'nai B'rith note that Lenin, Zinoviev, Radek and Sverdlov belonged to this Jewish lodge. Both Lenin and Trotsky participated in the 1910 International Masonic Conference in Copenhagen. A surprising text on the relationship of communism with Freemasonry and the Illuminati was written by Winston Churchill, who, before he himself joined the ranks of the conspiracy for good, confirmed in an article entitled "Zionism and Communism", published on 8 February 1920 in the *London Illustrated Sunday Herald*, that both Lenin and Trotsky belonged to the circle of Masonic and Illuminati conspirators. Churchill wrote: "From the days of 'Spartacus' Weishaupt to those of Karl Marx and on to those of Trotsky (Russia), Bela Kun (Hungary), Rosa Luxemburg (Germany) and Emma Goldstein (United States), this world-wide conspiracy for the overthrow of civilisation and for the reconstruction of a society based on restrained development, greedy malice and impossible equality has been steadily growing". Churchill acknowledged in this lengthy 1920 article that the group behind Spartacus-Weishaupt had driven all the subversive movements of the 19th century. While noting that Zionism and Communism competed for the soul of the Jewish people, Churchill was concerned about the role of Jews in the Bolshevik revolution and the existence of an international Jewish conspiracy.

Oleg Agranyants, an intelligence agent responsible for KGB operations in North Africa, worked under diplomatic cover in the Tunisian embassy until he defected to the United States in May 1986. It is to him that we owe the startling revelations about various "sacred cows" of Russian communism that appear in a work entitled *What is to be done? or the most important work of our time - The Deninisation of our Society* (London, 1989). Of particular interest here is one piece of information that clarifies the origin of the name Lenin. Agranyants explains that, contrary to popular belief, Lenin trusted Stalin. However, Lenin's Jewish wife, Nadezhda Krupskaya, had several clashes with Stalin before and after her husband's death: Krupskaya wanted Trotsky to be Lenin's successor and clashed with Stalin, who threatened to reveal publicly that Lenin's real wife was Stasova. According to Agranyants, Elena Stasova, a Bolshevik also of Jewish origin who lived for 93 years, repeatedly stated that Lenin had used her name, Lena, as his pseudonym. The encyclopaedia *Russipedia* corroborates Agranyants' information in an article in which it reproduces a telephone communication between Stalin and Krupskaya on 23 December 1922, when Lenin's health was already very poor. In this conversation Stalin severely insults her. Nadezhda Krupskaya, who defended the right to rape, knew about her husband's relations with other women and even with other men, since Lenin was bisexual.

Letters have recently come to light showing that she was in love with Grigory Zinoviev (Gerson Radomylsky). Jüri Lina quotes two excerpts from their correspondence, the source of which is the book *Hitlerism is terrible, but Zionism is worse*, published in 1999 in Moscow by Vladislav Shumsky. On 1 July 1917 Lenin wrote to Zinoviev: "Grigori! Circumstances have compelled me to leave Petrograd at once.... The comrades suggested a place. It is so boring to be alone. Come and stay with me and we'll spend wonderful days together, far away from everything..." In another letter Zinoviev addresses Lenin in these terms: "Dear Vova, you have not answered me. You have probably forgotten your Gershel (Grigori). I have prepared a nice hideaway for us... it is a wonderful house where we will live well and nothing will disturb our love. Travel here as soon as you can. I am waiting for you, my little flower. Your Gershel." Lenin's homosexuality was a secret that was kept hidden until the late 1990s.

On 4 April 1917 Lenin, who had gone into exile in Switzerland after the abortive coup d'état of 1905, informed the German government that he was ready to return to Russia. The trip, approved by Chancellor Theobald von Bethmann-Hollweg without the knowledge of Kaiser Wilhelm II, who found out all about it when Lenin was already in St. Petersburg, was theoretically part of a plan to get Russia out of the war and sign a peace treaty in order to gain commercial advantages later. That said, it is necessary to consider several relevant facts and to introduce the agents who coordinated Lenin's travel and financing.

First of all, the head of the German espionage services was the Jewish banker Max Warburg, whose brother, Paul, had been the mastermind behind the creation of the Federal Reserve cartel and had transferred to it from the United States large sums of money to cover the costs of the war with France. Working for Max Warburg was Alexander Parvus, Trotsky's mentor, with whom he had organised and directed the first act of the 1905 revolution. Parvus, an unscrupulous illuminati in the style of Adam Weishaupt, in addition to working for the conspiracy, was also paid by the Japanese in 1905. It was he who had brought Lenin, Rosa Luxemburg and Trotsky into contact with each other in Munich. Closely associated with Parvus in the operation to transfer Lenin to Russia was Jacob Fürstenberg, a Polish Jew whose real name was Ganetsky. He collaborated with another Bolshevik Jew of Polish origin, Karl Radek (Karol Sobelsohn), later one of the leaders of the Bavarian Soviet Republic. Radek, as an agent of the Comintern, appeared in a Soviet uniform at the founding congress of the Communist Party of Germany. Jacob Ganetsky, who had belonged to the Bolsheviks since 1896 and acted as a mediator between Lenin and the Germans, was, according to Wikipedia, "one of the financial wizards who organised the secret financing that saved the Bolsheviks." After the triumph of the revolution, Ganetsky acted as one of the heads of Soviet commercial banking and, before being executed by Stalin, was director of the USSR Museum of the Revolution.

It remains for us to introduce the third man, Count Brockdorff-Rantzau, the person who was used by Parvus to infiltrate the German secret service. Anthony Sutton mentions in *Wall Street and the Bolshevik Revolution* a letter dated 14 August 1915 in which Brockdorff-Rantzau informs the Under-Secretary of State about a conversation with Parvus and fervently recommends that he be used, as he considers him "an extraordinarily important man whose unusual powers I feel we must use during the war". The same text contains, however, a very significant caveat: "It may be risky to want to use the powers behind Helphand, but it would certainly be admitting our own weakness if we refused his services or feared we would not be able to direct them." This erratic character who naively pretended to control a conspiracy more than a hundred years in the making, was serving in 1917 as German ambassador in Copenhagen. After Germany's defeat, he was appointed foreign minister of the Weimar Republic and in March 1919 he represented his country as head of the German delegation at the Versailles Conference. In 1922 he was appointed ambassador to Moscow.

Lenin's trip to Russia received the approval of Chancellor Bethmann-Hollweg, who was descended from a family of Jewish bankers in Frankfurt am Main, where a park is named after the founder of the dynasty, Simon Moritz von Bethmann. Chancellor Bethmann-Hollweg had lost the support of the Reichstag and had been dismissed; but before handing over to Georg Michaelis, he gave the go-ahead for the operation, which was coordinated by Arthur Zimmermann, the secretary of state. If one considers that infiltration of the army, agitation and defeatism, techniques used in Russia by the revolutionaries, were used a year later in Germany, where the same men of the Lenin operation helped to establish communism in Bavaria, one can understand the error of judgement made by the Germans, who intended to control events. General Max Hoffman later wrote the following. "We never knew and never foresaw the danger to mankind resulting from this journey of the Bolsheviks to Russia".

On 9 April the train carrying the thirty-two revolutionaries, most of whom were Jewish extremists, left Berne. Among Lenin's principal companions were Zinoviev and his wife, Slata Radomylskaya; Moses Kharitonov, later head of the Petrograd militia; Grigory Sokolnikov (Brilliant), editor of *Pravda* and later Commissar for Banking Affairs; David Rosenblum, Alexander Abramovich and Nadezhda Krupskaya, who was accompanied by Inessa Armand, Lenin's consenting mistress. Before arriving in Stockholm the party met Ganetsky in Trelleborg. When the party arrived in Malmö, Ambassador Brockdorf-Rantzau immediately informed Berlin. Before ten o'clock on the morning of 13 April 1917, Lenin's train pulled into the Stockholm station. Waiting for them on the platform was the mayor of the city, the socialist Carl Lindhagen. Also the Freemason Hjalmar Branting, leader of the Swedish Social Democrats, helped the Bolsheviks to establish a base in Sweden to prepare terrorist actions in Russia.

Polish Freemason Karl Rádek (Sobelsohn) was on the train, but did not continue on to St. Petersburg, remaining in the Swedish capital to help his friend Ganetsky, who channelled German money to the Petrograd Bolsheviks through Nya Banken, founded in 1912 in Stockholm by the Jewish banker and Freemason Olof Aschberg (Obadiah Asch), described by the German press as the "Banker of the World Revolution" ("Bankier der

Weltrevolution"). Olaf Aschberg was part of the Rothschild banking network. In 1918 Aschberg changed the name of Nya Banken to Svensk Economiebolaget, whose London agent was the British Bank of North Commerce, chaired by Earl Grey, a former associate of Cecil Rhodes. In the same circle as Aschberg, associated with Nya Banken, was the Guaranty Trust Company of New York, controlled by J. P. Morgan. When in 1922 the Soviets founded their first international bank, the Ruskombank (Bank of Foreign Trade), it was headed by Olof Aschberg. The head of Ruskombank's foreign department was Max May, another Morgan Guaranty Trust man.

Lenin spent eight hours at the Regina Hotel, where he met Hans Steinwachs, representative of the German Foreign Ministry and head of German espionage in Scandinavia. At 6.30 p.m. on the same day, 13 April, he continued his journey to Haparanda. The tickets for the journey to Stockholm were paid for by the German Government, but from then on the expenses of the journey were borne by the Provisional Government, since Alexander Kerensky, the Minister of Justice, had directly invited Lenin and Trotsky. Finally, after 11.10 p.m. on the night of 16 April 1917, ten days after America's declaration of war on Germany and eighteen days before Trostsky's arrival, Lenin and his party set foot in Petrograd. Waiting for them with flowers was the chairman of the Soviet, the Menshevik Freemason Cheidze, who made a speech of welcome. Lenin climbed on top of a vehicle and also made a stirring speech before climbing into the waiting armoured car. Later he would be received at the Winter Palace by the Minister of Labour, the Menshevik Freemason Mikhail Skobelev. In May a new batch of 200 revolutionaries arrived from Switzerland, led by Menshevik Martov (Zederbaum) and Pavel Axelrod. All the actors arrived in Russia between April and May in order to perform the third and final act of the revolution.

Kerensky, Prime Minister: The countdown begins

When Lenin arrived, the Mensheviks and the revolutionary socialists, known as SRs, dominated the St. Petersburg Soviet and the Bolsheviks were in the minority. Both Chairman Cheidze and Vice-Chairmen Kerensky and Skobelev were Mensheviks and were initially in favour of continuing the war. But divisions within this faction of the Social Democrats grew with the arrival of Lenin. The leadership of the Mensheviks was entirely Jewish and at heart it was a family quarrel within the common house of the Social-Democratic Party. During the months of April, May and June, the Bolsheviks called for the destruction of the Provisional Government, which Lenin considered in his speeches to be an instrument of the bourgeoisie that had to be overthrown. However, the Provisional Government had promised to call elections for a Constituent Assembly which was to draft a constitution for Russia. On 3 June 1917 the soviets went ahead and convened the First All-Russian Congress of Soviets, which was held in St. Petersburg. After the

February/March revolution, the Marxist parties had organised hundreds of local soviets in Russia, and the purpose of the convocation was to unify the forces of the revolution. The Congress showed that Mensheviks and SRs were effectively in the majority and dominated an assembly with hundreds of delegates, of whom only forty were Bolsheviks. Before the Congress was dissolved, a date for a second meeting was agreed. Initially the date was set for 7/20 October, but then the date was changed to 25 October (7 November in the Gregorian calendar), which "coincidentally" coincided with the date of the revolution.

With fresh money at their disposal, Trotsky, who went over to the Bolsheviks, and Lenin circulated publications and pamphlets of all kinds. Already in May *Pravda* went from three thousand copies to three hundred thousand and was distributed free of charge. Although both Lenin and Trotsky sighed for civil war, for a merciless class war in which political opponents were to be exterminated, the slogan of the Bolsheviks was "Peace! Bread! Land! All power to the soviets!". Propaganda began to take effect among the factory workers and in the barracks near St. Petersburg. By July the Bolsheviks had won the support of the most radical elements in the city, and the uproar was growing. The return of the exiles, mostly Bolsheviks, also strengthened their position. All this agitation caused thousands of workers and soldiers to take to the streets on 3/16 July, emboldened by lower-ranking leaders eager to seize power. Trotsky himself restrained the Red Guards in front of the Taurid palace and told them to go home and calm down. On July 4/17, coinciding with a German offensive, the situation became explosive and an unscheduled uprising of thousands of workers and soldiers took place, putting Prince Lvov's government on the ropes and in readiness to resign. These days have gone down in Russian history as "July Days".

Some government Freemasons, unaware of what was at stake, on learning of the existence of documents implicating the Bolsheviks, removed their blindfolds and began to see the reality. On the same 4/17 July the French military attaché Pierre Laurent visited Colonel Boris Nikitin, then head of the Russian Secret Service, and handed him copies of twenty-nine telegrams from Lenin, Ganetsky, Zinoviev and others, as well as three letters from Lenin, which exposed the Bolshevik faction. This information was immediately leaked to sympathetic newspapers by patriots close to the government. Rumours that significant information about Lenin, Trotsky and Zinoviev was about to be published spread through the city. Stalin telephoned Cheidze and persuaded him to call the newspapers and forbid the publication of sensitive documents. The Provisional Government would have liked to bury the matter, but a small newspaper, *Zhivoe Slovo (The Living Word)*, ignored the ban and published on 5/18 July an article by the SRs Grigori Alexinsky and Vasily Pankratov on German financing of Lenin's party. The article contained excerpts showing that Lenin had received 315,000 marks through a Mr. Svenson who worked at the German

Embassy in Stockholm. Lenin had received money and instructions from trusted people such as Jacob Fürstenberg and Alexander Parvus. The published article contained the name of Eugenia Sumenson (Dora Simmons), who appears for the first time in this account. This woman of Jewish origin worked in Petrograd in a pharmaceutical business, *Fabian Klingsland*, run by Kozlovsky, an agent of Parvus who was on the executive committee of the Petrograd Soviet. The money was received by this firm, which served to launder it before depositing it in the banks from where it was withdrawn by Sumenson, who was a relative of Ganetsky. Here is a passage from the article, reproduced in *Wall Street and the Bolshevik Revolution:*

"According to the information just received, these trusted persons in Stockholm were: the Bolshevik Jacob Fürstenberg, better known by the name of Ganetsky, and Parvus (Dr. Helphand); in Petrograd: the Bolshevik lawyer M. U. Kozlovsky, a relative of Ganetsky's, Sumenson, engaged in speculation with Ganetsky and others. Kozlovsky was the main recipient of German money, which was transferred from Berlin through 'Disconto-Gesellschaft' to Stockholm 'via bank' and from there to the Bank of Siberia in Petrograd, where this account now has a balance of about 2,000,000 roubles. The military censorship has uncovered an uninterrupted exchange of telegrams of a political and financial nature between German agents and Bolshevik leaders".

As for Lenin's letters, the Provisional Government learned that Lenin had written on 12/25 April to Ganetsky and Radek, who were still in Stockholm, to confirm that he had received the money. A second letter to Ganetsky on 21 April/4 May confirmed another receipt of money. In addition, through correspondence with Ganetsky, it was also learned that an agent of the Provisional Government itself in Stockholm had helped the Bolsheviks smuggle the money in a mail sack. Ganetsky, who was travelling to Petrograd with important documents, learned of the scandal and called off the trip and returned to Stockholm. In *Under the Sign of the Scorpion* Jüri Lina adds that his representative, the Polish Jew Salomon Chakowicz, remained in Haparanda with his luggage and that the French military attaché Pierre Laurent sent an agent to the city in order to try to steal the luggage. Whether or not he succeeded in his aim is unknown. As for Parvus, he hastened to leave Copenhagen and return to Switzerland.

As soon as the article was published, Justice Minister Pavel Pereverzev became the scapegoat for leaking the documents to the press and was forced to resign. It was claimed that an investigation was needed to verify the alleged treachery of the Bolsheviks. By 6/19 July the agitation on the streets had subsided and Lenin published an article rejecting the accusations and calling them a "rotten fabrication of the bourgeoisie". Lenin's official biography refers to these accusations as a libel of agents provocateurs. Trotsky, for his part, maintained that the money came from workers' collections. Two months later, a certain Raphael Scholan (Schaumann) received in Haparanda a telegram from Jacob Fürstenberg, dated 21 September in Stockholm, the text of which shows who were the alleged "workers" giving money to Trotsky. In *The World at the Cross Roads* Boris Brasol reproduces the document[51], which is also quoted in other works. Its full text reads: "Dear Comrade: The branch of the banking house M. Warburg has opened in accordance with the telegram of the chairman of the Westphalian-Rhine Syndicate an account for Comrade Trotsky's project. The bank lawyer (agent) bought arms and has arranged for their transport and delivery to Luleo and Varde. In the name of the branch of Essen & Son in Luleo, receivers, and a person authorised to receive the money ordered by Comrade Trotzky. J. Fürstenberg."

Faced with the evidence, the Prosecutor's Office could not avoid opening an investigation which revealed that 180,000 roubles were in Eugenia Sumenson's bank account and that a further 750,000 roubles had been transferred over a six-month period by Nya Banken. Lenin was charged with treason and espionage. On July 7/20 the Provisional Government ordered the arrest of Lenin, Zinoviev and *Pravda* editor Lev Kamenev (Rosenfeld). Both bourgeois and revolutionary socialist (SR) newspapers called for Lenin to be put on trial. Kerensky, who was Minister of War, after having visited the front, offered on July 8/21 to assume the post of prime minister of a government of "salvation of the revolution". Kerensky intended to resolve the conflict "by peaceful means". The new prime minister, considered an excellent orator, immediately set about the task of whipping up enthusiasm for the new offensive against the Germans, another offensive-massacre that only favoured the Bolsheviks' strategy. Although initially moderately successful, it declined steadily in the months that followed, which was inevitable considering that the morale and discipline of the Russian troops had been undermined from within.

Lenin left St. Petersburg on the evening of 9/22 July. No one tried to arrest him and after a quiet tour of several Russian and Finnish cities he ended up a month later in Helsinki. Zinoviev also decided to go into hiding. On 13/26 July, the St. Petersburg Soviet itself called for Lenin and Zinoviev to stand trial. A group of comrades maintained that Lenin was innocent and that there was nothing to fear from the investigation. Lenin evidently did not share this view. Finally, under pressure from the hostile press, the main Bolshevik leaders still in town: Leon Trotsky, Anatoly Lunakarsky, Aleksandra Kollontai, Lev Kamenev, Eugenia Sumenson and several others were arrested, accused of maintaining contacts with Alexander Parvus, who was considered to be a German agent. The investigation produced thousands of pages that were archived without any action being taken against the

---

[51] Boris Brasol's source is the National Archives, specifically the Committee on Public Information in Washington D.C., where the document dated 27 October 1918 is from.

detainees. It was not until the fall of communism that all the documentation was made available.

Two months before the Bolshevik seizure of power, the Sixth Congress of the Russian Social-Democratic Labour Party opened on 26 July/8 August. Ten years had passed since the previous congress, held in London in 1907. Because the main leaders of the party were in hiding or in detention, it was organised by second-rank members, of whom Sverdlov was among the most prominent. Sverdlov, Olminsky, Lomov, Yurenev and Stalin held the chairmanship. In reality the congress was a Bolshevik affair, since the Menshevik faction had practically ceased to exist. It can therefore be called the Congress of the Bolshevik Party, which a year later was to be renamed the Communist Party. The most important event was the election of the 26-member Central Committee, which two months later led the October Revolution. Trotsky writes in his book *Stalin* that "owing to the semi-legality of the party the names of the persons elected by secret ballot were not announced at the congress, with the exception of the four who had received the largest number of votes." Lenin got 133 votes; Zinoviev, 132; Kamenev, 131; Trotsky, 131. If one accepts what was argued above about Lenin's mother, all four party leaders were Jews and married to women of the same race. During the congress V. Volodarsky (Moses Markovich Goldstein), one of the Trotskyists who had travelled from New York on the *Kristianiafjord*, led a group of delegates who wanted Lenin to stand trial. This is perhaps significant and will be discussed later, since Volodarsky was assassinated in June 1918.

Kerensky did not take long to start releasing the arrested Bolshevik leaders. The first to be released from prison in August was Kamenev, but soon they were all out on the streets. Trotsky was released on 4/17 September and in the same month the Moscow Soviet came under Bolshevik control. On 23 September/6 October Trotsky was elected chairman of the St. Petersburg Soviet, replacing the Menshevik Cheidze. From this point onwards the Bolsheviks also came to control the St. Petersburg Soviet, which on 12/25 October voted to transfer all military power to a Military Revolutionary Committee, headed by Trotsky.

Before turning to the seizure of power, mention must be made of the revolt of General Lavr Kornilov, who had been appointed commander-in-chief of the Russian army after the failure of the July offensive. Kornilov, one of the Masonic generals who had blindly supported the revolution that had overthrown the monarchy, had been charged with personally arresting the Tsar. Finally, tired of the shady manoeuvres of the Provisional Government, he set out to overthrow Kerensky, who was still freeing imprisoned Bolsheviks. On 19 August/1 September he ordered his Cossacks to attack the capital. On 25 August/7 September General Krymov's troops headed for St. Petersburg with orders to hang all soviets and traitors. On 26 August/8 September Kornilov issued a proclamation accusing the

Provisional Government of undermining the state and the army, and thus reclaiming power. Kerensky appealed for help from the Bolsheviks, who were all released from office and presented as the best defenders of democracy. To deal with the counter-revolution, a central committee was founded by the Bolsheviks and the SRs. Thousands of sailors from Kronstadt were ordered to Petrograd, the Red Guards were given back the weapons confiscated from them during the July days, the railwaymen were called upon to sabotage the tracks, and the workers were mobilised. The Soviets began to arrest thousands of officers suspected of sympathising with Kornilov, but also many civilians. In all about seven thousand people were arrested. General Krymov was invited to negotiate with Kerensky and after the interview was over he shot himself and ended his life. In short, by 30 August/12 September the revolt had been put down. The Bolsheviks, as has been explained, were able to make the most of the situation brought about by the revolt and took control of the soviets in the big cities.

... and Kerensky hands over power to the Bolsheviks.

From the telegram of Jacob Fürstenberg transcribed above, it is known that at the end of September the banking house of Max Warburg, in response to Trotsky's request, had placed arms and money at his disposal. This is clear evidence that preparations for the seizure of power were accelerating. Various authors agree that, according to information in the State Department archives, the American ambassador, David Francis, was well informed of the Bolsheviks' plans, and President Wilson knew a month and a half in advance that the Bolsheviks would seize power in October/November. The date chosen coincided exactly with Trotsky's birthday, 7 November in the Gregorian calendar. Both Wilson and Lloyd George knew that the triumph of the revolution in Russia would allow Germany to prolong the world war; but not only did they do nothing to prevent Russia's fall into the hands of international communism, they actually brought it about. Proof that the British government, too, knew what was coming is that a month and a half beforehand they advised all citizens to leave the country.

Lenin returned to St. Petersburg in early October and according to Margarita Fofanova lived in his flat until the moment of the seizure of power. The Kerensky government knew of this fact, but did nothing. Despite the fact that the Bolsheviks' plan was an open secret, even aired in the press, Kerensky rejected the suggestion to reinforce St. Petersburg with troops. The propaganda thesis that the revolution was spontaneous is nonsense. The Military Revolutionary Committee, to which the St. Petersburg Soviet officially handed over power on October 12/25, had already been operating secretly under Trotsky's orders for several days. On 22 October/4 November the Committee organised a huge demonstration in preparation for the imminent seizure of power. The next day the fortress of Peter and Paul declared itself in favour of the Bolsheviks. On 24 October/6 November, the day before giving up power, Kerensky staged his last farce, his last farce: he ordered the arrest of the Military Revolutionary Committee, banned all Bolshevik publications and ordered fresh troops to replace the St. Petersburg garrison. These measures, of course, were never taken.

Lenin's actions in the days before the coup remain a mystery. It has been confirmed that he was not at the Smolny Institute, which was the headquarters of the Military Revolutionary Committee from which Trotsky organised everything. As "coincidentally" scheduled in June, the Second Congress of Soviets of Russia met on 25 October/7 November at the same Smolny Institute from where the Military Revolutionary Committee directed operations. It was there that at 10.40 a.m. it was announced that the Provisional Government had been overthrown and that power had passed to the Soviets. The Congress of Soviets then accepted the request to form a new government: the Council of People's Commissars ("Sovnarkom" Soviet narodnij kommissarov). The proposal was approved by 390 votes out of a possible 650. The government that was formed was composed exclusively of Bolsheviks, and the leader of the Mensheviks, Martov (Zederbaum) left the congress with other members of the faction. The Council thus became the official government of Russia. All eighteen members of this Council of Commissars, which was chaired by Lenin, were Jews or married to Jews. Lenin himself considered it to be a provisional government, since the long-awaited elections for a Constituent Assembly, so often postponed by the Masonic cabinets, had already been scheduled. In fact they took place between 12/25 and 14/27 November.

As for the mythical seizure of the Winter Palace, supposedly stormed by five thousand sailors on the morning of 25 October/7 November, Sergei P. Melgunov states that it was only a few hundred revolutionaries and fifty Red Guards who quietly entered the palace, which in reality was never stormed because it was no longer necessary. The storming of the Winter Palace took place after the fall of the Provisional Government had already been announced at the Congress of Soviets. Trotsky had said hours before that "governmental power lay with the Military Revolutionary Committee". Before a few hundred dock and Putilova factory workers, who had been led there, and the Red Guards were ordered to enter the palace, Trotsky ordered thirty-five cannon shots to be fired from the fortress of Peter and Paul. Naturally, they never hit the supposed target of the Winter Palace. Surely their purpose was to enhance the drama and epicness of the revolution so that the history books they were to write themselves would not be lacking anything. In *The Bolshevik Seizure of Power* Melgunov states that the first Red Guards gathered around the palace at about 4.30 p.m., but that the head of the guards, Vladimir Nevsky, was ordered to wait. According to Melgunov, the forces on guard at the palace were withdrawn and only two companies of the women's battalion remained. Some sources claim that some of these women were raped, although the official version acknowledges that they offered no resistance and claims that they were simply disarmed and released. According to the narrative which tries to make the "glorious seizure of the Winter Palace" look like an epic, the Bolsheviks gave the Provisional Government an ultimatum which it refused to answer; but the truth is that the Government had not really existed for days, since it had voluntarily recognised de facto the power of Trotsky's Military Revolutionary Committee.

E. M. Halliday writes in *Russia in Revolution* that Kerensky, secretary of the Grand Orient in Russia, co-religionist and Freemason brother of Lenin and Trotsky, had left St. Petersburg the same morning of 25 October/7 November. The American Embassy placed at his disposal a car flying the American flag. Armed with false documents and money, the Bolsheviks escorted him to Murmansk, a naval base which had been occupied by the British. There he was received as a "white" refugee and sailed for England on an Italian ship. It is clear that everything had been planned in advance. After living quietly in Berlin and Paris, he moved years later to the USA, where he died in New York in 1970. However, the official version pretends that he disguised himself as a woman and fled to Gachino. In his memoirs, Kerensky, whom Trotsky considered an adventurer, insists that he tried to organise resistance in that city. As for the other members of the Provisional Government, some of whom were in the palace, their arrest was carried out by Antonov-Ovseyenko, a comrade of Trotsky. The arrest took place at exactly 2.10 a.m. on 26 October/8 November, when the Red Guards opened the door of the room where the ministers were assembled and announced, "Gentlemen, your time is up!

John Reed, the famous American communist to whose halo the Hollywood propaganda factory has contributed with the film *Reds* (1981), wrote *Ten Days That Shook the World, a* work published in 1919 by the Communist Party of the United States publishing house[52]. In it Reed, who happened to be there, recounts witnessing the Red Guards escorting half a dozen civilians, including Rutenberg, "who stared taciturnly at the ground", and Tereshchenko, "who glanced quickly around". According to Reed, they were taken to the fortress of Peter and Paul. This was in fact a parade, as they say colloquially, for the sake of appearances. All the detainees were released within a few months, and Rutenberg collaborated with the Bolsheviks before leaving Russia after the attempted assassination of Lenin. It has been reported earlier that Kerensky, as Minister of Justice, appointed Pyotr (Pinhas) Rutenberg, Chief of Police. It is impossible to think that Lenin and Trotsky could have taken action against this brother Freemason, who in 1905

---

[52] John Reed, reports Anthony Sutton, a member of the Executive Committee of the Third International, was backed by Eugene Boissevain, a New York banker. He was hired by Harry Payne Whitney's *Metropolitan* magazine, who was then a director of J. P. Morgan's Guaranty Trust Company.

was acting as a terrorist together with Parvus and Trotsky himself. In addition to being one of the founders of the Jewish Legion, Rutenberg also founded the "American Jewish Congress" with others. This Zionist obtained from the British the exclusive concession for the production and distribution of electricity in Palestine and founded what is today the Israel Electric Corporation. He was also involved in the creation of the *Haganah*, the embryo of the future Zionist army. He also served as chairman of the Jewish National Council. Another high-ranking Freemason who collaborated with the Bolsheviks was Nikolai Nekrasov, former Minister of Communications, who until 1920 worked in the Central Cooperative Union. As for Tereschchenko, the Rothschild-friendly finance minister, he was also released and died much later in Monaco in 1956.

Another witness, the army officer Mikhail Maslenninkov, who was exiled in 1919 and died at the age of ninety-eight in Madrid, confirms the fact that nobody was defending the Winter Palace, which was surrounded by a two-metre high wall of sandbags that did not cover the whole building. Maslenninkov tells how, out of curiosity, he arrived at one of the entrances to the palace and, after being greeted by a cadet on guard, quietly entered and climbed up to the first floor where a hundred or so Bolsheviks were moving from one place to another. A soldier was standing guard outside the door of a room where the ministerial cabinet was meeting. According to this officer, who was wearing a trench coat without rank insignia, a group of about thirty soldiers under the command of a lieutenant broke through. After entering the room, the door closed behind them. The account continues: "A few minutes later the door opened again and the government ministers appeared on the threshold, hastily putting on their coats... the next day I learned that they had been arrested and taken to the fortress of Peter and Paul". It was shortly afterwards that, according to this witness, two shots rang out from the cruiser *Aurora*, which had been making its way up the Neva to anchor near the palace, where it remains for tourists visiting the city to see the ship that took part in the "glorious October Revolution". From the square, shouts could be heard coming from the first-floor balcony: "Stop them, they will kill us! Tell them the palace is in our hands!"

Eighteen days after the coup d'état, between 12/25 and 14/27 November, the elections for the Constituent Assembly, so laboriously prepared by the Provisional Government and repeatedly postponed by Kerensky, were held. A little known fact is that eighty per cent of the Jews of Russia voted for Zionist parties, which had formed a united list of candidates. Lenin wrote that more than half a million Jews voted for the Jewish nationalists. The Balfour Declaration, made public weeks earlier, undoubtedly encouraged the rise of the Zionist parties. The Bolsheviks did not interfere, the results were against them and they were left in a minority. The Socialist Revolutionaries, the SRs, had more than twice as many seats as the Bolsheviks. The convocation of the Assembly was in the hands of a special commission which had been set up for the purpose. The Bolsheviks arrested the members of this body, which was replaced by a Commissariat for the Constituent Assembly, presided over by the Jew Uritsky, one of the New York Trotskyists. In this way they gave themselves the possibility of exercising their authority. Soon the arrests of SRs in Moscow began. In Petrograd, Lenin declared that the Assembly was less democratic than the Soviets and martial law was proclaimed.

When the Assembly finally met on 5/18 January 1918, the unelected Jew Sverdlov took charge of the proceedings. Outside, backed by the bourgeoisie and the officials, there was a massive peaceful demonstration in support of the Assembly, which was broken up by the Bolshevik troops with gunfire. Inside, following the example of the Jacobins, who paid the agitators who acted on their orders, the tribunes were filled with soldiers and sailors who heckled and booed the speakers opposed to the government. Ten hours later, confusion reigned inside the Taurid Palace. The Bolsheviks ended the session and left the hall. Shortly afterwards the troops entered, expelled the parliamentarians and locked the doors of the building. Thus ended the Constituent Assembly and the hope of a constitution and representative government in Russia. In March 1918 the Soviet government decided to move to Moscow, which thus became the new capital, and adopted the Gregorian calendar. On 8 March the Russian Social Democratic Party became the Communist Party. Meanwhile, the enemies of the new regime had been "organising" to try to put up resistance. Faced with this danger, Trotsky, after representing Russia at Brest-Litovsk, gave up his post as Foreign Commissar to another Jew, Georgi Chicherin (Ornatsky), and in March he became War Commissar, a position which enabled him to take command of all military resources and organise the Red Army, which in 1921 would eventually win the civil war.

The conspirators use the Red Cross

This section has as its main source the fifth and sixth chapters of *Wall Street and the Bolshevik Revolution,* in which Anthony Sutton certifies that Wall Street, the most representative banks of the Federal Reserve cartel, specifically, used the Red Cross as a front for a mission to support the Bolsheviks, whom they were financing. The man chosen for this task, William Boyce Thompson, was a high-level representative of Morgan, Rockefeller and Guggenheim, the Jewish bankers who aspired to big business, the ones who most coveted Russia's enormous wealth, which they sought to access through their Jewish-Bolshevik agents.

As early as 1910, J. P. Morgan had made a series of cash contributions to the American Red Cross that made him one of the leading "philanthropists" behind the organisation. During the Great War, the American Red Cross relied heavily on Morgan's Guaranty Trust. John Foster

Dulles acknowledges that, unable to cope with the demands of war, the Red Cross ended up in the hands of these bankers: "Viewing the American Red Cross as a virtual arm of the Government, they conceived of making an incalculable donation to the victory in the war. In doing so, they made a mockery of the Red Cross motto: Neutrality and Humanity". In return for increased funding, these bankers solicited the Red Cross War Council, of which Henry P. Davison, a partner of J. P. Morgan, was appointed chairman. Names working for Guggenheim, Morgan and Rockefeller banks and companies were added to the list of Red Cross administrators.

The matter of a Red Cross mission in Russia was introduced at a meeting of the reconstructed War Council, chaired by the aforementioned Davison, which was held at the Red Cross building in Washington D. C. on 29 May 1917. At that meeting, Alexander Legge of the International Harvester Company, a Rockefeller-owned farm machinery company, and Henry Davison himself were commissioned to explore the idea. At a subsequent meeting it was announced that William Boyce Thompson, head of the Federal Reserve Bank of New York, had already offered to pay all the expenses of the commission. The acceptance of the offer is recorded in a telegram: "Your willingness to pay the expenses of the commission to Russia is much appreciated and from our point of view very important". The American Red Cross mission, consisting of fifteen businessmen and lawyers, seven doctors and seven nurses and orderlies, arrived in Russia at the end of July 1917. As early as August, the seven doctors, after protesting indignantly at Thompson's political activities, left the mission and returned to the United States.

In the same month of August William B. Thompson had lunch at the American Embassy in Petrograd with Kerensky, Tereshchenho and Ambassador Francis. After lunch Thompson showed his Russian guests a cablegram he had sent to the New York office of J. P. Morgan, requesting a transfer of 425,000 roubles for a personal subscription to the Russian Liberty Loan, which was sent to a branch of Rockefeller's National City Bank. In addition, according to American Embassy records, the Red Cross gave Kerensky 10,000 roubles for assistance to political refugees. It is in the assistance to the Bolsheviks that the high historical and political significance of the American Red Cross mission in Russia is truly revealed. Thompson personally contributed a million dollars to the Bolshevik cause; but apart from the financial contributions, it is interesting to know the political connotations of the trip of the camouflaged Wall Street delegation, which immediately hired the services of three Russian interpreters, one of whom, Boris Reinstein, was later Lenin's secretary and head of the "Bureau of International Revolutionary Propaganda", which depended on Karl Radek's "Press Bureau" Rádek.

William B. Thompson left Russia in early December 1917 and left as his replacement at the head of the "Red Cross mission" Colonel Raymond

Robins, who organised with the Bolsheviks the implementation of a plan suggested by Thompson to spread communist propaganda throughout Europe. French documents confirm that Colonel Robins "was able to send a subversive mission of Russian Bolsheviks to Germany to start a revolution there". The overall plan included dropping propaganda from aeroplanes and smuggling Bolshevik literature through Germany. Shortly after the Bolshevik seizure of power, Robins received a telegram on behalf of President Wilson stating, "The President desires the maintenance of direct communications by representatives of the United States with the Bolshevik Government." Robins sent another telegram days later to the chairman of the Red Cross War Council, Henry Davison, asking, "Please convey to the President the necessity of our relations with the Bolshevik Government."

Before leaving Russia, Thompson had made preparations to sell the Bolshevik revolution in Europe and at home. From Petrograd he sent a telegram to Thomas W. Lamont, an associate of J. P. Morgan, who was in Paris with Colonel Edward Mandell House. He asked him to travel to London in order to coordinate his actions there. Thompson's ideas on the need to expand the revolution were conveyed months later to the American public through the *Washington Post.* On 2 February 1918, the Post reported:

> "William B. Thompson, who was in Petrograd from July until last December, has made a personal contribution of $1,000,000 to the Bolsheviks for the purpose of propagating their doctrine in Germany and Austria. Mr. Thompson, as head of the American Red Cross mission, whose expenses he has personally borne, had an opportunity to study the situation in Russia. He is of the opinion that the Bolsheviks constitute the greatest power against pro-Germanism in Russia and that their propaganda has been undermining the militaristic regimes of the empires. Mr. Thompson scorns American criticism of the Bolsheviks. He believes that they have been misunderstood and has made the financial contribution to the cause convinced that it will be money spent for the future of Russia and for the Allied cause."

In the biography *The Magnate: William B. Thompson and His time (1869-1930)* Hermann Hagedorn reproduces the cablegram sent by J. P. Morgan to William B. Thompson, received on 8 December 1917 in Petrograd, which reads: "New York Y757/5 24W5 Nil - Your second cable received. We have paid to the National City Bank one million dollars as ordered - Morgan". It may be added here that the Petrograd branch of the National City Bank was the only foreign bank left out of the Bolsheviks' nationalisation decree.

William B. Thompson left Petrograd in December 1917 to return to the United States, which he did via London, where he arrived on the 10th. There, accompanied by Thomas Lamont, a partner in the J. P. Morgan firm who would later become the Treasury representative at the Peace Conference and a member of the CFR (Council of Foreign Relations), a globalist body emanating from the Round Table, they visited Lloyd George. Thompson and Lamont tried to convince the British Prime Minister that the Bolshevik regime was here to stay, and that British policy should stop being anti-Bolshevik, should accept the new realities and should support Lenin and Trotsky. Lloyd George understood Thompson and Lamont's advice perfectly. His Foreign Office minister had just made the *Balfour Declaration* and, after a year as prime minister, he knew very well who was behind international events. Moreover, he was not a free man: he was beholden to those who had put him in office, whose man in the shadows was Lord Milner, the Rothschild agent who had founded the Round Table in 1909. Alfred Milner was then a member of the War Cabinet and director of the London Joint Stock Bank (now the Midland Bank), from where he provided cover for the arms dealings of Basil Zaharoff, a Greek-born Jew who was the main supplier to the Bolshevik side. Milner had turned down a fabulous offer in 1910 to fill the vacancy of J. P. Morgan junior, who was returning to New York with his father, and thus become one of the three partners of the Morgan Bank in London. In the end the new partner was E. C. Grenfell and the London branch became Morgan Grenfell & Company. Lord Milner preferred to become a director of a group of public banks, mainly the Joint Stock Bank.

The figure of Basil Zaharoff deserves a few paragraphs, at least. Zaharoff, Zedzed to his intimates, was a scoundrel of the worst kind. His life remains shrouded in mystery, as he himself took it upon himself to burn piles of confidential papers. He also burned a diary written over half a century that probably contained the most notorious episodes of his scandalous career. Born in Anatolia, perhaps in 1849, he was the son of a Greek merchant who imported rose essence. His family moved to Odessa, where he Russified his name. He is credited with inventing the "Zaharoff System", which consisted of selling arms to all parties involved in conflicts that he helped provoke. He made a fortune as an arms dealer for Vickers, Britain's largest armaments company, hence he was known as the 'Merchant of Death'. Recently declassified papers from 1917 show that he held secret negotiations with Greece to join the Allies and also with the Turks to betray the Germans. The highlight of this episode was his abortive trip to Switzerland, armed with ten million pounds in gold and with Lloyd George's authorisation, in order to buy Turkey out of the war and establish what was to become the State of Israel. These intrigues failed miserably, as he was stopped by the border police. Nevertheless, Zaharoff wrote to the British government to request "chocolate for Zedzed". In other words, he must have blackmailed Lloyd George, who reluctantly recommended him for the Knight's Grand Cross, allowing him to become "Sir Basil". Eustace Mullins writes *in New History of the Jews* that the Jews not only controlled Lloyd George with bribes, but that Zaharoff sent one of his former wives to have an affair with him. Mullins mentions among Zaharoff's agents in England a Hungarian Jew named

Trebitsch-Lincoln (we will get to know him better in the next chapter), who became a priest in the Anglican church and was a member of Parliament while working for Zaharoff. It is estimated that as a result of his business dealings during the Great War alone, the Merchant of Death amassed a fortune of $1.2 billion.

In 1963 a book by Donald McCormick, *The Mask of Merlin. A Critical Study of David Lloyd George*, showed that Lloyd George had become deeply mired in the quagmire of international intrigue over arms sales and was compromised by the international arms dealer Sir Basil Zaharoff. McCormick confirms that Zaharoff wielded enormous power behind the scenes and was consulted by Allied leaders. He claims that on more than one occasion Woodrow Wilson, Lloyd George and Georges Clemenceau met in Paris at the home of the Jew Zaharoff, whom they were 'obliged to consult before planning any attack'. British intelligence discovered documents that "incriminated servants of the Crown as secret agents of Sir Basil Zaharoff with the knowledge of Lloyd George". In 1917, Zaharoff was close to his Bolshevik co-religionists and had intervened in London and Paris on their behalf. He also used all his resources as a dealer to keep arms from reaching the anti-Bolsheviks.

The "secret papers" of the British War Office contain Lloyd George's account of his conversation with Thompson and Lamont. Because of its interest, we offer a transcription of a significant paragraph of the excerpt published by Anthony Sutton in his oft-mentioned book:

"The Prime Minister reported on a conversation he had had with Mr. Thompson - an American traveller and a man of considerable means - who had just returned from Russia and who had given him somewhat different impressions from what was generally believed about affairs in that country. The gist of his remarks was to the effect that the revolution was here to stay, that the Allies had not been sufficiently sympathetic to the revolution, and that Messrs. Trotsky and Lenin were not agents of Germany, the latter being a rather distinguished professor. Mr. Thompson had added that he felt that the Allies should conduct active propaganda in Russia by a sort of Allied Council composed of men specially selected for the purpose; moreover, considering the nature of the de facto Russian Government, he felt that, on the whole, the various Allied Governments were not adequately represented in Petrograd. From Mr. Thompson's point of view, it was necessary for the Allies to realise that the Russian army and people were out of the war, and that the Allies would have to choose between a friendly Russia or a hostile neutral."

Thompson thus made it clear that Trostky and Lenin were not agents of Germany, which is obvious, since they were agents of the MRM, organised and financed since the creation of the Bavarian Order of the Illuminati by the international Jewish bankers, i.e., by Mr. Thompson's direct bosses. It is quite another matter that they served Germany until their time came a year later. The World Revolutionary Movement, in order that the conspirators behind it might steal more and better, intended to use the platform gained in Russia to export the communist revolution to the whole world. It is understandable that Thompson would have personally contributed a million dollars for the spread of communism to Austria and Germany, since the MRM's ultimate goal was the establishment of a world-wide Soviet republic supposedly based on the dictatorship of the proletariat. Zinoviev himself wrote in an article published in *Pravda* in November 1919: "Our Third International now already represents one of the great factors in European history. And in a year, in two years, the Communist International will rule the whole world".

After hearing Lloyd George's report, the War Cabinet accepted William B. Thompson's approach to the Bolsheviks. Lord Milner immediately sent his agent, R. H. Bruce Lockhart, who had recently been British Consul in Moscow, to Russia with instructions to work informally with the Soviets. Maksim Litvinov (Meyer Hennokh Wallakh), the Jewish Freemason who in 1907 had robbed the State Bank of Tiflis with Stalin, served unofficially as the Bolsheviks' representative in Britain. This robber-turned-diplomat wrote for Bruce Lockhart a letter of introduction to Trotsky, in which he referred to the British agent as "a thoroughly honest man who understands our position and sympathises with us." In the War Cabinet documents, there is one dated 24 April 1918 denouncing Lockhart's collaboration with the Bolsheviks. General Jan Smuts reports a conversation with General Nieffel, head of the French Military Mission just returned from Russia, who alludes to Trotsky as "a consummate rascal who may not be pro-German, but he is absolutely pro-Trotsky and pro-revolutionary and cannot be trusted in any way. His influence is shown by the way he has come to dominate Lockhart, Robins and Sadoul, the French representative. He (Nieffel) advises great caution in negotiations with Trotsky, who, he admits, is the only really capable man in Russia."

When William B. Thompson returned to the United States in January 1918, he went on a tour to publicly call for recognition of the soviets, which must have come as a surprise to many considering that the propagandist was the head of the Federal Reserve Bank of New York. On 23 January Thompson received a telegram from Raymond Robins saying: "Soviet government stronger than ever. Its authority and power greatly consolidated after dissolution of Constituent Assembly". Robins stressed that it was very important that recognition should come soon. Among the conspirators surrounding Wodroow Wilson, the one who most insisted on this recognition of the Bolshevik government was, of course, Colonel Edward Mandell House, the President's closest adviser, the author of *Philip Dru: Administrator*, a political fantasy novel set in the United States that had just become a reality in Russia.

Trosky and Lenin, at loggerheads at Brest-Litovsk

In the previous section we have seen that the strategy of the international bankers who supported the Judeo-Bolsheviks was to export the revolution to Austria and Germany as soon as possible. If they succeeded, as they intended, the conspiracy could achieve all its aims at once. First they had obtained the issue and control of money in the United States through the Federal Reserve System. Then, in November 1917, they had achieved two long-sought goals: the *Balfour Declaration*, which gave them the right to rob the Palestinians of the "promised land", and, finally, the overthrow of the hated Christian monarchy of the Romanovs, who would not allow them to appropriate the coveted resources of the vast Russian empire. Now it was a question of imposing on Europe and then on the whole world the totalitarian system prophetically announced seventy-five years in advance by Heinrich Heine: "There will be only one fatherland, namely, the Earth". It is clear that the Jewish bankers aspired to expand the dictatorship of the proletariat, in reality the dictatorship over the proletariat, which would allow them to take possession of all the wealth of the planet. In this sense, the peace signed in the Belarusian city of Brest-Litovsk was a serious setback for the aims of the internationalists, today globalists.

Kerensky's July offensive had ended in disaster, not least because of the mass desertion of soldiers, to whom the revolutionaries had promised peace without Russia having to cede territory or pay war indemnities. Everyone knew that these were idyllic conditions, far removed from reality; but, as promised, when the Bolsheviks came to power, negotiations to get the country out of the war began immediately. Trotsky, the Bolshevik government's Commissar for Foreign Affairs, was Russia's top representative. Contacts for the signing of an armistice began on 1 December and the signing took place on 16 December. From this point on, war operations were suspended on the entire Eastern Front, from Lithuania to Transcaucasia, at.

Serious disagreements then arose in Moscow among the "comrades". These divergences, as we shall see, were to provoke fierce clashes which lasted for thirty-five years, until the assassination of Stalin and the execution of Beria in 1953. The assassination attempt on Lenin, the assassination of Trotsky and the Stalinist purges are the best known episodes of the struggle that began at Brest-Litovsk. Trotsky himself and his colleague at the *Novy Mir* newspaper in New York, Nikolai Bukharin (Dolgolevsky), who would be executed by Stalin during the Great Purge, led the section of the party that sought to use the negotiations to buy time until the Red Army was well organised. As for the Freemason Bukharin, who for a time was said not to be a Jew, it should be pointed out that the *Jewish Chronicle* of 9 October 1953 claims him to be a Jew. The speech of Bukharin and Trotsky consisted in arguing that the uprising of the workers of the Central Powers was only a matter of a short time. They believed that peace was incompatible with a capitalist state. Both he and Trotsky opposed any treaty and led the pro-war camp. On the other hand, Lenin, while recognising that the workers' revolution in Germany was imminent, was not in favour of continuing the war and was in favour of consolidating the revolution in Russia. Lenin was of the opinion that if socialist revolutions finally broke out in the rest of Europe there would then be an opportunity to regain the ground ceded to the Germans. In any case, all agreed that the negotiations should be dragged out as long as possible.

The talks began in Brest-Litovsk on 22 December 1917. Trotsky had as his interlocutors Richard von Kühlman, Foreign Secretary, and Max Hoffman, Commander of the Eastern Front, representing Germany. The highest Austro-Hungarian representative was the Czech Count Ottokar Czernin, Foreign Minister. The Turkish Empire was represented by the Gan Vizier Mehemet Talat. Trotsky tried to gain time and in his strategy was prepared to wait for the German ultimatum, which he intended to refuse. The Trotskyists were convinced that Russia's refusal to sign the treaty would provoke the refusal of the German soldiers and workers to continue fighting and thus the revolution would spread to the whole Continent. A million dollars to intensify propaganda to the maximum had just been donated by W. B. Thompson, a Wall Street representative, whose views were in agreement.

On 10 February 1918, pressure from the Central Powers was mounting and Trotsky withdrew from the negotiating table after rejecting the conditions demanded of him. The struggle in Moscow between supporters and opponents of peace was bitter, so much so that there were even plans to try to overthrow Lenin. The internationalists were an influential and powerful group within the party. All those who during the Great Purge were persecuted and liquidated by Stalin: Rakovsky, Kamenev, Zinoviev, Radek, Bukharin, etc. shared with Trotsky the theory that socialism in one country, national communism, was "opportunist". As early as February 1918, they already spoke out against a peace which they considered a mistake and a betrayal of the international revolution. What they really intended was to sit alongside the winners at the future Peace Conference, with a Red Army financed and strengthened by their banker partners, with Germany and Austria subjugated and in the hands of their co-religionists. In these circumstances, the post-war map would naturally have been that of a European Union of Soviet republics, i.e. a red Europe without independent nations. This was the scenario desired by the conspirators who financed international communism.

"Neither war nor peace" was Trotsky's surprising statement, which he pulled out of his hat in his eagerness to delay the talks. Naturally, the Germans were unwilling to accept any more ambiguity, and after Trotsky's rudeness, the expected ultimatum arrived: the Germans informed that the armistice would end on 17 February, which meant that on the 18th hostilities would resume. Lenin insisted on signature, Trotsky on refusal. Commenting on their strategy, Trotsky wrote sarcastically in 1925: "We began the peace negotiations in the hope that the workers' parties in Germany and the Austro-Hungarian Empire, as well as in the nations of the Triple Entente, would rise up. For this reason we were obliged to delay the negotiations as long as possible so that the European worker would have time to understand the main objective of the Soviet revolution and, particularly, its policy of peace."

The German advance came suddenly and caught the Russian soldiers, who were confident that the war was over, off guard. The Central Executive Committee met in St. Petersburg and Lenin, supported by Stalin and other Russian socialists, prevailed. On 24 February, after acrimonious debate, the CCE accepted Germany's terms by 112 votes to 86. There were, however, 25 abstentions, one of them strategic, that of Trotsky, who during the discussion had secluded himself in his room. Without having convinced the Trotskyists, who insisted on continuing the war, a telegram was sent to the Germans accepting their terms for peace. Germany's reply was delayed for three days. At last, informed that the Trotskyist faction dissented and wanted to continue the war, the Germans accepted the cessation of hostilities, but without withdrawing their troops, which had made substantial advances and had reached within two hundred kilometres of Petrograd.

The treaty was signed on 3 March 1918, in which Russia relinquished Ukraine, Poland, Lithuania, Estonia and Latvia to the Central Empires. Finland had declared its independence on 6 December 1917 and managed to consolidate it with German help. Bessarabia was ceded to Romania. Ardahan, Kars and Batumi were handed over to the Ottoman Empire. The second article of the Treaty read: "The signatory powers shall suspend propaganda against the other side". Ratification took place in Berlin on 15 March. Three days earlier, a Congress of all the Soviets meeting in Moscow had approved it. President Wilson, in his usual line of hypocritical altruism, addressed a message to the Congress of Soviets that purported to be in solidarity with the Russian people. In it he referred to Soviet totalitarianism as "the struggle for freedom". In the final excerpt, the rush he was in, under pressure from his clique of Jewish socialists and Zionists, to recognise the Communist dictatorship is evident: "While the American Government is not now, unfortunately, in a position to give the direct and effective aid which it would wish, I wish to assure the Russian people through the Congress that it will take every opportunity to secure their sovereignty and independence in their own affairs and the full restoration of their great role in European life and in the modern world. The heart of the American people is with the Russian people as they seek to free themselves forever from autocratic rule and become masters of their own lives."

The Congress also received a telegram from the president of the American Federation of Labor, the Jew Samuel Gompers, in which he asked the Soviets to tell them how they could help them. The text ended by saying that they "awaited your suggestions", read your instructions. In the United States the Jews were conducting a vociferous campaign to press Wilson to recognise Trotsky and Lenin and to propose that he become the world leader of the International. Rabbi Judas Magnes, president of the New York "Kahal" between 1906 and 1922, in the course of a conference in April 1918 declared that President Wilson intended to convene a Peace Conference at which he would call for "an immediate peace on the simple basis established by the Bolsheviks in Russia."

After the signing of the Treaty, the Bolsheviks announced the formation of a new Supreme War Council, of which Trotsky was appointed chairman. Trotsky did not attend the Congress of Soviets, as he was still in St. Petersburg (Petrograd). The Treatise of Brest-Litovsk was finally annulled eight months later as a result of Germany's defeat, as it was not recognised by the Allies in the Armistice of Compiègne, signed on 11 November 1918.

Talmudist Jews assassinate imperial family

The cold-blooded murder of the Russian imperial family was a despicable slaughter, a crime carried out by Jews who left for posterity at the site of the assassination various texts proudly vindicating their Talmudic vengeance. In 1920 *The Times* correspondent Robert Wilton was the first to denounce the events in a historical book, *The Last Days of the Romanovs*, through which the world learned in detail how it all happened. Before examining this brutal act, we will introduce Wilton, another master journalist who, like Douglas Reed, worked on the London paper in the days when Lord Northcliffe, the owner of the paper who insisted on airing *the Protocols of the Learned Elders of Zion*, was taken out of circulation. Wilton, who had been educated in Russia, knew the country well and spoke Russian fluently, was an exceptional witness to events from the spring of 1917 until he left Russia in 1920. He understood the true nature of what was happening and wanted to denounce the fact that a despotic Jewish regime had seized power in Russia; but he was not allowed to inform his readers about certain things.

In the course of 1918, the chancelleries in London and Paris received various reports secretly warning of the very thing that Robert Wilton intended to warn of in public through his journalistic works and plays. Thus, for example, there is a report in the British Government's *Collection of Reports on Bolshevism* sent to Lord Balfour by the Dutch ambassador to St. Peretsburg, Willem Jacob Oudendijk, which reads: "Bolshevism is organised and managed by Jews who have no nationality and whose sole aim is to destroy the existing order for their own ends". Also the American ambassador, David R. Francis, reported similarly, "The Bolshevik leaders here, most of whom are Jews and ninety per cent of whom are returned exiles, care very little about Russia or any other country, for they are internationalists and seek to set in motion a world revolution." Bertrand Russell, a Fabian socialist, acknowledged the truth in a private letter collected in *The Autobiography of Bertrand Russell* (London 1975). The epistle in question, dated 25 June 1920 in Stockholm, is addressed to Lady Ottoline Morell. B. Russell's words are not to be missed:

> "My dearest O.
> ... The days in Russia were infinitely painful to me, apart from being one of the most interesting things I have ever done. Bolshevism is a closed tyrannical bureaucracy, with a system of espionage more elaborate and terrible than that of the Tsar, and an equally insolent and insensitive aristocracy, composed of Americanised Jews. There is no trace of freedom left, neither of thought, nor of speech, nor of action. I was repressed and oppressed by the weight of the machine as if I were wearing a leaden cloak. Still, I think it is the right government for Russia at this time."

Obviously, the last sentence disqualifies the writer and discredits the Fabian Society, founded in 1883, whose emblem, eloquently, is a wolf in sheep's clothing. How can one claim that a tyrannical bureaucracy imposed by foreign Jews based on oppression and terror is right for Russia?[53] Yet this English philosopher who wished the Russian people so much good refers in his memoirs to Lenin as the worst person he had ever met and describes him talking about the peasants he had hanged and laughing as if he had told a joke.

Robert Wilton, unlike Russell, had no doubt that what was happening in Russia was bad for the Russians and for the whole world, and he tried to expose it. It was not easy for him because the conspirators using the puppet governments of the United States and Britain did not want the public to know the truth. Wilton's colleague Reed notes that in *The Times' Official History*, published in 1952, one can read praise for Robert Wilton's journalistic work, which was highly regarded until 1917. Suddenly, from that date onwards, the

---

[53] The Fabian Society, whose early names include such sacred cows as Bertrand Russell, H. G. Wells, Leonard and Virginia Wolf, George Bernard Shaw, William Morris and Annie Besant, successor to Helena Blavatsky in the leadership of the Theosophical Society, had John Ruskin as its spiritual leader. The Fabians are, as they recognise in their emblem, wolves hiding under the sheep's clothing of workerist and humanitarian slogans. The Fabian Society, linked to the Round Table, is a body integrated into the Committee of 300, i.e. it is part of the structures of the globalist conspiracy. In 1895, the Fabian Society published a manifesto advocating central government. The Fabian Socialists appear to the world as a group of independent intellectuals; but in reality they are hypocritical puppets whose strings are pulled from behind the scenes. Sidney Webb called the Soviet Union "a mature democracy". Playwright Bernard Shaw, in line with Bertrand Russell, considered the Judeo-Bolshevik terror that wiped out millions of innocent people "a necessary evil".

tone of the references assessing the work of the St Petersburg correspondent changes, and it is written about him that "he does not deserve the newspaper's confidence". In the pages of *Official History*, the journalist complained about the censorship and suppression of his reports. From this point on, *The Times* began to publish articles about Russia written by people with little knowledge of the country. The newspaper's editorials exasperated Wilton, who lost confidence for good. A few lines explain why he lost it: "It was unfortunate on Wilton's part that in Zionist circles and even in the Foreign Office the idea spread that his reporting showed him to be an anti-Semite".

What was regarded in "Zionist circles" as anti-Semitism was in reality the integrity of an honest journalist, whose love of the truth prevented the world from being sold yet another lie, the lie that the Romanovs had ended their days in the protective custody of the Bolsheviks. In the English and American editions of *The Last Days of the Romanovs*, the lists of the number of members of the various revolutionary organs were suppressed. However, the French edition did not censor this information, according to which the Central Committee of the Bolshevik Party (Communist Party from March 1918) was composed of ten Jews and two gentiles. The Central Committee of the Executive Committee (Secret Police) consisted of forty-two Jews and nineteen Russians. The Council of People's Commissars was composed of seventeen Jews and five other people. The Cheka was almost entirely controlled by Jews. Official information published in 1919 by the Bolsheviks themselves admits that of the five hundred and fifty-six high state commanders, four hundred and fifty-eight were Jews and one hundred and eight Gentiles. These figures are from 1920. Since then it has become known that behind many names that passed for Russian there was a Jew. Moreover, the few non-Jewish leaders were often married to Jewish women.

Having introduced the author, let us turn to the facts. The first to investigate the murder perpetrated on July 16, 1918, was M. Namëtkine, an examining magistrate of Ekaterinburg. He began the work at the end of July, shortly after the massacre; but in view of his manifest incapacity he was dismissed on the 8th of August and replaced by M. Sergueiev. This magistrate conducted for six months a hesitant investigation, blindly accepting the lies spread by the Bolsheviks, who claimed to have executed the Czar as a traitor and spread various stories placing the sons in one place or another. Their procedures and negligence turned the investigation of the case into a macabre comedy. Finally Admiral Kolchak, appointed Supreme Ruler of Russia in November 1918 by the anti-Bolshevik government in Omsk, entrusted the investigation to Nilolai Sokolov. Statements made before this judge by witnesses who lived with the royal family and the interrogation of some of the accused and regicides have made it possible to reconstruct the events since Nicholas II and his family were arrested by Kornilov after the coup d'état of February/March 1917. Notable among these statements is that of Colonel Kobylinsky, in whose custody the imperial family was held from 3 March 1917 to 26 April 1918. Two other statements of interest are those of Pierre André Gilliard, French teacher to the Tsar's daughters and deputy preceptor to Tsarevitch Alexis, and Sidney Gibbes, English teacher and preceptor to the Tsarevitch.

On 13 August 1917 the Imperial family, still detained at Tsarkoye Selo, was transferred by Kerensky's order to Tobolsk in Siberia. Robert Wilton states that during his stay in Tobolsk, the German ambassador, Count Mirbach, entered into negotiations with Sverdlov (Yankel-Aaron Salomon), a Freemason member of B'nai B'rith and Lenin's right-hand man. Wilton assumes that the Germans intended to bring Nicholas II to Moscow to sign the Treaty of Brest-Litovsk. If this is true, it suggests that the Germans were not sure that the Bolsheviks were in power to stay. Wilton's assumption is in turn based on another assumption, that of the Tsar himself, who according to witnesses commented: "It is to make me accept a treaty of the Brest-Litovsk type that I am being led to Moscow. I would rather have my right hand cut off". For her part, the Tsarina, alluding to the Tsar's abdication, made without consulting her, added: "They are trying to separate him from me in order to make him sign a shameful transaction." It is obvious that no historical value can be attached to these suppositions. Considering that Empress Alexandra was a first cousin of Wilhelm II, it is also conceivable that the Kaiser had other motives. The person chosen as the liaison for this top-secret mission was a former Russian naval officer, Vasily Yakovlev, who arrived unexpectedly in Tobolsk in the middle of the night on 23 April 1918. According to Colonel Kobylinski, obedience to his orders was demanded on pain of death, but no one knew why he had gone to Tobolsk.

The next day Yakovlev had a confrontation with the delegate of the Ural Soviet in the city, a Jew named Zaslavski, who suspected a hoax and tried to incite a mutiny against him among the soldiers. Zaslavski immediately went to Ekaterinburg, where he spread the news that the Romanovs intended to escape to Japan. According to witnesses, Yakovlev said that he had orders from the Central Committee to take the whole family, but when he realised that the thirteen-year-old Tsarevitch Alexis, a haemophiliac, was ill, he wanted to take Nicholas II with him. Tsarina Alexandra, however, insisted on accompanying her husband and agreed to leave her son in the care of Tatiana, her favourite daughter. According to Professor Gilliard's testimony before Judge Sokolov, Yakovlev made "a favourable impression" on the Tsar and confessed that he "thought him an honest, respectable man". Gilliard also stated that no one knew where the emperor was to be taken: "His Majesty asked Yakovlev, but Yakovlev's answers did not clarify anything. Kobylinski told us that he had first informed him that the destination was Moscow, then went on to say that he did not know where the emperor was to be taken". These words confirm the idea that Yakovlev's mission was a mystery to everyone.

They left Tobolsk on 26 April in peasant wagons. The couple's third daughter, Maria, accompanied her parents. Also in the party were Dr. Botkin, the court physician, Prince Dolgoruky, the attendant Chemodurov, the maid Anna Demidova, the valet Alexei Trupp, and the child Leonid Sednev, the Tsarevitch's playmate. It took them two days to reach Tyumen, a city three hundred kilometres to the southwest. There a special train was waiting for them, on which Yakovlev headed west, skipping the intermediate stations, but halfway to Ekaterinburg he learned that the train would be stopped by order of the Ural Soviet. He immediately reversed the train in order to proceed to Ufa, but the train was stopped by Omsk Soviet troops. Yakovlev had the locomotive uncoupled and went alone to Omsk to communicate with Sverdlov. He was then ordered to proceed to Ekaterinburg. For four days and four nights Yakovlev did not allow anyone to speak to the Tsar. He monopolised the conversation and probably told Nicholas II the real reasons for his mission. Later Yakovlev, back in Moscow, declared that the Red Jews had made a mockery of him and he went over to Kolchak's army. This fact became known to Judge Sokolov, who immediately sent a trusted officer to look for him, but Yakovlev had disappeared without trace and was never able to give a statement.

In Ekaterinburg the royal family was housed in the Ipatiev house, which had been requisitioned by the Soviet. The prisoners were led into the house by the Jews Golochtchekin and Diskovski, who ruthlessly searched them. Isaiah Golochtchekin headed the regional Soviet and was in charge of organising all the details of the massacre. This individual was a depraved sadist who enjoyed listening to detailed accounts of the tortures inflicted on the victims of the Extraordinary Commission. Prince Dolgoruki, who had all the money with him, was imprisoned on Golochtchekin's orders and later died a victim of his loyalty to the Tsar. On 23 May the members of the royal family who were still in Tobolsk were transferred to Ekaterinburg. Another Jew named Vilensky was in charge of the Soviet kitchen that fed the prisoners and their guards.

According to Robert Wilton the only non-Jew among the leaders of the Soviet was Beloborodov, a young worker who had been elected chairman of the regional Soviet in Ekaterinburg by his factory comrades. Jüri Lina, however, rectifies Wilton and claims that Beloborodov, whose real name was Yankel Weisbart, was also a Jew and a good friend of Trotsky. Specifically, he was the son of Isidor Weisbart, a fur trader. The first Romanov guards were indeed Russians. Their initial treatment of the family of Nicholas II was very inconsiderate, but as the days went by it became progressively milder. Anatole Yakimov, one of the jailers who fell into the hands of the White Army, implied to Judge Sokolov that the pity, gentleness and simplicity of the prisoners brought about a rapprochement. According to Yakimov, the obscene songs, the brutality of treatment and manners diminished until they ceased altogether.

Just two weeks before the assassination, the executioner made his appearance at the Ipatiev house. On 4 July Yankel Yurovski, the new commander, replaced the Russian Avdeiev, who, accused of robbery, was imprisoned. Yurovski, the leader of the assassins, the son and grandson of Jews, was a brutal and domineering man, feared even by his relatives. After several altercations with the police, he went into exile in Germany, where he had a relationship with a German woman who refused to marry him for religious reasons. He then decided to be baptised in Berlin in the Lutheran church. Speaking German and Yiddish, Yurovsky returned to Ekaterinburg well provided with money twelve months before the war. Since the beginning of the revolution he had left the city, but after the Bolshevik coup d'état he reappeared and immediately became a commissar in the regional Soviet. Under the new commander everything changed. The Russian guards were used for the outer guard and in their place ten "Latvians" entered the house, who came from the cheka, where worked as torturers and executioners. Among them were several Jews: the inscriptions written in Hebrew at the crime scene reveal their true nationality. The Russians generally called the mercenaries enrolled in the Red Army Latvians because they constituted the majority element. These "Latvians" were in fact Jews of Hungarian and German origin, did not speak Russian and communicated with Yurovsky in Yiddish or German.

On Monday, 15 July, the boy Leonid Sednev was lodged with the Russian guards in the Popov house across the street. On the same day Golochtchekin and Beloborodov took Yurovski by car to the place chosen for the disappearance of the corpses. At five o'clock in the afternoon they returned and began to prepare the crime. Of all the Russian guards, only Paul Medvedev, the only Russian who remained in the house, had been trusted. Medvedev, who had a conviction for the rape of a young girl on his criminal record, was eventually arrested. His statements are of great value not only because of his involvement in the assassination, about which he gave details that would never have been known, but also because he was part of the guard from the beginning and was aware of what was going on.

Since it gets dark very late in the summer in those latitudes, it was not until two o'clock in the morning of the 16th that the work was begun. Yurovsky entered the rooms, woke the members of the imperial family and ordered them to dress and leave the house. They hurriedly cleaned themselves, followed Yurovsky down the stairs leading to the courtyard and entered the ground floor. The Tsar carried his son in his arms. Behind the family followed Dr. Botkin and the servants Haritonov, Trupp and Demidova. The room chosen for the killing was a cellar with only one window, into which the victims went down fearlessly, as they thought they were going on a journey. Anastasia, the youngest of Nicholas II's daughters, was carrying her little Jemmy, a spaniel. The Tsar asked for chairs, as Alexis could not stand, and the request was granted. Everyone waited for the signal to depart. Before they got off, they had heard the sound of an engine in front of the door. It was the four-ton Fiat truck on which the bodies were to be transported. The executioners then entered the room. After Yurovski came three Russians, Medvedev and two others, Ermakov and Vaganov, who were to ride in the truck to help dispose of the corpses; Yurovski's assistant, an unknown man named G. Nikulin who belonged to the Cheka; and seven "Latvians". At this point the victims understood, but no one moved or said anything. Advancing towards the Tsar, Yurovsky said coldly: "Your relatives wanted to save you, but they did not have the chance. Now, in a moment we are going to kill you." Shocked, the Tsar barely had time to mutter: "What? What?". Twelve revolvers fired almost simultaneously. The salvos followed one after the other. The Tsar, the Tsarina and the three eldest daughters, Olga, Tatiana and Maria, were killed instantly. The Tsarevitch was dying and the youngest daughter, Anastasia, was still alive. Yurovsky shot Alexis with several shots. The executioners killed the young Anastasia, who struggled screaming, with bayonet shots. Haritonov and Demidova were killed separately. Yurovsky's words, the last ones the Tsar heard, about the attempt of Nicholas II's relatives to save his life are particularly striking, as they suggest that Yakovlev's mission may have been related to this end. It is surprising that Yurovsky, who did not have to explain anything, uttered them in the presence of the other people in the cellar.

When the killing was over, the bodies were loaded onto the truck and Yurovsky, Ermakov and Vaganov hurried out of the city before dawn. Medvedev was left in charge of cleaning the house. The destination was the iron mines of the Verkh-Issetsk plant, the shafts of which had long since been abandoned. The site was located fifteen kilometres north of Ekaterinburg, near the town of Koptiaki. During the 17th, 18th and 19th about one hundred and forty litres of petrol and another one hundred and seventy litres of sulphuric acid were transported to the site. Before being thrown down the well, the bodies were dismembered and incinerated. The most solid parts were subjected to the action of the acid. During this time, a guard was kept outside the Ipatiev house so that the inhabitants of the town would not suspect anything. In 1979, Soviet archaeologists announced to the world that they had found the remains of the Imperial family buried near Koptiaki, although, they said, those of Maria and Alexis were missing. This would call into question Wilton's version that they had been thrown down a well.

On 20 July the Ekaterinburg Soviet announced the execution of Nicholas "the Bloodthirsty". The Soviet was presided over by Beloborodov, who, being considered Russian, served as a screen to the miners opposed to Jewish power, but in reality was led by the Jews Golochtchekin, Volkov, Syromolotov and Safarov, another comrade close to Trotsky. Golochtchekin informed the population by means of speeches and posters, in which it was said that bands of Czechoslovaks were threatening the town and that "the crowned executioner could have avoided the trial of the people". At the same time, the government broadcast the news abroad on the radio. The official text published by the newspapers is as follows:

> "At the first session (July 20 or 21) of the Central Executive Committee, elected by the Fifth Congress of Soviets, a communiqué of the Ural Regional Soviet concerning the execution of Tsar Nicholas Romanov was read out: 'Lately the capital of the Urals was seriously threatened by the offensive of gangs of Czechoslovaks. At this time a plot of counter-revolutionaries was uncovered who intended to wrest the tyrant by force from the hands of the Soviet authority. Faced with this state of affairs, the chairmanship of the Urals Regional Soviet decided to shoot Tsar Nicholas Romanov. The decision was carried out on 16 July. Romanov's wife and children were sent to a safe place. Documents related to the uncovered plot have been sent to Moscow by special courier. Initially it was planned to bring the Tsar before a court in order to try his crimes against the people, but the above-mentioned circumstance forced to suppress the plan'.
> The presidency of the E.C.C., having studied the circumstances which led the Ural regional Soviet to the execution of Nicholas Romanov, concludes that:
> The E.C.C., in the person of its chairman, considers the resolution of the Urals Regional Soviet to be regular. At the disposal of the E.C.C. there is important documentation connected with the Romanov affair: the diary he wrote until the last day of his life, his wife's diary and those of his daughters, his correspondence, including Grigory Rasputin's letters to Romanov and his family. All these documents will be selected and published without delay".

Officially, a committee of enquiry into the death of the tsar was appointed, which consisted of ten people and was chaired by Sverdlov himself. In other words, the one who ordered the crime was the head of the investigation. Seven of the members of this committee were Jews: Sverdlov, Sosnovski, Teodorovitch, Smidovitch, Rosenholtz, Rosine and Vladimirski (Hirshfeldt). There were two Russians, Maximov and Mitrovanov, and an Armenian named Avanessov.

Two written texts were found on the walls of the room where the Romanovs and their closest servants were murdered. The most cryptic or mysterious is a Kabbalistic inscription of three letters and a dash. The letters are an 'L' written in three different languages: Hebrew, Samaritan and Greek. Deciphering the meaning of the message requires knowledge of the Kabbalah, which has been said to place numerical value on the letters (gematria). Leslie Fry (Paquita de Shishmareff) provides detailed study of the inscription in *Waters Flowing Eastwards*. In writing two pages commenting on her paraphrase of the interpretation of the meaning of the letters, Leslie Fry cites literature on the interpretation of dogmas and rituals of high magic, occult philosophy, tarot and the history of magic. Fry concludes that a passive principle is apparent in the text, which indicates that those who killed the Tsar did not do so of their own free will, but in obedience to a higher order. He adds that the person who made the inscription was versed in the secrets of ancient Jewish Kabbalism contained in the Kabbalah and the *Talmud*. This person, in performing the deed in obedience to a higher order, was carrying out a ritual of black magic. This is the reason, according to this author, why he commemorated his act by means of a coded message. Leslie Fry offers two possible translations of the text: "Here the king was struck through the heart in punishment for his crimes" or "Here the king was sacrificed to bring about the destruction of his kingdom". In 1989, issue 169 of the Vilnius newspaper *Konsomolskaya Pravda* deciphers the message as follows: "The Tsar was sacrificed here, by order of the secret forces, to destroy the state. This is announced to all nations".

The second text is a couplet in German by the poet Heinrich Heine, the prophet of communism, the friend of James Rothschild, Moses Hess and Karl Marx. The phrase "religion is the opium of the people" is generally attributed to Marx, but in reality it is Heine who wrote it. The content of the distich alludes to the fulfilment of Jewish law, i.e. Jewish vengeance as understood by the Levites. The author allows himself a figure of speech, a calambour, by changing the name Belshazzar[54] to **Belshazzar.** The English translation of the verses would be this: "**Belshazzar** was in the same night / by his own servants executed".

In 1924 the city of Ekaterinburg was renamed Sverdlovsk. This was intended to give eternal fame to this Jew who presided over the Central Executive Committee, the position from which he allegedly ordered the assassination of the Romanovs. Today it is known that the superior order came from higher up, from New York, from Jacob Schiff to be precise. Once again, it is Jüri Lina who dares to reveal this historical fact, which has been intentionally concealed. This is perhaps the most sensitive information in *Under the Sign of the Scorpion*. On 20 July 2011, Henry Makow, a Canadian writer of Jewish origin who unequivocally denounces Zionism and the illuminati bankers, transcribed on his website "henrymakow.com" the fragment in question (pp. 276-277). Makow believes that it is because of this extremely dangerous information that both the book and the author are being suppressed and that the few copies that are still available in North America and England are being sold at prohibitive prices on Amazon. According to Lina, it was from 1990 onwards that Jacob Schiff's role in the assassination

---

[54] Belshazzar or Balthasar was a Babylonian prince who, according to the *Book of Daniel*, used the vessels from the temple in Jerusalem, brought to Babylon as booty, as table service for his courtiers. This desecration prompted an invisible hand to write on the wall letters that no wise man of the court could decipher. Only the prophet Daniel understood the message and announced that the king's pride would be punished with the death of Belshazzar and the fall of his kingdom.

of the imperial family began to be explained in Russia, although the facts had already been revealed in 1939 *in Tsarky Vestnik*, a newspaper in exile.

The Estonian author claims that Lenin had very little involvement in the assassination. He explains that his hasty departure from Ekaterinburg in the face of the approach of the "Whites" was the reason for the failure to destroy the telegraph strips, which were seized by Judge Sokolov, who got hold of them without being able to decipher the telegrams. It was in 1922 that a group of experts in Paris deciphered the strips and Sokolov discovered that they were extremely revealing, as they related to the assassination of the Tsar and his family. It stated that the chairman of the E.C.C., Yakov Sverdlov, sent a message to Yakov Yurovsky that after he had informed Jacob Schiff about the approach of the White army, had received orders to liquidate the Tsar and his entire family. These orders were delivered to Sverdlov by the American Representation in the city of Vologda. To this city, halfway between Moscow and Archangel, all the European representations had retreated. Sverdlov instructed Yurovsky to carry out the order, but the next day Yurovsky wanted to confirm whether the whole family was to be killed or just the Tsar. Sverdlov confirmed the order to eliminate everyone and made him responsible for carrying it out. Jüri Lina rejects the claim by Edward Radzinsky, a Jewish historian, that it was Lenin who ordered the assassination. There is not a single document to support this thesis. In November 1924 Sokolov[55] told a close friend that his publisher was

---

[55] In March 1920, Judge Nicolas Sokolov and Pierre Gilliard, the French teacher of the Tsar's daughters, were in Kharbin (in the Russian Far East) trying to get the dossiers of the investigation into the Romanov assassination, contained in heavy suitcases, out of the country. Gillard himself recounted this adventure in *Le tragique destin de Nicolas II et de sa famille* (1922). They intended to reach the train of the French general Maurice Janin, parked a short distance from the platforms, but Bolshevik spies were swarming in and around the station. Gillard's account continues: "We suddenly saw some individuals emerge from the shadows and they approached us shouting: 'Where are you going? What are you carrying in those suitcases?' As we pressed on without replying, they showed an intention of stopping us and ordered us to open our suitcases. Fortunately, the distance to be covered was not very long and we ran. In a few moments we reached the General's carriage, whose sentries came to meet us. At last all the documents of the investigation were safe". Judge Sokolov refers to the same situation and describes it as "one of the most difficult." Sokolov makes it clear that, wanting to save the documents at any cost, he had written in February 1920 to the British ambassador in Peking, Mr. Lampson, asking for help in passing them on to Europe. The British government's reply was negative, and the British consul in Kharbin, Mr. Sley, was responsible for communicating this to the judge. Sokolov's account ends as follows: "On the same day, in the company of General Diterichs, I was to meet the French General Janin. He replied that he considered the mission we were entrusting to him as a debt of honour to a faithful ally. Thanks to General Janin, the documents were saved and taken to safety". General Janin himself later wrote a book, *My Mission in Siberia*, in which he explains that Sley, the English consul in Kharbin, "was a Jew about whom it was said that his wife was related to Trotsky." Judge Sokolov made for security reasons several copies of the investigation dossier. Robert Wilton claims that he had one of them.

afraid to publish these facts and wanted them suppressed. The judge reportedly then showed this friend the original strips and the deciphered translations. Sokolov, who was forty-two years old, died suddenly a month later. He was due to travel to New York to testify on behalf of Henry Ford, against whom Kuhn Loeb & Co, Jacob Schiff's bank, had filed a lawsuit for the publication of the book *The International Jew*. Judge Sokolov's book, *The Assassination of the Tsar's Family*, was published in Berlin in 1925 without the information in question.

The will to exterminate the Christian Romanov dynasty showed the hatred of those who ordered it. Between June 1918 and January 1919, the Talmudic revenge of the Bolshevik Jews claimed the lives of eighteen members of the imperial family. We will comment only on the assassination of Mikhail Romanov, since the Tsar had abdicated to him in 1917. On 12 June, a month before the Yekaterinburg massacre, the younger brother of Nicholas II was assassinated along with his secretary Brian Johnson by a gang of criminals under the orders of the Jew Markov. The assassins turned up at the hotel in Perm where they were staying. Under the pretext that they were going to take them to a safe place, they took them out of the city and killed them in a wooded area. The bodies were never found as they were burned. For many years one of the murderers carried the Englishman Johnson's watch as a souvenir.

Trotsky and the attempted assassination of Lenin

In every respect 1918 was a momentous year. During this ambiguous and uncertain year, among other things, the course of the revolution and the future of Russia and Germany were decided. After the signing of the Treaty of Brest-Litovsk there was an internal struggle between Trotskyists and Leninists which has been obscured by official historiography. In the summer of 1918, in addition to the massacre of the imperial family, there were a series of political assassinations that have never been adequately explained or understood. Between 20 June, the date of the assassination of V. Volodarsky (Moses Goldstein), and 30 August, the day on which an attempt was made to eliminate Lenin, there was an underhand struggle for power in Russia, which we will try to understand below. The attempted assassination of Lenin, about which a smokescreen was fabricated that has never faded, is one of the darkest episodes of the Bolshevik revolution. Against false versions interested in concealing the truth and blind partisan reasoning, we point out in this section the thesis that it was Trotsky who, manoeuvring in the shadows and using some and others, tried to kill Lenin in order to seize absolute leadership. We shall support this interpretation with facts and arguments, the logic of which the reader will be able to judge.

At this stage of our work, we consider that it has been demonstrated that Trotsky was an agent of international Jewish banking. At the age of only twenty-five, he had established himself alongside Parvus as the most important figure in the 1905 revolution, generated during the Russo-Japanese war, which had been financed by the bank Kuhn Loeb and Co. of Jacob Schiff. Even then Trotsky was related to the big financiers, having married Natalia Sedova, the daughter of the banker Givotovsky, who was linked to the Warburgs and Jacob Schiff. When Trotsky arrived in Russia with his Jewish revolutionaries from New York in 1917, he brought money and powerful international aid. Lenin, who had always despised his theory of "permanent revolution", was critical of him, but Nadezhda Krupskaya, his Jewish wife, knew very well what he meant Trotsky and was instrumental in Lenin's acceptance of him despite their bad relations.

In 1911 Lenin, referring to the internal struggle within the party, had alluded to Trotsky as a master in the use of "resonant but empty phrases" and lamented his continual changes of sides. He had then considered him "a scoundrel who minimised the party and exalted himself." On different occasions Lenin had complained about Trotsky's "swerves" and regretted that it was never possible to know where he stood. In a 1914 text on the right of nations to self-determination he stated: "Trotsky has never had a firm opinion on any important question of Marxism." Still in February 1917, in a letter written in February to Aleksandra Kollontái he exclaimed, "What a scoundrel that Trotsky is!" However much it pained Lenin, whose intransigence was an obstacle on many occasions, it was Trotsky who had the ability to rally around the Bolsheviks the entire revolutionary left wing, which included the revolutionary socialists and the anarchists. At bottom, the former Bund of Jewish proletarians was Trotsky's real party. The great majority of the leaders of the revolutionary parties came from the Bund, which had infiltrated them all.

The fact that it was President Wilson himself who provided Trotsky with a passport to travel to Russia for the purpose of revolution speaks volumes about the support he had in the United States. The British also knew that they had to go for him and not for Lenin, who was allegedly linked to the German secret services. No sooner had the British War Cabinet received the message from William B. Thompson, the Wall Street man, about the irreversibility of the revolution in Russia than Alfred Milner, spearhead of the international conspiracy in Britain, sent Robert Hamilton Bruce Lockhart to Trotsky's side. This agent has gone down in history for his alleged involvement in the attempt on Lenin's life. A plot that is known as "The Lockhart Plot". The problem is that the communist sources who relate the whole imbroglio claim that the intention was to destroy the revolution and not exclusively Lenin. In other words, an agent of Lord Milner, one of the magnates who had brought about the overthrow of the Tsar and financed the Bolsheviks, wanted months later to liquidate the revolution and undo all the work that had been done. It is easy to understand that the interpretation offered by these sources makes no sense. Of course, the British Government has always denied any involvement in the attempt to assassinate Lenin; but more than ninety years later, documents that could shed light on what happened are still classified as Official Secrets.

A key figure in the plot was the famous spy Sidney Reilly, an agent in the service of the conspiracy who made contact with Lockhart in May 1918. Presumably, Reilly, considered the best spy in the British Intelligence Service, was the man behind whom Trotsky himself was hiding, thus diverting all attention and responsibility for the attempt on Lenin's life onto England. In 1932 Robert Bruce Lockhart wrote his own version of events in *Memoirs of a British Agent*, in which, logically enough, he says nothing that could implicate him, his country or Trotsky in the plot. Precisely because of its apparent innocuousness, this interpretation was widely reported in the media and propaganda was quick to describe the book as "the greatest human document of the century". Hollywood, specifically Warner Brothers, made Lockhart's memoirs into a film in 1934. Lockhart's diplomatic career, however, was scarred as a result of this affair and, on the advice of Lord Milner, he left the Foreign Office.

His son Robin also published *Reilly Ace of Spies* in 1967, in which he tells what he wants to about his father's relationship with the spy. However, Robin Bruce Lockhart unwittingly provides very significant and valuable information of the utmost importance: two days before the outbreak of the war, Sidney Reilly temporarily left his job for the SIS (Secret Intelligence Service) because he "received a very attractive proposition from the Givotovsky brothers, who controlled the Russo-Asian Bank". In other words, Sidney Reilly worked for more than two years for the Givotovskys, the bankers related to Trotsky, who was married to the daughter of one of them, Natalia Sedova. The Givotovskys sent him as a bank representative first to Japan and then to the United States, to New York, where he lived until the end of 1916. *Reilly's Ace of Spies* also became a television serial. Ian Fleming was inspired by Sidney Reilly to create the famous James Bond. Certainly the real life of this spy far surpasses fiction. His multiple identities have confused investigators and intelligence services. According to Captain Mansfield Cumming, one of his bosses, Reilly was "a man of indomitable courage, a genius as an agent, but a sinister man to whom I could never fully give my trust." He was actually a Jewish bastard named Solomon (Shlomo) Rosenblum, the illegitimate son of a woman named Polina. His father was Dr. Mikhail Abramovich Rosenblum. He was born on 24 March 1873 in Kherson (Ukraine), although some sources place his birth in Odessa.

Robert Hamilton Bruce Lockhart, whose father may have been of Jewish origin (he himself writes that he received his first corporal punishment from his father for playing a cricket match on the Sabbath), nevertheless boasts in *Memoirs of a British Agent* of his mother's Scottish blood. His first contact with Alfred Milner came after the February/March coup, when Milner arrived in St Petersburg commissioned by the London government and infamously aborted any hope of British aid to its Russian ally. Lockhart, then British consul in Moscow, was summoned by the ambassador and travelled to St. Petersburg. Milner had probably received from George Buchanan, his Freemason brother, good reports from the Consul, who blatantly lies when he writes that the British Ambassador had nothing to do with the overthrow of the Tsar. Lockhart has only words of gratitude for Buchanan, whom he regards as an example of honesty, sincerity, etc. etc.. The contact between Lord Milner and the young Lockhart took place at the embassy, where after lunch they had "a long conversation" which continued in the evening: "I dined alone with him in his rooms at the Hotel Europa". A week later Alfred Milner travelled to Moscow, where Lockhart had arranged for him an interview with Prince Lvov, another Brother Mason who confirmed to Milner that "if there was no change in the Emperor's attitude there would be a revolution within three weeks." So it was. Six months later, in September 1917, Bruce Lockhart had an affair with a Jewish woman. By his own account, this prompted Ambassador Buchanan to advise the consul to return to London.

On 19 December 1917 Alfred Milner and Bruce Lockhart dined together in London at the home of Sir Arthur Steel-Maitland. The next day Lockhart was summoned from Downing Street, where Lord Curzon announced that the War Cabinet had decided to establish contact with the Bolsheviks. On 21 December Lord Milner introduced his agent to Prime Minister Lloyd George. Preparations for the journey began at once. Lockhart was to embark at Bergen (Norway) on the same cruise ship on which Ambassador Buchanan was returning to London. The plan was as follows: the British would give Maksim Litvinov, the Bolsheviks' unofficial ambassador to London, the same privileges that the Bolsheviks granted to Lockhart. The meeting between Litvínov (Meyer Hennokh Moisevitch Wallack-Finkelstein) and Lockhart came about through another Jew, Theodore Rothstein, a Trotskyite working as a translator in the War Ministry. Trotsky had initially thought of Rothstein as a semi-official representative of the Bolsheviks in Britain, but Radek observed that his position in the Ministry could be of greater use to them. Rothstein, writes Lockhart, explained that "Trotsky's ambition was not a separate peace, but a general peace. He pointed out that if he were Lloyd George he would accept Trotsky's offer of a conference without conditions, since England would be the main beneficiary." Litvinov and Rothstein on the Bolshevik side and Lockhart and Rex Leeper on the British side had lunch together in early January 1918. It was agreed that, without official recognition for the time being, both Litvínov and Lockhart would enjoy certain diplomatic privileges, including the use of codes and the right to diplomatic mail. It was on this occasion that Litvinov wrote for Lockhart the letter of introduction to Trotsky mentioned above.

Five days before the trip, Lockhart held daily meetings with Lord Milner. In his *Memoirs of a British Agent,* Lockhart provides extremely relevant information about these interviews for those who know how to read them. Let us look at for some of them. He writes, for example, that in the course of another dinner alone Milner expressed his bitterness about Foreign Office policy and referred to Lord Balfour as "a harmless old gentleman". Alfred Milner confessed to Lockhart that he wished to be at the head of the Foreign Office for six months. It would have been of great interest to know whether he told him what for. Milner, like Mandell House and Jacob Schiff, was part of the lobby calling for immediate recognition of the Bolshevik government. Trotsky's idea of the need to reject a separate peace with Germany was shared by Lord Milner and also by Lloyd George. Milner wanted something more: to see the Communists sitting at Versailles alongside the victors of the war, which required recognition of Lenin's government. Lockhart acknowledges, and this is extremely significant, that he had to do all he could to "put a stick in the wheels of a possible separate peace negotiation and was to strengthen as much as possible the Bolshevik resistance to German demands". Of Alfred Milner's thinking, he writes the following with absolute impudence: "He believed in a highly organised state, in whose service efficiency and hard work were more important than titles or money. He had little respect for the decadent aristocrat, and none for the financier who had made his money by manipulating the market." In his slavish adulation, Bruce Lockhart highlights Lord Milner's "nobility of thought and lofty idealism". What he does not mention, of course, is that he was a 33rd degree Freemason, an agent of the Rothschilds, the chief architect of the Boer War, the founder of the Round Table and the director of the London Joint Stock Bank, which profited from Basil Zaharoff's arms dealing. Lord Milner authorised Lockhart to telegraph directly to him in case of difficulty.

Once in Russia, Bruce Lockhart contacted Colonel Raymond Robins, his American counterpart who had been left in charge of the American Red Cross mission after the departure of William B. Thompson, and Captain Jacques Sadoul, a French socialist of Jewish origin, a former friend of Trotsky's who eventually switched to the Bolsheviks. Their missions were similar. Robins was the intermediary between the Wilson government and the Bolsheviks. This led them to be together on a daily basis for four months. Anthony Sutton quotes in *Wall Street and the Bolshevik Revolution* a paper on Bolshevik propaganda read in 1919 at a hearing before a Senate subcommittee. It quotes these words from Robins to Lockhart:

"You will hear that I am a representative of Wall Street, that I am in the service of William B. Thompson to get Altai copper for him, that I have already obtained 500,000 acres of timber forests in Russia, that I have already taken shares in the Trans-Siberian, that I have been granted a monopoly of Russian platinum, that this explains my work for the Soviets.... You will hear all these things. Now, I don't think this is true, commissioner, but let's assume it is. Let us accept that I am here to take Russia for Wall Street and for American businessmen. Let's assume that you are a British wolf and I am an American wolf, and that when this war is over we are going to devour each other for the Russian market. Let's do this in a frank way. But let's accept at the same time that we are pretty smart wolves, and that we know that if we don't hunt together right now the German wolf will devour us both, and then let's get to work."

Robins and Lockhart shared many meals together. Lockhart's loquacity is noted in his *Memoirs*, and he recalls an after-dinner conversation in which Robins went on to disparage the Allied politicians who opposed recognition of the Communists and demolished the ridiculous theory of those who claimed that they were working for the Germans. He went on to praise Trotsky, of whom he said that "he was a splendid son of a bitch, but the most important Jew after Christ."

After the signing of Brest-Litovsk, because of the proximity of the German troops, the government evacuated Petrograd[56] and settled in Moscow, where the formal ratification of the Treaty was to take place. Trotsky refused to attend and remained in the capital for another week. He proposed to Lockhart that he stay and offered to take him with him on his train when he travelled later to Moscow, where he personally arranged comfortable accommodation for him. The British agent, to whom Trotsky gave his private telephone, writes that they saw each other daily in those days. It was during this last week in Petrograd that Moura Budberg appeared in Bruce Lockhart's life. This woman, known as the Mata-Hari of Russia, later had intimate relations with Gorky and the Fabian socialist H. G. Wells, author of *The War of the Worlds*. It is likely that Moura was already a KGB agent at the age of 26: her biographer, Nina Berberova, suggests that she may have been a lover of the Latvian Chekist Yakov Peters. If so, it is unlikely that Lockhart ever suspected it.

On 24 April, as a consequence of the newly signed peace, the new German ambassador, Count Mirbach, who had been a counsellor at the German Embassy in St. Petersburg before the war, arrived in Moscow. He presented his credentials at the Kremlin on the 26th, but was received not by Lenin, but by Sverdlov, the chairman of the Central Executive Committee. During the months of the Brest-Litovsk negotiations, the opportunity for an understanding between the Bolsheviks and the Allies had been lost, and by early May Lenin's peace policy had been gaining ground. However, Trotsky, the new Commissar of War, continued to speak of war as inevitable and

---

[56] St. Petersburg's name was changed to Petrograd because the Tsar considered the name to be too German. He therefore decided to change it. Later, after Lenin's death in 1924, the city was renamed Leningrad.

sought to ensure that the Allies would not intervene in Russia's internal affairs, unless they did so as allies against Germany, as Robins, Mandell House and other agents lobbying President Wilson intended. In this connection, Trotsky proposed to London through Bruce Lockhart that they help them reorganise the Russian fleets and even offered to put an Englishman in charge of the railways. Lockhart, who regretted the disagreements between the Foreign Office and the War Cabinet, did not get a reply. The ambiguity in British and American decisions and actions would require a case study, as it was the consequence of serious internal divergences.

It was on 7 May that Sidney Reilly appeared. The staging recounted by Lockhart is almost unbelievable. The agent writes that, unbeknownst to him, Reilly arrived quietly at the Kremlin and asked to meet Lenin. Asked for his credentials, he said that he had been sent personally by Lloyd George to obtain first-hand information about the claims and ideals of the Bolsheviks. Lockhart writes that he understood that the government was dissatisfied with his reports and had moved another agent. Reilly evidently did not see Lenin, but met Bonch-Brouevitch, a personal friend of the Soviet leader. Lockhart settles the matter by saying that he asked Ernest Boyce, the new head of the Intelligence Service in Petrograd, for an explanation and was told that it was a new agent who had just arrived from England. Lockhart declares himself outraged and at the same time admiring the audacity of Reilly, who the next day showed up to explain himself to him.

From June onwards the internal struggle among the Bolsheviks intensified with a series of assassinations which have been interpreted in different ways. The most common ones attribute the responsibility to the revolutionary socialists. The first of these took place on 20 June, when Vladimir Volodarvsky (Moses Goldstein), Commissar of Press and Propaganda, was shot three times in the street, one of which struck him in the heart and killed him instantly. Moses Salomonovich Uritsky (Boretsky), head of the Petrograd Cheka, undertook the investigation of the attack; but, as we shall see, he too was eliminated two months later, on 30 August. Volodarvsky and Uritsky were two of Trotsky's most trusted men: they were part of the group that had arrived with him from New York on board the *Kristianiafjord*. Uritsky, known as the "butcher of Petrograd", had been with him in 1905 and had already led the Krasnoyarsk Soviet. He had also travelled with Trotsky from Barcelona to New York aboard the *Montserrat*. Volodarvsky's assassination took place on his way back from a meeting at the Obuchov factory. The car in which he was travelling stopped without petrol in a Petrograd street. Volodarvsky got out with three comrades and set out to complete the journey on foot to the nearby Soviet district. At this moment the terrorist appeared and shot him three times. Before fleeing, he threw a bomb to avoid pursuit. The fact that the car had stopped at the very spot where the assassin with gun and bomb was waiting aroused Uritsky's suspicions, and he concluded that the crime had been organised in the Moscow Cheka with the approval of Lenin and Felix Dzerzhinsky. The next day, Lenin accused the right wing of the revolutionary socialists of being behind the terrorist attack.

On 21 June, the day after Volodarvsky's assassination, Admiral Alexei Shchastny, commander of the Baltic Fleet imprisoned in the Kremlin, was shot. The admiral had refused to carry out the order to surrender to the Germans about 200 ships in Helsinki and, disobeying orders, moved the fleet to Kronstadt. The British had asked the Bolsheviks not to surrender the fleet, but to destroy it. Trotsky then ordered the ships to be dynamited in such a way that they would suffer as little damage as possible. This would have enabled the British to repair them for the Communists in the event of an understanding, as Trotsky wished, who, as seen above, proposed to Lockhart that England should help them to get the Russian fleets into operation. On 28 May Shchastny was summoned to the Kremlin and asked by Trotsky whether or not he wished to serve under the Soviet regime. The answer must not have pleased him and the admiral was imprisoned. On 20 June, only two hours after the charge of high treason had been announced, a farcical trial took place, with only the Russian sailor's sister allowed to attend. Trotsky, the only witness, presented the official accusation. The death sentence was carried out the next day.

Only two weeks later, on 6 July 1918, Wilhelm von Mirbach, the German ambassador who had been in office for just over two months, was assassinated. This was the trigger for the attempted coup d'état attributed to the revolutionary socialists led by Maria Spiridonova. Since the entry of the United States into the conflict, ten thousand American soldiers had been landing in Europe every day, which made it possible to foresee an accelerated outcome of the war. Trotsky, in a further attempt to abort the Treaty of Brest-Litovsk and resume the struggle against Germany, which would have allowed communist Russia to sit with the victors at Versailles, ordered Yakov Blumkin to kill Count Mirbach. The Finnish communist Aino Kuusinen confirms in her memoirs that Blumkin was the ambassador's assassin. As usual, the crime was blamed on the revolutionary socialists; but in reality they were being used by Trotsky.

Let us recall that in October 1917 Trotsky had rallied the most extremist section of the SRs around the Bolsheviks, which meant that he had the leverage and influence to manage them as he saw fit. Blumkin had begun his career as a rabbi in a synagogue in Odessa and like many Jewish extremists asked for a position in the Cheka after the Bolsheviks came to power. When he murdered Mirbach he was a member of the Social Revolutionary Party, but during the civil war he was already working as Trotsky's military secretary. In the preface to the first volume of the *Military Writings*, written between March 1918 and February 1923, Trotsky says: "As fate would have it, Comrade Blumkin, a former Left SR, who in July 1918 risked his life fighting us and is now a member of our party, is my collaborator in the preparation of this volume, one part of which reflects our all-out combat with the party of the Left SRs. The revolution is a consummate master at putting everyone in his place, and, if necessary, at taking his place. All that was most virile and consistent in the party of the Left Social-Revolutionaries is today in our ranks." We are of the opinion that the allusion to his "risking his life fighting us" is part of the blatant strategy of disassociating himself from Blumkin in order to continue to conceal his involvement in the Mirbach bombing and the attempted coup of the social-revolutionaries. Another crime to note in Comrade Blumkin's account is that of the poet Sergei Yesenin, who in 1912, at the age of seventeen, had married the famous dancer Isadora Duncan.[57]

Of course, in *Memoirs of a British Agent*, Lord Milner's agent to Trotsky, Bruce Lockhart, singles out the revolutionary socialists as the sole architects of Count Mirbach's assassination; yet in his account he acknowledges that, like the Trotskyist faction, these revolutionary socialists were opposed to the Brest-Litovsk peace, which they had never accepted. With an astonishing "naivety", Lockhart writes: "The Left Socialist Revolutionaries began to prepare fantastic plans to overthrow the Bolshevik Government in order to resume their war with Germany". Only very uninformed readers can swallow that members of the Left Sector of the SRs would single-handedly seek to seize power in Russia at a time of maximum complexity. It is much more logical to think that Trotsky was trying to build on this political and ideological coincidence and that he wanted to use it to seize control of the party and the government. Many members of the Jewish Bund had penetrated the revolutionary socialists and through these links

---

[57] Sergey Yesenin, considered Russia's most prominent poet of the 20th century, officially committed suicide. In *Under the sign of the scorpion* Jüri Lina comments that he could hardly have done so with a gash in his head through which his brain was coming out. The reason for his murder was a poem, *Land of Criminals*, in which he described a Jewish tyrant, Leibman Chekistov, who was a transcript of Trotsky himself. Yesenin initially believed in the revolution, but soon realised what was going on. In the poem, which he read to his friends, he described how American financiers had taken over Russia with the help of political gangsters. Informed of the poem, Trotsky could not forgive such an offence and ordered Blumkin, his enforcement arm, to eliminate the poet. A friend of Yesenin's, Alexei Ganin, was arrested on 25 March 1925 and executed under Articles 172 and 176 of the Criminal Code of Communist Russia, which condemned anti-Semitism with the death penalty. According to the secret police, the poets Oreshin, Klychkov, Ganin and Yesenin had publicly proclaimed in a bar at the end of 1923 that in Russia only Jews held power. On the night of 28 December 1925 Yakov Blumkin and one of his henchmen, Wolf Erlich, broke into the room of the *Angleterre* Hotel in Petrograd. The poet bravely resisted, but the murderers beat him violently on the head and then hanged him.

Trotsky had convinced them in 1917 to support the Bolsheviks, who had compensated them with various posts in different commissariats.

It was at the Fifth Congress of Soviets, which opened its sessions on July 4, two days before Mirbach's assassination, that the clash took place. In any case, it seems clear to us that the aim was not "to overthrow the Bolshevik Government", as Lockhart writes, but the Leninist section of the Party, which had imposed a line of action in international politics that neither the Trotskyists nor the Left SRs shared. The Congress was held in the Moscow Opera House. About one hundred and fifty members of the C.C.E., almost all of them Jews, presided over the sessions. On Sverdlov's right sat the revolutionary socialists: Cherepanov, the Jews Kamkov and Karelin, and at the far end was Maria Spiridonova, who had become famous in 1906 for having murdered Luzhenovsky, Inspector General of Police, whom she shot in the face on the platform of the Borisogliebsk station and then tried to kill herself, but failed to do so. On 5 July Maria Spirodonova took the floor to attack Lenin with extreme harshness. "I accuse you," she said, "of betraying the peasants, of using them for your own ends, and of not looking after their interests." Turning to his followers, he shouted, "In Lenin's philosophy you are only dung." A threat followed. Spiridonova warned Lenin that if he continued to humiliate and oppress the peasants he would still find in his hand "the same pistol and the same bomb" that he had used on another occasion. A burst of applause broke out at her last words, but she was immediately rebuked from the stalls by a Bolshevik delegate. There was a great uproar, and burly peasants rose to their feet, shaking their fists at the Bolsheviks.

Lenin, showing an irritating superiority, finally took the floor and calmly answered the accusations. Referring to the taunts concerning his servility towards the Germans and the desire of the Social-Revolutionaries to continue the war, he accused them in turn of carrying out the policy of the imperialist Allies, and defended the Treaty of Brest-Litovsk. The next to speak was the social-revolutionary Kamkov, who, addressing Mirbach and the German delegation attending the congress, roared: "The dictatorship of the proletariat has been transformed into the dictatorship of Mirbach. In spite of all our warnings, Lenin's policy remains the same and we have become not an independent power, but the lackeys of the German imperialists, who have the audacity to show their faces even in this theatre." Instantly the revolutionary socialists rose to their feet and showing their fists to the German box began to shout: "Down with Mirbach, out with the German butchers, out with the hangman's gallows of Brest." Hastily Sverdlov, ringing the bell, closed the session.

At a quarter to three on Saturday the 6th, Yakov Blumkin and another comrade arrived by car at the German Embassy, which was guarded by Bolshevik troops. They were allowed to enter without problem thanks to special passes signed by Alexandrovitch, vice-chairman of the Cheka, of which Blumkin himself was an officer. Trotsky's henchman told the embassy counsellor, Kurt Riezler, that he must see Mirbach personally, since the Cheka had uncovered an Allied plot to assassinate the ambassador. In view of Blumkin's credentials and considering the gravity of the situation, Riezler introduced him to Count Mirbach. When the ambassador asked him how the assassins intended to act, the terrorist pulled a Browning pistol from his pocket and replied: "This way". Blumkin then emptied the magazine into the diplomat's body. He then jumped out of a window and, before escaping, threw a hand grenade to ensure the ambassador's death.

At the same time the revolutionary socialists were gathering troops in the Pokrovsky barracks. Dmitri Popov, another Cheka agent, had brought a unit of two thousand men. There were also a few hundred sailors from the Black Sea Fleet and disaffected soldiers from other regiments. For the first hour it looked as if the coup might succeed: they arrested Dzerzhinsky, whom Lenin had charged in 1917 with the creation of the Cheka or Secret Police, of which he was the director, and captured the telegraph office, but failed to take advantage of it to send telegrams all over the country announcing the success of the coup d'état. When they tried to approach the Opera House to surprise Lenin and his men, they found that government troops had already surrounded the building. Seeing that the attempt had failed, the insurgents hurried back to their barracks. Trotsky, Lockhart says, had called up two regiments of Latvians from the suburbs and had the armoured cars ready. For what purpose? Most likely, he was keeping in wait for developments.

Bruce Lockhart himself, who had been there since four o'clock, gives his own version of what was going on at the Opera House in the meantime. As he recounts, "the afternoon was sweltering and the atmosphere in the theatre was like a Turkish bath". The stalls were full of delegates, but on the platform many of the seats of the Bolshevik leaders were empty. By five o'clock in the afternoon most of the members of the Central Executive Committee had disappeared. Nor was there anyone in the box assigned to the representatives of the Central Powers. Maria Spiridonova remained calmly in the theatre. Lockhart, who was in his box, succinctly explains in the *Memoirs* that at six o'clock in the evening Sidney Reilly arrived and announced that there had been fighting in the streets and that the theatre was surrounded by troops who had closed the exits. Something had gone wrong. Reilly and a French agent took several documents out of his pockets, tore them into very small pieces and stuffed them into the lining of the seats. "The most compromising ones," writes Lockhart, "were swallowed". At seven o'clock in the evening, Radek rescued them and explained that the Social Revolutionaries had assassinated the German ambassador with the intention of provoking the Germans to resume the war. Radek, according to the British agent's account, said that the murder of Count Mirbach was the signal for an uprising by the Social Revolutionaries, who, supported by Bolshevik dissidents, had planned to arrest the party leaders during the congress. In other words, a coup attempt had been aborted and the left SRs, who had been used, were the scapegoats. A few days later, a Red Army general, Muraviev, tried to move his troops from the Volga to Moscow, but the failure of the coup was known and his own soldiers arrested him. This general eventually shot himself in the presence of the Simbirsk Soviet. Spiridonova and Cherepanov were arrested and imprisoned in the Kremlin.

Yet another provocation was made to the Germans. On 30 July, Field Marshal Hermann von Eichhorn, one of the two commanders of the German troops occupying the Ukraine, was assassinated in Kiev in an attempt to push them into resuming the war. The new German ambassador, Karl Helfferich, who had recently arrived in Moscow to replace Count Mirbach, decided to leave Russia and return to Berlin. Dzerzhinsky, Lenin's man who headed the Cheka, responded to this attack with a wave of brutal terror: without trial he had more than a thousand people shot in Petrograd and as many in Moscow. Germany, despite the murders of Mirbach and Eichhorn, did not fall into the trap and found a way to coexist with Bolshevik Russia.

On 30 August the struggle among the Chekists reached its zenith. In the morning Moses Uritsky, who suspected Lenin and Dzerzhinsky of involvement in the Volodarsky bombing, was murdered. It was a visitors' day at the Commissariat of Internal Affairs and there were people waiting in the foyer. A young man wearing a leather jacket had arrived on a bicycle and, incomprehensibly, had entered the building without being searched. Sitting by the outer door, he awaited the arrival of Uritsky, chairman of the Cheka. The "Butcher of Petrograd", a bloodthirsty Trotskyite who had murdered five thousand officers, arrived at his Petrograd office at ten o'clock in the morning and made his way to the lift. Immediately the young man in the leather jacket approached him and shot him several times in the head and body. The killer then ran into the street, got on his bicycle and fled as fast as he could. As the cars of his pursuers caught up with him, he abandoned his bicycle and entered the headquarters of the British Representation. Shortly afterwards he came out wearing a long coat. Seeing the Red Guards waiting outside, he shot at them, but was soon captured. According to this official version, the terrorist was Leonid Kannegisser, a 22-year-old Jewish social revolutionary, a student at Petrograd University (Nina Berberova in *Histoire de la baronne Boudberg* reveals that Kannegisser wrote poems about Kerensky, his hero, whom he depicted on a white horse).

Most investigators consider the official version of the assassination "a tall tale". It is not credible that an armed man could enter the building without being searched by the guards, nor that he could approach the Cheka chairman without any obstacles, nor that he managed to leave the building and escape on a bicycle without being stopped by the guards at the gate. Unknown persons could not speak to Uritsky even on the telephone. It is most logical to think that the central organisation of the Secret Police, with Lenin and

Dzerzhinsky at its head, was behind the murder of Uritsky, who was a member of the C.C.E. It seems clear that the Cheka had no interest in the truth being known. Kannegisser, who admitted to being the perpetrator of the crime, declared that he had acted alone. The revolutionary socialists denied that he was a member of the party and rejected any connection with him. If Kannegisser really had been a revolutionary socialist, a trial would have served as propaganda for the regime. However, neither the revolver nor the ammunition used was analysed, nor was Kannegisser, who was killed illegally, brought to trial. Thus, the motive for Uritsky's murder was never known.

The war raging inside the Cheka had a second episode on 30 August, probably related to the first, which could have changed the course of the revolution. After ten o'clock that night, a Jewish terrorist, in this case a woman, Fanny Kaplan, also known as Dora Kaplan, although until the age of sixteen she kept the Jewish name of Feiga Roydman, fired three shots at Lenin. If she had succeeded in her aim, this attack would undoubtedly have been the final one. As usual, the SRs were singled out. But the pertinent question is now the one that Cicero asked in these circumstances: "Cui Bono? In other words, for whom is it good, for whom does it profit? Seneca offers an assertive answer to his predecessor's exhortative phrase: "Cui prodest scelus, is fecit", that is, whoever benefits from the crime, that is its author. It is unquestionable that Trotsky, according to Raymond Robins "the most important Jew after Christ", the agent of international Jewish banking who had essential backers in Washington and London, would have seized power in Russia if Lenin had died. By hook or by crook, Trotsky, to whom the Red Army he himself was building with the financing of the Warburgs and company obeyed, would have imposed his candidacy as successor. Stalin prevented this in 1924; but in 1918 there was no other leader with sufficient prestige to be able to replace Lenin.

The facts, as always when there is a desire to conceal the truth, have remained shrouded in a tangle of lies, misrepresentations, and contradictory versions,, which make it impossible to know for certain what happened. The official version explains that Lenin, after finishing a rally at the Michelson factory in Moscow, had gone out into the courtyard and was talking to the workers near his car. It was then in the darkness of the night that three shots rang out and Lenin fell to the ground with two bullets in his body: one penetrated his left lung above the heart, the other lodged in his neck, very close to the spine. The third went through his coat and slightly wounded a nurse at the Petropavlovsk hospital. Lenin's Jewish chauffeur, Stepan Gil, who was sitting in the vehicle, testified that a woman with a pistol was three steps away from Lenin and that when he got out of the car the woman threw the pistol at his feet and disappeared into the crowd. The wounded man was immediately put into the car and taken to the Kremlin. Lenin apparently feared a large-scale conspiracy and refused to leave his quarters to receive medical attention. Unable to remove the bullets, doctors rushed him to a hospital. Although he saved his life, his health was never again good, and the attack probably played a role in the subsequent strokes that took his life. In fact, strokes were frequent from May 1922 onwards. On 7 March 1923 he lost his ability to speak forever due to the penultimate stroke. The doctors decided to operate on him on 23 April to remove a bullet that had been lodged three millimetres from the carotid artery since the attack of 1918, as they considered that it could be one of the causes of the dangerous state of his blood circulation.

The person who captured Dora Kaplan was S. Batulin, deputy commander of the 5th Infantry Division in Moscow, who had attended the event and pursued the woman. According to this version, Batulin saw a strange woman carrying a briefcase and an umbrella under a tree and asked her what she was doing there. The answer was: "Why do you want to know? The deputy commissioner then searched her pockets, took the briefcase and umbrella from her and ordered her to follow him. On the way, Batulin asked her why she had shot Lenin. Again Dora Kaplan replied: "Why do you want to know? The commissar asked her directly: "Is it you who shot at Lenin? She answered in the affirmative. The investigation was conducted by the Latvian Jew Yakov Peters, who was not only vice-chairman of the Cheka but also chairman of the Revolutionary Tribunal. Peters would be executed by Stalin in 1942. Fanny Kaplan allegedly explained that the assassination attempt was a personal action. In the recorded statement are these words: "My name is Fanny Kaplan. Today I shot Lenin. I did it with my own means. I will not say who provided me with the gun. I will not give any details. I made the decision to kill Lenin a long time ago. I consider him a traitor to the revolution." Kaplan, like Kannegisser, was executed without trial. In 1958, Pavel Malkov, commander of the Kremlin in 1918, declared that he had personally killed the terrorist on 3 September.

The gaps in the official version are inexplicable. It is not logical that Dora Kaplan was carrying a briefcase and an umbrella in one hand while shooting with the other. Nor does it seem credible that the workers who were standing next to Lenin allowed him to escape. Why didn't Fanny Kaplan, in addition to the gun, throw the briefcase and umbrella? Where were Lenin's bodyguards? The driver Stepan Gil wrote in his memoirs that Lenin had no bodyguards. The Lenin Museum in Moscow exhibits the coat and jacket Lenin was wearing on the day of the attack. All the shots were fired from behind. Although the official version speaks of three shots, the garments are marked with four holes, two of which are red to indicate which ones penetrated his body.

At half past three in the morning of 31 August Bruce Lockhart opened his eyes and saw the barrel of a revolver pointed at him. Ten men had entered his room. When he asked for an explanation for the outrage, Mankov, the leader of the group, told him not to ask questions and to get dressed immediately. Moura Budberg, who lived with the British agent, was also arrested. Once in Lubyanka No. 11, the headquarters of the Moscow Cheka, Lockhart appeared before Yakov Peters, who politely warned him that this was a very serious matter. The Briton reminded him that he was in Moscow at the invitation of the Soviet Government and had been promised diplomatic privileges. He made a formal protest and asked to speak to Chicherin, the Foreign Affairs Commissioner. Peters ignored his words and asked: "Do you know a woman called Kaplan? Appearing calm, Lockhart warned him that he had no right to question him. The next question was, "Where's Reilly?" After advising him that it was better to tell the truth, he let him meet with one of his men, Captain Hicks, also arrested on the Lubianka. Moura, Lockhart and Hicks lived together in the same flat. The British realised that it was obvious that they were involved in Lenin's assassination attempt.

Lockhart goes on to explain how he got rid of an embarrassing notebook in a pocket of his coat: "Suddenly I felt in the inside pocket of my coat a notebook containing in coded form an explanation of the money I had spent. The Cheka agents had searched my flat. They were probably looking for it at the time, but they had not thought to search the clothes we had put on when we were arrested. The notebook was unintelligible to anyone but me, but it contained figures and, if it fell into the hands of the Bolsheviks, they would find a way to interpret them in a compromising way." Thinking of a way to get rid of the booklet, he asked the four guards for permission to go to the lavatory. Two of them accompanied him and as he was about to close the toilet door, they shook their heads negatively and standing in front of him ordered, "Leave it open." The unhygienic conditions of the place worked in the British agent's favour: there was no paper and the walls were stained with splashes of excrement: "With as much peace of mind as possible, I took the notebook, tore out the pages in question, used them as circumstances dictated and flushed the toilet. It worked. And I was saved. At six o'clock in the morning the Chekists brought Fanny Kaplan into the room where Lockhart and Hicks were. They were, of course, trying to see if the woman was reacting in any way that would show that she knew the detainees. Kaplan walked to the window and, without moving, without saying anything, rested her chin on her hand and stared at the light of dawn. Lockhart confirms that Fanny Kaplan was executed without trial before she could find out whether her attempt had succeeded. At nine o'clock in the morning Peters himself came in to announce that Chicherin had ordered them to be released.

The measure was momentary. On 3 September newspapers reported the discovery of a "sensational conspiracy to overthrow the Soviet Government". They attributed the plot to the Allies, who were accused of wanting to crush the revolution and re-establish tsarism, and a British diplomat was singled out as the main suspect. With the headline "Imperialist Allies' plot against Soviet Russia", *Izvestia* published the story in these terms:

"A plot organised by British and French diplomats was liquidated on 2 September. It was led by the head of the British mission Lockhart, the French consul-general Lavergne and others. This plot, with the help of bribed units of the armies of the Soviets, aimed at the arrest of the Council of People's Commissars and the proclamation of a military dictatorship in Moscow. The whole organisation, of a strictly clandestine type, with the use of false documents and corruption, has been unmasked.

In particular, documents were discovered which indicated that, in the event of a successful coup d'état, a false secret correspondence of the Russian Government with the German Government was to be published, and that false treaties were to be fabricated in order to create an atmosphere conducive to the resumption of war against Germany. The conspirators acted under cover of diplomatic immunity and on the basis of certificates signed by the head of the British mission in Moscow, Mr. Lockhart, of which the All-Russian Cheka now possesses numerous copies. It has been proved that in the space of the last ten days 1,200,000 roubles have passed through the hands of one of Lockhart's agents, the British secret service officer Reilly, for purposes of corruption. The plot was uncovered thanks to the firmness shown by the commanders of the units to whom the conspirators had addressed their offers of corruption.

An Englishman was arrested while in hiding with the conspirators. After being taken to the Cheka, he declared that his name was Lockhart, the diplomatic representative of Great Britain. After verifying his identity, the prisoner Lockhart was released without delay. The investigation is being vigorously pursued.

On 4 September, Yakov Peters received the order to arrest Bruce Lockhart for the second time, and he remained in prison for a month. On the 8th he was transferred from the Lubyanka to the Kremlin, where his conditions of imprisonment clearly improved. The reason for this was an immediate retaliatory action by the British government: Maksim Litvinov, Lockhart's counterpart, the unofficial representative of the Bolsheviks in London, was arrested and imprisoned. Negotiations for a prisoner exchange began immediately. Soon Moura was allowed to visit, sometimes accompanied by Yakov Peters himself, bringing goods such as books, coffee, clothes, tobacco, ham. These "luxuries" improved their daily lives. Moura Budberg had defined her lover in these terms: "Intelligent enough, but not intelligent enough; strong enough, but not strong enough; weak enough, but not weak enough". On 2 October 1918 Lockhart left Moscow by train and arrived at the Finnish border on Thursday evening, 3 October. There he waited for three days at the Bieloostrov station, until there was confirmation that Litvinov had arrived in Bergen. On the other hand, Sidney Reilly (in Russia there was always talk of the "Reilly Plot") was never arrested and months later the two were reunited in London.

Lockhart's conspiracy, "The Lockhart Plot", whose documents remain secret, has been interpreted in the sense expressed by the headlines of the Soviet press, i.e., in the sense of propaganda emanating from the regime. Stalin, however, knew that Lockhart and Reilly had been used and that Trotsky was hiding behind them. As is well known, Stalin succeeded Lenin to the detriment of Trotsky. After Lenin's death on 21 January 1924, Trotsky was to become the undisputed leader of the USSR and he had in his hands all the power necessary to achieve this. As will be discussed below, Lenin's wife, Nadehzda Krupskaya, tried by all means to prevent Stalin from seizing power from the Trotskyist faction. It was then that the fratricidal struggle within the party broke out again.

In 1938 the Trial of the Twenty-One took place, one of the famous Moscow trials that marked the purge of Trotskyism. We shall devote the whole of the sixth part of the next chapter to its study. Now, to conclude these pages on the struggle for power between Trotskyists and Leninists, we will anticipate that in the 1938 trial Nikolai Bukharin was accused of being the leader of the Trotskyist bloc, of having conspired to assassinate Lenin after the signing of the Treaty of Brest-Litovsk and of having organised the August assassination attempt. Another Trotskyite, Varvara Nikolaevna Yakovleva, testified against him. Also accused of other murders, including that of Gorky, Bukharin was convicted and executed. During the trial, five witnesses claimed that Bukharin had repeatedly proposed ideas and plans to arrest Lenin and physically destroy him. The prosecutor regretted that Bukharin had not even tried to refute the accusations of those who testified against him. In his closing argument before the court that tried him, Bukharin denied that he had failed to provide arguments against the accusations and admitted to the judges that the Trotskyists had used "the most criminal methods of struggle". He rejected the charge that he had conspired to kill Lenin. However, he admitted: "My counter-revolutionary accomplices and I at their head tried to assassinate Lenin's cause, which is being pursued with enormous success by Stalin. The logic of this struggle led us step by step into the darkest quagmire." Bukharin, who was trying to save his life, repeatedly pointed to Trotsky as the "main driving force" behind "highly developed methods of espionage and terrorism."

PART 4
THE REVOLUTION SPREADS
TO GERMANY AND HUNGARY

After the signing of the Treaty of Brest-Litovsk, Germany sought a decisive victory on the Western Front that would give it the final victory in the war. Britain, because of its commitment to Zionism and contrary to the opinion of some of its most prestigious generals, was engaged in a campaign in Palestine that endangered the stability of the French front. On 21 March 1918 the Germans launched the potentially decisive spring campaign. The British paid dearly for their recklessness and 175,000 soldiers were taken prisoner. In view of the gravity of the situation, the troops from Palestine were urgently redeployed to Europe. On 15 July, a momentous battle took place, the Second Battle of the Marne, in which 85,000 American troops were already engaged. The Germans managed to cross the Marne River near Dormans and came to within a little over 100 kilometres of Paris. On the 17th, French, British, American and Italian troops managed to halt the advance. On the 20th General Erich Ludendorff ordered a retreat, and on 3 August the Germans were at the point where the spring offensive had begun, between the Aisne and Vesle rivers.

While tens of thousands of soldiers were losing their lives on the front, the defeatist tactics used in Russia were reprised in Germany: strikes, which left the troops without supplies (in January 1918 half a million workers, mostly in the armaments factories, went on strike); campaigns in the Jewish press, the same press that in 1914 had enthusiastically cheered the war; propaganda in the barracks, where the seeds of defeatism were sown, feeding insubordination and undermining morale. And again, as in Russia, almost all the communist leaders who led the revolution in Germany and Hungary were Jews. As noted, Bolshevik propaganda in Germany was financed and organised by William B. Thompson and Raymond Robins. When Trotsky became Commissariat for Foreign Affairs, he set up a Press Department, headed by the Polish Jew Karl Rádek (Tobias Sobelsohn), to which was attached the Department of International Revolutionary Propaganda, headed by another Jew, Boris Reinstein. Through this Department, the German-language newspaper *Die Fackel (The Torch)*, of which half a million copies were published daily, was distributed to the fronts. Three agents of the Propaganda Department, Robert Minor, Philip Price and the aforementioned Jacques Sadoul, were sent to Germany by order of the Central Executive Committee. French, British and American intelligence services detected their activities and Scotland Yard reported that Price and Minor had also written pamphlets for British and American troops.

By autumn it was clear that Germany could not win the war, but neither did the Allies seem in a position to do so. The Eastern Front was still inactive and there were no foreign troops on German soil. There had been none at any time. When the armistice was signed on 11 November, German troops were well entrenched on French and Belgian soil. Berlin was 1,400 kilometres from the front, and the military considered itself capable of defending the country against a hypothetical Allied invasion. The Kaiser, as he had done in 1916, had again offered to negotiate a peace on terms acceptable to all sides. But treachery and propaganda were undermining the home front. Marxist trade unions and socialist politicians, allied with Zionist press magnates, were combining their efforts to demoralise the population and destabilise the country. Wilhelm II, although not a shot had been fired on German soil, was forced to abdicate.

The chronological sequence of events will help the reader to properly situate a series of historical events that took place at a dizzying pace. The first name to appear is that of General Ludendorff. It was he who convinced Marshal Hindenburg of the need for an armistice that would save the Army, which had not actually been defeated. Ludendorff, whom Hitler accused of being a Freemason in 1927, the year in which the General published the work *Destruction of Freemasonry by the Revelation of its Secrets*, agreed with Foreign Secretary von Hintze on a reform of the Constitution and a plan for a parliamentary majority to back the government in calling for an armistice. Hindenburg met with the Emperor, who accepted the proposal on 29 September 1918. On 3 October, Prince Maximilian of Baden was appointed Chancellor of the Empire and Prime Minister of Prussia to replace Georg Hertling, and remained in office until 9 November. The Prince of Baden formed a government with the participation of the main German parties, including the Socialists. Two days after his appointment, on 5 October, the new chancellor, naively thinking he could rely on President Wilson to broker an acceptable peace, addressed the Reichstag urging it to accept any democratic proposal emanating from the White House. Referring to the peace aspirations of the Imperial Government, he alluded to the famous fourteen points formulated on 8 January 1918 by Wilson in his speech to the US Congress, namely that of self-determination of peoples, and proposed the establishment of representative bodies in the Baltic provinces and in Poland. Prince Maximilian thus sought mediation from Woodrow Wilson to negotiate peace with the Allied nations. The response was a demand for unconditional surrender. Nevertheless, on 28 October Maximilian of Baden succeeded in passing a constitutional reform that established full democracy.

After learning of the demand for unconditional surrender, the military reacted angrily. On 26 October Ludendorff asked the Prince of Baden to break off negotiations. Failing to do so, he resigned. Two days earlier, at ten o'clock on the evening of the 24th, Hindenburg had signed the following order for his soldiers at the front:

"For the information of the troops:

Wilson says in his reply that he is prepared to propose to his allies that they should enter into negotiations for an armistice, but that the armistice must leave Germany so defenceless that she cannot take up arms again. He will only negotiate peace with Germany if Germany agrees to all the demands of America's allies on Germany's internal constitutional arrangements; otherwise there is no option but unconditional surrender. Wilson's reply is a demand for unconditional surrender. It is therefore unacceptable to us soldiers. It proves that our enemy desires our destruction..... It proves further that our enemies use the phrase 'Peace and Justice' only to deceive us and break our resistance. Wilson's reply can mean nothing to us soldiers but the challenge to continue our resistance with all our might. When our enemies know that no sacrifice will achieve the breaking of the German front, then they will be ready for a peace which will safeguard the future of our country for the majority of our people."

Seafarers' uprising in Kiel

Only the Royal Navy outnumbered the Imperial Navy, the world's second largest fleet, although due to the lack of allied ports it had not shown its full potential. Only submarines had circumvented the British blockade of the North Sea. Off the coast of South America the Battle of the Falkland Islands had been fought, but the only major naval battle had been the Battle of Jutland in 1916, where the British suffered the heaviest losses. At the time of Wilson's demand for unconditional surrender, Germany still had the most powerful army in the world, and the General Staff set out to launch a naval offensive against British ports to demonstrate its complete rejection of the American president's claim. This decision provided the ideal pretext for launching the seamen's rebellion against their officers. The revolutionary leaders had already accumulated a great deal of experience: at the height of the war against Japan in 1905, Mensheviks and Bolsheviks prepared simultaneous uprisings on all the ships of the Black Sea fleet. The failure was due to the impatience of the Potemkin's sailors. By 1917, however, the seamen's uprising had enabled the revolutionary to take control of the Cronstadt base and the Baltic Sea fleet. During the war, socialist and anarchist propaganda, repeating the methods used in Russia, had been spreading in the large German naval bases, and the sailors, imbued with revolutionary ideas, knew that their Russian colleagues had been instrumental in the triumph of the revolution. They, too, aspired to be so.

It all began in Wilhelmshaven, the main headquarters of the German fleet, where the ships were being assembled for the attack. On 29 October the crews of the ships *Thüringen* and *Helgoland* disobeyed the order to put to sea. On the night of the 29th to the 30th, the perfectly organised rebellion got underway. The seamen, after arresting their officers, seized several ships. The mutiny spread to the sailors ashore, who refused to embark on the naval units that were due to put to sea. The uprising may have been put down momentarily, but the high command was forced to postpone the attack. At the same time, there had been a mutiny within the units of the third squadron, which was already at sea. This synchronisation of actions leads to the conclusion that everything was planned in advance. About a thousand men were arrested and were to be disembarked to be court-martialled. On 1 November, the order was given to return to Kiel, where a delegation in solidarity with the detainees asked for their release, which was refused. On 2 November, in the union house ("Gewerkschafsthaus"), assemblies of shipyard workers and seamen drew up the plan for further action. The high command of the "Kaiserliche Marine", surprised and overwhelmed by the situation, was unable to react, and within a few hours the uprising had spread to the entire North Sea fleet. On 3 November, seafarers and workers abandoned the assemblies and held joint rallies. All sources attribute the responsibility for lighting the fuse of the ensuing explosion to naval lieutenant Steinhäuser. He reportedly ordered to open fire on the demonstrators, resulting in the death of nine of them. A marine shot and killed the officer. This triggered a general revolt, which took the form of a council (Soviet) of soldiers and workers on 4 November. The officers were disarmed and the Council took control of the naval base and the city of Kiel. The ships were occupied, red flags were hoisted on most of them, and the mutinous prisoners still held inside were released. In the afternoon, the army soldiers who had been sent to put down the rebellion joined the uprising. Forty thousand insurgent sailors, soldiers and workers demanding the abdication of Kaiser Wilhelm II had become masters of the situation.

In the evening, the SPD deputy Gustav Noske came to the city on behalf of the government of Maximilian Baden. Noske put forward various proposals that must have satisfied the workers' and soldiers' council, as he was appointed governor of the city. The events in Kiel had meanwhile spread like wildfire throughout the country, and demonstrations against the imperial regime and the continuation of the war took place in Berlin, Bavaria and the Ruhr area. Events moved at breakneck speed. The Socialists demanded the abdication of Wilhelm II.

On 6 November, Prince Maximilian of Baden was unable to convince the Emperor to abdicate to his grandson in order to save the monarchy. On the evening of November 7, trucks flying red flags patrolled the city of Munich, and on November 8 a soviet of workers' and peasants' soldiers led by the Jew Kurt Eisner proclaimed the Bavarian Republic. On 9 November, Chancellor Maximilian of Baden announced the abdication of the emperor and crown prince on his own. Afterwards, convinced by the Socialists, he resigned and handed over the office of chancellor to the Social Democratic leader Friedrich Ebert. On the same day Philipp Scheidemann proclaimed from the Reichstag what was later to be known as the Weimar Republic. Two hours later another Jew, Karl Liebknecht, proclaimed a second republic from the balcony of the imperial palace: the Free and Socialist Republic of Germany. Wilhelm II accepted the abdication after General Wilhelm Gröner replaced Ludendorff, whose plan, in the emperor's eyes, had caused the debacle. Gröner announced to the Kaiser that the army would obey Hindengurg's orders, who, embarrassed, advised the emperor to abdicate. On 10 November Wilhelm II crossed the border by train and went into exile in Holland. The November Revolution had achieved its first goal: to overthrow the monarchy. On 11 November another Jew, the socialist Paul Hirsch, became minister-president of Prussia.

From demobilisation to the Spartacist uprising

What had been years in preparation in Russia was intended to be done in a matter of weeks in Germany, where, by the way, there was no Kerensky willing to hand over power to the Communists when they demanded it. The German Social Democrats, as had been the case with the Masonic government in Russia, agreed with the Communists that the monarchy had to be done away with; but as the main party representing German society, it could not overnight surrender to the revolutionary forces. In the 1912 elections the SPD had won 35% of the seats in the Reichstag, and it was its responsibility to lead the process towards a democratic republic. However, in April 1917 there had been an internal split: the left wing of the party split and formed the Independent Social Democratic Party of Germany (USPD), known as the Independent Socialists. These, like the Mensheviks, accepted both parliamentarism and the revolutionary councils that were to oversee it.

Further to the left of the USPD was the Spartacist League, founded by Rosa Luxemburg and Karl Liebknecht. The name "Spartakusbund" or Spartacus League always refers to the leader of the slaves who revolted against Rome, but Spartacus was also the secret name behind Adam Weishaupt, founder of the Bavarian Enlightenment, the sect that sought to do away with all monarchies and religions. These two Jewish Marxists had chosen to leave the USPD and form a revolutionary party that aspired to follow the example of the Bolshevik revolution and establish the dictatorship of the proletariat. On 30 December 1918 the League joined the Comintern (Communist International) and became the Communist Party of Germany (KPD). At the founding congress of the KPD, Karl Radek appeared as an agent of the Comintern, wearing a Soviet uniform. The first Central Committee was headed by Jewish leaders. Among the most prominent alongside Rosa Luxemburg were Leo Jogiches, her close collaborator (they were lovers), August Thalheimer and Paul Levi. The latter declared in his speech that "the road of the proletariat to victory could only pass over the corpse of the National Assembly". Further proof of Jewish control over the

German Communist Party is the fact that almost all the secretaries of the leadership: Bertha Braunthal, Mathilde Jacob, Rosa Leviné, Rosi Wolfstein, Kathe Pohl (Lydia Rabinovich) were Jewish.

While Wilhelm II was leaving Germany, the Social Democrats decided on the same day, 10 November, to rely on the Independent Socialists to form a provisional government, which called itself the Council of People's Commissioners, consisting of six members, three Social Democrats and three Independent Socialists. On 11 November, barely three weeks after Hindenburg's order calling on his soldiers to resist, the government accepted the Armistice of Compiègne on the basis of Wilson's Fourteen Points. On the 12th a Provisional Executive Council, controlled by the SPD, was set up to serve as a link between the Provisional Government and the People's Councils. On 13 November, ignoring the demand for unconditional surrender, the government addressed a diplomatic note to the American president in which it nevertheless expressed faith in Wilson's demarche to the other Allies to safeguard German interests. The text concluded thus: "The German people, therefore, in this fateful hour, again address the President with the request that he use his influence with the Allied powers in order to mitigate these terrible conditions."

On 15 November the Provisional Government reached a pact with the trade unions, and the workers obtained the following guarantees: an eight-hour working day with no reduction in wages, renunciation of action by the employers against the trade unions, regulation of work by means of collective agreements. In imitation of the Pan-Russian congresses of the Soviets, a Pan-German Congress of Councils was convened in Berlin from 16 to 20 December. The Congress was attended by about five hundred delegates, only ten of whom were Spartacists, who pressed for the dismissal of General Hindenburg and the dissolution of the army in order to create a guard whose officers would be elected by their men. The Congress, however, supported the theses of the Social Democrats, who called for general elections for a National Constituent Assembly, which implied the disappearance of the Congress of Councils, which was dissolved.

The "terrible conditions" had been presented to Matthias Erzberger, who headed the German delegation that signed the Armistice of Compiègne in a railway carriage on 11 November. Germany was required to withdraw from France, Belgium, Luxembourg and Alsace-Lorraine, to remove troops from the eastern front, to renounce the Treaty of Brest-Litovsk, to hand over almost all war materiel: aircraft, guns, machine guns, mortars, locomotives, railway carriages, as well as the internment of the German fleet, which entailed its transfer to Scapa Flow. Months later, at the British base, Admiral Ludwig von Reuter ordered his officers to sink the ships to prevent them from being taken by the British. It should be noted that the armistice did not imply Germany's unconditional surrender, but rather the immediate cessation of hostilities on both sides and the withdrawal of troops to the pre-war borders as a preliminary step to negotiating a peace treaty. Incomprehensibly, however, while the German troops were withdrawing, the Provisional Government, under pressure from the Independent Socialists and the Spartacists, ordered the general demobilisation of the armed forces.

On 11 November Germany still had a powerful military machine, a month later it had nothing. This defenceless and prostrate Germany could no longer negotiate on Wilson's fourteen points, but had to accept humiliating conditions, befitting a defeated state, which were embodied in the Treaty of Versailles, which, as Lord Curzon declared, "was not a peace treaty, but a rupture of hostilities". Before the war, Germany was the leading industrial power in Europe and the country that invested the most in scientific research, which is why German science ranked first in the world and German was the scientific language par excellence. Many Germans, dumbfounded, could not understand how overnight Germany, whose economic, industrial and scientific potential was still intact, with an army whose troops still occupied parts of enemy territory and which had defeated Russia, had suddenly surrendered in offices. Hence the National Socialist thesis that Germany was not defeated on the battlefield, but stabbed in the back by Jewish-led communist traitors.

The connection of the German Jewish revolutionaries with the Judeo-Bolsheviks was an avowed fact which no one made any effort to conceal. Adolf Abramovich Joffe, the Jewish ambassador of the Soviet Government in Berlin, a staunch Trotskyite who, together with Kamenev and Radek, had been a member of the Bolshevik delegation to Brest-Litovsk, was absolutely convinced of the triumph of the revolution. On 2 November 1918, after hearing of the seamen's rebellion in Kiel, Joffe had announced to Karl Liebknecht that within a week the red flag would be flying at the Berlin Palace. In December 1918 Joffe publicly reminded Hugo Hasse, the Jewish leader of the "independent" socialists of the USPD, that he had received his financial help. In the same statement he revealed that he had placed ten million roubles at the disposal of Dr. Oskar Kohn, another SPD Jew who, in addition to being a member of Parliament, had been appointed on 11 November 1918 as Under-Secretary of State in the Ministry of Justice. Joffe was quoted as saying that he had "guaranteed Mr. Kohn the right to dispose of them in the interests of the German revolution". With absolute impudence, Oskar Kohn admitted that on the evening of 5 November he had indeed received this sum and that he had "gladly accepted" the financial aid. Naturally Oskar Kohn, who was legal adviser to the Russian Embassy in Berlin, must have considered that accepting the post of Under-Secretary of State for Justice was perfectly compatible with receiving foreign funding for the revolution. On 6 November, after it was established that the embassy was supplying the Spartacists with arms, propaganda material and money on a large scale, Joffe and the Soviet delegation were expelled on charges of planning a communist uprising. Joffe himself later admitted that the Soviet

Embassy in Berlin had been "the headquarters of the General Staff of the German revolution". After Joffe's expulsion, Karl Rádek (Tobias Sobelsohn), head of the International Propaganda Department set up by Trotsky, was sent to Germany. Under Radek's leadership, communist propaganda reached its peak in Munich.

Disorganisation and chaos in the army were the immediate consequence of the inconceivable order to demobilise. While soldiers were returning home as best they could, some from points two thousand kilometres away, the situation in Berlin was becoming increasingly tense. On 23 December, the People's Marine Division ("Volksmarinedivision"), newly formed in Kiel, seized the Reich Chancellery and held Chancellor Ebert in his office until the situation could be brought under control. It was only a foretaste of what was to come. After the decision to transfer power to a Constituent Assembly, 19 January 1919 was set as the date for the elections. The Spartacus League, now the KPD (Communist Party of Germany), realising that it had no chance in the electoral contest, asked not to take part in the process and tried to seize power by means of a coup d'état. The independent socialists, whose leader was the aforementioned Hugo Hasse, convinced after the skirmish of 23 December of the imminent triumph of communism, withdrew their three commissioners from the provisional government, which was thus left exclusively in the hands of the SPD.

On 4 January 1919 Chancellor Ebert, following the departure from the government of the three Independent Socialist commissars, dismissed Emil Eichhorn as head of the Police Department, a post he had held since 9 November 1918. Eichhorn, who in April 1917 had been one of the leftists who had formed the USPD and who had been the Berlin director of ROSTA (Soviet News Agency) since August 1918, did not accept Ebert's decision and claimed that he had been appointed by the Berlin workers and that only they could dismiss him. Supposedly protected by armed workers who occupied the building, he remained in his post. Along with Eichhorn, four Jewish socialists, Kurt Eisner (Kamonowsky) Karl Kautsky, Rudolf Hilferding and Paul Levi, had headed the group that led the SPD split. The latter, Levi, who had already joined the Communist Party, was the organiser of the protests against Eichhorn's dismissal: in addition to printing anti-government leaflets, a demonstration was organised in which independent socialists, the Communist Party and also social democratic militants took part. The demands were: annulment of Eichhorn's dismissal, disarmament of the counterrevolutionary forces and arming the proletariat.

On 5 January the People's Marine Division, under the orders of the communists and the most radical socialists, occupied the headquarters of the social-democratic newspaper *Vörwarts*, whose opinions the communists did not like. In this newspaper it had been written, for example, that "a certain Levi and the loud-mouthed Rosa Luxemburg, who have never stood next to a vise in a bank or in a workshop, are about to ruin everything our fathers have dreamed of:" Once liberated from occupation by a raid, on 12 January 1919 *Vorwärts* referred to Luxemburg, Trotsky and Radek, whom he quoted by their Jewish names of Bronstein and Sobelsohn, as "Asiatics and Mongols of Russia".

The general strike that paralysed Berlin on 6 January 1919 was to be the final blow against Friedrich Ebert's government. Communists and independent socialists turned the strike into an armed insurrection. A battle broke out in the streets of the capital, and the revolutionaries took control of the city centre. The Social Democrats failed to reach an agreement with the communists, and Karl Liebknecht called on the workers to take up arms to overthrow the government. The disastrous demobilisation of the armed forces had been demanded by the Spartacists, whose cells within the Provisional Government had skilfully manoeuvred to achieve this goal. Berlin and Germany were at the mercy of the insurrection. In view of the seriousness of the situation, Gustav Noske, the Minister of Defence, decided to turn to what remained of the army, namely the loyal Potsdam garrison and the "Freikorps", anti-republican organisations made up of former soldiers,. Rosa Luxemburg and Karl Liebknecht called on the soldiers of the soviets or councils to join the workers with their weapons. The urban fighting that ensued became known as the "bloody week". Finally, after five days of fighting, the Freikorps crushed the communist uprising and recaptured Berlin.

However, the civil war dragged on for several months in some places, as it had spread to Bremen, Saarland, Bavaria, Hamburg, Magdeburg and Saxony. The attempt to establish the dictatorship of the proletariat in Germany caused thousands of deaths, including Karl Liebknecht and Rosa Luxemburg, who were murdered. Rosa Leviné, who was married to two Jewish communist leaders, Eugen Leviné, then editor of *Rote Vorwärts*, and Ernst Meyer, was in hospital at the time. As she later wrote, an extra edition announced the murder of the KPD leaders and the news was greeted with jubilation: "everyone shouted and danced for joy". The two communist leaders, arrested at the Eden Hotel, were not brought before a court, but were executed practically on the spot on the night of 15 January 1919. Rosa Luxemburg's lifeless body was thrown from a bridge into a canal. On 31 May it was found by a lock and, after identification, was buried on 13 June.

After Rosa Luxemburg's death, her inseparable Leo Jogiches, whose nom de guerre was Tyscha, became the de facto new leader of the party until, arrested and imprisoned in early March, he was murdered by the Prussian police in the Moabit prison on 10 March 1919. Paul Levi, the son of Jewish bankers, was then elected successor to the murdered leaders as head of the KPD. Levi turned the KPD into a mass party, winning over many social democratic workers to the cause and winning a large section of the USPD to join the communists. August Thalheimer, the son of a Jewish manufacturer from Würtenberg and Radek's confidant, succeeded Rosa Luxemburg as editor-in-chief of *Rote Fahne* (*Red Flag*), which made him the new ideologue of the German Communist Party. Jogiches was replaced by his deputy Leo Flieg, who was descended from a Berlin Jewish family and served as organising secretary of the Central Committee. Flieg was also liaison between the Comintern's Secret Service (OMS) and administered the funds flowing in dollars to Germany from Moscow. In *Anti-Semitism, Bolshevism and Judaism,* Johannes Rogalla von Bieberstein explains that the millions were distributed by "Comrade Thomas ", another Jew trusted by Trotsky, Radek and Bukharin, whose real name was Jacob Reich, although he also used the surname Rubinstein. This money was used for the formation of a Red Army, organised in Proletarian Centuries, which was supposed to seize power in Germany in the very near future. For his contacts with Russia, "Comrade Thomas" had two chartered planes at his disposal.

Despite all this, the elections were held, with a voter turnout of 82.8 per cent. The Social Democrats of the SPD won 37.9% of the vote and 165 seats. The second party was the Catholic centrist ZP ("Zentrumspartei"), which won 19.7% of the vote and 91 seats. The DDP ("Deutsche Demokratische Partei"), left-wing democrats, won 18.6% and 75 seats. The fourth political force in terms of votes was the DVNP ("Deutsche Nationalen Volkspartei"), a conservative, anti-republican and pan-German party, which won 10.3% of the vote and 44 seats. Only in fifth place were the independent socialists of the USPD, who, unlike the communists of the KPD, took part in the elections and won only 7.8% of the votes, which translated into 33 seats. Finally, Gustav Stresemann's right-wing liberal DVP ("Deutsche Volkspartei") won 4.4% and 19 seats. The Social Democratic Party made a pact with the centrist parties and the so-called Weimar Coalition was formed. Friedrich Ebert was elected President of the Republic and Scheidemann was appointed head of government.

In view of the poor representativeness of the independent socialists, it is ridiculous that the leaders of the Communist Party should think themselves legitimised to use the manipulated masses who played along with them to stage a coup d'état and impose their dictatorship of the proletariat on Germany. In any case, as was shown in Russia, where the Bolsheviks dissolved the parliament by force of arms, democracy mattered little to them. In his famous *April Theses* Lenin had bluntly expressed his contempt for the parliamentary republic and the democratic process. It was rather a question of exterminating the class enemy. "Anyone who accepts class war," he wrote in 1916, "must accept civil war, which in every class society represents the natural continuation, development and accentuation of class war."

The Bavarian Soviet Republic

During 1918, when the war in France was still raging, Kurt Eisner (Salomon Kuchinsky), a high-ranking Freemason who called himself "Von

Israelovitch" in Polish and German lodges, had been organising strikes in munitions factories and promoting agitation, for which he had been imprisoned. Eisner frequented the Café Stefanie, where he and Gustav Landauer, Ernst Toller, Erich Mühsam and Edgar Jaffé, all Jewish writers or intellectuals, prepared their revolutionary strategy. In their lucubrations these sinister characters looked to the Russian system of soviets of soldiers and workers as the model to follow. On 7 November 1918, Kurt Esiner proclaimed the Free State of Bavaria in front of a people's assembly on the Theresienwiese in Munich, perched on a lorry. On the same day, the last Bavarian king, Ludwig III, resigned from the throne. The self-proclaimed Eisner, who had already become Bavaria's minister-president, wanted to pursue a foreign policy opposed to that of the German Foreign Office, and on 10 November he appealed to all nations, which was tantamount to a betrayal of his country. Among Eisner's first decisions was the appointment of his private secretary, a post he gave to the Jew Felix Fechenbach.

On the night of 6/7 December, Erich Mühsam, one of Eisner's colleagues, ordered revolutionary soldiers to occupy five bourgeois newspapers and declared them socialised. A few days later, on 12 December, the new minister-president of Bavaria rejected in a speech any power other than that of the soviets of soldiers and workers. Despite all these dictatorial displays, the provincial parliamentary elections on 12 January 1919 showed that those who had seized power were in a minority, winning only 2.5 percent of the vote. Kurt Eisner's career ended abruptly on 21 January when he was shot dead by Anton Graf Arco auf Valley. In Anti-Semitism, Bolshevism and Judaism Rogalla von Bieberstein points to the possibility that the young Graf was connected with the counter-revolutionary, anti-Semitic Thule Society. According to this author, it is possible that the Society did not accept him as a member because his mother came from the Jewish banking family Oppenheim. Because of this rejection, Anton Graf would have wanted to demonstrate his patriotic faith with a decisive act.

The removal of Eisner radicalised the situation. The Bavarian Diet (Landtag) that emerged from the elections was completely marginalised by the councils or soviets. On 7 April, the Jewish writer Ernst Toller, another of the Cafe Stefanie's fellow guests, proclaimed a councilist or Soviet republic at the instigation of Lenin's Russia and Bela Kun's Hungary. Alongside Toller, who was chairman of the Central Council of the Soviets and commander of the Red Army, the anarchists Gustav Landauer and Erich Mühsam were leaders. The Comintern, through the German Communist Party (KPD), immediately sent Eugen Leviné (Nissen Berg), Tobias Axelrod and Max Levien, three Jewish revolutionaries of Russian origin, to redirect and consolidate the situation. The third, Levien, was a personal friend of Trotsky and Lenin. These Comintern commissioners quickly seized power, and on 13 April the republic proclaimed by Toller was renamed the Bavarian Soviet Republic. With its own Red Army and Revolutionary Court, the new

Soviet Republic broke all ties with the Weimar Republic. Leviné became chairman of the Council of People's Commissars. In his speech he proclaimed: "Today Bavaria has finally established the dictatorship of the proletariat. Long live the world revolution!

The new dictatorship exasperated the population, who saw how a group of Jewish leaders, some of whom were not even German, had seized power. Naturally, hatred of the Jews, who were seen as the cause of all that was happening, was stoked, and violent clashes broke out in the city's streets and squares. The above-mentioned work by Johannes Rogalla von Bieberstein is a valuable source of information on little-known events in Munich. One of these took place on 18 April, when a group of Red Guards armed with rifles, pistols and grenades stormed the home of the Apostolic Nuncio Giovanni Pacelli, the future Pope Pius XII, and put a pistol to his chest. After his arrest, he was taken to the residence of Max Levien, who, as supreme leader, effectively ruled the city of Munich. The nuncio later described Levien's headquarters in a report sent to the Vatican, which he described as "Russian and Jewish". Giovanni Pacelli refers to a "gang of women of dubious appearance, Jewish, like all of them, of provocative behaviour." At the head of these "secretaries" was Levien's companion, a young Jewish divorcee.

The Berlin government finally decided to intervene, and between 30 April and 8 May 1919 the Soviet Republic was overthrown. Thirty thousand army and Freikorps troops were sent to Munich to subdue the revolutionary minority and restore legality. In the course of the operations some six hundred people were killed. Among the murders carried out by the Red Guards was the shooting of seven members of the *Thule Gesellschaft* (Thule Society), whose offices were raided. Among them were four aristocrats. Interestingly, one was Gustave von Thurn und Taxis; another, Countess Heila von Westarp, a beautiful young woman who served as the Society's secretary. Taken hostage, these noblemen were executed along with others in the *Luitpold Gymnasium*, which served as the barracks of the fourth detachment of the Munich Red Army, whose commander was Rudolf Egelhofer. In an attempt to prevent the seizure of the building, the commander ordered the imprisonment of twenty-two prisoners, and took revenge by murdering ten of them gratuitously, since they were innocent citizens.

The Freikorps, for their part, also carried out bloody acts of revenge, the most publicised of which was the murder of Gustav Landauer, who had served as commissioner of education. In the courtyard of Stadelheim prison, where he had been taken, a non-commissioned officer, emboldened by the soldiers calling for his execution, shot Landauer in the head. Despite the severity of the wound, Landauer was still alive, so he was shot again in the back while on the ground. Martin Buber at a Zionist conference referred to Gustav Landauer as "our secret driver". Eugen Leviné, who was considered "an intruder in Bavaria", was indeed brought before a court martial under the government of the Social Democratic Hoffman. Sentenced to death for high treason, he was executed on 5 June 1919. Ernst Toller and Erich Mühsam, however, were sentenced to fifteen years in prison, but by 1924 they were already free thanks to an amnesty for political prisoners decreed by the Weimar Republic, whose constitution, incidentally, was sanctioned on 11 November 1919 on the basis of a draft drawn up by the Jew Hugo Preuss. As for Max Levien, he managed to escape to Vienna, where he was arrested. The German authorities demanded his extradition, but this was not granted, and in 1920 Levien was released.

Bela Kun's Hungary

The dismemberment of the Austro-Hungarian Empire began as soon as the realisation that the war had been lost dawned. On 28 October 1918 a demonstration was held in Budapest to demand independence, and a few days later the Hungarian People's Republic was born. It was to last only four months, for on 21 March 1919 it became the Hungarian Soviet Republic, which in turn lasted just over four months, exactly one hundred and thirty-three days, until 4 August. During this period, soldiers, priests, landowners, merchants and professionals from all fields were murdered with impunity. Terror was widespread in Hungary, where tens of thousands of people, "enemies of the people", lost their lives under Bela Kun's regime.

Bela Kun (Aaron Kohn), born in 1866 in a Hungarian province, was the son of Mov Kohn and Rosalie Goldenberg. He used his Jewish name until 1909, when he changed it to Kun in order to Hungarianise it. A Master Mason of a lodge in Decebren, he was also a member of B'nai B'rith and the elite Shriner Lodge, which required the 32nd degree to join. In 1916 he was taken prisoner by the Russians, but in February 1917 he was released by his Masonic brother Kerensky, with whom he naturally made good friends. In 1918 he was already working in Petrograd with the Bolsheviks, who put him in charge of a propaganda school in Moscow, from which he was responsible for proselytising among the Hungarian sodalists detained in Russia. He personally met Lenin and Radek, with whom he negotiated the founding of the HCP (Hungarian Communist Party), which was founded in Budapest on 4 November 1918. It did not take Bela Kun long to become the leader of a Popular Front.

José-Oriol Cuffi Canadell narrates in Spanish in *La sombra de Bela Kun* the most relevant events that took place between 1918 and 1919. We will focus on the communist revolution, on the regime of terror imposed by Bela Kun and the Jewish clique that seized power in March 1919, but first we will comment in a few lines on the assassination of Count István Tisza, a supporter of the union with Austria, since his elimination was a clear sign of what was to come. After his last speech in Parliament, on 17 October 1918, his death was decided at a secret meeting of the opposition National Council. Cuffi Canadell gives the names of those involved in the assassination and explains how it happened.

The events began on 31 October 1918. During the early hours of the morning Nathan Kraus, a Jewish journalist known as Göndor, led a large group of assailants who managed to seize the capital's main barracks. This was the signal to set the ball rolling, as it led to the immediate fall of Prime Minister Sándor Wekerle and prompted Count Károlyi, the Hungarian Kerensky who led the opposition, to step in and take the lead. In the evening of the same day, the second act of the tragedy took place. Two members of the opposition National Council, Captain Cszerniak and the Jewish journalists Kéry and Fenyes, had offered 100,000 crowns to the criminals who accepted the commission to assassinate Count Tisza. A soldier named Dobo, the sailor Horvath Santa, Lieutenant Hüttner and two other Jews, Gärtner and Joseph Pogány, later Minister of Education, raided Tisza's home at night, armed with rifles. Three men entered the Count's rooms and, before the horrified eyes of his wife and his niece, Countess Almassy, shot him three times. István Tisza had been prime minister from 1913 to 1916.

The tactic for seizing power in Hungary was the usual one. On 16 November the Republic was proclaimed in Budapest and Károlyi became prime minister. From this point on, the process of creating the soviets began, followed by the convening of a congress of soviets to prepare for the communist revolution. At the beginning of 1919, already with a view to the seizure of power, about 300 professional agitators and secret agents arrived from Russia in order to reinforce the revolutionaries. Several Jewish sources admit that the Hungarian communists had at their disposal "inexhaustible financial means" from Russia. Thanks to this aid, the *Vörös Ujság* (*Red Newspaper*) was founded. As in Munich, the communists tried to take over the bourgeois and socialist newspapers in Budapest in order to control opinion. The police succeeded in preventing this, but in the raid on the social democratic newspaper *Nepzava* (*The Voice of the People*) eight people, some of whom were policemen, were killed and about a hundred injured. Bela Kun and his staff were arrested and imprisoned, despite the protest of two Jewish ministers, Sigismund Kunfi, whose real name was Kunstädter, and William Böhm, both Socialists. Meanwhile, the continued influx into Hungary of prisoners released by the Bolsheviks to spread the gospel of communism was plunging the country into a state of extreme turmoil.

Prime Minister Mihály Károlyi, the new Kerensky, gave Bela Kun every opportunity to forge the union of the socialist and communist parties with Kunfi and Böhm, which took place on 21 March and led to the resignation of Count Károlyi's government, which was supposedly overwhelmed by events. Bela Kun was immediately released and the Hungarian Soviet Republic was proclaimed. Already head of the government and undisputed leader of the new republic, Bela Kun saw himself as the man called upon to spread the world revolution in Europe. In fact, he proclaimed himself to be Lenin's top representative in Central and Western Europe. Among his priorities was the immediate spread of the revolution to Slovakia and Austria in order to promote the "world dictatorship of the proletariat". The Hungarian Red Army thus began by spreading communism in Slovakia, which was occupied during the spring. On 16 June 1919, the short-lived Slovak Soviet Republic was proclaimed, where it was soon plundered before being overthrown by the advancing Czechs and Romanians.

At the first meeting of the communist commissars in Hungary, the courts of justice were abolished and revolutionary courts were set up whose judges were to be elected by the people. Stéphan Courtois and Jean-Louis Panné write in *The Black Book of Communism* that Bela Kun was in constant telegraphic contact with Lenin from 22 March onwards. These authors give the figure of two hundred and eighteen messages exchanged. Lenin greeted Bela Kun as the head of the world proletariat and advised him to shoot the social democrats and petty bourgeois. One of the first measures was the mass release of prisoners convicted of property crimes. In a speech to the Hungarian workers on March 27, Bela Kun justified the use of terror in these words: "The dictatorship of the proletariat demands the exercise of unrelenting, prompt and resolute violence in order to put an end to the opposition of the exploiters, the capitalists, the big landowners and their henchmen. Whoever has not understood this is not a revolutionary."

Again, as in Russia, as in Berlin, as in Bavaria, most of the leaders of Soviet Hungary were Jews. The government was composed of a board of five people, four of whom were Jewish: Bela Kun; Bela Vago, one of the judges of the Revolutionary Court; Sigmund Kunfi, in charge of Croatian Affairs; and Joseph Pogany, the Commissioner for Education. The Commissioner for Trade, Mátyás Rákosi (Matthias Roth), was also Jewish. Captured during the war, Rákosi, like Bela Kun, had been indoctrinated in Russia and returned to Hungary. Eugen Varga, another Jew, was the Commissioner for Economic Affairs. The Political Investigation Department was headed by a hunchbacked Jew, Otto Korvin-Klein, a vengeful fellow responsible for thousands of deaths who amused himself by shoving a ruler down his victims' throats during interrogations. Jüri Lina quotes A. Melsky's *Bela Kun and the Bolshevik Revolution in Hungary* to denounce the crimes of another Jewish commissar, Isidor Bergfeld, who admitted to burning sixty Hungarians alive and boasted of killing another hundred with his bare hands.

Apart from the Jewish leadership of the commissariat, in *Roots of radicalism*, the Americans Stanley Rothman and Robert Lichter note that of two hundred top officials, one hundred and sixty-one were Jewish. In 1919 *The Times* of London referred to Bela Kun's regime as a 'Jewish mafia'. Bloodthirsty criminals predominated. Bela Vago explained the nature of the regime thus: "Nothing is obtained without blood. Without blood there is no terror, and without terror there is no dictatorship." Bela Kun himself corroborated these ideas: "We must inspire the revolution with the blood of the exploiting bourgeois." Another example of the ferocity of these sinister Jewish communists is the Minister of Education, Joseph Pogany, who is credited with the deaths of some one hundred and fifty people, mostly teachers and professors, eliminated during his educational inspection tours. For the post of Commissioner for Culture Bela Kun appointed a Jewish intellectual who was the son of the manager of the Rothschild Bank, the mythologised Georg Lukacs, whom many rank among the most important Marxist intellectuals of the 20th century. Lukacs was also political commissar of the 5th Division and had eight people shot by a war tribunal. He wore a leather uniform and was known to some as the "Robespierre of Budapest".

The "democratisation" of the army began in May with a very simple formula: officers were shot and replaced by agents from Moscow. The ruthless and savage war against Christian culture was one of the essential features of Bela Kun's policy. According to the book *Visegrader Straße* (*Visegrader Street*), the reasoning in the Soviet House in Budapest was as follows: "We communists are like Judas. Our bloody work is to crucify Christ. But this sinful work is, at the same time, our vocation." Religion was ridiculed and priests were murdered in the streets. On the socio-economic front, the measures soon dragged the country into general disarray. Soon enterprises with more than twenty workers were expropriated, although those with ten or even five or six workers were soon expropriated as well. Many private houses were confiscated and declared state property. Private bathrooms were nationalised and made public on Saturday nights, a measure which could only seriously damage the social and moral tone of Hungarian society. Banks not controlled by the international Jewish cartel were nationalised. Bank deposits were seized and more than £1 million in foreign currency was taken out of the country to be used for propaganda. The hunt for "goyim" who possessed wealth was constant. Huge amounts of gold were sent from Hungary to Jewish banks abroad. The claim that the resources of industry and agriculture should be socialised provoked a famine in the cities and the anger of the peasantry.

The terror unleashed by the agricultural commissar, the Jew Tibor Szamuely, who, like so many others, had been captured during the war and trained in Russia by Bela Kun himself and the communist leaders, deserves a special mention. Szamuely, who had participated with Rosa Luxemburg and Karl Liebknecht in the formation of the German Communist Party, was one of the most prominent leaders of the Hungarian Soviet Republic, where he held various posts, the last of which was that of Commissar for Military Affairs. As Commissar for Agriculture, he became one of the regime's greatest criminals. In order to terrorise peasants who did not submit to his dictates of collectivisation, he travelled in a red-painted train which became a mobile cheka. His henchmen, after torturing the victims, threw them out of the windows as they passed through villages and towns. He forced peasants condemned to death to dig their own grave in front of their relatives and then forced them to jump into it with a rope around their necks. Szamuely allied himself with József Czerny, the leader of a commando of terrorists who have gone down in history as "Lenin's boys". Arthur Koestler, the author of *The Thirteenth Tribe*, estimates the number of victims of Czerny and his henchmen to be around five hundred; however, other authors estimate the figure to be much higher.

A provisional government of real Hungarians was formed in Szeged. The Allied countries, unable, as in Russia, to react against the criminal totalitarianism of the communist regime, at least accepted Romania's intervention. On 31 July Bela Kun issued a manifesto calling for the support of the workers of the whole world. On 1 August, with the city in chaos and after transferring £50,000 to Basel, he left Budapest with his top lieutenants for Vienna. Before fleeing he declared that he would have liked the proletarians to give their lives on the barricades to defend the cause of the revolution. His last public words were these: "Are we to mount the barricades ourselves without masses to back us up? Happily, we would have sacrificed ourselves, but would this sacrifice benefit the cause of the international proletarian revolution? On 6 August 1919 the Romanian troops finally deposed the Hungarian communists. Kun was arrested in Austria, but the Jewish Freemason Friedrich Adler, whose father Victor Adler had been a good friend of Trotsky, arranged for his release. Friedrich Adler had been sentenced to death in 1916 for the murder of Austrian Prime Minister Count Karl von Stürghk, but his sentence was commuted to 18 years in prison. In 1918 he was released thanks to the revolution, which had also broken out in Austria, and became leader of the Austrian Communist Party.

Bela Kun returned to Russia in 1920 and was appointed political commissar of the Red Army on the southern front, where he worked with two other Jews, Roza Zemlyachka (Rozalia Zalkind), known as the 'fury of communist terror', and Boris Feldman. The three led the Red terror in a Crimean cheka, where they became ruthless mass murderers. Zemlyachka and Kun, who frequently raped his female victims, were a match made in heaven. In addition to their sadism and cruelty in killing, they were greedy and never missed an opportunity to accumulate great wealth. In Sevastopol, while appropriating huge amounts of gold, they murdered more than eight thousand people during the first week of November 1920. According to official sources, fifty thousand "enemies of the people" were executed in the Crimea, although some sources put the figure as high as 120,000. Bela Kun was sent to Germany in 1921, where he led a coup attempt, as will be seen in the next chapter. Before being imprisoned by Stalin on charges of Trotskyism, Kun travelled to Barcelona in 1936 with the task of exploring the political atmosphere and fomenting agitation.

The Jewish character of the Hungarian Soviet Republic was as evident as that of Bolshevik Russia; but while in the case of Russia there was and still is an attempt to cover up and falsify the reality, in the Hungarian case everyone agrees that Hungary had "a government of the Jews", "a Jewish republic" or, as Nathaniel Katzburg prefers, "to a large extent a Jewish enterprise". Certainly, Hungarians perceived it as such. Thus, predictably, after the collapse of Jewish rule, there was a violent reaction that some authors have described as "white terror". The Jewish community in Pest itself tried to avoid the hatred and reprisals of the Hungarian people by excluding those who had been associated in one way or another with Bela Kun's regime. According to some sources, between two and three thousand Jewish citizens lost their lives as a result of the numerous acts of revenge.

OTHER BOOKS

ꙨMNIA VERITAS

OMNIA VERITAS LTD PRESENTS:

It does not deny, but aims
to affirm more accurately.
Revisionists are not 'deniers'
or 'negationists'; they strive
to seek and find where, it
seems, there was nothing
left to seek or find".

ROBERT FAURISSON
REVISIONIST WRITINGS
I
1974-1983

ROBERT FAURISSON
REVISIONIST WRITINGS
I
1974-1983

Revisionism is a matter of method, not ideology

ꙨMNIA VERITAS

OMNIA VERITAS LTD PRESENTS:

Jewish and Zionist
organisations throughout
the world are experiencing a
tragedy. A myth, from which
they have sought to profit, is
being exposed: the myth of
the so-called 'Holocaust of
the Jews during the Second
World War'.

ROBERT FAURISSON
REVISIONIST WRITINGS
II
1984-1989

ROBERT FAURISSON
REVISIONIST WRITINGS
II
1984-1989

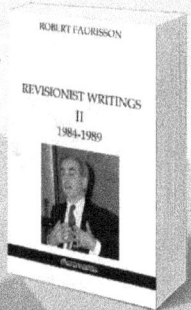

Revisionists have never denied the existence of the camps

ꙨMNIA VERITAS

OMNIA VERITAS LTD PRESENTS:

"By its very nature,
revisionism can only disturb
public order; where tranquil
certainties reign, the spirit of
free examination is an
intruder and causes a
scandal."

ROBERT FAURISSON
REVISIONIST WRITINGS
III
1990-1992

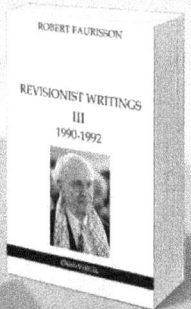

ROBERT FAURISSON
REVISIONIST WRITINGS
III
1990-1992

Every Frenchman has the right to say that gas chambers did not exist

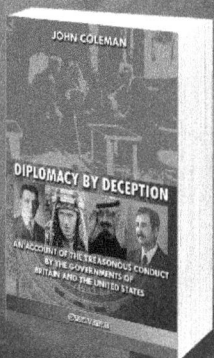

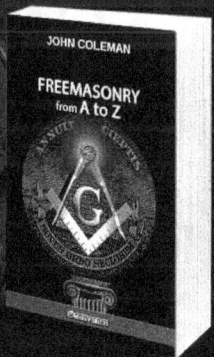

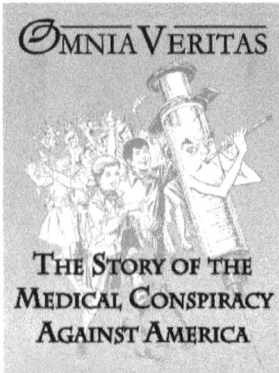

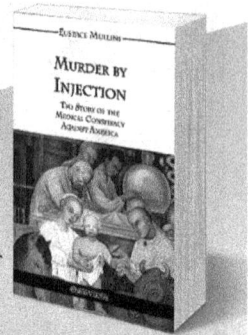

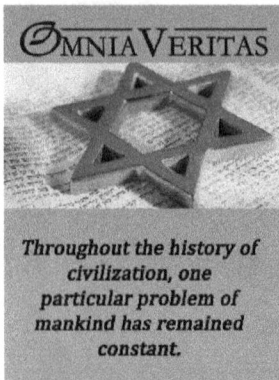

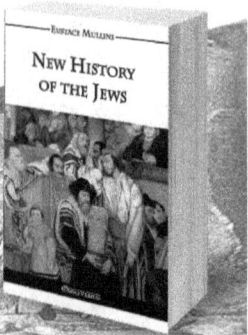

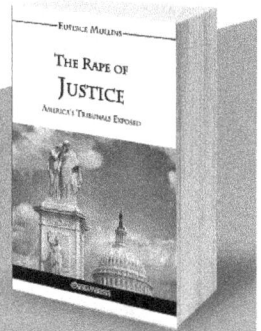

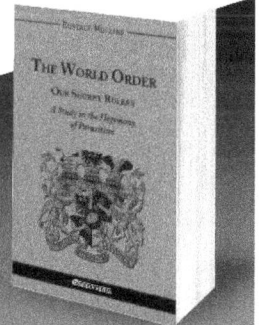

503

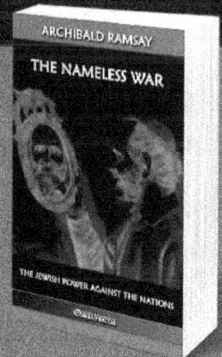

OMNIA VERITAS LTD PRESENTS:

SOLZHENITSYN

The Jews Before the Revolution

"The purpose that guides me throughout this work on the life common the Russians and the Jews consists of looking for all the points necessary for a mutual understanding, all the possible voices which, once we get rid of the bitterness of the past, can lead us towards the future."

The Jewish people is at the same time an active and passive element of History

Omnia Veritas Ltd presents:

An exclusive and unpublished work of EUSTACE MULLINS

BLOOD AND GOLD
HISTORY OF THE COUNCIL ON FOREIGN RELATIONS

The CFR, founded by internationalists and banking interests, has played a significant role in shaping US foreign policy

Revolutions are not made by the middle class, but by the oligarchy at the top

OMNIA VERITAS LTD PRESENTS:

THE TRACK OF THE JEW THROUGH THE AGES

One of the most characteristic and significant signs of the hostility of the Jews towards the Europeans is their hatred of Christianity

Indeed it is not surprising that the Church increasingly proscribed Jewish works

www.ingramcontent.com/pod-product-compliance
Lightning Source LLC
Chambersburg PA
CBHW050543270326
41926CB00012B/1891